An Introduction to Formal Logic

An Introduction to Formal Logic

Second edition

Peter Smith

LOGIC MATTERS

First edition, Cambridge University Press, 2003
Second edition, Cambridge University Press, 2020
Reprinted with corrections, Logic Matters, 2021

ISBN 978-1-916-90632-7 Hardback
ISBN 979-8-675-80394-1 Paperback

Additional resources for this publication at www.logicmatters.net.

Contents

Preface

The first and second printed editions   The world is not short of introductions to logic aimed at philosophy students. They differ widely in pace, style, coverage, and the ratio of formal work to philosophical commentary. Like other authors, my initial excuse for writing yet another text was that I did not find one that offered quite the mix that I wanted for my own students (first-year undergraduates doing a compulsory logic course).

Logicians are an argumentative lot and get quite heated when discussing the best route into our subject for beginners. But, standing back from our differences, we can all agree on this: in one form or another, the logical theory eventually arrived at in this book – *classical first-order quantification theory*, to give it its trade name – is a wonderful intellectual achievement by formally-minded philosophers and philosophically-minded mathematicians. It is a beautiful theory of permanent value, a starting point for all other modern work in logic. So we care greatly about passing on this body of logical knowledge. And we write our logic texts – like this one – in the hope that you too will come to appreciate some of the elements of our subject, and even want to go on to learn more.

This book starts from scratch, and initially goes pretty slowly; I make no apology for working hard at the outset to nail down some basic ideas. The pace gradually picks up as we proceed and as the idea of a formal approach to logic becomes more and more familiar. But almost everything should remain quite accessible even to those who start off as symbol-phobic – especially if you make the effort to read slowly and carefully.

You should check your understanding by tackling at least some of the routine exercises at the ends of chapters. There are worked answers available at the book's online home, www.logicmatters.net. These are often quite detailed. For example, while the book's chapters on formal proofs aim to make the basic principles really clear, the online answers provide extended 'examples classes' exploring proof-strategies, noting mistakes to avoid, etc. So do make good use of these further resources.

As well as exercises which test understanding, there are also a few starred exercises which introduce additional ideas you really ought to know about, or which otherwise ask you to go just a little beyond what is in the main text.

The first edition of this book concentrated on *logic by trees*. Many looking for a course text complained about this. This second edition, as well as significantly revising all the other chapters, replaces the chapters on trees with chapters on a *natural deduction* proof system, done Fitch-style. Which again won't please everyone! So the chapters on trees are still available, in a revised form. But to keep the length of the printed book under control, you will find these chapters – together with a lot of other relevant material including additional exercises – at the book's website.

This reprint   The second edition is now made freely available as a PDF download, and as an inexpensive reprint. Apart from altering this Preface to note the new publication arrangements, and taking the opportunity to correct a very small number of misprints, the book is unchanged. However, . . .

A third edition?   As just noted, in adding the chapters on natural deduction to the second edition, I had to relegate (versions of) the first edition's chapters on trees to the status of online supplements. But this was always a second-best solution. Ideally, I would have liked to have covered both trees *and* natural deduction (while carefully arranging things so that the reader who only wanted to explore one of these still had a coherent path through the book). I now hope over the coming months to be able to revert to that plan, and so eventually produce a third edition.

Thanks   Many more people have helped me at various stages in the writing and rewriting of this book than I can now remember.

   Generations of Cambridge students more or less willingly road-tested versions of the lecture handouts which became the first edition of this book, and I learnt a lot from them. Then Dominic Gregory and Alexander Paseau read and commented on full drafts of the book, and the late Laurence Goldstein did very much more than it was reasonable to expect of a publisher's reader. After publication, many people then sent further corrections which made their way into later reprintings, in particular Joseph Jedwab. Thanks to all of them.

   While writing the second edition, I have greatly profited from comments from, among many others, Mauro Allegranza, David Auerbach, Roman Borschel, David Furcy, Anton Jumelet, Jan von Plato, and especially Norman Birkett and Rowsety Moid. Exchanges on logical Twitter, a surprisingly supportive resource, suggested some memorable examples and nice turns of phrase – particularly from Joel D. Hamkins. Scott Weller was extremely generous in sending many pages of corrections. Matthew Manning was equally eagle-eyed, and also made a particularly helpful suggestion about how best to arrange the treatment of metatheory. At a late stage, David Makinson rightly pressed me hard to be clearer in distinguishing between types of rules of inference. And my daughter Zoë gave especially appreciated feedback and encouragement in the last phases of writing. I am again very grateful to all of them.

Most of all, I must thank my wife Patsy without whose love and support neither version of this book would ever have been finished.

1 What is deductive logic?

The core business of logic is the *systematic evaluation of arguments for internal cogency*. And the kind of internal cogency that will especially concern us in this book is *logical validity*.

But these brief headlines leave everything to be explained. What do we mean here by 'argument'? What do we mean by 'internal cogency'? What do we mean, more particularly, by 'logical validity'? And what kinds of 'systematic' evaluation of arguments are possible? This introductory chapter makes a gentle start on answering these questions.

1.1 What is an argument?

By 'argument' we mean a chain of reasoning, short or long, in support of some conclusion. So we must distinguish arguments from mere disagreements and disputes. The children who shout at each other 'You did', 'I didn't', 'Oh yes, you did', 'Oh no, I didn't' are certainly disagreeing: but they are not *arguing* in our sense – they are not yet giving any reasons in support of one claim or the other.

Reason-giving arguments are the very stuff of all serious inquiry, whether it is philosophy or physics, economics or experimental psychology. Of course, we also deploy reasoned arguments in the course of everyday, street-level, inquiry into the likely winner of next month's election, the best place to train as a lawyer, or what explains our team's losing streak. We want our opinions to be true; that means that we should aim to have good reasons backing up our opinions, so raising the chances of getting things right. This in turn means that we have an interest in being skilful reasoners, using arguments which really do support their conclusions.

1.2 Kinds of evaluation

Logic, then, is concerned with evaluating stretches of reasoning. Take this really simple example, and call it argument **A**. Suppose you hold

(1) All philosophers are eccentric.

I then introduce you to Jack, telling you that he is a philosopher. So you come to believe

1

(2)   Jack is a philosopher.

Putting these two thoughts together, you infer

(3)   Jack is eccentric.

And the first point to make is that this bit of reasoning can now be evaluated along two quite independent dimensions:

> First, we can ask whether this argument's *premisses* A(1) and A(2) are true. Are the 'inputs' to your inference step correct? A(1) is in fact very disputable. And perhaps I have made a mistake and A(2) is false as well.

> Second, we can ask about the quality of the *inference step*, the move which takes you from the premisses A(1) and A(2) to the *conclusion* A(3). In this particular case, the inference step is surely absolutely compelling: the conclusion really does follow from the premisses. We have agreed that it may be open to question whether the premisses are actually true. However, if they *are* assumed to be true (assumed 'for the sake of argument', as we say), then we have to agree that the conclusion is true too. There's just no way that A(1) and A(2) could be true and yet A(3) false. To assert that Jack is a philosopher and that all philosophers are eccentric, but go on to deny that Jack is eccentric, would be implicitly to contradict yourself.

Generalizing, it is one thing to consider whether an argument starts from true premisses; it is another thing to consider whether it moves on by reliable inference steps. Yes, we typically want our arguments to pass muster on both counts. We typically want *both* to start from true premisses *and* to reason by steps which can be relied on to take us to further truths. But it is important to emphasize that these are distinct aims.

The premisses of arguments can be about all sorts of topics: their truth is usually no business of the logician. If we are arguing about historical matters, then it is the historian who is the expert about the truth of our premisses; if we are arguing about some question in physics, then the physicist is the one who might know whether our premisses are true; and so on. The central concern of logic, by contrast, is not the truth of initial premisses but the way we argue from a given starting point – the logician wants to know when an argument's premisses, supposing that we accept them, do indeed provide compelling grounds for also accepting its conclusion. It is in this sense that logic is concerned with the 'internal cogency' of our reasoning.

1.3   Deduction vs. induction

(a)   Argument **A**'s inference step is absolutely compelling: if **A**'s premisses are true, then its conclusion is guaranteed to be true too. Here is a similar case:

> **B**   (1) Either Jill is in the library or she is in the bookshop.
> (2) Jill isn't in the library.
> So (3) Jill is in the bookshop.

Who knows whether the initial assumptions, the two premises, are true or not? But we can immediately see that the inference step is again completely watertight. If premises B(1) and B(2) are both true, then B(3) cannot conceivably fail to be true.

Now consider the following contrasting case (to illustrate that not all good reasoning is of this type). Here you are, sitting in your favourite café. Unrealistic philosophical scepticism apart, you are thoroughly confident that the cup of coffee you are drinking is not going to kill you – for if you weren't really confident, you wouldn't be calmly sipping as you read this, would you? What justifies your confidence?

Well, you believe the likes of:

C   (1)   Cups of coffee from GreatBeanz that looked and tasted just fine haven't killed anyone in the past.
(2)   This present cup of GreatBeanz coffee looks and tastes just fine.

These premises, or something rather like them, sustain your cheerful belief that

(3)   This present cup of GreatBeanz coffee won't kill you.

The inference that moves from the premises C(1) and C(2) to the conclusion C(3) is, in the circumstances, surely perfectly reasonable: other things being equal, the facts recorded in C(1) and C(2) do give you excellent grounds for believing that C(3) is true. However – and here is the quite crucial contrast with the earlier 'Jack' and 'Jill' examples – it is not the case that the truth of C(1) and C(2) absolutely guarantees C(3) to be true too.

Perhaps someone has slipped a slow-acting tasteless poison into the coffee, just to make the logical point that facts about how things have always been in the past don't guarantee that the trend will continue in the future.

Fortunately for you, C(3) is no doubt true. The tasteless poison is a fantasy. Still, it is a *coherent* fantasy. It illustrates the point that your grounds C(1) and C(2) for the conclusion that the coffee is safe to drink are strictly speaking quite compatible with the falsity of that conclusion. Someone who agrees to C(1) and C(2) and yet goes on to assert the opposite of C(3) might be saying something highly improbable, but they won't actually be contradicting themselves. We can make sense of the idea of C(1) and C(2) being true and yet C(3) false.

In summary then, there is a fundamental difference between the 'Jack' and 'Jill' examples on the one hand, and the 'coffee' example on the other. In the 'Jack' and 'Jill' cases, the premises absolutely guarantee the conclusion. There is no conceivable way that A(1) and A(2) could be true and yet A(3) false: likewise, if B(1) and B(2) are true then B(3) just has to be true too. Not so with the 'coffee' case: it is conceivable that C(1) and C(2) are true while C(3) is false. What has happened in the past is a very good guide to what will happen next (and what else can we rely on?); but reasoning from past to future isn't completely watertight.

(b)   We need some terminology to mark this fundamental difference. We will introduce it informally for the moment:

> If an inference step from premises to a conclusion is completely watertight, i.e. if the truth of the premises absolutely guarantees the truth of the conclusion, then we say that this inference step is *deductively valid*.
>
> Equivalently, when an inference step is deductively valid, we will say that its premises *deductively entail* its conclusion.

The inferential moves in **A** and **B** count as being deductively valid. Contrast the 'coffee' argument **C**. That argument involves reasoning from past cases to a new case in a way which leaves room for error, however unlikely. This kind of extrapolation from the past to the future, or more generally from some sample cases to further cases, is standardly called *inductive*. The inference in **C** might be inductively strong – meaning that the conclusion is highly probable, assuming the premises are true – but the inference is not deductively valid.

We should stress that the deductive/inductive distinction is *not* the distinction between good and bad reasoning. The 'coffee' argument is a perfectly decent one. It involves the sort of usually reliable reasoning to which we have to trust our lives, day in, day out. It is just that the inference step here doesn't completely guarantee that the conclusion is true, even assuming that the stated premises are true.

(c) What makes for reliable (or reliable enough) inductive inferences is a very important and decidedly difficult topic. But it is not our topic in this book, which is deductive logic. That is to say, we will here be concentrating on the assessment of arguments which aim to use deductively valid inferences, where the premises *are* supposed to deductively entail the conclusion.

We will give a sharper definition of the general notion of deductive validity at the beginning of the next chapter, §2.1. Later, by the time we get to §6.2, we will have the materials to hand to define a rather narrower notion which – following tradition – we will call *logical* validity. And this narrower notion of logical validity will then become our main focus in the remainder of the book. But for the next few chapters, we continue to work with the wider initial notion that we've called deductive validity.

1.4   Just a few more examples

The 'Jack' and 'Jill' arguments are examples where the inference steps are obviously deductively valid. Compare this next argument:

> **D**   (1) All Republican voters support capital punishment.
>   (2) Jo supports capital punishment.
>   So (3) Jo is a Republican voter.

The inference step here is equally obviously invalid. Even if D(1) and D(2) are true, D(3) doesn't follow. Maybe lots of people in addition to Republican voters support capital punishment and Jo is one of them.

How about the following argument?

E   (1)   Most Irish people are Catholics.

           (2)   Most Catholics oppose abortion on demand.

So (3)   At least some Irish people oppose abortion on demand.

Leave aside the question of whether the premisses are in fact correct (that's not a matter for logicians: it needs sociological investigation to determine the distribution of religious affiliation among the Irish, and to find out what proportion of Catholics support their church's teaching about abortion). What we can ask here – from our armchairs, so to speak – is whether the inference step is deductively valid: if the premisses are true, then must the conclusion be true too?

Well, whatever the facts of the case, it is at least conceivable that the Irish are a tiny minority of the Catholics in the world. And it could also be that nearly all the other (non-Irish) Catholics oppose abortion, and hence most Catholics do, even though *none* of the Irish oppose abortion. But then E(1) and E(2) would be true, yet E(3) false. So the truth of the premisses doesn't by itself absolutely guarantee the truth of the conclusion (there are possible situations in which the premisses would be true and the conclusion false). Hence the inference step is not deductively valid.

Here's another argument: is the inference step deductively valid this time?

F   (1)   Some philosophy students admire all logicians.

           (2)   No philosophy student admires anyone irrational.

So (3)   No logician is irrational.

With a little thought you should arrive at the right answer here too (we will return to this example in Chapter 3).

Still, at the moment, faced with examples like our last three, all you can do is to cast around hopefully, trying to work out somehow or other whether the truth of the premisses *does* guarantee the truth of the conclusion. It would be good to be able to proceed more systematically and to have a range of *general* techniques for evaluating arguments for deductive validity. That's what logical theory aims to provide.

Indeed, ideally, we would like techniques that work mechanically, that can be applied to settle questions of validity as routinely as we can settle simple arithmetical questions by calculation. We will have to wait to see how far this is possible. For the moment, we will just say a little more about what makes any kind of more systematic approach possible (whether mechanical or not).

1.5   Generalizing

(a)   Here again is our first sample mini-argument with its deductively valid inference step:

A   (1)   All philosophers are eccentric.

           (2)   Jack is a philosopher.

So (3)   Jack is eccentric.

Now compare it with the following arguments:

A' (1) All logicians are cool.
  (2) Russell is a logician.
  So (3) Russell is cool.

A'' (1) All robins have red breasts.
  (2) Tweety is a robin.
  So (3) Tweety has a red breast.

A''' (1) All post-modernists write nonsense.
  (2) Derrida is a post-modernist.
  So (3) Derrida writes nonsense.

We can keep going on and on, churning out arguments to the same pattern, all involving equally valid inference steps.

It is plainly no accident that these arguments share the property of being internally cogent. Comparing these examples makes it clear that the deductive validity of the inference step in the original argument **A** hasn't anything specifically to do with philosophers or with the notion of being eccentric. Likewise the validity of the inference step in argument **A'** hasn't anything specifically to do with logicians. And so on. There is a general principle involved here:

From a pair of premises, one saying that *all* things of a given kind have a certain property, the other saying that a particular individual is indeed of that given kind, we can validly infer the conclusion that this individual has the property in question.

(b) However, this wordy version is not the most perspicuous way of representing the shared inferential principle at work in the **A**-family. Focusing on arguments expressed in English, we can instead say something like this:

Any inference step of the form

  All F are G
  n is F
 So: n is G

is deductively valid.

Here the letters 'n', 'F', 'G' are being used to help exhibit a skeletal pattern of argument. We can think of 'n' as standing in for a name for some individual person or thing, while 'F' and 'G' stand in for expressions which pick out kinds of things (like 'philosopher' or 'robin') or properties (like 'eccentric'). A bit more loosely, we can also use 'is G' to stand in for other expressions attributing properties like 'has a red breast' or 'writes nonsense'. It then doesn't matter how we flesh out the italicized argument template or *schema*, as we might call it. Any sensible enough way of substituting suitable expressions for 'n', '(is) F' and '(is) G', and then tidying the result into reasonable English, will yield another argument with a deductively valid inference step.

Some forms or patterns of inference are deductively reliable, then, meaning that every inference step which is an instance of the same pattern is valid. Other forms aren't reliable. Consider the following pattern of inference:

Most G are H
Most H are K
So: At least some G are K.

(The choice of letters we use to display a pattern of inference is optional, of course! – a point we return to in §3.2(d).) This is the type of inference involved in the 'Irish' argument **E**, and we now know that it isn't trustworthy.

(c)   We said at the outset that logic aims to be a systematic study. We can now begin to see how to get some generality into the story. Noting that the same form of inference step can feature in many different particular arguments, we can aim to examine generally reliable forms of inference. And we can then hope to explore how such reliable forms relate to each other and to the particular arguments which exploit them, giving us a more systematic treatment. A lot more about this in due course.

1.6   Summary

We can evaluate a piece of reasoning along two different dimensions. We can ask whether its premisses are actually true. And we can ask whether the inference from the premisses is internally cogent – i.e., assuming the premisses are true, do they really support the truth of the conclusion? Logic is concerned with the second dimension of evaluation.

We are setting aside inductive arguments (and other kinds of non-conclusive reasoning). We will be concentrating on arguments involving inference steps that purport to be deductively valid. In other words, we are going to be concerned with deductive logic, the study of inferences that aim to strictly guarantee their conclusions, assuming the truth of their premisses.

Arguments typically come in families whose members share good or bad types of inferential move; by looking at such general patterns or forms of inference we can hope to make logic more systematic.

Exercises 1

By 'conclusion' we do not mean what concludes a passage of reasoning in the sense of what is stated at the end. We mean what the reasoning aims to establish – and this might in fact be stated at the outset. Likewise, 'premiss' does not mean (contrary to what the Concise Oxford Dictionary says!) 'a previous statement from which another is inferred'. Reasons supporting a certain conclusion, i.e. the inputs to an inference, might well be given *after* that target conclusion has been stated. Note too that the move from supporting reasons to conclusions can be signalled by *inference markers* other than 'so'.

What are the premisses, inference markers, and conclusions of the following arguments? Which of these arguments do you suppose involve deductively valid reasoning? Why? (Just improvise, and answer the best you can!)

(1) Most politicians are corrupt. After all, most ordinary people are corrupt – and politicians are ordinary people.

(2) Anyone who is well prepared for the exam, even if she doesn't get an A grade, will at least get a B. Jane is well prepared, so she will get at least a B grade.

(3) John is taller than Mary and Jane is shorter than Mary. So John is taller than Jane.

(4) At eleven, Fred is always either in the library or in the coffee bar. And assuming he's in the coffee bar, he's drinking an espresso. Fred was not in the library at eleven. So he was drinking an espresso then.

(5) The Democrats will win the election. There's only a week to go. The polls put them 20 points ahead, and a lead of 20 points with only a week to go to polling day can't be overturned.

(6) Dogs have four legs. Fido is a dog. Therefore Fido has four legs.

(7) Jekyll isn't the same person as Hyde. The reason is that no murderers are sane – but Hyde is a murderer, and Jekyll is certainly sane.

(8) All the slithy toves did gyre and gimble in the wabe. Some mome raths are slithy toves. Hence some mome raths did gyre and gimble in the wabe.

(9) Some but not all philosophers are logicians. All logicians are clever. Hence some but not all philosophers are clever.

(10) No experienced person is incompetent. Jenkins is always blundering. No competent person is always blundering. Therefore Jenkins is inexperienced.

(11) Many politicians take bribes. Most politicians have extra-marital affairs. So many people who take bribes have extra-marital affairs.

(12) Kermit is green all over. Hence Kermit is not red all over.

(13) Every letter is in a pigeonhole. There are more letters that there are pigeonholes. So some pigeonhole contains more than one letter.

(14) There are more people than there are hairs on anyone's head. So at least two people have the same number of hairs on their head.

(15) Miracles cannot happen. Why? Because, by definition, a miracle is an event incompatible with the laws of nature. And everything that happens is always consistent with the laws of nature.

(16) (Lewis Carroll) No interesting poems are unpopular among people of real taste. No modern poetry is free from affectation. All your poems are on the subject of soap bubbles. No affected poetry is popular among people of real taste. Only a modern poem would be on the subject of soap bubbles. Therefore none of your poems are interesting.

(17) 'If we found by chance a watch or other piece of intricate mechanism we should infer that it had been made by someone. But all around us we do find intricate pieces of natural mechanism, and the processes of the universe are seen to move together in complex relations; we should therefore infer that these too have a maker.'

(18) 'I can doubt that the physical world exists. I can even doubt whether my body really exists. I cannot doubt that I myself exist. So I am not my body.'

2 Validity and soundness

We have introduced the idea of an inference step being deductively valid and, equivalently, the idea of some premisses deductively entailing a conclusion. This chapter explores this notion of validity/entailment a bit further, though still in an informal way. We also emphasize the special centrality of deductive reasoning in serious inquiry.

2.1 Validity defined more carefully

(a) We said in §1.3 that an inference step is deductively valid if it is completely watertight – in other words, assuming that the inference's premisses are true, its conclusion is absolutely guaranteed to be true as well.

But talk of an inference being 'watertight' and talk of a conclusion being 'guaranteed' to be true is too metaphorical for comfort. So – now dropping the explicit 'deductively' – here is a less metaphorical definition, already hinted at:

> An inference step is *valid* if and only if there is no possible situation in which its premisses would be true and its conclusion false. Equivalently, in such a case, we will say that the inference's premisses *entail* its conclusion.

Take the plural 'premisses', here and in similar statements, to cover the one-premiss case too. Then this definition characterizes what is often called the *classical* concept of validity. It is, however, only as clear as the notion of a 'possible situation'. So we certainly need to pause over this.

(b) Consider the following bit of reasoning:

> **A**   Jo jumped out of a twentieth floor window (without parachute, safety net, etc.) and fell unimpeded onto a concrete pavement. So she was injured.

Let's grant that, with the laws of nature as they are, there is no way in which the premiss could be true and the conclusion false (assume that we are talking about here on Earth, that Jo is a human, not a beetle, etc.). In the actual world, falling unimpeded onto concrete from twenty floors up will always produce serious – very probably fatal – injury. Does that make the inference from **A**'s premiss to its conclusion valid?

No. It isn't, let's agree, *physically* possible in our actual circumstances to jump without being injured. But we can coherently, without self-contradiction, conceive of a situation in which the laws of nature are different or are miraculously suspended, and someone jumping from twenty floors up can float delicately down like a feather. We can imagine a capricious deity bringing about such a situation. In this very weak sense, it *is* possible that **A**'s premiss could be true while its conclusion is false. And that is enough for the inference to be deductively invalid.

(c) So our definition of validity is to be read like this: a deductively valid inference is one where it is not possible even in the most generously inclusive sense – roughly, it is not even coherently conceivable – that the inference's premisses are true and its conclusion false.

Let's elaborate. We ordinarily talk of many different kinds of possibility – about what is physically possible (given the laws of nature), what is technologically possible (given our engineering skills), what is politically possible (given the make-up of the electorate), what is financially possible (given the state of your bank balance), and so on. These different kinds of possibility are related in various ways. For example, something that is technologically possible has to be physically possible, but may not be financially possible for anyone to engineer.

But note that if some situation is physically possible (or technologically possible, etc.) then, at the very least, a description of that situation has to be internally coherent. In other words, if some situation is M-ly possible (for any suitable modifier 'M'), then it must be possible in the thin sense that the very idea of such a situation occurring isn't ruled out as nonsense. The notion of possibility we need in defining validity is possibility in this weakest, most inclusive, sense. And from now on, when we talk in an unqualified way about possibility, it is this very weak sense that we will have in mind.

(d) Kinds of possibility go together with matching kinds of necessity – 'necessary' means 'not-possibly-not'. For example, it is legally necessary for an enforceable will to be signed if and only if it is not legally possible for a will to be enforceable yet *not* signed. It is physically necessary that massive objects gravitationally attract each other if and only if it is not physically possible that those objects *not* attract each other. And so on. Generalizing, we can massage such equivalences into the standard form

It is M-ly necessary that C if and only if it is not M-ly possible that *not-C*,

where 'C' stands in for some statement, and '*not-C*' stands in for the *denial* of that statement (so asserting *not-C* is equivalent to saying it is false that C).

Likewise, our very weak inclusive notion of possibility goes with a correspondingly strong notion of necessity: it is necessary that C in this sense just in case it is not even weakly possible that *not-C*. Putting it another way,

It is necessarily true that C if and only if it is true that C in every possible situation, in our most inclusive sense of 'possible'.

10

From now on, when we talk in an unqualified way about necessity, it is this very strong sense that we will have in mind.

And yes, being necessarily true is a *very* strong requirement, as strong as can be. However, it is one that can be met in some cases. For example, it is necessary in this sense that Jill is not both married and unmarried (at the same time, in the same jurisdiction). It is necessary in our strong sense that all triangles have three sides (in any coherently conceivable situation, the straight-sided figures with three internal angles are three-sided). Again, it is necessary that whenever a mother smiles, a parent smiles.

It is equally necessary that if all philosophers are eccentric and Jack is a philosopher, then Jack is eccentric. And this last example illustrates a general point, which gives us an equivalent definition of deductive validity:

> An inference step is valid if and only if it is necessary, in the strongest sense, that *if* the inference's premisses are true, so is its conclusion. For short, valid inferences are *necessarily truth-preserving*.

2.2   Consistency and equivalence

We need a term for the kind of thing that can feature as a premiss or conclusion in an argument – let's use the traditional '*proposition*'.

We will return in §§7.3–7.5 to consider the tricky question of the nature of propositions: for the moment, we just assume that propositions can sensibly be said to be true or false in various situations (unlike commands, questions, etc.). That's all we need, if we are to introduce two more notions that swim in the same conceptual stream as the notion of validity – two notions which again concern the truth of propositions across different possible situations.

(a)   First, we will say:

> One or more propositions are (jointly) *inconsistent* if and only if there is *no* possible situation in which these propositions are all true together.

Or to put it another way, some propositions are (jointly) *consistent* if and only if there *is* a possible situation in which they are all true together. Both times, we mean 'possible' in the weakest, most inclusive, sense.

For example, taken together, the three propositions *All philosophers are eccentric, Jack is a philosopher* and *Jack is not eccentric* are jointly inconsistent. But any two of them are consistent, as is any one of them taken by itself.

Suppose that an inference is valid, meaning that there is no possible situation in which its premisses would be true and its conclusion false. Given our new definition, this is equivalent to saying that the premisses and the *denial* of the conclusion are jointly inconsistent. We can therefore offer another definition of the classical conception of validity which is worth highlighting:

An inference step is valid if and only if its premisses taken together with the denial of the conclusion are inconsistent.

This means that when we develop logical theory it matters little whether we take the notion of validity or the notion of consistency as fundamental.

(b)   Here is the second new notion we want:

Two propositions are *equivalent* if and only if they are true in exactly the same possible situations.

Again this is closely tied to the notion of a valid inference, as follows:

The propositions A and B are equivalent if and only if A entails B and B entails A.

Why so? Suppose A and B are equivalent. Then in any situation in which A is true, B is true – i.e. A entails B. Exactly similarly, B entails A. Conversely, suppose A entails and is entailed by B; then in any situation in which A is true, B is true and vice versa – i.e. A and B are equivalent.

2.3   Validity, truth, and the invalidity principle

(a)   To assess whether an inference step is deductively valid, it is usually not enough to look at what is the case in the actual world; we also need to consider alternative possible situations, alternative ways things might conceivably have been – or, as some say, alternative possible worlds.

Take, for example, the following argument:

B   (1) No Welshman is a great poet.
           (2) Shakespeare is a Welshman.
    So (3) Shakespeare is not a great poet.

The propositions here are all false about the actual world. But that doesn't settle whether the premisses of **B** entail its conclusion. In fact, the inference step here is valid; there is no situation at all – even a merely possible one, in the weakest sense – in which the premisses would be true and the conclusion false. In other words, any possible situation which *did* make the premisses true (Shakespeare being brought up some miles to the west, and none of the Welsh, now including Shakespeare, being good at verse) would also make the conclusion true.

Here are two more arguments stamped out from the same mould:

C   (1) No human being is a dinosaur.
           (2) Bill Clinton is a human being.
    So (3) Bill Clinton is not a dinosaur.

D   (1) No one whose middle name is 'William' is a Democrat.
           (2) George W. Bush's middle name is 'William'.
    So (3) George W. Bush is not a Democrat.

These two arguments involve valid inferences of the same type – in case **C** taking us from true premisses to a true conclusion, in case **D** taking us, as it happens, from false premisses to a true conclusion.

You might wonder about the last case: how can a truth be validly inferred from two falsehoods? But note again: validity is only a matter of internal cogency. Someone who believes D(3) on the basis of the premisses D(1) and D(2) would be using a reliable form of inference, but they would be arriving at a true conclusion by sheer luck. Their claimed grounds D(1) and D(2) for believing D(3) would have nothing to do with why D(3) in fact happens to be true. (Aristotle noted the point. Discussing valid arguments with false premisses, he remarks that the conclusion may yet be correct, but "only in respect to the fact, not to the reason".)

There can be mixed cases too, where valid inferences have some true and some false premisses. So, allowing for these, we have in summary:

A valid inference can have actually true premisses and a true conclusion, (some or all) actually false premisses and a false conclusion, or (some or all) false premisses and a true conclusion.

The only combination ruled out by the definition of validity is a valid inference step's having all true premisses and yet a false conclusion. Deductive validity is about the necessary preservation of truth – and therefore a valid inference step cannot take us from actually true premisses to an actually false conclusion.

That last point is worth really emphasizing. Here's an equivalent version:

The invalidity principle An inference step with actually true premisses and an actually false conclusion must be invalid.

We will see in Chapter 5 how this principle gets to do important work when combined with the fact that arguments come in families sharing the same kind of inference step.

(b) So much for the valid inference steps. What about the invalid ones? What combinations of true/false premisses and true/false conclusions can these have?

An invalid inference step can have any combination of true or false premisses and a true or false conclusion.

Take for example the following silly argument:

E   (1) My mother's maiden name was 'Moretti'.
        (2) Every computer I've ever bought is a Mac.
     So (3) The Pavel Haas Quartet is my favourite string quartet.

This is invalid: there is a readily conceivable situation in which the premisses are true and conclusion false. But what about the *actual* truth/falsity of the premisses and conclusion? I'm not going to say. *Any* combination of actually true or false premisses and a true or false conclusion is quite compatible with the invalidity of the hopeless inferential move here.

So note: having true premisses and a false conclusion is *enough* to make an inference invalid – in other words, it is a sufficient condition for invalidity. But that isn't *required* for being invalid – it isn't a necessary condition.

2.4 Inferences and arguments

(a) So far, we have spoken of *inference steps in arguments* as being valid or invalid. But it is more common simply to describe *arguments* as being valid or invalid. In this usage, we say that an argument is valid if and only if the inference step from its premisses to its conclusion is valid. (Or at least, that's what we say about one-step arguments like the toy examples we've been looking at: we'll consider multi-inference arguments later.)

Talking of valid arguments in this way is absolutely standard. But it can mislead beginners. After all, saying that an argument is 'valid' can sound like an all-in endorsement. So let's stress the point: to say that a (one-step) argument is valid in our sense is *only* to commend the cogency of the inferential move between premisses and conclusion, is only to say that the conclusion really does follow from the premisses. A valid argument must be internally cogent, but can still have premisses that are quite hopelessly false.

For example, take this argument:

F (1) Whatever Donald Trump says is true.
       (2) Donald Trump says that the Flying Spaghetti Monster exists.
   So (3) It is true that the Flying Spaghetti Monster exists.

Since the *inference step* here is evidently valid, this *argument* counts as valid, in our standard usage. Which might well strike the unwary as a distinctly odd thing to say!

You just have to learn to live with this way of speaking of valid arguments. But then we need, of course, to have a different term for arguments that *do* deserve all-in endorsement – arguments which both start from truths and proceed by deductively cogent inference steps. The usual term is 'sound'. So:

> A (one-step) argument is *valid* if and only if the inference step from the premisses to the conclusion is valid.
>
> A (one-step) argument is *sound* if and only if it has all true premisses and the inference step from those premisses to the conclusion is valid.

A few older texts use 'sound' to mean what we mean by 'valid'. But everyone agrees there is a key distinction to be made between mere deductive cogency and the all-in virtue of making a cogent inference *and* having true premisses; there's just a divergence over how this agreed distinction should be labelled.

(b) When we are deploying deductive arguments, we typically want our arguments to be sound in the sense we just defined. But not always! For we sometimes want to argue, and argue absolutely compellingly, from premisses that we *don't*

14

believe to be all true. For example, we might aim to deduce some obviously false consequence from premisses which we don't accept, in the hope that a disputant will agree that this consequence has to be rejected and so come to agree with us that the premisses aren't all true. Sometimes we even want to argue compellingly from premisses we believe are inconsistent, precisely in order to bring out their inconsistency.

(c)   Note three easy consequences of our definition of soundness:

(1)   any sound argument has a true conclusion;

(2)   no pair of sound arguments can have conclusions inconsistent with each other;

(3)   no sound argument has inconsistent premisses.

Why do these claims hold? For the following reasons:

(1′)   A sound argument starts from true premisses and involves a necessarily truth-preserving inference move – so it must end up with a true conclusion.

(2′)   Since a pair of sound arguments will have a pair of true conclusions, this means that the conclusions are true together. If they actually *are* true together, then of course they *can* be true together. And if they can be true together then (by definition) the conclusions are consistent with each other.

(3′)   Since inconsistent premisses cannot all be true together, an argument starting from those premisses cannot satisfy the first of the conditions for being sound.

Note though that if we replace 'sound' by 'valid' in (1) to (3), the claims become false. More about valid arguments with inconsistent premisses in due course.

(d)   What about arguments where there are intermediate inference steps between the initial premisses and the final conclusion (after all, real-life arguments very often have more than one inference step)? When should we say that they are deductively cogent?

As a first shot, we can say that such extended arguments are valid when each inference step along the way is valid. But we will see in §4.4 that more needs to be said. So we'll hang fire on the question of deductive cogency for multi-step arguments until then.

2.5   'Valid' vs 'true'

Let's pause for a brief terminological sermon, one which is important enough to be highlighted! The propositions that occur in arguments as premisses and conclusions are assessed for *truth/falsity*. Inference steps in arguments are assessed for *validity/invalidity*. These dimensions of assessment, as we have stressed, are fundamentally different. We should therefore keep the distinction carefully marked. Hence:

15

Despite the common misuse of the terms, resolve to *never* again say that a premiss or conclusion or other proposition is 'valid' when you mean it is true. And *never* again say that an argument is 'true' when you mean that it is valid (or sound).

2.6   What's the use of deduction?

(a)   As we noted before, deductively valid inferences are not the only acceptable inferences. Concluding that Jo is injured from the premiss she fell twenty storeys onto concrete is of course perfectly sensible. Reasoning of this kind is very often reliable enough to trust your life to: the premisses may render the conclusion a certainty for all practical purposes. But such reasoning isn't deductively valid.

Now consider a more complex kind of inference. Take the situation of the detective, Sherlock let's say. Sherlock assembles a series of clues and then solves the crime by an *inference to the best explanation* (an old term for this is 'abductive' reasoning). In other words, the detective arrives at some hypothesis that best accommodates all the strange events and bizarre happenings. In the ideally satisfying detective story, this hypothesis strikes us (once revealed) as obviously giving the right explanation – why didn't we think of it? Thus: why is the bed bolted to the floor so it can't be moved? Why is there a useless bell rope hanging by the bed? Why is the top of the rope fixed near a ventilator grille leading through into the next room? What is that strange music heard at the dead of night? All the pieces fall into place when Sherlock infers a dastardly plot to kill the sleeping heiress in her unmovable bed by means of a poisonous snake, trained to descend the rope through the ventilator grille in response to the snake-charmer's music. But although this is an impressive 'deduction' in one everyday sense of the term, it is not deductively valid reasoning in the logician's sense. We may have a number of clues, and the detective's hypothesis H may be the only plausible explanation we can find: but in the typical case it won't be a contradiction to suppose that, despite the way all the evidence stacks up, hypothesis H is actually false. That won't be an inconsistent supposition, only perhaps a very unlikely one. Hence, the detective's plausible 'deductions' are not (normally) valid deductions in the logician's sense.

Now, if our inductive reasoning about the future on the basis of the past is not deductive, and if inference to the best explanation is not deductive either, you might well ask: *just how interesting is the idea of deductively valid reasoning?* To make the question even more worrisome, consider that paradigm of systematic rationality, scientific reasoning. We gather data, and try to find the best theory that fits; rather like the detective, we aim for the best explanation of the actually observed data. But a good theory goes well beyond merely summarizing the data. In fact, it is precisely because the theory goes beyond what is strictly given in the data that the theory can be used to make novel predictions. Since the excess content isn't guaranteed by the data, however, the theory cannot be validly deduced from observation statements.

16

So again you well might very well be inclined to ask: if deductive inference doesn't feature even in the construction of scientific theories, why should it be particularly interesting? True, it might be crucial for mathematicians – but what about the rest of us?

(b) But that's far too quick! We can't simply deduce a scientific theory from the data it is based on. However, it doesn't at all follow that deductive reasoning plays no essential part in scientific reasoning.

Here's a picture of what goes on in science. Inspired by patterns in the data, or by models of the underlying processes, or by analogies with other phenomena, etc., we conjecture that a certain theory is true. Then we use the theory (together with assumptions about 'initial conditions', etc.) to deduce a range of testable predictions. The first stage, the conjectural stage, may involve flair and imagination, rather than brute logic, as we form our hypotheses. But at the second stage, having made our conjectures, we need to infer testable consequences; and now *this* does involve deductive logic. For we need to examine what else must be true if the hypothesized theory is true: we want to know what our theory deductively entails. Then, once we have deduced testable predictions, we can seek to test them. Often our predictions prove to be false. We have to reject the theory – or else we have to revise it to accommodate the new data, and then go on to deduce more testable consequences. The process is typically one of repeatedly improving and revising our hypotheses, *deducing* consequences which we can test, and then refining the hypotheses again in the light of test results.

This so-called *hypothetico-deductive* model of science (which highlights the role of deductive reasoning *from theory to predictions*) no doubt needs a lot of development and amplification and refinement. But with science thus conceived, we can see why deduction is absolutely central to the enterprise after all.

And what goes for science, narrowly understood, goes for rational inquiry more widely: deductive reasoning may not be the whole story, but it is an ineliminable core. Whether we are doing physics or metaphysics, mathematics or moral philosophy, worrying about climate change or just the next election, we need to think through what our assumptions logically commit us to, and know when our reasoning goes wrong. That's why logic, which teaches us how to appraise passages of reasoning for deductive validity, matters.

2.7   An illuminating circle?

Aristotle wrote in his *Prior Analytics* that "a deduction is speech (*logos*) in which, certain things having been supposed, something ... results of necessity because of their being so". Our own definition – an argument is valid just if there is no possible situation in which its premises would be true and its conclusion false – picks up the idea that correct deductions are necessarily truth-preserving. And we have tried to say enough to convey an initial understanding of this idea, and to give a sense of the central importance of deductively valid reasoning.

17

Note, though, that – as we explained how to understand our classical definition of validity – we in effect went round in a rather tight circle of interconnected ideas. We first defined validity in terms of what is possible, where we are to understand 'possible' in the weakest, most inclusive, sense. We then further elucidated this relevant weak notion of possibility in terms of what is coherently conceivable. But what is it for a situation to be coherently conceivable? A minimal condition would seem to be that a story about the conceived situation must not involve some hidden self-contradiction. Which presumably is to be understood, in the end, as meaning that we cannot validly deduce a contradiction from the story. So now it seems that we have defined deductive validity in a way that needs to be explained, at least in part, by invoking the notion of a valid deduction. How concerning is this?

This kind of circularity is often unavoidable when we are trying to elucidate some really fundamental web of concepts. Often, the best we can do is start with a rough-and-ready, partial, grasp of various ideas, and then aim to draw out their relationships and make distinctions, clarifying and sharpening the ideas as we explore the web of interconnected notions – so going round, we hope, in an *illuminating* circle. In the present case, this is what we have tried to do as we have illustrated and explained the notion of deductive validity and interrelated notions. We have at least said enough, let's hope, to get us started and to guide our investigations over the next few chapters.

Still, notions of necessity and possibility do remain genuinely puzzling. So – before you worry that we are starting to build the house of logic on shaky foundations – we should highlight that, looking ahead,

We will later be giving sharp technical definitions of notions of validity for various special classes of argument, definitions which do *not* directly invoke troublesome notions of necessity/possibility.

These definitions will, however, remain recognizably in the spirit of our preliminary elucidations of the classical concept.

2.8 Summary

Inductive arguments from past to future, and inferences to the best explanation, are not deductive; but the hypothetico-deductive picture shows why there can still be a crucial role for deductive inference in scientific and other empirical inquiry.

Our preferred definition of deductive validity is: an inference step is valid if and only if there is no possible situation in which its premises are true and the conclusion false. Call this the classical conception of validity.

The notion of possibility involved in this definition is the weakest and most inclusive.

Equivalently, a valid inference step is necessarily truth-preserving, in the strongest sense of necessity. NB: being 'necessarily truth-preserving' (this is a useful shorthand we will make much use of) is defined by a conditional: necessarily, *if* the premisses are true, so is the conclusion.

A one-step argument is valid if and only if its inference step is valid. An argument which is valid and has true premisses is said to be sound.

Exercises 2

(a)   Which of the following claims are true and which are false? Explain why the true claims hold good, and give counterexamples to the false claims.

(1)   The premisses and conclusion of an invalid argument must together be inconsistent.

(2)   If an argument has false premisses and a true conclusion, then the truth of the conclusion can't really be owed to the premisses: so the argument cannot really be valid.

(3)   Any inference with actually true premisses and a true conclusion is truth-preserving and so valid.

(4)   You can make a valid argument invalid by adding extra premisses.

(5)   You can make a sound argument unsound by adding extra premisses.

(6)   You can make an invalid argument valid by adding extra premisses.

(7)   If some propositions are consistent with each other, then adding a further true proposition to them can't make them inconsistent.

(8)   If some propositions are jointly inconsistent, then whatever propositions we add to them, the resulting propositions will still be jointly inconsistent.

(9)   If some propositions are jointly consistent, then their denials are jointly inconsistent.

(10)   If some propositions are jointly inconsistent, then we can pick any one of them, and validly infer that it is false from the remaining propositions as premisses.

(b*)   Show that

(1)   If A entails C, and C is equivalent to C', then A entails C'.

(2)   If A entails C, and A is equivalent to A', then A' entails C.

(3)   If A and B entail C, and A is equivalent to A', then A' and B entail C.

Can we therefore say that 'equivalent propositions behave equivalently in arguments'?

3 Forms of inference

We saw in the first chapter how arguments can come in families which share the same type or pattern or form of inference step. Evaluating this shareable form of inference for reliability will then simultaneously give a verdict on a whole range of arguments depending on the same sort of inferential move.

In this chapter, we say a little more about the idea of forms of inference and about the schemas we use to display them.

3.1 More forms of inference

(a) Consider again the argument:

> **A**   (1) No Welshman is a great poet.
>   (2) Shakespeare is a Welshman.
> So (3) Shakespeare is not a great poet.

This is deductively valid, and likewise for the parallel 'Clinton' and 'Bush' arguments which we stated in §2.3. The following is valid too:

> **A′**   (1) No three-year old understands quantum mechanics.
>   (2) Daisy is three years old.
> So (3) Daisy does not understand quantum mechanics.

We can improvise endless variations on this theme. And plainly, the inference steps in these arguments aren't validated by anything especially to do with poets, presidents, or three-year-olds. Rather, they are all valid for the same reason, namely the meaning of 'no' and 'not' and the way that these logical notions distribute in the premisses and conclusion (the same way in each argument). So:

> Any inference step of the form
>
> $$No\ F\ is\ G$$
> $$n\ is\ F$$
> $$So\!:\ n\ is\ not\ G$$
>
> is deductively valid.

As before (§1.5), 'n' in the italicized schema stands in for some name, while 'F' and 'G' (with or without an 'is') stand in for expressions that sort things into kinds or are used to attribute properties. We can call letters used in this way *schematic variables* ('schematic' because they feature in schemas, 'variable'

20

because they can stand in for various different replacements). Substitute appropriate bits of English for the variables in our schema, smooth out the language as necessary, and we'll get a valid argument.

That's rather rough. If we want to be a bit more careful, we can put the underlying principle or rule of inference like this:

> From a pair of propositions, one saying that nothing of some given kind has a certain property, the other saying that a particular individual is of the given kind, we can validly infer the conclusion that this individual lacks the property in question.

But surely the schematic version is easier to understand. It is more perspicuous to *display* the form of an inference by using a symbolic schema, rather than trying to *describe* that form in cumbersome words.

(b)   Here is another argument which we have met before (§1.4):

B   (1) Some philosophy students admire all logicians.
           (2) No philosophy student admires anyone irrational.
     So (3) No logician is irrational.

Do the premisses here deductively entail the conclusion?

Consider any situation where the premisses are true. Then by B(1) there will be some philosophy students who admire all logicians. Pick one, Jill for example. We know from B(2) that Jill (since she is a philosophy student) doesn't admire anyone irrational. That is to say, people admired by Jill aren't irrational. So in particular, logicians – who are all admired by Jill – aren't irrational. Which establishes B(3), and shows that the inference step is deductively valid.

What about this next argument?

B′   (1) Some opera fans buy tickets for every new production of *Tosca*.
           (2) No opera fan buys tickets for any merely frivolous entertainment.
     So (3) No new production of *Tosca* is a merely frivolous entertainment.

This too is valid; and a moment's reflection shows that it essentially involves the same pattern of valid inference step as before.

We can again display the general principle in play using a schema, as follows:

Any inference step of the following type

> *Some F are R to every G*
> *No F is R to any H*
> *So: No G is H*

is deductively valid.

Here we are using '*is/are R to*' to stand in for a form of words expressing a *relation* between things or people. So it might stand in for e.g. 'is married to', 'is taller than', 'is to the left of', 'is a member of', 'admires', 'buys a ticket for'. Abstracting from the details of the relations in play to leave just the schematic pattern, we can see that the arguments **B** and **B′** are deductively valid for the same reason, by virtue of sharing the same indicated pattern of inference step.

21

And just try describing the shared pattern of inference *without* using the symbols: it can be done, to be sure, but at what a cost in ease of understanding!

(c)   We have now used schemas to display three different types of valid inference steps. We initially met the form of inference we can represent by the schema

> *All F are G*
> *n is F*
> *So: n is G.*

And we have just noted the forms of inference

> *No F is G*
> *n is F*
> *So: n is not G*

> *Some F are R to every G*
> *No F is R to any H*
> *So: No G is H.*

Any argument instantiating one of these patterns will be deductively valid. The way that 'all', 'every' and 'any', 'some', 'no' and 'not' distribute between the premises and conclusion means that inferences following these schematic forms are necessarily truth-preserving – if the premises are true, the conclusion has to be true too.

For the moment, let's just note three more examples of deductively reliable forms of inference, involving different numbers of premises:

> *No F is G*
> *So: No G is F*

> *All F are H*
> *No G is H*
> *So: No F is G*

> *All F are either G or H*
> *All G are K*
> *All H are K*
> *So: All F are K.*

(Convince yourself that arguments which instantiate these schemas are indeed valid in virtue of the meanings of the logical words 'all', 'no', and 'or'.)

3.2   Four basic points about the use of schemas

We do not only use schemas to display patterns of reasoning in the logic class-room: it is also quite common to use schemas in a rough-and-ready way to clarify the structure of arguments in philosophical writing.

Later, from Chapter 8 on, we will also use schemas in a significantly more disciplined way when talking about patterns of reasoning in arguments framed in artificial formal languages – languages that logicians love, for reasons which will soon become clear. We pause next, then, to emphasize four initial points that apply to both the informal and the more formal uses of schemas to display types of inference step.

(a)   Take again the now familiar form of inference we can display like this:

> *All F are G*
> *n is F*
> *So: n is G.*

Does the following argument count as an instance of this schematic pattern?

C   (1) All men are mortal.
     (2) Tweety is a robin.
So (3) Donald Trump is female.

Well, of course not! But let's spell out why.

True enough, C(1) attributes a certain property to everything of a given kind; so taken by itself, we can informally represent it as having the shape *All F are G*. Likewise, C(2) and (C3) can, taken separately, be represented as having the form *n is F* or *n is G*. However, when we describe an inference as an instance of the three-line schema displayed above we are indicating that the *same* property-ascribing term *F* is involved in the two premises. Likewise, we are indicating that the name *n* and general term *G* that occur in the premises recur in the conclusion. This is worth highlighting:

> The whole point of using recurring symbols in schemas representing forms of inference is to indicate patterns of recurrence in the premises and conclusion. Therefore, when we fill in a schema by substituting appropriate expressions for the symbols, we must follow the rule: same symbols, same substitutions.

So, in the present case, in moving back from our displayed abstract schema to a particular instance of it, we must preserve the patterns of recurrence by being consistent in how we substitute for the '*F*'s and '*G*'s and '*n*'s.

(b)   What about the following argument? Does this also count as an instance of the last schema we displayed?

D   (1) All men are men.
     (2) Socrates is a man.
So (3) Socrates is a man.

Instead of filling in our schema at random, we have at least this time been consistent, substituting uniformly for both occurrences of '*F*', and likewise for both occurrences of '*G*'. However, we happen to have substituted in the same way each time.

We will allow this. So, to amplify, the rule is: same schematic variable, same substitutions – but different schematic variables need not receive different substitutions. In the present case, if the '*F*'s and '*G*'s are both substituted in the

23

same way, we still get a valid argument; **D** cannot have true premisses and a false conclusion!

Of course, **D** is no use at all as a means for persuading someone of the conclusion. An argument won't persuade you of the truth of its conclusion if you *already* have to accept the very same proposition in order to believe the argument's premisses. Still, being valid is one thing, and being usefully persuasive is something different. And keeping this distinction in mind, we can happily count **D** as a limiting case of a deductively watertight argument. After all, an inference step that covers no ground has no chance to go wrong.

(c)   And how about the following argument?

> **E**   (1) Socrates is a man.
> (2) All men are mortal.
> So (3) Socrates is mortal.

Compared with the displayed abstract schema, the premisses here are stated 'in the wrong order', with the general premiss second. *But so what?* An inference step is valid, we said, just when there is no possible situation in which its premisses are true and its conclusion false. Given that definition, the validity of an inference doesn't depend at all on the order in which the premisses happen to be stated. When we want to display a form of inference, the order in which the various premisses are represented in a schema is irrelevant. Hence we can take **E** as exemplifying just the same pattern of inference as before.

(d)   Last but not least, what is the relation between the symbolic schema presented at the beginning of this section and its three variants below?

All F are G	*All H are K*	*All Φ are Ψ*	*All ① are ②*
n is F	*m is H*	*α is Φ*	*$\star$ is ①*
So: n is G	*So: m is K*	*So: α is Ψ*	*So: $\star$ is ②*

Plainly, these four different schemas are alternative possible ways of representing the *same* form or pattern of inference (so don't confuse schemas with forms of inference!) Remember: what we are trying to reveal is a pattern of recurrence. The '*m*'s, '*n*'s, '*α*'s, and '*⋆*'s are just different arbitrary ways of indicating how names recur in the common pattern. Likewise the '*F*'s or '*Φ*'s or whatever are just different arbitrary ways of indicating where repeated property-ascribing expressions are to be substituted. We can use whatever symbols take our fancy to do the job. Later we will mainly be using Greek letters as schematic variables; but for our current informal purposes we will stick to ordinary italic letters.*

3.3   Arguments can instantiate many patterns

(a)   It can be tempting to talk about 'the' form or pattern of inference step exemplified by an argument. But we do need to be *very* careful here.

---

*If the letters of the Greek alphabet (starting *alpha, beta,* ...!) are not very familiar, now might be the time to start preparing the ground by looking at p. 412.

Consider again the hackneyed example of argument **E** with its two premisses *All men are mortal* and *Socrates is a man* and the conclusion *Socrates is mortal*.

This is, trivially, an instance of the entirely unreliable form of inference

(1)   *A, B, so C*

where '*A*' etc. stand in for whole propositions (contrast here, for example, the reliable form *A, B, so A*).

Exposing some structure in the individual propositions, but still ignoring the all-important recurrences, **E** also instantiates the equally unreliable form of inference

(2)   *All F are G, m is H, so n is K*

since it has the right sort of general premiss, a second premiss ascribing some property to a named individual, and a similar conclusion.

Next, and now filling in enough details about the structure of the inferential step to bring out an inferentially reliable pattern of recurrence, our 'Socrates' argument also instantiates, as we said before, the form

(3)   *All F are G, n is F, so n is G.*

But we can go further. **E** is also an instance of perfectly reliable types of inference like

(4)   *All F are G, Socrates is F, so Socrates is G,*

(5)   *All F are mortal, n is F, so n is mortal.*

(6)   *All men are G, Socrates is a man, so Socrates is G.*

And we could even, going to the extreme, take the inference to be the one and only example of the reliable type

(7)   *All men are mortal, Socrates is a man, so Socrates is mortal,*

which is (so to speak) a pattern with all the details filled in!

In sum, the 'Socrates' argument **E** exemplifies a number of different forms or patterns of inference, specified at different levels of generality. Which all goes to show that:

> There is no such thing as *the* unique form or pattern of inference that a given argument can be seen as instantiating.

Of course, this isn't to deny that the form of inference (3) has a special place in the story about **E**. For (3) is the most general but still reliable pattern of inference that the argument exemplifies. In other words, the schema *All F are G; n is F; so, n is G* gives just enough of the structure of **E** – but no more than we need – to enable us to see that the argument is in fact valid. So it is the reliability of *this* pattern of inference which someone defending argument **E** will typically want to appeal to. It is might be rather tempting, then, to fall into talking of the schema (3) as revealing 'the' pattern of inference in **E**; but, as we've just seen, that would be rather loose talk.

(b)   A terminological note:

It is common to refer to a universally reliable form or pattern of inference – i.e. one whose instances are all valid – as *itself* being 'valid'.

But if we fall in with this usage, we must emphasize again that, as just illustrated, an 'invalid' pattern of inference like (1) or (2) – meaning a pattern whose instances are not *all* valid – can still have *some* particular instances that do happen to be valid (being valid, of course, for some other reason than exemplifying the unreliable pattern).

3.4   Summary

Forms or patterns of inference can be conveniently represented by schemas using letters or other symbols as variables (the specific choice of symbols doesn't matter). The use of these symbols is governed by the natural convention that a symbol stands in for the same expression wherever it appears within a given argument schema.

There is strictly no such thing as the unique pattern or form exemplified by an argument.

But when we talk of 'the' form of a valid argument, we typically mean the most general reliable form of argument that it instantiates. Note, a valid argument can also be an instance of some other, 'too general', unreliable forms.

We can also say that a form of argument is valid, meaning that it is such that all its instances are valid.

Exercises 3

(a)   Which of the following patterns of inference are deductively reliable, meaning that all their instances are valid? (Here 'F', 'G', and 'H' hold the places for general terms.) If you suspect an inference pattern is unreliable, find an instance which has to be invalid because it has true premises and a false conclusion.

(1)   Some F are G; no G is H; so, some F are not H.
(2)   Some F are G; some H are F; so, some G are H.
(3)   All F are G; some F are H; so, some H are G.
(4)   No F is G; some G are H; so, some H are not F.
(5)   No F is G; no H is G; so, some F are not H.
(6)   All F are G; no G is H; so, no H is F.

(b)   What of the following patterns of argument? Are these deductively reliable?

(1)   All F are G; so, nothing that is not G is F.
(2)   All F are G; no G are H; some J are H; so, some J are not F.

(3) There is an odd number of F, there is an odd number of G; so there is an even number of things which are either F or G.

(4) All F are G; so, at least one thing is F and G.

(5) m is F; n is F; so, there are at least two F.

(6) Any F is G; no G are H; so, any J is J.

(c)   Arguments of the kinds illustrated in (a) are so-called (categorical) *syllogisms*, first systematically discussed by Aristotle in his *Prior Analytics*.

These syllogisms are formed from three propositions, each being of one of the following four forms, which have traditional labels:

A: All X are Y
E: No X is Y
I: Some X are Y
O: Some X are not Y.

By the way, these medieval labels supposedly come from the vowels of the Latin *affirmo* (I affirm, for the positive two) and *nego* (I deny, for the negative two).

A syllogism then consists of two premises and a conclusion, each having one of these forms. The two terms in the conclusion occur in separate premises, and then there is a third or 'middle' term completing the pattern – as in our six schematic examples above. Two questions arising:

(1) Which valid types of syllogism of this kind have a conclusion of the form A, 'All S are P'? (Use 'M for the 'middle' term in a syllogism.)

(2) Which have a conclusion of the form O, 'Some S are not P'?

(d)   Ancient Stoic logicians concentrated on a different family of arguments. Using 'A' and 'B' to stand in for whole propositions, and 'not-A' to stand in for the denial of what 'A' stands in for, they endorsed the following five basic forms of arguments. Indeed they held them to be so basic as to be 'indemonstrable':

(1) If A then B; A; so B.

(2) If A then B; not-B; so not-A.

(3) not-(A and B); A; so not-B.

(4) A or B; A; so not-B.

(5) A or B; not-A; so B.

Which of these principles are acceptable, which – if any – are questionable? Give illustrations to support your verdicts!

What about these further forms of argument? Which are correct?

(6) If A then B; not-A; so not-B.

(7) If A then B; B; so A.

(8) not-(A and B); so either not-A or not-B.

(9) A or B; so not-(not-A and not-B).

(10) not-not-A; so A.

What about these general principles?

(11) If the inference A *so* B is valid, and the inference B *so* C is valid, then the inference A *so* C is also valid.

(12) If the inference A, B *so* C is valid, then so is the inference A, *not-C so not-B*.

4 Proofs

In Chapter 1, we explained what it is for an inference step to be deductively valid, and then we noted that different arguments can share a common form or pattern of inference. Chapters 2 and 3 explored these ideas a little further.

We now move on to consider the following question: how can we establish that a not-obviously-valid inference is in fact valid? One answer, in headline terms, is: by giving a multi-step argument that takes us from that inference's premisses to its conclusion by simple, plainly valid steps – in other words, by giving a derivation or proof. This chapter explains.

4.1 Proofs: first examples

(a) Take a charmingly silly example from Lewis Carroll:

A   Babies are illogical; nobody is despised who can manage a crocodile; illogical persons are despised; so babies cannot manage a crocodile.

This three-premiss, one-step, argument is in fact valid. But how can we demonstrate the argument's validity if it isn't immediately clear? Well, consider the following two-step derivation:

A′   (1) Babies are illogical.   (premiss)
           (2) Nobody is despised who can manage a crocodile. (premiss)
           (3) Illogical persons are despised.   (premiss)
           (4) Babies are despised.   (from 1, 3)
           (5) Babies cannot manage a crocodile.   (from 2, 4)

Here, we have inserted an extra step between the three premisses and the target conclusion (and we can omit writing 'So' before lines (4) and (5), as the commentary on the right is already enough to indicate that these lines are the results of inferences).

The inference from two of the premisses to the interim conclusion (4), and then the second inference from the other original premiss and that interim conclusion (4) to the final conclusion (5), are both evidently valid. We can therefore get from the initial premisses to the final conclusion by a necessarily truth-preserving route. Which shows that the inferential step in the original argument **A** is valid.

(b) Here's a second quick example, equally daft:

B   Everyone loves a lover; Romeo loves Juliet; so everyone loves Juliet.

Take the first premiss to mean 'everyone loves anyone who is a lover' (where a lover is, by definition, a person who loves someone). Then this argument too is deductively valid! Here is a multi-step derivation:

B′   (1) Everyone loves a lover.   (premiss)
          (2) Romeo loves Juliet.   (premiss)
          (3) Romeo is a lover.   (from 2)
          (4) Everyone loves Romeo.   (from 1, 3)
          (5) Juliet loves Romeo.   (from 4)
          (6) Juliet is a lover.   (from 5)
          (7) Everyone loves Juliet.   (from 1, 6)

We have again indicated on the right the 'provenance' of each new statement as the argument unfolds. And by inspection we can see that each small inference step is valid, i.e. is necessarily truth-preserving. As the argument grows, then, we are adding new propositions which must also be true, assuming the original premisses are true. These new true propositions can then serve in turn as inputs to further valid inferences, yielding more truths. Everything is chained together so that, if the original premisses are true, each added proposition must be true too, and therefore the final conclusion in particular must be true. Hence the original inference step in **B** that jumps in one leap straight across the intermediate stages must be valid.

(c)   These examples illustrate how to establish the validity of an unobviously valid inference step, using a technique already familiar to Aristotle:

> One way of demonstrating that an inferential leap from some premisses to a given conclusion is valid is by breaking down the big leap into smaller inference steps, each one of which is clearly valid.

There is a familiar logician's term for a multi-step argument put together in such a way as to form a deductively cogent derivation – it's a *proof*.

(d)   One-step arguments can be merely valid (deductively cogent) or they can be sound (deductively cogent *and* proceeding from true premisses). Valid one-step arguments can have false conclusions; sound arguments, however, do establish the truth of their conclusions. There's a similar distinction to be made about multi-step arguments. They too can be merely valid (deductively cogent) or they can be sound (deductively cogent *and* proceeding from true premisses). In the logician's sense, then, there can be merely valid proofs and there can be sound proofs. It is only sound proofs that establish their conclusions as true.

So we have another potentially awkward departure from ordinary language here, for we ordinarily think of a proof as, well, *proving* something, establishing it as true! In other words, by 'proof' we ordinarily mean a *sound* proof. There would therefore be something to be said for using one term for a cogent multi-step argument, *derivation* (say), and reserving the term *proof* for an argument

29

which does indeed establish its conclusion outright. (Gottlob Frege, the founding father of modern logic, in effect adopts such a usage.) But like it or not, this isn't standard practice. And context should make it clear when we are talking about a 'proof' in the wider logician's sense of an internally cogent argument (usually multi-step), and when we are using 'proof' more narrowly to mean a sound argument, an outright demonstration of truth.

4.2 Fully annotated proofs

(a) In our first two examples of proofs, we have indicated at each new step which earlier statements the inference depended on. But we can do even better by also explicitly indicating what type or *form* of inference move is being invoked at each stage.

For use in our next example, then, let's repeat two principles that we have met before and now briskly label them:

Any inference step of either of the following two types is valid:

(R)   *No F is G*
          n is F
     So: n is not G

(S)   *No F is G*
     So: No G is F

So consider the following little argument:

C   No logician is bad at abstract thought. Jo is bad at abstract thought.
          So Jo is not a logician.

This hardly needs a proof! – but still, we *can* prove it, invoking (R) and (S), as follows:

C′   (1) No logician is bad at abstract thought.   (premiss)
          (2) Jo is bad at abstract thought.   (premiss)
          (3) No one bad at abstract thought is a logician. (from 1 by S)
          (4) Jo is not a logician.   (from 3, 2 by R)

(Why do you think we have mentioned steps (3) and (2) in that order in the annotation for line (4)?)

Note that in treating the move from (1) to (3) as an instance of (S) we are – strictly speaking – cutting ourselves a bit of slack, quietly massaging the English grammar. It's actually rather difficult to give strict rules for doing this sort of thing. Which is one good reason for eventually moving from considering arguments framed in messy English to considering their counterparts in more tidily rule-governed formalized languages.

(b) Of course, the validity of **C** has nothing especially to do with Jo, logicians, and abstract thought. Abstracting from its premisses and final conclusion, we can say, more generally:

Any inference step of the following type is valid:

(T)   *No F is G*
        n is G
     So: n is not F

Further, any instance of this pattern can be shown to be valid by using a proof parallel to **C′**. In other words, the general reliability of (T) follows from the reliability of (R) and (S).

So this little example nicely reveals another important sense in which logical inquiry can be systematic (compare §1.5). Not only can we treat arguments wholesale by considering together whole families relying on the same principles of inference, but we can systematically interrelate patterns of inference like (R), (S), and (T) by showing how the reliability of some ensures the reliability of others.

Logical theory can therefore give us much more than an unstructured catalogue of deductively reliable principles of inference; we can and will explore how principles of inference hang together. More about this later in the book!

(c)   Let's take another argument from Lewis Carroll, who is an inexhaustible source of silly examples (there is no point in getting too solemn at this stage!):

D   Anyone who understands human nature is clever; every true poet can stir the heart; Shakespeare wrote *Hamlet*; no one who does not understand human nature can stir the heart; no one who is not a true poet wrote *Hamlet*; so Shakespeare is clever.

The big inferential leap from those five premisses to the conclusion is in fact valid. For note the following:

Any inference step of either of the following two types is valid:

(U)   *Any/every F is G*
        n is F
     So: n is G

(V)   *No one who isn't F is G*
     So: Any G is F

Then we can argue as follows, using these two forms of valid inference step:

D′   (1) Anyone who understands human nature is clever.
                                                          (premiss)
       (2) Every true poet can stir the heart.   (premiss)
       (3) Shakespeare wrote *Hamlet*.   (premiss)
       (4) No one who does not understand human nature
           can stir the heart.   (premiss)
       (5) No one who is not a true poet wrote *Hamlet*. (premiss)
       (6) Anyone who wrote *Hamlet* is a true poet.   (from 5, by V)
       (7) Shakespeare is a true poet.   (from 6, 3, by U)

31

(8) Shakespeare can stir the heart.	(from 2, 7, by U)
(9) Anyone who can stir the heart understands human nature.	(from 4, by V)
(10) Shakespeare understands human nature.	(from 9, 8, by U)
(11) Shakespeare is clever.	(from 1, 10, by U)

That's all very *very* laborious. But now we have the provenance of every move fully annotated. Each of the inference steps is an instance of a clearly truth-preserving pattern, and together they get us from the initial premisses of the argument to its final conclusion. Hence, if the initial premisses are true, the conclusion must be true too. So our proof here really does show that the original argument **D** is deductively valid.

4.3 Glimpsing an ideal

(a) Using toy examples, we have now glimpsed an ideally explicit way of setting out one kind of regimented multi-step proof. Every premiss gets stated at the outset and is explicitly marked as such; and then we write further propositions one under another, each coming with a certificate which tells us what it is inferred from and what principle of inference is being invoked.

Needless to say, everyday arguments (and not-so-everyday proofs in mathematics) normally fall a long way short of meeting these ideal standards of explicitness! They rarely come ready-chunked into numbered statements, with each new inference step bearing a supposed certificate of excellence. However, faced with a puzzling multi-step argument, massaging it into something nearer this fully documented shape will help us to assess the argument. On the one hand, an explicitly annotated proof gives a critic a particularly clear target to fire at. If someone wants to reject the conclusion, then they will have to rebut one of the premisses, show an inference step doesn't have the claimed form, or come up with a counterexample to the reliability of one of the forms of inference that is explicitly called on. On the other hand, looking on the bright side, if the premisses are agreed and if the inference moves are uncontentiously valid, then the proof will establish the conclusion beyond further dispute.

(b) The exercise of regimenting an argument into a more ideally explicit form will reveal *redundancies* (premisses or inferential detours that are not needed to get to the final conclusion) and will also expose where there are *suppressed premisses* (i.e., premisses that are not stated but which *are* needed to get a well-constructed proof).

Traditionally, arguments with suppressed premisses are called *enthymemes*. Without worrying about that label, here's an example:

E   The constants of nature have to take values in an extremely narrow range (have to be 'fine-tuned') to permit the evolution of intelligent life. So the universe was intelligently designed.

As it stands this is plainly gappy: there are unspoken assumptions in the background. But it is instructive to try to turn this reasoning into a deductively valid argument, by making explicit the currently suppressed premisses. One such premiss will be uncontroversial, just noting that intelligent life has evolved. The other premiss will be much more problematic: roughly, intelligent design is needed in order for the universe to be fine-tuned enough. Only with some such additions can we get a deductively cogent argument.

4.4   Deductively cogent multi-step arguments

When is a multi-step argument internally cogent? The headline answer is predictable: when each inference step is cogent and also the steps are chained together in the right kind of way.

(a)   Consider first the following mini-argument:

F   (1) All philosophers are logicians.   (premiss)
         (2) All logicians are philosophers.   (from 1?!)

The inference here is horribly fallacious. It just doesn't follow from the premiss that all philosophers are logicians that only philosophers are logicians. (You might as well argue 'All women are human beings, hence all human beings are women'.)

Here's another really bad argument:

G   (1) All existentialists are philosophers.   (premiss)
         (2) All logicians are philosophers.   (premiss)
         (3) All existentialists are logicians.   (from 1, 2?!)

It plainly doesn't follow from the claims that the existentialists and logicians are both among the philosophers that any of the existentialists are logicians, let alone that all of them are. (You might as well argue 'All women are human beings, all men are human beings, hence all women are men'.)

But now imagine that someone chains this pair of rotten inferences together into a two-step argument as follows:

H   (1) All existentialists are philosophers.   (premiss)
         (2) All philosophers are logicians.   (premiss)
         (3) All logicians are philosophers.   (from 2?!)
         (4) All existentialists are logicians.   (from 1, 3?!)

Our reasoner first makes the same fallacious inference as in **F**; and then they compound the sin by committing the same howler as in **G**. So they have gone from the initial premisses H(1) and H(2) to their final conclusion H(4) by two quite terrible moves.

Yet note that in this case – despite the howlers along the way – the final conclusion H(4) in fact really does follow from the initial premisses H(1) and H(2). If the existentialists are all philosophers, and all philosophers are logicians, then the existentialists must of course be logicians!

What is the moral of this example? If we were to say that a multi-step argument is deductively cogent just if the big leap from the initial premisses to the final conclusion is valid, then we'd have to count the two-step argument **H** as a cogent proof. Which would be a *very* unhappy way of describing the situation, given that the two-step derivation involves a couple of nasty fallacies!

For a correctly formed proof – a deductively cogent multi-step argument, where everything is in good order – we should therefore require not just that the big leap from the initial premisses to the final conclusion is valid, but that the individual inference steps along the way are all valid too.

Exactly as you would expect!

(b)   But that is not the whole story. For deductive cogency, we also need a proof's valid inference steps to be chained together in the right kind of way.

To illustrate, consider the inference step here:

I   (1) Socrates is a philosopher.   (premiss)
          (2) All philosophers have snub noses.   (premiss)
          (3) Socrates is a philosopher and all philosophers have
               snub noses.   (from 1, 2)

That's trivially valid (since from A together with B you can infer A-*and*-B).

Next, here is another equally trivial valid inference step (since from A-*and*-B you can of course infer B):

J   (1) Socrates is a philosopher and all philosophers have
               snub noses.   (premiss)
          (2) All philosophers have snub noses.   (from 1)

And thirdly, here is another plainly valid inference step, one of a very familiar form which we've met before:

K   (1) Socrates is a philosopher.   (premiss)
          (2) All philosophers have snub noses.   (premiss)
          (3) Socrates has a snub nose   (from 1, 2)

(Note that **I** and **K** have the same premisses and different conclusions – but that's fine. We can extract more than one implication from the same premisses!)

Taken separately, then, those three little inference steps are entirely unproblematic. However, imagine now that someone chains these steps together to get the following unholy tangle:

L   (1) Socrates is a philosopher.   (premiss)
          (2) Socrates is a philosopher and all philosophers
               have snub noses.   (from 1, 3, as in **I**)
          (3) All philosophers have snub noses.   (from 2 as in **J**)
          (4) Socrates has a snub nose.   (from 1, 3 as in **K**)

By separately valid steps we seem to have deduced the shape of Socrates' nose just from the premiss that he is a philosopher! What has gone wrong?

The answer is plain. In the middle of the argument we have gone round in a circle. L(2) is derived from inputs including L(3), and then L(3) is derived from L(2). Circular arguments like this can't take us anywhere. Which shows that there is another condition for being a deductively cogent multi-step argument. As well as the individual inference steps all being valid, the steps must be chained together in a non-circular way. In particular, each step – unless a newly made assumption – must depend only on what's gone before. As you would expect.

4.5 Indirect arguments

(a) So far, so straightforward. But now we need to complicate the story, introducing an important new idea, namely that we often use *indirect* arguments. For example, we often try to establish a conclusion *not-S* by first supposing the opposite, i.e. *S*, and then showing that this leads to something absurd.

Return to the silly crocodile argument $\mathbf{A'}$ in §4.1. Imagine that someone has a momentary lapse and pauses over the final step (where we inferred *Babies cannot manage a crocodile* from the original premiss *Nobody is despised who can manage a crocodile* together with the interim conclusion *Babies are despised*). How could we convince them that this step really is valid?

We might try amplifying the argument so we get an expanded (not quite fully documented) proof which now runs as follows:

$\mathbf{A''}$ (1) Babies are illogical.   (premiss)
(2) Nobody is despised who can manage a crocodile.
                                                              (premiss)
(3) Illogical persons are despised.   (premiss)
(4) Babies are despised.   (from 1, 3)
      Suppose temporarily, for the sake of argument,
(5)   Babies *can* manage a crocodile.   (supposition)
(6)   Babies are not despised.   (from 2, 5)
(7)   Contradiction!   (from 4, 6)
      Our supposition leads to absurdity, hence
(8) Babies cannot manage a crocodile.   (from 5–7 by RAA)

What is going on in this expanded proof? We want to establish (8). But this time, instead of aiming directly for the conclusion, we branch off by temporarily supposing the exact opposite is true, i.e. we suppose (5). However, this supposition immediately leads to something that flatly contradicts an earlier claim. Hence the temporary supposition (5) has to be rejected. Therefore its denial (8) must be true after all.

The terse justification for the final step '(from 5–7 by RAA)' indicates that we have made a *reductio ad absurdum* inference, to use the traditional name – the supposition made for the sake of argument at (5) leads to absurdity at (7), so has to be rejected.

Note by the way that, in the indented part of the proof, we are working with our initial premisses plus the new temporary supposition all in play, assumptions which taken together are in fact inconsistent. By the end of the (short!) indented bit of the proof, we have exposed this inconsistency by showing that those assumptions together entail a contradiction. As we said back in §2.4, it is very important that we *can* in this way argue validly from inconsistent assumptions to expose their inconsistency.

(b)   Here is another quick example. Take the argument:

M   No girl likes any unreconstructed sexist; Caroline is a girl who likes anyone who likes her; Henry likes Caroline; hence Henry is not an unreconstructed sexist.

This is valid. Here is one way to see that it is, by using another reductio argument:

M′   (1) No girl likes any unreconstructed sexist.   (premiss)
     (2) Caroline is a girl who likes anyone who likes her.
                                                        (premiss)
     (3) Henry likes Caroline.   (premiss)
     (4) Caroline is a girl who likes Henry.   (from 2, 3)
     (5) Caroline is a girl.   (from 4)
     (6) Caroline likes Henry.   (from 4)
          Suppose temporarily, for the sake of argument,
     (7)   Henry is an unreconstructed sexist.   (supposition)
     (8)   No girl likes Henry.   (from 1, 7)
     (9)   Caroline does not like Henry.   (from 5, 8)
     (10)   Contradiction!   (from 6, 9)
          Our supposition leads to absurdity, hence
     (11) Henry is not an unreconstructed sexist.   (from 7–10 by RAA)

(c)   Let's now spell out the (RAA) principle invoked in these two proofs: the idea is surely a familiar one, even if we are now spelling it out more explicitly than you are used to seeing. We can put it like this:

> *Reductio ad absurdum*   If $A_1, A_2, \ldots, A_n$ (as background premisses) plus the temporary supposition S entail a contradiction, then $A_1, A_2, \ldots, A_n$ by themselves entail *not-S*.

Here, the 'A's and 'S' stand in for whole propositions; and entailing a contradiction is a matter of entailing some proposition C while also entailing its denial *not-C* (or equivalently, entailing the single proposition C *and not-C*).

It should be clear that the (RAA) principle is a good one. But it is worth spelling out carefully why it works:

Assume that the As plus S *do* entail a contradiction C *and not-C*. Now, whatever is entailed by truths must also be true (since entailment is truth-preserving). So suppose that the As plus S were all true together. Then C *and not-C* would have to be true too. But that's ruled out, as a contradiction can never be true. So the As plus S cannot all be true together.

Of course, just knowing that at least one of As plus S must be false doesn't tell us where to pin the blame! However, we *can* conclude this: in any situation in which the As *are* all true, the remaining proposition S must be the false one. Hence those propositions $A_1, A_2, \ldots, A_n$ entail *not-S*.

(Question: What happens when $n = 0$ and there are no background premisses?)

(d)   Reductio ad absurdum arguments are naturally called *indirect* arguments. We don't go straight from premisses to conclusion, but take a side step via some additional supposition which we temporarily add for the sake of argument and then eventually 'discharge'. (We have visually signalled the side step by indenting the column of argument to the right when we bring a new supposition into play, and going back left when the supposition is dropped again.)

As we will see later, there are other familiar kinds of indirect arguments. And to cover such indirect forms of reasoning, we will have to extend what we said before about cogent multi-step arguments. In particular, we must now permit steps which introduce new temporary suppositions 'for the sake of argument' (so long as they are clearly flagged). Then, as well as ordinary valid inference steps which depend on what we have previously established and/or some new assumption(s) currently in play, we will also allow inference steps like (RAA), which allow us to draw consequences when we have constructed appropriate 'subproofs' starting with temporary assumptions.

Our discussion in this section necessarily only gives a hint of what is to come: we will return to the topic of indirect arguments when we eventually start discussing formal 'natural deduction' proofs in Chapter 20. But it is worth noting one point straightaway. In an indirect argument, we make temporary assumptions or suppositions; and to *suppose* some proposition is true for the sake of argument is plainly not to *assert* its truth outright. Therefore propositions, the ingredients of arguments, do need to be distinguished from outright assertions. Propositions can be asserted, supposed, rejected, wondered about, and more.

4.6   Summary

To establish the validity of a perhaps unobvious inferential leap we can use deductively cogent multi-step arguments, i.e. proofs, filling in the gap between premisses and conclusion.

Simple, direct, proofs chain together inference steps that are valid – ideally, ones which are *obviously* valid – building up from the initial premisses to the desired conclusion, with each new step depending on what's gone before.

However, some common methods of proof like reductio ad absurdum are 'indirect', and involve making new temporary suppositions for the sake of argument, suppositions that are later discharged. (The availability of indirect modes of inference complicates the story about what makes for a deductively cogent multi-step argument; we return to this.)

37

Exercises 4

Which of the following arguments are valid? Where an argument is valid, sketch an informal proof. Some of the examples are enthymemes that need repair.

(1) Only logicians are good philosophers. No existentialists are logicians. Some existentialists are French philosophers. So, some French philosophers are not good philosophers.

(2) No philosopher is illogical. Jones keeps making argumentative mistakes. No logical person keeps making argumentative mistakes. All existentialists are philosophers. So, Jones is not an existentialist.

(3) No experienced person is incompetent. Jenkins is always blundering. No competent person is always blundering. So, Jenkins is inexperienced.

(4) Jane has a first cousin. Jane's father is an only child. So, if Jane's mother hasn't a sister, she has a brother.

(5) Every event is causally determined. No action should be punished if the agent isn't responsible for it. Agents are only responsible for actions they can avoid doing. Hence no action should be punished.

(6) Some chaotic attractors are not fractals. All Cantor sets are fractals. Hence some chaotic attractors are not Cantor sets.

(7) Something is an elementary particle only if it has no parts. Nothing which has no parts can disintegrate. An object that cannot be destroyed must continue to exist. So an elementary particle cannot cease to exist.

(8) Either the butler or the cook committed the murder. The victim died from poison if the cook was the murderer. The butler carried out the murder only if the victim was stabbed. The victim didn't die from poison. So, the victim was stabbed.

(9) Superman is none other than Clark Kent. The Superhero from Krypton is Superman. The Superhero from Krypton can fly. Hence Clark Kent can fly.

(10) Jack is useless at logic or he simply isn't ready for the exam. Either Jack will fail the exam or he is not useless at logic. Either it's wrong that he won't fail the exam or he is ready for it. So Jack will fail.

(11) Any elephant weighs more than any horse. Some horses weigh more than any donkey. Hence any elephant weighs more than any donkey.

(12) When I do an example without grumbling, it is one that I can understand. No easy logic example ever makes my head ache. This logic example is not arranged in regular order, like the examples I am used to. I can't understand these examples that are not arranged in regular order, like the examples I am used to. I never grumble at an example, unless it gives me a headache. So, this logic example is difficult.

Finally, an example that requires a minimal amount of arithmetical knowledge:

(13) $\sqrt{2}$ cannot be a rational number, i.e. a fraction. We can show this as follows. Suppose $\sqrt{2} = m/n$, where this fraction is in lowest terms. Then (i) $m^2 = 2n^2$, so m is even, and hence $m = 2k$. (ii) Then $n^2 = 2k^2$, so n is even, and hence m isn't (or else m/n wouldn't be in lowest term). Hence (iii) our supposition leads to contradiction.

Set this out as a line-by-line reductio proof more in the style of §4.5.

5 The counterexample method

Suppose we suspect that a particular one-step argument is invalid, but are unsure. If we can construct a multi-step argument from the given premisses to the claimed conclusion, relying on uncontentiously valid moves, then that settles it – the argument is valid after all. But what if we have tried to find such a proof and failed? What does that show? Maybe the argument *is* invalid. But maybe we have just not spotted a proof, and the argument is in fact valid. If failure to find a proof doesn't settle the matter one way or the other, how *can* we demonstrate that a dubious inference step really is invalid?

In this chapter we put together the invalidity principle (which we met in Chapter 2) and the observation that different arguments can depend on the same pattern of inference (as outlined in Chapter 3) to give us one method for showing that various invalid arguments are indeed deductively invalid.

5.1 'But you might as well argue . . . '

(a) In fact, we have already quietly used this method in passing in §4.4. We noted that the inference step in the mini-argument

A　　(1) All philosophers are logicians.
　　So (2) All logicians are philosophers.

is invalid. That should have been immediately clear. But, to press home the point, we remarked that you might as well argue

A′　　(1) All women are human beings.
　　So (2) All human beings are women.

What is the force of this brisk comparison? We can unpack it as follows:

> Argument **A′** has a true premiss and a false conclusion; hence by the invalidity principle of §2.3 it can't be valid. But the inferential move in argument **A** is no better. There is nothing to separate the cases. The arguments evidently share the same pattern of inference and stand or fall together as far as validity is concerned. Hence, **A** is invalid too.

And that's a simple illustration of the basic method we need. Roughly: to show an inference step is invalid, find an argument which relies on the same form of inference but which is clearly invalid by the invalidity principle.

(b)   We used the same method on a second example in §4.4. But let's next have a different illustration, this time revisiting an argument we met in §1.4:

> **B**   (1) Most Irish are Catholics.
> (2) Most Catholics oppose abortion on demand.
> So (3) At least some Irish oppose abortion on demand.

We persuaded ourselves that the inferential step here is invalid by imagining a situation in which its premises would be true and conclusion false. But equally, we could have brought out its invalidity by noting that you might as well argue

> **B′**   (1) Most chess grandmasters are men.
> (2) Most men are no good at chess.
> So (3) At least some chess grandmasters are no good at chess.

What is the force of the comparison this time?

> **B′**'s premises are true. Chess is still (at least at the top levels of play) a predominantly male activity, though one that few men are any good at. But **B′**'s conclusion is false. So **B′** is invalid by the invalidity principle. But the inferential move in argument **B** is no better. The arguments evidently stand or fall together as far as validity is concerned. Hence, **B** is invalid too.

(c)   There is nothing mysterious or difficult or even novel going on here. The 'But you might as well argue ...' technique for showing an inference step to be invalid is already noted and used by Aristotle, and we use it all the time in the everyday evaluation of arguments.

For example, some gossip says that Mrs Jones must be an alcoholic, because she has been seen going to the Cheapo Booze Emporium and everyone knows that is where the local alcoholics are to be found. You reply, 'But you might as well argue that Bernie Sanders is a Republican Senator, because he's been seen going into the Senate, and everyone knows that that's where the Republican Senators are to be found'. Which shows why the gossip's argument won't do.

5.2   The counterexample method, more carefully

(a)   Recall, however, a key point from §3.3. A pattern or form of inference F may be unreliable; yet it can still have some special instance which does happen to be valid (valid for some other reason than instantiating F). Hence we *can't* say, crudely, 'This inference I is an instance of the form F; but here's another instance J of the same form F which is plainly invalid. So I is invalid too.'

We therefore need to be a bit more careful in spelling out our 'counterexample method' for showing invalidity. The idea is this:

> *Stage 1*   Given a (one-step) argument whose validity is up for assessment, first locate a form of inference F which this argument is relying on, in the sense that F needs to be reliably truth-preserving if the inference in the argument is indeed to be valid.

> *Stage 2*   Show that this form of inference *F* is *not* a generally reliable one by finding a *counterexample*. In other words, find another argument having the same pattern of inference which is uncontroversially invalid, e.g. because it has actually true premisses and a false conclusion so we can apply the invalidity principle.

Note, by the way, that we do not here *require* a counterexample to be generated by the invalidity principle, i.e. to have actually true premisses and an actually false conclusion. Telling counterexamples don't *have* to be constructed from 'real life' situations. A merely imaginable but uncontroversially coherent counter-example will do just as well. Why? Because that's still enough to show that the inferential pattern in question is unreliable: it doesn't necessarily preserve truth in all possible situations. However, using 'real life' counterexamples does often have the great advantage that you don't get into any disputes about what is coherently imaginable.

(b)   In using this method for showing that a given argument is invalid, every-thing turns on picking out at Stage 1 a form of inference *F* which the challenged argument really does require to be reliable.

Often that is very easy to do. Take our initial example **A**: 'All philosophers are logicians. So all logicians are philosophers.' What form of inference move can this argument possibly be relying on, other than *All G are H; so all H are G*? And, as we saw, it is trivial to come up with a counterexample to the general reliability of *this* form of inference. Similarly for our second example **B**: 'Most Irish are Catholics. Most Catholics oppose abortion. So at least some Irish oppose abortion.' What form of inference can that argument be relying on, other than *Most G are H; most H are K; so at least some G are K*? Again, it is trivial to come up with a counterexample to the validity of that form of inference too.

Other cases, however, can be more problematic. Someone proposes an argu-ment. You challenge it by replying 'But you might as well argue …' (advancing a seemingly parallel but patently invalid argument). The proponent of the chal-lenged argument then seeks to show that your supposed counterexample isn't a fair one – the original argument didn't actually depend on the form of inference *F* you supposed. With arguments served up in ordinary prose, this might not be easy to settle. But, at the very least, challenge-by-apparent-counterexample will force the proponent of an argument to clarify what is supposed to be going on, to make it plain what principle of inference *is* being relied on.

5.3   A 'quantifier shift' fallacy

(a)   Let's have an example to illustrate the last point. Consider the following quotation (in fact, the opening words of Aristotle's *Nicomachean Ethics*):

> Every art and every inquiry, and similarly every action and pursuit, is thought to aim at some good; and for this reason the good has rightly been declared to be that at which all things aim.

At first sight, there is an argument here with this initial premiss:

C   (1) Every practice aims at some good.

And then a conclusion is drawn (note the inference marker 'for this reason'). An unkind reader might gloss the conclusion as:

So (2) There is some good ('*the* good') at which all practices aim.

This argument then has a very embarrassing similarity to the following one:

C′   (1) Every assassin's bullet is aimed at some victim.
      So (2) There is some victim at whom every assassin's bullet is aimed.

But every assassin's bullet has its target (let's suppose), without there being a single target shared by them all. Likewise, every practice may aim at some good end or other without there being a single good which encompasses them all.

Drawing out some logical structure, argument **C** relies on the inference form

Every F is R to some G
So: There is some G such that every F is R to it.

and then **C′** is a counterexample to the reliability of that form of inference.

(b)   Did Aristotle really use an argument relying on that disastrous form of inference? We have ripped the quotation from the *Ethics* out of all context, so there is room for debate about what his intended argument really is. We can't enter into such debates here. Still, anyone who wants to defend Aristotle must at least meet the challenge of saying why the supposed counterexample fails to make the case, and must tell us what principle of inference really is being used in his intended argument here. If Aristotle isn't to be interpreted as using a fallacious form of inference as in **C**, then what *is* he up to?

The same goes, to repeat, for other challenges by the counterexample method. Given an argument in a text apparently relying on some identified pattern of inference, finding a counterexample to the deductive reliability of that pattern delivers a potentially fatal blow. If you want to defend the author, then your only hope is to show that the text has been misunderstood and/or the relevant inference step mis-identified.

(c)   Expressions like 'every' and 'some' are standardly termed *quantifiers* by linguists and logicians (see Chapter 26): what we have just noted is that we cannot always shift around the order of quantifiers in a proposition.

It is perhaps worth briskly noting in passing that a number of naive arguments for the existence of God commit the same apparently tempting *quantifier shift fallacy*, using the same bad form of inference. Consider, for example,

D   (1) Every ecological system has an intelligent designer,
      So (2) There is some intelligent designer (God) who designed every ecological system.

Premiss (1) was exploded by Darwin; but forget that. The point we want to make now is that even if you grant (1), that does not establish (2). There may, consistently with the premiss, be no one Master Designer of all the ecosystems

– rather each system could be produced by a different designer. (No respectable philosopher of religion uses the rotten argument **D** as it stands; but you need to appreciate the fallacy in the naive argument here to see why serious versions of design arguments for God have to try a great deal harder!)

5.4 Summary

To use the counterexample strategy to prove that a target argument is invalid, (1) find a pattern of inference that the argument is depending on, and (2) then show that the pattern is not a reliable one by finding a counterexample to its reliability, i.e. find an argument exemplifying this pattern which has (or evidently could have) true premises and a false conclusion.

This method is familiar in the everyday evaluation of arguments as the 'But you might as well argue ...' gambit.

We used the counterexample strategy to show, in particular, that a certain (occasionally tempting?) quantifier shift fallacy is indeed a fallacy.

Exercises 5

An initial group of examples. Some of the following arguments are invalid. Which? Why?

(1) Many great pianists admire Glenn Gould. Few, if any, unmusical people admire Glenn Gould. So few, if any, great pianists are unmusical.

(2) Everyone who admires Bach loves the *Goldberg Variations*; some who admire Chopin do not love the *Goldberg Variations*; so some admirers of Chopin do not admire Bach.

(3) Some hikers are birdwatchers. All birdwatchers carry binoculars. Some who carry binoculars carry cameras too. So some hikers carry cameras.

(4) Anyone who is good at logic is good at assessing philosophical arguments. Anyone who is mathematically competent is good at logic. Anyone who is good at assessing philosophical arguments admires Bertrand Russell. Hence no one who admires Bertrand Russell lacks mathematical competence.

(5) Everyone who is not a fool can do logic. No fools are fit to serve on a jury. None of your cousins can do logic. Therefore none of your cousins is fit to serve on a jury.

(6) Most logicians are philosophers; few philosophers are unwise; so at least some logicians are wise.

(7) All logicians are rational; no existentialists are logicians; so if Sartre is an existentialist, he isn't rational.

(8) If Sartre is an existentialist, he isn't a logician. If Sartre isn't a logician, he isn't good at reasoning. So if Sartre is good at reasoning, he isn't an existentialist.

6 Logical validity

We now introduce a narrower notion of validity, namely (so-called) *logical* validity. All logically valid arguments are deductively valid in the sense of §2.1, but not vice versa.

Our discussion here will continue to be quite informal. But it will provide a useful stepping stone along the way to defining some more formal, precise notions of particular kinds of logical validity that will in fact be our topic in the rest of this book.

6.1 Topic-neutrality

Start by considering the following one-premiss arguments: are they valid?

A   (1) Jill is a mother.
    So (2) Jill is a parent.

B   (1) Jack has a first cousin.
    So (2) At least one of Jack's parents is not an only child.

C   (1) Jack is a bachelor.
    So (2) Jack is unmarried.

In any possible situation in which Jill is a mother, she must have a child, i.e. be a parent. In any situation in which Jack has a first cousin (where a first cousin is a child of one of his aunts or uncles) he must have or have had an aunt or uncle, so his parents cannot both have been only children. Necessarily, if Jack is a bachelor, he is unmarried. So these arguments all involve deductively valid inference steps, according to our characterization of validity in §2.1.

In each of these cases, we can again abstract from some of the details, and see the argument as an instance of a schema all of whose other instances are valid too. For plainly, our arguments are not made valid by something peculiar to Jill or Jack; rather, what matters are the concepts of a mother, a first cousin, a bachelor. Therefore any inference of the following kinds is valid:

> *n is a mother*
> *So: n is parent*
>
> *n has a first cousin*
> *So: n's parents are not both only children*

n is a bachelor
So: n is unmarried.

So these are further examples of reliable principles of inference. But these principles are evidently less abstract than those we have highlighted previously.

Here is a – rather loose – definition:

> Vocabulary like 'all' and 'some', 'and' and 'or', 'not' and 'if' etc. (plus the likes of 'is', 'are') – vocabulary which doesn't refer to specific things or properties or relations, etc., but which is useful in discussing any topic – is *topic-neutral.*

The schemas we used in earlier chapters to display some inferential patterns involved only schematic variables and topic-neutral vocabulary. By contrast, the new schemas we have just introduced involve concepts which belong to more specific areas of interest – these first examples in fact all concern familial relations. The new patterns of inference are none the worse for that; their instances are perfectly good valid inferences by our informal definition in §2.1. But their validity does not rely merely on the distribution of topic-neutral vocabulary in the premises and conclusions.

Let's add a few similar examples:

D   (1) Cambridge is north of Oxford.
   So (2) Oxford is south of Cambridge.

E   (1) Siena is in Tuscany,
      (2) Tuscany is in Italy,
   So (3) Siena is in Italy.

F   (1) Kermit is green.
   So (2) Kermit is chromatically coloured.

The inference steps here are also all valid. We can again abstract to get shareable principles of inference that can recur in other arguments. But again, the schemas revealing these shareable principles will involve concepts which aren't topic-neutral (for example, the related concepts of *north of* and *south of*).

6.2   Logical validity, at last

(a)   Having noted that there are arguments whose deductive validity depends on features of special-interest concepts such as those to do with family connections or geographical relations etc., we will now put them aside. Throughout this book, we will be concentrating on the kinds of valid arguments illustrated in our earlier examples – i.e. arguments whose load-bearing principles of inference can be laid out using only topic-neutral notions. Such arguments involve patterns of reasoning that can be used when talking about any subject matter at all. And these universally applicable patterns of reasoning are the special concern of logic as a discipline (yet another idea that goes back to Aristotle).

(b)   It is useful to have some terminology to mark off these core cases of valid arguments which rely on topic-neutral principles of inference. Acknowledging the traditional focus of logic, we will say:

> An inference step is *logically valid* if and only if it is deductively valid in virtue of the way that topic-neutral notions occur in the premisses and conclusion.
>
> We likewise say that some premisses *logically entail* a certain conclusion if the inference from the premisses to the conclusion is logically valid.

Let a *purely logical schema* be one involving only schematic variables and topic-neutral vocabulary. (For convenience, we will allow limiting cases such as '*A, so A*', which is a schema built just from variables. We will also allow limiting cases like '*There is something; so there is not nothing*' which lacks variables and only features topic-neutral vocabulary; this can count as a purely logical schema whose only instance is itself.) Then we can equivalently say: a logically valid inference is an instance of a purely logical schema all of whose instances are necessarily truth-preserving.

In this usage, the inferences in arguments **A** to **F** in this chapter, although deductively valid in our original sense, do not count as *logically* valid. Contrast our bold-labelled examples of valid arguments in earlier chapters; apart from one possible exception to which we return in a moment, those *are* logically valid.

(c)   How can we show that an unobviously valid inference is logically valid? By a suitable proof, of course – meaning a proof where the pattern of inference used at each step can be displayed using a purely logical schema. See for example our fully annotated proof labelled **D′** in §4.2: by inspection, this not only shows that the inference from the initial premisses to the final conclusion is deductively valid but also that it is, more specifically, logically valid.

How can we demonstrate that an argument is *not* logically valid? If we can show that the argument is not deductively valid (by a counterexample, say), then that settles the question. But this point won't help us assess an example like the Kermit argument which *is* deductively valid. However, in the case of that argument, we can note that the most structure we can expose with a purely logical schema is *n is F, So n is G*; and *that* is not a reliable pattern of inference! So the Kermit argument is indeed not *logically* valid. Similar reasoning can be used in many other cases.

(d)   Our wider concept of *deductive validity* as defined in §2.1 and our new narrower concept of *logical validity* are both standard, and the distinction between the two has a long history. For example, the medieval logician John Buridan similarly distinguishes between what he would call a *consequence* (a necessarily truth-preserving inference) and a *formal consequence* (meaning an inference which is necessarily truth-preserving just in virtue of its form – where he thinks of form narrowly, in terms of the distribution of logical words like 'and' and 'or', 'some' and 'all'). Most logicians use *logical consequence* to mean what Buridan does by formal consequence.

Note, however, that the *labels* attached to the wider and narrower concepts of validity by different writers vary. In particular, those writers who foreground just one of these two concepts will tend to call that one, whichever it is, simply 'validity' (unqualified). So care is needed when comparing different textbook treatments.

6.3   Logical necessity

We say that an inference step is logically valid if and only if it is necessarily truth-preserving in virtue of how topic-neutral logical notions feature in its premisses and conclusion. Similarly, we will say:

> A proposition is *a logically necessary truth* (or more simply, is *logically necessary*) if and only if it is necessarily true in virtue of how topic-neutral notions feature in it.

So compare *Whatever is green is coloured* with *Whatever is both green and square is green*. The first proposition is true of every possible situation, so is necessarily true in the sense of §2.1(d). But it is not *logically* necessary in our sense, for its truth depends on the internal connection between being green and being coloured. But the second proposition is an example of the schematic pattern 'Whatever is F and G is F', any of whose instances has to be true just in virtue of the meanings of the topic-neutral logical notions 'whatever', 'is', and 'and'. For that reason, the second proposition is said to be *logically* necessary.

Generalizing, a logically necessary truth will be an instance of a type of proposition which can be specified by a purely logical schema using just schematic variables and topic-neutral vocabulary, where all of the instances of that schema are necessarily true.

As noted back in §2.1, the notions of deductive validity and necessary truth are tied tightly together. Thus, the single-premiss inference *A, so C* is valid if and only if it is necessarily true that *if A, then C*. We should now remark that, exactly similarly, the notions of logical validity and logical necessity also fit tightly together: *A, so C* is logically valid if and only if it is logically necessary that *if A, then C*.

6.4   The boundaries of logical validity?

We can say, in a summary slogan, that an argument is logically valid just if it is valid in virtue of its topic-neutral form.

But, on second thoughts, how secure is our grasp on the notion of topic-neutrality here? We started making a list of topic-neutral vocabulary like 'all' and 'some', 'and' and 'or', etc.; but exactly how do we continue the list, and where do we stop?

It in fact isn't entirely obvious what is to count as suitably topic-neutral vocabulary (without going into details, there are various stories on the market, but no agreed one). Hence it is not obvious what counts as a purely logical, topic-neutral, schema in our sense. Hence it is not obvious either just what will count as a *logically* valid inference, valid in virtue of its form as captured by a purely logical schema.

Here's a case to think about. Take the argument

G   (1) Bill is taller than Chelsea,
   (2) Chelsea is taller than Hillary,
So (3) Bill is taller than Hillary.

This is valid, and our first attempt at exposing a relevant general pattern of inference here might be

> *m is taller than n*
> *n is taller than o*
> *So: m is taller than o.*

And this isn't a purely logical, topic-neutral, schema.

But hold on! Can't we expose some more abstract inferential structure here? – like this, perhaps:

> *m is F-er than n*
> *n is F-er than o*
> *So: m is F-er than o.*

Here *is F-er than* is the comparative of *F* (in other words, it is equivalent to *is more F than*). And *this* pattern of valid inference using the comparative-forming construction arguably *is* topic-neutral and so purely logical.

But hold on again! We in fact can only talk of one thing being more *F* than another thing, when *F* stands in for the kind of property that comes in degrees, as in *tall, wise, heavy, dark, flat*, etc. But we can't take comparatives of other properties like *even* and *prime* (of numbers), *dead* (of people), *valid* (of arguments), and so on. So arguably the comparative construction *is* ... *-er than* is not an entirely topic-neutral device after all: it depends on what we apply it to whether it makes sense.

So is our last schema fully topic-neutral or not? We can't pursue this issue further here; we will have to leave the question hanging, and so leave it unsettled whether **G** counts as *logically* valid. We will similarly leave it unsettled whether the deductively valid 'Everyone loves a lover' argument **B** in §4.1 also counts as *logically* valid (that will depend on how you think of the link between 'is a lover' and 'loves someone').

Fortunately, that's no problem. We just don't need to worry about the outer boundaries of the notion of logical validity: our concern will only be with some clear central cases. We will be considering various ways in which validity can depend on limited selections of quite uncontroversially topic-neutral vocabulary like 'all' and 'some', 'and' and 'or', etc. And *these* cases will be absolutely clear examples of logical validity. Likewise, we will be focussing on clear central cases of logical necessity. Much more on this in due course, starting in real earnest in Chapters 14 and 15.

6.5 Definitions of validity as rational reconstructions

How well does the definition of logical validity in §6.2(b) tally with our initial hunches about what counts as a completely watertight, absolutely compelling inference step that depends on topic-neutral logical notions?

There are a number of potential issues here (apart from the question about what exactly counts as 'topic-neutral'). Let's focus on just one central issue. In fact, we could have raised this same issue about our earlier definition of the wider notion of deductive validity back in §2.1; but it would have been far too distracting to mention it there, right at the very beginning.

To bring out the worry, consider the following argument:

H   Jack is married. Jack is not married. So the world will end tomorrow!

Plainly, just in virtue of the role of 'not' here, there is no possible situation in which the premises of this argument are true together (being married and being not married rule each other out). Hence there is no possible situation in which the premises of this argument are true together and the conclusion is false. Hence, applying our definition, the inference step in **H** counts as logically valid (as is any inference of the form *A, not-A, so C*, for any propositions *A* and *C*). Which might well seem a *very* unwelcome verdict. How can we think of this inference as compelling, as 'necessarily truth-preserving'?

There are two possible lines of response. The first runs like this:

Recall Aristotle's appealing definition of a correct deduction as one whose conclusion "results of necessity" from the premises. And surely the conclusion of any compelling deduction should have *something* to do with the premises: so how could some claim about the end of the world really follow from propositions about Jack's marital status? Argument **H** commits a gross fallacy of irrelevance.

Our definition of deductive validity in §2.1(a), and our derived definition of the narrower notion of logical validity in §6.2(b), therefore both overshoot – they count too many inferences as logically cogent. So, the definitions need to be revised: they need to be tightened up by introducing some kind of relevance-requirement in order to rule out such daft examples as the apocalyptic **H** counting as 'valid'. Back to the drawing board!

The trouble is that when we get back to the drawing board, we find it is very difficult to respect the hunch that **H** is not a cogent argument without offending against *other*, equally basic, intuitions (see §20.9). And this prompts a different response to that initially unwelcome implication of our definition of validity:

Arguably, *no* crisp definition of deductive validity (or of the special case of logical validity) can be made to fit all our untutored hunches about what is and what isn't an absolutely compelling inference. The aim of definitions of validity, then, is to give tidy 'rational reconstructions' of our everyday concepts which at least smoothly capture the uncontroversial core cases. The classical definitions of the notions of deductive and logical validity do this very neatly and naturally.

True, we do get some odd results like the verdict on **H**. But this is a small price to pay when tidying up the notion of validity. After all, **H**'s premisses can never be true together; so we can't ever *use* this type of officially valid inference step to establish the irrelevant conclusion as true (it is, as we might put it, only 'vacuously' truth-preserving because there can be no truth in the premisses together to preserve). Our definition therefore sanctions an entirely harmless extension of the intuitive idea of an absolutely compelling inference step. Similarly (we hope!) we can live with a few other initially odd-looking implications of our classical definitions.

So which line shall we take? Shall we revise our definitions of deductive and logical validity, or swallow their initially unwelcome consequences?

We will take the second line (and this is very much the majority response among modern logicians). Later we will define technical notions of validity like Chapter 15's 'tautological validity'; these definitions will similarly count arguments like **H** as valid. Again, we will take the majority line that it is worth paying this price to get otherwise neat and natural notions into play.

It is important to emphasize that official definitions of logical notions are quite typically arrived at on the basis of cost-benefit assessments like this; we will meet other examples later. The best logical theory isn't handed down, once and for all, on tablets of stone. We repeatedly have to balance, say, a certain natural simplicity or smoothness of theory over here against a corresponding artificiality over there. And the best choices for definitions, i.e. the best choices for rational reconstructions of informally messy ideas, can depend on our particular theoretical priorities in a given context.

6.6 Summary

Vocabulary like 'all' and 'some', 'and' and 'or', etc. (plus the likes of 'is' and 'are'), not about particular things or properties, but useful in discussing any topic, is said to be topic-neutral.

A purely logical schema is one involving only schematic variables and topic-neutral vocabulary.

A logically valid inference is an instance of a purely logical schema all of whose instances are necessarily truth-preserving.

A logically necessary proposition is an instance of a purely logical schema all of whose instances are necessarily true.

It isn't altogether clear what counts as topic-neutral vocabulary, so it is not clear either where to draw the boundaries of logical validity.

Exercises 6

(a)   Which of the following arguments are deductively valid? Which are logically valid? (Defend your answers, as best you can.)

(1)   Only logicians are wise. Some philosophers are not logicians. All who love Aristotle are wise. Hence some of those who don't love Aristotle are still philosophers.

(2)   The Battle of Hastings happened before the Battle of Waterloo. The Battle of Marathon happened before the Battle of Hastings. Hence the Battle of Marathon happened before the Battle of Waterloo.

(3)   Jane is no taller than Jill, Jill is no taller than Jo, Jo is no taller than Jane. So Jane, Jill, and Jo are the same height.

(4)   Jane is taller than Jill, Jill is taller than Jo, Jo is taller than Jane. So Jane, Jill, and Jo are the same height.

(5)   Someone loves Alex, but Alex loves no one. The person who loves Dr Jones, if anyone does, is Dr Jones. So Alex isn't Dr Jones.

(6)   Whoever respects Socrates respects Plato too. All who respect Euclid respect Aristotle. No one who respects Plato respects Aristotle. Therefore Jo respects Euclid if she doesn't respect Socrates.

(7)   Jill is a good logician only if she admires either Gödel or Gentzen. Jill admires Gödel only if she understands his incompleteness theorem. Whoever admires Gentzen must understand his proof of the consistency of arithmetic. No one can understand Gentzen's proof of the consistency of arithmetic without also understanding Gödel's incompleteness theorem. So if Jill is a good logician, then she understands Gödel's incompleteness theorem.

(8)   All the Brontë sisters supported one another. The Brontë sisters were Anne, Charlotte, and Emily. Hence Anne, Charlotte, and Emily supported one another.

(9)   There are exactly two logicians at the party. There is just one literary theorist at the party. No logician is a literary theorist. Therefore, of the party-goers, there are exactly three who are either logicians or literary theorists.

(10)   There are no unicorns. Hence the set of unicorns is the empty set.

(11)   There is water in the cup. Hence there is liquid H_2O in the cup.

(12)   Necessarily, water is H_2O. Hence it is not possible that water isn't H_2O.

(13)   It is possible that it is cold. It is possible that it is rainy. Hence it is possible that it is cold and rainy.

(14)   This argument is valid. Hence this argument is invalid.

(b)   'We can treat an argument like "Jill is a mother; so, Jill is a parent" as having a suppressed premiss: in fact, the underlying argument here is the *logically* valid "Jill is a mother; all mothers are parents; so, Jill is a parent". Similarly for the other examples given of arguments that are supposedly deductively valid but not logically valid; they are all enthymemes, logically valid arguments with suppressed premisses. The notion of a logically valid argument is all we need.' Is that right?

7 Propositions and forms

One last general topic before we get down to formal business. *Propositions* – the ingredients of arguments – are, we said, the sort of thing that can be true or false (as opposed to commands, questions, etc.). But what is their nature?

7.1 Types vs tokens

We begin with two sections introducing relevant distinctions. Firstly, we want the distinction between *types* and *tokens*. This is best introduced via a simple example.

Suppose then that you and I take a piece of paper each, and boldly write 'Logic is fun!' a few times in the centre. So we produce a number of different physical inscriptions – perhaps yours are rather large and in blue ink, mine are smaller and in black pencil. Now we key the same encouraging motto into our laptops, and print out the results: we get more physical inscriptions, first some formed from pixels on our screens and then some formed from printer ink.

How many different sentences are there here? We can say: many, some in ink, some in pencil, some in pixels, etc. Equally, we can say: there is one sentence here, multiply instantiated. Evidently, we must distinguish the many different sentence-instances or sentence *tokens* – physically constituted in various ways, of different sizes, lasting for different lengths of time, etc. – from the one sentential form or sentence *type* which they are all instances of.

We can of course similarly distinguish word tokens from word types, and distinguish book tokens – e.g. printed copies – from book types (compare the questions 'How many books has J. K. Rowling sold?' and 'How many books has J. K. Rowling written?').

What makes a physical sentence a token of a particular type? And what exactly is the metaphysical status of types? Tough questions that we can't answer here! But it is very widely agreed that we need *some* type/token distinction, however it is to be elaborated.

7.2 Sense vs tone

Next, we will say that the *sense* of a sentence – or at least the sense of a sentence apt for propositional use in stating a premiss or conclusion – is that aspect or ingredient of its meaning that is relevant to questions of truth or falsity. This use of 'sense' is due to the great nineteenth-century German logician Gottlob Frege (translating his 'Sinn').

In other words, *the sense of a sentence fixes the condition under which it is true*. Distinguish this from the 'colouring' or 'flavour' or *tone* which the choice of different words might give a sentence.

For example, if I refer to a particular woman as 'Lizzie' rather than 'Elizabeth', the familiar tone may reflect my closeness (or my lack of respect). Similarly, to adapt an example of Frege's, whether I refer to her mount as a 'horse' or 'steed' or 'nag' or 'gee-gee' may reflect how I regard the beast (or depend on whether I'm talking to a child). But these differences of tone need not affect the truth or falsity of 'Elizabeth's/Lizzie's horse/steed/nag/gee-gee is black' – the various permutations can have the same truth-relevant sense and be true in just the same worldly situations. Or at least, so goes a very natural story. And we don't have to buy any particular theory about sense to acknowledge that we do need to make *some* such distinction between core factual meaning and its embellishments.

Now, as far as logic is concerned, questions of colouring or tone aren't going to matter – those aspects of the overall meaning of claims don't affect their logical properties. What matters for validity is preservation of unvarnished truth. So it is the *sense* of interpreted sentences that we will care about.

7.3 Are propositions sentences?

Return, then, to the question we posed at the beginning of the chapter. What is a proposition? Here is one initially appealing view:

> Propositions – potential premises and conclusions and the bearers of truth and falsity – are *declarative sentences* (i.e. sentences like 'Jack kicks the ball' as opposed to interrogatives like 'Does Jack kick the ball?' or imperatives like 'Jack, kick the ball!').

But having made the type/token distinction, how are we now to gloss this seemingly straightforward suggestion?

(a)   Harry and Hermione are taking a logic course. As they read the first chapter of their respective copies of this book, they meet different *tokens* of the types

> All philosophers are eccentric. Jack is a philosopher. So Jack is eccentric.

But it seems very odd to say that Harry and Hermione are thereby tangling with different *arguments*. It is surely the very same argument, with the same premises and conclusion, which they both encounter and both get to think about.

Generalizing, we surely want to say that the same argument can appear in the many different printed copies of this book, and in the e-copies too. So it seems that we naturally think of arguments as types which can have many instances, rather than as tokens. And what goes for arguments then goes for the constituent propositions which are their premises and conclusions.

53

Hence, the view that propositions are declarative sentences seems to be more naturally glossed as claiming that propositions are sentence *types*.

(b)   But, even with that clarification, a naive identification of propositions with declarative sentences won't do as it stands. Here are some problems:

(1)   Don't some grammatically acceptable declarative sentences lack sense? Take, for example, 'Purple prime numbers sleep furiously' (it is arguably just nonsense to talk of numbers as either coloured or sleeping, and also nonsense to talk of sleeping furiously). And it seems wrong to say that a senseless sentence can be an ingredient of a real argument, i.e. can be a contentful proposition.

(2)   Other grammatical sentences have too many senses. Take, for example, 'Visiting relatives can be boring'. This sentence can say two different things, one of which may be true and the other false: so, same sentence, different truth-evaluable messages conveyed, hence – it seems natural to say – different possible ingredients of arguments, different propositions.

(3)   The converse situation to (2): different sentences can surely express the same premisses/conclusions. Adopting an example of Frege's, consider the arguments 'The Greeks defeated the Persians at Plataea. So the Persians were defeated at least once' and 'The Persians were defeated by the Greeks at Plataea. So the Persians were defeated at least once.' Aren't these the same argument, with the active and passive versions of the premiss just stylistic variants expressing the same thought? Or take the arguments 'Jack is both tall and slim. So, Jack is tall' and 'Jack is tall and is slim. So, he is tall.' These strictly speaking involve distinct pairs of sentences; yet again it seems odd to say that the minor stylistic variation gives us different arguments.

(4)   We may use a sentence like 'He is tall' in framing an argument, as we've just done. But this sort of sentence has – as it were – an incomplete sense, i.e. it won't by itself express a determinate proposition which can be a premiss or conclusion. We need context to fix who is being referred to.

In sum, the same declarative sentences can be used to express different arguments, and different sentences can be used to express the same arguments. And context can matter. So we can't *simply* identify propositions, the ingredients of arguments, with declarative sentences.

Still, we can perhaps work around these initial difficulties for the sentential view of propositions by adding some qualifications (see §7.5). But there is a more radical problem which we have saved for last. In (3) we suggested that sentences which are stylistic variations of each other can express the same premiss or conclusion. But can't sentences that are *entirely* different also count as expressing the same proposition?

(5)   Surely the very same argument can be discussed by Aristotle, by medieval logicians, and then by Frege. And the very same argument can

now appear both in this book and in its Italian translation, with the same premises and conclusions again expressed by *entirely* different sentences. So what makes this the same argument all along, it now can seem natural to claim, has to be what is said rather than how it is said – i.e. must be the *messages expressed*, whether in Greek, Latin, German, English, or Italian.

7.4 Are propositions truth-relevant contents?

Considerations like those we have just been discussing seem, then, to push us towards a second view, along the following lines:

> Propositions, potential premises and conclusions and the bearers of truth and falsity, are not declarative sentences but rather the *messages* that declarative sentences can be used, in context, to express.

Some would talk of 'thoughts' rather than 'messages' as what are expressed by declarative sentences – meaning possible thought-contents as opposed to acts of thinking. And some talk just of 'contents'. So the idea is that a proposition is something language-independent, a content that can be shared by sentences in different languages which have the same sense.

(An annoying terminological aside. We have from the outset been using the word 'proposition' in a non-committal, theory-neutral, way – leaving it as an open question what propositions are. Confusingly, many philosophers instead use 'proposition' quite specifically to refer to these putative truth-relevant thought-contents that can be expressed by sentences in various languages. Though just to complicate things further, many medieval logicians and those modern writers most influenced by them use 'proposition' in exactly the opposite way, specifically to refer to declarative sentences themselves. Sorry about that! – you just have to be alert when reading other authors.)

Whatever the terminology, however, the trouble with our second view about the bearers of truth and falsity is that it tells us what premises and conclusions are *not* – they aren't sentences – but their positive nature is now quite mysterious. In fact it is entirely unclear what kind of theory to offer about messages or contents when thought of as language-independent. We can't stop to review a hundred years of arguments about this: let's just say that no particular attempt to give a theory of propositions-as-contents has ever commanded very wide support.

7.5 Why we can be indecisive

(a) So maybe we should after all try to rescue the less puzzling first view – propositions are sentences – by fine-tuning it. Consider, then, the revised suggestion that propositions are *fully interpreted* declarative sentences – i.e. they are disambiguated sentences parsed as having one determinate sense, with context supplying the references of pronouns etc. Then we may equate 'Jack is tall' and 'he is tall' when the pronoun refers to Jack; and we can perhaps also allow minor grammatical massaging, e.g. equating active and passive versions of the same sentence. In this way, we might hope to deal with difficulties (1) to (4). On the other hand, we can and should perhaps just bite the bullet, and respond to (5) by insisting that the premisses and conclusions of an argument in this book and the corresponding premisses and conclusions in its Italian translation are *not* strictly speaking the same after all, because the sentences are quite different – rather, there will be two distinct arguments which are more or less smooth translations of each other.

How, though, are we to nail down some version of this revised suggestion, based on the idea that propositions are fully interpreted sentences (allowing for minor grammatical variations)?

(b) We will have to leave that question hanging. Having flagged up two different ways of thinking about propositions – as sentences and as contents – we aren't going to develop either approach any further, let alone decide between them.

Now, sitting on the fence about the nature of ordinary propositions, i.e. about the nature of premisses and conclusions in everyday arguments, may sound irresponsible; how can we possibly leave unresolved such a very basic question as *what are arguments made of?* For our purposes in this book, however, it turns out that we happily won't need to adjudicate this tricky issue in 'philosophical logic'. Why so? Because – spoiler alert! – our key technique for assessing everyday arguments will involve (a) rendering them into artificial formalized languages, and then concentrating our logical efforts on (b) assessing arguments once tidily formalized. Stage (a) won't require us to say that the formal versions are the very same arguments, just that they are close-enough translations. And crucially, *the sentences of our artificial formalized languages explored at stage (b) will by design be free of ambiguities and context dependence* – they will come already fully interpreted, stipulated to have a determinate sense. This means that formalized sentence types and the messages they convey will be neatly aligned, and for our purposes we needn't fuss too much about distinguishing them.

Hence, in sum, it will do our project no harm to take arguments framed in *formalized* languages to be simply made up of formal sentences.

7.6 Forms of inference again

(a) We have just asked how we should think of the premisses and conclusions of everyday arguments: are they sentences or are they the messages expressed by sentences (i.e. thought-contents)? We can now raise a related issue: when we talk about forms of inference in everyday arguments, are we referring to patterns to be found at the surface level of the sentences used to state the argument, or should we primarily be thinking of patterns at the level of messages expressed (whatever exactly that means)?

In fact, we have been cheerfully casual about this. On the one hand, we have discussed patterns of inference to be found in arguments couched in English by using schemas in which we are to systematically substitute English expressions for the schematic variables – allowing for some grammatical tidying. Which chimes with the policy of thinking of the ingredients of arguments as sentences, and with thinking of patterns of inference as patterns to be found on the surface, at sentence level.

On the other hand, when we laboriously stated in words the principles underlying our first couple of examples of reliable inference schemas (in §1.5 and §3.1), we found ourselves talking about what premisses and conclusions *say*, and this looks to be at the level of messages expressed. It is very natural to slide into this way of speaking. After all, weren't the great dead logicians – who were considering arguments couched in entirely different sentences from (say) Greek, Latin, or German – in some sense discussing the very same forms of inference that occur in our arguments couched in English?

(b)   Leaving aside arguments in other languages, the issue already arises within a single language. Take for example the argument

All dogs have four legs. Fido is a dog. Fido has four legs.

And now consider the variants with the alternative first premisses 'Every dog has four legs', 'Any dog has four legs', and 'Each dog has four legs'.

Thinking at the level of sentences, these four arguments exemplify different forms of inference, because they involve the distinct logical words 'all', 'every', 'any', and 'each'. However we might well be inclined to suppose that the differences in these cases are only superficial and that the underlying inferential structure is in some sense really the same. The respective first premisses of these arguments are just stylistically different ways of expressing the very same thought-content; and then the rest of the arguments are the same. It is tempting, then, to suppose that although these various versions may differ in surface sentential form, they in *some* way share the same underlying 'logical form' – so, thinking at the level of the messages expressed by the various sentences, the inferences are all instances of a single form.

We might even recruit the familiar schema '*All F are G, n is F, so n is G*' to represent this supposed underlying shared form. And in fact schemas are very often used in this way in philosophical writing, i.e. they are treated as fitting the surface form of arguments only quite loosely.

(c)   So which should it be, when thinking about the forms of inference in everyday arguments? Should we be looking for patterns at sentence level, or for underlying patterns in the messages expressed?

As we have seen, the second line can be tempting. But do we really understand what it comes to – for what kind of theory of the nature of messages would be needed for it to make sense? As we have already noted, there is no widely agreed account of propositions-as-messages that we can appeal to for help.

Fortunately, at an introductory level, it doesn't matter much whether we say that Aristotle was discussing the very same forms of argument as we might use, or whether we instead say that he was considering the Greek equivalents of our forms of argument. And much more importantly – another spoiler alert! – when we start to consider arguments regimented into formalized languages, things become very clean and simple. As we said, formal arguments can be thought of as made up of formal sentences; and then the inferential forms of such arguments can be understood quite unproblematically as formal patterns at the sentential level. More about this soon.

7.7 Summary

There are two main types of view on the nature of the propositions in ordinary arguments: they are sentences (perhaps fully interpreted sentence-types) or alternatively they are the messages or thought-contents that sentences can be used to express.

We need not adjudicate: our focus from now on will be on propositions in formalized arguments, and these can unproblematically be treated as sentences.

Likewise, there are differing views about what forms or patterns of inference are patterns in – sentences or messages? Again we do not need to adjudicate: our focus from now on will be on forms of inference in formalized arguments, and these can unproblematically be treated as patterns in the surface form of formal sentences.

Exercises 7

Consider the following exchange:

> Jack: Mary took her picnic to the bank.
> Jill: Mary took her picnic to the bank.

And assume that context makes it clear that Jack means *bank* in the sense of the river side, and Jill means *bank* in the sense of a financial institution.

In this particular exchange, then, we have instances of *one* sentence type (as identified by its surface form). These instances have *two* different senses (different truth-relevant literal meanings). And these instances are used to express *two* different messages or thoughts (or propositions, in one sense of that overused word).

There are potentially *eight* different kinds of exchanges between Jack and Jill with one utterance each as in our example; they can involve instances of one or two different sentence types, having one or two different senses (literal meanings), expressing one or two different messages or thoughts or propositions.

Give an example of each combination which is in fact possible.

Interlude: From informal to formal logic

(a) What have we done so far? In bare headlines,

We have explored, at least in an introductory way, the (classical) notion of a valid inference step, and the corresponding notions of a deductively valid/sound (one-step) argument.

We have seen how to distinguish deductive validity from other virtues that an argument might have (like being a highly reliable inductive argument).

We have noted how different arguments can share the same form of inference. And we have seen how to exploit this fact in using the counterexample method for demonstrating invalidity.

We have seen some simple examples of direct multi-step proofs, where we show that a conclusion really can be validly inferred from certain premisses by filling in the gap between premisses and conclusion with evidently valid intermediate inference steps. We in addition briefly looked at one kind of indirect method of proof, reductio ad absurdum.

We have also met the narrower notion of logical validity – where an inference step is valid in this narrower sense if it is deductively valid in virtue of the way that topic-neutral notions feature in the premisses and conclusion.

Along the way, we have had to quietly skate past a number of issues, leaving more needing to be said. But hopefully you will have gained at least a rough-and-ready preliminary understanding of some key logical concepts. And you need such an understanding if you are to see the *point* of the more formal investigations which follow.

(b) So what next? One good option would be to spend more time on techniques for teasing out the arguments involved in passages of extended prose argumentation, to develop further methods of informal argument analysis, explore how to reason with a range of key logical notions like 'if' and 'all', and then catalogue a variety of common ways in which everyday arguments can go wrong. This kind of study in *informal logic* (as it is often called) can be a highly profitable exercise.

But our focus in this book – as its title suggests! – will be rather different. Instead of going for breadth of coverage, we aim for depth; we will develop systematic and rigorous treatments for some highly important but limited classes of arguments. Moreover – and this is a crucial move – the arguments we focus on will be *formalized* arguments, framed in purpose-designed formalized languages. These formalized languages will be written in special symbols, but that is really just a convenience. The essential thing is that these artificial languages are governed by simple grammatical rules which fix which expressions are sentences and which aren't, and by simple semantic rules which fix sharp and unambiguous truth-conditions for those expressions which are sentences. This way we don't have to tangle with all the complexities of ordinary language. Rather, we can evaluate arguments after they have been rendered into a tidier shape, by translation into suitable formalized languages. More on this key policy decision very soon.

(c)   The resulting *first-order quantification theory* – the main branch of formal logic which we will eventually be introducing – is (as we said in the Preface) one of the great intellectual achievements of formally-minded philosophers and of philosophically-minded mathematicians. It is beautiful in itself, and it opens the door onto a very rich and fascinating field. (In this introductory book, there will only be very occasional glimpses further through that door; but we will at least get to the threshold.)

Quantification theory explores the logic of arguments involving *quantifiers* (expressions of generality like 'all', 'some', and 'none' etc.) and explains how these expressions interact with the so-called propositional or sentential *connectives* ('and', 'or', 'if', 'not'). It gives us a framework in which most, perhaps all, of the deductive reasoning needed in science and mathematics can be conducted. We will take things slowly, however. Before turning to the full theory, we are going to be spending a *lot* of time on the limited fragment of this logical system which deals just with the connectives: this is *propositional logic*.

Why so much effort exploring propositional logic? Because this makes for a relatively painless introduction to our subject, by allowing us to meet a whole range of basic ideas and strategies of formal logic in a very accessible context. This will very considerably ease the path into full quantification theory.

Let's get straight to work!

8 Three connectives

We start our more formal work by looking at length at a *very* restricted class of arguments, namely those whose relevant logical structure turns simply on the presence in premises and/or conclusions of 'and', 'or', and 'not' (used as so-called sentential or propositional connectives). We begin by explaining the great advantage of working in artificial formalized languages, even when exploring the logic of arguments relying on just these three sentential connectives.

8.1 Two simple arguments

We met the following trivially valid argument in the first chapter:

A (1) Either Jill is in the library or she is in the coffee bar.
   (2) Jill isn't in the library.
So (3) Jill is in the coffee bar.

We can represent this as having the form

> *Either A or B*
> *Not-A*
> *So: B.*

Here, the symbols '*A*', '*B*' stand in for suitable sentences, and – as we have already informally done in e.g. §2.1(d) and §4.5(c) – we are using '*not-A*' to indicate a sentence that expresses the denial of what '*A*' says (so is true just when *A* is false). Evidently, any inference of this form will be valid.

Here is another valid argument:

B (1) It's not the case that Jack played lots of football and also did well in his exams.
   (2) Jack played lots of football.
So (3) Jack did not do well in his exams.

This also instantiates a reliable pattern of inference, which we might represent:

> *Not-(A and B)*
> *A*
> *So: Not-B.*

Any inference of the same type will again be valid, this time just in virtue of the meaning of 'and' and the way denial works.

Why did we use brackets in representing the structure of **B**'s first premiss? Because we plainly need to distinguish between a claim of the form

$$Not\text{-}(A \text{ and } B)$$

which denies that A and B both hold together, and a claim of the form

$$(Not\text{-}A) \text{ and } B$$

which denies A, but then adds that B does hold. Suppose we put

A: The President will order an invasion.

B: There will be devastation.

Then the first schema yields the hopeful thought that we won't get an invasion with devastation; while the second schema yields the depressing claim that although the President will not order an invasion, there will still be devastation.

Arguments **A** and **B** are trite, but do illustrate a couple of types of inference whose validity depends on the distribution in the premises and conclusion of 'and', 'or', and 'not'. Our task is to explore such arguments more systematically.

8.2 'And'

(a) How does 'and' work in ordinary language? Note first that it can be used to conjoin a pair of matched expressions belonging to almost any grammatical category – as in 'Jack is fit and tanned', 'Jill won quickly and easily', 'Jack and Jill married', or 'Jo smoked and coughed', where 'and' conjoins pairs of adjectives, adverbs, proper names, and verbs. But leave aside all those uses, and consider only the cases where 'and' operates at sentence level, i.e. it acts as a *sentential connective* and joins two whole sentences to form a new one.

For example, take the sentences 'Lyon is in France' and 'Turin is in Italy'; we can conjoin them to get 'Lyon is in France and Turin is in Italy'. This resulting compound sentence is then true (or, if you prefer, expresses a truth) exactly when both of the constituent sentences are true, and it is false otherwise.

Let's use '$\diamond$' to stand in for some expression which works as a binary connective (i.e. one that connects two sentences to form another). Then we will say:

$A \diamond B$ is a *conjunction* of A and B just if $A \diamond B$ is true when both of A and B are true, and is false when at least one of A and B is false.

(b) In our sample sentence 'Lyon is in France and Turin is in Italy', the connective 'and' serves to form a conjunction in this sense. But English has other ways too of forming conjunctions. For note that 'Lyon is in France but Turin is in Italy' is also true just when Lyon is in France and Turin is in Italy. And more generally, pairs of claims of the form A *but* B and A *and* B do not differ in what it takes for them to be true. Rather, in the Fregean terms of §7.2, the sentences differ in colour or tone, not sense – the contrast between 'but' and the colourless 'and' is (*very* roughly) that A *but* B is typically used when the speaker takes it that there is some kind of contrast between the truth or the current relevance of A and of B.

So we can use 'but' to form conjunctions. And for other ways of forming conjunctions consider, for example, 'Lyon is in France, though Turin is in Italy', 'Paris is in France; moreover Lyon is in France too'.

(c)   You might wonder: doesn't *A and B* often express more than simply the joint truth of *A* and *B*? For example, compare

(1)   Eve became pregnant and she married Adam.
(2)   Eve married Adam and she became pregnant.

Using one of these sentences rather than the other would normally be taken as conveying a message about the temporal order of events. So does this show that 'and' in English sometimes signifies temporal succession as well as the truth of the conjoined sentences? Does 'and' sometimes mean the same as 'and then'?

It has often been claimed so. But compare the two mini-stories

(1′)   Eve became pregnant. She married Adam.
(2′)   Eve married Adam. She became pregnant.

The divergent implications of temporal succession surely *still* remain, because of our default narrative practice of telling a story in the order in which the events happened. Since the implications of temporal order remain even without the use of 'and', there is no compelling need to treat temporal succession as one possible meaning built into the connective. Perhaps even in (1) and (2) the role of 'and' itself is still just to form a bare conjunction.

However, we can't expand here on the sort of issues we have just touched on. So let's be conciliatory. Let's agree that there is at least a prima facie issue about whether 'and', when used as a sentential connective in ordinary language, sometimes forms more than a bare conjunction. When we turn to considering arguments involving 'and', we will therefore want to make it absolutely clear how the connective *is* being used.

8.3   'Or'

(a)   Like 'and', we can use 'or' to combine a pair of matched expressions belonging to almost any grammatical category – as in 'Jack is walking or cycling', 'Jack or Jill went up the hill', etc. However, let's just consider the cases where 'or' (with or without 'either') is used as a binary operator at sentence level, i.e. is used as a sentential connective to disjoin two whole sentences.

Here is Jack who has failed his logic test. I say 'Jack didn't work or he isn't any good at abstract thought'. This is true if Jack didn't work, and also true if Jack is not good at abstract thought. But I don't mean to rule out that he is both a slacker and hopelessly illogical. The 'or' here is inclusive.

Using '∘' to stand in for another binary connective, let's say

> $A \circ B$ is an (inclusive) *disjunction* of A and B just if $A \circ B$ is true when at least one of A and B is true, and is false when both of A and B are false.

'Or' in English often serves to form an inclusive disjunction in this sense. Another example: 'We are now bound to win the cup. Surely we will beat the Lions or we will beat the Tigers' – again, note that I don't rule out our beating both.

(b)   You might wonder: isn't it part of the meaning of *A or B* to signal that the speaker doesn't definitely know that *A* is true or know that *B* is true?

But why so? Of course, unless there is a special context (like giving a child a hint in a game), it would be oddly uncooperative of me to assert the bare disjunction *A or B* when I know perfectly well e.g. that *A* is in fact true. So for *that* reason, if I merely assert *A or B*, you will normally expect me not to know which. However, there is no linguistic oddity in saying '*A or B* – I know which, but I'm not telling you!'.

(c)   The main complication about the use of 'or' is that it seems, at least at first sight, that claims of the type *A or B* can in fact have two different meanings. Often, 'or' forms a disjunction in the *inclusive* sense we defined above (meaning *A or B or both*). But can't it equally well form an *exclusive* disjunction (meaning *A or B but not both*)? For a possible example of an exclusive disjunction, consider

(1)   A peace treaty will be signed this week or the war will drag on a year.

The thesis that 'or' is ambiguous between inclusive and exclusive senses used to be popular. But maybe it is wrong (many linguists would say so); it could be that 'or' in fact has a single, inclusive, literal meaning, with any implication of exclusiveness in a particular case being due to extraneous clues of one sort or another. For note that implications of exclusiveness can usually be coherently cancelled. Thus, without any sense of linguistic oddity, we *can* surely say

(2)   A peace treaty will be signed this week or the war will drag on a year; indeed – given the fragility of the peace process – maybe both.

This would be unhappy if the initial disjunction in (2) were genuinely exclusive, ruling out the 'both' case (as we'd then be saying 'not both; maybe both'). So it seems that the 'or' in (2) can't be exclusive. But it seems odd to say that this 'or' changes its literal meaning if we now drop the last part of (2) and revert to (1). Arguably, then, the presumption of exclusiveness for the original claim (1) comes not from a special exclusive sense of 'or' but from our background knowledge that peace treaties and wars don't usually go together.

But that's contentious and there is more to be said. And there are other sorts of example to consider. So this is another area of debate we can't pursue any further. Being conciliatory again, we can at least agree that when we turn to considering the logic of arguments involving 'or' we will want to make it absolutely clear whether inclusive or exclusive disjunctions are in play.

8.4   'Not'

(a)   To *deny* a claim *A* outright is equivalent to asserting some strict *negation* of *A* (meaning a sentence which is true when *A* is false and false when *A* is true).

Earlier, we represented a negation of A very informally by '*not-A*'.

English has various ways of forming negations. For the simplest kind of case, consider 'Jo is married' vs 'Jo is not married', 'Jack smokes' vs 'Jack does not smoke', 'Jill went to the party' vs 'Jill did not go to the party'. In these examples, we negate a sentence by simply inserting a 'not' and then making any needed grammatical changes.

By contrast, inserting a 'not' into the truth 'Some students are good logicians' at the only grammatically permissible place gives us another truth, namely 'Some students are not good logicians'; hence inserting 'not' doesn't always produce the negation of a sentence. Instead, we can negate 'Some students are good logicians' by changing 'Some' to 'No'. Similarly, we can negate 'Alexander sometimes lost a battle' by changing 'sometimes' to 'never'. Again, we can negate an inclusive disjunction of the form A *or* B by the corresponding *Neither A nor B*.

As well as these brisk but varied ways of forming negations, English has a more cumbersome but more uniform way of forming negations – namely, we can prefix 'It is not the case that' (or equivalently, 'It is not true that'). Thus we can negate 'Some students are good logicians' by saying 'It is not the case that some students are good logicians'. We can negate 'Alexander sometimes lost a battle' by saying 'It is not the case that Alexander sometimes lost a battle'. And we can negate A *or* B by asserting *It is not the case that A or B*, so long as it is clear that the negation-prefix applies to the whole of what follows it (a point we will return to in just a moment).

(b)   Let's focus on the uniform construction. Now using '$\triangleright$' to stand in for some expression which is prefixed to a single sentence, we will say

> $\triangleright A$ is a *negation* of A just if $\triangleright A$ is true when A is false, and is false when A is true.

As we will see, although a prefixed negation operator doesn't connect different sentences, there are enough other similarities with the behaviour of conjunction and disjunction signs to encourage us to treat them all together. It is therefore entirely standard to count a negation operator as an honorary sentential 'connective', a one-place or unary one.

8.5   Scope

(a)   A prefixed 'It is not the case that' typically works as a negation in the sense just defined. But not always. Consider, for example, the following pairs:

(1)   Jack loves Jill, or Jill is much mistaken about Jack's feelings.

(1′)   It is not the case that Jack loves Jill, or Jill is much mistaken about Jack's feelings.

(2)   Jack loves Jill and it is not the case that Jill loves Jack.

(2′)   It is not the case that Jack loves Jill and it is not the case that Jill loves Jack.

Here, (1′) results from prefixing 'It is not the case that' to (1). But on the natural way of reading (1′), only the clause 'Jack loves Jill' is governed by – or is in the *scope* of – the initial negation. Which means that both (1) and the natural reading of (1′) are *true* if Jill is much mistaken. Hence (1′) isn't unambiguously a negation of (1).

We can make this clear by helping ourselves to brackets again, and using '*Not*' as a negation prefix. Then if (1) is represented by *A or B*, then (1′) is naturally read as having the form *(Not-A) or B*. But a negation of (1) needs to be equivalent to *Not-(A or B)*.

Similarly (2′) results from prefixing 'It is not the case that' to (2). But on the natural reading of (2′), again only the clause 'Jack loves Jill' is in the scope of the initial negation. Which means that both (2) and (2′) are *false* if Jill loves Jack. Hence again one isn't a negation of the other. In symbols, if (2) is represented by *A and Not-B* then (2′) is naturally read as having the form *Not-A and Not-B*. But a negation of (2) needs to be equivalent to *Not-(A and Not-B)*.

So, to form an unambiguous negation of some sentence in English it may not be enough simply to prefix it with 'It is not the case that'; we may also need to indicate somehow the intended *scope* of the prefix.

(b) The implicit rules about how much of a sentence an ordinary-language logical operator applies to are complicated, and don't settle a unique reading for every sentence. They permit ambiguities to arise. Consider

(3) Either Jack took Jill to the party or he took Jo and he had some fun.

No individual word in this sentence is ambiguous, we may suppose. But there are still two possible messages here, because we can construe the sentence as being put together in two different ways. Does this say that either Jack went to the party with Jill or else Jack had fun going to the party with Jo? Or does it say, differently, that he took Jill or Jo to the party and either way enjoyed himself?

There is an ambiguity in how to group together the clauses in (3) – and we can think of this as a *scope ambiguity*. For what is the scope of the 'and'? Does the connective just conjoin 'he took Jo' with 'he had some fun'? Or is its scope wider, so that the whole of 'either Jack took Jill to the party or he took Jo' is being conjoined with 'he had some fun'? In speech, intonation and little pauses can tell us what is intended. In writing, adding punctuation will help, as in:

(4) Either Jack took Jill to the party, or he took Jo and he had some fun.
(5) Either Jack took Jill to the party or he took Jo, and he had some fun.

When it comes to considering sentences with multiple connectives in logical contexts, we evidently need *some* device to block scope ambiguities.

8.6 Formalization

To sum up so far: even when considering only their uses as sentential connectives, we find that natural-language 'and', 'or' and 'not' behave in quite complex ways. There are similar intricate complexities in the use of other logically salient constructions. Treating the logic of arguments couched in ordinary English therefore really requires taking on two tasks simultaneously; we need *both* to negotiate the many vagaries of English *and* to deal with the logical relations of the premises and conclusions once we have correctly construed them.

How are we going to handle this dual task? Let's *divide and rule*, and separate the two tasks as far as possible. We will sidestep the complexities of natural language by reformulating the arguments we want to discuss; we will render them into more austere and regimented *formalized languages*, languages which are designed from the start to be very well-behaved, entirely clear and quite free of ambiguities and shifting meanings – at least as far as their logical apparatus is concerned. And then we can much more easily assess the resulting formalized arguments. Applied to the present case, where just the sentential connectives are in focus, this means:

> We will assess an argument involving the English 'and', 'or', and 'not' as sentential connectives by a two-step process:
>
> (1) We render the given vernacular argument into a well-behaved artificial language with tidied-up versions of those three connectives.
>
> (2) We then investigate the validity or otherwise of the now tidily formalized version.

The first step may raise more or less tricky issues of interpretation, as we try to reformulate the English propositions, imposing the logical straightjacket of a sharply defined formalism. But most of our logical attention will then be on the second step. For even given the premises and conclusion now rendered into a sufficiently perspicuous and unambiguous formalized language, the central question still remains: is the resulting argument deductively valid?

The divide-and-rule strategy has its roots as far back as Aristotle, whose logical works are the logician's Old Testament. But the strategy really came of age in the nineteenth century with Frege's New Testament. In his *Begriffsschrift* (1879), Frege presented a 'concept-script' designed for the perspicuous representation of a rich class of propositions. His own notational choices didn't win much favour; but the idea of using a formalized language to regiment arguments into a more manageable shape quickly became central to the whole project of modern formal logic.

In the rest of this book, we are going to follow the divide-and-rule strategy. The justification of this approach is its richly abundant fruitfulness, though *that* can only become fully clear as we go along.

8.7   The design brief for PL languages

For our immediate purposes, then, we want to design a formalized language – or rather, a whole *family* of languages – for regimenting arguments involving our three sentential connectives as their relevant logical apparatus. We will call such a language a PL *language* – with the label meant to suggest 'propositional logic'.

We can usefully carve up the design brief for a PL language into three parts. But first, a new convention which we will say more about in Chapter 11:

> When we want to generalize *about* sentences of artificial languages such as PL languages by the use of symbols in schemas, instead of again using italic letters like '*A*', '*B*', '*C*', we will now use Greek letters like 'α', 'β', 'γ'.

(a)   We start, then, by giving our languages symbols for 'and' and 'or' as sentential connectives, and a symbol for sentence-negation. So:

> We give a PL language a connective '$\wedge$' (some use '&') which is stipulated to invariably form a bare *conjunction*, no more and no less: i.e. in all cases, for all sentences α, β of the language, the sentence $(\alpha \wedge \beta)$ is true when α and β are both true, and is false when one or both of α and β are false.
>
> We add a connective '$\vee$' which is stipulated to invariably form an *(inclusive) disjunction*, no more and no less. So the sentence $(\alpha \vee \beta)$ is true when one or both of α and β are true, and is false when α and β are both false.
>
> Finally we add a prefixed '$\neg$' (some use '$\sim$') which is stipulated to work as 'It is not the case that' usually works. So the sentence $\neg\alpha$ forms a *negation* of α, and is true just when the sentence α is false, and false when α is true.

(The inclusive disjunction sign '$\vee$' is supposed to be suggestive of the initial 'v' of 'vel', the Latin for 'or'. Later, we will see how to deal with exclusive disjunction.)

By all means, pronounce '$\wedge$', '$\vee$', and '$\neg$' as *and*, *or*, and *not*. But these new symbols shouldn't be thought of as mere equivalents of their ordinary-language counterparts. For true equivalents would simply inherit the complexities of their originals! The PL connectives are better thought of as cleaned-up *replacements* for the vernacular connectives.

(b)   We next need to avoid any structural scope ambiguities of the kind illustrated by 'Either Jack took Jill to the party or he took Jo and he had some fun'. Ambiguous expressions of the pattern $\alpha \vee \beta \wedge \gamma$ must therefore be banned.

How do we achieve this? Compare arithmetic, where we can form potentially ambiguous expressions like '$1+2\times 3$' (is the answer 7 or 9?). To disambiguate, we can use brackets, writing '$1 + (2 \times 3)$' or '$(1 + 2) \times 3$', which each have unique values. We will insist on the same bracketing device in our PL languages:

> Every occurrence of '$\wedge$' to join two sentences α and β is to come with a pair of brackets to yield the sentence $(\alpha \wedge \beta)$, thereby clearly demarcating the scope of the connective and showing what it connects. Similarly for '$\vee$'.
>
> But the negation sign '$\neg$' only combines with a single sentence, and we don't need to use brackets to mark its scope.

This way, we are allowed sentences of the shape $(\alpha \vee (\beta \wedge \gamma))$ or $((\alpha \vee \beta) \wedge \gamma)$, but not the unbracketed $\alpha \vee \beta \wedge \gamma$. And a negation sign binds tightly to the sentential PL-expression that immediately follows it. So:

(1) In a sentence of the form $(\alpha \vee (\neg\beta \wedge \gamma))$, just β is being negated.

(2) In $(\alpha \vee \neg(\beta \wedge \gamma))$, the bracketed conjunction $(\beta \wedge \gamma)$ is negated.

(3) And in $\neg(\alpha \vee (\beta \wedge \gamma))$, the whole of $(\alpha \vee (\beta \wedge \gamma))$ is negated.

(c) Finally, what do these three connectives '$\wedge$', '$\vee$', and '$\neg$' (ultimately) connect? Simple, connective-free, sentences; we can think of these as the *atoms* from which we build more complex *molecular* sentences using the connectives.

So we'll need to give each PL language a base class of 'atomic' sentences – and it is just here that the various PL languages will differ, in what atomic sentences are available, and in what these atomic sentences mean. However, since for present purposes we are not interested in further analysing these atomic sentences, we will waste as little ink on them as possible. Therefore, for brevity, we can start by using single letters as atoms, as in 'P', 'Q', 'R', 'S'.

Note, using single letters like this does *not* imply that the atoms of our PL language are meaningless. Formalized languages, on our account of them, may differ from natural languages in many ways; but they will resemble them in containing genuine meaningful sentences, with which we can frame genuine arguments.

8.8   One PL language

(a) Take a PL language with just the four letters from 'P' to 'S' as atoms. And suppose our meaning-giving *glossary* for the language looks like this:

> P: Jack loves Jill.
> Q: Jill loves Jack.
> R: Jo loves Jill.
> S: Jack is wise.

Then let's render the following into this miniature formalized language:

(1) Jack doesn't love Jill.

(2) Jack is wise and he loves Jill.

(3) Either Jack loves Jill or Jo does.

(4) Jack and Jill love each other.

(5) Neither Jack loves Jill nor does Jo.

(6) It isn't the case that Jack loves Jill nor does Jill love Jack.

(7) Either Jack is not wise or both he and Jo love Jill.

(8) It isn't the case that either Jack loves Jill or Jill loves Jack.

(b) The first four are very easily done:

(1′) $\neg P$

(2′) $(S \wedge P)$

(3′) $(P \vee R)$

(4′) $(P \wedge Q)$.

Just three quick comments:

(i) Note that rendering the English as best we can into our PL language isn't a matter of mere phrase-for-phrase transliteration or mechanical coding. For example, in rendering (2) we have to assume that the 'he' refers to Jack; likewise we need to read (3) as saying the same as 'either Jack loves Jill or Jo loves Jill' – and assume too that the disjunction here is inclusive.

(ii) We are insisting that whenever we introduce an occurrence of '∧' or '∨', there needs to be a pair of matching brackets. To be sure, the brackets in (2') to (4') are strictly speaking redundant; if there is only one connective in a sentence, there is no possibility of a scope ambiguity. No matter; our official bracketing policy will be strict.

(iii) Note too that it is customary *not* to conclude sentences of our PL languages by full stops or periods. There is no such punctuation mark in the languages. (However, we *will* add full-stops to displayed material when it helpfully completes the surrounding English.)

To continue: We do not have a built-in 'neither ..., nor ...' connective in our language. But we can render (5) into our PL language in two equally good ways:

(5') ¬(P ∨ R)
(5″) (¬P ∧ ¬R).

Next, the natural reading of the English (6) treats it as the conjunction of 'It is not the case that Jack loves Jill' and 'It is not the case the Jill loves Jack':

(6') (¬P ∧ ¬Q).

And proposition (7) is to be rendered as follows:

(7') (¬S ∨ (P ∧ R)).

(Why are the brackets placed as they are?) Finally, we can translate (8) as

(8') ¬(P ∨ Q).

So far, so easy. But now that we've got going, we can translate ever more complicated sentences. For just one more example, consider the rather laboured claim

(9) Either Jack and Jill love each other or it isn't the case that either Jack loves Jill or Jill loves Jack.

This is naturally read as the disjunction of (4) and (8); so we can render it into our PL language by disjoining the translations of (4) and (8), thus:

(9') ((P ∧ Q) ∨ ¬(P ∨ Q)).

8.9 Summary

Our aim is to consider arguments whose logical structure depends on the presence of 'and', 'or', and 'not' in the premises and conclusion.

There are many quirks and ambiguities in the way ordinary-language 'and', 'or', and 'not' behave (even when we just consider their uses as sentential connectives). To avoid the vagaries of the vernacular, we are going to use special-purpose languages, PL languages, to express arguments without ambiguities or obscurities.

A PL language has a base class of 'atomic' symbols which can be used to express whole messages, and which might as well be as simple as possible, e.g. single letters. More complex, 'molecular', symbolic formulas are then built up using '∧', '∨', and '¬' (unambiguously expressing bare conjunction, inclusive disjunction, and negation), bracketing carefully.

Exercises 8

(a) Usually, we can ambiguously negate a statement by prefixing it with 'It is not the case that'. Can you think of any exceptions (in addition to the kinds described in §8.4)?

(b) Give negations of the following in natural English:

(1) It is not the case that both Jack and Jill went up the hill.

(2) Neither Jack nor Jill went up the hill.

(3) No one loves Jack.

(4) Only tall men love Jill.

(5) Everyone who loves Jack admires Jill.

(6) Someone loves both Jack and Jill.

(7) Some who love Jill are not themselves loveable.

(8) Jill always arrives on time.

(9) Whoever did that ought to pay for the damage.

(10) Whenever it rains, it pours.

(11) No one may smoke.

(c) Two propositions are *contraries* if they cannot be true together; they are *contradictories* if one is true exactly when the other is false. (Example: 'All philosophers are wise' and 'No philosophers are wise' are contraries – they can't both be true. But maybe they are both false, so they are not contradictories.) Give examples of propositions which are contraries but not contradictories of the propositions in (b).

(d) Render the following as best you can into the PL language we introduced in §8.8:

(1) Jack is unwise and loves Jill.

(2) Jack and Jo both love Jill.

(3) It isn't true that Jack doesn't love Jill.

(4) Jack loves Jill but Jo doesn't.

(5) Jack doesn't love Jill, neither is he wise.

(6) Either Jack loves Jill or Jill loves Jack.

(7) Either Jack loves Jill or Jill loves Jack, but not both.

(8) Either Jack is unwise or he loves Jill and Jo loves Jill.

9 PL syntax

In the previous chapter, we explained why we will be using artificial PL languages to regiment arguments involving connectives for conjunction, disjunction, and negation. This chapter now pins down the grammar or *syntax* of such languages.

9.1 Syntactic rules for PL languages

The syntax of a language tells us, which strings of symbols count as grammatical sentences. In our case, introducing some standard terminology,

> The syntax of a PL language defines what counts as a *well-formed formula* or, for brevity, *wff* of that language.

We will explore PL syntax in three stages: (a) we fix the alphabet of symbols we can use in a PL language; (b) we stipulate what count as the 'atomic' wffs of a given language; finally, (c) we explain how other, 'molecular', wffs are built up from the atoms. (I pronounce 'wff' either as *woof* or simply as *formula*.)

(a)   First, then, we need to specify the *alphabet* of PL languages. We have already met the propositional letters 'P', 'Q', 'R', 'S', the three connectives '∧', '∨', '¬', plus brackets '(', ')'. But we now add a few more symbols.

(1)   In some cases, we will need more than a mere four basic atomic wffs. We will use a *prime* "'" for making as many additional atoms as we want. We can then form the likes of these: P', P'', Q', R'', S''', ...

(2)   We want to be able to formalize not just individual propositions but whole arguments. So we will want to be able to list premisses, separated by punctuation. Let's provide a *comma* to do the job.

(3)   We will also want an inference marker to signal when a conclusion is being drawn after a list of premisses. We can adopt '∴', the familiar *therefore* sign.

So, in summary, we stipulate that:

> The *alphabet* of a PL language is: P, Q, R, S, ', ∧, ∨, ¬, (,), ∴, plus the comma.

Or at least, that's our initial alphabet. We will add two more symbols in due course (in particular, if you have met propositional logic before, you'll notice that '→' is missing so far: but there is a reason for delaying its introduction).

(b)   Next, each PL language must have a stock of atomic wffs formed from this alphabet, atoms which provide the basic building blocks for the language.

How many atoms we need in a particular language will depend on the complexity of the argument(s) we want to use it to formalize. Perhaps we need, say, ten atoms. (We can safely assume in this book that we will never need more than a *finite* number of atoms!) Now, at the end of §8.7, we said that 'P', 'Q', 'R', 'S' can serve as atoms; but we left it open how we are to continue that list. But we don't want any ambiguity about what counts as an atomic wff of a particular language. So how do we get a determinate ten atoms? What if we want thirty atoms (more than there are letters in the alphabet)? As we've just said, we will use primes to form as many atoms as we want. So:

> A PL language has a (finite) supply of one or more *atomic wffs*. We will assume that each is formed from one of the four basic propositional letters followed by zero or more primes. We specify the atoms of a particular language simply by listing them. For example, if we want exactly ten atoms, we can choose these: P, Q, R, S, P′, Q′, R′, S′, P″, Q″.

(c)   Having fixed the finite class of atomic wffs for a language, we now need to give the rules for building up more complex wffs out of simpler ones using connectives, to arrive at the language's full class of wffs, atomic and molecular.

While the atomic wffs can vary between PL languages, the rules for constructing more complex wffs from them are constant. We outlined these rules in §8.7. Recalling our insistence that the connectives '∧' and '∨' always come with a pair of brackets to indicate their scope, we can sum things up like this:

> The *wffs* of a particular PL language are determined as follows. Having explicitly specified its atomic wffs, then
>
> (W1)   Any atomic wff of the language counts as a wff.
> (W2)   If α and β are wffs, so is $(\alpha \wedge \beta)$.
> (W3)   If α and β are wffs, so is $(\alpha \vee \beta)$.
> (W4)   If α is a wff, so is $\neg\alpha$.
> (W5)   Nothing else is a wff.

It should be immediately clear how to understand these rules. But, at the risk of labouring the obvious, let's spell out two points.

First, W2 is to be read as telling us that the result of writing a left-hand bracket '(' followed by the wff α followed by a conjunction sign '∧' followed by the wff β followed by a right-hand bracket ')' is also a wff. And naturally we will say that a wff constructed like this *has the form* $(\alpha \wedge \beta)$. Similarly, of course, for W3 and W4.

73

Second, note that the rules W1 to W4, taken by themselves, don't stop Julius Caesar from also counting as a wff. That's why we need to add the *extremal clause* W5 to delimit the class of wffs and thereby block Caesar along with other intruders. In W5, 'nothing else' means that the only wffs are the strings of symbols that can be proved to be wffs using the preceding rules W1 to W4.

(d)   For the record, in the context of discussing wffs of PL (and similar) languages, when we talk about *the* negation of a wff α we will from now on always mean the wff $\neg\alpha$, rather than some possible equivalent (compare §8.4, where we talked of *a* negation). Similarly when we talk about *the* conjunction or disjunction of the wffs α and β we will mean the corresponding wffs $(\alpha \wedge \beta)$ or $(\alpha \vee \beta)$ rather than any equivalents.

9.2   Construction histories, parse trees

(a)   Assume we are dealing with a PL language whose atoms are 'P', 'Q', 'R', 'S'. Let's use our stated W-rules to prove that the sequence of symbols

$$\neg((P \vee Q) \wedge \neg(\neg Q \vee R))$$

is a wff of this language. We can laboriously lay out an annotated derivation in the style of §4.1. Premisses are supplied by our assumption about atoms together with W1; and then at further steps we appeal to the other W-rules:

A		
(1)	'P' is a wff.	(premiss)
(2)	'Q' is a wff.	(premiss)
(3)	'R' is a wff.	(premiss)
(4)	'(P ∨ Q)' is a wff.	(from 1, 2 by W3)
(5)	'¬Q' is a wff.	(from 2 by W4)
(6)	'(¬Q ∨ R)' is a wff.	(from 5, 3 by W3)
(7)	'¬(¬Q ∨ R)' is a wff.	(from 6 by W4)
(8)	'((P ∨ Q) ∧ ¬(¬Q ∨ R))' is a wff.	(from 4, 7 by W2)
(9)	'¬((P ∨ Q) ∧ ¬(¬Q ∨ R))' is a wff.	(from 8 by W4)

This reveals what we might call a *construction history* for our wff. However, the vertical presentation of the proof here is perhaps not the most illuminating way of setting things out. We can rather more perspicuously re-arrange the derivation like this:

A^T

```
                                              'Q' is a wff
                                         ──────────────────
                                         '¬Q' is a wff     'R' is a wff
                                         ───────────────────────────────
        'P' is a wff     'Q' is a wff         '(¬Q ∨ R)' is a wff
        ─────────────────────────────        ───────────────────
             '(P ∨ Q)' is a wff              '¬(¬Q ∨ R)' is a wff
        ─────────────────────────────────────────────────────────
               '((P ∨ Q) ∧ ¬(¬Q ∨ R))' is a wff
        ───────────────────────────────────────────────
              '¬((P ∨ Q) ∧ ¬(¬Q ∨ R))' is a wff
```

This is essentially the same proof as **A**, but now presented in the form of a *tree*. At the tips of the branches we have our premisses telling us that various atoms are wffs (the premiss that 'Q' is a wff gets repeated on different branches because it is used twice). The horizontal lines then mark inferences. So as we move down the tree $\mathbf{A}^T$, we derive further facts about wffs in accordance with the rule W4 (which keeps us on the same branch), or in accordance with the rules W2 and W3 (when we join two branches). We impose the natural convention for building this construction history in tree form: when we apply the joining rules, the wffs immediately above the horizontal line appear in the same left-to-right order as they appear inside the wff below the line.

(b)   Here is another way of presenting exactly the same information as is given by $\mathbf{A}^T$. First, turn everything upside down: that obviously doesn't make a significant difference! Second, reduce clutter by omitting all those occurrences of the repeated frame '…' *is a wff* (since the same frame surrounds every wff, it can safely be left as understood). Then we get

$\mathbf{A}^P$

$$\neg((P \vee Q) \wedge \neg(\neg Q \vee R))$$
$$|$$
$$((P \vee Q) \wedge \neg(\neg Q \vee R))$$

$(P \vee Q)$ $\neg(\neg Q \vee R)$

P   Q $(\neg Q \vee R)$

      $\neg Q$ R

      Q

Or rather this is what we get when – following convention – we change the decorative style a bit, and replace each horizontal line with a short vertical line (when going from one wff to another) or with a joined pair of sloping lines (when going from one wff to two).

Reading upwards, we can still think of this as a construction tree, which now more economically displays how our wff is constructed stage by stage in accordance with our W-rules. Reading downwards, we have what linguists might call a *parse tree*. For, read this way, our tree displays how the wff at the top can be parsed, i.e. how it can be disassembled into its component wffs or subformulas stage by stage until we reach its ultimate atomic components.

(c)   Let's take another example. We will show that

$$(((S \wedge Q) \wedge \neg\neg R) \vee \neg(\neg(P \vee P) \wedge Q))$$

is also a wff of our current PL language. Here is a construction history in a neat tree version, $\mathbf{B}^T$:

'P' is a wff   'P' is a wff
'(P ∨ P)' is a wff

'R' is a wff   '¬(P ∨ P)' is a wff   'Q' is a wff

'S' is a wff   'Q' is a wff   '¬R' is a wff
'(S ∧ Q)' is a wff   '¬¬R' is a wff   '(¬(P ∨ P) ∧ Q)' is a wff

'((S ∧ Q) ∧ ¬¬R)' is a wff   '¬(¬(P ∨ P) ∧ Q)' is a wff

'(((S ∧ Q) ∧ ¬¬R) ∨ ¬(¬(P ∨ P) ∧ Q))' is a wff

Pause to check which W-rule is being applied at each inference step. And note that there is nothing in the rule W3 for constructing a disjunction of the form $(\alpha \lor \beta)$ which says that the schematic variables here have to be substituted for by *different* expressions. So, in particular, given that 'P' is a wff, we can use W3 to infer that '(P ∨ P)' is a wff.

Inverting and omitting the clutter of those repeated frames '. . .' *is a wff* appearing in the construction history $\mathbf{B}^T$, we get the following parse tree, $\mathbf{B}^P$:

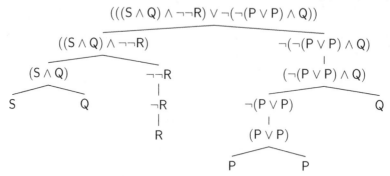

Again, we can read this upwards, as showing us how to construct the wff at the top by building it up stage by stage from its atoms. Or we can read the same tree downwards, as showing us how to parse the top wff by disassembling it stage by stage into ever-shorter subformulas. (The idea of a parse tree is simple; but it is worth pausing to try some of this chapter's Exercises to test understanding.)

9.3 Wffs have unique parse trees!

(a) By rule W5, the wffs of a PL language are exactly those strings of symbols that can be assembled from atomic wffs by using the three building rules W2–W4. And so we must be able to disassemble wffs back into their component atoms. Hence each wff must have *at least one* construction history/parse tree showing how it can be built up from or dissembled back into atomic wffs.

Now, suppose our wff-building rules W2 and W3 had *not* insisted on conjunctions and disjunctions being delimited by brackets. What would have happened? We would get expressions which have *more than one* parse tree, as in

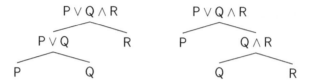

This would give us a structurally ambiguous expression on a par with our ordinary-language example from §8.5(b), 'Either Jack took Jill to the party or he took Jo and he had some fun'. However, *our formal bracketing rules are in place precisely to prevent such structural scope ambiguities.* For example, here is a parse tree for one properly bracketed version of that last expression:

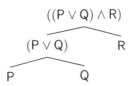

Read upwards, this tree shows that '∨' here serves first to form '(P ∨ Q)' (so this subformula is therefore the connective's scope in the intuitive sense which we sharpen in the next section); '∧' then forms the whole wff (so the whole wff is the scope of *that* connective). And, having constructed the wff '((P ∨ Q) ∧ R)', now note there is only one way of disassembling it again – there is only one possible parse tree for the wff.

(b)   The point generalizes. Fix the convention that the wffs immediately below a fork on a parse tree occur in the same left-to-right order as they appear inside the wff just above the fork. Then, crucially, our bracketing rules ensure that

Every wff of a PL language has a *unique* parse tree.

Experimentation with a few examples will quickly convince you that this claim is true – and such experimentation will probably be much more enlightening than an official proof. But, for the sceptical, we do outline a proof in the Exercises.

(c)   A quick observation. As we walk up a parse tree, brackets always get introduced into a wff in left-right pairs. So note that every genuine wff must be *balanced,* i.e. have the same number of left-hand and right-hand brackets.

9.4   Main connectives, subformulas, scope

(a)   The following should now seem an entirely natural definition:

The *main connective* of a molecular wff is the first connective to be removed as we go down the wff's parse tree.

Equivalently, the main connective of a molecular wff is the last connective introduced in a construction history for the wff. Then:

If a wff has the form ¬α, then its main connective is that initial '¬'.

If a wff has the form (α ∧ β) for wffs α, β, then its main connective is that '∧'. We define (α ∧ β)'s *conjuncts* to be α and β.

Similarly, if a wff has the form (α ∨ β), then its main connective is that '∨'. Its *disjuncts* are again α and β.

A molecular PL wff can only have one main connective. In particular a wff can't both be of the form (α ∘ β) for wffs α, β and ∘ a binary connective, and also of the form (γ ⋄ δ) for wffs γ, δ and ⋄ a binary connective – unless α = γ, ∘ = ⋄, and β = δ. For if a wff did have distinct forms (α ∘ β) and (γ ⋄ δ), it would have two distinct parse trees – and we have said that that's impossible.

(b) The main connective of a wff determines its key logical properties – which is why it matters. For example, given the intended meanings of '∨' and '¬', any instance of the following pattern of inference is valid (compare §8.1):

$$(\alpha \lor \beta), \neg \alpha \therefore \beta.$$

But to apply this principle to warrant a particular argument in some PL language, we need to know whether the longer premiss in the argument really is a disjunction, i.e. really has the form $(\alpha \lor \beta)$ with '∨' as its main connective.

(c) Here next is the official definition for a notion we've already used:

A wff β is a *subformula* of a wff α just if β appears on the parse tree for α.

This is provably equivalent to saying that a subformula is a string of symbols occurring in a wff which could equally stand alone as a wff in its own right. Note, our definition allows a wff α trivially to count as a subformula of itself. But that is a convenient convention (if you know about sets, compare how it is convenient to allow a set X to trivially count as one of its own subsets).

(d) Our final definition in this section sharpens another intuitive idea – the idea of the *scope* of a connective, which we first met in §8.5. Roughly speaking, the scope of a given occurrence of some connective in a wff is the part of the wff which that connective governs. So take another parse tree, $\mathbf{C}^P$:

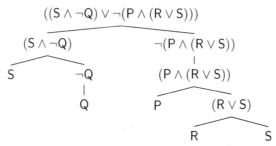

Working up the tree reveals how each particular occurrence of a connective gets into the final wff. Thus the first conjunction '∧' is introduced to form '(S ∧ ¬Q)'. So we can rather naturally say that this subformula is the scope of the connective – and then, as we intuitively want, 'S' and '¬Q' and 'Q' too are *in* the scope of that conjunction. Similarly, the second negation is first introduced on the tree in the subformula '¬(P ∧ (R ∨ S))': so we can say that *that* subformula is the scope of this second occurrence of '¬'. And so on:

The *scope* of an occurrence of a connective in a wff is the subformula where that occurrence first gets introduced, reading up the wff's parse tree.

An expression is in the scope of a particular connective in the intuitive sense if it is literally *in*, is part of, that connective's scope as we have just defined it (a connective counts as being in its own scope by our definition, but again that's harmless). This implies, in particular, that

An occurrence of a connective is in the scope of some other occurrence of a connective in a wff if the first is introduced before the second as we go *up* the relevant branch of the parse tree for the wff (i.e. go up the branch which contains those two occurrences).

So the first negation in our example is in the scope of the first conjunction; the second conjunction is in the scope of the second negation, and so on.

(e)   Note, we have just slipped into referring to an occurrence of the conjunctive connective as simply a 'conjunction' (and similarly for the other connectives). This is handy shorthand; it should always be clear from context when we are using e.g. 'a conjunction' to mean a *wff* formed using '∧', and when we mean an occurrence of that *connective*.

9.5   Bracketing styles

Finally, a quick suggestion about how we can occasionally make long wffs rather more readable: use some way of marking pairs of left and right brackets which belong together, to reveal more clearly how the wff is constructed.

In this spirit, we will occasionally aid the eye by making use of the different available styles of brackets. Take, for example, the following mildly unreadable string of symbols:

$$(\neg((P \lor (R \land \neg S)) \lor \neg(Q \land \neg P)) \land \neg(P \lor \neg(\neg Q \lor R))).$$

It is perhaps not immediately evident that this is a wff (in a language with the right atoms, of course). But suppose we bend some of the matching pairs of round brackets into curly ones '{', '}' and straighten other pairs into square ones '[', ']' to get

$$[\neg\{(P \lor (R \land \neg S)) \lor \neg(Q \land \neg P)\} \land \neg\{P \lor \neg(\neg Q \lor R)\}].$$

The string now looks rather more obviously a wff. Give a parse tree for it!

9.6   Summary

The syntax of a PL language, after fixing the basic alphabet, first defines the class of atomic wffs, and then gives rules for constructing legitimate molecular wffs out of simpler ones using the three connectives '∧', '∨', and '¬', bracketing as we go.

Each wff has a unique construction/parse tree displaying how it is constructed ultimately from atomic wffs and equally how it can be disassembled back down into atomic wffs.

A subformula of a wff α is a wff that appears somewhere on α's parse tree.

The main connective of a (non-atomic) wff is the first connective to be removed as we go down the wff's parse tree.

The scope of a particular occurrence of a connective in a wff is the subformula where it is introduced going up the wff's parse tree (this will be the shortest subformula including that occurrence).

Exercises 9

(a) Show the following expressions are wffs of a PL language with suitable atoms by producing parse trees. Which is the main connective of each wff? What is the scope of each connective in (3) and of each disjunction in (4)? List all the subformulas of (5). Use alternative styles of brackets in (5) and (6) to make them more easily readable.

(1) $((P \land P) \lor R)$

(2) $(\lnot (R \land S) \lor \lnot Q)$

(3) $\lnot\lnot((P \land Q) \lor (\lnot P \lor \lnot Q))$

(4) $((((P \lor P) \land R) \land Q) \lor (\lnot (R \land S) \lor \lnot Q))$

(5) $(\lnot(\lnot(P \land Q) \land \lnot(P \land R)) \lor \lnot(P \land (Q \lor R)))$

(6) $(\lnot((R \lor \lnot Q) \land \lnot S) \land (\lnot(\lnot P \land Q) \land S))$

(b) Which of the following expressions are wffs of a PL language with the relevant atoms? Repair the defective expressions by adding/removing the minimum number of brackets needed to do the job. Show the results are now wffs by producing parse trees.

(1) $((P \lor Q) \land \lnot R))$

(2) $((P \lor (Q \land \lnot R) \lor ((Q \land \lnot R) \lor P))$

(3) $\lnot(\lnot P \lor (Q \land (R \lor \lnot P))$

(4) $(P \land (Q \lor R) \land (Q \lor R))$

(5) $(((P \land (Q \land \lnot R)) \lor \lnot\lnot\lnot(R \land Q)) \lor (P \land R))$

(6) $((P \land (Q \land \lnot R)) \lor \lnot\lnot\lnot((R \land Q) \lor (P \land R)))$

(7) $(\lnot(P \lor \lnot(Q \land R)) \lor (P \land Q \land R)$

(c*) Show that parse trees for wffs are unique, in the following stages.

(1) Suppose that a wff has the form $(\alpha \land \beta)$ or $(\alpha \lor \beta)$. Then show that the relevant occurrence of the connective '$\land$' or '$\lor$' is preceded by exactly one more left-hand bracket than right-hand bracket. And show that any *other* occurrence of a binary connective in the wff is preceded by at least two more left-hand brackets than right-hand brackets.

(2) You know that if a wff starts with a negation, it must have the form $\lnot \alpha$. And if it starts with a left bracket, you now have a method of parsing it uniquely as having either the form $(\alpha \land \beta)$ or $(\alpha \lor \beta)$: what method?

(3) Now develop this into a method of disassembling a complex wff stage by stage, building a parse tree as you go. Confirm that there are no choice points in this process, and if we start with a wff, the result is the only possible one, and therefore parse trees are unique.

(4) As a bonus result, show how the same basic method applied to any string of symbols can be used to decide whether it is a wff or not (because either the process will freeze, or will generate a parse tree).

10 PL semantics

Having described the syntax of PL languages, we now turn to consider their *semantics*; in other words, we discuss questions of *meaning* and of *truth*. In particular, we introduce the crucial notion of a truth-value *valuation*.

10.1 Interpreting wffs

(a) Recall from §8.6 our 'divide-and-rule' plan for tackling arguments involving connectives. We first render a vernacular argument into a well-behaved artificial PL language. Then we investigate the validity or otherwise of the reformulated argument. But if the reformulated version is still to be a genuine *argument* whose premises and conclusion are contentful, the wffs of the relevant PL language cannot be left as mere uninterpreted symbols. They must be interpreted, i.e. must be assigned meanings.

A little more carefully – since, as we remarked in §7.2, questions of colouring or tone don't matter for logic – when interpreting a formal PL language, what we need to do is assign sufficiently clear and unambiguous truth-relevant *senses* to its wffs. We do this by assigning senses to the atomic wffs – these atoms form the basic *non-logical vocabulary* of a given language. We have already indicated the intended meanings of connectives, which form the topic-neutral *logical vocabulary* which stays constant across PL languages. We can then work out the senses of arbitrarily complex molecular wffs.

(b) So, first step:

> We specify the senses of a PL language's atoms by a glossary that fixes the atoms' truth-conditions.

We might compare this with one of those lists at the end of a tourist guide, giving the local equivalents of various English phrases (except that the guide-book does aim to get tone approximately right, whereas here we really care only about truth-relevant sense).

For a mini-example, take the three-atom language with the glossary

     P :   Alun loves Bethan.
     Q :   Bethan is Welsh.
     R :   Alun is married to Bethan.

Note, atoms need not have very *simple* readings like these: the messages that they are stipulated to convey can be as complex as you like. However, they do need to have truth-conditions which are *determinate* enough, in a sense to be explained shortly.

(c) We have already explained in §8.7 the meanings of the three connectives which are common to any PL language. To repeat:

> (1) '∧' invariably forms a conjunction, no more and no less; it trans-
> lates as 'and' (or 'and also' or 'both ... and ...'), so long as it is
> clear – perhaps from contextual clues – that the English rendition
> should be read as forming a bare conjunction (and not as meaning
> e.g. 'and then').
>
> (2) '∨' invariably forms an inclusive disjunction, no more and no less;
> it translates as 'either ... or ... or both', or 'and/or' – or in-
> deed as plain 'or', so long as context again makes it clear that the
> disjunction is to be understood as inclusive.
>
> (3) '¬' invariably negates the whole wff that follows; it can be trans-
> lated by 'It is not the case that ...', or often by a judiciously
> inserted 'not'.

So, for trivial examples, we will have

(R ∨ ¬Q) :	Either Alun is married to Bethan or she isn't Welsh.
(Q ∧ ¬P) :	Bethan is Welsh and Alun doesn't love her.
((R ∧ P) ∧ ¬Q) :	Alun is married to Bethan and he loves her, and she isn't Welsh.
¬(¬P ∧ R) :	It's not the case that Alun both doesn't love Bethan and yet also is married to her.
¬¬Q :	It isn't the case that Bethan is not Welsh.

Note the last case. In relaxed ordinary language, multiple negatives can remain emphatically negative ('We don't need no education'). But in classical logic double '¬'s always cancel each other out: hence '¬¬Q' tells us that Bethan *is* Welsh.

(d) There's more to do in interpreting molecular wffs than simply plugging in the interpretations of the atoms, translating the connectives, and tidying the English; we also need to respect the relative scopes of the connectives as determined by the compulsory bracketing in a PL wff. For example, consider a language with the same three atoms 'P', 'Q', 'R', but where these are now interpreted as follows:

> P: Jack took Jill to the party.
> Q: Jack took Jo to the party.
> R: Jack had some fun.

Note then that it won't do to interpret

$$(P \lor (Q \land R))$$

as, for example,

> Either Jack took Jill to the party or he took Jo and he had some fun.

For that English version has exactly the kind of potential ambiguity which the careful bracketing in the PL language is there to eliminate – see §8.7(b). A rendition that better expresses the correct interpretation of the wff might, for example, be

> Either Jack took Jill to the party, or he took Jo and had some fun, or both.

10.2 Languages and translation

(a) In the last section, we described two alternative dictionaries or glossaries for the same collection of atoms 'P', 'Q', 'R'. Do these define, as it were, two dialects of the *same* PL language? Or shall we say that we have characterized two *different* languages?

Some writers in effect define a formalized language by its syntax alone, and so they say that the same language can have many interpretations. But we'll prefer to take a language to be defined by its syntax *and* semantics: hence, to our way of thinking, different dictionaries will give us different formal languages (which perhaps coheres better with how we ordinarily think of languages).

So, on our approach, arguments on different topics will get translated into different PL languages – usually these will be languages set up ad hoc, for the special purposes at hand. But, as we will see, arguments in different formalized languages can still have the same form: that's how the desired generality gets into our story.

(b) Given the glossary for the atoms of a PL language, translation to and from this language shouldn't be too problematic. We won't pause for more examples now, as there are plenty of translation Exercises at the end of this and later chapters. However, we should perhaps say a word straight away about the notion of 'translation' here.

Some prefer to talk instead of 'paraphrasing' or 'rendering' or 'transcribing' ordinary language into PL. But, however described, what matters is that we aim for a wff of the relevant formalized language which captures, as closely as possible in that language, the sense, i.e. the truth-relevant meaning, of the English claim being translated. Tone and colour can be ignored.

Others prefer to talk of 'symbolizing' the English. But *this* way of putting it could mislead. For 'symbolizing' might suggest a mere exercise of introducing symbolic shorthand for bits of English; and such renditions would have all the ambiguities and obscurities of their originals. PL languages are not mere *shorthand code* for bits of English; their whole point is to be usefully tidied-up *replacements* for the messy vernacular.

10.3 Atomic wffs are true or false

It is up to us what the atom 'P' means in a particular PL language. To take the last mini-language we considered, we stipulated that 'P' there says that Jack took Jill to the party. But having fixed the meaning by settling which Jack and Jill are in question, etc., and therefore fixed the conditions under which 'P' is true, it is then up to how things are in the world whether 'P' *is* true (or if you prefer, whether what 'P' expresses is true). If Jack did take Jill to the party, then 'P' is true; if not, 'P' is false.

And we'll now make the idealizing and simplifying assumption that the world *will* always settle the matter, one way or the other. More generally, we will assume:

> *Determinacy* For any PL language, once we have stipulated the senses of its atoms – fixed their truth-conditions – each of these atoms will be determinately true or determinately false in any possible situation.

Now, it seems that there are various ways this idealizing assumption could go wrong and an interpreted atomic wff could fail to be either true or false. For example:

(1) Perhaps our glossary entry for some atom 'P' is something like *Jane is a philosopher*, but given in a context which somehow fails to pin down which Jane we are referring to. Or the entry is 'It is raining', and it isn't clear where or when we are talking about. As we might put it, in such cases, 'P' is not yet *fully* interpreted. In other words, the wff doesn't yet express a determinate truth-relevant content – there is, so to speak, part of the message still waiting to be filled in by context – and hence 'P' doesn't yet get to the starting line for being assessable for truth or falsehood.

(2) Perhaps, as in an example above, 'P' means that Alun loves Bethan. Suppose Alun's feelings are mixed, on the border of love. So maybe it is neither definitely true that he loves Bethan nor on the other hand definitely false.

(3) Perhaps 'P' is interpreted as one of those paradoxical 'Liar' sentences which says of itself that it is false. So if 'P' is false, it is true; and if it is true it is false. So again, it must be wrong to say that it is true and wrong to say that it is false (assuming it can't be both).

And perhaps there are other possibilities too where we will want to allow for claims that are neither true nor false.

But we will keep things simple. Our crucial *Determinacy* assumption is that such issues don't arise for atoms of our PL languages. In particular, we can pretend that the atoms have fully determinate, context-independent content, so as to avoid problem (1). We suppose too that we can ignore (2) issues of vagueness (perhaps we imagine any vague boundaries to be artificially sharpened when we render ordinary-language propositions into our formalized language).

We will also assume that we will not get entangled with (3) the likes of the Liar Paradox.

Certainly, there are deep problems about context-dependence, about vagueness, and about liar-style paradoxes. Many whole books have been written on each of these topics. However, just as we have to start our study of dynamics by ignoring friction and air-resistance, we have to start our study of logic by simply sidestepping all these problems, leaving them for another day.

So, to repeat: we henceforth assume that the basic building blocks of our PL languages can for our purposes be taken to have complete, sharp, and unambiguous senses, and that they are determinately true or false in every possible situation.

(Usually, whether a wff is true will *depend* on the situation; but not always. An atom could express a necessary truth or necessary falsehood and so come out true or come out false independently of the situation in the world – as would be the case if, for example, we stipulated that 'P' means *Anyone who is a mother is a parent* or 'Q' means *Anyone who is a bachelor is married*, making them respectively true and false, just by definition.)

10.4 Truth values

Another bit of terminology. It is absolutely standard to talk of *truth values* (a notion first explicitly introduced into logic by Frege). To explain:

> If a wff (or indeed a sentence of an ordinary language) is true in a given situation, we say it then has the truth value *true*; and if it is false, it then has the truth value *false*. For brevity, we denote these truth values by simply 'T' and 'F'.
>
> We call an assignment of truth values to some wffs of a PL language a *valuation* of those wffs.

But what *are* truth values? Well, we don't really *have* to suppose there are such things – we could take our talk of them simply to be a colourful idiom. However it makes life a bit easier if we construe talk of values literally and identify truth values with suitable objects. A standard choice is to identify the truth value T with the number 1, and the truth value F with the number 0. We are then, in effect, thinking of these truth-values-as-numbers as codes for the truth-status of sentences or wffs.

With this new way of talking in play, our crucial assumption in the last section therefore can be rephrased like this:

> *Determinacy* The atoms of a PL language are to be interpreted so that they have determinate truth values, exactly one of T and F, in any possible situation.

10.5 Truth tables for the connectives

It is useful to have some brisk notation – added to logicians' English – to talk about the assignment of a truth value to a wff. So we will write

$$P := T, \quad Q := F, \quad (P \wedge Q) := F, \quad ((P \wedge \neg Q) \vee (\neg P \wedge Q)) := T, \ldots$$

to say that the value of 'P' is T, the value of 'Q' is F, the value of '$(P \wedge Q)$' is F, etc. (The symbol ':=' suggests itself because it is used in some programming languages for the assignment of values.)

Now, in §8.2, we characterized a conjunction of two claims A and B as being true when both of A and B are true, and false when at least one of A and B is false. Then in §8.7 we stipulated that the connective '$\wedge$' always forms a bare conjunction in a PL language. Hence the following four conditions apply to any PL-wffs α, β:

> If $\alpha := T$ and $\beta := T$, then $(\alpha \wedge \beta) := T$.
> If $\alpha := T$ and $\beta := F$, then $(\alpha \wedge \beta) := F$.
> If $\alpha := F$ and $\beta := T$, then $(\alpha \wedge \beta) := F$.
> If $\alpha := F$ and $\beta := F$, then $(\alpha \wedge \beta) := F$.

Since we are assuming that PL wffs always have one or other truth value, one of the four conditions on the left must apply. Whatever the situation, it will fix the truth values of given wffs α and β; hence we can apply the relevant condition to determine the truth value of their conjunction $(\alpha \wedge \beta)$.

Likewise, in §8.3 we defined an inclusive disjunction of two claims A and B to be true when at least one of A and B is true, and to be false when both A and B are false. But '$\vee$' always forms an inclusive disjunction in a PL language. Hence, for any wffs α, β,

> If $\alpha := T$ and $\beta := T$, then $(\alpha \vee \beta) := T$.
> If $\alpha := T$ and $\beta := F$, then $(\alpha \vee \beta) := T$.
> If $\alpha := F$ and $\beta := T$, then $(\alpha \vee \beta) := T$.
> If $\alpha := F$ and $\beta := F$, then $(\alpha \vee \beta) := F$.

And thirdly, 'negation flips truth values'; that is to say, a negation of A is true when A is false and is false when A is true. The prefixed connective '$\neg$' serves as a negation operator in a PL language. So in our new notation, for any wff α:

> If $\alpha := T$, then $\neg\alpha := F$.
> If $\alpha := F$, then $\neg\alpha := T$.

Conventionally, we sum up these three lists of conditions in tabular form:

The truth tables for the PL connectives:

α	β	$(\alpha \wedge \beta)$
T	T	T
T	F	F
F	T	F
F	F	F

α	β	$(\alpha \vee \beta)$
T	T	T
T	F	T
F	T	T
F	F	F

α	$\neg\alpha$
T	F
F	T

Just read across the lines of these truth tables in the natural way, and you will recover the lists of conditions above. So these tables can be thought of as a vivid way of giving the senses, i.e. the truth-relevant meanings, of the PL connectives.

10.6 Evaluating molecular wffs: two examples

(a)   Consider now the following wff of some PL language:

$$\neg((P \lor Q) \land \neg(\neg Q \lor R)).$$

Suppose that the interpretations of the atoms in this language and the facts of the matter conspire to generate assignments of truth values to the three atoms involved as follows:

$$P := T, \ Q := T, \ R := F.$$

Then we can easily work out, by a plodding calculation, that the whole wff is false in this circumstance.

The key point to bear in mind when evaluating complex wffs is that we need to do our working 'from the inside out', exactly as in arithmetic. Here is a step-by-step semantic evaluation presented as a derivation in rather gruesome detail:

$\mathbf{A}^S$

(1)	$P := T.$	(premiss)
(2)	$Q := T.$	(premiss)
(3)	$R := F.$	(premiss)
(4)	$(P \lor Q) := T,$	(from 1, 2 by the table for '$\lor$')
(5)	$\neg Q := F.$	(from 2 by the table for '$\neg$')
(6)	$(\neg Q \lor R) := F.$	(from 5, 3 by the table for '$\lor$')
(7)	$\neg(\neg Q \lor R) := T.$	(from 6 the table for '$\neg$')
(8)	$((P \lor Q) \land \neg(\neg Q \lor R)) := T.$	(from 4, 7 by the table for '$\land$')
(9)	$\neg((P \lor Q) \land \neg(\neg Q \lor R)) := F.$	(from 8 by the table for '$\neg$')

However, this linear version isn't really the most illuminating way of presenting the derivation. As in §9.2, we can rather more perspicuously re-arrange our reasoning as a tree, like this:

$\mathbf{A}^{ST}$

$$
\dfrac{
\dfrac{P := T \qquad Q := T}{(P \lor Q) := T}
\qquad
\dfrac{\dfrac{\dfrac{Q := T}{\neg Q := F} \qquad R := F}{(\neg Q \lor R) := F}}{\neg(\neg Q \lor R) := T}
}{
\dfrac{((P \lor Q) \land \neg(\neg Q \lor R)) := T}{\neg((P \lor Q) \land \neg(\neg Q \lor R)) := F}
}
$$

Simple vertical steps correspond to applications of the rule for evaluating a negation; while steps where two branches of the tree join correspond to applications of the rule for evaluating a conjunction or disjunction.

But now note the *exact* parallelism between these *semantic* derivations $\mathbf{A}^S$ and $\mathbf{A}^{ST}$ and the old *syntactic* derivations $\mathbf{A}$ and $\mathbf{A}^T$ in §9.2(a) which showed that the same wff is well-formed. *This is no accident!*

We have designed PL languages so that the syntactic structure of a wff, i.e. the way that the symbols are put together into grammatical strings, is a perfect guide to its semantic structure, and in particular to the way the truth value of the whole will depend on the truth values of the atoms.

Replacing the frames '...' *is a wff* in the construction history $\mathbf{A}^T$ by the appropriate assignments of truth values gives us the semantic derivation $\mathbf{A}^{ST}$.

As with construction histories, we can also write this tree the other way up, like a parse tree. Then the values assigned to the atoms at the bottom of branches determine the values of wffs immediately above them on the parse tree, which in turn determine the values of wffs above them, all the way up. Looking at things this way, we can say that *semantics chases truth up the tree of grammar* (to adapt a neat phrase of the American philosopher W. V. O. Quine).

(b)   For a second example, take the following wff:

$$(((S \wedge Q) \wedge \neg\neg R) \vee \neg(\neg(P \vee P) \wedge Q)).$$

We showed that this *is* a wff by the tree proof $\mathbf{B}^T$ in §9.2(c). And consider the following valuation of its atoms:

$$P := F, \quad Q := T, \quad R := T, \quad S := T.$$

Again, we can work out the value of the wff on the given valuation by assigning truth values like this:

$\mathbf{B}^{ST}$

$$
\begin{array}{l}
\hspace{6cm} P := F \qquad P := F \\
\hspace{6.5cm} \underline{(P \vee P) := F} \\
\hspace{4cm} \underline{R := T} \hspace{1.3cm} \neg(P \vee P) := T \qquad Q := T \\
\underline{S := T \quad Q := T} \quad \underline{\neg R := F} \hspace{1.2cm} \underline{(\neg(P \vee P) \wedge Q) := T} \\
\underline{(S \wedge Q) := T} \hspace{1.2cm} \neg\neg R := T \hspace{1.2cm} \neg(\neg(P \vee P) \wedge Q) := F \\
\hspace{1cm} \underline{((S \wedge Q) \wedge \neg\neg R) := T} \\
\hspace{2cm} (((S \wedge Q) \wedge \neg\neg R) \vee (\neg(P \vee P) \wedge Q)) := T
\end{array}
$$

(c)   Note that we can do these two calculations of the truth values of complex wffs in $\mathbf{A}^{ST}$ and $\mathbf{B}^{ST}$ once we know the initial valuations of their atoms, just using the truth tables for the connectives. We don't at all need to know what their constituent atoms are supposed to mean. That's because the truth values of wffs in PL depend only on the *truth values* of their atomic parts, and not on the *interpretation* of those parts. More on this hugely important point in Chapter 12.

10.7   Uniqueness and bivalence

(a)   Recall from §9.3 that our strict bracketing convention prevents us from forming structurally ambiguous expressions like 'P ∨ Q ∧ R'.

Imagine that we did allow such expressions, and suppose P := T, Q := T, R := F. Then consider the following pair of calculations of truth values, reflecting the two ways of constructing the ambiguous expression:

$$\frac{\dfrac{P := T \quad Q := T}{P \lor Q := T} \quad R := F}{P \lor Q \land R := F} \qquad \frac{P := T \quad \dfrac{Q := T \quad R := F}{Q \land R := F}}{P \lor Q \land R := T}$$

Here the final valuations differ because, on the left, the final expression is read with '∧' having wider scope than '∨', and on the right it is read with '∨' having wider scope. The syntactic structural ambiguity in this case leads to a semantic ambiguity: in other words, fixing the truth values of the atoms does not uniquely fix the truth value of the whole unbracketed expression. The bracketing rules are in place precisely to ensure that this sort of thing can't happen. (Our strict bracketing policy is not the only one on the market: but any policy must similarly prevent structural ambiguities.)

(b)   Now to generalize. Suppose that we have a valuation of the atoms of a given wff α (perhaps the valuation arising from the real-world truth values of interpreted atoms, perhaps another possible valuation). We can then work out the consequent unique truth value taken by α on that valuation.

Look at it this way (turning the likes of $\mathbf{A}^{ST}$ and $\mathbf{B}^{ST}$ upside down). We take the unique parse tree for α. We feed in the truth values of whichever atoms we find at the bottom of the branches. Then we go up the branches calculating the values of the larger and larger subformulas of α we meet, at each stage applying the truth tables for the connectives. We must then end up with a unique truth value for the wff α.

And note, the fact that we evaluate α by chasing values up its parse tree means that the values of atoms that *don't* appear on its parse tree can't affect α's value. In other words, unsurprisingly, the truth value of a wff depends only on the assignment of values to the atoms it actually contains.

It follows, then, that we have:

A valuation of the atomic wffs in a PL wff *uniquely* determines a resulting valuation of the wff.

A valuation of all the atomic wffs of a PL language uniquely determines a resulting valuation of *every* wff of the language, however complex.

(c)   Put that last observation together with our assumption that the atoms of a PL language will in any possible situation have a definite valuation, and it follows that *every* wff of a PL language is determinately either true or false whatever the situation. Hence:

Our formalized PL languages are *bivalent* – i.e. are two-valued, with every wff always taking one (though not both!) of the values T and F, in any possible situation.

In studying the logic of arguments regimented in these languages, we can therefore be said to be studying *classical two-valued logic* – 'classical' not in the sense of ancient but in the sense of basic and mainstream. (And, regrettably, we can only touch on one non-classical logic in this book: see §24.8.)

10.8 Short working

(a) The last two sections have explained the basic principles of evaluating PL wffs given a valuation of its atoms. In this section, we will introduce a way of presenting truth-value calculations considerably more snappily.

In practice, of course, it isn't necessary to go through all the palaver of chasing truth values down construction histories/up parse trees. Simple calculations of truth values, like simple arithmetic calculations, can very easily be done in our heads. And more complex ones can be set out in a *much* more economical style, in a mini-table, as we will now show.

So compare $\mathbf{A}^S/\mathbf{A}^{ST}$ with the following. We begin constructing our mini-table by setting down the same wff as before on the right. And on the left we display the same initial assignment of values to its atomic subformulas:

P	Q	R	$\neg((P$	$\vee$	$Q)$	$\wedge$	$\neg(\neg Q$	$\vee$	$R))$
T	T	F							

Next, we copy the values of atoms across to the right, writing the appropriate value under each atom again:

P	Q	R	$\neg((P$	$\vee$	$Q)$	$\wedge$	$\neg(\neg Q$	$\vee$	$R))$
T	T	F	T		T		T		F
			1		2		2		3

(To aid comparison with the linear derivation in $\mathbf{A}^S$, we have started to number the sequence of stages at which values are calculated by the corresponding line number in that derivation.)

We then continue by calculating the values of more and more complex subformulas of the final formula: and at each step *we write the resulting value under the main connective of the subformula being evaluated* – in other words, we write the value under the connective whose impact is being calculated at each stage. For example, in a few steps we get to,

P	Q	R	$\neg((P$	$\vee$	$Q)$	$\wedge$	$\neg(\neg Q$	$\vee$	$R))$
T	T	F	T	T	T		F T	F	F
			1	4	2		5 2	6	3

And in a few more steps we arrive at:

P	Q	R	$\neg((P$	$\vee$	$Q)$	$\wedge$	$\neg(\neg Q$	$\vee$	$R))$
T	T	F	<u>F</u> T	T	T	T	T F T	F	F
			9 1	4	2	8	7 5 2	6	3

For clarity, we have underlined the final value we get when we evaluate the impact of the main connective.

Let's take a second example, revisiting the wff in $\mathbf{B}^{ST}$, with the valuation of atoms as before. We lay out the working as a mini-table again. But this time, to speed things up, we won't bother to copy across the values of atoms from the left-hand part of the table to the right-hand part – after all, how much trouble is it to look up the values of atoms when we need them by glancing back to the left? So we get:

P	Q	R	S	(((S ∧ Q) ∧ ¬¬R) ∨ ¬(¬(P ∨ P) ∧ Q))
F	T	T	T	T T TF T F T F T
				1 4 3 2 9 8 6 5 7

Here, the numbers suggest *one* possible order in which to work things out. So check the steps in that order, at each stage evaluating the subformula whose main connective is written above the step-number.

(b) This standard way of setting out working is neat and tidy. But we can speed things up further by noting three elementary facts:

> Once one of two conjuncts α and β has been shown to be false, it is redundant to evaluate the other conjunct: the whole conjunction $(\alpha \wedge \beta)$ must be false.
>
> Once one of two disjuncts α and β has been shown to be true, it is redundant to evaluate the other disjunct: the whole disjunction $(\alpha \vee \beta)$ must be true.
>
> We can jump straight from the truth value of a wff α to the value of its double negation $\neg\neg\alpha$, since these wffs always have the same value.

For instance, in the last example, we can skip step 2. And once we have completed step 4 and evaluated the first disjunct '$((S \wedge Q) \wedge \neg\neg R)$' as true, we can skip the next four steps and immediately conclude that the whole disjunction is true.

    Here is another quick example, showing our suggested short cuts in operation. We take the same wff again, but with a different assignment of values to its atoms:

P	Q	R	S	(((S ∧ Q) ∧ ¬¬R) ∨ ¬(¬(P ∨ P) ∧ Q))
T	F	F	T	T T F
				3 2 1

Since the conjunct 'Q' is false, the conjunction '$(\neg(P \vee P) \wedge Q)$' must be false (here we use the first of our shortcuts). Therefore the conjunction's negation '$\neg(\neg(P \vee P) \wedge Q)$' is true. But that wff is the second disjunct of the complete disjunctive wff. Therefore the whole wff must be true too (that's the second shortcut at work). Just three steps of working, and we are done!

    One more example. Take the rather longer wff that we met in §9.5 (we used different bracketing styles to make it more readable). And suppose we want to work out the truth value of this wff on the valuation of atoms stated on the left:

P	Q	R	S	[¬{(P ∨ (R ∧ ¬S)) ∨ ¬(Q ∧ ¬P)} ∧ ¬{P ∨ ¬(¬Q ∨ R)}]
T	T	F	T	F T T F
				3 1 2 4

Since the disjunct 'P' is true, the disjunction '$(P \vee (R \wedge \neg S))$' is true. Hence the longer disjunction '$\{(P \vee (R \wedge \neg S)) \vee \neg(Q \wedge \neg P)\}$' must also be true. So the negation of this curly-bracketed expression has to be false. But *this* false wff is the first conjunct of the whole conjunctive wff. Therefore the whole wff is false too. That's all the working we need.

(c)   The business of evaluating wffs on various assignments of values to their atoms, and fully setting out all the working in our brisk tabular form, is entirely mechanical and straightforward, even though potentially very tedious. As we have just seen, however, we can often considerably reduce the tedium. It will only take a little practice to learn to spot when we can use our shortcuts.

10.9   Summary

The atomic wffs – the basic non-logical vocabulary – of a PL language are interpreted by a glossary which gives the truth-relevant senses of the atoms, and the same atoms can get different interpretations in different languages. However, the connectives '∧', '∨', and '¬' – forming the logical vocabulary constant across PL languages – always get the same meanings, respectively expressing bare conjunction, inclusive disjunction, and strict negation.

Having fixed the truth-relevant content of an atomic wff, the situation in the world will then determine whether this atom is true or false. Or at least, it will do so assuming that we have in fact assigned a determinate meaning to the atom, and are setting aside cases of context-dependence, vagueness, paradoxical sentences, etc.

The truth or falsity of each of the wffs α and β will also determine the truth or falsity of the conjunction $(\alpha \wedge \beta)$, the disjunction $(\alpha \vee \beta)$, and the negation $\neg\alpha$. Simple truth tables display the ways that the truth values of the molecular wffs of those forms depend on the values of the relevant subformulas α and β.

Applying those tables, a valuation of the atoms in a wff of a PL language (i.e. an assignment of the value *true* or *false* to each of its atoms) will determine a valuation for the whole wff, however complex it is; and this valuation will be unique because of the uniqueness of the wff's construction/parse tree.

A calculation of the truth value of a wff given a valuation of its atoms can be set out in various styles – e.g. as a vertical linear derivation, or by a tree decorated with truth values. Most economically, we can set out the working in a mini-table (the basic rule is to write the value of a subformula under its main connective).

Exercises 10

(a)   Suppose we are working in a PL language where 'P' means *Fred is a fool*; 'Q' means *Fred knows some logic*; 'R' means *Fred is a rocket scientist*. Translate the following sentences into this formal language as best you can. What do you think is lost in the translations, if you can only use the 'colourless' connectives '∧', '∨' and '¬'?

(1) Even Fred is a rocket scientist.

(2) Fred is a rocket scientist, but he knows no logic.

(3) Fred is a rocket scientist, moreover he knows some logic.

(4) Fred's a fool, even though he knows some logic.

(5) Although Fred's a rocket scientist, he's a fool and even knows no logic.

(6) Fred's a fool, yet he's a rocket scientist who knows some logic.

(7) Fred is a fool despite the fact that he knows some logic.

(8) Fred is not a rocket scientist who knows some logic.

(9) Fred knows some logic unless he is a fool.

(b)   Confirm that the following strings are wffs by producing parse trees. Suppose that P := T, Q := F, R := T. Evaluate the wffs first by chasing values up the trees. Then do the working again in the short form (i.e. as a mini-table, skipping redundant working when you can).

(1) $((R \lor \neg Q) \land (Q \lor P))$

(2) $\neg(P \lor ((Q \land \neg P) \lor R))$

(3) $\neg(\neg P \lor \neg(Q \land \neg R))$

(4) $(\neg(P \land \neg Q) \land \neg\neg R)$

(5) $(((P \lor \neg Q) \land (Q \lor R)) \lor \neg\neg(Q \lor \neg R))$

Work out, in short form, the truth values of the following wffs on the assignment of values P := F, Q := F, R := T, S := F

(6) $\neg((P \lor Q) \land \neg(\neg Q \lor R))$

(7) $\neg\neg((P \land Q) \lor (\neg S \lor \neg R))$

(8) $(((S \land Q) \land \neg\neg R) \lor \neg Q)$

(9) $(((P \land (Q \land \neg R)) \lor \neg\neg\neg(R \land Q)) \lor (P \land R))$

(10) $(\neg((P \lor (R \land \neg S)) \lor \neg(Q \land \neg P)) \land \neg(P \lor \neg(\neg Q \lor R)))$

(c*)   In this book we have taken a maximalist line about the use of brackets in PL wffs. What conventions for dropping brackets could we have adopted (while still writing '∧' and '∨' *between* the wffs they connect) in order to reduce the numbers of brackets in a typical wff while not reintroducing semantic ambiguities?

(d*)   *Polish notation* for the propositional calculus – introduced by Jan Lukasiewicz in the 1920s – is a bracket-free notation in which connectives are written *before* the wffs they connect.

Traditionally, for the Negation of α we write $N\alpha$; for the Konjunction of α and β we write $K\alpha\beta$; for the disjunction of the Alternatives α and β we write $A\alpha\beta$. Since capital letters are used for connectives, it is customary in Polish notation to use lower case letters for propositional atoms. Hence '$(\neg P \land Q)$' becomes '$KNpq$', '$\neg(P \land Q)$' becomes '$NKpq$', '$\neg((P \land \neg Q) \lor R)$' becomes '$NAKpNqr$', etc.

(1) Rewrite the syntactic rules of §9.1(c) for a language using Polish notation.

(2) Render the Polish wffs $KNpNq$, $KNNpq$, $NKpNq$, $AKpqr$, $ApKqr$, $AANpNqNr$, $AKNpqKpNq$, $ANKKpqKqrNArs$ into our notation.

(3) Render the wffs (1) to (5) from (b) into Polish notation.

(4) (Difficult!) Show that Polish notation, although bracket-free, introduces no semantic ambiguities (every Polish wff can be parsed in only one way).

11 'P's, 'Q's, 'α's, 'β's – and form again

In this chapter, we pause to make it clear how our 'P's and 'Q's, and 'α's and 'β's, are being used, and why it is crucial to differentiate between them.

We also need to explain the standard convention governing the use of quotation marks (though we will very soon start avoiding their use when convenient). We then add some more remarks about the idea of a wff's form.

11.1 Styles of variable: object languages and metalanguages

(a)   Recall the use of '*n*' and '*F*' which we introduced in a rough and ready way to stand in for everyday names and general terms right back in §1.5. These are handy augmentations of logicians' English, particularly useful when we want to talk perspicuously about general patterns of inference.

We have similarly used '*A*' and '*B*' in a rough and ready way to stand in for whole sentences; and again the role of these symbols is to help us speak snappily about forms of sentences, patterns of inference, etc. For example, in §8.1 we used them to enable us to discuss forms of ordinary-language arguments involving conjunction and disjunction.

Then in §8.7 we started using '*α*' and '*β*' in order to talk briskly and clearly – but still in augmented English – about wffs in a PL language.

The use of symbolic letters as schematic variables in these ways is always dispensable. At the expense of long-windedness, we could use plain English prose instead. Rather than using the likes of '*A*' and '*B*' or '*α*' and '*β*' in *displaying* patterns of inference, we could *describe* the same patterns using expressions such as 'the first proposition' and 'the second wff'. And note too that, just as 'the first proposition' and 'the second wff' don't themselves express propositional messages, neither do English-augmenting schematic variables like '*A*' or '*α*'.

(b)   By contrast, our recently introduced 'P', 'Q', etc. do not belong to English, augmented or otherwise. Instead they are atomic wffs (in effect, basic sentences) of one of our new artificial PL languages. Unlike the schematic variables, these new symbols *do* potentially express complete propositional claims; they can be used to convey whole messages, as it might be about Alun's loving Bethan, or Jack's taking Jill to the party, or whatever.

The letters 'P', 'Q', etc. are available to express different messages in different PL languages (what stays constant across languages is the meaning of the connectives). In this sense, the atomic wffs can perhaps also be thought of as another kind of 'variable', i.e. they are potentially open to various interpretations in different languages. But within a fixed language, we suppose they are assigned a fixed meaning. And the crucial contrast remains: Greek-letter variables like 'α', 'β', etc. are used in augmented English to *talk about* PL wffs and arguments; while sans serif 'P', 'Q', etc. belong to various PL languages and can themselves *express* messages on all kinds of subject matter, depending on the glossary or interpretation manual in force.

(c)   Here is some standard terminology:

> The *object language* is the language which is the object of logical investigation at a particular point. The *metalanguage* is the language in which we conduct our investigation and discuss what is going on in the current object language.

In the last few chapters, PL languages have been the object of investigation. Our metalanguage has been English augmented with variables like 'α', 'β', etc. (hence those are often also called *metalinguistic variables*). In an Italian translation of this book, the object language might at some point be the same PL language, but the metalanguage in which we would be discussing it would now be augmented Italian.

(Of course, we might well want to discuss facts about logical features of English sentences in English, as we ourselves did earlier in the book; and then the metalanguage subsumes the object language. But in general, in logical investigations, the object language and metalanguage are distinct.)

(d)   To avoid confusion, it is more or less essential to mark typographically, one way or another, the distinction between (i) elements of the formalized languages like PL languages which are (from now on) the primary objects of our investigation and (ii) the informal metalinguistic apparatus which we use 'from outside' in discussing these object languages. Here are our conventions:

> In this book, the constituents of formalized languages such as PL languages will always be printed in sans-serif type, like 'P', 'Q'.

> Symbols printed in *serif italics*, like 'A', 'n', 'F', etc., or Greek letters like 'α', 'β', etc., are always augmentations of our English metalanguage. We reserve Greek letters for when we are talking about PL wffs and arguments, or about expressions and arguments in other artificial languages.

11.2   Quotation marks, use and mention

(a)   We now turn to talk about one key role for quotation marks.

If we want to refer to a certain *man*, we may of course simply use his name, as in the sentence

95

(1) Socrates was snub-nosed.

However, sometimes we want to discuss not the philosopher himself but his (English) *name*. There are various ways of referring to this name. We can very laboriously use this expression:

> The name consisting of the nineteenth letter of the alphabet, followed by the fifteenth letter, followed by the third letter, ...

Or more indirectly, we could use

> The name which begins the sentence (1).

But, much more economically, we can use quotation marks, thus:

> 'Socrates'

This whole expression refers to our philosopher's name, by the default logicians' convention governing the use of such quotation marks:

> Given an expression beginning with an opening quotation mark and ending with a matching closing quotation mark, the whole expression *including* the quotation marks is to be construed as referring to the word, sentence, or other expression displayed *inside* the quotes.

There are other uses of quotation marks, for example as so-called 'scare quotes' – as now in this very sentence. Such quotes highlight an expression perhaps as novel, or perhaps as being used in a contentious way. But this section is about the primary use of quotes round an expression as a device for *mentioning* that expression.

(b) Compare, then,

(1) Socrates was snub-nosed.
(2) Socrates contains the first letter of the alphabet.
(3) 'Socrates' is snub-nosed.
(4) 'Socrates' contains the first letter of the alphabet.
(5) 'Socrates was snub-nosed' is an English sentence.
(6) 'Snub Socrates nosed was' is not an English sentence.

The first is famously true; the second false (people don't contain letters of the alphabet). The third is false too (names don't have noses to be snub or otherwise); the rest are true.

Again, consider the following:

(7) Charles is called Chuck by his friends and Dad by his children.

If we strictly observe the convention of using quotation marks when we are mentioning or talking about an expression, this needs to be marked up as follows:

(7') Charles is called 'Chuck' by his friends and 'Dad' by his children.

And since Socrates is a man, not an expression, how should we insert quotes in the following in order to yield a truth?

(8) The initial referring expression in example (3) is Socrates.

We need the following:

(8′)   The initial referring expression in example (3) is ' 'Socrates' '.

That's because, in order to denote the referring expression at the beginning of (3), which already involves quotation marks, we need to put that whole expression in another pair of quotation marks – hence the double ration. Or for clarity's sake, to make it plain that there *are* two pairs of quotation marks here, we could/should use two different styles of quotation marks as we have done a few times before, like this:

(8″)   The first referring expression in example (3) is " 'Socrates' ".

(c)   Let's have another series of examples. Consider *this* wff:

(P ∨ Q)

(and here we refer to a type of expression by another common device which we have often used before; i.e. we display a sample token and use a demonstrative to 'point through' to the type instantiated by the token). In one PL language we've met, that wff says that either Jack took Jill to the party or he took Jo. And in an argument deploying that wff, the PL disjunction sign is simply *used* to express this disjunctive claim.

But sometimes we want to talk about the disjunction sign itself, i.e. to *mention* it in English. We can do this in various ways. We could use, as we have just done, the description 'the disjunction sign'. We can call it, as some do, 'the vel symbol'. Or we can use quotation marks again, as we have already often done, and refer to the disjunction sign via *this* expression:

'∨'

This quotation expression is then available for use *in our extended English*, as when we report that '∨' is a binary connective in PL languages. (Compare: the word 'soleil' is not part of English. However we can use its quotation in an English sentence – as we have just done, or as when we say that the French word 'soleil' is used to refer to the sun.)

Similarly for the atomic wffs of PL languages. Given their interpretations in a particular language, we can *use* them to report Bethan's love affairs or Jack's party-going or whatever. But we will also want to *mention* the atoms, i.e. talk about them in English, our metalanguage. Again the easy way of referring to them is to do what we have been doing all along – i.e. to use quotation marks to form expressions (augmenting English!) to refer to wffs. Thus consider:

(9)   'P' is an atomic wff of some PL languages.
(10)   'P' is a sentence of English.
(11)   " 'P' " is an expression which can occur in PL wffs.
(12)   " 'P' " is an expression which can occur in English sentences.
(13)   The atomic wff 'P' is a subformula of the molecular wff '¬(P ∨ ¬Q)'.

(9) is true, but (10) is false; (11) is false too (since PL languages don't contain quotation marks). (12), however, is true; for example, (9) and (13) provide instances of true English claims where the quotation of 'P' occurs.

(d)   A word of caution. Of course, when we *mention* an expression by putting it in quotes, we are still in one perfectly good sense *using* that expression! So when philosophers contrast 'use' vs 'mention', this has to be understood as standard shorthand for something a bit more complicated: 'use of an expression to talk about something other than itself' vs 'talking about that expression (which could still involve a special use of that very expression)'.

11.3   To Quine-quote or not to Quine-quote?

(a)   The distinction between directly *using* an expression to say something and *mentioning* that expression (i.e. referring to the words or symbols) is evidently crucial. We therefore need some convention for marking the distinction between use and mention. The logicians' usual convention is to use quotation marks explicitly to signal when expressions are being mentioned.

However, strictly abiding by this convention does lead to unsightly rashes of quotation marks, and most logicians adopt a more relaxed policy when no confusion will result. And we have in fact already done so, forgivably cutting ourselves some slack in various cases. For example, in giving a glossary for a formalized language, instead of writing something like

   (1)   'P' means *Jack loves Jill,*

we simply put

   (2)   P: Jack loves Jill.

Again, when making assignments of truth values to wffs, instead of writing

   (3)   'P' := T,

(i.e., 'P' takes the value T), we simply wrote

   (4)   P := T,

allowing ':=' to, so to speak, generate its own invisible quotation marks on the left.

(b)   Let's also note another – rather more subtle – sort of case where we have already been relaxed about quotation. Recall that in §9.1(c), we briskly stated one of the wff-building rules using schematic variables as follows:

(W2)   If α and β are wffs, so is $(\alpha \wedge \beta)$.

Strictly speaking, this mixes augmented English (the metalinguistic variables 'α' and 'β') with PL expressions (the conjunction sign, of course, but also the two brackets as well). So we seem to have an unholy mixture of languages here, and no quotation marks to keep things well-behaved. And note that we can't untangle things simply by writing

         If α and β are wffs, so is '$(\alpha \wedge \beta)$',

for what is inside the quotation marks there is *not* a wff of a PL language (remember, the Greek letters 'α' and 'β' are *not* symbols of that type of language).

What to do? As we explained before, W2 is to be understood as saying

(W2′)   If α and β are wffs, so is the expression formed from '(' followed by α followed by '∧' followed by β followed by ')'.

So, if we want to be super-punctilious, we will have to introduce a new species of quotation marks – corner quotes, often called *Quine quotes* after their inventor – and write

(W2″)   If α and β are wffs, so is $\ulcorner(\alpha \wedge \beta)\urcorner$,

where the corner quotes are defined so as to make this equivalent to W2′. We will see in the Exercises how to define Quine quotes.

However, there is surely no real risk of muddle in using W2 as it stands, undecorated by any kind of special quotation marks. For us, then, insisting on using Quine quotes is a fussy step too far.

11.4   How strict about quotation do we want to be?

In earlier chapters, we quietly followed a fairly strict policy on the use of quotation marks, although – as noted – we have occasionally taken a more relaxed line. But now we are alert to the use/mention distinction, why not be even more relaxed about omitting quotation marks when it is safe to do so?

Consider the following:

(1)   The wff $(P \vee \neg P)$ contains the connective $\vee$, and is an instance of the schema $(\alpha \vee \neg\alpha)$.

It is obvious from the phrases 'the wff $(P \vee \neg P)$', 'the connective $\vee$', 'the schema $(\alpha \vee \neg\alpha)$', that we are *mentioning* a wff, a connective, and a schema in (1). We are not *using* the wff to express a message, using the connective to express a disjunction, or using the schema to do some generalizing work. Now, if we were following the logicians' default quotation policy, we would write

(2)   The wff '$(P \vee \neg P)$' contains the connective '$\vee$', and is an instance of the schema '$(\alpha \vee \neg\alpha)$';

But this begins to look like overkill, since (1) was already perfectly clear. Consider too

(3) $(P \vee Q)$ is a subformula of $((P \vee Q) \wedge R)$.

What are these PL expressions doing as parts of an English sentence? Well, even though we haven't written 'the wff $(P \vee Q)$' or 'the wff $((P \vee Q) \wedge R)$', we again know that these formal expressions in (3) must be being mentioned or referred to. If we are being strict about quotation marks, we should therefore write, as we did in §9.3,

(4)   '$(P \vee Q)$' is a subformula of '$((P \vee Q) \wedge R)$'.

But again this begins to seem excessively fastidious, given that (3) is again already entirely clear as it stands. Just how pernickety do we want to be?

Some introductory logic texts, including the first edition of this book, do take a pretty strict line throughout, and insist on surrounding all mentioned formal expressions with inverted commas (unless displayed on a separate line), even when omitting the quotation marks would cause no confusion at all. But from now on we are going to incline towards the more usual mathematical practice of minimizing the use of quotation marks around symbolism. In particular,

> We can drop explicit quotation marks around expressions prefixed by 'the wff', 'the connective', 'the schema', 'the symbol', etc.
>
> More generally, when sans serif expressions from some formal language appear in an English sentence, they can be understood as being mentioned (and so can be thought of as accompanied by invisible quotation marks).

However, we will still use explicit quotation marks round formal expressions when it is helpful. For example, we will usually mention single lower-case letters by putting them in quotes – as here, 'x' – simply because this aids the eye. And sometimes, when we want to mention more than one expression in the same sentence, if one expression is put in quotes to help the eye, it is then natural to balance things by putting other mentioned expressions in quotes too.

It is a judgement call. But arguably it is better to aim to be locally clear than to stick religiously to either a global maximalist or a global minimalist policy about quotation marks.

11.5 Why Greek-letter variables?

Let's now return to comment on the use of Greek-letter variables when talking about PL wffs. Why are we using these, instead of continuing with the familiar 'A', 'B', etc., which we had used earlier when talking about informal propositions? The danger is that sprinklings of Greek letters can make a logic text look dauntingly mathematical (even when it isn't). But here are three reasons that, on balance, tip the scales in favour of their use – though this is another judgement call.

(1) It is a *widely adopted* convention to use Greek letters as metalinguistic variables like this. So, like it or not, you might as well get accustomed to it!

(2) It is a *helpful* convention. Once formalized languages are in play, we need to be able to keep track of the distinction between symbols from these languages and any metalanguage symbols we might use. And yes, in print, we can easily enough distinguish italic letters (in our metalanguage) from upright sans serif letters (in formal object languages). But in handwriting on the blackboard or in notebooks, that distinction can get lost, and it is much easier to distinguish metalinguistic Greek letters from object-language Roman letters.

(3) But most importantly, our convention *marks a difference*. Our earlier use of 'A', 'B', etc. was rough and ready, and the rules for the use of such metalinguistic variables were intentionally left unclear. By contrast,

there is a very clean and crisp story to be told about our use of Greek-letter metalinguistic variables.

To expand the third point, our practice of using schemas with schematic variables like 'n', 'F', 'A' etc. can be pretty casual. Look again how free and easy we were in allowing different sorts of English expression as substitutions for the likes of '(is) F' and then grammatically tidying up the results – we cheerfully allowed 'is wise' but also 'is a philosopher' or even (without an 'is') 'understands quantum mechanics' to count as instances. Or consider our relaxed use of '$not\text{-}A$' in §2.1(d), §4.5(c), etc., where we really didn't pin down what would count as an allowable instance. Informal schemas are often treated like this, as corresponding quite loosely to the details of surface form. Now, this lack of precision, the need for more than a bit of charity in applying the symbolism, was no real problem given our earlier introductory purposes: as they say, 'Sufficient unto the day is the rigour thereof.' But it does leave us with some messy questions about just how relaxed and flexible we want to be in using schemas with italic variables.

By contrast, when it comes to the use of Greek-letter variables in talking about formal wffs and formal arguments, everything will be crystal clear and rigorous (as we announced in §7.6). For example, when we say that a wff has the form $(\alpha \wedge \beta)$, we are talking about nothing other than its surface shape. We of course just mean that, for some wffs α, β of the relevant PL-language, the wff in question has the form of a left-hand bracket followed by α followed by the conjunction sign followed by β followed by a right-hand bracket. No charitable tidying-up is required!

11.6   The idea of form, again

That last point is simple but important. The idea is that a formal Greek-letter schema gives a kind of template or pattern for constructing PL expressions; and a wff counts as having the form displayed by some schema when the wff is built exactly to the required pattern. Let's spell this out, in two steps.

(a)   Start, then, with the following definition:

A *substitution instance* of a Greek-letter schema is the result of systematically replacing the metalinguistic variables in the schema with wffs.

Here, 'systematic' replacement means replacing the same Greek-letter variable with the same wff throughout; recall from §3.2(a), the whole point of using recurring metalinguistic symbols is to indicate patterns of recurrence. And note, the replacement wff may be atomic or molecular.

For example, the wff $((\mathsf{P} \wedge \mathsf{Q}) \vee \neg(\mathsf{P} \wedge \mathsf{Q}))$ is a substitution instance of the schema $((\alpha \wedge \beta) \vee \neg(\alpha \wedge \beta))$. But note too that the same wff is *also* a substitution instance of the different schemas $(\alpha \vee \neg\alpha)$ and $(\alpha \vee \beta)$. It is also, of course, a substitution instance of the minimally informative schema α!

(b)   We can now say:

> A PL wff has the form displayed by a schema using Greek-letter variables if and only if it is a substitution instance of that schema.

In this sense, the wff $((P \wedge Q) \vee \neg(P \wedge Q))$ has the form displayed by the schema $((\alpha \wedge \beta) \vee \neg(\alpha \wedge \beta))$ – or for brevity, we can more simply say: it has the form $((\alpha \wedge \beta) \vee \neg(\alpha \wedge \beta))$. But the wff *also* has the form $(\alpha \vee \neg\alpha)$, and the form $(\alpha \vee \beta)$, and also has the trivial form α.

(c)   When we speak of a wff as having a certain form, then, we are making use of a notion that can be characterized purely syntactically, in terms of the surface shape of a wff. Of course, this notion of form is of interest principally because, in PL and other formalized languages, syntactic form reflects relevant semantic structure. However, it remains the case that we can define form quite unproblematically in terms of surface syntax.

But note again that, as we have just seen, we can no more talk about *the* form of a wff than we can talk about *the* form of an argument – see §3.3.

However, taking the same example wff, there is a sense in which the schema $((\alpha \wedge \beta) \vee \neg(\alpha \wedge \beta))$ gives its *basic* form: the schema captures all the structure of the wff $((P \wedge Q) \vee \neg(P \wedge Q))$, right down to its atomic level. So:

> Suppose we systematically replace the atoms in a wff with schematic variables – the same atoms (i.e. atoms which are tokens of the same letter-type) to be replaced by the same schematic variable, different atoms (atoms of different types) to be replaced by different schematic variables. Then we can call the resulting schema a *basic* schema for the wff.

Basic schemas aren't unique, because we still have a choice of which schematic variables to use to indicate places in the pattern. Both $(\alpha \vee \beta)$ and $(\gamma \vee \delta)$ will do as basic schemas for the wff $(P \vee Q)$. But basic schemas for a given wff will just be trivial alphabetical variants. In due course, we will occasionally need to put the notion of a basic schema to work.

11.7   Summary

> We need in general to distinguish the *object language* under discussion (whether it is a PL language, some later formal language, or some natural language) from the *metalanguage* that it is being discussed in (in this book, our metalanguage is slightly augmented English).

> A key convention: we use sans-serif type as in 'P', 'Q', etc., for expressions belonging to some artificial formalized object language like a PL language.

> Italicized letters like 'A', 'n', 'F' belong to our metalanguage of augmented English, as do Greek-letter variables like 'α' and 'β'. They are in principle

dispensable devices; but they help us to speak briskly about general patterns of argument, or formation rules for wffs, etc.

So there is a key distinction between the sans-serif symbols of PL languages and the Greek-letter variables which we add to English specifically to help us talk about and generalize over formal expressions of PL languages (and of other formalized languages).

When we want to *mention* a particular expression, rather than *use* it in the ordinary way, quotation marks give us a standard way of doing this. But, from now on, we will be fairly relaxed about the use of quotes in contexts where it is transparently clear that we are indeed mentioning a formal expression rather than using it. (Our policy will be more or less: if no confusion is likely to result, drop the quotes.)

Exercises 11

(a)   Where necessary, insert quotation marks into the following in accord with the strict convention for quotation, to make the resulting sentences come out true.

(1)   The first word in this sentence is the.

(2)   This is not a verb, but is is.

(3)   George Orwell is the same person as Eric Blair.

(4)   George Orwell was Eric Blair's pen-name.

(5)   The Evening Star and The Morning Star denote the same planet, namely Venus.

(6)   Sappho is the name of a Greek poet.

(7)   If we want to refer not to Sappho but her name, we need to use the expression Sappho.

(8) $\wedge$ means much the same as and.

(9)   P can be interpreted as meaning that grass is green.

(10)   P is a subformula of $(Q \wedge \neg P)$.

(11)   If $(Q \wedge \neg P)$ is a subformula of a wff α so is P.

(12)   If α and β are PL wffs, so is their conjunction.

(13)   The result of substituting the atomic wff P for the schematic letter in $\neg\neg\alpha$ is $\neg\neg$P.

(14)   The schema $(\alpha \wedge \beta)$ is formed from Greek letters, the connective $\wedge$, and the brackets (and).

(15)   If a wff has the form $(\alpha \wedge \neg\alpha)$ it is self-contradictory.

(b*)   In his *Mathematical Logic*, Quine defines what he calls *quasi-quotes* and what we call *Quine quotes*. Slightly changing his example he says that the expression $\ulcorner(\alpha \wedge \beta)\urcorner$ "amounts to quoting the constant contextual backgrounds, '( )' and ' $\wedge$ ', and imagining the unspecified expressions α and β written in the blanks." Guided by what Quine says about this particular example, explain more carefully the use of Quine quotes, with further examples.

103

12 Truth functions

We saw in §10.7 that any assignment of truth values to the atoms of a PL wff will determine the truth value of the whole wff. This chapter expands on that key result.

12.1 Truth-functional vs other connectives

As before, we will call an expression which can combine with one or more sentences to form a compound sentence a sentential connective. Then:

> A sentential connective is *truth-functional* if and only if the overall truth value of a compound sentence formed using the connective is always determined by the truth values of the connected constituent sentences.

We will say more about the label 'truth-functional' in the next section. For now, the thing to note is that some ordinary-language connectives are truth-functional in this sense – such as 'and' in its core use – while many others are not.

Consider the two-place connective 'because'. And suppose both of the following are true:

(1) The bridge fell down.
(2) There was a storm yesterday.

This plainly does not settle the truth value of

(3) The bridge fell down *because* there was a storm yesterday.

The joint truth of (1) and (2) is compatible with the truth of (3); but it is equally compatible with the falsehood of (3). Hence fixing the truth values of the constituent sentences (1) and (2) is not always enough to determine the truth value of the compound sentence (3).

Of course, if A is false or B is false, A *because* B will be false too. For example, (3) must be false if the bridge in fact didn't fall down, or if there wasn't a storm. But for full truth-functionality, as we have just defined it, *any* assignment of truth values to the constituents must determine a corresponding truth value for the compound whole.

Many (most?) ordinary-language connectives are not truth-functional. By contrast, the only connectives built into PL languages *are* truth-functional – fixing the truth values of any wffs α and β will of course determine the truth values of the corresponding wffs $(\alpha \wedge \beta)$, $(\alpha \vee \beta)$, and $\neg\alpha$.

12.2 Functions and truth functions

Why 'truth-functional'? This section explains.

(a)   You will be familiar with the idea of an arithmetical *function* which takes as input one or more numbers, and spits out a unique value. For example, 'x^2' signifies a one-place or unary function mapping a single number x to a definite value, the result of multiplying x by itself; '$x + y$' signifies the binary function which maps two numbers to their sum. And 'x^y' (i.e. 'x multiplied by itself y times') signifies another binary arithmetic function; and since in general $x^y \neq y^x$, this example reminds us that it usually matters which input is fed into which place in a function.

We can now generalize the idea of a function to cover any mapping that takes one or more inputs and outputs a single determinate result (we'll ignore for now the possibility of partial functions which are undefined for some inputs, and the possibility of multi-value functions which deliver more than one output). For example, 'the biological mother of [the living person] x' denotes a function mapping each living person to someone else. 'The winner of the Wimbledon women's tennis championship in the year y' denotes a function mapping dates (from the right range) to women. 'The distance in metres between a and b at time t' gives us a function mapping two spatially located objects and a time to a number.

(b)   We should pause for a word of clarification.

Consider '$(x + 2)(x - 2)$' and '$x^2 - 4$', as used to signify arithmetical functions. The two expressions have different *senses*, different truth-relevant interpretations. The first, in effect, tells us to take a given input, calculate the result of adding two and the result of subtracting two, and then multiply these results; the second expression tells us to take the input and square it, then subtract four. However, in this case it doesn't matter which of the two different procedures we follow; the same *correlation* between inputs and outputs will result either way.

Now, what really matters about a function is indeed the way that inputs are correlated with outputs, not how the correlation is specified. Hence, if f and g are functions with the same 'look-up table' listing inputs against outputs, then we will count f and g as being the *same* function. Or in terminology which we will meet properly later, if f and g have the same *extension* – the same input-output pairings – then they count as the same function. Note: this is the standard mathematical way of thinking about functions.

Going back to our example, then: while the expressions '$(x + 2)(x - 2)$' and '$x^2 - 4$' have different senses, they do denote the same function.

(c)   Among the functions, we are going to be especially interested in those which map truth values to truth values.

105

A *truth function* is a function which takes truth values as inputs and outputs a truth value. (An n-place truth function requires n inputs.)

In fact – when we recall that we are officially thinking of truth values as numbers (see §10.4) – we can think of a function mapping truth values to truth values as an ordinary kind of mathematical function. It is then just a function in a cut-down, two-number, arithmetic.

(d)   So now consider, for example, the familiar table

α	β	$(\alpha \land \beta)$
T	T	T
T	F	F
F	T	F
F	F	F

We introduced this in §10.6 as a way of displaying how the truth value of a wff $(\alpha \land \beta)$ is fixed by the truth values of its conjuncts α and β. So this table records that the conjunction is *truth-functional* in the sense of the previous section. But of course, the very same table can be read as defining a *truth function*, since it correlates the various possible combinations of input truth values given on the left with the corresponding output values given on the right.

(e)   Let's have another example. We introduce a new ternary (three-place) truth-functional connective that we imagine to be added to a PL-type language, and which we will symbolize using '$\$(\ ,\ ,\ )$', so we can form the likes of $\$(P, Q, R)$, $\$((P \land R), \neg Q, \neg S)$, $(\$(\neg P, Q, R) \lor \$(P, Q, (P \land Q)))$, etc.

Since we are assuming that this new connective is truth-functional, we must be able to display in a table how the value of a complex wff of the form $\$(\alpha, \beta, \gamma)$ depends on the values of the constituent wffs α, β, and γ. Perhaps the table goes as follows:

α	β	γ	$\$(\alpha, \beta, \gamma)$
T	T	T	F
T	T	F	T
T	F	T	F
T	F	F	T
F	T	T	F
F	T	F	F
F	F	T	T
F	F	F	F

But again, this table can equally well be read as defining a three-place truth function, which maps the three values given in order on the left of the table to the corresponding value on the right. This 'dollar' truth function might not be terrifically *interesting* – I have chosen it more or less at random. Still, it is an example of another perfectly well-defined truth function, the one which we can say is *expressed* by the truth-functional dollar connective.

12.3 Truth tables for wffs

(a) In §12.1, we defined truth-functionality for single sentential connectives. Now we can generalize:

Any way of forming a compound sentence out of constituent sentences is truth-functional if and only if fixing the truth values of the constituents is always enough to fix the truth value of the resulting compound sentence.

But recall: any valuation of the atoms in a PL wff fixes a corresponding value for the whole wff. So *a PL wff is always a truth-functional compound of its atoms.*

Next, note that the truth-functional dependency of the value of a whole PL wff on the value of its atoms can be displayed in a standard tabular form. For example, take the wff

A   ¬((P ∨ Q) ∧ ¬(¬Q ∨ R))

belonging to some PL language. In §10.6(a) we calculated the truth value of the same wff for the valuation P := T, Q := T, R := F. We first gave an explicit line-by-line derivation $\mathbf{A}^S$ following the wff's construction history; and in $\mathbf{A}^{ST}$ we reorganized the same derivation into a tree. Then in §10.8(a) we showed how to lay out that working in a much more economical way. However, that was to take just a single valuation of the atoms. But there are in all eight alternative ways of assigning the values T and F to three atoms. There are two ways we can assign a value to the atom P, each of these can combine with either value for Q, while each of these combinations can combine with either value for R – and $2 \times 2 \times 2 = 8$.

Running through these eight valuations in turn, we can mechanically compute the truth value of our sample wff in each case. And we can then lay out the stages of the calculation, in rather painful detail, as follows:

```
P  Q  R │ ¬((P  V  Q)  ∧  ¬(¬Q  V  R))
T  T  T │ T  T  T  T   F   F FT   T  T
T  T  F │ F  T  T  T   T   TFT   F  F
T  F  T │ T  T  T  F   F   F TF   T  T
T  F  F │ T  T  T  F   F   F TF   T  F
F  T  T │ T  F  T  T   F   F FT   T  T
F  T  F │ F  F  T  T   T   TFT   F  F
F  F  T │ T  F  F  F   F   F TF   T  T
F  F  F │ T  F  F  F   F   F TF   T  F
        │ 9  1     4   2   8  7 5 2  6  3
```

On the left, we systematically display the eight possible valuations of the atoms. On the right, for each valuation in turn, we calculate the truth value of the wff – we show our working in short form, recording the value of each subformula under its main connective, and underlining the overall value of the whole wff. The supplementary numbers at the foot of the columns indicate one order in which we can tackle the calculation.

(b) Putting all that detail on the right-hand side of the table is, however, quite excessive! For a start, we need not repeat on the right the assignments of truth values to atoms. Moreover, we can start omitting redundant working. Just remember those rather handy shortcuts from §10.8(b) – if one conjunct is false, we immediately know the whole conjunction is false without looking at the other conjunct; if one disjunct is true, we immediately know the whole disjunction is true. Cutting things down in this way halves the required writing:

P	Q	R	¬((P	∨	Q)	∧	¬(¬Q	∨	R))
T	T	T	T̲	T		F	F	T	
T	T	F	F̲	T		T	T	F	
T	F	T	T̲	T		F	F	T	
T	F	F	T̲	T		F	F	T	
F	T	T	T̲	T		F	F	T	
F	T	F	F̲	T		T	T	F	
F	F	T	T̲	F		F			
F	F	F	T̲	F		F			
			6	1		2/5	4	3	

At step 1, evaluate (P ∨ Q) on each line. It is false on the last two lines; so this already fixes the last two values of ((P ∨ Q) ∧ ¬(¬Q ∨ R)) at step 2.

Then at step 3 work out the value of (¬Q ∨ R) on the other six lines. At step 4, we can now write down the value of ¬(¬Q ∨ R), on the same six lines. So at step 5 we work out the value of ((P ∨ Q) ∧ ¬(¬Q ∨ R)) on those six lines.

We now know the value of that conjunction on all eight lines, and finally – at step 6 – we flip values to get the value of its negation on each line.

(c) Let's have another example. So this time take the wff

B   ((P ∧ (Q ∨ ¬R)) ∨ (R ∧ ¬(P ∧ Q))).

And here again is a table, giving the value of the wff on every possible valuation of its three atoms. This time we'll do more of the working in our heads:

P	Q	R	((P ∧ (Q ∨ ¬R))	∨	(R ∧ ¬(P ∧ Q)))
T	T	T	T	T̲	
T	T	F	T	T̲	
T	F	T	F	T̲	T
T	F	F	T	T̲	
F	T	T	F	T̲	T
F	T	F	F	F̲	F
F	F	T	F	T̲	T
F	F	F	F	F̲	F
			1	2/4	3

Here we start by evaluating the conjunction (P ∧ (Q ∨ ¬R)). This will be false whenever P is false, i.e. on the last four lines. When P is true, the conjunction's truth value depends on the value of (Q ∨ ¬R), which is easily calculated. So at step 1, we can write down the value of (P ∧ (Q ∨ ¬R)) at each line. Hence at step

2, we already know that the whole wff has to be true at the three lines where that first disjunct is true.

Next, at step 3, calculate the value of the second disjunct $(R \land \neg(P \land Q))$ on the remaining five lines.

So we now know the value of both disjuncts of the whole wff on the five as-yet-unsettled lines. We can immediately finish the table at step 4.

(d) One more worked example, where we can use multiple shortcuts. Consider

C $(((S \land Q) \land \neg\neg R) \lor \neg(\neg(P \lor P) \land Q))$.

We evaluated this in short form for just two valuations of its atoms in §10.8(a). But there are sixteen possible ways of assigning T or F to four atoms. Let's now give a table for the wff, evaluating it for each possible assignment:

P	Q	R	S	(((S ∧ Q) ∧ ¬¬R)	∨	¬ (¬(P ∨ P)	∧	Q))
T	T	T	T		T	T		F
T	T	T	F		T	T		
T	T	F	T		T	T		
T	T	F	F		T	T		
T	F	T	T		T	T		F
T	F	T	F		T	T		
T	F	F	T		T	T		
T	F	F	F		T	T		
F	T	T	T	T	T	F		T
F	T	T	F	F	F	F		
F	T	F	T	F	F	F		
F	T	F	F	F	F	F		
F	F	T	T		T	T		F
F	F	T	F		T	T		
F	F	F	T		T	T		
F	F	F	F		T	T		
				5	4/6	2/3		1

(1) Consider first the subformula $(\neg(P \lor P) \land Q)$. In a four-line block where the values of P and Q stay constant, the value of this subformula stays constant. Therefore we only need to calculate the value of this subformula on the first line of each block!

(2) We then flip that subformula's values to get the truth value of its negation $\neg(\neg(P \lor P) \land Q)$ on the first line of each block.

(3) We can next copy those values into the rest of each block. So the subformula $\neg(\neg(P \lor P) \land Q)$, the second disjunct of the whole wff, comes out true on twelve lines.

(4) That means we can already settle the value of the *whole* disjunctive wff on those twelve lines, with no further work needed.

(5) We now only need evaluate the *first* disjunct on the remaining four lines.

109

(6) Finally, we use the values of the first disjunct to work out the value of the whole wff on those four lines, and so complete the table

Irrespective of how much working we show, we will call any table which records the overall value of a PL wff for *every* possible valuation of its atoms a *truth table* for the wff.

A truth table for a wff can also be read as defining a corresponding *truth function*, namely the function which correlates the values given in order (on the left, in our formatting) with the output overall value (given on the right).

(e) If we use our shortcuts and are alert to cases where we can repeat results on different lines, constructing truth tables for shortish wffs with a smallish number of atoms need not be *too* painful. There are some tame Exercises to practise on, so we won't give more examples now. But two final remarks in this section:

(1) If the wff α involves n different atoms, there will be $2 \times 2 \times \ldots \times 2$ (n times) $= 2^n$ different possible valuations of these atoms. We can still mechanically construct a truth table for α, working out the truth values of the increasingly large subformulas of α until we reach the overall value of α, for each of the 2^n possible valuations of the atoms. But as n increases, the amount of labour required will explode exponentially. No wonder that we will in practice stick to small examples!

(2) Note that we have fallen into using the following systematic way of setting out all the assignments of values to a sequence of atoms such as P, Q, R, S. The *last* atom in the sequence gets alternating Ts and Fs; the previous one gets alternating blocks of two Ts and two Fs; moving leftwards, we next get alternating blocks of four Ts and four Fs; and so it goes. This system is guaranteed to cover all the possible valuations.

Any other systematic way of running through all the valuations of the relevant atoms will do equally well, of course. But ours is pretty much the standard convention when constructing full truth tables.

12.4 'Possible valuations'

Every PL wff has a truth table giving its truth value on every possible valuation to its atoms: this table defines a corresponding truth function. In the next chapter, we will show the converse: for every truth function, there is a PL wff which defines it.

For the moment, however, we pause for clarification. We need to distinguish two senses in which we can talk about 'possible valuations' of some given atoms.

(a) In the last section, as we worked out the full truth tables, we considered all the different combinations of values T or F that can be assigned to some atoms, quite regardless of what those atoms mean (in fact, we didn't even specify an interpretation for the atoms). In a phrase, we ran through all the *combinatorially* possible assignments of values. Call these the *c-possible* valuations, for short. And note, the notion of possibility here seems quite unproblematic.

But now bring meanings back into the picture. The atoms from a properly interpreted PL language express propositions. These atoms, given their meanings, are then true or false depending on how things are in the world. Take the world as it actually is: then there will be one resulting assignment of truth values to these interpreted atoms. And then, as we consider different possible situations, i.e. consider different ways the world might have been, the atoms with their given meanings will take on various other corresponding values. Let's say an assignment of values to some atoms is *realizable*-in-some-situation if there is indeed a possible situation in which these atoms, with their given meanings, would take those values. Call this an *r-possible* valuation for short.

The different short labels mark a real distinction. For not all combinatorially possible assignments of values to interpreted atoms may be realizable. In other words, in some cases not all c-possible valuations are r-possible valuations. Why?

For an easy example, suppose that – in our current PL language – P means *Jack is married*, and Q means *Jack is single*. Combinatorially, we can assign both these atoms the value T. But with their given interpretations, there can be no situation in which these atoms are true together. So in this case there is no realizable, meaning-respecting, r-possible valuation of P and Q which gives them both the value T. For an even easier example, suppose that R means *all mothers are parents*, so expresses a necessary truth, and therefore takes the value T whatever the situation. Then there is no r-possible valuation, no assignment of values which respects the meaning of R, which assigns it the value F.

(b) Return to our sample wff **A**, $\neg((P \lor Q) \land \neg(\neg Q \lor R))$. We set down all eight c-possible valuations for its three atoms – and the truth-functionality of the connectives means that we can then work out the value of the wff in each case without worrying about the interpretations of atoms. Still, depending on the interpretations of the atoms, perhaps not every line of the table is a realizable valuation corresponding to a way the world might be – i.e. perhaps not every line gives an r-possible valuation. But then, when setting out the truth table for the wff, shouldn't we really only care about realizable, meaning-respecting, valuations (distributions of truth values reflecting situations that could obtain)?

It depends! But looking forward, our particular aim is going to be to give an account of those arguments whose validity turns only on the distribution of the connectives 'and', 'or' and 'not' in their premises and conclusions, and doesn't turn on the topics of the sentences they connect. In other words, our concern is going to be with some questions about topic-neutral *logical* validity.

And the plan is that we avoid the vagaries of English by regimenting an argument up for assessment into a suitable PL language, thereby cleaning up the connectives, making their scopes explicit, etc. At this first stage we still care about the interpretation of the PL atoms we use, because we do want to be still talking about a contentful argument, a tidied-up version of the natural language original. However, at the second stage, when we now focus on validity-in-virtue-of-the-connectives, we will want to temporarily ignore the facts about the meaning of individual atoms. We will temporarily abstract away from those facts in order to reveal those PL arguments whose validity depends only on the truth-functional meanings of the topic-neutral connectives ∧, ∨, and ¬.

Hence, given *this* context in which we are going to be using truth tables, we will not want to restrict ourselves to considering only meaning-respecting possible valuations of atoms. Rather, we will treat any combinatorially possible assignment of T or F to the atoms P, Q, etc., as equally relevant for our purposes, whether it is realizable or not.

In sum, we will treat every assignment of values for the atoms as needing to be considered (all the c-possible assignments, in our unproblematic sense). We say rather more about this in §§14.3 and 15.2(b).

12.5 Summary

A truth function is a function sending one or more truth values as inputs to a single truth value as output.

A way of forming a complex sentence or wff out of one or more constituent sentences/wffs is truth-functional if fixing the truth values of the constituents is always enough to determine the truth value of the complex whole.

All wffs of a PL language are truth-functional combinations of their atoms. We can calculate and set out in a truth table the values that the wff takes on each combinatorially possible assignment of values to its atoms (so defining a truth function). This is tedious mechanical labour – though there are shortcuts which, if judiciously used, can reduce the work en route to the final result in many cases.

Exercises 12

Give truth tables for the following wffs of a PL language – i.e. calculate the value of the wff for every assignment of values to the atoms. (Use the recommended shortcuts.)

(1) (P ∧ ¬(P ∧ Q))
(2) ((R ∨ Q) ∨ ¬P)
(3) (¬(P ∧ ¬S) ∧ ¬¬R)
(4) ((P ∧ Q) ∨ (¬P ∨ ¬Q))
(5) ¬((P ∧ ¬Q) ∨ (¬R ∨ ¬(P ∨ Q)))
(6) (((P ∨ ¬Q) ∧ (Q ∨ R)) ∨ ¬¬(Q ∨ ¬R))
(7) (¬(¬P ∨ ¬(Q ∧ ¬R)) ∨ ¬¬(Q ∨ ¬P))
(8) (¬((R ∨ ¬Q) ∧ ¬S) ∧ ¬((¬P ∧ Q) ∧ S))
(9) (¬(¬(P ∧ Q) ∧ ¬(R ∧ S)) ∨ ¬(S ∧ (Q ∨ R)))

13 Expressive adequacy

We now fulfil a promise made back in §8.7; we show that PL languages can handle exclusive disjunctions, using just the three built-in connectives. Indeed, *any* truth-functional combination of PL wffs can be expressed using just the familiar connectives.

13.1 Conjunction and disjunction interrelated

First, though, we begin by noting two of *De Morgan's Laws*, a family of principles interrelating conjunction, disjunction, and negations:

> For any wffs α, β in a PL language, $(\alpha \lor \beta)$ has the same truth table as $\neg(\neg\alpha \land \neg\beta)$.
>
> Similarly, $(\alpha \land \beta)$ has the same truth table as $\neg(\neg\alpha \lor \neg\beta)$.

The first formalizes the obvious truth that a disjunction holds when it isn't the case that both disjuncts fail. And the second formalizes the equally elementary observation that a conjunction holds when neither conjunct fails.

These interrelations mean that we *could* set up our PL languages with just $\land$ and $\neg$ as built-in connectives, and then introduce $\lor$ by the rule that an expression of the form $(\alpha \lor \beta)$ is a mere *abbreviation* for the corresponding expression of the form $\neg(\neg\alpha \land \neg\beta)$. Likewise we could set up our languages with just $\lor$ and $\neg$ as basic – as in fact Bertrand Russell and A. N. Whitehead did in their great *Principia Mathematica*.

However, it is nowadays customary to treat the connectives $\land$ and $\lor$ on a par, as equally basic, even if they *are* interdefinable using negation. This is both more convenient and also more revealing of important logical relations.

13.2 Exclusive disjunction

(a) Suppose that we want to translate 'Either Jack drank beer or he drank cider (but not both)' into a PL language. Using P for *Jack drank beer* and Q for *Jack drank cider*, we want a wff which comes out true when exactly one of P and Q is true. Consider then the following pair of truth tables:

P	Q	((P ∨ Q) ∧ ¬(P ∧ Q))			((P ∧ ¬Q) ∨ (¬P ∧ Q))		
T	T	T	F̲	F	F	F̲	F
T	F	T	T̲	T	T	T̲	F
F	T	T	T̲	T	F	T̲	T
F	F	F	F̲	T	F	F̲	F

Our two displayed wffs have truth tables defining the same overall truth functional combination of atoms, with the same desired correlation of input values to outputs. Both wffs will therefore serve equally well to render the exclusive disjunction of P and Q.

(b)   Now generalize. Whatever wffs α and β we choose, if they take the values on the left in the next table, then the more complex wffs on the right take the values shown:

α	β	((α ∨ β) ∧ ¬(α ∧ β))	((α ∧ ¬β) ∨ (¬α ∧ β))
T	T	F	F
T	F	T	T
F	T	T	T
F	F	F	F

So, for every α and β, either of those equivalent complex wffs will serve to render the exclusive disjunction of α and β.

(c)   We could have built a third binary connective $\oplus$ into the basic syntax of our formal languages from the start, and then adopted the semantic rule that a wff of the form $(\alpha \oplus \beta)$ is true just so long as exactly one of α and β is true. In such an augmented language, the new truth-functional $\oplus$ would live alongside the inclusive disjunction $\vee$, and could be used to render an exclusive disjunction. However, as we have just seen, instead of using a new wff of the form $(\alpha \oplus \beta)$ we can equally well render the exclusive disjunction of α and β by using the corresponding wff $((\alpha \vee \beta) \wedge \neg(\alpha \wedge \beta))$ or the wff $((\alpha \wedge \neg\beta) \vee (\neg\alpha \wedge \beta))$.

So we can manage perfectly well without a new connective to express exclusive disjunction. And if we *do* want the convenience of having such a connective to hand, we don't have to build it into the language's basic syntax. Instead, we can define expressions of the form $(\alpha \oplus \beta)$ to be *shorthand* for e.g. the corresponding $((\alpha \vee \beta) \wedge \neg(\alpha \wedge \beta))$. In brief, $\oplus$ can be *defined* in terms of the standard three connectives.

13.3   Another example: expressing the dollar truth function

We will now prove a parallel result about the dollar connective which we met in §12.2(e). It would again be redundant to add to a PL language a special connective to express the corresponding dollar truth function.

(a)   First, though, a minor notational matter. To reduce clutter, we are temporarily going to be more relaxed about bracketing. For example, we are going to be writing down some expressions like these

$$(\alpha \wedge \beta \wedge \gamma)$$
$$\alpha \vee \beta \vee \gamma \vee \delta \vee \eta$$

when strictly speaking – remembering our rule that each occurrence of $\wedge$ and $\vee$ comes with its own pair of brackets – we ought to write expressions like

$$((\alpha \wedge \beta) \wedge \gamma)$$
$$((((\alpha \vee \beta) \vee \gamma) \vee \delta) \vee \eta).$$

Still, the particular choice of internal bracketing for multiple conjunctions doesn't affect the truth value of the resulting wffs – they are true if and only if *all* the conjuncts are true. Similarly, it doesn't matter how we bracket multiple disjunctions – they are true if and only if *at least one* disjunct is true. Hence leaving out the internal bracketing in the special cases of unmixed conjunctions and unmixed disjunctions can do no harm, and will make for readability. It also doesn't matter if we leave off the outermost brackets.

(b)   Suppose, then, that we start with some wffs. Now take each of these wffs in turn, and either leave it as is or negate it: then (if we have started with more than one wff) conjoin the results. This gives us a *basic conjunction* formed from those wffs. For example, start with just three wffs, α, β, γ. Here are three sample basic conjunctions formed from those wffs:

$$(\alpha \wedge \beta \wedge \neg\gamma)$$
$$(\alpha \wedge \neg\beta \wedge \neg\gamma)$$
$$(\neg\alpha \wedge \neg\beta \wedge \gamma).$$

And now we observe that a basic conjunction like one of these will evidently be true on *one and only one* corresponding assignment of values to its ingredient wffs α, β, γ. Thus our three samples are true exactly when, respectively,

$$\alpha := T, \ \beta := T, \ \gamma := F,$$
$$\alpha := T, \ \beta := F, \ \gamma := F,$$
$$\alpha := F, \ \beta := F, \ \gamma := T.$$

It is simple: to get the valuation corresponding to a true basic conjunction, naked constituent wffs get assigned T, the negated ones get assigned F. And conversely, given a valuation of some wffs, there is a basic conjunction true on just that valuation, which conjoins the wffs assigned T and the negations of the wffs assigned F.

(c)   With these preliminaries out of the way, we can get down to the main business of this section and briskly prove our claim that, in any language which includes the wffs α, β, γ and the standard three connectives, there is already a way of truth-functionally combining these wffs which has the same truth table as $\$(\alpha, \beta, \gamma)$.

Start with a specific example (as we did when discussing exclusive disjunction). Here then is the truth table for $\$(P, Q, R)$. And for each assignment of values to the constituent wffs where $\$(P, Q, R)$ gets the value T, we've added the corresponding basic conjunction on the right:

P	Q	R	(P, Q, R)	
T	T	T	F	
T	T	F	T	$(P \land Q \land \neg R)$
T	F	T	F	
T	F	F	T	$(P \land \neg Q \land \neg R)$
F	T	T	F	
F	T	F	F	
F	F	T	T	$(\neg P \land \neg Q \land R)$
F	F	F	F	

And we now see that (P, Q, R) is true just when one of those three basic conjunctions is true. In other words, (P, Q, R) is true exactly when

$$(P \land Q \land \neg R) \lor (P \land \neg Q \land \neg R) \lor (\neg P \land \neg Q \land R)$$

is true.

The observation generalizes. By just the same reasoning, for any α, β, γ, the corresponding (α, β, γ) is true exactly when

$$(\alpha \land \beta \land \neg \gamma) \lor (\alpha \land \neg \beta \land \neg \gamma) \lor (\neg \alpha \land \neg \beta \land \gamma)$$

is true. Re-inserting the officially required brackets, we therefore have a way of constructing a wff built up from wffs α, β, γ using the built-in connectives which has the same truth table as (α, β, γ).

Job done! We have shown it would be redundant to adopt the $ connective as new basic apparatus to be added to a PL language. And if, for some obscure reason, we *did* want a symbol for the dollar truth function, we can just treat (α, β, γ) as shorthand for an expression of the shape just displayed. In other words, to put it briskly again, we can simply *define* the $ connective in terms of the standard three connectives.

13.4 Expressive adequacy defined

The results about $\oplus$ and $ now generalize – predictably enough, there is nothing special about these cases:

> Given *any* possible new truth-functional connective – which combines with one or more wffs to form a new wff – we can already define it using the existing resources of a PL language (just as we can define the connectives $\oplus$ and $).

And to show this, we just deploy again the sort of reasoning we used about the dollar connective, with one new tweak.

Spelling out the argument:

(1) Imagine that we are planning to add to a PL language an n-place truth-functional connective % which takes n wffs $\alpha, \beta, \ldots, \lambda$ to form a wff $\%(\alpha, \beta, \ldots, \lambda)$. Since, by assumption, the connective is truth-functional, we can set out a 2^n-line truth table for %, just as we set out a truth

table for \$. Now look at this table to find the lines giving valuations of $\alpha, \beta, \ldots, \lambda$ where $\%(\alpha, \beta, \ldots, \lambda)$ comes out true.

There are then two cases to consider:

(2a) Assume first that there is at least one such line. For each of these lines, i.e. for each valuation of $\alpha, \beta, \ldots, \lambda$ where $\%(\alpha, \beta, \ldots, \lambda)$ is true, write down a corresponding basic conjunction. Then disjoin these basic conjunctions, if there is more than one (and tidy up brackets). Exactly as before, the resulting wff – built up from $\alpha, \beta, \ldots \lambda$ using no more than the three standard connectives – will be true on exactly the lines where $\%(\alpha, \beta, \ldots, \lambda)$ is true. So the new wff will have exactly the same truth table as $\%(\alpha, \beta, \ldots, \lambda)$.

(2b) But now (this is the new tweak) we also need to consider the exceptional case where $\%(\alpha, \beta, \ldots, \lambda)$ is false on every valuation of its components. In this case take e.g. the wff $(\alpha \wedge \neg\alpha) \vee (\beta \wedge \neg\beta) \vee \ldots \vee (\lambda \wedge \neg\lambda)$. This too is always false, so will have the same truth table as $\%(\alpha, \beta, \ldots, \lambda)$.

Hence, either way,

(3) We can construct an expression from $\alpha, \beta, \ldots, \lambda$ using just the connectives $\wedge$, $\vee$, $\neg$ which has the same truth table as $\%(\alpha, \beta, \ldots, \lambda)$ – in other words, as we put it before, we can now *define* the new truth-functional connective $\%$ in terms of just the old three basic connectives.

(4) But $\%$ was an arbitrarily chosen truth-functional connective: so the result is, as announced, a general one.

Let's introduce some natural terminology.

> Some sentential connectives, when taken together, are *expressively adequate* – alternatively, are *functionally complete* – if and only if you can define *any* possible truth-functional connective using only those connectives (in the way that $\oplus$ and \$ can be defined using only the PL connectives).

Equivalently, some sentential connectives are expressively adequate just if, using only those connectives, you can construct a wff with any desired truth table. Then, in summary, what we have now shown is that

> The basic connectives $\wedge$, $\vee$, $\neg$ are together expressively adequate. In particular, then, any truth-functional combination of PL atoms can already be expressed by a PL wff.

13.5 Some more adequacy results

(a) The key adequacy result is the one we have just proved. But it is worth noting that we can do even better.

One of De Morgan's Laws (as noted in §13.1) tells us that the disjunction connective can be defined in terms of conjunction and negation; hence the connectives $\wedge$ and $\neg$ together are already expressively adequate. We already know that we can express any truth-functional combination of wffs using just $\wedge$, $\vee$, and $\neg$. Go through replacing the disjunctions with equivalent negation/conjunction combinations. We will then end up with a wff with the same table built up using just the connectives $\wedge$ and $\neg$.

Exactly similarly, using another of De Morgan's Laws, we can show that $\vee$ and $\neg$ together are expressively adequate.

However, $\wedge$ and $\vee$ together are *not* expressively adequate. Any wff built using just conjunction and disjunction must be true when its atoms are all true (why?). So using just conjunction and disjunction we can never get a wff with the same table as $(\neg P \vee \neg Q)$ which is false when its atoms are true.

(b)   The result that any truth function can be expressed using just *two* connectives is enough to satisfy any sensible taste for economy! But let's now show that there is at least one connective which is expressively adequate just by itself.

Since $\wedge$, $\neg$ are together expressively adequate, it is enough to find a single connective in terms of which these two connectives can both in turn be defined. It must be at least a two-place connective, and one candidate is the 'neither ... nor ...' connective which is often abbreviated 'NOR' and which we will symbolize '$\downarrow$':

α	β	$(\alpha \downarrow \beta)$
T	T	F
T	F	F
F	T	F
F	F	T

To see that $\downarrow$ can be used to define negation, consider what happens when we give it the same wff twice: $(\alpha \downarrow \alpha)$ – neither α nor α – is true just when $\neg\alpha$ is true. And $(\alpha \wedge \beta)$ is equivalent to (neither $\neg\alpha$ nor $\neg\beta$), so is true just when $(\neg\alpha \downarrow \neg\beta)$, and hence will have the same truth table as $((\alpha \downarrow \alpha) \downarrow (\beta \downarrow \beta))$, as you can quickly check. Which gives us the following result:

> The down-arrow connective $\downarrow$ can be used to define negation and conjunction and so is expressively adequate just by itself.

13.6   Summary

> The previous chapter showed that every wff of a PL language expresses a truth function of its atoms (namely the truth function given by the wff's truth table). This chapter proves the converse result that every truth function of atoms can be expressed by a PL wff (i.e. there is a wff with the right truth table).
>
> In a phrase, the standard three connectives taken together are expressively adequate (i.e. can be used to define any truth-functional connective).

Indeed, any truth function can be defined using just $\wedge$ and $\neg$, or using just $\vee$ and $\neg$, or even using just the down-arrow $\downarrow$ by itself.

Exercises 13

(a) We could introduce a new *four*-place connective '$\bigsqcup$', where $\bigsqcup(\alpha, \beta, \gamma, \delta)$ is true when exactly two of $\alpha, \beta, \gamma, \delta$ are true, and is false otherwise. Show that doing this would be redundant because we can already define the new connective using the standard three connectives.

(b) More on expressive adequacy:

(1) Compare the truth tables for the down-arrow '$\downarrow$' and '$\vee$': one is formed from the other by swapping 'T's and 'F's in the last column. Define an up-arrow connective '$\uparrow$' (also symbolized '$|$', and then known as the 'Sheffer stroke') whose table stands in the same relation to the table for '$\wedge$'. Show that, like the down-arrow, this up-arrow connective ('NAND') taken just by itself is expressively adequate.

(2) Show that the up-arrow and down-arrow connectives are the only *binary* connectives that, taken by themselves, are expressively adequate.

(3) Define a *ternary* connective which, taken by itself, is expressively adequate. You are supposed to spot that the answer is trivial, given what you already know. Just define e.g. $\Downarrow (\alpha, \beta, \gamma)$ so that on any line of its truth-table it's value depends on just α, β and equals $(\alpha \downarrow \beta)$ (so the third input is an idle wheel). Then $\Downarrow (\alpha, \beta, \beta)$ will do as well as $(\alpha \downarrow \beta)$ to define any truth function!

(4) Are '$\oplus$' and '$\neg$' taken together expressively adequate? What about '\$' and '$\neg$'?

(c*) Assume that we are working in some PL language. Then:

(1) Show that pairs of wffs of the forms $(\alpha \wedge (\beta \vee \gamma))$ and $((\alpha \wedge \beta) \vee (\alpha \wedge \gamma))$ have the same truth table.

(2) Show that pairs of wffs of the forms $((\alpha \wedge \beta) \wedge \gamma)$ and $(\alpha \wedge (\beta \wedge \gamma))$ have the same truth table. Generalize to show that any way you bracket an unmixed conjunction $\alpha \wedge \beta \wedge \gamma \wedge \ldots \wedge \lambda$ to give a properly bracketed wff expresses the same truth function. Check the comparable results for disjunctions.

(3) Show that pairs of wffs of the forms $\neg(\alpha \wedge \beta)$ and $(\neg\alpha \vee \neg\beta)$ also have the same truth tables. Generalize to show that a negated unmixed conjunction $\neg(\alpha \wedge \beta \wedge \ldots \wedge \lambda)$ has the same truth table as $(\neg\alpha \vee \neg\beta \vee \ldots \neg\lambda)$, however we insert brackets to get wffs. What are the comparable results for negated disjunctions?

(4) Say that an atom or the negation of an atom is a *basic* wff. A wff is in *disjunctive normal form* if it is, ignoring bracketing, of the form $\alpha \vee \beta \vee \ldots \vee \lambda$ for one or more disjuncts, where each disjunct is a conjunction of one or more basic wffs. Show that any wff has the same truth table as a wff in disjunctive normal form.

(5) Define an analogous notion of being in *conjunctive normal form*. Show that any wff α has the same truth table as a wff in conjunctive normal form. (Hint: consider a wff in disjunctive normal form which is equivalent to $\neg\alpha$ and take negations.)

14 Tautologies

In this short chapter, we note a particularly important class of wffs formed using our truth-functional PL connectives, namely the wffs that are necessarily true 'in virtue of their logical form' (as we might put it).

14.1 Tautologies and contradictions

(a)   As we have seen, given any wff of a PL language, we can calculate its truth value for any combinatorially possible valuation of its atoms. Usually, the wff will be true on some of these valuations and false on others. However, we occasionally get a uniform result:

> A PL wff is a *tautology* if and only if it takes the value *true* on every combinatorially possible valuation of the atoms in the wff.
>
> A wff is a *contradiction* if and only if it takes the value *false* on every such valuation.

Trivial two-line tables show that the following are tautologies (assume here and later that we are working in PL languages with the relevant atoms):

(1) $(P \lor \neg P)$
(2) $\neg(P \land \neg P)$.

And a moment's reflection shows that these wffs *ought* invariably to be true, whatever their interpretation and however the world is.

The fact that (1) is a tautology reflects our stipulation that, however the world is, a given PL atom is determinately either true or false. There is no middle option. So this is a formal instance of the *Law of Excluded Middle*: for any proposition, either it or its negation is true.

The fact that (2) is a tautology reflects our stipulation that in PL languages negation flips values and hence a wff and its negation are never true together. So this is a formal instance of Aristotle's *Law of Non-contradiction*: for any proposition, it can't be the case that both it and its negation hold.

Here is another tautology:

(3) $((P \land Q) \lor (\neg P \lor \neg Q))$.

Again, this *ought* to be inevitably true. Given our assumption that atoms have determinate values, then – for any two – either they are both true, or at least

120

one of them is false and so its negation is true. For future reference, though, here is a truth table to show that this wff is indeed a tautology:

P	Q	((P ∧ Q)	∨	(¬P ∨ ¬Q))
T	T	T	T̲	F
T	F	F	T̲	T
F	T	F	T̲	T
F	F	F	T̲	T

(b)   However, tautologies need not be quite as obvious as our first three! For example, take the wff

(4)   [¬{¬(P ∧ Q) ∧ ¬(P ∧ R)} ∨ ¬{P ∧ (Q ∨ R)}].

For readability, we have varied the styles of brackets to make it clear that this is a disjunction, both of whose disjuncts are of the form '¬{...}'. We can then construct a truth table, using our shortcuts and also doing some of the working in our heads. We quickly arrive at

P	Q	R	[¬{¬(P ∧ Q) ∧ ¬(P ∧ R)}	∨	¬{P ∧ (Q ∨ R)}]
T	T	T	T F	T̲ F	T
T	T	F	T F	T̲ F	T
T	F	T	T F	T̲ F	T
T	F	F		T̲ T	F
F	T	T		T̲ T	F
F	T	F		T̲ T	F
F	F	T		T̲ T	F
F	F	F		T̲ T	F
			5 4	3/6 2	1

Here, we evaluate the second curly-bracketed subformula first (just because it's simpler – step 1); then we flip values to evaluate its negation (2); and that enables us to fix the value of the whole disjunction on the last five lines (3). Next, we evaluate the first curly-bracketed subformula on the three lines we still need to examine (4); then we evaluate its negation (5). That enables us to complete the table for the whole disjunction (6).

(c)   If a wff α takes the value true on every valuation of its atoms, then $\neg\alpha$ will always take the value false; and vice versa. Hence:

> The negations of tautologies are contradictions. Conversely, the negations of contradictions are tautologies.

Hence ¬((P ∧ Q) ∨ (¬P ∨ ¬Q)), the negation of the tautology (3) above, counts as a contradiction. Therefore, in our stretched usage of the term, not all contradictions will have the form $(\alpha \wedge \neg\alpha)$, where a wff is directly conjoined with its negation (compare §4.5(c)).

However, every contradiction in our wide sense *will* have the same truth table as an explicit contradiction in the sense of a wff of the form $(\alpha \wedge \neg\alpha)$ – see the Exercises.

121

14.2 Generalizing examples of tautologies

(a)   Let's introduce some standard symbolic shorthand for use in our meta-language, logicians' English:

We abbreviate the claim that γ is a tautology as follows: $\vDash \gamma$.

(As a mnemonic, you can for the moment think of the double turnstile symbol '$\vDash$' as a stylized superposition of the two 't's from 'tautology'.) So, we know that

(1) $\vDash (P \lor \neg P)$
(2) $\vDash \neg(P \land \neg P)$
(3) $\vDash ((P \land Q) \lor (\neg P \lor \neg Q))$
(4) $\vDash (\neg(\neg(P \land Q) \land \neg(P \land R)) \lor \neg(P \land (Q \lor R)))$.

As we've already noted, these claims are implicitly general. They hold for any PL language with the right atoms – i.e. (1) to (4) are true irrespective of the interpretation of the atoms.

(b)   But of course, there is nothing special about the choice of atoms appearing in our initial samples of tautologies. For example, the wffs $(R \lor \neg R)$ and $(P'' \lor \neg P'')$ are equally good instances of the law of excluded middle. So too are $((P \land Q) \lor \neg(P \land Q))$ and $((R \lor (\neg Q \land S)) \lor \neg(R \lor (\neg Q \land S)))$, where we disjoin a more complex wff with its negation. In fact, *any* substitution instance of the schema $(\alpha \lor \neg \alpha)$ will be a tautology. So there's further level of generality here: for *any* wff α, whether atomic or molecular, we have

(1′) $\vDash (\alpha \lor \neg \alpha)$.

The same goes for other tautologies, of course. Take any tautology, and form a basic schema from it (in the sense of §11.6(c)); in other words, form a schema that gives the tautology's structure down to the level of atoms. Then any substitution instance of this schema is also a tautology. So, for example, for *any* wffs α, β, γ,

(2′) $\vDash \neg(\alpha \land \neg \alpha)$
(3′) $\vDash ((\alpha \land \beta) \lor (\neg \alpha \lor \neg \beta))$.
(4′) $\vDash (\neg(\neg(\alpha \land \beta) \land \neg(\alpha \land \gamma)) \lor \neg(\alpha \land (\beta \lor \gamma)))$.

(c)   *Why* can we generalize claims about tautologies in this way? Let's slowly think through an example:

Consider $((P \land Q) \lor (\neg P \lor \neg Q))$, because in the previous section we showed that this wff is a tautology by writing out its truth table. The table showed the particular way in which the truth value of our wff (and of its main subformulas) depends on a valuation of its constituent atoms. We can now generalize by writing down a schematic version of the table:

α	β	$((\alpha \land \beta)$	$\lor$	$(\neg \alpha \lor \neg \beta))$
T	T	T	$\underline{T}$	F
T	F	F	$\underline{T}$	T
F	T	F	$\underline{T}$	T
F	F	F	$\underline{T}$	T

This tells us how the truth value of a wff of the form $((\alpha \wedge \beta) \vee (\neg\alpha \vee \neg\beta))$ similarly depends – in just the same particular way – on a valuation of *its* constituent wffs α and β. So whatever truth values α and β take, the corresponding wff of the form $((\alpha \wedge \beta) \vee (\neg\alpha \vee \neg\beta))$ is true. Hence whatever values the *atoms* inside α and β take, the wff $((\alpha \wedge \beta) \vee (\neg\alpha \vee \neg\beta))$ will come out true. Therefore that wff is a tautology.

This line of argument can be applied to any tautology. So here it is again, a bit more abstractly – just bear in mind that (a) forming a basic schema from a wff and then taking an instance of that schema is the same as (b) directly replacing the atoms in the original wff with some wffs (same atom, same replacement).

(i) Start with a tautology whose constituent atoms are (say) P, Q, ... By assumption, whatever values these atoms have, the wff in question is true.

(ii) Now systematically replace P, Q, ..., throughout our tautology with the wffs α, β, ..., respectively.

(iii) Then the truth value of the resulting new wff will depend on the truth values of these new constituent wffs α, β, ..., exactly as the truth value of the original wff depends on the values of their original atoms. So whatever values these new constituents have, the new wff is also true.

(iv) So whatever values of the atoms inside the wffs α, β, ... have, the new wff is true. It is therefore a tautology.

Hence, whenever we show that a particular wff is a tautology, we get an implicitly general result. Buy one tautology, and you get indefinitely many more for free.

(d) It is natural to say that, if we start from a particular tautology and construct a basic schema for it, what we get is a *tautological schema*. Then what we've shown in this section can be neatly summed up as follows:

Any substitution instance of a tautological schema is also a tautology.

Note, however, an important contrast: not every instance of a *non*-tautological schema need be a non-tautology. For a simple example, the schema $(\alpha \vee \neg\beta)$ is of course not a tautological schema! But now consider the special case where we substitute the same way for both α and β.

14.3 Tautologies, necessity, and form

(a) To repeat, the tautologies of a PL language are the wffs which we can mechanically determine to be true, even while ignoring the particular meanings of the atoms, and while ignoring the situation in the world.

Since they come out true however the world might be, tautologies express *necessary* truths in the strong sense of §2.1(d). Moreover, since the topics of the atoms will be irrelevant (it is the distribution of the topic-neutral connectives which makes a tautology a tautology), it is also natural to say that tautologies are *logically* necessary in the sense of §6.3.

Now, the general notion of necessity – the idea of something's being true in all possible worlds – has its very puzzling aspects. What *are* these possible worlds of which we speak? If they are a mere metaphor, how do we cash out this *façon de parler*? How can we possibly know what is true in *all* possible worlds? But whatever the broader worries here, the necessary truth of PL tautologies seems relatively unmysterious. We stipulated that PL atoms get meanings which ensure that they have determinate truth values in any situation (this was our *Determinacy* assumption in §10.3). We then stipulated the meanings of the three connectives precisely in order to make PL wffs truth-functional (in §10.5). It is then a side effect of these stipulations that certain special wffs, the tautologies, must come out true on every combinatorially possible valuation, and hence however things might be in the world.

Tautologies are sometimes said to be 'true by definition' – or are said to be 'vacuously true', echoing Wittgenstein's claim that tautologies 'say nothing' (in fact, we owe our logical use of the word 'tautology' to his *Tractatus Logico-Philosophicus*). But these claims are best understood as just variations on the basic theme that you don't have to know how things are in this world or in any other world in order to determine the truth value of a tautological wff.

(b)   Take a language where the atom R says that Rosalind is a mother, while S says that all mothers are parents. Then note that

(1)   S expresses a necessary truth. But trivially it is not a tautology, for no atom can be a tautology.

(2)   (R ∨ S) also expresses a necessary truth. But again it is not a tautology, though this time we do need to use the truth table for disjunction in showing that it must be true given that S has to be true.

(3)   (S ∨ ¬S) is also a necessary truth – and this is overdetermined. It is a necessary truth because S has to be true and hence so must be the disjunction of S with anything else. It is also a necessary truth because it is a substitution instance of the tautological schema (α ∨ ¬α).

It is worth pausing over (2). So think again about the truth table for the wff (R ∨ S). As we go through all the combinatorially possible valuations for the atoms, our table includes the line where R := F, and S := F; and on *that* line (R ∨ S) := F – which is why the wff isn't a tautology.

But this doesn't stop the wff, with its given interpretation, being necessarily true. For the *combinatorially* possible valuation R := F, S := F, is not a *realizable* valuation, since there is no possible way that the world can be, keeping the sense of the atoms fixed, where S := F (see §12.4). That's why there is no possible way that the world can be, with the sense of the atoms as given, which can make (R ∨ S) := F. So that wff is necessarily true even if not tautologous.

(c)   The tautologies, to repeat, are the wffs of a PL language whose truth can be derived purely from the meaning and distribution of the connectives, without attending to the meaning of the atoms. For example, $((P \land Q) \lor (\neg P \lor \neg Q))$ is a tautology; and it is the pattern in which the connectives appear with their given meanings which explains why this wff is always true. This pattern or logical form in which the connectives appear can be displayed using $((\alpha \land \beta) \lor (\neg \alpha \lor \neg \beta))$, a basic schema for the tautology. And there's a good sense in which it is *because* the wff has that form that it's a tautology.

In §11.6(b), we stressed the general point that we can't talk in an unqualified way about 'the' form of an individual wff – a wff can instantiate different schematic forms at different levels of detail. But it is natural to fall into saying that *the* logical form of a wff is the form which gets displayed by a basic schema for the wff (because that schema will show all the wff's structural detail apart from the particular choice of atoms). And so, generalizing the point in the last paragraph, we can say:

A PL tautology is true in virtue of its logical form.

(d)   Our official definition of a tautology applies to wffs of PL languages. Later, we will carry over the notion to apply to the wffs of richer formal languages which still contain some truth-functional connectives.

By extension, we can also describe certain claims in ordinary English as tautologies, if they involve what are naturally construed as truth-functional connectives and a PL rendition is a tautology. And these ordinary-language claims too might then be said, rather more loosely, to be true in virtue of their logical form – but we won't attempt to give a really sharp sense to this idea.

14.4   Tautologies as analytically true

We finish the chapter by noting that there is an interestingly deep philosophical question waiting in the wings here.

Tautologies are true because of the meanings of the connectives and how the connectives are put together. Let's follow convention, and say that a proposition is *analytically* true if it is true because of (i) the meanings of (some of) the words involved in expressing it and (ii) how these words are put together. The idea is that an analytically true proposition can be seen to be true just by analysing it and reflecting on that analysis. Then, in another traditional slogan, tautologies are *analytic*, i.e. analytically true.

Now for the lurking question. Not every necessary truth – in the strongest sense of 'necessary' – is a truth-functional tautology. But we might wonder all necessary truths are similar to tautologies at least in being analytic? That would be a quite beautifully demystifying theory about the nature of necessity. And it seems plausible, perhaps, for the likes of 'No bachelor is married' and 'Every mother is a parent': these too are surely in some sense true in virtue of the meaning of the words involved. But moving beyond relative trivia, does the theory apply, say, to the necessary truths of arithmetic? Are *they* analytic?

We will have to leave this last question hanging: it deserves a book in itself.

14.5 Summary

Wffs of a PL language which are true on every valuation of their atoms are tautologies. Wffs that are false on every valuation are contradictions. And note that contradictions do not have to be of the form $(\alpha \wedge \neg\alpha)$.

We abbreviate the claim that γ is a tautology as: $\vDash \gamma$.

A PL tautology remains a tautology whatever the meaning of the atoms; and any wff instantiating its basic form will also be a tautology.

PL tautologies are necessary truths: but not all the necessary truths expressible in some PL language need be tautologies. The tautologies can be said to be true in virtue of logical form.

The necessary truth of tautologies is unpuzzling, a spin-off from the semantic rules governing the connectives.

Exercises 14

(a)   Which of the following wffs are tautologies, which are contradictions, and which are neither?

(1) $\neg((\neg\neg Q \wedge \neg\neg P) \vee \neg(P \wedge Q))$

(2) $(P \vee ((\neg P \vee Q) \wedge \neg Q))$

(3) $(\{P \vee \neg(Q \wedge R)\} \vee \{(\neg P \wedge Q) \wedge R\})$

(4) $(\{P \vee (Q \wedge \neg R)\} \vee \neg\{(\neg P \vee R) \vee Q\})$

(5) $(\{P \wedge (\neg Q \vee \neg R)\} \vee \neg\{(P \vee \neg R) \vee \neg Q\})$

(6) $\neg(\{(P \wedge \neg(Q \wedge S)) \vee \neg R\} \wedge \neg\{(P \wedge \neg(Q \wedge S)) \vee \neg R\})$

(7) $\neg(\{\neg(P \wedge \neg R) \wedge \neg(Q \wedge \neg S)\} \wedge \neg\{\neg(P \vee Q) \vee (R \vee S)\})$

(b*)   Which of the following claims are true about PL wffs, and why?

(1)   The conjunction of a contradiction and any another wff is still a contradiction.

(2)   The conjunction of a tautology and any another wff is still a tautology.

(3)   The disjunction of two tautologies is a tautology.

(4)   All the tautologies in a PL language express the same truth function as each other.

(5)   Every contradiction in a PL language has the same truth table as a wff of the form $(\alpha \wedge \neg\alpha)$.

If a wff is neither a tautology nor a contradiction, it is said to be *contingent*. Which of the following claims are true, and why?

(6)   The negation of a contingent wff is contingent.

(7)   The disjunction of two contingent wffs is contingent.

(8)   The conjunction of two contingent wffs is contingent.

(9)   The disjunction of two contingent wffs is never a contradiction.

15 Tautological entailment

In this pivotal chapter, our work on PL languages at last gets put to use in the assessment of arguments! We introduce the crucial *truth-table test* for the validity of inferences which rely on the connectives 'and', 'or', and 'not'.

15.1 Three introductory examples

(a)   Consider the everyday argument

A   Jack is logical. It isn't the case that he is logical while Jill isn't. Hence Jill is logical.

Now construct an ad hoc PL language where P means *Jack is logical* and Q means *Jill is logical* (we ignore any potential vagueness here). Then we can render **A** into this language, capturing the argument's essential structure:

A′   P, ¬(P ∧ ¬Q) ∴ Q.

Here we use the symbol '∴' as an inference marker, and use the comma to separate premises. But that's fine: both the 'therefore' sign and the comma do belong to the official alphabet of our PL languages (see §9.1).

Now let's evaluate the premises and the conclusion of **A′** for each possible assignment of values to their atoms, setting out the results in a table:

P	Q	P	¬(P ∧ ¬Q)	Q
T	T	T	T	T
T	F	T	F	F
F	T	F	T	T
F	F	F	T	F

We use a double line to separate off the list of possible valuations of atoms on the left from the part of the table which records the values of the premises on each valuation. Then we use another double line before giving the corresponding values of the conclusion. In this mini-example, one of the premises and the conclusion is an atom (so we can simply copy their values across). And to reduce clutter, we have omitted working and simply given the overall value of the remaining complex wff, written as usual under its main connective.

Now look along the rows of this truth table. *We find, by inspection, that there is no valuation of the atoms that makes the premises true and the conclusion false*. Hence, however the world might be with respect to the truth values of P and Q – and the four listed combinations of values are the only possible ones – there is no situation in which the premises will be true and conclusion false. So argument **A′** is valid.

That **A′** is valid was no doubt clear from the start! However – and this is the crucial advance – we have now *proved* the argument's validity. By a simple calculation, we have shown than in any possible situation, if the premises of **A′** are true, the conclusion is true too just because of the meanings of the connectives.

And since **A′** is valid, the original argument **A** is valid, for the arguments plainly stand or fall together.

(b)   Consider next the argument

B   Jack or Jill or both went up the hill. But it isn't the case that Jack *and* Jo went up the hill. Hence Jo and/or Jill went up the hill.

Take a different ad hoc PL language, this time one where P means *Jack went up the hill*, Q means *Jill went up the hill*, and R means *Jo went up the hill*. Then we can translate the argument **B**, capturing its logical structure, as follows:

B′ $(P \lor Q)$, $\neg(P \land R) \therefore (R \lor Q)$.

And now we work out the following truth table:

P	Q	R	$(P \lor Q)$	$\neg(P \land R)$	$(R \lor Q)$
T	T	T	T	F	T
T	T	F	T	T	T
T	F	T	T	F	T
T	F	F	T	T	F
F	T	T	T	T	T
F	T	F	T	T	T
F	F	T	F	T	T
F	F	F	F	T	F

Inspection reveals that there *is* a valuation of atoms which makes the premises of **B′** true and the conclusion false, namely $P := T$, $Q := F$, $R := F$. Moreover, this combinatorially possible valuation *does* in this case represent a way the world could really be (i.e. Jack's going up the hill alone). This possible situation makes the premises of **B′** true and conclusion false (and also makes the premises of **B** true and conclusion false). So the argument, in both its PL and English versions, is invalid.

No doubt the invalidity of **B/B′** was also obvious from the beginning. But we have again arrived at our assessment of the argument based on a mechanical search through the relevant possibilities.

(c)   Let's have one more introductory example. Consider this argument:

C   Jack is useless at logic or he simply isn't ready for the exam. Either Jack will fail the exam or he is not useless at logic. Either it's wrong that he won't fail the exam or he is ready for it. So Jack will fail.

Is it valid? Perhaps this time the answer isn't quite so evident.

So, first tidy up the argument by rendering into a suitable PL language, where P means *Jack is useless at logic*, Q means *Jack is ready for the exam*, and R means *Jack will fail the exam*. How should we handle the disjunctions? Well, for now assume the disjunctions are all inclusive. We then get the formal version

C′ $(P \vee \neg Q)$, $(R \vee \neg P)$, $(\neg\neg R \vee Q)$ ∴ R.

There are three different atoms and so again eight different possible assignments of values to the atoms. So we can construct the following truth table:

P	Q	R	$(P \vee \neg Q)$	$(R \vee \neg P)$	$(\neg\neg R \vee Q)$	R
T	T	T	T	T	T	T
T	T	F	T	F	T	F
T	F	T	T	T	T	T
T	F	F	T	F	F	F
F	T	T	F	T	T	T
F	T	F	F	T	T	F
F	F	T	T	T	T	T
F	F	F	T	T	F	F

However the world might be, the three atoms P, Q and R must take one of the eight listed assignments of values; and each assignment fixes the values of the given wffs. Inspection then reveals that, however the world might be, the resulting valuation of the atoms makes the conclusion of **C′** true whenever it makes the premises true. Hence argument **C′** must be valid. Hence **C** is valid, at least if the disjunctions are inclusive.

(As a follow-up exercise, it is illuminating to consider what happens if we treat some of the disjunctions as exclusive.)

15.2   Tautological entailment defined

(a)   Motivated by the examples in the last section, let's introduce a crucial new notion. When working in a PL language, we will say:

An *inference step* is *tautologically valid* if and only if there is no valuation of the atoms involved (i.e. no combinatorially possible valuation) which makes the premises all true and the conclusion false.

Also, the premises of an inference *tautologically entail* its conclusion if and only if the inference step from the premises to the conclusion is tautologically valid.

A (one-step) *argument* is tautologically valid when its premises tautologically entail its conclusion.

We have just shown, then, that the PL arguments **A′** and **C′** are tautologically valid in this sense, and the argument **B′** isn't.

129

Our terminology here should seem quite natural. Compare: a wff is a tautology if it is true on any valuation at all; a wff is tautologically entailed by given premises if it is true on any valuation which makes all the premises true.

(b) The sharply defined notion of tautological validity for PL arguments is evidently closely related to the informal notion of deductive validity (as characterized in §2.1), and also to the narrower informal notion of logical validity (from §6.2).

To make the first connection, we can simply generalize the line of thought we used above in discussing $\mathbf{A}'$:

Suppose the PL inference step from the wffs $\alpha_1, \alpha_2, \ldots, \alpha_n$ to the wff γ is tautologically valid. Then, by definition, there is no valuation of the relevant atoms which makes the αs true and γ false. Hence no possible situation can give the relevant interpreted atoms values which make the αs true and γ false. Therefore the inference is deductively valid.

We can also rephrase this argument using the terminology of §12.4. A tautologically valid PL inference is truth-preserving (*if* the premises are true, so is the conclusion) on every c-possible valuation of its atoms. But the r-possible valuations are c-possible. So a tautologically valid PL inference will be, in particular, truth-preserving on every r-possible valuation of its atoms. Which makes this PL inference deductively valid (according to our original definition of validity).

Now, we did worry in §6.4 whether the narrower notion of logical validity might be somewhat indeterminate, because the notion is defined in terms of topic-neutrality and it isn't clear exactly what does and what doesn't count as topic-neutral. However, the sentential connectives certainly count as topic-neutral if anything does. So:

Suppose again that the argument $\alpha_1, \alpha_2, \ldots, \alpha_n \therefore \gamma$ is tautologically valid. Then, by definition, this is just in virtue of the way that the topic-neutral connectives appear in the premises and conclusion. Hence the argument is valid (by our previous argument) and valid just in virtue of the way that the topic-neutral connectives appear. Hence the argument is *logically* valid.

In summary then:

If a (one-step) PL argument is tautologically valid, then it is logically valid.

But tautological invalidity does *not* always imply (logical) invalidity – see §15.5.

15.3 Brute-force truth-table testing

(a) How do we determine whether some PL wffs tautologically entail a stated conclusion? There is more than one way of doing this. But for now, we will continue to use the most direct method of settling the matter – namely, a *brute-force truth-table calculation*, exactly as in our earlier examples. This certainly isn't very pretty; but it works!

Here then is the general principle:

Given a PL inference, set out a composite truth table for the inference by listing every (combinatorially) possible valuation of the various atoms that appear in its premisses and conclusion, and then calculate the values of the premisses and the conclusion on each of the successive valuations.

Let's say that a line on a truth table for an inference is 'bad' if, on its valuation of the relevant atoms, the premisses are true and conclusion false. Otherwise a line is 'good'.

Then an inference is tautologically valid just in case its corresponding truth table has no bad lines.

(b)   We will give more examples in the next section. But first let's note that, brute-force though it is, truth-table testing for tautological validity need not be too onerous if we make judicious use of some obvious shortcuts. Just remember, we are searching all the time for bad lines on a table because whether an inference is tautologically valid turns on whether there are any such lines. Hence:

(1)   If we find the conclusion is true on a particular valuation, we can declare the line to be 'good', without worrying about the truth values of the premisses. For *a line where the conclusion is true cannot be a bad line*, i.e. cannot be a line with true premisses and a false conclusion! Therefore one tactic is to evaluate the conclusion first (when this is not too complex), and we then need do no further work evaluating the premisses on lines with true conclusions.

(2)   Similarly, if we find that a premiss is false on a particular valuation, we can suspend work on that line, and not worry about the truth values of the other premisses or conclusion. For *a line where a premiss is false cannot be a bad line*. Therefore another tactic is to prioritize evaluating any very simple premiss, and we then need do no further work evaluating the other premisses and conclusion on lines where that simple premiss is false.

(3)   Finally, *one bad line is enough to prove tautological invalidity*. So, as soon as we hit a bad line, we can stop.

Now let's put these handy shortcuts to work!

15.4   More examples

(a)   Consider again the PL argument

  C′ $(P \lor \neg Q), (R \lor \neg P), (\neg\neg R \lor Q) \therefore R.$

We did a calculation of the values of *all* the premisses and the conclusion on *each* of the eight possible assignments of values to its atoms. But taking advantage of the shortcuts suggested in the last section, we could have significantly cut down the labour, like this:

P	Q	R	(P ∨ ¬Q)	(R ∨ ¬P)	(¬¬R ∨ Q)	R
T	T	T				T
T	T	F	T	F		F
T	F	T				T
T	F	F	T	F		F
F	T	T				T
F	T	F	F			F
F	F	T				T
F	F	F	T	T	F	F
			2	3	4	1

At step (1), following the first of our tactics to cut down working, we start off by evaluating the simple conclusion. Immediately we see that the first, third, fifth, and seventh lines of our truth table can't be bad lines (i.e. can't be lines with true premises and a false conclusion). So at step (2) we need only evaluate the first premiss on the four remaining lines; and we immediately find that one more line, the sixth, is no longer potentially bad. At step (3) we evaluate the second premiss. And this leaves only the final line as still potentially bad (i.e. as possibly having all true premises and false conclusion).

Therefore at step (4) we only have to evaluate the remaining premiss on this *one* remaining potentially bad line; the premiss turns out to be false.

Hence there is *no* bad line at all – showing, rather more speedily than before, that **C′** is tautologically valid.

(b) For another example, consider next the following argument.

D (¬P ∨ R), (P ∨ Q), ¬(Q ∧ ¬S) ∴ (R ∨ S).

This argument too is tautologically valid. For consider the following truth table:

P	Q	R	S	(¬P ∨ R)	(P ∨ Q)	¬(Q ∧ ¬S)	(R ∨ S)
T	T	T	T				T
T	T	T	F				T
T	T	F	T				T
T	T	F	F	F	T		F
T	F	T	T				T
T	F	T	F				T
T	F	F	T				T
T	F	F	F	F	T		F
F	T	T	T				T
F	T	T	F				T
F	T	F	T				T
F	T	F	F	T	T	F	F
F	F	T	T				T
F	F	T	F				T
F	F	F	T				T
F	F	F	F		F		F
				3	2	4	1

Step (1): evaluating the conclusion first, we find it to be true on no fewer than twelve lines. That leaves only *four* potential bad lines to examine further. At step (2), evaluate the simplest premiss on those four lines. That leaves us just three candidate bad lines. Evaluating the next simplest premiss at step (3) eliminates two more. Finally, step (4), we knock out the last candidate bad line, showing that there are no bad lines and hence that argument **D** is tautologically valid.

Note the implicit generality here. We haven't specified how to interpret the atoms in this case. The argument is tautologically valid however the atoms are interpreted (i.e. whichever PL language we are using).

(c) Let's for the moment consider just one more PL argument:

E   ¬((¬S ∧ Q) ∧ R) , (P ∧ R) , ¬(Q ∧ S) ∴ ((P ∨ Q) ∧ ¬(R ∨ S)).

(Again, interpret the atoms however you like.) We evaluate the wffs in order of increasing complexity; then – stopping work on any line as soon as we find a false premiss or true conclusion, showing that the line can't be bad – we get:

P Q R S	¬((¬S ∧ Q) ∧ R)	(P ∧ R)	¬(Q ∧ S)	((P ∨ Q) ∧ ¬(R ∨ S))
T T T T		T	F	
T T T F	F T T	T	T	F T
T T F T		F		
T T F F		F		
T F T T	T F F	T	T	F T
T F T F	?	T	T	F T
T F F T		F		
T F F F		F		
F T T T		F		
F T T F		F		
F T F T		F		
F T F F		F		
F F T T		F		
F F T F		F		
F F F T		F		
F F F F		F		
	4	1	2	3

Step (1) already finds twelve lines to be good. At step (2), evaluating the next simplest premiss, another line turns out to be good. Next, we have recorded in miniature that (R ∨ S) is true on each remaining line; so its negation – the second conjunct of the conclusion – is false; so step (3) the whole conclusion is then false. That leaves three lines still in the running as to be bad. So, at step (4), we start work evaluating the first premiss on those three lines.

On our first potentially bad line, this premiss comes out false, hence the line is good after all. So we turn to the next potentially bad line, the fifth line of the table. This time the first premiss *is* true: hence we *have* found a bad line where the premisses are all true and conclusion false. And now we can stop, for one bad line is enough. Argument **E** is not tautologically valid.

15.5 Ordinary-language arguments again

Suppose we translate an ordinary-language (one-step) argument *Arg* into some suitable PL language to get a formal version Arg. Let's review what we can learn about the (in)validity of *Arg* from the tautological (in)validity of Arg.

(a) In translating from ordinary language into PL, we will typically be ignoring any concerns about vagueness, context-dependence, etc., when we tidy *Arg*'s component clauses into the PL atoms used in Arg. And we may also be tidying up some ordinary-language connectives when we render them using PL's crisply defined truth-functional connectives. But let's assume that the tidying isn't too drastic. In other words, let's assume that Arg renders *Arg* well enough for us to be able to assume that the two versions stand or fall together at least as far as deductive validity is concerned. Then the fundamental result is this:

> If the formal version Arg is tautologically valid, the original argument *Arg* will be valid too.

We know from §15.2 that if Arg is tautologically valid then Arg is valid, indeed logically valid; and we are assuming that if Arg is valid so is *Arg*.

(b) Suppose next that *Arg* is valid in virtue of the way that connectives 'and', 'or' and 'not' are distributed in its premisses and conclusion, and suppose the translation Arg captures those connectives. Then Arg will also be valid in virtue of the way that its connectives are distributed, i.e. will be tautologically valid.

It follows that, if Arg *isn't* tautologically valid, then (still assuming our translation picks up all the connectives in *Arg*), the original *Arg* isn't valid in virtue of the distribution of connectives in premisses and conclusion.

But Arg and *Arg* can still be valid for some other reason. Consider

Arg   All men are mortal and Socrates is a man; so Socrates is mortal.

Famously valid! Imagine, then, that we have constructed an ad hoc PL language where the atom P is stipulated to mean *All men are mortal*, Q means *Socrates is a man*, R means *Socrates is a mortal*. In *that* language the inference

Arg $(P \wedge Q) \therefore R$

is then necessarily truth-preserving and so deductively valid. But Arg is plainly not *tautologically* valid, as there's a combinatorially possible valuation making the premisses true and conclusion false. So here we have a formal PL argument Arg which is not tautologically valid, but where Arg and the corresponding informal argument *Arg are* valid. In sum:

> If Arg is *not* tautologically valid, then it doesn't follow that Arg or *Arg* aren't valid. However, if Arg captures all the connectives in *Arg*, then it will at least follow that *Arg* isn't valid in virtue of the distribution of connectives in premisses and conclusion.

15.6 Tautological consistency and tautological validity

(a) In Chapter 2, we noted that an inference is deductively valid just if its premisses taken together with the denial of its conclusion are inconsistent. Similarly, we can alternatively define tautological validity in terms of a very natural notion of tautological inconsistency. Let's say:

> One or more PL wffs are *tautologically consistent* if and only if there is some valuation of the atoms in the wffs which makes these wffs all true together. These wffs are otherwise *tautologically inconsistent*.

Note: to say of a *single* wff that it is tautologically inconsistent is just to say that it is a contradiction (in the wide sense introduced in §14.1).

To work out directly whether some PL wffs are tautologically (in)consistent, we can just run a truth-table test. Take the atoms in the wffs; draw up a table of every possible assignment of values to those atoms; and work out the value of each wff on each assignment. If there is a row of the table on which all the wffs come out true together, then the wffs are tautologically consistent: and if not, then not. For a trivial example, any two of the following wffs

$$(P \vee Q), \neg P, \neg Q$$

are tautologically consistent; but all three taken together are inconsistent. While for another example, check that the following wffs

$$(P \vee (\neg Q \wedge \neg R)), ((P \wedge Q) \vee R), (P \wedge \neg R) \vee \neg Q))$$

taken together are consistent.

(b) Given our definitions of tautological entailment and tautological inconsistency, we immediately get the following key relationship:

> The premisses $\alpha_1, \alpha_2, \ldots, \alpha_n$ tautologically entail the conclusion γ if and only if the wffs $\alpha_1, \alpha_2, \ldots, \alpha_n, \neg \gamma$ are tautologically inconsistent.

For recall that $\alpha_1, \alpha_2, \ldots, \alpha_n$ tautologically entails γ just when there is no valuation of the relevant atoms on which the αs are all true and γ false. And that means there is no valuation on which the αs plus $\neg \gamma$ are all true – which is exactly what it takes for those wffs to be tautologically inconsistent.

15.7 Summary

> A (one-step) argument couched in a PL language is tautologically valid if and only if there is no 'bad' valuation of the relevant atoms which makes the premisses true and conclusion false.
>
> We can decide whether an argument is tautologically valid by a brute search for bad valuations, setting out our working in a truth table. (We can speed

up the search by ignoring any line on a table once it becomes clear that it won't give a bad valuation.)

The tautological validity of a PL argument implies its plain validity. Tautological invalidity does not always imply invalidity, but means that the PL argument, if valid, must depend for its validity on the meanings of its atoms.

Take an ordinary-language argument. Then if a matching PL translation of this argument – capturing the truth-relevant content of premises and conclusion, and reflecting the distribution of truth-functional connectives in the original argument – is tautologically valid, then the original is valid. While, if the translation is not tautologically valid, we can at least conclude that the original argument is not valid in virtue of the way that 'and', 'or', and 'not' are distributed in the premises and conclusion.

Exercises 15

(a)   Practice makes perfect! Use the truth-table test to determine which of the following arguments are tautologically valid:

(1) $(P \land S), \neg(S \land \neg R) \therefore (R \lor \neg P)$

(2) $P, \neg(P \land \neg Q), (\neg Q \lor R) \therefore R$

(3) $(\neg P \lor \neg(Q \lor R)), (Q \lor (P \land R)) \therefore (\neg P \lor Q)$

(4) $(P \lor Q), \neg(Q \land \neg\neg R) \therefore \neg(R \lor P)$

(5) $P, (Q \lor R) \therefore ((P \land Q) \lor (P \land R))$

(6) $(P \lor (\neg P \land Q)), (\neg P \lor R), \neg(Q \land S) \therefore \neg(\neg R \land S)$

(b)   Assess the following arguments for validity:

(1) Either Jack went up the hill or Jill did. Either Jack didn't go up the hill or the water got spilt. Hence, either Jill went up the hill or the water got spilt.

(2) Either Jack didn't go up the hill or the water got spilt. Why? Because it isn't the case that Jack went up the hill and Jill didn't. Moreover, it isn't the case that Jill went up the hill and the water got spilt.

(3) Either Jill hasn't trained hard or she will win the race. It isn't true that she'll win the race and not be praised. Either Jill has trained hard or she deserves to lose. Hence either Jill will be praised or she deserves to lose.

(4) Veronika and Marek are both violinists. Veronika and Peter are married but aren't both violinists. And likewise, Marek and Jiří aren't both violinists. So neither Jiří nor Peter are violinists.

(5) Jill is a mother. Either Jack and Jill are both parents, or neither are. Either Jack isn't a parent at all, or he is a proud father. Therefore Jack is a proud father.

(6) Either Popper is a logician or Quine is; moreover it isn't the case that either Russell or Sellars are logicians. Why so? Well, for a start, Popper and Russell are logicians. But not both Quine and Sellars are. And finally, this much is ruled out: Sellars not being a logician while Quine is one, and at the same time Russell being a logician too!

16 More about tautological entailment

In this chapter, we continue to explore the twin concepts of tautological validity and tautological entailment.

16.1 Extending the notion of tautological entailment

In §1.4 we said that, ideally, we would like techniques for determining whether an argument is valid that work mechanically, so that we can settle questions of validity as routinely as we can settle arithmetical questions by calculation. We have now seen that we can determine whether a PL argument is *tautologically* valid by a brute-force test.

And now let's note that the idea of tautological entailment – and of truth-table testing – extends in an entirely natural way to apply to arguments in other languages with truth-functional connectives. What matters is that fixing the values of the relevant atoms still fixes the values of the wffs.

For a toy example, suppose that we are working in a PL-like language which has as its built-in connectives just the familiar negation and the dollar connective we defined in §13.3. Then we can easily check that the argument

A $(P, Q, R), \neg P \therefore \neg Q$

in this language is tautologically valid. Here's a truth table:

P	Q	R	(P, Q, R)	$\neg P$	$\neg Q$
T	T	T	F		
T	T	F	T	F	
T	F	T	F		
T	F	F	T	F	
F	T	T	F		
F	T	F	F		
F	F	T	T	T	T
F	F	F	F		

We have filled in the value of the first premiss on each line just by looking up the definition of the dollar connective. Completing lines where necessary is trivial. This shows that the argument is tautologically valid, as announced.

Of course, this example has no special interest. But there is a general moral:

As long as we are dealing with a language with truth-functional connectives, we can talk of arguments framed in the language as being tautologically valid, and can use a truth table to test for validity in this sense.

16.2 Can there be a more efficient test?

(a)   Is the following argument tautologically valid,

B $\neg P, \neg P', \neg P'', \ldots, \neg P''^{\cdots''} \therefore Q,$

where there are *fifty* similar premises, each the negation of a different atom?

Of course not. As you no doubt immediately saw. And I *know* that you didn't base your verdict on a mechanical truth-table test! For suppose you *had* set off mindlessly to construct a truth table for **B** (with all the Ps listed on the left before the Q in the usual way). Then you would have had to write down a 2^{51} line truth table. And it won't be until the very last line, which assigns F to all the Ps and also assigns F to Q, that you get to the lone 'bad' valuation making all the premises true and the conclusion false. Even if you could write down a line of the table in just a couple of seconds, it would take *a million years* before you got to that decisive final line.

So how can we know – straight off, without waiting for millennia – that argument **B** is tautologically invalid?

Well, instead of working through all the combinatorially possible valuations of its atoms waiting for a 'bad' line to turn up, we can approach things from the other end. In other words, we suppose that there *is* a bad valuation, i.e. one where the premises are true and the conclusion is false; i.e. a valuation where

$$\neg P := T, \neg P' := T, \neg P'' := T, \ldots, \neg P''^{\cdots''} := T, Q := F.$$

We then *work backwards* to see what such a valuation must look like if it exists. And in this case, the job is *very* easily done – it takes no work to spot the bad valuation. As you no doubt did immediately on being presented with **B**.

(b)   We can generalize this idea of working backwards to test any given argument for tautological validity. We suppose that there *is* a bad valuation, and then systematically unravel the implications of this supposition. We will either eventually find a bad valuation (showing the inference step is invalid), or we will get embroiled in contradictions every way we turn (showing that there is no bad valuation after all, hence that the inference is valid). This strategy can be developed into the so-called *truth tree* method for testing for validity. 'Trees' get into the story because we may have to explore branching paths of alternatives.

Approaching our toy example **B** by working backwards saves a ludicrous amount of time compared with working forwards through a truth table! But there's bad news. Systematically working backwards through a truth tree is neat and quick in simple classroom cases: but just as with a truth table, the amount of work required can still grow exponentially as we deal with more complex examples. In fact, there is no *known* way of testing arguments for tautological validity that isn't exponentially costly in unfavourable cases. (The issue whether there *could* in principle be a more efficient test is a fundamental unsolved question in the theory of computational complexity.)

16.3   Truth-table testing and the counterexample method

We now highlight a not-quite-obvious connection between old and new ideas. We can best do this via an example.

Suppose we are working in a PL language where P means *Paris is the capital of France*, Q means *Rome is bigger than Turin*, P′ means *Lyon is the capital of France*, and Q′ means *Venice is in Italy*. Then consider

>   **C**   (P ∨ Q) ∴ P.

This argument is certainly not valid! But how can we show its invalidity from very first principles? It has a true premiss and a true conclusion, so we can't directly apply the Invalidity Principle of §2.3.

Can we show **C** is invalid by using the counterexample method of §5.1? A counterexample, remember, is another argument with the same logical structure but which *does* have a true premiss but a false conclusion. So consider

>   **D**   (P′ ∨ Q′) ∴ P′,

which has the same form. Given the meaning of the atoms, this *does* have a true premiss and false conclusion, so is invalid. Since the arguments stand or fall together as far as validity is concerned and **D** is invalid, **C** is invalid too.

But now note that – as with any PL wffs – the truth values of the premiss and conclusion in **D** are completely fixed by the values of the atoms, P′ := F, Q′ := T. It is that valuation of atoms which makes **D** the counterexample we are looking for. So instead of substituting new atoms for old in **C**, with the *new* atoms having truth values which make the (revised) premiss true and (revised) conclusion false, we could simply take the same values and assign them to the corresponding *original* atoms, i.e. we could consider the valuation P := F, Q := T. This will now make the (original) premiss true and (original) conclusion false. In other words, if we transfer the values of the new atoms in the *counterexample* **D** to become the values of the corresponding old atoms in **C**, then we get a *bad line* on the truth-table testing **C** for tautological validity, i.e. a line specifying what we can call a *countervaluation* making the premisses true and conclusion false.

So we can think of looking for a bad line or *countervaluation* on a truth table as a stripped-down version of looking for a *counterexample* to tautological validity. It's just that in looking for a countervaluation we go straight for what matters in counterexamples for PL arguments, namely the valuation of the atoms.

16.4   '⊨' and '∴'

(a)   Let's now redeploy the double turnstile symbol which we introduced in §14.2:

We abbreviate the claim that the premisses $\alpha_1, \alpha_2, \ldots, \alpha_n$ tautologically entail the conclusion γ as follows: $\alpha_1, \alpha_2, \ldots, \alpha_n \vDash \gamma$.

So an expression of the form $\alpha_1, \alpha_2, \ldots, \alpha_n \vDash \gamma$ says that γ is true on every valuation which makes the αs all true. Applying that to the special case where there are zero premisses, an expression of the form $\vDash \gamma$ will say that γ is true on every valuation, with no further condition to meet. Which of course tallies with our earlier use of $\vDash \gamma$ to abbreviate the claim that γ is a tautology. In fact, there's a general point here: it is sometimes useful to think of a tautology as the conclusion of a tautologically valid argument which has zero premisses!

(b) Note, as we did before, that the turnstile is being added to *English*. It is metalinguistic shorthand. This status can get obscured because, as is entirely standard, we write the likes of

(1) $(P \lor Q), \neg P \vDash Q$

rather than write

(2) '$(P \lor Q)$', '$\neg P$' $\vDash$ 'Q'

which would then unpack as

(3) The premisses '$(P \lor Q)$' and '$\neg P$' tautologically entail the conclusion 'Q'.

But we will follow convention and use the pared-down (1), letting the sign $\vDash$ generate its own invisible quotation marks – again like $:=$ (see §11.3 and §14.2).

(c) Be careful, then! There is a fundamental difference between the symbols $\vDash$ and $\therefore$, and hence between (1) and

(4) $(P \lor Q), \neg P \therefore Q$.

(4) is an *argument* couched in some PL language. If put to serious use, it makes *three* assertions in that language, with the PL inference marker signalling that the third assertion is being inferred from the other two. By contrast, (1) is not an argument at all. It is used to make a *single assertion* in shorthand English, a metalinguistic claim *about* the PL argument (4).

16.5   Generalizing examples of tautological entailment

(a) Using our new notation, here are a few elementary examples of tautological entailments to add to those in the last chapter (check them using truth tables!):

(1) $\neg(P \land Q) \vDash (\neg P \lor \neg Q)$
(2) $(P \lor Q), \neg P \vDash Q$
(3) $(P \land (Q \lor R)) \vDash ((P \land Q) \lor (P \land R))$
(4) $(P \lor Q), \neg(P \land \neg R), \neg(Q \land \neg R) \vDash R$.

These claims are already general, applying across languages, since they are true irrespective of the meanings of the atoms. What we need to stress now is that they can also be generalized further. For *any* PL wffs α, β, and γ, we have:

(1') $\neg(\alpha \wedge \beta) \vDash (\neg\alpha \vee \neg\beta)$
(2') $(\alpha \vee \beta), \neg\alpha \vDash \beta$
(3') $(\alpha \wedge (\beta \vee \gamma)) \vDash ((\alpha \wedge \beta) \vee (\alpha \wedge \gamma))$
(4') $(\alpha \vee \beta), \neg(\alpha \wedge \neg\gamma), \neg(\beta \wedge \neg\gamma) \vDash \gamma$.

And the proof that we can generalize tautological entailments like this is basically the same as the proof in §14.2(c) which showed that we can generalize tautologies.

   (i)   Start with a tautologically valid argument whose constituent atoms are P, Q, ... By assumption, whatever values these atoms have, we can't make the argument's premises all true and the conclusion false.

  (ii)   Now systematically replace P, Q, . . . , as they appear throughout the given argument with the wffs α, β, . . . , respectively.

 (iii)   The truth values of the resulting new wffs will depend on the truth values of these new constituent wffs α, β, . . . , exactly as the truth values of the old wffs in our original argument depend on the values of their atoms. So whatever values these new constituents have, we can't make the new premises all true together and the conclusion false.

 (iv)   So whatever values of the atoms *inside* the wffs α, β, . . . , have, we can't make the new premises all true together and the conclusion false. The new argument is therefore tautologically valid.

Hence, as with tautologies, buy one tautological entailment, and you get indefinitely more for free. There is an implicit generality then in claims about tautological entailment.

(b)   Here is another way of putting the point, again echoing what we said about tautologies in §14.2(d). Take any (one-step) argument in a PL language. Rewrite all its atoms as schematic variables. Follow the strict rule, same atom same replacement variable, different atom different replacement – and then the schematic version shows all the structure of the relevant wffs down to the atomic level. Call the resulting schema a *basic schema for the argument*. If the argument we start off from is tautologically valid, call the resulting basic schema a *tautological argument schema*. (1') to (4') are examples.

   A substitution instance of an argument schema is, of course, the result of going in the opposite direction and systematically replacing schematic variables with wffs (as usual, same variable, same replacement). What we have shown in this section can then neatly be summed up as follows:

> Any substitution instance of a tautological argument schema is tautologically valid.

Note again, however, that the claim that an argument is *non*-valid does *not* unrestrictedly generalize. For a very trivial example, the argument P $\therefore$ Q is not tautologically valid. And most instances of the corresponding basic schema $\alpha \therefore \beta$ will of course be non-valid. *But not all.* Consider, for example, the special case when we substitute (R $\wedge$ S) for α and R for β!

16.6   Tautological entailment and form

(a)   A tautology is a PL wff whose truth is fixed simply by the pattern in which the connectives appear in it – we can determine that the wff has to be true without knowing the actual truth values of the relevant atoms. That's why we can say that a tautology is true in virtue of its logical form, in the sense explained in §14.3(c).

Exactly similarly, a tautologically valid argument in a PL language is an argument whose inference step is truth-preserving simply because of the pattern in which any connectives appear in its premisses and conclusion (understand that to cover trivially valid arguments like P ∴ P where there are no connectives).

For example, (P ∨ Q), ¬P ∴ Q is tautologically valid because the connectives appear where they do, i.e. because of what the argument shares with any argument of the form $(\alpha \vee \beta)$, $\neg\alpha$ ∴ β. We can sensibly sum that up by saying the argument is tautologically valid in virtue of having this form.

(b)   Now, as long ago as §3.3 we stressed the general point that we can't talk in an unqualified way about 'the' form of an argument – an argument can instantiate different schematic forms at different levels of detail. But it is natural to fall into saying that *the* logical form of a PL argument is the form which gets displayed by a basic schema for the argument (because that schema will show all the structural detail down to the atomic level). And then, generalizing the point in the last paragraph, we can say:

A tautologically valid PL argument is valid in virtue of its logical form.

The validity of such an argument results, then, from the stipulated meaning of the cleaned-up connectives and the way they are distributed in the relevant wffs. Validity-in-virtue-of-form for tautologically valid arguments is as unmysterious as truth-in-virtue-of-form for tautologies.

16.7   Tautological equivalence as two-way entailment

(a)   Finally, we introduce an important concept which sharpens up the intuitive notion of equivalence which we met back in §2.2(b):

If $\alpha \vDash \beta$ and $\beta \vDash \alpha$, then for brevity we will write $\alpha \approx \beta$.

The PL wffs α and β are *tautologically equivalent* if and only if $\alpha \approx \beta$.

When is α tautologically equivalent to β? When, for every valuation of the relevant atoms (i.e. all the atoms which appear in at least one of them), if α is true, so is β, and if β is true so is α. This means that if α and β are equivalent and share the same atoms, their truth tables will be the same. And recall, the idea of sharing a truth table was pivotal when we were discussing the ideas of defining one connective in terms of others and of expressive adequacy in §§13.2–13.4.

142

(Fine print: we should note, however, that wffs can be tautologically equivalent without having the same truth tables. For example, the wffs ¬P and (¬P ∧ (Q ∨ ¬Q)) don't share all their atoms so have different tables. But these wffs *do* have the same values on each valuation of *all* the atoms which appear in at least one of them, and so are tautologically equivalent.)

Gathering together a few elementary examples, we have:

(1) (P ∧ Q) ≈ (Q ∧ P)
(2) (P ∧ (Q ∧ R)) ≈ ((P ∧ Q) ∧ R)
(3) (P ∧ (Q ∨ R)) ≈ ((P ∧ Q) ∨ (P ∧ R))
(4) ¬(P ∧ Q) ≈ (¬P ∨ ¬Q)
(5) ((P ∧ ¬Q) ∨ (¬P ∧ Q)) ≈ ((P ∨ Q) ∧ ¬(P ∧ Q)).

Some write '⫤⊨' for '≈'. And either way, note that this is *not* a connective added to PL languages. Again, it is a metalinguistic symbol added to logicians' English.

(b)   Just as claims about tautologies and about one-way tautological entailment generalize, so too do claims about two-way tautological entailment.

Hence, for any wffs α, β, and γ of a PL language, we have:

(1′) (α ∧ β) ≈ (β ∧ α)
(2′) (α ∧ (β ∧ γ)) ≈ ((α ∧ β) ∧ γ)
(3′) (α ∧ (β ∨ γ)) ≈ ((α ∧ β) ∨ (α ∧ γ))
(4′) ¬(α ∧ β) ≈ (¬α ∨ ¬β)
(5′) ((α ∧ ¬β) ∨ (¬α ∧ β)) ≈ ((α ∨ β) ∧ ¬(α ∧ β)).

(c)   Why does tautological equivalence matter? Because – picking up a theme from Exercises 2(b) – we have:

Two tautologically equivalent wffs can be used interchangeably as premisses or as conclusions without affecting the tautological validity of an argument.

For example, suppose the wffs β and β′ are tautologically equivalent, i.e. are such that β ≈ β′. Then, for any wffs α, γ

(i)   α ⊨ β if and only if α ⊨ β′
(ii) β ⊨ γ if and only if β′ ⊨ γ.

Check that you understand why these claims certainly *ought* to be true. We can leave their proofs, though, to the Exercises.

16.8   Summary

Looking for a bad line on a truth table can be thought of as a stripped-down version of looking for a counterexample to the validity of a PL argument.

We (re)introduce the symbol ⊨ as an augmentation of English, so α ⊨ β says that α tautologically entails β. It is important to distinguish the metalinguistic ⊨ from the PL inference marker ∴.

If a PL argument is tautologically valid, so too is any argument generated from it by systematically substituting wffs for its atoms (same atom, same replacement wff).

There is a good sense in which tautologically valid arguments are logically valid, and are valid in virtue of logical form.

We then introduced the notion of tautological equivalence, symbolized in our metalanguage by $\approx$: so $\alpha \approx \beta$ just in case $\alpha \vDash \beta$ and $\beta \vDash \alpha$. Tautologically equivalent wffs have the same logical powers.

Exercises 16

(a*) Our §15.2 definition says that $\alpha_1, \alpha_2, \ldots, \alpha_n \vDash \gamma$ if and only if there is no valuation of the atoms *involved in the relevant wffs* which makes the αs all true and γ false. Show that we could equivalently have said: The wffs $\alpha_1, \alpha_2, \ldots, \alpha_n \vDash \gamma$ if and only if there is no valuation of *all the language's atoms* which makes the αs all true and γ false. (Hint: see §10.7(b).)

(b*) Why are the following true? (Hint: make use of the previous exercise.)

    (1) Any two tautologies are tautologically equivalent.

    (2) If $\alpha \vDash \gamma$, then $\alpha, \beta \vDash \gamma$.

    (3) If $\alpha, \beta \vDash \gamma$ and β is a tautology, then $\alpha \vDash \gamma$.

    (4) If $\alpha \vDash \beta$ and $\beta \vDash \gamma$, then $\alpha \vDash \gamma$.

    (5) Suppose $\beta \approx \beta'$. Then for any wffs α, γ both (i) $\alpha \vDash \beta$ if and only if $\alpha \vDash \beta'$, and (ii) $\beta \vDash \gamma$ if and only if $\beta' \vDash \gamma$.

    (6) Replacing a subformula of a wff by an equivalent expression results in a new wff equivalent to the original one.

(c*) Some new notation. Alongside the use of lower-case Greek letters for individual wffs, it is common to use upper-case Greek letters such as 'Γ' (*Gamma*) and 'Δ' (*Delta*) to stand in for some wffs – zero, one, or many.

    Further, we use 'Γ, α' for the wffs Γ together with α. We also use 'Γ ∪ Δ' for the wffs Γ together with the wffs Δ.

    Now prove these generalized versions of the some of the claims in (b):

    (1) If Γ $\vDash \gamma$, then Γ, $\alpha \vDash \gamma$.

    (2) If Γ, $\alpha \vDash \gamma$ and α is a tautology, then Γ $\vDash \gamma$.

    (3) If Γ $\vDash \beta$ and Δ, $\beta \vDash \gamma$, then Γ ∪ Δ $\vDash \gamma$.

    (4) Prove the more general version of (b5) which is highlighted at the very end of the chapter.

We will normally be interested in cases where we are dealing with only finitely many wffs Γ. But would (1) to (3) still be true if Γ and/or Δ were infinitely many?

(d*) In the light of §16.7, (1'), (2'), and (3'), it can be said 'conjunction is commutative', 'conjunction is associative', 'conjunction distributes over disjunction'. Investigate and explain. What parallel claims apply to disjunction?

(e*) Find out more about the idea of 'working backwards' (touched on in §16.2) by looking at the online supplement on propositional truth trees.

17 Explosion and absurdity

We start this chapter by noting that tautological entailment, as we have defined it, is explosive! What does that mean? Can we live with this consequence?

We then introduce the *falsum* or absurdity sign to our PL languages, and get some more explosive inferences.

17.1 Explosion!

Here is another general result about tautological entailment.

> *Explosion* For any wffs α, γ in a given PL language, $\alpha, \neg\alpha \vDash \gamma$.

The entailments of a contradictory pair of wffs explode everywhere!

Why? Because no valuation of the atoms in the wffs α and γ can possibly make α and $\neg\alpha$ true together. Hence no relevant valuation can possibly make α and $\neg\alpha$ true together and also make γ false. Hence $\alpha, \neg\alpha \vDash \gamma$.

Explosion for tautological entailment is, of course, a formal analogue of the result that we remarked on in §6.5, when we noted that – according to our official general definition of deductive validity – arguments of the form *A, not-A, so C* count as deductively valid. Now, as we remarked at the time, this consequence of our official definition may well strike us as a reason to reject the definition. Arguments of the form *A, not-A, so C* just don't look compelling. However, as we went on to say, it is in fact unclear whether there is *any* consistent way of accommodating all our untutored hunches about what is and what isn't an absolutely compelling inference. So official definitions of entailment – as with many other definitions of logical concepts – are best thought of as rational reconstructions of our messy pre-theoretic ideas. We try to fit a range of informal desiderata as best we can, balancing considerations of theoretical simplicity and ease of use against the cost of some departures from our initial intuitions.

It is the same here. The notion of tautological validity is an elegantly simple and powerful reconstruction of the intuitive notion of validity as applied to arguments whose essential logical ingredients are truth-functional connectives. We get a sharply defined concept of validity which no longer relies on a troublesome notion of necessity, or on the idea of premises 'absolutely guaranteeing' a conclusion; we trade in those murky notions for the crystal clear idea of being truth-preserving on all combinatorially possible valuations of atoms (meaning that on every valuation, *if* the given premisses are true, so is the conclusion). Yes, on this reconstruction of the notion of validity, a formal PL version of 'Jack is married, Jack is not married, so the world will end tomorrow' gets counted as valid. But, in other respects, our reconstruction is so *very* neat and elegant that most logicians recommend that we learn to cheerfully live with this apparent oddity. (We return to this theme in §20.9.)

17.2 The falsum as an absurdity sign

(a)   A binary truth-functional connective like conjunction takes two wffs to form a wff; the truth value of a resulting wff $(\alpha \wedge \beta)$ then depends on the values of α and β. A unary connective like negation takes just one wff to form a wff; the truth value of a resulting wff $\neg\alpha$ depends on the value of α. Going another step, what would be the zero case – a 'nullary' connective? It would be a symbol which takes zero wffs to form a wff, so it must *already* be a wff! And its truth value will depend on nothing – hence its truth value must be fixed once and for all.

So, there can only be two logical symbols of this kind, the one which always evaluates as true, and the one which always evaluates as false. Traditionally these special wffs are called the *verum* and the *falsum*, and they are symbolized $\top$ and $\bot$ respectively.

As we go from one PL language to another, the interpretation of ordinary atomic wffs can vary, but the interpretation of the three connectives stays the same. The connectives are said to be *logical constants*. If we do add the verum and the falsum to a PL-style language, we are then adding two more logical constants, two more symbols which again retain the same interpretation from language to language. Obviously, the always-false wff $\bot$ is equivalent to the negation of the always-true $\top$, and likewise $\top$ is equivalent to the negation of $\bot$. For some purposes, it is nice to have both symbols in our formal language. Equally, for many purposes we can manage perfectly well without either symbol.

(b)   Suppose, though, that we do add the falsum to our formal languages. Using the equivalence symbol introduced in §16.7, for any wff α we will have

(1) $\bot \approx (\alpha \wedge \neg\alpha)$,

(2) $\bot \vDash \alpha$.

To show (1), pick either side of the equivalence. There is no way it can be true. And hence there is no way it can be true and the other side false. So $\bot$ is equivalent to any explicit contradiction. And (2) is just another version of explosion: from the falsum, anything can be inferred – or as the common Latin tag has it, *ex falso quodlibet*.

(1) tells us that we can regard $\bot$ as a kind of all-purpose contradiction, though one without any specific content. Which encourages us to simply read the symbol as 'Contradiction!' or 'Absurd!'. Which in turn gives us a clue about why it will be useful to have the symbol in our formal languages. For one type of argument we will want to be able to regiment formally is reductio ad absurdum arguments

– i.e. arguments where we prove $\neg\alpha$ by showing that supposing α leads to some absurdity. We will now be able to recruit our new sign to indicate that a line of reasoning yields absurdity: we will meet $\bot$ starring in this role in Chapter 20.

17.3   Adding the falsum to PL languages

We will, from now on, take the falsum $\bot$ to be built in to PL languages.

We have two ways to think about $\bot$. We can think of it in the slightly tricksy way in which we first introduced it, i.e. as the limiting case of a connective – one that connects nothing. Or we can think of it as a special wff (like an atomic wff in not being built out of other wffs) – a wff that has no specific content, a sort of abstract contradiction. There is nothing to choose between these characterizations.

Either way, we formally handle the symbol by adding a clause to the syntactic definition of a PL wff that allows $\bot$ by itself to count as a wff. And we add a semantic rule which constrains this new wff to be false on any valuation. But let's wait until §18.7 before we set that out more carefully. In the next chapter we will also add another binary connective to our formal languages. And it will be neater to give a single official account of our extended PL languages after we have made both additions.

17.4   Summary

Explosion holds for tautological entailment – a contradictory pair of wffs entails any conclusion you like.

The symbol $\bot$ will be added to PL languages as a special wff which always evaluates to false, and which can be informally read as 'Contradiction!' or 'Absurd!'. This wff also entails any conclusion you like.

Exercises 17

(1) Show that for any wff α, $(\alpha \wedge \bot) \approx \bot$ and $(\alpha \wedge \neg\bot) \approx \alpha$. What are the analogous results for wffs of the form $(\alpha \vee \bot)$ and $(\alpha \vee \neg\bot)$?

(2) Show that any wff including one or more occurrences of $\bot$ is equivalent to a wff without any absurdity signs or to $\bot$ or to $\neg\bot$.

(3) Find a binary connective % such that a language with just that connective is *not* expressively complete, but a language with % plus $\bot$ *is* expressively complete.

Recalling the notation introduced in Exercises 16(c*), where 'Γ' stands in for some wffs – zero, one, or many:

(4*) Show that $\Gamma \vDash \bot$ if and only if the wffs Γ are tautologically inconsistent.

(5*) Show that $\Gamma, \alpha \vDash \bot$ if and only if $\Gamma \vDash \neg\alpha$.

18 The truth-functional conditional

We have seen (at some length!) how to evaluate arguments whose essential logical materials are the three connectives 'and', 'or', and 'not'. We now ask: can the techniques that we have developed be smoothly extended to deal with arguments involving that other quite fundamental connective, 'if'?

18.1 Some arguments involving conditionals

Consider the following elementary arguments:

A   If Jack bet on Eclipse, he lost his money. Jack did bet on Eclipse. So Jack lost his money.

B   If Jack bet on Eclipse, he lost his money. Jack did not lose his money. So Jack did not bet on Eclipse.

C   If Jack bet on Eclipse, he lost his money. So if Jack didn't lose his money, he didn't bet on Eclipse.

D   If Jack bet on Eclipse, then he lost his money. If Jack lost his money, then he had to walk home. So if Jack bet on Eclipse, he had to walk home.

E   Either Jack bet on Eclipse or on Pegasus. If Jack bet on Eclipse, he lost his money. If Jack bet on Pegasus, he lost his money. So, Jack lost his money.

Each of these first five arguments involving *conditionals* is intuitively valid. Contrast the next three arguments:

F   If Jack bet on Eclipse, he lost his money. Jack lost his money. So Jack bet on Eclipse.

G   If Jack bet on Eclipse, he lost his money. Jack did not bet on Eclipse. So Jack did not lose his money.

H   If Jack bet on Eclipse, he lost his money. So if Jack did not bet on Eclipse, he did not lose his money.

These are plainly fallacious. Suppose foolish Jack lost his money by betting not on Eclipse but on Pegasus, an equally hopeless horse. Then in each of the three cases, the premises of the argument can be true and conclusion false.

148

The validity or invalidity of the arguments **A** to **H** has nothing specifically to do with Jack or betting, but is evidently due to the meaning of the conditional construction introduced by 'if'. We would therefore like to have a general way of handling arguments like these which rely on conditionals. Now, 'if' seems often to behave as a binary connective – it seems like 'and' and 'or', at least in respect of combining two propositions to form a new one. So the next question is: can we carry over our methods for evaluating arguments involving those other binary connectives to deal with conditionals as well?

18.2   Four basic principles

As we will see in the next chapter, conditionals come in importantly different flavours; but in this chapter let's concentrate on simple cases like those in the previous section (leaving it wide open for now what counts as 'simple').

We will regard *if A, C* and *if A then C* as stylistic variants, treating the 'then' as usually no more than helpful punctuation (perhaps 'then' does more work in some contexts; but put any such cases aside). And we now introduce some standard terminology:

> Given a conditional *if A then C*, we refer to the 'if' clause *A* as the *antecedent* of the conditional, and to the other clause *C* as the *consequent*.
>
> The *converse* of *if A then C* is the conditional *if C then A*.
>
> The *contrapositive* of *if A then C* is the conditional *if not-C then not-A*.

We will also use the same terminology when talking about conditionals in our formal languages.

Generalizing from the examples **A** and **B**, the following pair of basic principles of conditional reasoning evidently hold good (at least for simple conditionals):

> (MP)   An inference step of the form *A, if A then C, so C* is valid. This mode of inference is traditionally referred to as *modus ponens*.
>
> (MT)   An inference step of the form *not-C, if A then C, so not-A* is valid. This mode of inference is traditionally referred to as *modus tollens*.

Another intuitively correct principle is the *falsehood condition*:

> (FC)   A conditional *if A then C* must be false if in fact *A* is true and *C* is false.

Note that both (FC) and (MT) are immediate consequences of (MP). Take three propositions of the form (i) *A*, (ii) *if A then C*, (iii) *not-C*. These are inconsistent since, by (MP), (i) and (ii) imply *C*, which contradicts (iii). Hence, if we keep (ii) and (iii) we have to reject (i), which is the principle (MT). And if we keep (i) and (iii) we have to reject (ii), which is the principle (FC).

Later, in §18.8, we will meet another core principle about conditionals: roughly, if we can infer C from the temporary supposition A, then we can drop the supposition and assert *if A then C*. But let's put that idea on hold for the moment, and note instead another basic fact about conditionals – namely, that they are usually non-reversible:

> (NR) From a conditional premiss of the form *if A then C*, we usually can't infer the converse conditional *if C then A*.

No doubt, if I have won a Nobel prize, then I am clever. But it doesn't follow that if I am clever, then I have won a Nobel prize.

18.3   Introducing the truth-functional conditional

(a)   In headline terms, our Chapter 15 technique for evaluating arguments involving 'and', 'or' and 'not' has two stages, (1) translation into a PL language and (2) assessing the translated version for tautological validity by using a truth-table test. Step (1) presupposes that the ordinary-language connectives are close enough in their core meanings to the corresponding connectives of PL for logically important features of the original argument to get carried over by the translation. Step (2) then depends on the fact that the PL connectives are truth-functional. That's needed to ensure that, given any valuation of the relevant atoms, we can work out whether it makes the premisses of the PL argument true and the conclusion false.

Hence, if our truth-table technique is to be straightforwardly extended to cover arguments involving the conditional, we need to be able to render conditional propositions using a suitable truth-functional connective, and to do this in a way which preserves enough of the core meaning of the conditional.

(b)   It is quite easy to see that there is only one truth-functional connective which satisfies inferential principles parallel to the four headlined principles (MP) to (NR) which apply to ordinary conditionals. Why so?

α	γ	$(\alpha \rightarrow \gamma)$
T	T	?
T	F	F
F	T	?
F	F	?

Suppose we add the arrow symbol '$\rightarrow$' to our PL languages in order to represent a connective which is intended to be both truth-functional and conditional-like. The issue is how to fill in its truth table.

With an eye on (FC), we have already completed the second line: the supposed truth-functional conditional has to be false when it has a true antecedent and false consequent. So how does the rest of the table go?

(c)   Taking it slowly, step by step, note that the first line on the truth table has to be completed with 'T'. Otherwise $(\alpha \rightarrow \gamma)$ would always be false when α is true. But of course there can be true conditionals with true antecedents – else we'd never be able to use (MP) with two true premisses $(\alpha \rightarrow \gamma)$ and α in order to prove that γ.

The last line also has to be completed with 'T'. Otherwise $(\alpha \to \gamma)$ would always be false when γ is false. But of course there can be true conditionals with false consequents – else we'd never be able to use (MT) with two true premisses $(\alpha \to \gamma)$ and $\neg\gamma$ to prove that $\neg\alpha$.

α	γ	$(\alpha \to \gamma)$
T	T	T
T	F	F
F	T	?
F	F	T

Which just leaves one entry for the truth table to be decided. But if we put 'F' on the third line, then $(\alpha \to \gamma)$ would have the same truth table as $(\gamma \to \alpha)$, making our supposed conditional reversible, contrary to the requirement that a conditional-like connective satisfies the analogue of (NR). Hence:

The only candidate for a conditional-like truth function is the one defined by the following truth table:

α	γ	$(\alpha \to \gamma)$
T	T	T
T	F	F
F	T	T
F	F	T

(d)   For a fast-track argument, take the wff $((P \land Q) \to P)$. Assuming the arrow is conditional-like, this wff should *always* be true (since necessarily, if P and Q are both true, then P in particular is true). But the values of the antecedent/consequent in this wff can be any of T/T, or F/T, or F/F (depending on the values of P and Q). And we've just said that our conditional needs to evaluate as T in each of those three cases. So that forces the same completion of the table for our conditional-like truth function.

(e)   The Stoic logician Philo (fourth century BC) claimed, in effect, that the ordinary-language conditional has this truth table. So the truth-functional connective here is sometimes still referred to as the *Philonian* conditional. It was reintroduced into modern logic by Frege in the nineteenth century, and then taken up by Bertrand Russell who called it – for rather bad reasons that need not detain us – *material implication*. The connective is now commonly known as the *material conditional* or simply as the *truth-functional conditional*.

18.4   Ways in which '→' is conditional-like

(a)   Since PL languages are expressively complete, they can already express the material conditional. But it is conventional to add a special symbol for this truth function, appropriately extending the syntactic and semantic rules of our formal languages. The official way to do this is *exactly* as you would now expect, as you will see in §18.7. For the moment, then, let's simply assume that the arrow symbol for the material conditional is now part of our formal languages. How well does this arrow conditional behave as a formal counterpart to the ordinary-language conditional?

We make a start on discussing this troublesome issue by first confirming that if we transcribe the various examples in §18.1 using the arrow conditional, and run truth-table tests, we do get the right verdicts. (Remember from §16.1 that we can extend the notion of tautological entailment and the use of truth-table tests beyond our original PL languages, so long as we are still dealing with truth-functional connectives.)

(b) Start with the modus ponens inference in

A   If Jack bet on Eclipse, he lost his money. Jack did bet on Eclipse. So Jack lost his money.

Rendered into an extended PL language with a suitable glossary, this goes into

A′ $(P \to Q)$, P ∴ Q.

And running a full truth-table test (not exactly hard!), we get

P	Q	$(P \to Q)$	P	Q
T	T	T	T	T
T	F	F	T	F
F	T	T	F	T
F	F	T	F	F

There are no bad lines with true premises and false conclusion. Therefore argument **A′** is tautologically valid. Hence it is valid – as was the original **A**.

We will skip the modus tollens argument **B** – it is a trivial exercise to confirm that a formal rendition is tautologically valid too. So let's next look at

C   If Jack bet on Eclipse, he lost his money. So if Jack didn't lose his money, he didn't bet on Eclipse.

This can be rendered as

C′ $(P \to Q)$ ∴ $(\neg Q \to \neg P)$.

Running another truth-table test, this time we get

P	Q	$(P \to Q)$	$(\neg Q \to \neg P)$
T	T	T	T
T	F	F	F
F	T	T	T
F	F	T	T

So the inference in **C′** is tautologically valid and hence valid. And note that our table shows that a material conditional not only tautologically *entails* its contrapositive, but is tautologically *equivalent* to it. But this result still tracks the behaviour of ordinary-language conditionals, for the following is also true:

Simple ordinary-language conditionals are equivalent to their contrapositives.

For example, 'If Jack bet on Eclipse, he lost his money' not only entails but is entailed by 'if Jack didn't lose his money, he didn't bet on Eclipse'.

Next example:

D   If Jack bet on Eclipse, then Jack lost his money. If Jack lost his money, then Jack had to walk home. So if Jack bet on Eclipse, Jack had to walk home.

This goes into one of our formal languages as, say,

D′ $(P → Q)$, $(Q → R)$ ∴ $(P → R)$.

Making a truth table using the now familiar shortcuts (evaluating the conclusion first, and then the premises in turn but only as needed), we very quickly get

P	Q	R	$(P → Q)$	$(Q → R)$	$(P → R)$
T	T	T			T
T	T	F	T	F	F
T	F	T			T
T	F	F	F		F
F	T	T			T
F	T	F			T
F	F	T			T
F	F	F			T

There are no bad lines, so the argument is tautologically valid, and therefore plain valid, corresponding again to an intuitively valid vernacular argument.

Our fifth example illustrates another common form of valid inference, a version of what is called *proof by cases* (discussed later in §21.2(b)):

E   Either Jack bet on Eclipse or on Pegasus. If Jack bet on Eclipse, he lost his money. If Jack bet on Pegasus, he lost his money. So, Jack lost his money.

Using the material conditional, we can transcribe this as follows:

E′ $(P ∨ Q)$, $(P → R)$, $(Q → R)$ ∴ R.

You won't be surprised to learn that this too is tautologically valid. Here's a truth table to confirm that (again, we evaluate the conclusion first, ignore good lines, and then look at the premises in order, as needed).

P	Q	R	$(P ∨ Q)$	$(P → R)$	$(Q → R)$	R
T	T	T				T
T	T	F	T	F		F
T	F	T				T
T	F	F	T	F		F
F	T	T				T
F	T	F	T	T	F	F
F	F	T				T
F	F	F	F			F

(c)   So much, then, for our first five example arguments **A** to **E**: they are both intuitively valid and valid by the truth-table test when rendered into suitable PL languages. Let's turn, then, to the argument

F   If Jack bet on Eclipse, he lost his money. Jack lost his money. So Jack bet on Eclipse.

The form of inference *If A then C, C, so A* is evidently unreliable! – the fallacy here is traditionally called *affirming the consequent*.

   Take a translation of **F** using the material conditional, for instance

F′ $(P \rightarrow Q)$, Q ∴ P.

This inference is tautologically invalid. Just consider the following trivial truth table:

P	Q	$(P \rightarrow Q)$	Q	P
T	T	T	T	T
T	F	F	F	T
F	T	T	T	F
F	F	T	F	F

And now note that the bad line here evidently corresponds to a possible state of affairs – i.e. Jack's not betting on Eclipse yet losing his money all the same. The possibility of that situation confirms that the original argument is plain invalid. So the tautological invalidity of **F′** directly reveals the invalidity of **F**.

   Similarly, consider again:

G   If Jack bet on Eclipse, he lost his money. Jack did not bet on Eclipse. So Jack did not lose his money.

This inference step of the form *If A then C, not-A, so not-C* commits another fallacy (traditionally called *denying the antecedent*). Transcribing into our formal language using the material conditional and running a truth-table test confirms this.

   Finally note example **H**. Rendered into our extended PL language, this goes into the tautologically invalid

H′ $(P \rightarrow Q)$ ∴ $(\neg P \rightarrow \neg Q)$.

Be *very* careful to distinguish the fallacious **H′** from the perfectly valid inference from the same conditional to its contrapositive $(\neg Q \rightarrow \neg P)$ as in **C′**!

(d)   Examples **A** to **H** show that rendering some elementary arguments involving conditionals into a PL language augmented with a symbol for the truth-functional conditional, and then using the truth-table test, can yield just the right verdicts about the validity or invalidity of the original arguments. And in the now familiar sort of way, we can generalize from those examples. So we see that – as intended – the material conditional satisfies the principles (MP), (MT), (FC), and (NR) from §18.2 (when we rephrase replacing 'if' by the arrow).

   In interim summary, then:

The logical behaviour of '→' in (extended) PL languages is indeed parallel to that of the vernacular 'if', in at least *some* simple cases.

18.5 'Only if'

(a) Up to now, we have been discussing conditionals of the form

(1) If A then C.

(with or without the 'then'). We can also write these 'if' conditionals in the form

(1′) C, if A.

Without further ado, we will take (1) and (1′) to be mere stylistic variants.

However, there is another basic kind of conditional which needs to be discussed, namely 'only if' conditionals. Consider the pair

(2) A only if C.
(2′) Only if C, A

Again, we will take (2) and (2′) to be just stylistic variants of each other.

So the interesting question concerns the relation between (1) *if A then C* and (2) *A only if C*. But consider the following two-part argument:

Suppose we are given *if A then C*. This means that A's truth implies C, so we will only have A if C obtains as well . Hence *A only if C*.

Conversely, suppose we are given *A only if C*. This means that if A is true then, willynilly, we get C as well. Hence *if A then C*.

It seems then that (1) and (2) imply each other. So, plausibly,

In many cases, propositions of the form *if A then C* and *A only if C* are equivalent.

Consider for example the following conditionals:

(3) Einstein's theory is right only if space-time is curved.
(4) If space-time isn't curved, Einstein's theory isn't right
(5) If Einstein's theory is right, space-time is curved.

(3) and (4) are surely equivalent. (4) and (5) are also equivalent (a conditional is equivalent to its contrapositive). So indeed (3) is equivalent to (5).

(As so often, however, ordinary language has its quirks: so can you think of examples where a proposition of the form *if A then C* seems *not* to be straightforwardly equivalent to the corresponding *A only if C*?)

(b) Concentrate on cases where *A only if C* and *if A then C* do come to the same. Then if we want to render them into a formal language with only truth-functional connectives, we will have to translate them the same way, by using the material conditional. So in particular, *A only if C* will be rendered by the corresponding wff of the form $(\alpha \to \gamma)$, where α is the formal translation of A, and γ the translation of C.

155

Do be careful: translating 'only if' conditionals gets beginners into a tangle surprisingly often. But the basic rule is easy: first put an 'only if' conditional into the form *A only if C* and then replace the 'only if' with the arrow, to get the corresponding $(\alpha \to \gamma)$.

(c)   For a simple example, consider the following argument:

I   Jack came to the party only if Jo did. Also Jill only came to the party if Jo did. Hence Jo came to the party if either Jack or Jill did.

(Note how the 'only' can get separated in ordinary English from its associated 'if'.)

This is valid (think about it!). What about its correlate in a PL language? Using P to render the claim *Jack came to the party*, Q for *Jill came to the party*, and R for *Jo came to the party*, we can transcribe the argument as follows:

I′ $(P \to R)$, $(Q \to R)$ ∴ $((P \lor Q) \to R)$.

A truth table shows that this formal version is tautologically valid:

P	Q	R	$(P \to R)$	$(Q \to R)$	$((P \lor Q) \to R)$
T	T	T			T
T	T	F	F		F
T	F	T			T
T	F	F	F		F
F	T	T			T
F	T	F		T F	F
F	F	T			T
F	F	F			T

18.6   The biconditional

(a)   What about the so-called *biconditional*, i.e. *A if and only if C?*

Plainly, this two-way conditional says more than either of the separate one-way conditionals *A if C* and *A only if C*. Which doesn't stop careless authors sometimes writing *A if C* when they really mean *A if and only if C*. And it doesn't stop careless readers understanding the one-way *A if C* as the two-way *A if and only if C* even when only the one-way conditional is intended. So do take care!

The biconditional *A if and only if C* is the conjunction of *A if C* and *A only if C*. The second conjunct we have just suggested should be translated into our formal language by the relevant $(\alpha \to \gamma)$. The first conjunct, equivalently *if C, then A*, is rendered by $(\gamma \to \alpha)$. Hence the whole biconditional can be rendered by $((\gamma \to \alpha) \land (\alpha \to \gamma))$.

Now, that is just a little cumbersome. So it is quite common to introduce another new symbol, the two-way arrow '↔', for the two-way conditional. We can either treat this as a fifth basic ingredient of PL languages, exactly on a par with the other connectives. Or, our preference, we can introduce it for occasional use as follows (swapping the order of the conjuncts for aesthetic reasons!):

An expression of the form $(\alpha \leftrightarrow \gamma)$ is defined to be simply an abbreviation of the corresponding expression of the form $((\alpha \to \gamma) \wedge (\gamma \to \alpha))$.

The truth table of a wff abbreviated as $(\alpha \leftrightarrow \gamma)$ will be as displayed: this is the truth table of the so-called *material biconditional*.

α	γ	$(\alpha \leftrightarrow \gamma)$
T	T	T
T	F	F
F	T	F
F	F	T

You really should know about this biconditional truth function and its most basic properties, and be able to recognize symbols for it when you see them elsewhere. However, we will rarely deploy '$\leftrightarrow$' in the main text of this book; instead, we will mostly relegate its use to a few examples in various end-of-chapter Exercises.

(b)   An important footnote. As well as the *formal* symbol for the biconditional, there is a widely used *informal* abbreviation that you should certainly know about:

> Logicians (and others) often write the ordinary-language biconditional *A if and only if C* as simply *A iff C*.

18.7   Extended PL syntax and semantics, officially

(a)   The material conditional – like any truth-functional way of combining wffs – can be expressed using the resources of a PL language in its unaugmented form. It is easily seen that, for any wffs α and γ, both $(\neg\alpha \vee \gamma)$ and $\neg(\alpha \wedge \neg\gamma)$ have the same truth table as $(\alpha \to \gamma)$. (Check this! We return to these equivalences in §19.2.)

Hence, as we said before, we certainly do not *need* to add a new basic symbol for the material conditional. However, there are trade-offs between various kinds of simplicity here. On the one hand, if we add a symbol for the conditional, we thereby get smoother 'translations' (if we can call them that). On the other hand, it complicates our story a little: for example, in developing formal apparatus for regimenting proofs involving our languages' basic logical constants, we will need additional inference rules to govern each new connective.

On balance, however, it *is* worth adding the new symbol for the material conditional to our propositional languages. But since adding this symbol doesn't change the expressive powers of our formal languages, we don't get anything essentially new. Nor do we really add to the power of our languages by including the absurdity sign introduced in the last chapter (the new symbol is just, as we put it before, an all-purpose contradiction). So it is reasonable enough to continue calling our slightly augmented languages 'PL languages' (rather than insist on a distinctive new name for them).

(b)   For the record, then, the official syntax of our augmented PL languages is therefore as follows (compare the panel in §9.1):

The alphabet of a PL language is as before, but with the symbols $\rightarrow$ and $\bot$ added.

The definition of atomic wffs remains the same.

The rules for forming PL wffs are now

(W1)   Any atomic wff counts as a wff. Also $\bot$ counts as a wff.
(W2)   If α and β are wffs, so is $(\alpha \wedge \beta)$.
(W3)   If α and β are wffs, so is $(\alpha \vee \beta)$.
(W4)   If α and β are wffs, so is $(\alpha \rightarrow \beta)$.
(W5)   If α is a wff, so is $\neg\alpha$.
(W6)   Nothing else is a wff.

Results like the uniqueness of parse trees, and definitions like that of a main connective, etc., will of course continue to apply.

(c)   A comment on the choice of symbolism for the material conditional. Most logicians do now use the arrow. But you will also encounter the old-school symbol '$\supset$', due to the nineteenth-century mathematician Giuseppe Peano and popularized by Bertrand Russell. Since the arrow is also used for different conditional-like connectives in other formal languages, there is something to be said for sticking to the old horseshoe notation when the truth-functional material conditional is specifically intended. But we will follow modern notational practice. (You will also find '$\equiv$' used as an alternative symbol for the material biconditional.)

(d)   As for the semantic story about the now extended PL languages, it is a highly contentious question just how well the arrow connective captures the core meaning of even the simplest ordinary 'if's. We will say more about this in the next chapter.

However, it is entirely straightforward to extend the story about *valuations* for full PL languages to cover the additional wffs, given our explanation of the arrow connective and of the absurdity sign.

A valuation for a language starts, as before, with an assignment of truth values to the atoms of the language. And the falsum or absurdity sign is always assigned the value F. We then determine the truth value of molecular wffs by a stage-by-stage calculation, applying the truth tables for the connectives, old and new, in the now familiar way:

The truth tables for the PL connectives:

α	β	$(\alpha \wedge \beta)$	$(\alpha \vee \beta)$	$(\alpha \rightarrow \beta)$
T	T	T	T	T
T	F	F	T	F
F	T	F	T	T
F	F	F	F	T

α	$\neg\alpha$
T	F
F	T

18.8   Contrasting '∴' and '⊨' and '→'

(a)   Recall that in §16.4 we drew a very sharp distinction between the object-language inference marker and the metalinguistic sign for the entailment relation. We now have another sign which we must also distinguish very clearly from *both* of these, namely the object-language conditional. Let's finish this chapter by sorting things out carefully.

As we stressed before,

(1) $(P \wedge Q) \therefore Q$

is a mini-argument expressed in a PL language. Someone who asserts (1), assuming that the atoms have been given some content, is asserting the premiss, asserting the conclusion, and indicating that the second assertion is derived from the first one. Compare, for example, the English *Jack is a physicist and Jill is a logician. Hence Jill is a logician.*

By contrast

(2) $((P \wedge Q) \rightarrow Q)$

is a single proposition in a PL language. Someone who asserts (2) asserts the whole material conditional in that language (whose content will depend on the content we have given the atoms); but they do not assert the antecedent $(P \wedge Q)$, nor do they assert the consequent Q. Compare the English *If Jack is a physicist and Jill is a logician, then Jill is a logician.*

By contrast again

(3) $(P \wedge Q) \vDash Q$

is another single proposition, but this time it is a proposition in our extended English metalanguage, and the wffs here are not used but mentioned. For (3) just abbreviates

(3') '$(P \wedge Q)$' tautologically entails 'Q'.

Compare *'If Jack is a physicist and Jill is a logician' logically entails 'Jill is a logician'.*

(b)   There is an unfortunate practice that – as we said – goes back to Russell of talking, not of the 'material conditional', but of 'material *implication*', and reading something of the form $(\alpha \rightarrow \gamma)$ as α *implies* γ. If we also read $\alpha \vDash \gamma$ as α *(tauto)logically implies* γ, this makes it sound as if an instance of $(\alpha \rightarrow \gamma)$ is the same sort of claim as an instance of $\alpha \vDash \gamma$, only the first is a weaker version of the second. But, as we have just emphasized, these are in fact claims of a quite different status, one in the object language, one in the metalanguage. Talk of 'implication' can blur the very important distinction.

(Even worse, you will often find the symbol $\Rightarrow$ being used in informal discussions so that $\alpha \Rightarrow \gamma$ means either $\alpha \rightarrow \gamma$ or $\alpha \vDash \gamma$, and you have to guess from context which is intended. *Never* follow this bad practice!)

(c)   However, we can link 'logical implication' in the sense of entailment to 'material implication' in the sense of the material conditional as follows:

Let α, γ be wffs from a PL language: then $\alpha \vDash \gamma$ if and only if $\vDash (\alpha \to \gamma)$.

In plain words: a PL argument $\alpha \therefore \gamma$ is tautologically valid if and only if (iff) the corresponding material conditional $(\alpha \to \gamma)$ is a PL tautology. Why so?

By definition, for any wffs α and γ, $\alpha \vDash \gamma$ iff there is no assignment of values to the atoms which appear in the wffs which makes α true and γ false, i.e. which makes $(\alpha \to \gamma)$ false. Hence $\alpha \vDash \gamma$ iff every assignment of values to the relevant atoms makes $(\alpha \to \gamma)$ true, i.e. iff $\vDash (\alpha \to \gamma)$.

Similarly, a logical equivalence holds iff the corresponding material biconditional is a tautology:

Let α, γ be wffs from a PL language: then $\alpha \approx \gamma$ if and only if $\vDash (\alpha \leftrightarrow \gamma)$.

(d)   Finally, let's note that by similar reasoning we can show that $\Gamma, \alpha \vDash \gamma$ if and only if $\Gamma \vDash (\alpha \to \gamma)$ – where Γ stands in for the wffs we are using as background assumptions. This is the formal analogue of the following principle governing reasoning to a conditional conclusion:

Suppose, using some background premises, that we can argue from the additional temporary assumption A to the conclusion C. Then, keeping those background premises fixed, we can infer from them that *if A then C*.

We will return to discuss this important rule of inference in Chapter 22.

18.9 Summary

The only truth-functional connective that is a candidate for translating the conditional of ordinary discourse is the so-called material conditional. Although this is definable in terms of negation and conjunction or disjunction, it is convenient to represent this by its own arrow symbol. Then $(\alpha \to \gamma)$ is false just when α is true and γ is false, and is true otherwise.

At least some ordinary-language arguments using conditionals can be rendered into PL languages using $\to$ while preserving their intuitive validity or invalidity. However, the exact relation between ordinary 'if's and the material conditional is very contentious, as we will see in the next chapter.

Many conditionals of the form *A only if C* are equivalent to the corresponding conditional of the form *if A then C*; so both sorts of conditional can be rendered into PL languages equally well (or equally badly!) by something of the form $(\alpha \to \gamma)$.

It is imperative to sharply distinguish '$\to$' from both '$\therefore$' and '$\vDash$'.

Exercises 18

(a) Suppose we are working in a PL language where 'P' means *Putnam is a philoso-pher*, 'Q' means *Quine is a philosopher*, etc. Translate the following as best you can:

(1) If either Quine or Putnam is a philosopher, so is Russell.
(2) Only if Putnam is a philosopher is Russell one too.
(3) Quine and Russell are both philosophers only if Sellars is.
(4) Russell's being a philosopher is a necessary condition for Quine's being one.
(5) Russell's being a philosopher is a sufficient condition for Quine's being one.
(6) Putnam is a philosopher if and only if Quine isn't.
(7) Provided that Quine is a philosopher, Russell is one too.
(8) Quine is not a philosopher unless Russell is one.
(9) Only if either Putnam or Russell is a philosopher are both Quine and Sellars philosophers.

(b) Assuming that we are dealing with a suitable PL language. Which of the following arguments *ought* to come out valid, assuming that '→' is a reasonably good surrogate for 'if ..., then ...'? Which is tautologically valid?

(1) $P, (P \rightarrow Q), (Q \rightarrow R) \therefore R$
(2) $\neg R, (P \rightarrow R), (Q \rightarrow P) \therefore \neg Q$
(3) $(P \rightarrow \neg(Q \vee R)), (Q \rightarrow R), (\neg R \rightarrow P) \therefore (P \rightarrow R)$
(4) $(P \vee Q), (P \rightarrow R), \neg(Q \wedge \neg R) \therefore R$
(5) $(R \rightarrow (\neg P \vee Q)), (P \wedge \neg R) \therefore \neg(\neg R \vee Q)$
(6) $(\neg P \vee Q), \neg(Q \wedge \neg R) \therefore (P \rightarrow R)$
(7) $(P \wedge \neg R), (Q \rightarrow R) \therefore \neg(P \rightarrow Q)$
(8) $\neg(\neg S \rightarrow (\neg Q \wedge R)), (P \vee \neg\neg Q), (R \vee (S \rightarrow P)) \therefore (P \rightarrow S)$

(c) Which of the following are true for all α, β, γ in a PL language and why? Which of the true claims correspond to true claims about the vernacular (bi)conditional?

(1) If $\alpha, \beta \vDash \gamma$ then $\alpha \vDash (\beta \rightarrow \gamma)$.
(2) $((\alpha \wedge \beta) \rightarrow \gamma) =\!\!\vDash\!\!= (\alpha \rightarrow (\beta \rightarrow \gamma))$.
(3) $((\alpha \vee \beta) \rightarrow \gamma) =\!\!\vDash\!\!= ((\alpha \rightarrow \gamma) \vee (\beta \rightarrow \gamma))$.
(4) If $\vDash (\alpha \rightarrow \beta)$ and $\vDash (\beta \rightarrow \gamma)$, then $\vDash (\alpha \rightarrow \gamma)$.
(5) If $\vDash (\alpha \rightarrow \beta)$ and $\vDash (\alpha \rightarrow \neg\beta)$, then $\vDash \neg\alpha$.
(6) $\vDash (\alpha \leftrightarrow \alpha)$
(7) $(\alpha \leftrightarrow \beta) \vDash (\beta \leftrightarrow \alpha)$.
(8) $(\alpha \leftrightarrow \beta), (\beta \leftrightarrow \gamma) \vDash (\alpha \leftrightarrow \gamma)$.
(9) If $\vDash \alpha \leftrightarrow \beta$ then α and β are tautologically consistent.
(10) If $\vDash \alpha \leftrightarrow \neg\beta$ then α and β are tautologically inconsistent.

(d*) On alternative languages for propositional logic:

(1) Suppose the language PL_1 has just the connectives → and ¬ (with the same interpretation as before). Show that disjunction and conjunction can be expressed in PL_1. Conclude that PL_1 has an expressively adequate set of built-in connectives.

(2) Consider too the variant language PL_2 whose only logical constants are → and the absurdity constant ⊥. Show that in PL_2 we can introduce a negation connective so that ¬α is shorthand for $(\alpha \rightarrow \bot)$. Conclude that PL_2 is also expressively adequate.

19 'If's and '→'s

We saw in the last chapter that the logical behaviour of the material conditional is parallel to that of the ordinary vernacular conditional, in at least some simple cases. But just how close is the parallel? Is it close enough to justify our adopting the material conditional as a tidy formal substitute for (some) ordinary conditionals? The story quickly becomes a very tangled one, and we can only briefly touch on some of the issues in this chapter.

19.1 Types of conditional

(a)   We are discussing the biodynamics of kangaroos (as one does). You say:

   (1) If kangaroos had no tails, they would topple over.

How do we decide whether you are right? Kangaroos do have tails. So we have to proceed by imagining a possible world very like our actual world, with the same physical laws, and where kangaroos are built much the same except now for the lack of tails. We then work out whether the poor beasts in such a world would be unbalanced and fall on their noses.

   In short, we have to consider not the actual situation where kangaroos have tails, but other possible ways things might have been. So let's call a conditional that invites this kind of evaluation – i.e. evaluation which requires thinking, not necessarily about the world as it is but about other ways things might have been – a *possible-world conditional*. (Another common label is *counterfactual conditional*; but for various reasons this label can be misleading, and we won't be using it.)

(b)   Here is a memorable pair of examples (again from David Lewis):

   (2) If Oswald didn't shoot Kennedy in Dallas, someone else did.
   (3) If Oswald hadn't shot Kennedy in Dallas, someone else would have.

Let's assume, for the sake of the example, that we agree that Kennedy was definitely shot in Dallas, and we also believe that Oswald did it, acting alone. What should we then think about (2) and (3)? Evidently, since in the actual world Kennedy was shot, someone must have done it. Hence, if (to our surprise) not Oswald, someone else. So we'll take (2) to be true.

   But to decide whether (3) is true, we have to consider a non-actual possible world, a world like this one except that Oswald missed. Keeping things as similar as we can to the actual world (as we believe it to be), Oswald would still have been acting alone. There would still be no back-up marksmen. In such a situation, Kennedy would have left Dallas unscathed. Hence we'll take (3) to be false.

Since they take different truth values, (2) and (3) must have different contents. Which reinforces the intuition that a 'would have' possible-world conditional like (3) means something different from a simple 'did' conditional like (2).

(c)   The logic of possible-world conditionals is beyond the scope of this book, but one thing is clear:

> Possible-world conditionals are not truth-functional, and cannot even approx-imately be rendered by the material conditional.

The truth value of a material conditional asserted about the actual world is fixed by the actual truth values of its constituent sentences. By contrast, the actual-world truth value of a conditional like (1) or (3) will typically depend on what happens in non-actual situations. Uncontroversially, then, the truth-functional rendition can at most be used for conditionals like (2), and not for those like (1) or (3).

(d)   So far, so good. What is controversial, though, is the range of conditionals that *are* appropriately like (2) and which are not like (1) or (3).

Conditionals grammatically like (1) and (3) have conventionally been called *subjunctive* conditionals, for supposedly they are couched in the subjunctive mood (some linguists would dispute this). By contrast, (2) – and all the conditionals in examples **A** to **H** at the beginning of the last chapter – are conventionally called *indicative* conditionals, being framed in the indicative mood. So does the traditional grammatical subjunctive/indicative distinction mark the distinction between the possible-world conditionals which are definitely not truth-functional and the rest?

Arguably not. But the story gets complicated and we really don't want to get entangled here with contentious issues about the classification of conditionals. We'll just say that from now on we are setting aside possible-world conditionals whichever exactly those are, and will be concentrating on core cases of indicative conditionals.

(e)   More specifically, we concentrate on *singular* indicative conditionals.

For note that conditionals like 'If you heat an iron bar, it expands' or 'If a number is even and greater than two, then it is the sum of two primes' are in fact generalizations, equivalent to 'Any iron bar is such that, if you heat it, it expands' or 'Any number is such that, if it is even and greater than two, then it is the sum of two primes'. So we will temporarily put such cases aside and consider only singular, i.e. ungeneralized, indicative conditionals.

Our question then is: how well does the material conditional work in capturing the logical content of at least these conditionals (*simple* ones, as we arm-wavingly called them in the previous chapter)?

19.2 Simple conditionals as truth-functional: for

As we saw, the indicative conditionals in arguments **A** to **H** from §18.1 can be rendered into PL using the material conditional in a way that preserves facts about validity and invalidity. Here then is a hopeful proposal:

> (*if* = →)   '→' stands to *some* 'if's as '∧' stands to 'and' and '∨' stands to 'or'; for the material conditional does at least capture the core logical role of those 'if's which feature in singular indicative conditionals.

In this and the next section, we briskly argue *for* this attractively easy position; then in §19.4 we give an even brisker argument *against* it.

(a)   Let's ask: how does an ordinary-language simple (i.e. singular indicative) conditional *if A then C* relate to the propositions *either not-A or C* and *it isn't the case that both A and not-C*? Here is a pair of two-part arguments:

X (i)   The claim *if A then C* rules out having *A* true and *C* false. So *if A then C* implies *it isn't the case that both A and not-C*. (This is just the falsehood condition (FC) which we met in §18.2.)

  (ii) Conversely, suppose we are given that *it isn't the case that both A and not-C*. Then we can infer that if *A* is true we can't have *not-C* as well: in other words *if A then C*.

Y (i)   Suppose *if A then C*. So we either have *not-A*, or we have *A* and hence *C*. So *if A then C* implies *either not-A or C*.

  (ii) Conversely, suppose we are given *either not-A or C*. Then if not the first disjunct, then the second. So we can infer *if A then C*.

The two-part argument **X** implies that *if A then C* is equivalent to the truth-functional *it isn't the case that both A and not-C*. The two-part argument **Y** implies that *if A then C* is equivalent to the truth-functional *not-A or C*. Therefore – using α, γ to stand in for formal translations of the English clauses A, C – we can render the truth-relevant content of indicative conditionals *if A then C* by something of the form $\neg(\alpha \land \neg\gamma)$ and equally by something of the form $(\neg\alpha \lor \gamma)$.

But, by trivial truth tables, both those are of course tautologically equivalent to $(\alpha \to \gamma)$, as we noted in passing at the beginning of §18.7. So we can indeed render the core content of simple conditionals using the material conditional.

(b)   That argument for (*if* = →) is brisk but it is entirely abstract. So let's amplify one of the steps by giving a realistic concrete illustration of what looks like an equivalence between something of the form *if A then C* and the corresponding *not-A or C* – or, what comes to the same, between *if not-B then C* and the corresponding *B or C*.

Suppose I vividly remember that Jack and Jill threw a party together last Easter, but can't recall whose birthday it was celebrating. On this basis, I believe

(1)   Either Jack has a birthday in April or Jill does.

Now, you tell me – a bit hesitantly – that you think that maybe Jack has an October birthday. I agree that you might, for all I know, be right; but I will still infer from (1) that

(2) If Jack was not born in April, then Jill was.

In the context, deriving (2) is surely perfectly acceptable. And note, it doesn't commit me for a moment to supposing that there is any causal or other intrinsic connection between the facts about Jack and Jill's birth months. I just think that at least one of the propositions *Jack was born in April* and *Jill was born in April* happens to be true, and thus if not the first, then the second.

So (1) entails (2); and since (2) unproblematically entails (1), these two therefore are equivalent. Hence perfectly acceptable conditionals like (2) can be no-more-than-material in what they commit us to.

(c) Of course, when we assert an ordinary conditional, we often *do* think that there is a causal connection, for example, between the matters mentioned in the antecedent and the consequent ('If ice was applied, the swelling went down'). But equally, when we assert a disjunction, it is quite often because we think there is some mechanism ensuring that one disjunct or the other is true ('Either the temperature was normal or the warning light went on'). However, even if our *ground* for asserting that disjunction is our belief in an appropriate mechanism, what we actually *say* is true just so long as one or other disjunct holds. Likewise, our *ground* for asserting a conditional may be a belief in some mechanism that ensures that if the antecedent holds the consequent does too. But the birthdays example shows that such a causal mechanism doesn't have to be in place for a conditional to be true.

19.3   Another kind of case where 'if' is truth-functional

We should next note a very important family of cases where simple 'if's apparently do behave just like '→'s (as far as truth conditions are concerned).

Consider again Goldbach's Conjecture, the claim that

(1) If a number is even and greater than two, then it is the sum of two primes

(where 'number' means 'positive integer'). As already noted, *this* is of course not a straightforward singular conditional of the form *if A then C*, with A and C whole propositions. It is a *generalized* conditional, equivalent to

(2) Any number is such that, if it is even and greater than two, then it is the sum of two primes.

Is Goldbach's Conjecture true? No one knows: it is still unproved. But (2) will be true if and only if *every* particular instance C of the form

(3) If n is even and greater than two, then n is the sum of two primes

is true, where 'n' gets replaced in turn by '1', '2', '3', ...

Now ask: *what kind of 'if' is involved in all the singular instances C of the form (3)?*

   (i) Suppose the antecedent of an instance C is *false* (so n is either 2 or is an odd number). The consequent of C can be either true or false depending on n. *But either way, we want the whole conditional C to be true.* Why? Because if this instance C were false, (2) would be false. However, Goldbach's Conjecture can't be falsified by considering facts about two or about some odd number! Hence, when the antecedent of C is *false*, we need the whole conditional to come out true irrespective of whether the consequent is true or false.

  (ii) Consider now the cases where the antecedent of C is *true* (so n is an even number greater than two). Then all that is required for Goldbach's Conjecture to be true is that the consequent of C is true in each case. Hence, when the antecedent of an instance C is *true*, we need the whole conditional to come out true so long as the consequent is true.

In sum: we need the particular instances C to behave just like material conditionals. And this isn't a special case. It seems that the particular instances of generalized conditionals should usually behave just like material conditionals.

19.4   Simple conditionals as truth-functional: against

So far, then, so favourable for the proposal (*if* = →) for singular indicative conditionals. Now for an argument that goes flatly in the opposite direction.

    There are a number of cases where treating ordinary indicative conditionals as material conditionals leads to strongly counter-intuitive claims about validity. But we will concentrate here on a central type of case. Compare, then, the following three arguments – where, for vividness, we start borrowing '→' to express the material conditional truth function in English:

  (1) Bacon didn't write *Hamlet*. So, either Bacon didn't write *Hamlet* or he was a bad dramatist.

  (2) Bacon didn't write *Hamlet*. So, (Bacon wrote *Hamlet* → Bacon was a bad dramatist).

  (3) Bacon didn't write *Hamlet*. So, if Bacon wrote *Hamlet*, then he was a bad dramatist.

(1) is trivially valid (as is any inference of the form *not-A, so either not-A or C* for inclusive 'or'). By definition, the conclusion of (2) is just another way of writing the conclusion of (1), and hence (2) must be trivially valid too. By contrast, doesn't the inference in (3) look absurd? (3)'s conclusion, it will be said, is quite unacceptable (being the author of *Hamlet* makes you a good dramatist, if anything does). So how can the apparently absurd conclusion validly follow from the sensible premiss?

    Let's generalize. The inference pattern

 (M) *not-A, so not-A or C*

is unproblematically reliable. So too, borrowing the arrow again, is the inference

(M′) *not-A*, so $A \rightarrow C$.

On the other hand, with the indicative conditional, most inferences of the type

(V) *not-A*, so *if A then C*

strike us as unacceptable. Surely, it will be said, we *cannot* correctly argue 'I won't buy a lottery ticket; hence if I buy a ticket I will win', or argue 'Jill has not got a broken leg. So if Jill has a broken leg, she is now skiing'. Nor can we argue 'It's not freezing cold. So if it's freezing cold, it's boiling hot.' And so on.

Yet $(if = \rightarrow)$ equates the content of the vernacular indicative conditional *if A then C* in (V) with the material conditional expressed in English by *not-A or C* in (M). But that implies that inferences of the type (V) should be as reliable as inferences of type (M). Which looks absurd.

19.5 Three responses

So the situation is this. On the one hand, §§19.2–19.3 offer strong-looking arguments in favour of the view that simple conditionals are equivalent to material conditionals. On the other hand, §19.4 exposes what seems to be an entirely unwelcome upshot of this view. We have a problem! What to do?

We consider two initial responses which try to rescue the proposal $(if = \rightarrow)$ as it stands; then we offer a third response which suggests a friendly amendment.

(a) The first response simply asks us to think again and then to revise our initial antipathy to (V):

> Suppose I'm entirely confident that Bacon didn't write *Hamlet*. Then, I'll happily assert 'If Bacon wrote *Hamlet*, then I'm a Dutchman', 'If Bacon wrote *Hamlet*, then pigs can fly', 'If Bacon wrote *Hamlet*, then Donald Trump wrote *Pride and Prejudice*'. In the same spirit, we can also conclude 'If Bacon wrote *Hamlet*, then …' for any other completion, however silly the result. Why not?

Some logicians find this line satisfactory. But others object, claiming that 'Dutchman' conditionals – as we can call them – are a jokey idiom. To say 'If Bacon wrote *Hamlet*, then I'm a Dutchman', they will say, seems too much like going through a *pretence*, playing at asserting a conditional as a dramatic way of inviting you to draw the obvious modus tollens conclusion that Bacon didn't write *Hamlet*. Can we safely erect a theory of conditionals on the basis of apparent outliers like this?

(b) The second response we will consider is more conciliatory, allows that (V) not only looks absurd at first sight but continues to do so on further reflection, but still tries to reconcile this with $(if = \rightarrow)$.

> It would, we can agree, be uncooperative of me to assert something equivalent to $A \rightarrow C$ when I already know that A is simply false. For I could

much more informatively simply tell you, straight out, that *not-A*. That's why you can normally expect me to have grounds for asserting $A \to C$ other than belief in the falsity of the antecedent.

Assuming (*if* $=$ $\to$), it will be the same for the equivalent ordinary-language proposition *if A then C*. Even though it is really a material conditional as far as its truth conditions go, you will reasonably expect me to have some grounds for asserting it other than belief in *not-A*. Because of that default expectation, inferences of the form (V) will strike us as peculiar, even though strictly speaking correct.

But does this response do enough? Yes, it would usually be oddly unhelpful of me to assert a bare disjunction when I believe that the first disjunct is definitely true. So, yes, in many contexts, it would be odd simply to assert the disjunction *not-A or C*, or equivalently assert $A \to C$, when my reason is that I think that *not-A*. However, granted all that, nothing strikes us as odd about the explicit inference (M) *not-A; so not-A or C*. Likewise, there is nothing odd about the equivalent inference (M') *not-A; so A → C*, once we understand the symbol. That's because in this case the default presumption that I might have grounds for $A \to C$ (i.e. *not-A or C*) other than belief in *not-A* is plainly being *cancelled*: I am here quite frankly and explicitly offering *not-A* as my grounds!

In sum, there is nothing odd about (M'), even allowing for what can be expected from co-operative conversationalists. And if the ordinary conditional is merely the material conditional again, then there should equally be nothing odd about (V), still allowing for what can be expected from co-operative conversationalists. Yet surely the cases *are* different.

(c)   It still seems, then, that an unqualified identification of 'if' and the material conditional can't explain the radical difference in plausibility between inferences (M) and (V). So that strongly suggests that, even concentrating on simple cases, there is *something* more to the meaning of 'if' than a merely material conditional. But what? Here is a new outline proposal:

Recall our brief discussion in §8.2(b) about the difference between *A but B* and *A and B*. We suggested that these two claims don't differ in what it takes for them to be true. Rather, the contrast between 'but' and the colourless 'and' is (very roughly) that *A but B* is typically reserved for use when the speaker presumes that there is some kind of contrast between the truth or the current relevance of *A* and of *B*.

Well, could it be similar for a pair of claims for the form *if A then C* and $A \to C$? Perhaps again these two don't differ in what it takes for them to be true. But still, there *is* a difference between 'if' and the colourless material conditional. For *if A then C* is reserved for use when the speaker is – as it were – promising to endorse a modus ponens inference to the conclusion *C* should it turn out that *A* is true.

This seems a friendly amendment of the bald equation (*if* $=$ $\to$). For it keeps the core idea that the assertions *if A then C* and $A \to C$ (i.e. *not-A or C*) come to the same as far as their logic-relevant truth conditions are concerned. That explains why the arguments **X** and **Y** in §19.2 do look compelling. But we also get an explanation for why the inferential move from *not-A* to *if A then C* typically seems quite unacceptable (even though truth-preserving).

How so? The plausible suggestion is that the use of 'if' signals that the conditional it expresses can be used in an inference to its consequent. Now, suppose that I start off by believing *not-A*. Then, I will accept *not-A or C* or equivalently $A \to C$. But of course, I *won't* in this case be prepared to go on to infer C should I later come round to accepting A. Instead, because I have changed my mind about the truth value of A, I will now *take back* my earlier endorsement of $A \to C$. In other words, if my only reason for accepting $A \to C$ is a belief in *not-A*, I won't be prepared to go on to endorse using the conditional in a modus ponens inference to the conclusion C. And that is why, according to our suggestion about the role of 'if', I won't be prepared to assert *if A then C* just on the ground that *not-A*.

Which is the beginning of a neat and attractive story. If it is right, then we can regiment simple conditionals using the arrow, confident that informal conditional claims and their formal regimentations can match at least on their core truth-relevant aspects of meaning, which is what logic cares about. But *is* our story right?

19.6 Adopting the material conditional

We are going to have to leave that last question hanging. The many-stranded debates in the vast literature on conditionals are sophisticated and intriguing but frustratingly inconclusive. We have only scratched the surface, and we certainly can't review the ramifying arguments any further here.

However, for our purposes in this book, we can perhaps side step all these debates. Let's finish this chapter by explaining how.

(a) Suppose we decide that the story at the end of the last section doesn't work, despite its initial attractions, and that the behaviour of everyday 'if' is too complex to be accommodated by any such neat and simple theory (that's what the inconclusive philosophical literature about conditionals might seem to show). Well, in this case, should we even be *trying* to reflect those complexities in a formal language?

As we have seen, rendering arguments involving conditionals into a formal language by using the material conditional will get things right in a range of simple core cases – i.e., will get things right as far as verdicts on validity are concerned. So perhaps we should be content with that. In other words, perhaps we should regard the material conditional as a suitable surrogate or partial *substitute* for the vernacular conditional, one which is sufficiently conditional-like to be happily adopted for some important formal purposes, while being elegantly clear, perfectly understood, and very easy to work with.

This is in fact the line typically taken by mathematicians who want an easily managed logic for regimenting their arguments. Indeed, this is exactly how the truth-functional conditional was introduced by Frege in his *Begriffsschrift*. Frege's aim was to provide a setting in which ordinary mathematical reasoning, in particular, could be reconstructed entirely rigorously – and for him, clarity requires departing significantly from what he calls "the peculiarities of ordinary language". So he introduces a formalized framework which then takes on a life of its own. Choice of notation apart, the central parts of Frege's formal apparatus including his truth-functional conditional, together with his basic logical principles (bar one), turn out to be exactly what mathematicians need.

That's why modern mathematicians – who do widely use logical notation for clarificatory purposes – often introduce the material conditional in textbooks as part of their 'mathematical English', and then cheerfully say (in a Fregean spirit) that this tidy notion is what *they* are going to mean by 'if'. It serves them well when giving their semi-formal theories of arithmetic or set theory or whatever. It works well, in particular, when regimenting general claims like 'if a number is even and greater than two, then it is the sum of two primes'. Further, as we will see in Chapter 22, the inference rules that the material conditional obeys are just the rules that mathematicians and others already use by default in reasoning with conditionals. So '→' is sufficiently conditional-like for their purposes, even if it remains debatable whether it captures all the truth-relevant content of other ordinary 'if's.

This gives us, then, more than enough reason to continue exploring what happens when we adopt '→' as a clean substitute for 'if' in our formal languages – a substitute which serves many of the central purposes for which we want conditionals, especially in mathematical contexts.

(b) However, a word of warning. If the material conditional does not always capture all the content of vernacular conditionals, if we are thinking of it more as a substitute apt for use in some (but not all) contexts, then we'll have to be correspondingly cautious in using the now familiar two-stage, divide-and-rule, procedure for evaluating ordinary-language arguments.

The idea, recall, is that (1) we render a vernacular argument involving conditionals into an appropriate PL language, and then (2) we evaluate the corresponding PL argument by running the truth-table test. But we now will have to ask ourselves, case by case, whether the rendition of the vernacular argument into PL using the truth-functional conditional at stage (1) really hits off enough of the conditional content of the premises and conclusion for the verdict on the PL version to carry back to a verdict on the original argument.

Our motto has to be: *proceed with caution.*

19.7 Summary

As we saw in the previous chapter, a number of ordinary-language arguments using conditionals can be rendered using '→' while preserving their intuitive validity/invalidity. However this only works for some singular indicative conditionals – and not for so-called subjunctive conditionals.

There are serious issues about how far, even in the best cases, '→' can capture all of the core meaning of everyday 'if'. Identifying the two leads to oddities like the acceptability of arguments of the form *Not-A; so if A, then C.*

However, the material conditional can still be recommended as a perfectly clear *substitute* for the ordinary-language conditional, with a perfectly determinate logic, suitable for use by mathematicians and others.

Exercises 19

(a)   Show that the following hold for PL languages with the relevant atoms:

(1) $\vDash ((P \to Q) \lor (Q \to P))$
(2) $((P \land Q) \to R) \vDash ((P \to R) \lor (Q \to R))$
(3) $((P \to Q) \to R), \neg P \vDash R$

Do these results raise more problems for equating '→' with 'if'?

More generally, the pattern of inference $\gamma \therefore (\alpha \to \gamma)$ is valid. What about a corresponding ordinary-language inference of the form *C; so if A then C*?

The pattern of inference $(\beta \to \gamma) \therefore ((\alpha \land \beta) \to \gamma)$ is also valid. What about a corresponding ordinary-language inference of the form *C, if B; so C, if A and B*?

(b)   Assess the following arguments for validity:

(1)   Beth is a logician, provided that Amy is one too. And given that Beth is a logician, Chloe is a philosopher. But, hold on! – Chloe *isn't* a philosopher. So Amy isn't a logician.
(2)   Jo went up the hill. Why so? Because Jo went up the hill if Jack and Jill did. While Jack went up the hill if Jane did, and either Jane didn't go or Jill did. But Jane *did* go up the hill!
(3)   If Angharad speaks Welsh, so does either Bryn or Carys. But Bryn doesn't speak Welsh. So if Carys doesn't speak Welsh, neither does Angharad.
(4)   Veronika is a violinist only if Peter plays the cello. Marek is a violinist if and only if Jiří plays the viola. Veronika doesn't play the violin if Marek doesn't. Jiří doesn't play the viola only if Peter doesn't play the cello. Hence either Veronika isn't a violinist or Marek isn't.
(5)   It isn't the case that Popper is a good philosopher and Quine isn't. But in fact, Quine isn't a good philosopher, unless Russell is one too. And if Russell is merely a wordy fool, then he isn't a good philosopher. Hence if Popper is a good philosopher, then it isn't the case that either Russell is a wordy fool or isn't himself a good philosopher.
(6)   If the switch had been flipped, the light would have been on. If the light had been on, the burglar would have been discovered. So, if the switch had been flipped, the burglar would have been discovered.

Interlude: Why natural deduction?

(a)   Let's review our explorations since the last Interlude:

We explained the 'divide-and-rule' approach to logic. We sidestep having to deal with the quirks of ordinary language by rendering vernacular arguments into well-behaved artificial languages. We can then investigate the validity or otherwise of the resulting formalized arguments.

We then set off to explore formalized arguments involving (tidied versions of) 'and', 'or', and 'not' as their essential logical materials.

We defined the *syntax* of our PL languages (which initially have just these three connectives built in). We learnt how wffs of such languages are built up (in ways that can be displayed using parse trees). We also defined the notion of scope, the notion of a main connective, and related ideas.

Next, *semantics*. We discussed the *interpretation* of PL languages: we assign truth-relevant contents (senses) to atoms, and read the connectives as expressing bare conjunction, inclusive disjunction, and negation – understanding these in a way that makes the connectives truth-functional.

Given the truth-functional interpretation of the connectives, it follows that the truth value of a wff is determined by a *valuation* of its atoms.

We showed that there is a good sense in which we can define *any* truth-functional connective using just the three built-in connectives.

This got us to the position where we could take a pivotal step, and define the notions of a tautology and of tautological validity:

A tautology is a PL wff true on every combinatorially possible valuation of its atoms, while a contradiction is false on every such valuation.

A PL argument is tautologically valid if *every* possible valuation of the relevant atoms which makes the premisses true makes the conclusion true.

We discussed the relation between this notion of validity and the informal notion of logical validity. We argued that the notion of tautological validity gives us a cleanly defined rational reconstruction for the notion of logical validity as applied to inferences relying on truth-functional connectives.

We introduced *one* way of establishing tautological validity, namely by a brute-force truth-table test. We can in this way decide, quite mechanically, which PL inferences are tautologically valid.

Finally – after adding the absurdity constant for later use – we considered the prospects for dealing with arguments involving 'if' in the same way:

> We met the material conditional, which is the only possible conditional-like truth function, and we added a special symbol for this to the formal apparatus of PL languages.

> However, the material conditional is at best a surrogate for the 'if' in just some indicative conditionals; and, even in these cases, there remains a serious issue about how far it captures all the meaning of 'if'.

(b)   In Chapters 4 and 5, we talked about *two* informal ways of assessing arguments – namely, showing validity by giving a step-by-step *proof*, and showing invalidity by finding a *counterexample*. We have seen that a truth-table test is in effect a systematic search through all the possibilities for a counterexample to the validity of a PL argument (see §16.3). Our next task is to pick up the idea of step-by-step proofs, and to consider how to construct such proofs inside our formalized PL languages. Take, for example, the argument

$$(P \land (Q \land R)), (S \land P') \therefore (P' \land Q).$$

We can run up a thirty-two-line truth table to validate this little argument. But it is surely *much* more natural simply to reason as follows. We note:

(i)   Given a conjunction, we can derive each conjunct.
(ii)   Given a pair of propositions, we can derive their conjunction.

Deploying these two rules of inference for conjunctions, we can use (i) to infer $(Q \land R)$ and hence Q from the first premiss of our argument above and then also use (i) to infer P' from the second premiss. And we can use (ii) to put these interim consequences together to get the desired conclusion.

We can go on to introduce rules of inference similarly governing negations, disjunctions, and conditionals, and also explain how to put together natural-looking step-by-step PL deductions using these rules. And we can do all this while aiming to follow reasonably closely the modes of argument that we already find in everyday informal reasoning. In a phrase, we can aim to develop a *natural deduction proof system* for propositional logic.

So this gives us a second approach to showing the validity of a correct PL argument – namely, via a proof. Is it overkill to explore a proof system as well as the truth-table approach to propositional logic? Well, natural deduction proofs for PL inferences *are* well worth knowing about for their own sake. But a key point is that, unlike the truth-table approach, *natural deduction methods can be extended from propositional logic in a smooth way to validate arguments with quantifiers*. And that's our ultimate target, to be able to deal with formal QL (quantificational logic) arguments turning on 'all', 'some', 'no', etc. As with many other logical ideas, however, the general conception of a formal proof system is *much* more easily grasped if we meet it first in the tame context of propositional logic. So this is why we will be spending more time on PL over the next few chapters before finally moving on.

20 PL proofs: conjunction and negation

Outside the logic classroom, when we want to convince ourselves that an inference really *is* valid, we often try to find an informal *proof*. When working in a formal language – as just noted in the Interlude – we can similarly aim to construct step-by-step formal derivations to warrant inferences. We now start developing a framework for constructing such derivations in PL languages. We begin in this chapter by looking at derivations using rules of inference for conjunction and negation.

One important point at the outset. We will be laying out our formal proofs in the vertical column-shifting style which we first met in Chapter 4. We won't complicate matters by considering other options in this book (such as tree-shaped proofs like $\mathbf{A}^T$ in §9.2). But we should certainly emphasize that there is no single 'right' way of laying out natural deduction proofs.

20.1 Rules for conjunction

(a) We start by officially adopting the following proof-building rules for arguing to and from wffs which have '∧' as their main connective.

> ∧-*Introduction*: Given α and β, we can derive $(\alpha \wedge \beta)$.
>
> ∧-*Elimination*: Given $(\alpha \wedge \beta)$, we can derive α. Equally, we can derive β.

Here, α and β are of course arbitrary PL wffs.

Informally, we can infer a bare conjunction given both its conjuncts; and we can infer each conjunct from a conjunction. So our two proof-building rules are faithful to the intended meaning of the connective '∧' as (tidied up) 'and'.

Our names for the rules are standard and reasonably self-explanatory. Two particular comments on the first rule:

(i) The inputs α and β used when inferring $(\alpha \wedge \beta)$ don't have to be distinct – so we are allowed, for instance, to appeal to a premiss P twice over to derive $(P \wedge P)$.

(ii) The order in which α and β appear earlier in a proof doesn't matter: we can infer $(\alpha \wedge \beta)$ either way.

With these points understood, we can display our rules diagramatically and give them brief labels like this:

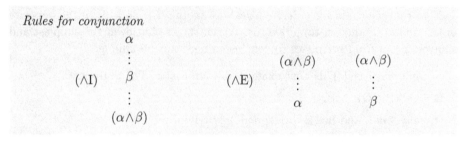

Rules for conjunction

Note how the two rules fit together beautifully. In an obvious sense, the elimination rule can be used to reverse an application of the introduction rule – applying (∧E) twice after invoking (∧I) takes us back to where we started.

(b)   Let's have a first simple example of these rules at work. So consider

A   Popper is a philosopher, and so are Quine and Russell. Sellars is a philosopher and Putnam is one too. Hence both Putnam and Quine are philosophers.

Regimenting this into an appropriate PL language (where P means *Popper is a philosopher*, Q means *Quine is a philosopher*, and so on), **A** can be rendered as

A′ $(P \land (Q \land R))$, $(S \land P') \therefore (P' \land Q)$.

We met this argument a few pages ago in the Interlude. So here again is the truth-preserving derivation of the conclusion from the premises that we informally sketched there, now presented in what will be our official style:

(1)	$(P \land (Q \land R))$	(Prem)
(2)	$(S \land P')$	(Prem)
(3)	$(Q \land R)$	(∧E 1)
(4)	Q	(∧E 3)
(5)	P′	(∧E 2)
(6)	$(P' \land Q)$	(∧I 5,4)

This proof illustrates two basic stylistic choices:

(i)   We have used a *vertical line* against which to align our column of reasoning.

(ii)   And we have used a *horizontal bar* to draw a line under the premises at the beginning of our argument.

Both these visual aids are conventional.

As an optional extra, we have also introduced on the right a rather laconic style of annotation, again pretty standard in form. 'Prem' doesn't need explanation. Then at later lines which result from the application of a derivation rule, we give the label for the relevant rule, followed by the line number(s) of its input(s). In the case of an application of (∧I) resulting in a wff of the form $(\alpha \land \beta)$, we give the line numbers of the relevant preceding wffs α and β in that order.

Note that we could have derived the wffs at lines (4) and (5) in the opposite order, and still gone on to derive (6). Which shows that even the simplest and shortest proof from premisses to conclusion need not be unique.

(c) That was easy! This next example is even easier. The argument

B $(P \land Q) \therefore (Q \land P)$

is trivially valid, and has a correspondingly trivial proof:

(1)	$(P \land Q)$	(Prem)
(2)	P	($\land$E 1)
(3)	Q	($\land$E 1)
(4)	$(Q \land P)$	($\land$I 3, 2)

And the pattern of proof here can be generalized. Just replace each P by α, each Q by β, where α and β are any PL wffs however complex. The result will be a derivation from the wff $(\alpha \land \beta)$ to the corresponding wff $(\beta \land \alpha)$.

For example, here is another proof with the same pattern of inference steps:

(1)	$((R \to S) \land (Q \lor \neg(P \land R)))$	(Prem)
(2)	$(R \to S)$	($\land$E 1)
(3)	$(Q \lor \neg(P \land R))$	($\land$E 1)
(4)	$((Q \lor \neg(P \land R)) \land (R \to S))$	($\land$I 3, 2)

(d) We have so far adopted just two basic rules for arguing with conjunctions. But we could, with equal justification, have added other basic rules. For example, consider the rule ($\land$C) reflecting the fact that conjunction 'commutes':

$\land$-*Commutes*: Given $(\alpha \land \beta)$, we can derive $(\beta \land \alpha)$.

However, we now know that *this* third rule would be redundant. Any application of ($\land$C) at any point in a proof could evidently be replaced by a little three-step dance involving ($\land$I) and ($\land$E).

Of course, there would be nothing *wrong* about adding to our proof system the truth-preserving but unnecessary rule ($\land$C). Economy of basic rules is one virtue for a proof system, but it isn't the only virtue; as we will see later, there can be countervailing reasons for adding a strictly-speaking redundant rule. However, there aren't any strong reasons for adding any other $\land$-rules, perfectly natural and reliable though they might be. So we won't.

20.2 Rules for negation

(a) We next introduce rules governing negation – and things now do get a little more interesting! So consider the following informal argument:

C   Popper didn't write a logic book. Hence it isn't the case that Popper and Quine each wrote a logic book.

This is valid. Why? Here is a natural line of reasoning, spelt out in painful detail:

Our premiss is that Popper didn't write a logic book. Now temporarily suppose that Popper and Quine each wrote a logic book. Then, trivially, we'll also be committed to saying Popper in particular *did* write a logic book. But that directly contradicts our premiss. Hence our temporary supposition leads to absurdity and has to be rejected. So it *isn't* the case that Popper and Quine each wrote a logic book.

Here we are, of course, deploying a *reductio ad absurdum* (RAA) inference of the kind we first met back in §4.5. In other words, we are making a temporary assumption or supposition S for the sake of argument. We find that S leads to absurdity, given our background premiss. So we drop or discharge that temporary supposition S, and conclude from our background premiss that S can't be true.

(b)   Let's transpose all this into a formal mode. Argument **C** can be rendered into a PL language with the obvious glossary, giving us

C′   ¬P ∴ ¬(P ∧ Q).

And now we can replicate the natural line of reasoning we used a moment ago:

(1)	¬P	(Prem)
(2)	(P ∧ Q)	(supposed for the sake of argument)
(3)	P	(∧E 2)
(4)	⊥	(absurd! – 3 and 1 are contradictory)
(5)	¬(P ∧ Q)	(by RAA, using the subproof 2–4)

It should be pretty clear what is going on here. But let's spell things out carefully:

(i)   In a formal derivation, we can at any step make a new temporary supposition for the sake of argument, so long as we clearly signal what we are doing. (This supposition can be anything we like – it doesn't have to be related to what's gone before.) If this new supposition isn't to become a permanent new premiss, we will later need to drop that supposition. And when we drop a supposition, we can of course no longer use it or its implications as inputs to further inference steps.

(ii)   The overall layout of our proof follows the convention already informally introduced in §4.5. So when we make a new supposition or additional temporary assumption for the sake of argument, we mark this by *indenting the line of argument* one column to the right. We thereby start a derivation-within-a-derivation, i.e. a *subproof*, as at (2).

When we decide to finish or close off a subproof, *we shift the line of argument back* one column to the left, as at (5). At this point, we say the supposition at the head of the subproof has been *discharged*.

This elegant column-shifting layout for handling temporary suppositions is primarily due to Frederic Fitch in his *Symbolic Logic* (1952).

(iii)   We have decorated the proof by using another *vertical line* to mark the new column for our indented subproof. This line starts against our new supposition, and continues for as long as the supposition remains in play. (The initial premiss is in play throughout the argument, and so the vertical line starting against it continues for the length of the whole proof.) We have also used another *horizontal bar* to draw a line under the temporary supposition at the beginning of the indented subproof.

Now a comment on the role of the absurdity sign:

(iv) In our proof, we reach a blatant contradiction, with a pair of wffs of the form α and $\neg\alpha$ both in play. So we have reached an absurdity. We highlight this by adding $\perp$ to our derivation. This is the absurdity constant which we introduced to the resources of PL languages in §§17.3 and 18.7, and which we have already noted is tautologically entailed by any contradictory pair.

The (RAA) rule can now be characterized like this:

(v) Suppose we have a subproof which starts with a wff α, temporarily supposed true for the sake of argument, and in this subproof we derive $\perp$. We can terminate this subproof by moving back a column to the left, thereby discharging the temporary supposition α. The rule (RAA) then allows us to appeal to this finished subproof and derive $\neg\alpha$.

So here, then, is another proof cut to just the same pattern as the last one:

(1)	$\neg(R \vee S)$	(Prem)
(2)	$\quad ((R \vee S) \wedge (P \wedge \neg Q))$	(Supp)
(3)	$\quad (R \vee S)$	($\wedge$E 2)
(4)	$\quad \perp$	(Abs 3, 1)
(5)	$\neg((R \vee S) \wedge (P \wedge \neg Q))$	(RAA 2–4)

We have added to our repertoire of laconic annotations in a straightforward way. 'Supp' marks, unsurprisingly, a temporary supposition starting a subproof. 'Abs' marks that we are declaring an absurdity on the basis of a blatant contradiction, and we give the line numbers of the relevant contradictory wffs α and $\neg\alpha$, in that order. And a reductio inference is marked by 'RAA' together with the line numbers of the beginning and end of the relevant subproof.

(c) For another example, one requiring a slightly longer proof, consider the argument

D Popper is from Vienna. It isn't the case that both Popper and Quine are Viennese. The same goes for Popper and Russell: they aren't both from Vienna. Hence both Quine and Russell are not Viennese.

This is valid. For suppose Quine were from Vienna – then both Popper and Quine would be Viennese, contradicting the second premiss. So Quine isn't Viennese. Similarly suppose Russell were from Vienna – then both Popper and Russell would be Viennese, contradicting the third premiss. So Russell isn't Viennese either. Hence, as we want, both Quine and Russell are not Viennese.

With the obvious glossary for P, Q and R, we can transcribe our informal argument into a PL language as follows:

D′   P, ¬(P ∧ Q), ¬(P ∧ R) ∴ (¬Q ∧ ¬R).

And we can then mirror our easy informal proof as a formal PL derivation:

(1)	P	(Prem)
(2)	¬(P ∧ Q)	(Prem)
(3)	¬(P ∧ R)	(Prem)
(4)	Q	(Supp)
(5)	(P ∧ Q)	(∧I 1, 4)
(6)	⊥	(Abs 5, 2)
(7)	¬Q	(RAA 4–6)
(8)	R	(Supp)
(9)	(P ∧ R)	(∧I 1, 8)
(10)	⊥	(Abs 9, 3)
(11)	¬R	(RAA 8–10)
(12)	(¬Q ∧ ¬R)	(∧I 7, 11)

Two important comments about the significance of the layout here.

(i)   Note that we *are* allowed to derive (P ∧ Q) at line (5) even though we have shifted columns. When we moved a column to the right, we *added* the new temporary supposition Q; but we remain committed to the three original premises including P, so we can still invoke it.

(ii) It is when moving columns in the other direction that we have to be really careful; for then we are *dropping* the commitment to an additional temporary assumption and its implications. For example, our supposition Q made at line (4) is discharged after line (6) – and then it is no longer in play, no longer available to be used as an input to further inferences. But later at line (8) the new supposition R is made and becomes available to be used, e.g. in the derivation step which gets us to line (9).

For more about how wffs can go in and out of play in a proof as temporary suppositions are made and discharged, see §20.6.

(d)   Let's summarize the negation rules which we have met so far.

> *Reductio ad absurdum*: Given a finished subproof starting with the temporary supposition α and concluding ⊥, we can derive ¬α.
>
> *The absurdity rule*: Given wffs α and ¬α, we can derive ⊥.

(RAA) is our basic rule for arguing *to* a conclusion with negation as its main connective. So we could equally well have called it the ¬-*introduction* rule (and this alternative label is common). Similarly, (Abs) is our rule for arguing *from* an input with negation as its main connective. In this sense it can be said to be a ¬-*elimination* rule. But we will stick to our more memorable labels.

And note how these two rules again fit together beautifully. (Abs) reverses (RAA) in the sense that (Abs) recovers *from* ¬α the essential input that would be needed for arguing *to* ¬α by (RAA) (this input is the fact we can derive absurdity from α) – because (Abs) tells us that, given we have ¬α, then indeed from α we can derive absurdity.

20.3   A double negation rule

Our first two ¬-rules are intuitively faithful to our understanding of negation. Do we need any other rules?

Given our so-called *classical* conception of negation as truth-value-flipping, a wff and its double negation are equivalent. So we will want to be able to establish this equivalence in our PL proof system. Two questions arise: (a) is there a proof of ¬¬P from P using our current rules? (b) Is there a proof of P from ¬¬P?

(a)   The first of these questions is quickly answered.

As a generally useful rule of thumb, if we want to prove ¬α, the thing to do is to suppose α and then aim to expose a contradiction so we can use (RAA). So let's do that here, with ¬P for α:

(1)	P		(Prem)
(2)		¬P	(Supp)
(3)		⊥	(Abs 1,2)
(4)	¬¬P		(RAA 2–3)

Which couldn't have been more straightforward!

And again the proof generalizes: we can always derive a wff of the form ¬¬α from the corresponding α (wherever α appears in a proof). So it would be redundant to add a new basic rule to allow us to *introduce* double negations.

(b)   However, a little experimentation should quickly convince you that we *do* need a new rule if we are to go in the opposite direction and derive P from ¬¬P.

In §24.8 we will return to consider why this derivation can't yet be warranted by our existing rules. But for now we just state our additional ¬-rule, which reflects our classical understanding of negation. Thus, for any PL wff α,

Double negation: Given ¬¬α, we can derive α.

Note: this rule only allows us to eliminate double negations at the very start of a wff. For example, the argument (P ∧ ¬¬Q) ∴ (P ∧ Q) is valid; but to prove this, we have to apply (∧E) *before* we are in a position to apply (DN).

To introduce another simple example where we need to invoke (DN), consider the following argument:

> **E**   Popper is a philosopher. It isn't the case that Popper is a philosopher while Quine isn't. Therefore Quine is a philosopher.

This is valid. Why? Here's a simple informal derivation:

The first premiss tells us that Popper is a philosopher. Now temporarily suppose that Quine *isn't* a philosopher. Then we'll be committed to saying Popper is a philosopher while Quine isn't. But that directly contradicts the second premiss. Hence our temporary supposition leads to absurdity and has to be rejected: so it can't be that Quine *isn't* a philosopher. Hence he *is* one.

Two comments about this:

(i)   This example illustrates that sometimes, even if your target conclusion *isn't* a negated proposition, it may still be natural to establish it by a reductio argument.

(ii) But note, our reductio arguments do always end with the *negation* of some previous temporary supposition. So if that supposition is already a negated proposition, the reductio argument will yield a *doubly* negated proposition. Formally, we will need an application of our new Double Negation rule if we want to remove the double negation.

We can now render **E** into a suitable PL language like this:

E′   P, ¬(P ∧ ¬Q) ∴ Q.

And we can regiment the informal line of reasoning just sketched into a formal proof as follows (with the obvious short-form annotation):

(1)	P	(Prem)
(2)	¬(P ∧ ¬Q)	(Prem)
(3)	¬Q	(Supp)
(4)	(P ∧ ¬Q)	(∧I 1, 3)
(5)	⊥	(Abs 4, 2)
(6)	¬¬Q	(RAA 3–5)
(7)	Q	(DN 6)

(c)   We will soon see more examples of our three negation rules at work. But, for the moment, let's just finish this section with a diagrammatic summary of these natural derivation rules with their short-form labels.

Rules for negation

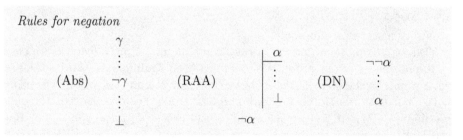

Note, though, that we have already learnt that the inputs for the application of a rule like (Abs) can appear in either order, and needn't be in the same column (the inputs just need to be 'available' in the sense to be spelt out in §20.6).

181

20.4 A more complex proof: thinking strategically

(a) Our five derivation rules tell us how we *can* extend a formal proof, not how we *must* extend it – the rules give us permissions, not instructions. And permissions can allow us to do pointlessly silly things. We therefore need to keep our wits about us if we are not to waste time and effort when proof-building.

Consider for example this slightly messy argument:

> **F**   It isn't true that Putnam is a logician while Quine isn't. Also, it isn't the case that both Ryle and Quine are logicians. Hence it isn't true that both Putnam and Ryle are logicians.

This is valid (can you see why?). Translated into an appropriate PL language, the argument becomes

> **F′** $\neg(P \wedge \neg Q)$, $\neg(R \wedge Q)$ $\therefore$ $\neg(P \wedge R)$

So how do we get from the premises to the conclusion? The only rule that applies to our two premises (separately or jointly) is $(\wedge I)$. And yes, we could derive e.g. $(\neg(P \wedge \neg Q) \wedge \neg(R \wedge Q))$. But given our target conclusion, it would be no help at all. The permissive nature of our derivation rules allows us to ramble off on pointless detours like this. So, a bit of strategic thinking is needed.

(b) Since we want to establish $\neg(P \wedge R)$ from the premises, the inviting strategy is to assume the opposite, i.e. to suppose $(P \wedge R)$, and then try to show that this leads to absurdity. So our proof should take the following shape:

$$
\begin{array}{|l}
\neg(P \wedge \neg Q) \\
\underline{\neg(R \wedge Q)} \\
\quad \begin{array}{|l}
\underline{(P \wedge R)} \\
P \\
R \\
\vdots \\
\bot
\end{array} \\
\neg(P \wedge R)
\end{array}
$$

We therefore now have an easier problem. How are we going to argue towards absurdity inside that subproof?

Well, only two of our derivation rules can be applied to the five wffs we have at the beginning of our proof. We could use $(\wedge E)$ again on the third wff – but what would be the point of *that*? Or we could conjoin any two of the wffs using $(\wedge I)$ – but that would also be quite pointless again. So it seems that the only sensible way forward is to make a judiciously chosen *further* supposition. But this looks promising: an obvious option is to chose Q, as this will combine with R to give us a contradiction.

So, let's make this further temporary supposition, indenting the line of proof again accordingly, and we get

(1)	¬(P ∧ ¬Q)	(Prem)
(2)	¬(R ∧ Q)	(Prem)
(3)	(P ∧ R)	(Supp)
(4)	P	(∧E 3)
(5)	R	(∧E 3)
(6)	Q	(Supp)
(7)	(R ∧ Q)	(∧I 5 6)
(8)	⊥	(Abs 7, 2)
(9)	¬Q	(RAA 6–8)

And *now* we can see our way home! Another contradiction has come into view, and we can easily finish our proof:

(10)	(P ∧ ¬Q)	(∧I 4, 9)
(11)	⊥	(Abs 10, 1)
(12)	¬(P ∧ R)	(RAA 3–11)

Do note the column-shifting discipline imposed in our Fitch-style proof system. In this proof, we make two temporary suppositions, with the second one introduced while the first is still active. That is why, at line (6), the column of reasoning has to be indented a second time. Then we eventually discharge our suppositions one at a time, as we jump back leftwards just one column at a time. (And do compare this proof with the proof for **D′**, which also involves two reductio arguments. Make sure you understand why, in the proof for **D′**, those arguments appear one *after* the other, while here in the proof for **F′**, they appear one *inside* the other.)

20.5 Understanding proofs, discovering proofs

An important general remark, before proceeding. *This is a logic book for philosophers, not a mathematics book.* So your aim should be to *understand* the concepts and principles behind the construction of Fitch-style proofs, and to be able to *follow* a proof when one is presented to you. Being able to *discover* proofs like the last one for yourself is much less important.

We will work through many more examples, often talking strategies for finding proofs as we go. But if you still find proof-discovery a bit challenging, don't panic! Philosophically speaking, it is *not* the crucial thing: so don't get bogged down in tackling Exercises if you find them hard going. Just read on and make sure you at least grasp the general *principles* at stake in these chapters about proofs.

20.6 'Given'

Our summary statements of the five derivation rules so far all have the form 'Given ..., we can derive ...'. We need to say more about that 'given'.

(a)   Suppose we are working in a language where P means *Hillary Clinton is a Democrat* and Q means *Donald Trump is a Democrat*. Consider this argument:

G $\neg(P \wedge Q) \therefore \neg P$

This has a true premiss and false conclusion, so it is of course invalid! Yet here is a 'proof' which purports to derive **G**'s conclusion from its premiss:

(1)	$\neg(P \wedge Q)$	(Prem)
(2)	P	(Supp)
(3)	Q	(Supp)
(4)	$(P \wedge Q)$	($\wedge$I 2, 3)
(5)	$\bot$	(Abs 4, 1)
(6)	$\neg Q$	(RAA 3–5)
(7)	Q	($\wedge$E 4)
(8)	$\bot$	(Abs 7, 6)
(9)	$\neg P$	(RAA 2–8)

Since **G** is invalid, something must be badly amiss with this putative 'proof'. But what? Everything before line (7) is fine. We make a first temporary supposition at line (2), indenting the line of proof; and then we make another supposition at (3), so we indent the proof a second time. The inner proof-within-a-proof then tells us that the supposition Q at (3) leads to absurdity; so we can discharge that supposition and correctly appeal to (RAA) to derive $\neg Q$ at line (6).

However, note that by the time we get to line (6), we have discharged the supposition (3). Hence, from (6) onwards, *the wff (3) and the wffs it implies are no longer being assumed to be true*. Once a subproof is finished or closed off, its innards are, so to speak, all 'packed away'. In particular, by the time we get to line (7), the wff $(P \wedge Q)$ from line (4) is no longer available to be used as an input to a further inference. So we *can't* now appeal to it in order to derive Q.

(b)   *What happens in subproofs, stays in subproofs* – we could call this the Vegas rule! And for another example of what can go wrong if you flout the Vegas rule, here is a second 'proof' for **G**:

(1′)	$\neg(P \wedge Q)$	(Prem)
(2′)	Q	(Supp)
(3′)	P	(Supp)
(4′)	$(P \wedge Q)$	($\wedge$I 3′, 2′)
(5′)	$\bot$	(Abs 4′, 1′)
(6′)	$(Q \wedge Q)$	($\wedge$I 2′, 2′)
(7′)	$\neg P$	(RAA, 3′–5′)

This time the howler is at line (7′). Why? Everything is unproblematic up to and including line (5′). Then we terminate the inner subproof, and basically ignore it at the next step: but that's fine too – we don't go *wrong* by not immediately applying reductio and by applying another rule instead. We then terminate the subproof from $(2')$ to $(6')$. We are allowed to do this too. We can't actually go wrong by closing off a subproof whenever we want – so long as we no longer rely on anything we deduced while that supposition was in force.

But now note that, when we close off the subproof from $(2')$ to $(6')$, by the Vegas rule all its contents are to be considered as 'packed away', *including the inner sequence of wffs from $(3')$ to $(5')$*. That's why we can't *now* apply (RAA) to that subproof in order to derive $(7')$.

(c)   With these two examples vividly in mind, here is the key idea we need if we are to avoid howlers like those in our last two 'proofs':

> After a subproof is finished and its initial temporary supposition is discharged, its contents become *unavailable*.

> So, at a given line, the *available* wffs are the earlier ones which are not in a finished subproof. And an earlier subproof is *available* at that line if it isn't itself nested inside a finished subproof.

> When extending a proof by applying a derivation rule, the rule can *only* invoke as its inputs previous wffs and/or subproofs that are still *available* at that stage in the proof.

In sum, when we talk of the *given* inputs to a derivation rule, these inputs must still be available, not-packed-away-inside-a-finished-subproof, at the point when the rule is applied. Do note, by the way, how our Fitch-style structuring of proofs makes it transparently clear when subproofs are finished, and hence when their contents become unavailable.

20.7   'We can derive'

(a)   To repeat, the summary statements of our derivation rules all have the form 'Given ..., we can derive ...'. We now need to say more about 'we can derive'.

On the surface, we simply mean in each case that (given appropriate available inputs from earlier in the derivation), we can add another wff of the right kind to the current column of our derivation in our Fitch-style layout.

But digging a bit deeper, we can see that our formulation in fact covers two rather different sorts of rules. We should pause to highlight the difference.

(1)   Take for example half our ($\wedge$E) rule: given $(\alpha \wedge \beta)$ we can derive α. The formal derivation rule here corresponds to a *logical relation between wffs*: we can validly infer one of the conjuncts from a conjunction, in an entirely straightforward sense.

(2)   Now compare our formal (RAA) rule. The rule comes to this:

> Suppose, given some background assumptions plus α, we can derive $\bot$. Then from the same background assumptions alone we can derive $\neg\alpha$.

So the formal derivation rule this time corresponds to a *logical relation between entailments*. Think back to our informal version of (RAA) in §4.5(c), which said

> Suppose some background assumptions plus the temporary supposition S entail a contradiction. Then those background assumptions by themselves entail *not-S*.

We can helpfully think of the informal rule here as a 'second-level' rule, because it in effect tells us how to move from one valid inference to another valid inference.

Derivation rules like (∧E) and derivation rules like (RAA) are both standardly called, simply, *rules of inference*. That's fine – so long as we realize that the shared label does cover both (1) rules that reflect ground-level inferences from one or more wffs to a wff, and (2) rules that reflect second-level inferences between entailments.

(b) It is worth noting very briefly that the first recognizably modern formal logics starting with Frege's *Begriffsschrift* in effect managed with just a few rules of the first, ground-level, type. It isn't until the nineteen-thirties, in particular in the work of Gerhard Gentzen, that we get formal systems that aim to mirror those everyday patterns of reasoning where we can make temporary assumptions for the sake of argument, and then make use of the resulting subderivations by using second-level principles like (RAA).

It is characteristic of what we now call *natural deduction* proof systems that they use rules of both types. Different systems handle the two types of rules in significantly different ways, with various costs and benefits. Our Fitch-style version with its column-indenting for subproofs at least has the merits of being visually neat, quickly grasped by beginners, and relatively easy to use.

20.8   Putting things together

And how do we assemble inference steps into a Fitch-style proof? Roughly:

> An array of wffs counts as a Fitch-style derivation from $\alpha_1, \alpha_2, \ldots \alpha_n$ as premisses to the conclusion γ if it starts with the premisses in the 'home' column, and perhaps after jumping to and fro between columns, ends back in the home column with γ as the final wff. Each step along the way either applies a rule of inference to extend the current column, or else starts or finishes a subproof, as previously illustrated.

We will give a much more careful definition of a PL derivation in §24.2, when we know about arguing using disjunctions and conditionals. For the moment, let's just stress that while the *motivation* for the rules of our PL proof-system is *semantic* (so far, they are justified by the *meaning* of 'and' and 'not'), the rules themselves are in fact *syntactically* defined in terms of patterns in arrays of wffs. This becomes important later, particularly in §§24.6 and 24.7.

186

20.9 Explosion and absurdity again

(a) Now for a surprise, perhaps. Consider the following two arguments:

C″   ¬P ∴ ¬(P ∧ ¬Q),
E′   P, ¬(P ∧ ¬Q) ∴ Q.

Both are valid. The first is a minor variant of **C′**, and is proved in the same way. The second we have met before. Here are the (natural-seeming) proofs:

(1)	¬P	(1)	P
(2)	(P ∧ ¬Q)	(2)	¬(P ∧ ¬Q)
(3)	P	(3)	¬Q
(4)	⊥	(4)	(P ∧ ¬Q)
(5)	¬(P ∧ ¬Q)	(5)	⊥
		(6)	¬¬Q
		(7)	Q

Now, we normally assume that we can chain together correctly constructed proofs so that the conclusion of one becomes a premiss for the next, and the result will be a longer, equally correct, proof. That's how mathematics works. And more generally, this is how logical inference can contribute massively to knowledge. We chain together relatively obvious pieces of reasoning into something less obvious, but still reliably truth-preserving; and this way we get to warrant some new and perhaps surprising conclusions.

Our formal deduction system will allow us to combine proofs in this way. So let's in particular chain together our two compelling derivations above (just moving the right-hand proof's initial premiss to the top, since – merely as a matter of style – we insist on listing premisses at the outset). We then get **H**:

(1)	P	(Prem)
(2)	¬P	(Prem)
(3)	(P ∧ ¬Q)	(Supp)
(4)	P	(∧E 3)
(5)	⊥	(Abs 4, 2)
(6)	¬(P ∧ ¬Q)	(RAA 3–5)
(7)	¬Q	(Supp)
(8)	(P ∧ ¬Q)	(∧I 1, 7)
(9)	⊥	(Abs 8, 6)
(10)	¬¬Q	(RAA 7–9)
(11)	Q	(DN 10)

So from P and ¬P, we can derive Q. And the proof idea generalizes. Replacing P throughout by α and Q throughout by γ, we will get a proof from any contradictory pair α, ¬α to an arbitrary conclusion γ. Explosion! (Compare §17.1.)

(b) When we first met this sort of explosive inference in §6.5, it was as a probably unwelcome upshot of our informal definition of validity. We then asked: should we revise the definition because of this consequence? Or should we learn to live with the idea that a contradiction entails anything?

In that early discussion, we said – then without explanation – that rejecting explosion comes at a high price. We can now see one reason why. In order to block our particular formal proof **H**, we have just three options:

(1) We can reject the proof which we took to validate the inference **C″**.

(2) We can reject the proof which we took to validate the inference **E′**.

(3) We can drop the assumption that we can chain correct inferences together to get another correct inference.

None of these options looks very attractive at all. Which is why the great majority of logicians take the remaining option and accept explosion.

Philosophers being the contentious bunch that they are, there exists a vocal minority who resist, insisting that explosion is a fallacy of irrelevance. We can't here investigate the ways that have been suggested for escaping **H** and similar explosive arguments – though, if forced to choose, I'd tinker with option (3). It is fair to say, though, that no escape route has gained very wide acceptance.

(c) Now for another explosive inference. We have officially added the absurdity sign to our PL languages as a special wff, and it has featured in our formal (RAA) arguments as the conclusion of some subproofs. But, like any other wff, it can also in principle appear elsewhere, even as a premiss in an argument.

(An aside here. We could – with only relatively minor adjustments – have arranged things so that the absurdity sign *only* gets used to conclude subproofs. And then we could downgrade the sign to being something like an exclamation mark signalling that you have hit a contradiction. But we will continue along the more well-trodden path of treating $\bot$ as a wff.)

Since $\bot$ is like a generalized contradiction, we will now expect to be able to argue from it to any conclusion we want. And we can: consider derivation **I**:

(1)	$\bot$	(Prem)
(2)	$\neg P$	(Supp)
(3)	$(\neg P \land \bot)$	($\land$I 2, 1)
(4)	$\bot$	($\land$E 3)
(5)	$\neg\neg P$	(RAA 2–4)
(6)	P	(DN, 5)

Needless to say, this line of argument also generalizes. Replace P by any wff α, and we will get a derivation from $\bot$ to α. This corresponds to the explosive tautologically valid inference we tagged *ex falso quodlibet* in §17.2.

(d) The availability of formal derivations like **I** means that it is strictly speaking redundant to add the following an additional rule of inference:

Ex falso quodlibet   Given ⊥, we can derive any wff α.

However, despite the redundancy, it *is* usual to include this (EFQ) rule in the basic package of rules for a Fitch-style proof system for a propositional logic which uses the absurdity sign. There are a number of reasons for this. A shallow one is that it makes some proofs neater. But the deep reason is that (EFQ) tells us just what it is to be an all-purpose absurdity (it defines '⊥') – it is something such that if *that* is true, then really *anything* goes!

So we *will* now adopt (EFQ) into our proof system. Using this rule we get a *much* snappier proof than **H** taking us from P and ¬P to Q, namely **J**:

(1)	P	(Prem)
(2)	¬P	(Prem)
(3)	⊥	(Abs 1, 2)
(4)	Q	(EFQ 3)

Quite often, the (EFQ) rule is presented right at the very start of an exposition of a proof system for propositional logic. And then the beginner is immediately faced with proofs like this last one which can seem far too much like suspicious trickery. That's why we have left adding the (EFQ) rule right until the end of this chapter, *after* the explosive consequence P, ¬P ∴ Q has *already* been proved. The derivation **J** which uses (EFQ) just allows us to get more quickly to a destination that we can equally well get to the long way round, invoking only our initial package of rules.

20.10   Summary

We have adopted five basic rules for arguing with conjunctions, negations, and the absurdity sign. (∧I) and (∧E) tell us that we can argue from conjuncts to conjunctions and back again. (Abs) tells us how to mark that we have got entangled in the absurdity of blatant contradiction. (RAA) tells us that if a supposition leads to absurdity, then we can infer its negation. (DN) allows us to eliminate (initial) double negations.

In general terms, these basic rules seem entirely natural and compelling – they seem true to the core meanings of 'and' and 'it is not the case that'. So we indeed ought to be able to use them to construct genuine *proofs* which show that the eventual conclusion will be true if the premisses are.

But we have choices about how to implement the rules in detail. We have adopted a *Fitch-style* vertical layout, whose distinctive feature is that we indent the line of reasoning when we make a new temporary supposition, and cancel the indent when we drop that supposition again.

It is crucial that the inputs invoked in applying a rule of inference are still available to be used, i.e. they are not buried inside a subproof which is already finished. What happens in a subproof, stays in the subproof.

We noted that, if we are allowed to chain proofs in the standard sort of way, then our rules – natural though they are – warrant the explosive inference from contradictory wffs to any conclusion we like. We also in effect get for free the further rule (EFQ) which tells us that we can infer anything from absurdity – though we will now officially add this as a rule in its own right.

Exercises 20

(a) Show that the following inferences (in suitable languages, of course) can be warranted by proofs using our rules for conjunction and negation:

(1) P, Q, R $\therefore$ $(P \wedge (P \wedge (Q \wedge Q)))$

(2) $(P \wedge (Q \wedge R))$ $\therefore$ $((Q \wedge \neg\neg P) \wedge R)$

(3) $(P \wedge Q)$, $\neg(P \wedge R)$, $\neg(Q \wedge S)$ $\therefore$ $(\neg R \wedge \neg S)$

(4) $\neg(P \wedge \neg Q)$, $\neg(Q \wedge \neg\neg R)$ $\therefore$ $\neg(P \wedge \neg\neg R)$

(5) $\neg((P \vee R) \wedge \neg\neg(\neg S \wedge Q))$, $\neg\neg(\neg S \wedge Q)$ $\therefore$ $\neg(P \vee R)$

(6) $\neg(P \wedge S)$, $\neg(\neg S \wedge Q)$ $\therefore$ $\neg((P \wedge R) \wedge Q)$

(7) $\neg(P \wedge \neg(S \wedge Q))$, $(\neg R \wedge \neg\neg P)$ $\therefore$ $(Q \wedge \neg\neg\neg R)$

(8) $\neg(P \wedge S)$, $\neg(\neg S \wedge Q)$, $((P \wedge R) \wedge Q)$ $\therefore$ P'

(9) $\neg(P \wedge \neg\neg\neg\bot)$ $\therefore$ $\neg P$

(10) $(P \to Q)$ $\therefore$ $((P \to Q) \wedge \neg\bot)$

(b*) Recall the 'Γ' notation from Exercises 16(c*), introduced to indicate some wffs (zero, one, or many), with 'Γ, α' indicating those wffs together with α. And recall the use of 'iff' introduced in §18.6. We now add a new pair of definitions

Γ are *S-consistent* – i.e., are consistent as far as the proof system S can tell – iff there is no proof in system S of $\bot$ from Γ as premisses.

Γ are *S-inconsistent* iff there is an S-proof of $\bot$ from Γ as premisses.

Let S be the current proof system with our conjunction and negation rules. Show:

(1) α can be derived in S from Γ as premisses iff Γ, ¬α are S-inconsistent.

Now for three results (for eventual use in the Appendix) about what we can *add* to S-consistent wffs while keeping them S-consistent. First, note that if Γ, α are S-inconsistent, Γ proves ¬α; so if Γ, α are S-inconsistent and ¬¬α is one of the wffs Γ, then Γ must already be S-inconsistent. (Explain why!) Conclude that

(2) If the wffs Γ are S-consistent and ¬¬α is one of them, then Γ, α are also S-consistent.

We use 'Γ, α, β' to indicate the wffs Γ together with α and β. Show that

(3) If the wffs Γ are S-consistent and $(α \wedge β)$ is one of them, then Γ, α, β are also S-consistent.

Note too that if Γ, ¬α and Γ, ¬β are both S-inconsistent, we can derive both α and β from Γ, and hence can derive $(α \wedge β)$. So if Γ, ¬α and Γ, ¬β are both S-inconsistent and these wffs Γ already include $\neg(α \wedge β)$, then Γ are S-inconsistent (why?). Conclude

(4) If the wffs Γ are S-consistent and $\neg(α \wedge β)$ is one of them, then either Γ, ¬α or Γ, ¬β (or both) are also S-consistent.

21 PL proofs: disjunction

In the previous chapter, we showed how to argue using conjunctions and negations in our Fitch-style system. Now we see how to argue using disjunctions.

21.1 The iteration rule

First, however, consider the following little argument which involves *none* of the sentential connectives:

A   Popper was born in 1902. Quine was born in 1908. Russell was born in 1872. Hence, Quine was born in 1908.

Given our understanding of what makes for validity, this counts as trivially valid, for there is certainly no possible situation in which our premisses are all true and the conclusion false – see §3.2(b).

Correspondingly, in a suitable PL language,

A′   P, Q, R ∴ Q

is also trivially valid. We will therefore want to be able to construct a derivation of the conclusion from the premisses in our PL proof system – a proof using the layout where premisses appear above a horizontal bar and the conclusion (eventually) below. A simple way is to adopt a new rule:

Iteration: At any inference step, we can reiterate any available wff.

This just reflects our structural understanding of how proofs work: if a wff is available at a given step, repeating it can't involve any new commitment.

Using our iteration rule, call it '(Iter)' for short, we can now construct the required miniature proof for the inference in **A′**:

(1) | P   (Prem)
(2) | Q   (Prem)
(3) | R   (Prem)
(4) | Q   (Iter 2)

Note, though, that we *could* have managed without using any iteration rule. For – assuming that we can use the usual rules for conjunction – our rule is strictly speaking redundant. In the present case, we could argue as follows:

$$
\begin{array}{lll}
(1) & P & \text{(Prem)} \\
(2) & Q & \text{(Prem)} \\
(3) & R & \text{(Prem)} \\
(4) & (Q \wedge Q) & (\wedge\text{I 2, 2)} \\
(5) & Q & (\wedge\text{E 4)}
\end{array}
$$

Recall, we said in §20.1(a) that we can appeal to the same input twice when applying (∧I), as in (4). And the trick here generalizes: in other words, whenever we are tempted to use (Iter), we could use the two conjunction rules instead.

Still, it does seem perverse to invoke the conjunction rules in a little two-step dance in order to derive a conclusion which contains no conjunction from premisses which equally contain no conjunctions. And so, because it directly reflects our understanding of how proofs work, we will explicitly adopt the trivially safe additional rule (Iter) – though it is worth stressing that there is no right or wrong policy here.

21.2   Introducing and eliminating disjunctions

(a)   We move on, then, to introduce two principles for reasoning with disjunctions (take all disjunctions in this chapter to be inclusive).

Consider first the following little argument:

B   Quine is a logician. Therefore either Popper or Quine is a logician, or Russell is one.

This is of course trivially valid. You can infer an inclusive disjunction from either disjunct. So from the premiss that Quine is a logician you can infer that Popper or Quine is a logician. And from that interim conclusion you can now infer that either Popper or Quine is a logician, or Russell is one.

Going formal, the inferential principle for arguing *to* a disjunction becomes:

∨-*Introduction*: Given a wff α, we can derive $(\alpha \vee \beta)$ for any wff β. Equally given β, we can derive $(\alpha \vee \beta)$ for any α.

With P meaning *Popper is a logician*, etc., our everyday argument **B** can be rendered into a suitable PL language as

B′   Q ∴ ((P ∨ Q) ∨ R).

And we can then mirror our informal proof which shows that **B** is valid by a direct – and truth-preserving! – formal PL derivation:

$$
\begin{array}{lll}
(1) & Q & \text{(Prem)} \\
(2) & (P \vee Q) & (\vee\text{I 1)} \\
(3) & ((P \vee Q) \vee R) & (\vee\text{I 2)}
\end{array}
$$

(We use the natural label for our new rule in the commentary, and indicate the line number of the wff which an application of the rule appeals to.)

192

(b)   To introduce the corresponding ∨-elimination rule, let's start by considering an informal one-premiss argument:

> **C**   Either Popper and Quine are both logicians, or Quine and Russell are both logicians. Therefore Quine is a logician.

This is valid. Why? Here's an informal proof, spelt out in very laborious detail:

> Suppose for the sake of argument that the first disjunct of our premiss is true, so Popper and Quine are both logicians. Then, on that assumption, Quine in particular is a logician.
>
> Suppose alternatively that the second disjunct of our premiss is true, so Quine and Russell are both logicians. It follows on that assumption too that Quine is a logician.
>
> Both disjuncts of our initial premiss imply Quine is a logician. Therefore – since we are told at least one disjunct is true – we get our desired conclusion.

The principle here is a version of *proof by cases*. We are given that (at least) one of two cases A and B holds. We show that in the first case C follows. We show that, equally, in the second case C follows. Since C follows in either case, and we are given that (at least) one of the cases holds, we can conclude C outright.

(c)   Going formal, this principle is captured by the following derivation rule in our Fitch-style system. Suppose α, β, and γ are any wffs, then:

> ∨-*Elimination*: Given $(\alpha \lor \beta)$, a finished subproof from the temporary supposition α to γ, and also a finished subproof from the temporary supposition β to γ, we can derive γ.

The informal argument **C** can be rendered into a suitable PL language as

> **C′** $((\mathsf{P} \land \mathsf{Q}) \lor (\mathsf{Q} \land \mathsf{R}))$ ∴ Q.

So now we can closely mirror our informal proof for **C** with the following formal proof for **C′** using our new rule:

(1)	$((\mathsf{P} \land \mathsf{Q}) \lor (\mathsf{Q} \land \mathsf{R}))$	(Prem)
(2)	$(\mathsf{P} \land \mathsf{Q})$	(Supp)
(3)	Q	(∧E 2)
(4)	$(\mathsf{Q} \land \mathsf{R})$	(Supp)
(5)	Q	(∧E 4)
(6)	Q	(∨E 1, 2–3, 4–5)

Putting $(\mathsf{P} \land \mathsf{Q})$ for α, $(\mathsf{Q} \land \mathsf{R})$ for β, and Q for γ, the final line is a correct application of the (∨E) rule. And note:

(i)   At line (2) we suppose for the sake of argument that the first disjunct of (1) is true, indenting our proof a column rightwards as we do so. When we finish this first subproof after line (3), we head back a column leftwards. However, we *immediately* make the alternative supposition that the second disjunct of (1) is true, giving us a new supposition at line (4) to start the second subproof. And therefore we indent our column of reasoning rightwards again. Hence the proof layout as displayed.

(ii) There is therefore a little *gap* between the vertical lines marking the extents of the two different finished subproofs – but it helps the eye if we put a short bar in the gap to mark the break between the subproofs.

(iii) Our short-form annotation of the final step records the *three* inputs to the final ∨-elimination inference; we give the line number of the relevant disjunction, and then give the extents of the two relevant subproofs.

(d) Consider next the informal argument

D Popper is a clear writer. Either Quine or Russell is a clear writer. Hence either Popper and Quine are clear writers, or both Popper and Russell are.

Valid again, as is shown by considering cases, using the second premiss.

Take the case where Quine is clear. Then Popper and Quine are clear – so, it will be true that C, either Popper and Quine are clear or Popper and Russell are. Similarly in the other case, where Russell is clear; then Popper and Russell are clear and C again follows. So either way, C follows.

Going formal, here is a corresponding PL argument:

D′ P, (Q ∨ R) ∴ ((P ∧ Q) ∨ (P ∧ R)).

This can be shown to be valid by the following proof:

(1)	P	(Prem)
(2)	(Q ∨ R)	(Prem)
(3)	Q	(Supp)
(4)	(P ∧ Q)	(∧I 1, 3)
(5)	((P ∧ Q) ∨ (P ∧ R))	(∨I 4)
(6)	R	(Supp)
(7)	(P ∧ R)	(∧I 1, 6)
(8)	((P ∧ Q) ∨ (P ∧ R))	(∨I 7)
(9)	((P ∧ Q) ∨ (P ∧ R))	(∨E 2, 3–5, 6–8)

(e) Let's have another example. So consider this argument:

E Polly and Quentin are both married. So it isn't the case that either Polly is unmarried or that Quentin is.

This too is valid. How can we informally show that? We could argue like this.

Suppose for the sake of argument that the opposite of the conclusion holds, i.e. suppose that either Polly is unmarried or Quentin is unmarried.

The first disjunct leads to absurdity; it is contradicted by our premiss telling us that Polly *is* married. The second disjunct also leads to absurdity; it is contradicted by our premiss telling us that Quentin is married.

194

So either way, whichever disjunct of our supposition holds, we get absurdity. Since that supposition leads to absurdity, it has to be rejected.

Again, in the middle of this informal proof we use a version of proof by cases. We suppose for the sake of argument that (at least) one of two cases A and B holds. We show that in the first case absurdity follows. We show that, equally, in the second case absurdity follows. Since we can infer an absurdity in either case, the supposition that one of the cases A and B holds is itself absurd.

Using the obvious glossary, here is a formal version of **D** (giving us an instance of one of De Morgan's Laws – see §13.5):

E′ $(P \land Q) \therefore \neg(\neg P \lor \neg Q)$.

And we can replicate our informal line of reasoning for **D** as follows:

(1)	$(P \land Q)$	(Prem)
(2)	$(\neg P \lor \neg Q)$	(Supp)
(3)	$\neg P$	(Supp)
(4)	P	($\land$E 1)
(5)	$\bot$	(Abs 4, 3)
(6)	$\neg Q$	(Supp)
(7)	Q	($\land$E 1)
(8)	$\bot$	(Abs 7,6)
(9)	$\bot$	($\lor$E 2, 3–5, 6–8)
(10)	$\neg(\neg P \lor \neg Q)$	(RAA 2, 9)

(f)   For our last example in this initial group, take the trivial argument

F $(P \lor P) \therefore P$.

We can prove the conclusion from the premisses here by another proof by cases:

(1)	$(P \lor P)$	(Prem)
(2)	P	(Supp)
(3)	P	(Iter 2)
(4)	P	(Supp)
(5)	P	(Iter 4)
(6)	P	($\lor$E 1, 2–3, 4–5)

(Minor point: we could also allow the same subproof to be invoked twice by ($\lor$E), just as we allow the same wff to be invoked twice e.g. in applying ($\land$I).)

Note our use of the iteration rule (Iter) to get us from the supposition P at (2) to the subproof's conclusion P at (3). As we remarked in the previous section, we could equally derive the same conclusion by introducing and then eliminating a conjunction. But this would again seem rather unnatural. We want to be able to warrant the conjunction-free **F** without invoking conjunction rules, and (Iter) enables us to do that.

21.3   The disjunction rules, a diagrammatic summary

(a)   Let's review the basics. Reasoning *informally* with disjunctions, one obviously safe inferential principle is simply this: given some proposition, we can infer its (inclusive!) disjunction with any proposition. Another safe informal mode of reasoning is proof by cases. We can spell out the underlying principle like this:

> Suppose three things: (i) Given some background assumptions, we can infer a disjunction A or B. (ii) Given the same background plus A, we can infer C. (iii) Given that same background plus B, we can also infer C. Then: from the same background, we can infer C outright.

Looking at it like this, we see that we can think of informal proof by cases as another 'second-level' principle like (RAA), licensing an inference on the basis of some other correct inferences (compare §20.7).

These two informal principles of inference are then reflected by our two *formal* rules which we can display like this:

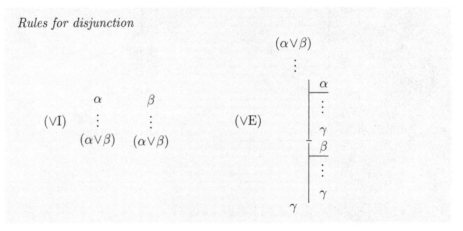

Rules for disjunction

Strictly speaking, we do not *require* the three elements for an application of (∨E) to appear in the order diagrammed, nor do we require one subproof to appear immediately after the other. But in practice, that's the usual layout.

(b)   We noted in §20.1(a) that (∧E) allows us to recover *from* a conjunction $(\alpha \land \beta)$ the inputs that (∧I) requires in arguing *to* that conjunction. We might say: (∧E) can be used to 'reverse' an application of (∧I).

Now, we obviously can't reverse an application of (∨I) in quite the same way. For of course we cannot argue back from a disjunction $(\alpha \lor \beta)$ to recover whichever input (∨I) might use in arguing to that disjunction. Still, (∨E) can be used to undo an application of (∨I) in a closely related sense. For (∨E) allows us to argue *forwards* from $(\alpha \lor \beta)$ to any conclusion we could already have derived equally from α and β before we used (∨I). If we can already infer γ from α, and also infer γ from β, then (∨E) allows us *still* to get to γ, now from $(\alpha \lor \beta)$.

So our (∨I) and (∨E) rules also do still seem to fit together very nicely – as it is often put, they are in *harmony*.

21.4 Two more proofs

(a) Consider the following argument (interpret the atoms however you like):

G $\neg(\neg P \vee \neg Q) \therefore (P \wedge Q)$.

This is valid, being an instance of another of De Morgan's Laws.

How can we show this to be a valid inference by a PL proof in our system? Given that our conclusion is a conjunction, a natural strategy is first to derive one conjunct from our given premiss, and then to derive the other conjunct. Which breaks down the proof into two simpler tasks.

How then can we prove P from our premiss? There's no rule we can directly apply to the premiss. (Reality check: why would it be a howler to try to infer P from $\neg(\neg P \vee \neg Q)$ by a straight application of (DN)?) What else can we do, then, but suppose ¬P, and aim for a contradiction?

(1)	$\neg(\neg P \vee \neg Q)$	(Prem)
(2)	$\neg P$	(Supp)
(3)	$(\neg P \vee \neg Q)$	(∨I 2)
(4)	$\bot$	(Abs 3, 1)
(5)	$\neg\neg P$	(RAA 2–4)
(6)	P	(DN 5)
(7)	$\neg Q$	(Supp)
(8)	$(\neg P \vee \neg Q)$	(∨I 7)
(9)	$\bot$	(Abs 8, 1)
(10)	$\neg\neg Q$	(RAA 7–9)
(11)	Q	(DN 10)
(12)	$(P \wedge Q)$	(∧I 6, 11)

(b) Now let's show the following is valid by another Fitch-style derivation of the conclusion from the premiss:

H $(P \vee (Q \vee R)) \therefore ((P \vee Q) \vee R)$.

We have a disjunctive premiss. We need to use it in a proof by cases. So we can already sketch out the shape of our hoped-for proof:

$(P \vee (Q \vee R))$	
P	(Suppose first disjunct of initial premiss is true)
⋮	
$((P \vee Q) \vee R)$	(Target conclusion)
$(Q \vee R)$	(Suppose second disjunct is true)
⋮	
$((P \vee Q) \vee R)$	(The same target conclusion)
$((P \vee Q) \vee R)$	(∨E from initial premiss and two subproofs)

197

How is the first subproof to go? Plainly, we can use (∨I) twice to arrive at ((P ∨ Q) ∨ R). How is the second subproof to go? This time we have a disjunctive temporary supposition (Q ∨ R). Hence we will now have to embed *another* proof by cases (*inside* the main one), with two new subproofs starting with Q and R and each aiming at the same conclusion ((P ∨ Q) ∨ R).

With these guiding thoughts in mind, a finished proof is quite easily found:

(1)	(P ∨ (Q ∨ R))	(Prem)
(2)	P	(Supp)
(3)	(P ∨ Q)	(∨I 2)
(4)	((P ∨ Q) ∨ R)	(∨I 3)
(5)	(Q ∨ R)	(Supp)
(6)	Q	(Supp)
(7)	(P ∨ Q)	(∨I 6)
(8)	((P ∨ Q) ∨ R)	(∨I 7)
(9)	R	(Supp)
(10)	((P ∨ Q) ∨ R)	(∨I 9)
(11)	((P ∨ Q) ∨ R)	(∨E 5, 6–8, 9–10)
(12)	((P ∨ Q) ∨ R)	(∨E 1, 2–4, 5–11)

21.5   Disjunctive syllogisms

(a)   We turn next to discuss so-called *disjunctive syllogism* inferences. Informally, these are inference steps where we take a disjunction and the negation of one disjunct, and then infer the other disjunct. Thus from *A or B* and *Not-A* we can infer *B*; and equally, from *A or B* and *Not-B* we can infer *A*. Given our standard understanding of negation and disjunction, such inferences are certainly valid (see argument **B** in §1.3). So consider a formal instance such as

I   (P ∨ Q), ¬P ∴ Q.

How can we derive the conclusion from the premises by a PL proof, using just our current rules of inference? We will need a proof by cases, shaped like this:

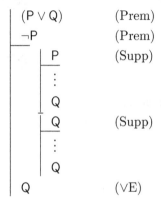

Filling in the *second* subproof takes no work at all – it is just an iteration step. But what about the *first* subproof? In that subproof, the initial premiss ¬P and the temporary supposition P are both available. So we can now appeal to some explosive argument to get us to Q.

There are various options. We could for example borrow the long-way-round proof **H** from the last chapter. But having the fast-track explosive rule (EFQ) to hand enables us to give the following much snappier proof:

(1)		(P ∨ Q)	(Prem)
(2)		¬P	(Prem)
(3)			P	(Supp)
(4)			⊥	(Abs 3, 2)
(5)			Q	(EFQ 4)
(6)			Q	(Supp)
(7)			Q	(Iter)
(8)		Q	(∨E 1, 3–5, 6–7)

(b)   What we have just given is the kind of derivation for a disjunctive syllogism that you standardly meet in Fitch-style proof systems. But on reflection, isn't it really a little peculiar? Return to informal argumentation for a moment. Assume you believe that *A or B* holds. Then suppose you realize that the first disjunct is inconsistent with something else you already accept, *X*. In this case, don't you now simply *rule out the first option A*, and immediately conclude that *B* without any further fuss? You don't ordinarily think that you have to pause to show, by some explosive inference, that *A* plus *X* together entail *B*!

If we want to stay closer to ordinary ways of reasoning, making a minimal change, then we should liberalize our (∨E) rule by *adding* a further clause:

Given (α∨β), a subproof from one of the disjuncts as temporary supposition to the wff γ and also a subproof from the other disjunct to absurdity, we can infer γ.

And then our proof for **I** could be completed by appeal to this additional clause, without any unnatural play with explosion:

(1)		(P ∨ Q)	(Prem)
(2)		¬P	(Prem)
(3)			P	(Supp)
(4)			⊥	(Abs 3, 2)
(5)			Q	(Supp)
(6)			Q	(Iter 6)
(7)		Q	(Liberalized ∨E 1, 3–4, 5–6)

But is it worth liberalizing our (∨E) rule like this? You might say that being able to shorten a proof by just one line is neither here nor there! On the other hand, it could be argued that our liberalized rule is really the natural version that we should have adopted from the start. The usual line, however, is to stick to the original version of (∨E). And on balance it is probably unwise to depart significantly from the conventional wisdom in an introductory text like this. So – with some regrets – we will retain our (∨E) rule in its austere standard form.

This, of course, leaves open the option of adding a Disjunctive Syllogism rule to be built into our system as a new basic rule: *from* (α∨β) *and* ¬α *you can infer* β; *from* (α ∨ β) *and* ¬β *you can infer* α. But we now know that this rule would be redundant; any application of it can be replaced by a short proof modelled on our proof for **I**. It is another judgement call whether to add a (DS) rule: but arguably this redundant rule doesn't have the fundamental character of the strictly-speaking redundant rules we *have* added, (EFQ) and (Iter). So we won't add it. (But there is no right or wrong policy here.)

(c)   Let's have another example where we need to use (EFQ) in order to massage a proof to conform to our standard (∨E) rule. So consider:

J   Either Popper and Quine were both born in the twentieth century or Quine and Russell were both born in the twentieth century. But Russell wasn't born in the twentieth century. So Popper was.

Why is this valid? Informally,

Consider cases from the disjunctive premiss. The second case – Quine and Russell both being born in the twentieth century – is quickly ruled out by the premiss that Russell *wasn't* born in the twentieth century. So that leaves only the first case in play: and in that case, Popper was indeed born in the twentieth century.

Using a language with the obvious glossary, **J** can be formally rendered as

J′ $((P ∧ Q) ∨ (Q ∧ R)), ¬R ∴ P.$

And then here is a formal approximation of our sketched proof:

(1)	$((P ∧ Q) ∨ (Q ∧ R))$	(Prem)
(2)	¬R	(Prem)
(3)	$(P ∧ Q)$	(Supp)
(4)	P	(∧E, 3)
(5)	$(Q ∧ R)$	(Supp)
(6)	R	(∧E, 5)
(7)	⊥	(Abs 6, 2)
(8)	P	(EFQ 7)
(9)	P	(∨E 1, 3–4, 5–8)

The supposition (5) leads to absurdity at (7), as in the intuitive proof. But to shoehorn our formal proof into the standard form of a (∨E) argument, we need (5) to lead eventually to P. We bridge the gap again by appealing to (EFQ).

(d)   Just for the fun of the ride, let's finish this section with a more compli-cated example, where our ∨-elimination rule is appealed to twice over (with one occurrence inside another, as in the proof of **H**). So take the following argument:

K   Either Polly is unmarried or Roland is married. But at least one of Polly and Quentin is married. And it's not true that Quentin is married while Sebastian isn't. So either Roland or Sebastian is married.

This is valid. Informally,

Consider cases from the second premiss.
     Suppose Polly is married – then, by disjunctive syllogism using the first premiss, Roland is married; and hence Roland or Sebastian is married.
     Suppose alternatively that Quentin is married. Combined with the third premiss that implies that Sebastian is married too. So again it is then im-mediate that Roland or Sebastian is married.
     In both cases we get our conclusion.

And now let's argue formally. **K** can be regimented into a PL language like this:

K′ $(\neg P \vee R)$, $(P \vee Q)$, $\neg(Q \wedge \neg S) \therefore (R \vee S)$.

Note, we have in fact already met this argument – it was **D** in §15.4 where we showed it to be valid by the truth-table test. But now we can turn our informal proof by cases for **K**'s validity into a Fitch-style proof warranting **K′** as follows:

(1)	$(\neg P \vee R)$	(Prem)
(2)	$(P \vee Q)$	(Prem)
(3)	$\neg(Q \wedge \neg S)$	(Prem)
(4)	P	(Supp)
(5)	$\neg P$	(Supp)
(6)	$\bot$	(Abs 4, 5)
(7)	R	(EFQ 6)
(8)	R	(Supp)
(9)	R	(Iter 8)
(10)	R	(∨E 1, 5–7, 8–9)
(11)	$(R \vee S)$	(∨I 10)
(12)	Q	(Supp)
(13)	$\neg S$	(Supp)
(14)	$(Q \wedge \neg S)$	(∧I 12, 13)
(15)	$\bot$	(Abs 14, 3)
(16)	$\neg\neg S$	(RAA 13–15)
(17)	S	(DN 16)
(18)	$(R \vee S)$	(∨I 17)
(19)	$(R \vee S)$	(∨E 2, 4–11, 12–18)

Note how we are inserting now familiar patterns of reasoning at (4) to (10), and at (12) to (17): our complex proof, not untypically, is built up from re-usable simpler modules. Also note that the application of (∨E) at line (10) is quite correct, even though the subproofs are indented more than one column in from the original disjunction at line (2). All that matters is that, at line (10), (P ∨ Q) plus the two subproofs are indeed all available.

Finally, though, let's remind ourselves that what really matters for us here is proof-understanding, not proof-discovery. Just make sure you appreciate what is going on in proofs like this!

21.6 Summary

In this chapter, we have added to our Fitch-style proof system the introduction and elimination rules (∨I) and (∨E) for dealing with disjunctions.

These new rules again seem entirely compelling, and true to the ordinary core meaning of 'or' (at least when used inclusively).

If we restrict ourselves to the standard (∨E) rule, some proofs – for disjunctive syllogisms, for example – can look rather unnatural, needing to appeal to (EFQ). We could, for example, tinker with the (∨E) rule by adding another clause: but we follow the usual practice and keep our rule simple.

Exercises 21

(a) Show that the following inferences can be warranted by proofs using the derivation rules introduced over the last two chapters:

(1) (P ∨ (Q ∧ R)) ∴ ((P ∨ Q) ∧ (P ∨ R))
(2) (P ∨ Q) ∴ ¬(¬P ∧ ¬Q)
(3) ¬(P ∧ Q) ∴ (¬P ∨ ¬Q)
(4) (P ∨ Q), (P ∨ R) ∴ (P ∨ (Q ∧ R))
(5) (P ∨ ⊥), (Q ∨ ⊥) ∴ (P ∧ Q)
(6) ¬(Q ∧ P), ((R ∧ Q) ∨ (P ∧ Q)) ∴ R
(7) (P ∨ ¬Q), (R ∨ ¬P), (¬¬R ∨ Q) ∴ R.
(8) (P ∧ (Q ∨ R)), ¬((P ∧ Q) ∧ S), (¬(P ∧ S) ∨ ¬R) ∴ ¬S

(b*) Revisit Exercises 20(b*). Let S be the proof system with our rules for conjunction, negation and now disjunction as well.

(1) Do results (1) to (4) from those previous exercises still obtain now we have revised what counts as the proof system S?

Use similar arguments to those outlined in those previous exercises to show:

(2) If the wffs Γ are S-consistent and $(\alpha \vee \beta)$ is one of those wffs, then either Γ, α or Γ, β (or both) are also S-consistent.

(3) If the wffs Γ are S-consistent and $\neg(\alpha \vee \beta)$ is one of those wffs, then Γ, $\neg\alpha$, $\neg\beta$ are also S-consistent.

22 PL proofs: conditionals

We started Chapter 18 by saying (in effect) 'It would be nice if we can treat "if" as another truth-functional connective. For then we'll be able to carry over our familiar apparatus of truth-table testing, etc.' However, in Chapter 19 we noted problems with simply identifying 'if' and '→'. Though we did end that chapter by suggesting that, all the same, the truth-functional conditional will serve as a stripped-down *substitute* for the ordinary conditional for many purposes.

Let's now start from a different thought: 'Suppose we treat the conditional as another connective governed by intuitively compelling inference rules, and extend our Fitch-style proof system to cover arguments involving conditionals. Perhaps this will give us a more appealing way of handling the logic of "if"!'

So set aside for a moment the official truth-functional semantics for the arrow symbol in PL languages. Keep the same syntax, but regard the arrow as standing in for a conditional governed by the two natural-seeming rules of inference we are about to introduce. Where does this take us?

22.1   Rules for the conditional

(a)   As we saw in Chapter 18, the fundamental principle for arguing *from* a conditional is (MP), modus ponens. So here is one inference rule we'll want:

> *Modus ponens*   Given α and $(\alpha \to \gamma)$, we can derive γ.

What about arguing *to* a conditional proposition? Well, here is Jo considering a particular given triangle Δ. She wants to prove the conditional *if Δ is isosceles, then Δ's base angles are equal*. What does Jo do? She supposes for the sake of argument that Δ is isosceles – *Let Δ be isosceles, ...* Then, on the basis of that supposition, she establishes that Δ's *base angles are equal*. And she takes it that doing this warrants the desired conditional assertion.

The ('second-level') inferential principle that Jo is relying on is this:

> Suppose that – given some background assumptions – we can argue from the additional temporary supposition A to the conclusion C. Then – given the same background – we can infer *if A then C*.

In fact, we often hardly notice the difference between (i) making a supposition A and drawing a conclusion C and (ii) asserting a conditional *if A then C*.

So now for a formal version of this inferential principle:

Conditional proof Given a finished subproof starting with the temporary supposition α and ending γ, we can derive $(\alpha \to \gamma)$.

Immediately putting these two rules into diagrammatic form, we have:

Rules for the conditional

$$\begin{array}{ccc}
& & \alpha \\
& & \vdots \\
(\text{MP}) & (\alpha \to \gamma) & (\text{CP}) \\
& \vdots & \\
& \gamma &
\end{array}
\qquad
\begin{array}{c}
\alpha \\
\vdots \\
\gamma \\
\hline
(\alpha \to \gamma)
\end{array}$$

We can think of (CP) as our $\to$-introduction rule. What then is the matching $\to$-elimination rule that extracts from a conditional wff just what the introduction rule requires us to put in? (CP) grounds $(\alpha \to \gamma)$ in a proof from α to γ; so the corresponding elimination rule should say that, given $(\alpha \to \gamma)$, then if we do have α we should be able to conclude γ. Which is exactly what (MP) says.

(b) The various intuitively valid arguments involving conditionals that we met in §18.4 can now be warranted by proofs using our new conditional rules plus our existing rules for conjunction, disjunction, and negation.

Start with the modus tollens argument

A $(P \to Q), \neg Q \therefore \neg P.$

The proof strategy should be obvious – we want to prove the negation of something, and so we appeal to (RAA), as in:

(1)	$(P \to Q)$	(Prem)
(2)	$\neg Q$	(Prem)
(3)	$\quad P$	(Supp)
(4)	$\quad Q$	(MP 3, 1)
(5)	$\quad \bot$	(Abs 4, 2)
(6)	$\neg P$	(RAA 3–5)

Here we annotate the application of (MP) in the predictable way.

And note that the proof-strategy here generalizes: whenever we have $(\alpha \to \gamma)$ and $\neg\gamma$, we can of course use a proof of the same shape to derive $\neg\alpha$. It would therefore be redundant to add a separate modus tollens rule to our repertoire of rules for the conditional.

Next, we noted that the informal counterpart of the argument

B $(P \to Q), (Q \to R) \therefore (P \to R)$

is intuitively correct for simple conditionals. And here is how to derive the conclusion from the premises, using our conditional rules. The proof strategy is the default one when the target conclusion is a conditional. We temporarily assume the antecedent for the sake of argument and then aim for the consequent, so we can use the introduction rule (CP).

(1)	$(P \rightarrow Q)$	(Prem)
(2)	$(Q \rightarrow R)$	(Prem)
(3)	P	(Supp)
(4)	Q	(MP 3, 1)
(5)	R	(MP 4, 2)
(6)	$(P \rightarrow R)$	(CP 3–5)

The way we annotate the application of the conditional proof rule (CP) by giving the extent of the relevant subproof is also just as you would predict.

Next consider the contraposition inference (i.e. the inference from a conditional to its contrapositive) in

C $(P \rightarrow Q) \therefore (\neg Q \rightarrow \neg P)$.

Again, we are aiming to prove a conditional. So again the strategy is to temporarily suppose the antecedent $\neg Q$ is true and aim to derive to consequent $\neg P$ with a view to using (CP). But this just sets us off on the same modus tollens inference as in **A** after line (2):

(1)	$(P \rightarrow Q)$	(Prem)
(2)	$\neg Q$	(Supp)
(3)	P	(Supp)
(4)	Q	(MP 3, 1)
(5)	$\perp$	(Abs 4, 2)
(6)	$\neg P$	(RAA 2–5)
(7)	$(\neg Q \rightarrow \neg P)$	(CP 2–6)

And now for the variant kind of proof by cases that we met in §18.4:

D $(P \lor Q), (P \rightarrow R), (Q \rightarrow R) \therefore R$.

To argue from the disjunctive first premiss, we have to use (∨E). And then the proof goes in the predictable way.

(1)	$(P \lor Q)$	(Prem)
(2)	$(P \rightarrow R)$	(Prem)
(3)	$(Q \rightarrow R)$	(Prem)
(4)	P	(Supp)
(5)	R	(MP 4, 2)
(6)	Q	(Supp)
(7)	R	(MP 6, 3)
(8)	R	(∨E 1, 4–5, 6–7)

205

Let's have one more example in this initial group. So consider the argument

E $(P \rightarrow (Q \rightarrow R))$ ∴ $(Q \rightarrow (P \rightarrow R))$.

This argument intuitively *ought* to be valid (why?). So how do we derive the conclusion from the premiss?

The target conclusion is a conditional, so the obvious thing to do is assume the antecedent Q and aim for the consequent $(P \rightarrow R)$, preparing to use (CP). Our new target then is *another* conditional, and to prove this we again assume its antecedent P and aim for its consequent R, preparing to invoke (CP) again.

With that plan in mind, the proof is then easily completed:

(1)	$(P \rightarrow (Q \rightarrow R)$	(Prem)
(2)	Q	(Supp)
(3)	P	(Supp)
(4)	$(Q \rightarrow R)$	(MP 3, 1)
(5)	R	(MP 2, 4)
(6)	$(P \rightarrow R)$	(CP 3–5)
(7)	$(Q \rightarrow (P \rightarrow R))$	(CP 2–6)

22.2   More proofs with conditionals

Let's work through a few more proofs – starting with two desirable results, but ending in a perhaps unexpected place.

(a)   In §19.2, we met these informal arguments (keeping the same labels):

X(i) The claim *if A then C* rules out having *A* true and *C* false. So *if A then C* implies *it isn't the case that both A and not-C.*

Y(i) Suppose *if A then C.* So we either have *not-A*, or we have *A* and hence *C*. So *if A then C* implies *either not-A or C.*

Using our new derivation rules for conditionals, we can now provide proofs for corresponding formal arguments. Take these particular examples:

F $(P \rightarrow Q)$ ∴ $\neg(P \wedge \neg Q)$
G $(P \rightarrow Q)$ ∴ $(\neg P \vee Q)$.

The strategy for the first proof is straightforward; we just follow the implied reductio in the informal argument **X**(i):

(1)	$(P \rightarrow Q)$	(Prem)
(2)	$(P \wedge \neg Q)$	(Supp)
(3)	P	(∧E 2)
(4)	Q	(MP 3, 1)
(5)	¬Q	(∧E 2)
(6)	⊥	(Abs 4, 5)
(7)	$\neg(P \wedge \neg Q)$	(RAA 2–6)

As for **G**, our informal argument in **Y**(i) quietly appeals to the law of excluded middle – but we won't meet the formal version of that until the next chapter. So let's instead suppose the opposite of the conclusion, and aim to reduce that to absurdity. Our proof will then have the shape

$(P \rightarrow Q)$	(Prem)
$\neg(\neg P \vee Q)$	(Supp)
$\vdots$	
$\bot$	
$\neg\neg(\neg P \vee Q)$	(RAA)
$(\neg P \vee Q)$	(DN)

How do we join up the dots? We can't yet apply a conditional rule to the initial premiss, nor can we apply a negation rule to the supposition. There's only one sensible thing to do! Namely, make *another* supposition. So try assuming 'P', which sets up a modus ponens inference. Things then go smoothly enough:

(1)	$(P \rightarrow Q)$	(Prem)
(2)	$\neg(\neg P \vee Q)$	(Supp)
(3)	P	(Supp)
(4)	Q	(MP 3, 1)
(5)	$(\neg P \vee Q)$	(VI 4)
(6)	$\bot$	(Abs 5, 2)
(7)	$\neg P$	(RAA 3–6)
(8)	$(\neg P \vee Q)$	(VI 7)
(9)	$\bot$	(Abs 8, 2)
(10)	$\neg\neg(\neg P \vee Q)$	(RAA 2–9)
(11)	$(\neg P \vee Q)$	(DN 10)

(b)   As we noted before, **X**(i) is just a version of the basic falsehood condition (FC) from §18.2. Hence any good rules for arguing with a conditional should certainly allow us to show that $(P \rightarrow Q)$ entails $\neg(P \wedge \neg Q)$ (and should also allow us to show that it entails the equivalent $(\neg P \vee Q)$). So far, then, so good.

But what about the other two informal arguments we met in §19.2, namely

X(ii) Suppose we are given that *it isn't the case that both A and not-C*. Then we can infer that if A is true we can't have *not-C* as well: in other words *if A then C*.

Y(ii) Suppose we are given *either not-A or C*. Then if not the first, then the second. So we can infer *if A then C*.

Well, these two arguments can also be mirrored using our formal derivation rules for conditionals. For example, we can warrant the following arguments:

H	$\neg(P \wedge \neg Q) \therefore (P \rightarrow Q)$
I	$(\neg P \vee Q) \therefore (P \rightarrow Q).$

For the first of these we can argue simply as follows:

(1)	¬(P ∧ ¬Q)		(Prem)
(2)		P	(Supp)
(3)			¬Q	(Supp)
(4)			(P ∧ ¬Q)	(∧I 2, 3)
(5)			⊥	(Abs 4, 1)
(6)		¬¬Q	(RAA 3–5)
(7)		Q	(DN 7)
(8)	(P → Q)		(CP 2–8)

And for the second we just echo the informal disjunctive syllogism in **Y**(ii):

(1)	(¬P ∨ Q)		(Prem)
(2)		P	(Supp)
(3)			¬P	(Supp)
(4)			⊥	(Abs 2, 3)
(5)			Q	(EFQ 4)
(6)			Q	(Supp)
(7)			Q	(Iter 5)
(8)		Q	(∨E 1, 3–5, 6–7)
(9)	(P → Q)		(CP 2–8)

(c)   Put together the trivial proof from ¬P to (¬P ∨ Q) with a proof for **I** and we get a proof warranting the inference in

J   ¬P ∴ (P → Q).

Compare our discussion in §19.4. But note that there is also a much quicker proof for this inference, again using explosion:

(1)	¬P		(Prem)
(2)		P	(Supp)
(3)		⊥	(Abs 2, 1)
(4)		Q	(EFQ 3)
(5)	(P → Q)		(CP 2–4)

22.3   The material conditional again

(a)   In §18.4, we saw that the material conditional satisfies the modus ponens principle (MP). In §18.8, we saw that, if α together with background premises entails γ, then those premises entail (α → γ), where the arrow is specifically the material conditional. So the material conditional satisfies the conditional proof principle (CP). That's unsurprising. What is perhaps more surprising is a converse point.

Suppose we add an arrow connective to our Fitch-style PL logical system for the other connectives. Suppose we initially require only that this connective is governed by the two intuitively compelling principles (MP) and (CP). Then, generalizing from the examples we met in the last section, a wff of the form $(\alpha \to \gamma)$ will imply and be implied by the corresponding truth-functional wff $\neg(\alpha \land \neg\gamma)$. Similarly, $(\alpha \to \gamma)$ will imply and be implied by $(\neg\alpha \lor \gamma)$.

We wondered whether we could avoid the problems of identifying 'if' with the material conditional by introducing a conditional into our logic via intuitively appealing inference rules. But we now see this is no help, at least if we start from a standard logic for the other connectives. Add to that basis a conditional connective obeying the natural rules (MP) and (CP), and this connective will end up behaving exactly like the material conditional again.

(b)   Return, then, to our remarks in §19.6 about adopting the material conditional. Nearly all mathematicians cheerfully accept the usual logic for the other connectives. And mathematicians reason all the time using a conditional which unrestrictedly obeys (CP) as well as (MP) – it is absolutely standard in informal mathematical reasoning to prove a conditional by assuming the antecedent and aiming for the consequent. Therefore, these mathematicians are indeed reasoning with a conditional which behaves like the material conditional.

22.4   Summary

We add to our PL proof system two inference rules for the conditional – namely (MP) and (CP), i.e. modus ponens and conditional proof. Once more, the rules we are adding to our system seem intuitively very natural.

However, these intuitive rules make a wff of the form $(\alpha \to \gamma)$ interderivable with the corresponding wffs $\neg(\alpha \land \neg\gamma)$ and $(\neg\alpha \lor \gamma)$. In other words, when added to our core PL system, our rules make a conditional behave like the material conditional.

Exercises 22

(a)   Warrant the following inferences by PL natural deduction proofs:

(1) $((P \land Q) \to R) \; \therefore \; (P \to (Q \to R))$

(2) $(P \to (Q \to R)) \; \therefore \; ((P \land Q) \to R)$

(3) $((P \lor (Q \land R)) \to \bot) \; \therefore \; \neg(P \lor (Q \land R))$

(4) $(P \to \bot), (P \lor \neg Q) \; \therefore \; (Q \to \bot)$

(5) $(P \land (\neg Q \to \neg P)) \; \therefore \; (\neg P \lor (Q \land P))$

(6) $((P \land Q) \to (Q \land R)), (R \to \neg P) \; \therefore \; (P \to \neg Q)$

(7) $(\neg S \to \neg R), ((P \land Q) \lor R), (\neg S \to \neg Q) \; \therefore \; (\neg P \lor S)$

(8) $(\neg P \to (Q \land R)), \neg(R \lor P) \; \therefore \; \neg Q$

Also give proofs warranting the following inferences:

(9) $Q \; \therefore \; (P \to Q)$

(10) $\neg(P \rightarrow Q)$ $\therefore$ P
(11) $\neg(P \rightarrow Q)$ $\therefore$ $\neg Q$
(12) $(P \rightarrow (Q \vee R))$ $\therefore$ $((P \rightarrow Q) \vee (P \rightarrow R))$

(b)   Following the general definition in Exercises 20(b*), let's say in particular

Some wffs are PL-consistent if we cannot use premisses from among them to prove $\bot$.

In each of the following cases, show that the given wffs are PL-*inconsistent*, i.e. show that there *is* a PL proof of absurdity from them as premisses:

(1) $(P \rightarrow \neg P)$, $(\neg P \rightarrow P)$
(2) $(\neg P \vee \neg Q)$, $(P \wedge Q)$
(3) $((P \rightarrow Q) \wedge (Q \rightarrow \neg P))$, $(R \rightarrow P)$, $(\neg R \rightarrow P)$
(4) $(P \vee (Q \rightarrow R))$, $(\neg R \wedge \neg(P \vee \neg Q))$
(5) $(\neg P \vee R)$, $\neg(R \vee S)$, $(P \vee Q)$, $\neg(Q \wedge \neg S)$.

Note: the idea of PL-consistency is defined in terms of what we can do by symbol-shuffling in a PL proof. Compare the notion of tautological consistency which is defined in terms of valuations. They are different notions, differently defined (see Chapter 24).

(c)   Suppose that we use '$\leftrightarrow$' as introduced in §18.6, so that an expression of the form $(\alpha \leftrightarrow \gamma)$ is simply an *abbreviation* of the corresponding expression of the form $((\alpha \rightarrow \gamma) \wedge (\gamma \rightarrow \alpha))$. Warrant the following inferences by PL natural deduction proofs:

(1) $(P \leftrightarrow Q)$ $\therefore$ $(Q \leftrightarrow P)$
(2) $(P \leftrightarrow Q)$ $\therefore$ $(\neg P \leftrightarrow \neg Q)$
(3) $(P \leftrightarrow Q)$, $(Q \leftrightarrow R)$ $\therefore$ $(P \leftrightarrow R)$

Suppose alternatively that we introduce '$\leftrightarrow$' to PL as a basic built-in biconditional connective. Give introduction and elimination rules for this new connective (rules which, like the rules for '$\rightarrow$', *don't* mention any other connective). Use these new rules to warrant (1) to (3) again. Also give proofs to warrant the following:

(4) P, Q $\therefore$ $(P \leftrightarrow Q)$
(5) $\neg(P \leftrightarrow Q)$ $\therefore$ $((P \wedge \neg Q) \vee (\neg P \wedge Q))$
(6) $(P \leftrightarrow R)$, $(Q \leftrightarrow S)$ $\therefore$ $((P \vee Q) \leftrightarrow (R \vee S))$

Use a truth-table to confirm that the following wffs are tautologically equivalent:

(7) $(P \leftrightarrow (Q \leftrightarrow R))$, $((P \leftrightarrow Q) \leftrightarrow R)$.

For a trickier challenge, outline a proof deriving the second from the first.

(d*)   First show

(1) There is a proof of $(\alpha \rightarrow \gamma)$ from the premisses Γ if and only if there is a proof of γ from Γ, α.
(2) There is a proof of $(\gamma \rightarrow \bot)$ from the premisses Γ if and only if there is a proof of $\neg \gamma$ from Γ.

And now show the following:

(3) The results of Exercises 20(b*) and 21(b*) still obtain when S is the whole PL proof system.
(4) If Γ are PL-consistent and $(\alpha \rightarrow \gamma)$ is one of those wffs, then either $\Gamma, \neg \alpha$ or Γ, γ (or both) are also PL-consistent.
(5) If Γ are PL-consistent and $\neg(\alpha \rightarrow \gamma)$ is one of those wffs, then $\Gamma, \alpha, \neg \gamma$ are also PL-consistent.

23 PL proofs: theorems

A proof in our Fitch-style system has to start from *something*. But it doesn't have to start from a permanent premiss. A mere temporary supposition is good enough. This short chapter illustrates this simple but important new idea.

23.1 Theorems

(a) Consider the following proof. We start with *no* premisses, but make a supposition for the sake of argument, and then continue to get proof **A**:

(1)		
(2)	(P ∧ ¬P)	(Supp)
(3)	P	(∧E 2)
(4)	¬P	(∧E 2)
(5)	⊥	(Abs 4, 5)
(6)	¬(P ∧ ¬P)	(RAA 2–5)

Let's adopt a standard bit of terminology:

> A wff which is provable in our Fitch-style proof system from *no* premisses is said to be a *theorem* of the system.

Then we have just shown that one formal instance of Aristotle's Law of Non-Contradiction is a theorem. And the proof strategy can be generalized: *any* wff of the form ¬(α ∧ ¬α) is a theorem. Put α for P throughout the proof, and we will get a derivation of the corresponding ¬(α ∧ ¬α) from no premisses.

Is this some dubious sleight of hand, as we apparently pull truths out of an empty logical hat? No. In fact, on reflection, our result is exactly what we would hope for! We can intuitively establish that any instance of Aristotle's Law is true just by reflecting on how the connectives appear in it. So the rules governing the connectives *ought* to be enough by themselves to generate instances of the Law.

(b) We can also show that an instance of the Law of Excluded Middle like (P ∨ ¬P) is a theorem. How will the proof go? We can't get the disjunctive conclusion using (∨I), as we plainly can't get either P or ¬P from no premisses. So our only hope is to suppose the opposite, ¬(P ∨ ¬P), and aim for a contradiction.

But now note that we can't usefully apply our negation or disjunction rules to this supposition either: so it seems that we will need to make *another* supposition in order to move on.

In fact, the simplest further supposition will do the trick. Here is how, **B**:

(1)		
(2)	¬(P ∨ ¬P)	(Supp)
(3)	P	(Supp)
(4)	(P ∨ ¬P)	(∨I 3)
(5)	⊥	(Abs 4, 2)
(6)	¬P	(RAA 3–5)
(7)	(P ∨ ¬P)	(∨I 6)
(8)	⊥	(Abs 7, 2)
(9)	¬¬(P ∨ ¬P)	(RAA 2–8)
(10)	(P ∨ ¬P)	(DN 9)

Check that you understand how the proof almost writes itself. Once again, the proof-idea generalizes. Any wff of the form $(\alpha \lor \neg\alpha)$ is a theorem.

(c) Now for a couple of examples involving conditionals. Firstly, we will show that $(P \to (Q \to (P \land Q)))$ is a theorem – as you would expect, since it is in general a trivial logical truth that if A is true, then if B is true as well, we will have A *and* B! Here's a proof, **C**:

(1)		
(2)	P	(Supp)
(3)	Q	(Supp)
(4)	(P ∧ Q)	(∧I 2, 3)
(5)	(Q → (P ∧ Q))	(CP 3–4)
(6)	(P → (Q → (P ∧ Q)))	(CP 2–5)

That was easy! But our next example is more interesting and decidedly trickier. Take the wff

D $(((P \to Q) \to P) \to P)$

This is an instance of what is known as Peirce's Law. If we interpret the arrow as the material conditional then, as can be easily checked, it is a tautology.

To prove it, we will evidently need a proof of the following shape:

	((P → Q) → P)	(Supp)
	⋮	
	P	
	(((P → Q) → P) → P)	(CP)

But how do we fill in the dots? We will need to apply (MP) if we are to make use of the temporary supposition. But that means we will must first derive the antecedent of our supposition, i.e. (P → Q). And how are we going to do *that*?

Well, we can make another supposition ¬P, and then derive (P → Q) as in the short proof for **J** in the last chapter. We then get the (non-obvious!) proof:

(1)		
(2)	((P → Q) → P)	(Supp)
(3)	¬P	(Supp)
(4)	P	(Supp)
(5)	⊥	(Abs 4, 3)
(6)	Q	(EFQ 5)
(7)	(P → Q)	(CP 4, 6)
(8)	P	(MP 7, 2)
(9)	⊥	(Abs 8, 3)
(10)	¬¬P	(RAA 3–9)
(11)	P	(DN 10)
(12)	(((P → Q) → P) → P)	(CP 2–11)

It is interesting to note that this theorem of our system only involves the conditional; yet we do need to use more than our two conditional rules in order to prove it. (In particular, we have invoked (DN) at line (11): and it can be shown that we *have* to use (DN) or some equivalent to derive instances of Peirce's Law in our proof system.)

23.2 Derived rules

(a) Let's take one more example of a theorem. Back in §14.1 we saw that

E $((P \land Q) \lor (\neg P \lor \neg Q))$

is a PL logical truth. So we will want to be able to prove it from no premises. Here is an outline proof:

(1)		
(2)	((¬P ∨ ¬Q) ∨ ¬(¬P ∨ ¬Q))	(Excluded middle, as in **B**)
(3)	(¬P ∨ ¬Q)	(Supp)
(4)	((P ∧ Q) ∨ (¬P ∨ ¬Q))	(∨I 3)
(5)	¬(¬P ∨ ¬Q)	(Supp)
(6)	(P ∧ Q)	(from 5, as in **G** §21.4)
(7)	((P ∧ Q) ∨ (¬P ∨ ¬Q))	(∨I 6)
(8)	((P ∧ Q) ∨ (¬P ∨ ¬Q))	(∨E 2, 3–4, 5–7)

Filling in the details, that's a twenty-five line proof. But we have kept things a lot shorter by allowing ourselves to 'plug in' derivations from two earlier proofs.

(b)   Picking up that last point, here is a general observation. Suppose we want to cope with increasingly messy PL proofs. Then:

(i)   We can generalize from particular proofs that we have already produced, and build up a library of *derived rules* of inference (rules that must be truth-preserving if our original rules are).

(ii)   We can then invoke these derived rules in order to speed up new proofs.

For example, we could officially adopt the Law of Excluded Middle, as described in the next section. Or we could adopt versions of De Morgan's Laws like *From* $\neg(\neg\alpha \lor \neg\beta)$ *you can infer* $(\alpha \land \beta)$. Or we could adopt the Disjunctive Syllogism rule mentioned in §21.5(b). And then we can allow ourselves to appeal to one of our derived rules at any point in a formal proof.

And that is how introductory logic texts often proceed. But not us. For we are not going to make a fetish of producing lots of complex PL proofs. Once you have got the hang of how to use our formal logics here and later in the book, and understand their role as ideal models of explicit rigour, then there is little point in making it easier to produce more and yet more proofs inside our various systems. For us, as stressed before in §20.5, understanding the basic motivations and guiding principles of our logical systems is *much* more important.

23.3   Excluded middle and double negation

Having mentioned theorems and derived rules, we finish the chapter with a simple observation. Consider these two rules of inference, one old, one new:

Double negation (DN): Given $\neg\neg\alpha$, we can infer α.

Law of excluded middle (LEM): At any point in a derivation, we can add a wff of the form $(\alpha \lor \neg\alpha)$, where α is any wff.

Now, (DN) is built into our proof system as a basic rule. (LEM) isn't. But we have seen how any instance of $(\alpha\lor\neg\alpha)$ *can* be proved at any point by using (DN) (along with other rules). In other words, we could add (LEM) to our system as a derived rule, and it would make no difference to what we can establish.

Suppose, however, that we *hadn't* adopted the rule (DN), but had *instead* adopted the rule (LEM) as basic alongside the other rules. Then, in this revised system, we have the following short proof, by disjunctive syllogism:

(1)	$\neg\neg$P	(Prem)
(2)	$(P \lor \neg P)$	(LEM)
(3)	P	(Supp)
(4)	P	(Iter 3)
(5)	$\neg$P	(Supp)
(6)	$\bot$	(Abs 5, 1)
(7)	P	(EFQ 6)
(8)	P	($\lor$E 2, 3–4, 5–7)

And of course this proof idea generalizes too. In our revised system, we can still always get from $\neg\neg\alpha$ (whether as a premiss or as a wff in the middle of a proof) to α by using (LEM) and other background rules. So in our new system (DN) would be a derived rule.

In short, taking the other rules – i.e. (Iter), (EFQ), and the pairs of introduction and elimination rules – as fixed background, *it doesn't matter whether we adopt (DN) as our additional negation-involving rule or adopt (LEM) instead*. The resulting proof systems will be equivalent, in the obvious sense of warranting just the same conclusions from given premisses.

We will say something about the significance of this observation at the end of the next chapter.

23.4   Summary

A theorem of our proof system is a wff which can be proved from no premisses at all. Intuitively, theorems will be logical truths.

We saw that, given the other inference rules, having the rule (DN) in place is equivalent to having the rule (LEM) that allows us to invoke an instance of the law of excluded middle at any point in a proof.

Exercises 23

(a)   Show that the following wffs are theorems of our PL proof system (in a suitable language).

(1) $(\neg((P \wedge Q) \to R) \vee ((P \wedge Q) \to R))$

(2) $(((P \wedge Q) \to R) \to (Q \to (P \to R)))$

(3) $((P \to (Q \to R)) \to ((P \to Q) \to (P \to R)))$

(4) $(\neg(P \wedge (\neg P \vee Q)) \vee Q)$

(5) $((P \to Q) \vee (Q \to P))$

(6) $(((P \wedge Q) \to R) \to ((P \to R) \vee (Q \to R)))$

(7) $(((P \to Q) \to P) \to ((Q \to P) \vee P))$

(b*)   More on negation and alternative rules of inference. The following rule is often called *Classical Reductio*, to be carefully distinguished from our (RAA):

Given a finished subproof starting with the temporary supposition $\neg\alpha$ and concluding $\bot$, we can derive α.

And the following is a form of *Peirce's Law* (analogous to (LEM)):

We can invoke an instance of $((\alpha \to \beta) \to \alpha) \to \alpha)$ at any stage in a proof.

Show that the new proof system which results from our PL proof system by replacing the double negation rule (DN) with either (i) Classical Reductio or (ii) Peirce's Law is equivalent to our current system.

24 PL proofs: metatheory

We have now worked through a range of proofs *inside* our Fitch-style natural deduction system. In this chapter we mostly stand *outside* this system in order to note some important results about it. In a word, we do some . . .

24.1 Metatheory

We have already remarked on some small 'metatheoretic' results. For example, having shown that we could argue from $(P \land Q)$ to $(Q \land P)$ in our proof system, we then noted that – by replacing P and Q with α and β throughout the little proof – we can similarly get a proof from any wff $(\alpha \land \beta)$ to $(\beta \land \alpha)$. So we concluded that it would be redundant to add to our system a further rule ($\land$C) allowing us directly to swap the order of conjuncts in a conjunction – see §20.1(d). This redundancy result is not itself a theorem in the sense of a wff derived inside our PL proof system: it is, as they say, a *metatheorem* about our system.

For another example, at the end of the last chapter we proved the metatheorem that, keeping the other rules fixed, we could replace the rule (DN) with the rule (LEM) without changing what can be proved in the system.

As we will see, however, the most basic metatheorems about our Fitch-style proof system are the *soundness* and *completeness* results – our system is sound in the sense of always warranting genuine tautological entailments, and complete in the sense of warranting all such entailments. More about this soon.

Our Fitch-style system is certainly not the only sound and complete one for arguing in PL languages with their truth-functional connectives. There are other frameworks for proof-building on the market; and even within a natural deduction framework, there are various choices both for layout and for the fundamental rules. Still, for brevity's sake, we will continue to refer to a derivation in our particular Fitch-style PL natural deduction system as simply a 'PL proof'.

24.2 Putting everything together

Before discussing some metatheorems, let's bring together in one place the PL rules of inference that have been scattered through the last four chapters. And then we will officially specify the ways in which we are allowed to chain inference steps together to form proofs.

(a)   First, then, the inference rules again. We start with the rule which allows us to simply repeat ourselves when it is useful to do so:

(Iter)   At any inference step, we can reiterate any available wff.

Next we have a rule governing the absurdity sign, plus four pairs of introduction/elimination rules. (We explained in §20.2(d) why we can think of the negation rules as forming a pair of this kind. And we explained in §22.1(a) why we can think of the conditional rules as forming an introduction/elimination pair.) As usual, α, β and γ are arbitrary PL wffs, and then:

(EFQ)   Given $\bot$, we can derive any wff α.

(RAA)   Given a finished subproof starting with the temporary supposition α and concluding $\bot$, we can derive $\neg\alpha$.

(Abs)   Given α and $\neg\alpha$, we can derive $\bot$.

($\wedge$I)   Given α and β, we can derive $(\alpha \wedge \beta)$.

($\wedge$E)   Given $(\alpha \wedge \beta)$, we can derive α. Given $(\alpha \wedge \beta)$, we can derive β.

($\vee$I)   Given α, we can derive $(\alpha \vee \beta)$ for any β. Given β, we can derive $(\alpha \vee \beta)$ for any α.

($\vee$E)   Given $(\alpha \vee \beta)$, a finished subproof from α as supposition to γ and also a finished subproof from β as supposition to γ, then we can derive γ.

(CP)   Given a finished subproof starting with the temporary supposition α and ending γ, we can derive $(\alpha \rightarrow \gamma)$.

(MP)   Given α and $(\alpha \rightarrow \gamma)$, we can derive γ.

Finally, we have the additional negation rule – an outlier, which is independent of the basic introduction/elimination pairs (as we will confirm in §24.8):

(DN)   Given $\neg\neg\alpha$, we can derive α.

The 'given' inputs for the application of any rule of inference must be *available*, occurring earlier in the proof but not inside an already finished subproof.

(b)   Now we review how to put together inference steps in order to construct complete PL proofs. Two preliminary decisions:

(i)   Line numbers on the left of a derivation, and commentary on the right, are helpful optional extras, but won't count as part of the proof itself. But what about the vertical lines marking columns of reasoning? And what about the horizontal bars separating premises and temporary suppositions from what follows? These do carry important information, so let's retain them. So when we talk about 'columns' we will take these as marked as before by a vertical line, one for the whole 'home' column, and others lasting for the duration of a subproof.

217

(ii) We repeat a point that we have made before. Consider:

(1) | P   (Prem)
(2) | Q   (Prem)
(3) | | R   (Supp)
(4) | | (P ∧ R)   (∧I 1, 3)
(5) | (P ∧ Q)   (∧I 1, 2)

This proof contains a correctly formed subproof which then turns out to be an irrelevant digression. We finish the subproof, but then make no later use of it in reaching our final conclusion.

Now, we *could* require proofs to be written economically, so that the *only* subproofs which appear along the way are ones which are actually used as inputs to later rules of inference. However, we can afford to be relaxed about this. After all, digressions may be inefficient: but we do not ordinarily regard them as fallacious. Hence we will allow subproofs to be completed and then, in effect, abandoned. For us, being a correct proof is one thing: being elegantly minimal is something else!

We can now give an official summary of the principles for building PL proofs. We take it as understood that a proof in our system is a snaking vertical line of wffs, arranged in marked columns and jumping at most one column left or right at each step. Then:

A PL proof begins with zero or more wffs as premisses, entered at the top of the *home* (left-most) column of the proof, followed by a horizontal bar.

Then at each further step we do one of the following (keeping going until we eventually end the proof):

(1) We remain in the current column, and apply a PL rule of inference to add a wff. In applying a rule, *the 'given' inputs to the rule must be available*, i.e. must occur earlier but *not* inside an already finished subproof.

(2) We move one column to the right and add a wff (which becomes a new temporary supposition) followed by a horizontal bar. This starts a new subproof.

(3) We move one column to the left (only if we are *not* in the home column). This ends the current subproof.

(4) We end the whole proof (only if we *are* in the home column).

These moves are subject to the following condition:

(5) After stating the premisses, or after stating a temporary supposition, or after moving a column left, we must next do (1) or (2).

The constraint in rule (4) means that we can't get a properly completed proof if we stop in the middle of a subproof, with some undischarged temporary supposition left dangling. The constraints in (5) stop us putting down premisses or a temporary supposition and doing *nothing* with them, and ensure that every proof and subproof has some concluding wff.

Just check through some of our earlier examples, to convince yourself that they do conform to our now official proof-building rules.

(c) One important remark. Look again at our derivation rules and at our rules for using them in forming PL proofs. These rules are *motivated* by semantic thoughts about truth-preservation. But the rules nowhere *mention* anything semantic; they just describe permissible symbol-shuffling moves. A computer can be programmed to check whether an array of symbols constitutes a PL proof just by checking the syntactic patterns in the expressions involved (without considering valuations, for example). In short:

It is a purely syntactic matter whether an array of wffs is put together in such a way as to form a properly constructed PL proof.

24.3 Vacuous discharge

The guiding ideas behind our PL proof system are, we can agree, very natural and attractive. This section pauses over one bothersome point of detail.

(a) Consider, for example, the following derivation, **A**:

(1)	P	(Prem)
(2)	¬P	(Prem)
(3)	¬Q	(Supp)
(4)	⊥	(Abs 1, 2)
(5)	¬¬Q	(RAA 3–4)
(6)	Q	(DN 5)

Our (Abs) rule tells us that given P and ¬P we can declare an absurdity. At line (4), both P and ¬P *are* available. So we can indeed correctly put down ⊥ at that line. Our (RAA) rule tells us that, given an available subproof starting with the temporary supposition ¬Q and concluding ⊥, we can discharge the supposition and infer ¬¬Q. At line (5) just such a subproof *is* available, so (RAA) allows us to infer ¬¬Q at that line. Hence, with a final (DN) step, we get another proof in our system warranting the explosive inference P, ¬P ∴ Q.

Isn't there something odd here, though? For note that the supposition ¬Q at line (3) is not actually invoked in arriving at the absurdity at line (4). But isn't the idea behind a reductio proof that, if an assumption *A* leads to or *generates* a contradiction, we can infer *not-A*? By contrast, our official (RAA) rule allows what is known by the rather unprepossessing name of 'vacuous discharge'. Which means that we are allowed to discharge the temporary supposition α at the top of a subproof ending in absurdity and infer ¬α, *even if α is not actually involved in deriving the absurdity.*

(b) Here is an even simpler derivation, **B**:

(1)	Q	(Prem)
(2)	P	(Supp)
(3)	Q	(Iter 1)
(4)	(P → Q)	(CP 2–3)

To infer a wff of the form $(\alpha \to \gamma)$ by (CP), all we need is an available finished subproof starting α and ending γ; and that's what we have here at line (4).

Again, you might be suspicious. The supposition P at line (2) in **B** is not used in deriving (3), the final wff Q of the subproof. But isn't the idea behind a 'conditional proof' that, if an assumption A *leads to* or *generates* a derived conclusion C, then we are entitled to infer *if A then C*? By contrast, our official (CP) rule also allows vacuous discharge. Which means that we are allowed to discharge the temporary supposition α at the top of a subproof ending in γ and derive $(\alpha \to \gamma)$, *even if α is not actually involved in deriving γ*.

(c) So the question arises: is allowing vacuous discharge as in these cases a bug in our proof system? Or is it an acceptable feature?

Concentrating on the slightly simpler second example, it might be suggested that we should make the conditional proof rule stricter, along the following lines:

(CP$_2$) Given an available subproof starting with the temporary supposition α and ending with γ, *where α is actually used in deriving γ*, then we can infer $(\alpha \to \gamma)$.

Consider, however, the following proof, **C**:

(1)	Q	(Prem)
(2)	P	(Supp)
(3)	(P ∧ Q)	(∧I 2, 1)
(4)	Q	(∧E, 3)
(5)	(P → Q)	(CP$_2$ 2–4)

Here the wff officially appealed to in deriving (4), namely (3), is itself derived from (2). So we do still get a proof even with our revised rule (CP$_2$).

To avoid (CP$_2$) in effect collapsing back into our original rule (CP), should we *also* try to block the sort of two-step dance involved at lines (3) and (4) in **C**? Shall we ban using an introduction rule and then simply 'undoing' the result by using the corresponding elimination rule? The trouble with this suggestion is that such little detours strike us as typically redundant rather than wrong, so an outright ban would – at least initially – seem hard to motivate.

(d) There's a lot more to be said. But we must leave matters here. The headline news is that other natural deduction systems for standard propositional logic also permit vacuous discharge when applying rules using temporary suppositions like (RAA), (VE), and (CP), so this isn't only a feature of our system. And this feature doesn't enable us to prove anything that we can't prove otherwise, so it isn't a vicious bug. The path of least resistance, then, is simply to continue to allow vacuous discharge of 'unused' temporary suppositions as a special case.

24.4 Generalizing PL proofs

We now pick up again a point which we have already noted: PL proofs generalize.

Suppose we take an array of PL wffs which are interrelated by our rules of inference so as to form a correctly formed proof. And suppose we systematically swap out the atoms in this proof for other wffs (obeying the crucial rule – same atom, same replacement throughout). Then we will get an array of new wffs.

Now, nothing in our rules for PL proof-building gives a special role to atomic wffs. So given that the old wffs in the old array were originally related to each other in the right way to make them a proof, then the new wffs in the new array will *still* be related in the right way to make them a proof. Any derivation built up the same way as our original proof will also be a correctly formed proof.

We can put the same point like this (compare §16.5). Take a correct PL proof. Show its structure down to the atomic level by systematically replacing its atoms with schematic variables (same atom, same replacement; different atoms, different replacements). Call the result a *(basic) proof schema*. Then

Any substitution instance of a proof schema is also a proof.

We get a substitution instance, of course, by systematically replacing schematic variables with wffs again.

24.5 '⊨' and '⊢'

(a) We introduced a useful notational convention in exercises, starting with Exercises 16(c*). We will be using it frequently, so let's now headline it:

Alongside the use of lower-case Greek letters for individual wffs, it is common to use upper-case Greek letters such as 'Γ' (*Gamma*), 'Δ' (*Delta*) to stand in for some wffs, zero, one or many. Further, we use 'Γ, α' for the wffs Γ together with α.

Unless explicitly indicated, you can take the wffs Γ to be finitely many in number.

(b) Recall now some standard metalinguistic notation from §14.2 and §16.4. Assuming the wffs Γ and γ all belong to some PL language, then:

We abbreviate the claim that the wffs Γ tautologically entail the conclusion γ as follows: Γ ⊨ γ.

We abbreviate the claim that γ is a tautology as follows: ⊨ γ.

We now add new, equally standard, companion notation:

We abbreviate the claim that there is a PL proof from premisses Γ to the conclusion γ as follows: $\Gamma \vdash \gamma$.

We abbreviate the claim that γ is a PL theorem – i.e. the claim that γ can be derived from zero premisses – as follows: $\vdash \gamma$.

The double turnstile is the *semantic* turnstile, defined in terms of the semantic property of being a truth-preserving inference. Correspondingly, the single turnstile is the *syntactic* turnstile, defined in terms of the syntactic property of being a well-constructed PL proof. So the turnstiles have quite different definitions.

(c)   Still, despite their quite different definitions, it is easy to see that the semantic and syntactic turnstiles march in step in many particular cases. For example, we know from §§14.2, 16.5, and 17.1 that for any PL wffs α, β, γ, we have

(1) $\vDash (\alpha \lor \neg\alpha)$,
(2) $(\alpha \lor \beta), \neg\alpha \vDash \beta$,
(3) $\alpha, \neg\alpha \vDash \gamma$.

And we now know from §§23.1, 21.5, and 20.9 respectively that these semantic facts are exactly matched by the syntactic facts that for any α, β, γ,

(1′) $\vdash (\alpha \lor \neg\alpha)$,
(2′) $(\alpha \lor \beta), \neg\alpha \vdash \beta$,
(3′) $\alpha, \neg\alpha \vdash \gamma$.

Likewise, we noted the following semantic principles in Exercises 16:

(4)   If $\alpha \vDash \gamma$, then $\alpha, \beta \vDash \gamma$,
(5)   If $\alpha \vDash \beta$ and $\beta \vDash \gamma$, then $\alpha \vDash \gamma$.

We now have parallel results about provability:

(4′)   If $\alpha \vdash \gamma$, then $\alpha, \beta \vdash \gamma$,
(5′)   If $\alpha \vdash \beta$ and $\beta \vdash \gamma$, then $\alpha \vdash \gamma$.

For the first, note that adding an unused premiss to a proof still gives us a correctly formed proof. For the second, we just take a derivation from α to β and splice that together with a proof from β to γ to get a proof from α to γ.

We can multiply such examples of how particular facts about provability match facts about tautological entailment. But we won't enumerate any more. That's because we will now see that, globally, the two sorts of fact must *always* march in step – as shown by this chapter's two major metatheorems.

24.6   Soundness

(a)   The first of these metatheorems is this:

Our PL proof system is *sound*: if $\Gamma \vdash \gamma$, then $\Gamma \vDash \gamma$.

As a special case, if $\vdash \gamma$ then $\vDash \gamma$.

Reading the turnstiles, if Γ *prove* γ, then Γ (tautologically) *entail* γ. In other words, our proof system really is trustworthy: a completed derivation of a wff from given premises is always a genuine proof showing that the conclusion is tautologically entailed by the premises. And if a wff is derivable from no premises, then it is a tautology. (It is only a very mild annoyance that 'sound' is used in elementary logic in two different ways – to say of a particular argument that it has true premises and makes a valid inference move, and to say of a formal proof system that its derivations are reliably truth-preserving.)

(b) A general comment on the very idea of soundness.

So far we have introduced just *one* family of formal languages, PL languages. And we defined a suitable notion of validity-in-virtue-of-logical-structure for inferences framed in a PL language, namely tautological validity. We have since introduced a Fitch-style framework for proving conclusions from premises in a PL language. The aim of this PL proof system all along has been to enable us to establish that various inferences are truth-preserving without trudging through a truth-table test. And certainly, we have chosen proof-building rules that intuitively *seem* reliable in virtue of the meaning of the connectives. So it would be Very Bad News if our proof system can after all lead us astray and purport to validate inferences that are *not* tautologically valid!

We are soon going to introduce another family of formal languages, QL languages, designed for regimenting quantificational arguments. And we will extend our Fitch-style framework to enable us to prove conclusions from premises in a QL language. We will eventually define a suitable notion of validity-in-virtue-of-logical-structure for arguments framed in a QL language, namely q-validity. Again, we will want to be able to rely on the so-called proofs – i.e. we will require every derivation of a conclusion from premises to be q-valid, making our QL proof system sound in the relevant sense.

And so it goes. Beyond the scope of this book, there are other formal languages equipped with different topic-neutral vocabularies, and there will be correspondingly different definitions of validity-in-virtue-of-logical-structure for arguments in such languages. We will typically want to design deductive systems for arguing formally in such languages. There will be many options other than Fitch-style deduction systems. But however they are structured, we will *always* require our deductive systems to be sound, i.e. we will require a 'proved' conclusion to validly follow from the given premises.

(c) Back to PL. You need to take away from this chapter an *understanding* of the claim that our proof system is sound. You *don't* need to know how to prove this claim. Still, the basic proof idea is quite straightforward. Let's have some terminology that we will highlight because we will want it later anyway:

> For brevity, premises and suppositions will now both be called *assumptions*.
>
> The *live* assumptions at a line of a proof are any available earlier assumptions, plus the wff on that line if it is itself an assumption.

And now say that the line of a PL proof is *good* if the wff on that line is tauto-logically entailed by the live assumptions at that line (if any).

A proof starts with a good line (a premiss is tautologically entailed by the live assumption at that line, itself!). As we can check, the allowed proof-building moves all take us from good lines to another good line. So every line of a proof is good. In particular the last line, where all temporary suppositions have been discharged, must be good – which is just to say the final conclusion will indeed be entailed by the initial premisses. For more details, see the Appendix, §A1.

24.7 Completeness

(a)   Now for the converse of the soundness theorem:

> Our PL proof system is *complete*: if $\Gamma \vDash \gamma$, then $\Gamma \vdash \gamma$.
>
> As a special case, if $\vDash \gamma$ then $\vdash \gamma$.

In other words, there are no 'missing rules' in our PL system. Given a tautolog-ically valid inference from PL wffs Γ, we can always derive its conclusion from Γ as premisses by a derivation in the system as it stands.

(b)   A general comment on the very idea of completeness. Of course, it is very welcome when we *can* find a complete proof system for inferences framed in a given class of logical languages, a system in which it is in principle possible to warrant all the logically valid inferences by correctly formed derivations.

We can do this in the present case. Our PL proof system is complete. And note, this isn't just *obvious*. A completeness proof will be non-trivial.

It turns out that we can similarly construct a complete proof system that captures all the q-valid inferences in QL languages. However, complete proof systems aren't always available. Some logical languages are too 'infinitary' for the relevant notion of validity to be fully captured by a finitely specifiable formal deductive system – though this has to be a story for another time. For the moment, we will just say: completeness in a proof system is highly desirable, but may not be obtainable once we go beyond the elementary cases considered in this book.

(c)   Again, what you should take away from this chapter is an *understanding* of the claim that our PL proof system is complete in the sense defined. You *don't* need to know how we establish this claim to be true.

There is more than one type of strategy for a PL completeness proof. In the Appendix, we will explain one strategy, whose leading ideas can then be devel-oped to give an analogous completeness proof of our future QL proof system. But these ideas are somewhat trickier to grasp than the simple idea underlying the soundness proof; so trying to summarize them here would not be very en-lightening. Let's therefore leave the details for enthusiasts to explore at the end of book, in §§A3, A4.

224

24.8   Double negation and excluded middle again

We finish this chapter by revisiting the double negation rule and its equivalent, the law of excluded middle. As we will see, these have a distinctive status that sets them interestingly apart from the other PL rules.

(a)   Start from the PL proof system which we codified in §24.2. Now simply omit the rule (DN). Call the resulting cut-down system IPL – the reason for the label will become clear in a moment. In the light of §23.3, we see that adding the rule (DN) to IPL is equivalent to adding the rule (LEM) which allows us to invoke an instance of the law of excluded middle at any stage in a proof. And the point we want to emphasize is that (DN) or (LEM) *are* substantive additions to IPL, enabling us to derive conclusions that do not follow if we can only use the rules of the cut-down system. To put it another way, (DN) – or equivalently, (LEM) – is independent of the other rules of the original system PL.

(b)   How do we *prove* the independence result? Here is a strategy. We find some new way of interpreting IPL and its connectives, an interpretation on which the rules of our cut-down deductive system would still be acceptable, but on which (DN) or (LEM) would plainly *not* be acceptable. It then follows that buying the rules of IPL can't commit us to (DN) or (LEM). Now, as we said when we first introduced it, the (DN) rule reflects the classical understanding of negation as truth-value-flipping. So an interpretation on which (DN) or (LEM) *doesn't* hold will have to revise the interpretation of negation. How can we do that?

It is natural to think of a correct assertion as one that corresponds to some realm of facts (whatever that means exactly). But suppose for a moment that we instead think of correctness as a matter of being informally provable or being fully justified or (for short) being *warranted*. Then here is a quite natural four-part story about how to characterize the connectives in this new framework:

(i) $(\alpha \land \beta)$ is correct, i.e. warranted, iff α and β are both correct, i.e. are both warranted.

(ii) $(\alpha \lor \beta)$ is correct, i.e. warranted, iff at least one disjunct is correct, i.e. there is a warrant for α or a warrant for β.

(iii)   A correct conditional $(\alpha \rightarrow \beta)$ must be one that, together with the warranted assertion α, will enable us to derive another warranted assertion β by using modus ponens. Hence $(\alpha \rightarrow \beta)$ is correct iff there is a way of converting a warrant for α into a warrant for β.

(iv)   Finally, $\neg\alpha$ is correct iff we have a warrant for ruling out α as leading to something absurd (given what else is warranted).

Now, suppose that – in keeping with this approach – we think of a correctness-preserving inference as one that preserves warranted assertibility. We can then still accept (EFQ) as essentially defining the absurdity constant – so the absurd can't be warrantedly assertible (or else everything would be assertible). And the familiar four *introduction* rules for the connectives will *still* be acceptable, for they will be warrant-preserving (think through why this is so). But – as we saw

– the various elimination rules in effect just 'undo' the effects of the introduction rules: so they should come along for free once we have the introduction rules.

Hence, in short, thought of as warrant-preserving rules, all our IPL rules can remain in place.

However (DN) will *not* be acceptable in this framework. We might have a good reason for ruling out being able to rule out α, so we can warrantedly assert $\neg\neg\alpha$. But that doesn't put us in a position to warrantedly assert α. We might just have to remain neutral. Likewise (LEM) will *not* be acceptable. On the present understanding, $(\alpha \lor \neg\alpha)$ would be correct, i.e. warranted, just if there is a warrant for α or a warrant for ruling out α. But again, must there always be a way of justifiably deciding a conjecture α in the relevant area of inquiry one way or the other? Some things may be beyond our ken.

Hence, if we want a proof system as a framework for arguments preserving warranted assertability, we shouldn't endorse (DN) or (LEM). (Be careful here. It is one thing to stand back from endorsing (LEM). It would be something else to actually *deny* some instance of (LEM). In fact, it is an easy exercise to show that, even in IPL, any wff of the form $\neg(\alpha \lor \neg\alpha)$ entails a contradiction!)

(c) So now we see the significance of the fact that the built-in (DN) rule is an outlier, not one of the introduction/elimination rules. Its special status leaves room for an interpretation on which the remaining rules – the rules of IPL – hold good, but (DN) doesn't. Hence (DN) is independent of the other rules.

True, our version of the argument might seem a bit too arm-waving for comfort; after all, the notions of warrant or informal proof are not ideally clear. But let's not fuss about that. For we can in fact develop a rigorous story inspired by these notions which gives us an entirely uncontroversial technical proof that (DN) and its equivalents are, as claimed, independent of the other rules of PL.

Things *do* get controversial when it is claimed that in some particular domain of inquiry (DN) and (LEM) really don't apply, because in this domain there can be no more to correctness than warrant or informal provability. For example, so-called *intuitionists* hold that mathematics is a case in point. Mathematical truth, they say, doesn't consist in correspondence with facts about objects laid out in some Platonic heaven (after all, there are familiar worries: what kind of objects could these ideal mathematical entities be? how could we possibly know about them?). Rather, the story goes, being mathematically correct is a matter of being assertible on the basis of a proof – meaning not a proof in this or that formal system but any proof satisfying informal mathematical standards. Take, then, a proposition like G, Goldbach's Conjecture that every even number (other than two) is the sum of two primes. We have no proof to warrant an assertion of G; we have no disproof which warrants ruling out G; and there's no guarantee that we can ever get a warrant, either way. So the intuitionist will say we are not in a position to hold $(G \lor \neg G)$ to be correct.

This view is radical and highly contentious – taken seriously, it involves having to reject swathes of standard mathematics, because it changes the logic we can use. For an intuitionist, the appropriate propositional logic for arguing with the connectives is not the full *classical* two-valued logic PL where (DN) and (LEM) hold, but rather the cut-down *intuitionist* logic we have already labelled IPL, because *this* is the right logic for correctness-as-informal-provability.

(d)   In an introductory logic book, we obviously can't even begin to discuss those intriguing issues about the nature of truth and provability in mathematics. But we have said enough to raise some horribly difficult questions. Are there really domains where we can't apply the full classical PL apparatus (even when we set aside such troublesome issues as vagueness and the proper treatment of paradoxical sentences like the Liar – see §10.3)? More generally, is there One True Logic, or should we be pluralists allowing different principles to govern reasoning in different areas of inquiry? Is a pluralist approach consistent with whatever is true in the thought that logic should be topic-neutral?

We can't pursue such weighty questions here. We will just have to follow standard practice and concentrate on the *classical* logic which includes the law of excluded middle, reflecting the classical understanding of negation as truth-value-flipping. For this is the logic which is routinely deployed by mathematicians – along with the rest of us, at least most of the time. Classical logic is, so to speak, the baseline against which alternative logics are usually measured: so it is – on almost everyone's view – the logic you need to understand first.

24.9   Summary

We have reviewed our Fitch-style proof system, restating the inference rules, and now specifying the permissible ways of assembling inferences together into correctly structured proofs.

In fixing the details of our system, various choices have had to be made. We noted in particular that we allow 'vacuous discharge'.

We defined the syntactic turnstile '⊢' (indicating provability) to go alongside the semantic turnstile '⊨' (indicating entailment). We noted particular cases where properties of '⊢' match properties of '⊨'.

But the properties of provability and entailment march in step in a more general way too. Our PL proof system is sound and complete. A conclusion derived from some premisses by a PL proof really is tautologically entailed by those premisses. And conversely, a conclusion tautologically entailed by some premisses can be derived from them by a PL proof. Proofs of these two key results do, perhaps, go rather beyond what you really need to know at an introductory level. However, we give outline versions in the Appendix.

We saw that (DN) and equivalents stand aside from the other PL rules, and encapsulate a so-called classical conception of negation. Intuitionists would argue that full classical logic overshoots, and only the cut-down propositional logic IPL which lacks (DN) and equivalents can be applied in general to mathematical reasoning.

Interlude: Formalizing general propositions

(a)   Propositional logic has provided us with a simple and approachable setting in which we can first encounter a whole range of absolutely fundamental logical ideas. So:

(1)   In Chapters 8 to 13 we saw why we might want to regiment some informal arguments into tidily formalized languages; and we then explored the syntax and semantics of the family of PL languages.

And since then we have approached questions of validity for PL inferences in two rather different ways.

(2)   In Chapters 15 to 16 we defined tautological validity and we explored the truth-table method for determining validity in this sense.

And then, having added the absurdity sign and the material conditional to our story about PL languages,

(3)   In Chapters 20 to 24, we have developed a natural deduction framework for showing the validity of inferences depending on the core sentential connectives, using intuitively correct step-by-step derivations.

Happily, we can show that the two approaches (2) and (3) validate just the same inferences. Our proof system doesn't overshoot by allowing us to construct proofs which aren't truth-preserving (the system is sound). And it doesn't undershoot by failing to validate some correct reasoning with the connectives (the system is complete).

(b)   And now, after all this work on propositional logic, we must at last move on. So where next? Consider the following logically valid arguments:

(1)   Felix is a cat. All cats are scary. So, Felix is scary.
(2)   Ludwig envies anyone Alma loves. Alma loves Fritz. So, Ludwig envies Fritz.
(3)   Each great philosopher is worth reading. Some logicians are also great philosophers. So some logicians are worth reading.
(4)   Some philosophers admire every logician. No philosopher admires any charlatan. So, no logician is a charlatan.

If we expose no more structure than the way in which whole propositional clauses are related by connectives (if any), then each of these arguments can only be assigned the utterly unreliable inferential form *A, B, so C.*

228

To explain the validity of these arguments, we will therefore have to dig deeper inside their premises and conclusions. What is crucial here is the presence of expressions of generality – i.e. *quantifiers* such as 'all', 'any', 'every', 'each', not to mention 'some' and 'no'. If we are to make any headway tackling the logic of general statements, we are therefore going to need a way of handling sub-propositional structure, and of explaining in particular the roles of quantifiers.

(c)   Ordinary language has a rich multiplicity of quantifiers. For example, 'all', 'any', 'every', and 'each' can *all* be used to express a general claim about everything of some kind. Though, as we will soon see, these four quantifiers also behave in significantly different ways. And this is just one of the complications we encounter with vernacular quantifiers. But we surely don't want to get bogged down in all the linguistic niceties.

So we will again follow the 'divide-and-rule' strategy we have already used to deal with propositional arguments. Just as we sidestepped the quirks of ordinary language by going formal in order to deal with the sentential connectives, the plan will be to introduce some well-behaved formal languages for regimenting ordinary-language quantified arguments, and then to investigate the logic of the neatly formalized arguments.

However, formalization in this case is a non-trivial task. The design brief for PL languages as explained in §8.7 is very simple and the resulting languages are correspondingly easy to work with. By contrast, the design rationale for our formal languages for quantifier logic is less immediately obvious. The resulting QL languages depart more from the structures of ordinary language. So we need to spend quite some time explaining carefully why these new languages have the form they do. And it will require a little effort to become fluent at handling them.

(d)   We go slowly. Take the 'Felix' argument again. As we said, this argument's validity depends on the internal sub-propositional structures of its premises and conclusion. And apart from the quantifier 'all', it is also crucial how the name 'Felix' recurs, and the way that '(is a) cat' and '(is/are) scary' recur.

When we formalize this sort of argument in a QL language we will therefore need some way of representing the internal structure of the relevant propositions by using formal *names* and *predicates*. So, to guide the syntax and semantics of our formalization, we need some preliminary remarks about proper names and logical predicates in ordinary language and about the simple sentences built from them. That's the business of the next chapter, Chapter 25.

Following this, in Chapters 26 and 27, we motivate and explain the general idea of a *quantifier-variable notation* for expressing general propositions in a disciplined way. Then in Chapter 28 we learn how to implement this pivotal Fregean idea in the formal setting of QL languages.

That won't be the end of the story (for example, we will eventually want to add a special *identity predicate* and *function expressions* to our languages for quantificational logic). But for the next chapters, we concentrate on the basics.

25 Names and predicates

As just indicated in the Interlude, before turning to consider the proper treatment of quantifiers in our formal languages, we need to start with some preliminary remarks about names and predicates.

25.1 Names and other 'terms'

(a) A language like English (here we include mathematical English) has a variety of devices for referring to particular objects. These include:

(i) *Proper names* – e.g. 'Alice', 'Socrates', 'Kilimanjaro', 'Vienna', '0', 'π', etc. (Ordinary proper names can of course be widely shared, as anyone called 'Peter Smith' can tell you. So context will be needed to fix *which* Peter Smith is being referred to by a particular use of that name.)

(ii) *Demonstratives* or demonstratively used *pronouns* – e.g. 'this', 'that guy', or simply 'she' (relying on context to fix the intended reference).

(iii) So-called *definite descriptions* of the form 'the F' – e.g. 'the tallest girl in the class' or 'the hardest logic problem'. (Once again, some context might be needed in these cases to fix the reference: which class, which set of problems?).

(iv) *Functional terms* – where we use an expression for a function like 'the mother of', 'the population of', 'the positive square root of', in combination with some other referring expression, to form a complex term like 'the mother of Alice', 'the mother of the mother of Alice', 'the father of that guy', 'the population of this town', 'the positive square root of π', '$\pi/2$', '$\sin(\pi/2)$'.

Rather differently, we also use what are variously called temporary names, quasi-names, arbitrary names, or

(v) *Dummy names* – consider, for example, legal uses of 'John Doe' and 'Jane Roe' ('If Jane Roe is the executor of John Doe's will, then ...'). Or consider the mathematician's use of 'a' in 'Let a be an arbitrary real number, ...'.

(b) In contrast to ordinary language, the logical languages in this book will not have *any* referring expressions which rely on context for their reference. But we will add expressions of type (i), (v), and then (iv) in stages, while setting aside definite descriptions for special treatment. So:

(1) Initially, our QL languages will only have the equivalent of unstructured *proper names* which unambiguously always refer to a fixed thing.

(2) Next, we will add *dummy names* to our formal languages, as these will play a key role in regimenting arguments with quantifiers.

(3) Eventually, we will also be able to form *functional terms* in our QL languages.

There is a standard label that generically covers expressions of these three types:

Proper names, dummy names, and functional terms are all *terms*.

More specifically, these are *singular terms* as opposed to plural terms (like 'the Alps', 'the wives of Henry VIII', 'the fifth roots of i' which refer to more than one thing), and also as opposed to general terms for kinds of thing (like 'mountain' or 'woman' or 'complex number').

We concentrate first on those singular terms which are proper names, and for both informal and formal cases we say (unsurprisingly!):

The object referred to by a proper name is the name's *reference.*

25.2 Predicates and their 'arity'

(a) According to school-room grammar, simple sentences can be parsed into 'subject' and 'predicate' (roughly, the subject tells us what/who the sentence is about, the predicate then tells us something concerning that subject-matter). For example, the following sentences are traditionally divided into subject then predicate as shown:

(1) Socrates / is wise
(2) Socrates / loves Plato
(3) Some philosopher / is wise

But modern logicians see things differently. First, we will insist that there is a deep difference between the roles of names like 'Socrates' and of quantifier-involving expressions like 'some philosopher', and so resist classifying them together as 'subjects'.

Second – the point emphasized in this section – we will generalize the school-room notion of a predicate. For us, a predicate is an expression which can combine with one *or more* singular terms or other expressions to form a sentence. For example, 'loves' in 'Socrates loves Plato' counts as a predicate in the logician's sense: it is a binary predicate taking two suitable expressions to form a sentence.

(b) It is convenient to have a device to use when we want to mark explicitly *where* one or more names can be attached to a predicate to form a sentence (let's for now take simple combinations with names to be the most basic case). We can use dots and dashes, as in '... is a cat', '... loves —'. But here's another standard device: we can use numbered counters to mark slots where names can go, as in '① is a cat', '① loves ②', '① is between ② and ③', etc.

To be clear: earlier, we informally used an expression like '*n* is a man' to represent a *whole* sentence, with the schematic letter standing in for some particular name (see for example §3.3). By contrast, '① is a man' represents just *part* of a sentence, a predicate, with the counter indicating where a name (or other expression) would need to be added to get a sentence.

So: the ordinary-language predicates '① is a cat', '① is scary', '① mews', '① killed themself' (for example) take one name or other suitable completion to form a sentence. While '① loves ②', '① is a pupil of ②', '① took ② to task', '① and ② are married to each other' all take two names, different or the same, to form a sentence. And similarly, '① is between ② and ③' takes three names. Call these unary, binary, ternary predicates respectively (or less formally, one-place, two-place, three-place predicates). And generalizing:

A *k*-ary predicate is an expression which takes *k* names (or other suitable expressions) to form a sentence.

The number of names that a predicate takes to form a sentence is its *arity*.

(c) Consider, however, the English sentences

(1) Tom and Dick cowrote a book,
(2) Tom, Dick, and Harry cowrote a book,
(3) Tom, Dick, Harry, and Jo cowrote a book,

and so on. Or for a logical example (using quotation marks for clarity), consider

(1′) 'P' and 'Q' entail '(P ∧ Q)',
(2′) 'P', 'Q', and 'R' entail '((P ∧ Q) ∧ R)',
(3′) 'P', 'Q', 'R', and 'S' entail '(((P ∧ Q) ∧ R) ∧ S)',

and so on. Do such examples show that some ordinary-language predicates like 'cowrote a book' (or 'entail') can combine with *varying* numbers of singular terms for people (or terms for wffs) to form a sentence? Arguably so.

However, when we go formal, we will – as is usual – insist that our built-in QL predicates are tidily behaved and each has a definite arity; so in particular, each combines with a *fixed* number of terms to make an atomic wff.

(d) Now to refine our notation and the associated notion of arity. There is a useful convention that places attached to predicates which are marked in the same way are to be filled in the same way – for example, we can fill out '① killed ①' to get 'Seneca killed Seneca' and 'Mark Anthony killed Mark Anthony' but not 'Nero killed Poppaea'. So we can say that '① killed ①' takes *one* name, albeit twice over; and it is naturally classed as another *unary* predicate because it is equivalent to '① killed themself'.

Understood this way, the arity of a predicate is represented by the number of *different* counters that get attached in our notation. (We do, however, allow different slot-marking counters to be filled out the same way – compare §3.2(b). So 'Seneca killed Seneca' counts as one way of filling out the binary predicate '① killed ②' alongside 'Nero killed Poppaea'.)

25.3 Predicates, properties and relations

(a) What do predicates *do*, semantically? Informally: unary predicates express properties, binary predicates express relations between two things (or between a thing and itself), ternary predicates express three-way relations, and so on.

For example, in the sentence 'Socrates is snub-nosed', the unary predicate '① is snub-nosed' is used to ascribe the property of being snub-nosed to Socrates. In the sentence 'Romeo loves Juliet', the binary predicate '① loves ②' is used to say that the binary relation of loving holds between Romeo and Juliet taken in that order, with the first loving the second. Life and love being what they are, it matters which name goes into which slot attached to the predicate here: for Romeo can stand in the relation of loving to Juliet without, conversely, Juliet loving Romeo. Similarly, in the sentence 'York is on the rail line between London and Edinburgh', the predicate '① is on the rail line between ② and ③' expresses a ternary relation between the three cities – again, the order in which their names appear matters.

(b) So far, so good. Except that the notion of a property/relation does come freighted with a *lot* of unwanted baggage. For example, many philosophers urge us to distinguish what they take to be genuine properties like *being human* and *being wise* and *having zero mass* from trumped-up fakes like *being either a logician or a neutrino* and *being green if it is Tuesday and tasting like coffee otherwise*. And philosophers argue about where to draw the genuine/fake line.

By contrast, logicians are generous souls who talk about properties and relations in a cheerfully inclusive way (we certainly don't want to get entangled in the philosophers' metaphysical debates). For us, then, talk about predicates expressing properties/relations will officially mean no more than this:

A unary predicate *expresses a condition* that an object o has to meet if the predicate is to be true of o; a binary predicate expresses a condition that the objects o_1, o_2 taken in that order have to meet if the predicate is to be true of them; and so on – where any condition, however complex or gerrymandered, is countenanced.

(c) Now for some useful terminology:

If an object o meets the condition expressed by a given unary predicate, then – for short – we will say that o *satisfies* that predicate.

233

Likewise, suppose that the two objects o_1 and o_2, taken in that order, meet the condition expressed by a binary predicate, then we will say that the ordered pair of o_1 and o_2, notated $\langle o_1, o_2 \rangle$, satisfies the predicate.

After ordered pairs come ordered triples, quadruples, quintuples, etc. There is nothing very mysterious about finite ordered sequences of objects: the traditional general term for them is *tuples*. So a k-tuple is just a finite ordered sequence of k objects $\langle o_1, o_2, \ldots, o_k \rangle$ – and we can take a 1-tuple to be an object by itself. The angled bracket notation for tuples is, by the way, pretty standard. Then:

If a k-tuple of objects meets the condition expressed a k-ary predicate, then the k-tuple *satisfies* the predicate.

25.4 Predicates: sense vs extension

(a) We said in §7.2 that the sense of a declarative sentence is the aspect or ingredient of its meaning that fixes the condition under which the sentence is true. Similarly, the *sense of a unary predicate* – to start with that case – *is the aspect of its meaning which fixes the condition which some object must meet if the predicate is to be true of it*. So, to borrow a Fregean example, compare the predicates '(is a) horse/steed/nag/gee-gee'. The use of these alternative expressions will no doubt give a different colouring to the sentences which contain them. However, these predicates arguably share the same sense, i.e. they can be taken to mean the same in truth-relevant respects and express the same property. In other words, they express the same equine condition that an object has to meet if the predicate is to be true of it.

(b) The sense of a sentence is, to repeat, the truth-relevant aspect of its meaning. But knowing the sense of a sentence isn't, in general, enough to tell us whether the sentence actually *is* true; that usually depends on how things are in the world. And it is exactly similar with predicates. The sense of a unary predicate is the truth-relevant aspect of its meaning. But knowing the sense of a predicate – i.e. knowing the condition it expresses – isn't, in general, enough to tell us which objects *do* satisfy the predicate. That usually depends on how things are in the world. Let's say that

The objects which *do* satisfy a unary predicate form the predicate's *extension*.

Then the point we have just made is that the extension of a predicate will in general depend on the situation in the world.

Take for example the unary predicate 'is a philosopher'. In the world as it is, Socrates is in the predicate's extension, along with Plato and Aristotle. But he might not have been. For example, there is another way the world might have been in which Socrates, that man, opts for a quiet life and doesn't hang around the agora corrupting the youth. And perhaps Socrates in that possible world has an argumentative sister (who doesn't exist in the actual world), and *she* satisfies 'philosopher' there.

(c)   Evidently, then, a predicate with a fixed sense can acquire different extensions as we consider different possible ways the world might be. Conversely, predicates with different senses can have the same actual extension.

For example, the two sentences 'Jo is a human' and 'Jo is a terrestrial featherless biped' express different thoughts, because the predicates 'is a human' and 'is a terrestrial featherless biped' express different conditions. Something could in theory satisfy one condition without satisfying the other: in some possible worlds, there are humans who are not terrestrial (humans could move to Mars), and there are terrestrial featherless bipeds who aren't human (suppose Neanderthals had survived). But still, these two predicates do happen to have the same extension as things actually stand – or so our traditional example assumes.

For another example, the predicates 'is a unicorn' and 'is a dragon' plainly do not have the same sense – satisfying the condition for being a unicorn is not the same thing as satisfying the condition for being a dragon, and you could have a world with creatures of the one kind but not the other. That's why to ask whether dragons ever roamed the earth is not to ask whether unicorns ever roamed the earth. But these two predicates in fact happen to have the same empty or null extension in the world as it is.

(d)   The sense of a binary relational predicate is likewise that aspect of its meaning which fixes the condition which an ordered pair of objects must meet in order to satisfy the predicate. And pairs which satisfy the condition will form the predicate's extension. Generalizing, the sense of a k-ary predicate fixes the condition on which k-tuples of objects satisfy the predicate. And

The k-tuples which satisfy a k-ary predicate form the predicate's extension.

Again, k-ary predicates with different senses can have the same extension. While, keeping its sense fixed, a k-ary predicate can have different extensions in different possible situations.

25.5   Sets

We have just talked of some objects (or ordered pairs of objects, etc.) as 'forming' the extension of a predicate, and we have talked too of an object as being 'in' the extension of a predicate. It very natural, therefore, to speak of an extension as a *set* of objects (or a *set* of ordered pairs of objects, etc.). But just what does this commit us to?

For example, do we really need to think of the extension of '① is a philosopher' as a distinct new object in its own right, over and above the people who satisfy the predicate? Or can we take talk of a set of philosophers here just as a *façon de parler* – a handy way of speaking in the singular about the philosophers, plural?

A lot of elementary talk of sets can be construed in the lightweight second way. Saying that n is in the set of Fs is frequently just another way of saying that n is one of the Fs, i.e. is an F. Still, the non-committal set idiom is still useful. In ordinary language we often find it natural to use singular talk of a collection, class, group, bunch, and the like when talking about some things, plural: and it can seem rather artificial to try strenuously to avoid it.

Up to now, we *have* avoided talk of sets – so, for example, we preferred to talk of some wffs, plural, tautologically entailing a conclusion rather than of a *set* of wffs entailing the conclusion (which is the more usual idiom). Still – partly for convenience, partly to align ourselves with other treatments – we will start occasionally talking of sets or collections. However, unless explicitly signalled, *this is to be interpreted in the non-committal lightweight way that can in principle be paraphrased away into plural talk.* (When apparent reference to some objects can be paraphrased away, some philosophers talk of these as being merely *virtual* objects: in this sense, unless otherwise indicated, our sets can be treated as virtual sets.)

25.6   Names: sense vs reference

It is pretty much agreed on all sides that we need a sense vs extension distinction for predicates. Do we need an analogous sense vs reference distinction for proper names? Frege famously thought so, but the issue is hotly contended.

Here, just to think about, is an argument for the view that we *do* need some sense vs reference distinction for names.

> For vividness, we can take an engaging fictional example. 'Superman' and 'Clark Kent' are two different names for the same person. It is evidently possible for someone to have both names in their vocabulary but not to know that these *are* two names for the same person. Lois Lane is initially in this state. And these names are then associated by her with very different Fregean 'modes of determination' – i.e. very different ways of picking out what is, as it happens, the same person. So, roughly speaking, she thinks of Superman as the handsome superhero in tights, and of Clark Kent as the bespectacled reporter. *That* is why Lois can rationally assert 'Superman can fly' yet deny 'Clark Kent can fly' even though, in the circumstances, these sentences attribute the same property to the same person and therefore must in fact have the same truth value. And that's also how 'Superman *is* Clark Kent' can be quite startlingly informative for her.
>
> Hence, for the purposes of interpreting Lois's talk about 'Superman' and 'Clark', and in order to make her related behaviour comprehensible, it seems that we need to know more than merely the reference of the name she uses. We do need to distinguish her two different ways of thinking about the man, the different 'modes of determination' which Lois associates with the different names – and so, as Frege would put it, we need to distinguish the different *senses* the names have for her. Which is why, just as two predicates

with the same extension can have different senses, we need to recognize that two names with the same reference can have different senses.

Or so, in the very briefest terms, a Fregean argument begins. However, all this is contentious, and we certainly can't follow the twists and turns of the debates here. Fortunately, for our purposes we don't need to. Why so?

25.7   Reference, extension, and truth

(a)   When is a basic name/predicate sentence true? When the named object meets the condition expressed by the predicate. Or equivalently:

A sentence formed from a name and a unary predicate is true if and only if the reference of the name is in the predicate's extension.

The sense of a predicate combines with how things are in the world to fix the extension of the predicate: but it is this extension which then does the work of determining the truth values of basic sentences involving that predicate. Similarly, whether or not names have senses, it is the reference of a name which determines the truth values of basic name/predicate sentences involving that name. Generalizing to cover basic sentences with any number of names:

A sentence built from a k-ary predicate and k names in order is true if and only if the k-tuple of objects referred to by the names is in the extension of the predicate.

For example, the extension of the predicate '① loves ②' (defined over people) comprises those ordered pairs of people such that the first of them loves the second. And a sentence of the form 'm loves n' is true just when the pair of objects denoted by 'm' and 'n', in that order, is in the extension of the predicate.

(b)   How should we read this in the special case where a name is 'empty', i.e. lacks a reference? Ordinary language can acquire proper names which fail to refer: for example, 'Vulcan' was introduced as the name of a postulated planet closer to the sun than Mercury, and it turned out that there is no such planet.

What should we say about the truth values of simple name-predicate sentences involving 'Vulcan'? One view is that we should say that they are false. Another view is that we should say that they are neither true nor false, because there is no reference to be either in or not in the relevant predicate's extension – the empty name produces a 'truth value gap'. We won't need to decide, however: for when we turn to consider formalized languages, we will simply ban empty names – the proper names in our QL languages will always have a reference.

(c)   Let's introduce some standard terminology:

Two names are *co-referential* iff they have the same reference.

Two predicates are *co-extensional* iff they have the same extension.

> A sentence provides an extensional context for names and predicates – in short, is *extensional* – iff swapping a name in it for a co-referential name and/or swapping a predicate in it for a co-extensional predicate cannot change the truth value of the sentence.

Basic name/predicate sentences are extensional. Since what determines the truth value of a basic sentence as far as a name is concerned is its reference, swapping a name for a co-referential one can't change the truth value of the sentence. Co-referential names can be intersubstituted *salva veritate* (i.e., preserving the truth). Likewise, since what determines the truth value of a basic sentence as far as a predicate is concerned is its extension, swapping a predicate for a co-extensional one can't change the truth value of the sentence. Co-extensional predicates can also be intersubstituted salva veritate.

(d)   What goes for the simplest sentences formed from just names and predicates goes for plenty of other ordinary-language sentences. However, English is not a *fully* extensional language: in other words, some sentence constructions yield *intensional*, i.e. non-extensional, contexts.

For example, compare the claims

(1)   Daisy believes that Dobbin is a unicorn.
(2)   Daisy believes that Dobbin is a dragon.

Little Daisy may believe that Dobbin, dressed up for the fête, is a real unicorn without believing him to be a dragon. Which shows that (1) and (2) can have different truth values even though the predicates '① is a unicorn' and '① is a dragon' have the *same* null extension. Here, co-extensional predicates cannot be intersubsituted salva veritate.

How can this be so? Plainly, what makes (1) true and (2) false are facts about the contents of Daisy's beliefs, facts about how she is thinking about things. And a Fregean will say that these contents are given by the respective *senses* of 'Dobbin is a unicorn' and 'Dobbin is a dragon' and these sentence-senses are determined by the *senses* of the predicates here. So, in this case, it isn't the shared null extension of the predicates which contributes to fixing the truth values of (1) and (2) but rather the predicates' different senses.

Similarly, compare

(3)   Lois believes that Superman can fly.
(4)   Lois believes that Clark Kent can fly.

Still going along with the familiar fiction, initially (3) is true while (4) is false. Here, co-referential names cannot be intersubsituted salva veritate.

How can this be so? A Fregean will say that (3) and (4) make claims about the contents of Lois's beliefs, and these different contents are given by the respective senses of 'Superman can fly' and 'Clark Kent can fly', and hence are determined by the senses of 'Superman' and 'Clark Kent'. So in these cases, the shared reference of the names isn't what determines truth values. (Relatedly, the expression 'Lois believes that ① can fly' can't attribute a genuine property to what's named by a term filling the gap, otherwise we'd have to say Superman/Clark Kent both has and doesn't have the property. So that gappy expression won't count as a property-ascribing expression either, i.e. it isn't a real predicate.)

(e) We need not worry here whether the Fregean gives the right diagnosis for these cases: what is uncontroversial is that English provides many non-extensional contexts like these. And the important point is that, in contrast, our QL languages will lack any contexts like the ordinary-language 'n believes that ...'. In QL languages, the truth values of sentences will be fixed (so far as the contributions of names and predicates goes) by references and extensions alone – in short, QL *languages are fully extensional.*

But if senses don't have to enter the story about what fixes the truth values of QL sentences, they also won't have to enter into the story about what makes for the validity of QL arguments (since validity is defined in terms of truth preservation). So – as far as our logical inquiry into QL arguments goes – we won't need to have a developed theory of sense.

Which is a relief. We should be grateful for small mercies!

25.8 Summary

The non-logical building blocks of QL languages – at least at the initial stage – are names and predicates (only later will we add function expressions). This chapter prepares the ground for moving to these formalized languages by saying something about names and predicates in ordinary language.

We distinguish proper names from other ways of picking out particular objects (unlike definite descriptions and functional terms, they are not internally complex and, unlike demonstratives, names can be treated as context-independent).

A logical predicate is an expression that can, in particular, combine with some names to form a sentence, and which expresses a condition which the named objects have to meet if the sentence is to be true.

We need to distinguish the sense of a predicate from its extension. Arguably, we need a parallel distinction between the sense and reference of a name.

It is the references of names and the extensions of predicates that determine the truth values of simple sentences built from names and logical predicates, both in ordinary language and in QL languages. But in QL languages, as we will see, this applies to all the complex sentences too – what matters about names and predicates in fixing the truth values of complex sentences will still be just references and extensions.

For convenience, we will talk of extensions as being *sets*: but don't over-interpret this.

26 Quantifiers in ordinary language

We now turn to consider how we are going to express general propositions in our formal languages. Expressions of generality in a natural language like English behave in complex ways: this chapter explores just some of the tangles. The following chapter then explains a strategy for handling quantification in formalized languages so as to avoid these many vagaries of ordinary language by using a so-called quantifier-variable notation.

26.1 Which quantifiers?

As we noted in Exercises 3, Aristotle in his *Prior Analytics* concentrates on four forms of quantified propositions corresponding to the English 'All F are G', 'No F are G', 'Some F are G', and 'Some F are not G'.

But that's just a handful among many ordinary-language constructions involving expressions which quantify. Consider, for example:

> Every/any/each F is G,
> At most one/at least three/exactly five F are G,
> Finitely/infinitely many F are G,
> There are exactly as many F as G,
> Few/many/almost all F are G,
> Half/a quarter of the F are G,
> Numerous/a lot of/several/enough F are G.

And perhaps, as we'll see in Chapter 40,

> The F is G

belongs on the list too.

Those constructions all take two general terms (replacing 'F' and 'G') to form a sentence. By contrast, consider

> Everything/something/nothing is G,
> Everyone/everybody/someone/somebody/no one/nobody is G,
> There is/there exists a G,
> There exist two/at least four/many Gs,
> There are infinitely many Gs.

In these cases we have to replace just the one schematic letter 'G' with a general term to get a sentence.

We can naturally speak, then, of *binary* vs *unary* quantifier constructions. And a first question is: which of these varied binary and unary constructions are we going to care about in developing our logical quantification theory?

We will in fact be focusing on so-called *universal* ('every'/'any'/'all'/'each') and *existential* ('some'/'there is') quantifiers. These both come in binary and unary versions: we'll consider in the next chapter how the two versions are related. We will also get a treatment of 'no' quantifiers for free because we will have negation in our formal languages and 'no' is equivalent to 'not some'. Later, when we add an identity predicate to our formal languages, we will be able to cope with numerical quantifiers like 'at least five/exactly five/at most five' and we can also give a formal treatment of 'the'. This way, we arguably get all the quantifiers we need for core mathematical and scientific purposes, and for a great amount of common-or-garden reasoning too.

26.2   Every/any/all/each

(a)   Consider the following English sentences, used as stand-alone claims:

(1) Every play by Shakespeare is worth seeing.
(2) Any play by Shakespeare is worth seeing.

These surely come to the just same, expressing the same generalization about all the plays. Yet compare how (1) and (2) embed in wider contexts. For example, contrast

(3) If every play by Shakespeare is worth seeing, I'll eat my hat.
(4) If any play by Shakespeare is worth seeing, I'll eat my hat.

Some find (4) ambiguous. But on the natural reading – expressing a general dismissal of the Bard's plays – (4) says something quite different from (3). Similarly for the following:

(5) I don't believe that every play by Shakespeare is worth seeing.
(6) I don't believe that any play by Shakespeare is worth seeing.

On the natural reading of (6), it says something quite different from (5).

So the quantifiers 'every' and 'any' are certainly not *always* interchangeable. For another example to show this, consider the following pair (a 'Monro' is a Scottish mountain over 3,000 feet):

(7) If Jack can climb every Monro, he can climb every Monro.
(8) If Jack can climb any Monro, he can climb every Monro.

The first is a tautology; the second could well be false on the reading which says that, if Jack can climb any one Monro, then he can climb them all, even the most challenging.

(b)   What about 'all' and 'each'? Take for example

(9) All plays by Shakespeare are worth seeing.
(10) Each play by Shakespeare is worth seeing.

As stand-alone claims, these again seem to convey just the same message as (1) and (2). And now consider

(11) If all plays by Shakespeare are worth seeing, I'll eat my hat.

(12) I don't believe that all plays by Shakespeare are worth seeing.

(11) is equivalent to (3), and (12) to (5). So, at least in these cases, sentences containing 'all' behave like sentences with 'every' rather than 'any'. Similarly for the corresponding 'each' sentences.

So can we perhaps say this: 'all', 'each', and 'every' are just stylistic alternatives, the main difference being that 'all' goes with a plural construction while 'each' and 'every' go with the corresponding singular form? Well, we will also have to allow some other grammatical adjustments (for example, 'All my books are blue' corresponds to 'Each of my books is blue' and 'Every one of my books is blue'). But now compare

(13) You can fit all (of) Jane Austen's novels into a single ordinary-sized book.

(14) You can fit each of Jane Austen's novels into a single ordinary-sized book.

I take the first to be false, the second true; 'all' here is naturally read as 'all, taken together', 'each' is more naturally read as 'each, taken separately'. Similarly, compare

(15) Jill can legally marry all (of) Bill's brothers.

(16) Jill can legally marry each of Bill's brothers.

By my lights, the second may be true, while the first isn't, given our laws against polygamy.

But if you disagree (perhaps you find the sentences in each of the last pairs to be ambiguous between the taken-together/taken-separately readings), then no matter: your view equally reinforces the point that these English expressions of generality do behave in complex ways. And we haven't yet mentioned other complications – for example, the way that 'all' but not 'every/each' can go with so-called mass terms: thus we can say 'All snow is white' but not 'Every/each snow is white'.

(c) Given that we are interested in the logic of arguments involving ideas of generality, but are not especially interested in theorizing about the tangled English usage of 'every/any/all/each', or similar complications, what to do?

As announced in the last Interlude, we will follow the same strategy that we introduced to cope with the connectives. We will explain how to construct QL languages which avoid the complex multiplicity of the English 'every/any/all/each' quantifiers by having just *one*, simply-behaved, way of forming universal generalizations of this type. These formalized languages will also replace 'some' and its close relations 'there is at least one' and 'there exists' with a single simply-behaved substitute. We can now divide and rule again (see §8.6); in other words, we can tackle the assessment of many quantificational arguments in two stages. We translate a given argument into a suitable QL language, enabling us

242

to represent quantified messages in a uniform, tidy, and easily understood way. And *then* we assess the resulting formalized argument for validity.

26.3   Quantifiers and scope

Wanting to sidestep the tricky multiplicities of English usage is one major motivation for going more formal. However, there is another, rather deeper, reason for adopting an artificial language to regiment quantified propositions for logical purposes. For we need to avoid the structural ambiguities which beset English quantified sentences. Let's explore.

(a)   For a warm-up exercise, compare the following sentences:

(1)   Some senior Republican senators took cocaine in the nineteen-nineties.
(2)   Some women died from illegal abortions in the nineteen-nineties.

As a shock headline, (1) can be read as saying, of some present Republican senators, that they have a dark secret in their past (namely that they dabbled in illegal drugs in the nineties). But (2) is not to be read, ludicrously, as saying of some present women that they have a secret in *their* past (namely that they earlier died of an illegal abortion). The intended claim is of course that some women living in the nineties died then from illegal abortions.

With some mangling of tenses, and adding brackets for clarity, we might represent the intended readings of the two sentences respectively as follows:

(3)   (Some senior Republican senators are such that)(in the nineteen-nineties it was true that) they use cocaine.
(4)   (In the nineteen-nineties it was true that)(some women are such that) they die from illegal abortions.

Here the final verbs are now deemed to be tenseless.

So a compelling way of describing the situation is to say that the tense modifier and the quantification are understood as having different *scopes* in the messages intended by (1) and (2) – compare §8.5 on the idea of scope. But note that the shared surface form of the two original sentences doesn't explicitly mark this difference. We implicitly rely on context and plausibility considerations in order to arrive at the natural readings. These two readings are, however, represented unambiguously by (3) and (4): in these sentences the relative scopes of the tense modifier and quantifier phrase are now fixed by the obvious rule that the first bracketed modifier has wider scope, and applies to what follows.

Now consider

(5)   Some philosophers used to be enthusiastic logical positivists.

Are we saying that some current philosophers went through a positivist phase in their brash younger days? Or are we saying that, once upon a time, some then philosophers were keen positivists? The intended message could be

(6)   (Some philosophers are such that)(it used to be true that) they are enthusiastic logical positivists,

or alternatively we could be claiming

(7) (It used to be true that)(some philosophers are such that) they are
enthusiastic logical positivists.

Without any context to help us construe (5), the claim is simply ambiguous.
And the ambiguity is structural (the individual words aren't ambiguous). The
issue is: which has wider scope, i.e. which governs more of the sentence, the
generalizing operator or the tense modifier?

(b) Mixing together ordinary expressions of generality and tense-modifying
operators is therefore prone to produce scope ambiguities. So too is mixing vernacular quantifiers with what logicians call *modal* operators – i.e. with expressions of necessity and possibility.

Consider, for example, that notorious philosophical claim

(8) Every perceptual experience is possibly delusory.

Does this mean that each and every perceptual experience is one which, taken
separately, is open to doubt, i.e.

(9) (Every perceptual experience is such that)(it is possible that) it is delusory?

Or is the thought that the whole lot could be delusory all at once, i.e.

(10) (It is possible that)(every perceptual experience is such that) it is delusory?

These claims are certainly different, and it is philosophically important which
reading is meant in arguments for scepticism about the senses. Even if (9) is
true, (10) doesn't follow. Compare, for example,

(11) Every competitor might win first prize,

and the following two readings:

(12) (Every competitor is such that)(it is possible that) they win first prize,
(13) (It is possible that)(every competitor is such that) they win first prize.

It could be that (12) is true because it's a fairly run competition of skill with
very well matched entrants, while (13) is false because the rules governing the
knock-out rounds ensure that only one ultimate winner can emerge.

Now, some English-speakers rather firmly claim that (8) means (9); others
equally firmly say it means (10). I take that as some evidence for a third view,
namely that in ordinary use (8) is dangerously ambiguous. In what order is
the intended message built up using the quantifier and the modality? Surface
grammar doesn't fix this. (Again, you don't have to agree. Even if you think that,
in correct usage, (8) and (11) are unambiguous, you must still acknowledge the
key point, namely that the interpretation of such quantified sentences crucially
involves paying attention to questions of scope.)

(c) Exploring the logic of tense operators and of modal operators is beyond the
scope(!) of this book. So, let's turn to the sorts of cases that more immediately
concern us. First, consider what happens when we mix everyday expressions of

generality with *negation*.

Here is one kind of example. A statement of the form 'Some *F*s are not *G*s' is usually heard as being entirely consistent with the corresponding 'Some *F*s are *G*s'. For example, 'Some students are not keen on logic' is no doubt sadly true; but it is consistent with the happier truth 'Some students are keen on logic'.

But now suppose Jack says 'Some footballers deserve to earn five million a year'. Jill, in response, takes a high moral tone, expostulates about the evils of huge wages in a world of poverty and deprivation, and emphatically concludes: 'Some footballers do *not* deserve to earn five million a year'. Jill plainly does not intend to be heard as saying something compatible with Jack's original remark! Which shows that, although vernacular English sentences of the form 'Some *F*s are not *G*s' are more usually construed as meaning

(14) (Some *F*s are such that)(it is not the case that) they are *G*s,

in some contexts the negation can be understood to have wide scope, with the resulting message being

(15) (It is not the case that)(some *F*s are such that) they are *G*s.

Another example. In the *Merchant of Venice*, Portia says

(16) All that glisters is not gold,

which is naturally construed in context as meaning that not everything that glisters (i.e. glitters) is gold. So what Portia intends to say is equivalent to

(17) (It is not the case that)(all that glisters is such that) it is gold.

But now compare the following sentence which in surface form is just like (16):

(18) All that perishes is not divine.

This is more naturally read with the quantifier and the negation scoped the other way around, i.e. as equivalent to

(19) (All that perishes is such that)(it is not the case that) it is divine.

In sum: like the logical operation of negation, quantifying may be thought of as an operation which can govern more or less of a complex sentence. And when an assertion mixes a negation and a quantifier, we may not be able to read off the intended relative scopes of the two logical operators simply from the surface form of the sentence being used – unless we set out to be very ploddingly explicit in the manner of (17) and (19). We can again be left with a scope ambiguity – as in these examples, perhaps:

(20) Jill didn't finish every book.
(21) Everyone's not yet arrived.
(22) I would not give that to anyone.

(d) Consider next some sentences containing more than one quantifier (Joel Hamkins's nice example):

(23) On Mother's Day, every mother will get some gift.
(24) At the Crack of Doom, the clouds will part and every human will look up to see some angry and jealous god.

The first is surely to be read as saying that every mother will get her own present; the second is more naturally read as saying that the same angry and jealous god will reveal itself to all alive that dread day. We can express the core parts of these claims respectively as follows:

(25) (Every mother is such that)(there is some gift such that) she will get it.

(26) (There is some angry and jealous god such that)(every human is such that) they will look up to see it.

So on the obvious reading of (23), the 'every' quantifier has the wider scope, i.e. governs more of the sentence, while we read (24) with the 'some' quantifier having wider scope.

Here is another example of an 'every/some' sentence, this time one which can quite reasonably be read with the quantifiers scoped either way:

(27) Everyone loves a certain someone.

Is the claim that each person (perhaps in some contextually indicated group) has their own beloved? Or is the claim that there is someone who is the apple of every eye?

Given an English sentence involving more than one quantifier, context and plausibility considerations may indeed often serve to privilege one particular reading and prevent misunderstanding – as is the case with (23) and (24). But there is always the potential for unresolved ambiguity, as perhaps in (27). And the two readings of (27) *do* express different propositions – you can't infer one from the other (compare §5.3).

(e) Note, by the way, that these four kinds of scope ambiguity, arising when everyday quantifiers are mixed with tense, modality, negation, or with other quantifiers, do not occur when *proper names* are used instead of the quantifiers. Consider, for example:

(28) Jack took cocaine in the nineteen-nineties.
(29) Jill might possibly win.
(30) Michael does not deserve five million a year.
(31) Romeo loves a certain someone.

We need to fix who is being talked about and the unit of currency. But none of these claims is *structurally* ambiguous – issues of scope do not arise. Which is why it is often said that, unlike quantifiers, genuine names are *scopeless*.

(f) Finally, having introduced the notion of quantifier scope, let's revisit a pair of examples from the previous section:

(32) If every play by Shakespeare is worth seeing, I'll eat my hat.
(33) If any play by Shakespeare is worth seeing, I'll eat my hat.

The difference between these can now be seen as involving issues of scope. In (32), the generalization is definitely confined inside the antecedent of the conditional – if this narrow-scope generalization is true, I'll eat my hat. By contrast, the more natural reading of (33) gives the generalization wider scope, outside the conditional – any play by Shakespeare is such that, if that one is worth seeing, I'll eat my hat.

There might be some mileage in the view that (in the absence of other indications) 'every' defaults to narrow scope with respect to other logical operators, and 'any' defaults to wide scope. But everyday usage really doesn't seem to be consistent in this respect: I continue to find (8) scope-ambiguous, for example.

(g) We have said enough. Yes, we can argue about the interpretation of particular examples: but, there is no question that ordinary-language expressions of generality can generate scope ambiguities. Part of the design brief for our formal QL languages, therefore, must be that – as with PL languages – the scope of logical operators, now including the quantifiers, is always clear and unambiguous.

26.4   Fixing domains

Suppose that, at the beginning of class, I ask 'Is everyone here?'. Plainly I am not asking about everyone now living. I have in mind those who have signed up for the logic class, and I am asking if all of *them* are present. I continue: 'I am impressed: someone solved that extremely tricky optional homework problem!'. Again, I am not talking about some student in another college or in another year, let alone just some random person; I mean that there is someone among the current logic class who solved the problem. So, although not explicitly restricted, 'everyone' and 'someone' here are naturally understood as ranging over a rather particular group of people; these people form the intended current *domain* of the quantifiers – or, in rather grander terminology, they make up the *universe of discourse*. (An 'every/any/all/each' quantifier is then universal in the sense of making a claim about every object in the relevant universe of discourse.)

As in our logic class example, we often leave it up to the context to fix the domain which the quantifiers are ranging over, i.e. to determine who or what currently counts as 'everyone' or 'everything'. For more examples, consider e.g. 'Everyone enjoyed the concert', 'Make sure everyone has a glass of wine', 'Everything fitted into two suitcases', 'Can you finish everything this morning?'.

Even if we use a binary quantifier with a general term qualifying the quantifier, what we are quantifying over can still vary with context: consider e.g. 'Every seat is booked', 'All passengers have now boarded', 'Any laptops should now be switched off', 'Each baby started crying' – which seats, which passengers, which laptops, which babies?

Moreover, we are adept at following mid-conversation *shifts* in the intended domain of our quantifiers, using contextual cues and common sense to follow implicit changes in who counts as 'everyone' or what counts as 'everything' (or who/what counts as a relevant 'someone'/'something'). To continue with our logic class example, suppose I go on to say: 'As we saw, everyone agrees that modus ponens is a good form of inference for the ordinary-language conditional'.

You immediately pick up that I am this time generalizing not over the members of the class but over the mainstream logical authors whom we were explicitly discussing last week. And when I later remark, 'Someone, however, has denied that modus ponens is always reliable', you don't take me to be contradicting myself: you charitably suppose that I am now moving on to cast the generalizing net rather wider, beyond the standard authors we've already mentioned, to include logical outliers and mavericks.

Ordinary discourse, then, often leaves it merely implicit who or what we are quantifying over. But when we start regimenting arguments for logical purposes – with the aim of making everything ideally clear and determinate – we won't want to rely on contextual clues or interpretative charity. We will need a policy for explicitly and clearly fixing the domains of quantifiers in QL languages.

26.5 Summary

Ordinary English expressions of generality include both unary and binary quantifiers. These behave in complicatedly tangled ways. Consider for example the availability of 'all', 'every', 'any', and 'each' to express universal generalizations, and compare the different behaviour of these quantifiers in various contexts.

Note too how sentences involving quantifiers and other logical operators are prone to scope ambiguities.

Quantifiers like 'everything/everyone' will range over different things from case to case. In ordinary usage, we typically need extraneous input to fix the current domain of quantification.

This gives us good reason to introduce formal QL languages with a more restricted number of simply-behaved quantifiers, where there aren't scope ambiguities, and where domains of quantification are clearly fixed.

Exercises 26

The following are not questions with straightforward answers. But, before reading on, you should pause to consider:

(1) What further complexities in the behaviour of ordinary-language quantifiers like 'all', 'any', 'every', 'each', 'some', 'no', etc. strike you?

(2) We saw that some quantifiers (apparently) come in both unary and binary forms. Is there any reason to suppose one form is more fundamental than the other?

(3) What might be the limitations of a logic of quantifiers which focuses just on Aristotle's four main forms of quantified sentences, as noted at the beginning of this chapter?

27 Quantifier-variable notation

The discussion in the last chapter suggests three desiderata for formal languages apt for exploring the logic of generality. We want to avoid the complicated multiplicity of ordinary-language ways of expressing general claims. We want to devise our notation so that the scope of a quantifying operation is always unambiguous. And we want to clearly fix what our quantifiers range over. This chapter explains how to design our QL languages to meet these requirements.

27.1 Quantifier prefixes and 'variables' as pronouns

(a)   First, how are we going to avoid scope ambiguities? Well, as we saw in §26.3, we can usually keep things unambiguous even in ordinary language by rephrasing using *quantifier prefixes* like 'everyone is such that', 'some senior Republican senators are such that', 'there is some gift such that', 'every perceptual experience is such that', etc., where these are linked to later pronouns such as 'they' and 'it'. For example, we can disambiguate 'Every student admires a certain book' by offering the alternative readings

  (1) (Every student is such that)(there is a book such that) they admire it,
  (2) (There is a book such that)(every student is such that) they admire it.

These paraphrases are unambiguous – the order of the two quantifier prefixes in these sentences determines their relative scope, with the first one having wider scope (and so governing what follows it).

  So we immediately have an attractive and quite natural model to emulate in designing languages for use in quantificational logic:

  In our formal QL languages, we will unambiguously render general propositions by using quantifier prefixes linked to later pronouns.

(b)   How are we going to handle pronouns formally? Note that there are different uses of ordinary-language pronouns. There are, for example, demonstrative uses – as when I point across the room and say '*She* is a great logician' (I could have equivalently used a demonstrative and said '*That* woman is a great logician'). For my use of the pronoun here to be in good order, I must successfully pick out a particular woman. Contrast the claim 'No woman is such that she is immortal'. In this case, 'she' plainly doesn't denote a particular woman! Nor does

249

it in 'Every woman is such that she is mortal'. In these cases, the pronouns are not doing straightforwardly referential work but rather link back to, are 'bound' to, the previous quantifier prefix. Pronouns like this are classed as one kind of *anaphoric* pronoun (literally, they 'carry back'). But we will call them simply *bound* pronouns.

So let's sharpen our question: what shall our formal languages use as bound pronouns tied to quantifier prefixes?

(c) Suppose we want to unambiguously render the more natural reading of

(3) Everyone loves a certain someone,

by using quantifier prefixes linked to later pronouns. Our gender-neutral singular pronoun is 'they'; but it plainly won't do to write

(4) (Everyone is such that)(there is someone such that) they love them.

For that is again ambiguous. Who is doing the loving?

We need, therefore, some way to indicate which pronoun is bound to which quantifier prefix. In examples (1) and (2) we could exploit the difference between the person-including 'they' and the impersonal 'it' to link them to the personal and impersonal quantifier prefixes respectively. But what can we do more generally? One ordinary-language option is to use something like

(5) (Everyone is such that)(there is someone such that) the former loves the latter.

But that's not a very useful model to adopt – if only because it isn't easy keeping track of what counts as 'the former' or 'the latter' as we manipulate propositions while working through an argument. So here's a neat alternative trick:

We will henceforth use single letters as additional pronouns: $x, y, z, \ldots$.

We then explicitly tag our quantifier prefixes with these new pronouns – as in '(Everyone x is such that)', '(Someone y is such that)' – in order to make it entirely clear which quantifier is bound to which later pronoun.

Hence instead of (5) we can write

(6) (Everyone x is such that)(there is someone y such that) x loves y.

Similarly, the other reading of (3) – as in 'Everyone loves a certain someone, namely Kylie' – gets unambiguously rendered as

(7) (There is someone y such that)(everyone x is such that) x loves y.

Compare and contrast

(8) (There is someone x such that)(everyone y is such that) x loves y.

which unambiguously says that someone (Jesus?) loves us all.

Of course, we have borrowed our new pronoun symbols from the mathematicians, following *one* use they make of so-called *variables*. Consider, for example, the arithmetical truism

(9) For every number x, $x + 1 = 1 + x$.

What does this say? The same as: 'every number is such that it plus one equals one plus it'. So we see that in this sort of case the mathematician's 'x' is essentially doing the work of a pronoun like 'it'. And while using 'x's etc. as pronouns tied to more or less explicit quantifier prefixes may be most familiar from the maths classroom, there is nothing irredeemably mathematical about this usage.

(d)   Quine wrote "Logic is an old subject, and since 1879 it has been a great one." Why that date? It is when the *Begriffsschrift* was published. And it is to Frege there that we owe the key insight that we can make the scope of quantifiers unambiguously clear by using a *quantifier-variable* notation where quantifier prefixes get linked to variables-as-pronouns. This will be our notation too.

27.2   Unary vs binary quantifiers

We have already said in §26.1 that we are going to build just two kinds of quantifiers into our QL languages, corresponding to 'every/all' and 'some/there is'. But we also noted that the ordinary-language versions of these come in two forms, unary and binary. And this still applies when we use quantifier prefixes linked to variables. So compare these two:

> (Everything x is such that) x is physical,
> (Every philosopher x is such that) x is wise.

Or, generalizing, compare the schematic forms

> (Everything x is such that) x is G,
> (Every F, x, is such that) x is G.

The first quantifier construction takes one general term G, the second takes two general terms F, G to form a sentence. Again, we can call the first form of quantifier unary, the second binary. We might also say the second form involves a *restricted* quantifier, as the role of the F term here is to restrict what the initial quantifier prefix ranges over.

What, then, is the relationship between the unary and binary forms of quantifier here? A natural view might be that binary/restricted quantifiers are in fact the basic case. The apparently unary 'Everything is G' is really a special case of 'Every F is G', where F is replaced by the colourless, all-inclusive, 'thing'. Similarly, for example, 'Somebody is G' is a special case of 'Some F is G', where F is replaced by 'body' (meaning *person*).

However, it seems we can also go in the other direction, and instead treat the unary versions of the 'every' and 'some' quantifiers as basic. Thus consider

(1)   Every elephant has a trunk,

or the regimented version in quantifier-variable form

(2)   (Every elephant x is such that) x has a trunk.

These look to be equivalent to the *quantified conditional*

(3)   (Everything x is such that)(if x is an elephant, then x has a trunk),

where now the quantifier is unary. Likewise, consider the generalization

(4) Some elephant trampled the grass,

or the regimented version

(5) (Some elephant *x* is such that) *x* trampled the grass.

These look to be equivalent to the *quantified conjunction*

(6) (Something *x* is such that)(*x* is an elephant and *x* trampled the grass).

We will need to say more about these claimed equivalences. But for the moment, let's assume that we can – without mangling content too much – exchange binary 'every' and 'some' for unary quantifiers plus connectives.

So which way shall we jump? Do we develop our formal quantifier-variable treatment of 'every/some' general propositions in a way that treats the binary versions as basic? Or do we treat the unary quantifiers as basic?

Taking the second line means being less faithful to the surface forms of natural language. However, it *does* keep our formal apparatus particularly simple, and this is the line adopted by most logicians ever since Frege. So:

> We will only build *unary* quantifiers into our QL languages – just formal versions of '(everything *x* is such that)' and '(something *y* is such that)', etc. We then express restricted quantifications by using conditionals and conjunctions inside the scope of these unary quantifiers.

Note though that treating unary quantifiers as basic *is* an independent move, over and above the fundamental decision to adopt a quantifier-variable notation.

27.3 Domains

(a) We have decided then that our formal QL languages will only have built-in 'every' and 'some' quantifiers in their unary forms. What do these quantifiers range over? As we noted in the last chapter, ordinary discourse often leaves it up to context and interpretative charity to settle what counts as 'everything' or 'everyone'. And the universe of discourse is often allowed to shift as conversation progresses. By contrast, we will want everything in our formal languages to be explicit and stable, with nothing left to guesswork.

The standard approach is to take the quantifiers in a particular QL language to all run over the *same* unshifting domain. And a further standard stipulation is that domains always contain at least one object. Hence

> To interpret a QL language, we fix at the outset, once and for all, one common non-empty domain for its quantifiers. We do this by giving a description *D* of the domain in the glossary for the language (where at least one thing satisfies *D*).

For convenience we can think of this domain, the objects the quantifiers of a language run over, as forming a set: but don't over-interpret the lightweight set talk here (see §25.5).

252

(b)   The one-common-domain convention buys us clarity and simplicity, though at the cost of some artificiality, including some departure from mathematical practice. For mathematicians using semi-formal language often use different quantifiers with different domains, associated with different sorts of variables. For example, an arithmetician might typically use lower case variables for numbers, and upper case variables for sets of numbers; an algebraist might typically use letters from early in the alphabet for scalars, and letters from the end of the alphabet for vectors. Simultaneously using quantifiers tied to distinct sorts of variables to range over distinct domains is very natural. However – and to repeat, this is the logician's initial convention – our QL languages will have just *one* sort of variable ranging over *one* inclusive domain. Hence, when we want to quantify over different sorts of things in a single QL language, we will again have to explicitly restrict our all-inclusive quantifiers using connectives.

(c)   Domains can be small – comprising just, say, *the students signed up to the logic class*. However, as we said, we will ban completely empty domains. In other words, we assume that a QL language isn't talking about nothing at all (but see Chapter 34).

Domains can also be very large – as when our quantifiers range over *everyone now living*, or over *all elementary particles* or *all positive integers*. The quantifiers of standard set theories range over a wildly infinitary universe of sets (fully caffeinated sets, treated as objects in their own right; compare §25.5).

Can we allow a language's universe of discourse to be absolutely everything – every object there is, of any sort? Yes, *if* that idea makes sense. However, that's a big 'if'! (To get the flavour of *one* reason why there might be a problem here, consider this thought, plausible if we take sets seriously. Given any universe of objects, however many there are, there is always *another* object, namely the set of all the objects collected together so far. So any proposed totality of objects is always further extensible by another object, and so we can never determinately pin down '*all* objects' in a stable way. Or so one story goes. But we can't tangle with this troublesome line of argument here.)

27.4   Quantifier symbols

(a)   We now take one more step, moving from stilted-English-using-variables-as-pronouns towards something even closer to a standard logical QL language. We introduce the *quantifier symbols* ∀ *and* ∃, as follows:

> Instead of writing '(everything/everyone x is such that)', we will simply use the very terse notation '$(\forall x)$', with the rotated 'A' reminding us that this can also informally be read as 'for all x'.
>
> And instead of '(something/someone y is such that)' or '(there is something/someone y such that)' we will use '$(\exists y)$'. Here, the rotated 'E' reminds us that this can also informally be read as 'there exists y such that'.

Assume that we are working in a context where the quantifiers range over, say, all people. Then our three examples from §27.1, there numbered

(6) (Everyone x is such that)(there is someone y such that) x loves y
(7) (There is someone y such that)(everyone x is such that) x loves y
(8) (There is someone x such that)(everyone y is such that) x loves y,

can now be very neatly abbreviated in turn as follows:

(6′) $(\forall x)(\exists y)$ x loves y
(7′) $(\exists y)(\forall x)$ x loves y
(8′) $(\exists x)(\forall y)$ x loves y.

Note that you obviously can't infer (7′) from (6′). That would indeed what we called a quantifier shift fallacy in §5.3 – and now it is clear why the label is apt!

(b)   Keeping the same universe of discourse, now consider how we can express restricted generalizations using our new notation. Take for example

(1) Everyone in the class has arrived.

Then, following the suggestion made in §27.2, we can render this as

(2) (Everyone x is such that)(if x is in the class, then x has arrived),

which now becomes

(3) $(\forall x)$(if x is in the class, then x has arrived),

where '$(\forall x)$' still ranges over all people. Taking another step of symbolization by borrowing the symbol for the material conditional, this is arguably equivalent to

(4) $(\forall x)(x$ is in the class $\rightarrow x$ has arrived).

The next sentence, however, is potentially ambiguous

(5) Everyone in the class has not arrived.

We can, in some contexts, understand this with 'not' having wide scope, i.e. we can understand (5) as conveying the message unambiguously expressed by

(6) $\neg(\forall x)(x$ is in the class $\rightarrow x$ has arrived).

But in other contexts, we will understand (5) as meaning

(7) $(\forall x)(x$ is in the class $\rightarrow \neg x$ has arrived).

In (6) and (7) the relative scopes of the negation and quantifier are now transparently clear.

Likewise,

(8) Some footballer deserves great riches,

which we can render using a prefixed unary quantifier as

(9) (Someone x is such that)(x is a footballer and x deserves great riches),

can now be partially symbolized as

(10) $(\exists x)(x$ is a footballer $\wedge x$ deserves great riches).

And what about the following sentence, which taken out of context is ambiguous?

254

(11)   Some footballer does not deserve great riches.

We can unambiguously render the two possible readings like this:

(12) $(\exists x)(x$ is a footballer $\wedge \neg\; x$ deserves great riches),

(13) $\neg(\exists x)(x$ is a footballer $\wedge\; x$ deserves great riches).

(c)   The sort of unholy mixture of English and logical symbolism in our examples in this section is often called *Loglish*. It is easily understood, given a grasp of the connectives and a grasp of the new quantifier symbols in their abbreviatory role. As we will see in the coming chapters, going via varieties of Loglish as a halfway house greatly eases the transition between ordinary language and fully formalized QL languages.

27.5   Unnamed objects

Now a simple point, but one that we should stress: not everything in a domain need have a fixed proper name! This has two important implications.

(a)   Let's use $(\forall v)A(v)$ informally to represent a Loglish sentence starting with the quantifier prefix $(\forall v)$, where $A(v)$ is an expression with one or more occurrences of the variable v. Let $A(n)$ be the result of replacing all the occurrences of v in $A(v)$ with the proper name n. Then we will say that $A(n)$ is an *instance* of the quantified sentence $(\forall v)A(v)$. For example '(Ludwig is in the class → Ludwig has arrived)' might be an instance of '$(\forall x)(x$ is in the class → x has arrived)'.

Now, what holds of everything in a domain holds for any particular named thing (we assume names in use do refer to things in the current domain). So from $(\forall v)A(v)$ we can infer any corresponding particular instance $A(n)$.

But the reverse is false. It could be that for any available name n in the language, $A(n)$ is true but $(\forall v)A(v)$ is still false because some unnamed object fails to satisfy the condition expressed by A. For example, it may be that – as the Psalmist sings – the Lord "telleth the number of the stars; he calleth them all by their names". But *we* certainly don't have names for all the stars. And if we say 'All stars contain iron' (for example) – i.e. '$(\forall x)\; x$ contains iron', where the quantifier ranges over stars – then our claim wouldn't be made true just by the fact that the *named* stars all happen to contain iron.

(b)   Similarly, let $(\exists v)A(v)$ informally represent a Loglish sentence starting with the quantifier prefix $(\exists v)$. And we will say that $A(n)$ is an instance of the quantified sentence $(\exists v)A(v)$ too.

Now, since what holds of a particular named thing holds of something in the domain (keeping the assumption that names currently in use do refer to things in the current domain), from any instance $A(n)$, we can infer $(\exists v)A(v)$.

Again the reverse is false. It could be that $(\exists v)A(v)$ is true, even if each particular instance $A(n)$ is false (where n is a name already in our language). Consider, for example, the true claim '$(\exists x)\; x$ is a nameless star'!

255

27.6   A variant notation

(a)   The quantified sentence

(1) $(\forall x)(\exists y)$ x loves y

corresponds to one reading of 'Everyone loves a certain someone'. It is now important to emphasize that the particular choice of variables here is quite arbitrary. The role of the variables is simply to tie the quantifier prefixes to the places either side of 'loves'. To express the same message we could therefore equally well use

(2) $(\forall y)(\exists z)$ y loves z, or $(\forall y)(\exists x)$ y loves x, or $(\forall z)(\exists y)$ z loves y, or ...

Here is a variant notation which ties quantifier prefixes to places graphically. Take the predicate '① loves ②'. Then instead of (1) or (2) we could write simply

(3) $\forall \exists$ ① loves ②

And similarly, instead of using

(4) $(\exists y)(\forall x)$ x loves y

to express the other reading of 'Everyone loves a certain someone', we could write

(5) $\exists \forall$ ① loves ②

For another example, consider again

(6) $(\forall x)$(if x is in the class, then x has arrived).

We can think of this as involving the complex predicate 'if ① is in the class, then ① has arrived' (using a repeated counter to indicate that the gaps are to be filled in the same way – see §25.2(d)). And we could alternatively express the message that everyone satisfies this predicate by writing

(7) $\forall$ (if ① is in the class then ① has arrived)

Of course, this braces-and-gaps graphical notation is difficult to typeset, and it gets difficult to read when more than one prefixed quantifier symbol gets tied to multiple later gaps. No wonder, then, that we will stick to the now conventional quantifier/variable notation. Still, note that the use of a variable to link a quantifier to some place(s) in an expression is really just a variant on our graphical notation. For example,

(1) $(\forall x)(\exists y)$ x loves y,

(3) $\forall \exists$ ① loves ②

are to be explained as ultimately meaning just the same. This re-emphasizes that the particular choice of variable-letters is irrelevant, so long as we keep fixed the pattern of ties from quantifier prefixes to places-occupied-by-variables.

(b)   The graphical notation also vividly brings out another important point. In the graphical notation, the quantifier symbol $\forall$ by itself doesn't yet implement a generalization – it needs to be tied to slots in the following gappy expression. It is ∀-plus-the-ties which does the work.

It is exactly similar when we use variables. ∀ without its variable does not yet implement a generalization. Nor does the quantifier prefix (∀x) by itself. It is the prefixed quantifier plus the later linked variable(s) – the combination that together forms what we can call a quantifier operator – which does the work.

Now, linguists use 'quantifier' to mean expressions in ordinary language like 'every' and 'some' etc. The nearest equivalent in Loglish – i.e. the simple expressions which determine the *kind* of generalization we are making – are the quantifier symbols ∀ and ∃: and some writers do indeed call these simply 'quantifiers'. If we alternatively hijack the word 'quantifier' for the operator that does the work of forming a generalized claim, then – as we've just noted – it is the quantifier prefix *plus* its linked variables which really deserves the label. However, it is also quite usual to call the quantifier prefix (∀x) by itself a 'quantifier', even though that arguably labels the wrong thing.

But let's not get hung up on the terminological point. Let's relax and agree to cheerfully use the word 'quantifier' in whichever way is convenient in context.

27.7 Summary

At the beginning of the chapter, we listed three desiderata to guide the design of our formal QL languages. We can now indicate how we are going to meet each one in the following chapter.

A primary goal is to devise our notation so that the scope of a quantifying operation is always clear and unambiguous. We will meet this central requirement by using quantifier prefixes tied to variables-as-pronouns in our QL languages.

It is also important to avoid the complex multiplicity of ordinary-language ways of expressing general claims. So we are going to restrict ourselves to just two types of quantifier prefixes in QL languages, corresponding to the ordinary-language 'every' and 'some' in their unary versions. We will symbolize these using '∀' (tagged with a variable) for 'every', and '∃' for 'some'.

We want to clearly fix what our quantifiers range over. We will do this by the crude-but-effective method of simply stipulating, when setting up a formal QL language, the common domain of quantification for all its quantifiers.

So our QL languages have only unary quantifiers, and the quantifiers in a particular language all run over the same domain. It remains to be seen just how expressive the resulting formal languages are. How well, for example, can we capture the content of ordinary-language binary or restricted quantifications?

28   QL languages

The previous chapter motivated and explained the crucial new idea of a quantifier-variable notation for expressing generality. In this pivotal chapter, we see how to construct QL languages which incorporate this sort of notation.

28.1   QL languages – a glimpse ahead

The informal Loglish of §27.4 introduces a symbolic quantifier-variable notation and recycles the familiar symbols for the connectives. But it keeps English for non-logical vocabulary. Our more formal QL languages will now use symbols for names and predicates too. So we will symbolize

(1)   Romeo loves Juliet

by the likes of

(2)   Lrj,

using lower case (sans serif) letters like 'r' and 'j' for names, upper case letters like 'L' for predicates, and following a standard convention where we write predicates *before* the names or variables they apply to. And instead of

(3)   (Everyone x is such that)(there is someone y such that) x loves y

or the Loglish version

(4) $(\forall x)(\exists y)$ x loves y,

in a QL language we will, for example, write

(5) $\forall x \exists y$ Lxy.

Similarly, instead of

(6)   (Everyone x is such that)(if x is in the class then x has not arrived)

or the Loglish version

(7) $(\forall x)(x$ is in the class $\rightarrow \neg x$ has arrived),

a QL language will provide something like

(8) $\forall x(Cx \rightarrow \neg Ax)$.

with the one-place predicates having the obvious interpretations.

Let's take one more initial example. The claim

(9)   Every philosopher admires some logician

258

is potentially ambiguous. But the more natural reading can be unambiguously rendered like this, using unary quantifier prefixes:

(10) (Everyone x is such that)(if x is a philosopher, then (there is someone y such that)(y is a logician and x admires y)).

Using Loglish shorthand, this becomes

(11) $(\forall x)(x$ is a philosopher $\rightarrow (\exists y)(y$ is a logician $\wedge x$ admires y)).

And this goes into a suitable QL language – with the predicate letters appropriately (re)interpreted – as

(12) $\forall x(\mathsf{P}x \rightarrow \exists y(\mathsf{L}y \wedge \mathsf{A}xy))$.

Once you have grasped the quantifier-variable notation in its informal Loglish guise, then, it really is quite a small step to understand formal QL languages. The rest of this chapter now introduces these languages, in three main stages.

28.2   Names, predicates and atomic wffs in QL: syntax

(a)   The atomic wffs of a QL language are formed from *predicates* with fixed arities combined with the right number of *terms* – see §25.1(b) and §25.2(b). The only terms we are going to be introducing in this chapter are *proper names*. (It will be important that QL languages also have an unlimited supply of further terms in the guise of so-called dummy names. But we don't really need to introduce them until §32.1. Much later, we also introduce functional terms.)

So, for now, the *non-logical* vocabulary of a QL language – the vocabulary which can vary from language to language – will comprise just names and predicates. We want to keep our symbolism uncluttered. So we will use *single letters* (perhaps with primes) for these non-logical building blocks of QL languages, just as we used single letters for the non-logical building blocks of PL languages.

As noted, we normally use *lower-case* letters from mid-alphabet for proper names and use *upper-case* letters for predicates (compare our earlier informal use of letters like 'n' to stand in schematically for names and the likes of '(is) F' to stand in for predicates). Hence, in summary:

> The built-in non-logical vocabulary of a QL language can include
>
> > *proper names*, usually letters like: m, n, o, ...;
> > *predicates*, usually letters like: F, G, ..., L, M, ..., R, S, ...
>
> Proper names are *terms*.
>
> Each predicate is assigned a fixed arity and will take a fixed number of terms to form an atomic wff.

(b)   In English we can put predicates *after* names (as in 'Felix is scary') or *between* names (as in 'Romeo loves Juliet' or 'Jo prefers Jack to Jill'). And in the informal notation introduced in Chapter 1, we represented the simplest name/predicate sentences by the likes of 'n is F', again following the order of ordinary language, and inserting an 'is' for readability. In QL languages, by the convention we announced, we put the predicate *before* the names (or other terms), and we don't need the equivalent of 'is' to glue them together:

> In a QL language, a predicate of arity k followed by k terms from the language forms an atomic wff – perhaps, for example: Fm , Lnm , Loo , Rnmo , ...

Note, however, that this way of structuring atomic wffs *is* no more than a default convention, blessed by tradition. Later we will allow some exceptions to the predicates-first rule. We can also allow the use of non-letter symbols for names and/or predicates.

28.3 Names, predicates, and atomic wffs in QL: interpretation

(a) Now for interpreting the QL symbolism we have so far. Proper names refer to objects (in that broad sense of 'object' that can include people and mountains, stars and molecules, numbers and metric spaces, etc.). Predicates express conditions for objects, or tuples of objects, to satisfy.

And how do we fix the reference of a name or fix the condition expressed by a predicate? By giving a glossary, which for us will be in English. So:

> A glossary for a QL language interprets a QL proper name by associating it with an English name or other expression which (in context) unambiguously refers to some unique object.
>
> A glossary interprets a QL predicate of arity k by associating it with some English expression giving the condition which a k-tuple of objects needs to satisfy if the formal predicate is to be true of those objects.
>
> An atomic QL wff formed by a k-ary predicate followed by k proper names says that the named objects taken in order satisfy the condition expressed by the predicate.

As in the PL case, glossaries here fix interpretations, not truth values. Whether an interpreted QL atomic wff is true will depend, in particular, on the extension of the relevant predicate, and *that* is up to the world. See §25.7 again.

(b) An important proviso: *the condition expressed by a predicate must be sharp enough for it to be quite determinate whether or not an object satisfies the condition.* This ensures that the sentences of QL languages will be like the wffs of PL languages in having definite truth values (compare §10.3). Ordinary language has vague predicates with borderline cases: it is natural to say, for example, that it can be indeterminate whether Bill is bald, neither true nor false. By our determinacy assumption, QL languages must lack such predicates.

So, when we interpret a formal predicate by associating it with an English predicate, we have to quietly assume that any vagueness in the English has been tidied away or can for current purposes just be ignored.

(c)   Now a neat little dodge. *We will allow the case where a formal predicate has arity zero.* By our syntactic rule, a predicate of arity zero followed by zero terms forms an atomic wff. So a predicate of arity zero just *is* already an atomic wff, comparable to an atom of PL. Hence we will interpret a predicate of arity zero by assigning it a sentence in a glossary, again just like a PL atom.

It obviously makes no real difference whether we say (i) a QL language can have predicates of various arities from one up, and can also have propositional letters as well, or (ii) a QL language can have predicates of various arities from zero up. The second way of putting it is just rather appealingly neater.

28.4   One example: introducing QL$_1$

That's the first stage of language-building done. At the level of syntax, we specify the non-logical vocabulary of a QL language by listing its built-in proper names and listing its built-in basic predicates, fixing the arity of each predicate as we go. Then, at the level of semantics, we give a glossary for these names and predicates. We then have rules which tell us how to form and interpret atomic wffs using these names and predicates.

Let's take a particular example, the language we will call QL$_1$. We can neatly package the syntactic and semantic stories together, like this:

> In the language QL$_1$, the *proper names* are just
>
> > m: Socrates,
> > n: Plato,
> > o: Aristotle;
>
> and the *predicates* are just
>
> > F: ① is a philosopher,
> > G: ① is a logician,
> > H: ① is wise,
> > L: ① loves ②,
> > M: ① is a pupil of ②,
> > R: ① prefers ② to ③.

Read this in the obvious way. The arity of the interpreting informal predicate fixes the arity of the corresponding formal predicate. And then match the *j*-th place after the formal predicate to the informal predicate's place marked with the *j*-th counter. For example, the predicate R followed by three names says that the first named individual prefers the second to the third.

So here are seven atomic wffs from QL$_1$ (formed according to our construction rule in §28.2) together with their interpretations (following our interpretation rule in §28.3, given the language's glossary):

> Fm: Socrates is a philosopher.
> Hn: Plato is wise.
> Lnm: Plato loves Socrates.

Loo: Aristotle loves himself.
Mon: Aristotle is a pupil of Plato.
Rnmo: Plato prefers Socrates to Aristotle.
Romo: Aristotle prefers Socrates to himself.

28.5   Adding the connectives

(a)   The second stage of QL language-building is very straightforward. We simply take over from PL languages the familiar connectives plus the absurdity sign.

> If α and β are wffs of a given QL language, so too are $\neg\alpha$, $(\alpha \wedge \beta)$, $(\alpha \vee \beta)$, and $(\alpha \rightarrow \beta)$. The absurdity sign $\bot$ is also a wff of any QL language.
>
> The connectives are to be interpreted as before – as (tidied-up) negation, conjunction, inclusive disjunction, and the material conditional.
>
> The absurdity sign can be thought of as before as expressing a non-specific contradiction.

Given these newly added rules for wff-building with connectives, the following are therefore also wffs of QL_1, with their associated interpretations:

¬Fm: Socrates is not a philosopher.
(Go → Ho):   If Aristotle is a logician, he is wise.
(Hn ∧ Lmn):   Plato is wise and Socrates loves him.
(Rnmo → (Lom ∧ ¬Lon)): If Plato prefers Socrates to Aristotle,
                   then Aristotle loves Socrates but not Plato.

(b)   We should strongly emphasize that connectives in a QL language do remain essentially sentential connectives. So we must render 'Plato and Aristotle are philosophers' into QL_1 as

(Fn ∧ Fo)

and not, repeat *not*, as the ill-formed

F(n ∧ o).

In English, as we noted in §8.2, 'and' can connect two names as well as two sentences; but in QL languages it is quite different – '∧' cannot connect names.
   Similarly, to render 'Aristotle is a logician and is wise' into QL_1, we must use

(Go ∧ Ho)

and not, repeat *not*, the ill-formed

(G ∧ H)o.

Again, unlike the English 'and', the QL connective cannot connect predicates.

28.6   Syntax for the quantifiers

(a)   Now for the key third stage, adding quantifiers to our formal languages. First, then, we need to add to the logical vocabulary of QL languages as follows:

Every QL language has an unlimited supply of *variables*, starting

x, y, z, ...

It also contains the two *quantifier symbols* (read, roughly, 'for all', 'for some')

∀, ∃.

We tag a quantifier symbol with a variable to get a quantifier prefix, or *quantifier* for short, as in

∀x, ∀y, ∀z, . . . ;

∃x, ∃y, ∃z, ...

Quantifiers of the first kind are called *universal* quantifiers; quantifiers of the second kind are called *existential* quantifiers.

Note that, unlike in our informal Loglish, we will *not* put brackets round quantifier prefixes in our official QL languages (we don't really need them, and the more austere bracket-free notation is nowadays at least as common).

When we come to specifying QL languages more carefully, we will want to be a bit more definite about what counts as a variable. But for now the key point is that symbols for variables are to be sharply distinguished from symbols for terms like proper names.

(b)   How, then, do we form quantified QL wffs? Variables serve as bound pronouns, and must always be introduced along with the quantifier prefixes which bind them. So the idea is this. We take a wff containing one or more occurrences of some term – for now, that means some proper name. Then, in one step, we replace all the occurrences of that term with a variable not already in the wff, and prefix a quantifier using the same variable. The result is a new QL wff.

Let's restate the rule symbolically using a couple of new conventions (following our policy of using Greek letters for schematic letters):

τ (*tau*, the Greek *t*) will be used to stand in for a term.

ξ, ζ (*xi*, *zeta*, the Greek *x*, *z*) will be used to stand in for formal variables.

Then here is our syntactic rule for forming quantified wffs.

Suppose $\alpha(\tau)$ stands in for a QL wff involving one or more occurrences of the term τ, and $\alpha(\xi)$ is the expression which results from replacing the term τ throughout $\alpha(\tau)$ by a variable ξ new to that wff.

Then $\alpha(\xi)$ is *not* a wff. However, $\forall\xi\alpha(\xi)$ and $\exists\xi\alpha(\xi)$ *are* QL wffs.

Schematic notation like $\alpha(\tau)$ is common. But note, it *doesn't* signify that the represented expression contains brackets, only that it contains the term τ!

Some handy shorthand: we will say that a wff $\forall\xi\alpha(\xi)$ formed from $\alpha(\tau)$ in this way is formed by *universally quantifying on* τ. Similarly, $\exists\xi\alpha(\xi)$ is formed from $\alpha(\tau)$ by *existentially quantifying on* τ.

263

(c)   To make all this clear, we will step slowly through some very easy examples, sketching how to construct quantified wffs. Start with the QL_1 wff

(1) (Fm → Hm).

Think of this as $\alpha(m)$. Now universally quantify on the only term, the name 'm'. We replace the term by the variable 'x' (say) and prefix the result with the quantifier symbol '∀' tagged with the same variable. We get $\forall x \alpha(x)$, i.e.

(2) ∀x(Fx → Hx).

Equally, starting from

(3) (Fm ∧ Lmn)

we can existentially quantify on 'm' to get e.g.

(4) ∃z(Fz ∧ Lzn).

Now think of this new wff as $\alpha(n)$. We can then proceed another step, and replace the name 'n' here with a variable. We have to choose a variable that doesn't occur in the wff we are building from, so we can't use 'z' again. But we could pick, e.g., 'x'. Then we prefix a quantifier symbol tagged with *this* new variable. Which gives us, say, the wff $\exists x \alpha(x)$:

(5) ∃x∃z(Fz ∧ Lzx).

Similarly, starting from the QL_1 wff

(6) Lmn

we can quantify first on 'n' and then on 'm' to form in turn

(7) ∃y Lmy,

(8) ∀x∃y Lxy.

Or – starting from (6) again – we can replace names in a different order and/or use different variables and/or use different quantifier symbols. We could form

(9) ∀x Lxn,

(10) ∃y∀x Lxy.

Equally, we could get from (6) to

(11) ∃y∀x Lyx, ∀y∀x Lyx, ∃z∃y Lzy, ...

Note though that our construction rule doesn't allow us to get from (6) to

(12) ∃y Lyy, ∀z Lzz, ...

(Think why not!) However, those expressions *are* wffs, as they can be formed by quantifying on the name in the wff

(13) Lmm.

Next, since Hm is a wff as well as (7), we can use a connective to construct

(14) (Hm → ∃y Lmy).

Then, universally quantifying on the name 'm', we get for example

(15) ∀x(Hx → ∃y Lxy).

264

And since ∀x Mxn is of course a wff alongside (9), so too is their disjunction

(16) (∀x Lxn ∨ ∀x Mxn);

and existentially quantifying on the name 'n' we can get the wff

(17) ∃y(∀x Lxy ∨ ∀x Mxy).

(d) Now for some non-wffs. Expressions like the following

(18) Fz, Lzn, Myx, Rxoy, (Fm → Gz), ∃x Lxy

are *not* QL₁ wffs. Expressions with variables dangling free, not bound to preceding quantifiers, do *not* count as wffs according to our construction rules.

 And, given our ban on reusing variables already in a given wff when applying a quantifier, we *can't* get from (7) to the expression

(19) ∃y∃y Lyy.

Note too that we can't prefix another quantifier to (8). We can't form an expression with a dangling quantifier, not tied to any later variable, as in

(20) ∀z∀x∃y Lxy.

Neither of the expressions (19) and (20) will count as wffs for us.

 And because the wff (14) already contains the variable y, we can't quantify it using the same variable again. So this is another non-wff:

(21) ∀y(Hy → ∃y Lyy).

(e) To repeat, Fz and Lzn are *not* wffs. So inside the wff (4) ∃z(Fz ∧ Lzn) the conjunction does *not* connect wffs. How does this square with our stern words in §28.5(b) about QL connectives still being essentially sentential connectives? Well, note that (4) is constructed by quantifying on a name in a wff like (3) (Fm ∧ Lmn). And in (3) the connective *does* connect wffs.

 The point generalizes. In building up a wff, a connective will always be first introduced as connecting whole wffs. See §35.2 for more on this.

28.7 An aside on scope again

We just noted that the QL₁ wff ∃z(Fz ∧ Lzn) can be constructed by quantifying on 'm' in the wff (Fm ∧ Lmn). But, of course, it can equally well be constructed by quantifying on 'o' in the wff (Fo ∧ Lon). Hence – at least on the story so far – a quantified wff will *not* have a unique possible construction history/parse tree in the sense of §9.2. Does this matter?

 No. Exploring a few simple examples will show you that different possible routes to constructing a quantified wff will structurally all look the same; they will just differ in the proper names that occur earlier in the history of a wff and which then get quantified away. Therefore our syntactic story still doesn't allow structurally ambiguous wffs. In particular, the relative order in which logical operators are introduced into a quantified wff in a possible construction history remains determinate. Hence, as when discussing PL wffs in §9.4(d), we can still say this (as a first rough version): an occurrence of a logical operator (connective or quantifier) is in the *scope* of some other occurrence of an operator in a wff if the first operator is introduced *before* the second as we build up the wff.

Other definitions of syntactic ideas can similarly be carried over from our discussion of PL languages to our new QL languages. For more on this, put more carefully, see §35.2.

28.8   Interpreting the quantifiers

(a)   Now to interpret quantified wffs. As we said:

> To interpret a QL language we must specify its (non-empty) domain. We do this in the glossary for the language by giving some *domain description*.

We can then continue as follows, drawing on our understanding of the quantifier prefixes in their Loglish guise:

> Suppose that the term τ refers to the object o and suppose that, given the interpretation of other vocabulary, the wff $\alpha(\tau)$ involving that term says that this object o satisfies a certain condition, says that o is C. Then:
>
> Universally quantifying on τ, $\forall \xi \alpha(\xi)$ says that everything is C – meaning everything in the relevant language's domain, of course.
>
> Existentially quantifying on τ, $\exists \xi \alpha(\xi)$ says that something, at least one thing, is C – meaning something in the relevant domain again.

(b)   The assigned domain for a QL language can be any definite set of objects, large or small (so long as there is at least one object in the domain), subject to one important constraint:

> The domain of quantification for a language must include the objects referred to by any proper names of that language.

Why? This constraint is to ensure that, given as premiss a wff saying that everything (in the domain) is C, we can indeed infer that any particular named object is C. And likewise, given that a named object is C, we can infer the quantified wff saying that something (in the domain) is C.

(c)   We will illustrate this interpretative scheme by working through a few examples from our mini-language QL_1.

First, however, we need to complete the interpretation key for this language by fixing what its quantifiers range over. So let's add a domain description to the language's glossary:

> The domain of quantification for QL_1: people, past and present.

Start off, then, with the wff

(1) (Fm → Hm).

Given our glossary for the language, this says that if Socrates is a philosopher, then Socrates is wise. In other words, Socrates is such that if he is a philosopher, then he is wise – or for short (using 'C' for this condition), Socrates is C. Then

(2) ∀x(Fx → Hx)

says that *everyone* (i.e. everyone past and present) is C: i.e. everyone is such that if they are a philosopher then they are wise. Equivalently, all philosophers are wise. Similarly,

(3) (Fm ∧ Lmn)

says that Socrates is a philosopher and Socrates loves Plato. In other words, it says Socrates is such that he is a philosopher and he loves Plato – for short (now using 'C'' for this new condition), Socrates is C'. And then

(4) ∃z(Fz ∧ Lzn)

says that there is *someone* who is C': i.e. there is someone who is a philosopher and loves Plato. Equivalently, some philosopher loves Plato.

Next, take the simple wff

(5) Lmn.

This of course says that Socrates loves Plato. Hence, when we existentially quantify into the place occupied by the second name as in

(6) ∃y Lmy,

this says that someone has the property which (5) ascribes to Plato. So, someone is loved by Socrates, i.e. Socrates is such that he loves someone.

By universally quantifying into the place occupied by Socrates's formal name, we can then say the same about everyone. Therefore

(7) ∀x∃y Lxy

means that everyone is such that they love someone.

Needless to say, however, we don't really need to build up to the interpretation of (7) laboriously like this! In practice, since the QL and the Loglish quantifiers effectively mean the same, *we can just directly transcribe (7) into Loglish as*

(8) (Everyone x is such that)(there is someone y such that) x loves y.

And, once we've fixed the domain, this stilted not-quite-English is already perfectly understandable as it is.

(d) Let's work through another series of examples.

(9) (Fm ∧ Romn)

says that Socrates is a philosopher and Aristotle prefers him to Plato. So

(10) ∃y(Fy ∧ Royn)

says that someone has the property that (9) attributes to Socrates, i.e. there is someone who is a philosopher whom Aristotle prefers to Plato. Hence

(11) (Go → ∃y(Fy ∧ Royn))

267

says that if Aristotle is a logician, then there's some philosopher he prefers to Plato. And next

(12) $\forall x(Gx \rightarrow \exists y(Fy \land Rxyn))$

says about everyone what (11) says about Aristotle: everyone is such that, if they are a logician, then there's some philosopher they prefer to Plato. In other words, every logician prefers some philosopher to Plato.

But again, we needn't in practice go through all this step-by-step interpretative palaver when faced with a wff such as (12). *The quick thing to do is just to transcribe (12) into Loglish as a halfway house*, as in

(13) $(\forall x)$(if x is a logician, then $(\exists y)(y$ is a philosopher and x prefers y to Plato))

which in turn unpacks as

(14) (Everyone x is such that)(if x is a logician, then (there is someone y such that)(y is a philosopher and x prefers y to Plato)),

which is, to be sure, very stilted not-quite-English; but it is surely still entirely understandable.

28.9 Quantifier equivalences

(a) Given our glossary for QL_1 and the rule for interpreting universally quantified wffs,

(1) $\forall x \neg Fx$

says that everyone is a non-philosopher – i.e. no one is a philosopher. Therefore its negation

(2) $\neg \forall x \neg Fx$

says that it isn't the case that no one is a philosopher – in other words, there is someone who *is* a philosopher. Hence this says the same as

(3) $\exists x Fx$.

Similarly, since

(4) $\exists x \neg Fx$

in QL_1 means that someone is not a philosopher, its negation

(5) $\neg \exists x \neg Fx$

says that it isn't the case that there is someone who is not a philosopher – in other words, everyone *is* a philosopher. Hence (5) is equivalent to

(6) $\forall x Fx$.

The two equivalences here obviously generalize. Let's use 'ξ' as before to indicate a variable; and now for brevity use 'ψ' (*psi*) for some suitable wff-completing expression (containing that variable). Then:

In QL languages, wffs of the forms $\neg\forall\xi\neg\psi$ and $\exists\xi\psi$ (with the same completing expression ψ) are equivalent, i.e. are true in just the same circumstances.

Likewise, wffs of the forms $\neg\exists\xi\neg\psi$ and $\forall\xi\psi$ are equivalent.

(b)   So universal and existential quantifiers are interdefinable using negation, just as conjunction and disjunction are interdefinable using negation (see §13.1).

The parallel shouldn't be surprising. If we imagine for a moment that we are dealing with a case where everything has a name (compare §27.5), then we can think of $\exists xFx$ as in effect a big disjunction like $Fm \lor Fn \lor Fo \lor \ldots$. But by a version of one of De Morgan's Laws, this big disjunction is equivalent to the *negation* of the big conjunction $\neg Fm \land \neg Fn \land \neg Fo \land \ldots$ (why?). Given the same pretence that everything has a name, this big conjunction is in effect equivalent to $\forall x\neg Fx$. Whence $\exists xFx$ is equivalent to the negation of that, i.e. $\neg\forall x\neg Fx$. (By a similar arm-waving argument, $\forall xFx$ should be equivalent to $\neg\exists x\neg Fx$.)

We could therefore do quantificational logic using a language with only one of the two interdefinable types of quantifiers just as we could do propositional logic using only one of conjunction or disjunction alongside negation. Frege's *Begriffsschrift* used just the universal quantifier. However, just as it is customary and convenient to use both conjunction and disjunction in PL languages, so it is now customary and convenient to use both types of quantifier in QL languages.

(c)   The whole point of the quantifier-variable notation is to encode the relative scope of quantifiers, so we can (say) render the two different readings of 'Everyone loves a certain someone' quite unambiguously by the QL_1 wffs $\forall x\exists yLxy$ and $\exists y\forall xLxy$. We plainly cannot swap the order of quantifiers here without changing the meaning of the wff. And that holds in general: quantifier order matters.

But there *are* exceptions that we should finish by noting. Thus consider

(1) $\forall x\forall yLxy$

which says of everyone what $\forall yLmy$ says of Socrates. So (1) says that everyone loves everyone. While, swapping round the quantifiers,

(2) $\forall y\forall xLxy$

says that everyone has the property which $\forall xLxn$ attributes to Plato, i.e. the property of being loved by everyone. So (2) also says that everyone is loved by everyone. Hence (1) and (2) are equivalent. Likewise

(3) $\exists x\exists yLxy$
(4) $\exists y\exists xLxy$

are also equivalent, both saying that someone loves someone.

The point generalizes. Suppose ξ and ζ are (distinct) variables. Then:

Adjacent quantifiers of *the same type* can be interchanged. That is to say, pairs of wffs of the form $\forall\xi\forall\zeta\psi$ and $\forall\zeta\forall\xi\psi$ are equivalent. Similarly, pairs of wffs of the form $\exists\xi\exists\zeta\psi$ and $\exists\zeta\exists\xi\psi$ are equivalent.

28.10   Summary

The atomic wffs of QL languages are built from predicates and terms; proper names are the most basic kind of term (later we will introduce dummy names and functional terms). Predicates come with fixed arities. An atomic wff is formed by taking a predicate of arity k and following it by k terms.

We give the interpretations of proper names and predicates by glossaries associating the expressions with vernacular equivalents. Then, roughly, a predicate-name(s) wff says that the named object(s) satisfy the condition expressed by the predicate.

Connectives in QL languages still basically behave as sentential connectives, as in PL languages.

We next add variables and quantifier symbols to the logical vocabulary of QL languages. Expressions like $\forall x$, $\forall y$, ..., are now available as universal quantifiers: expressions like $\exists x$, $\exists y$, ..., are existential quantifiers.

A wff with an initial quantifier can then be formed by taking a wff $\alpha(\tau)$ with one or more occurrences of a name or other term τ, replacing the term throughout by a variable ξ new to the wff to form $\alpha(\xi)$, and prefixing a quantifier involving the same variable to get $\forall \xi \alpha(\xi)$ or $\exists \xi \alpha(\xi)$.

We interpret quantified wffs by fixing the domain or universe of discourse for the relevant language. Suppose $\alpha(\tau)$ says the object referred to by τ is C. Then a wff of the form $\forall \xi \alpha(\xi)$ renders *everything is C*, while $\exists \xi \alpha(\xi)$ renders *something is C* – where the things in question in the relevant domain.

Exercises 28

Which of the following expressions are wffs of the language QL_1?

(1) $(Lnn \land (Lmn \rightarrow Lnm))$
(2) $\forall x(Fx \rightarrow Lxm)$
(3) $(Go \land \neg \exists x(Gx \land Hx))$
(4) $\forall x(Fx \rightarrow Gx \land Hx)$
(5) $(\exists xFx \lor \exists xGx)$
(6) $\exists x(Fx \lor \exists xGx)$
(7) $(Fx \lor \exists yGy)$
(8) $\exists x(Fx \lor \exists yGy)$
(9) $\forall y \exists x\, Rxyx$
(10) $\exists x \forall y \exists x\, Rxyx$
(11) $(Lmn \land \forall x(Lmx \rightarrow Lxn))$
(12) $(Gn \rightarrow \exists z(Fz \land Lnz))$
(13) $\forall y(Gy \rightarrow \exists z(Fz \land Lyz))$
(14) $\neg \exists y(Fy \land \forall xRxoy)$

In each case, give one possible construction history for those expressions which are wffs, and indicate which logical operators (connectives or quantifiers) are in the scope of which other logical operators. What do those expressions which are wffs mean?

270

29 Simple translations

The striking novelty of QL languages is that they use a *quantifier/variable* notation to express generality. However, as we have seen, this notation is in fact
modelled quite closely on two familiar devices found in ordinary English and/or
in mathematician's English (namely prefixed quantifiers tied to pronouns, and
variables serving as pronouns). So the basics of the notation are actually not
hard to grasp. What will cause the translational headaches is the additional
sparseness that we have imposed on our formalized languages:

(i)   Each QL language has just a single sort of variable, with all variables
      ranging over the same domain.
(ii) QL languages don't have any special apparatus for expressing restricted
      quantifiers. They don't have binary quantifiers taking two predicates –
      perhaps notated as in $(\forall x: Fx)\, Gx$ – to say that all Fs in the domain are
      G. We have to make do with the now-familiar unary quantifiers, plus
      connectives.
(iii) QL languages only have two built-in kinds of unary quantifier.

These restrictions are absolutely standard, and you have to learn to negotiate
them. But we should emphasize that they are not really intrinsic to the basic
Fregean conception of quantifiers that underlies modern logic.

29.1   Restricted quantifiers revisited

(a)   Suppose we are working in a language like QL_1 where the quantifiers range
inclusively over all people, past and present. Then, given the sparse resources of
this language, if we want to translate

(1)   All logicians are wise,
(2)   Some logicians are wise,

our only option is to follow the lead of §27.2, and restrict our quantifiers using
connectives. Therefore (1) and (2) will get translated by

(3) $\forall x(Gx \rightarrow Hx)$,
(4) $\exists x(Gx \wedge Hx)$.

And let's stress that the connectives do have to go this way round – i.e. we need
to translate (1) using a conditional and (2) using a conjunction, and not vice
versa. Why?

(i) Translating (1) into QL_1 as $\forall x(Gx \wedge Hx)$ would plainly be wrong. For that formal wff says, quite differently, that everyone is a wise logician!

(ii) Translating (2) as $\exists x(Gx \to Hx)$ would also be wrong. Socrates is not a logician, and Gm is false. Hence $(Gm \to Hm)$ is *true*, being a material conditional with a false antecedent. But if $(Gm \to Hm)$ is true, so is $\exists x(Gx \to Hx)$. So the mere existence of a non-logician like Socrates makes $\exists x(Gx \to Hx)$ true. But obviously that's not enough to make (2) true, i.e. it's not enough to make it true that some logicians are wise.

Further, we want the translations of intuitively equivalent propositions to come out as equivalent formal sentences. Translating restricted 'all' with a conditional and restricted 'some' with a conjunction makes this happen:

(iii) 'Not all logicians are unwise' is equivalent to 'Some logicians are wise'. So their QL_1 translations should be equivalent.

Translating restricted 'all' with a conditional, the negated 'all' proposition gets rendered $\neg\forall x(Gx \to \neg Hx)$, or equivalently $\exists x\neg(Gx \to \neg Hx)$. But something of the form $\neg(\alpha \to \neg\beta)$ is equivalent to $(\alpha \wedge \beta)$; and still because of the meaning of the connectives, $\exists x\neg(Gx \to \neg Hx)$ is equivalent to $\exists x(Gx \wedge Hx)$.

Putting things together, 'Not all logicians are unwise' is rendered as $\neg\forall x(Gx \to \neg Hx)$, which comes out as equivalent to $\exists x(Gx \wedge Hx)$, which translates 'Some logicians are wise'. As required.

(b) How good is our translation of (1) as (3)? In particular, what about the use of the material conditional here? Informally, we might suggest that

(1) All logicians are wise

can be paraphrased along the lines of

(1$'$) Everyone is such that, if they are a logician, they are wise.

Suppose we accept this. Then note that we have already discussed the kind of 'if' which is involved in contexts like (1$'$) in §19.3. Using a different example, we argued that the 'if' here does need to be a material conditional. So if we accept the equivalence of (1) and (1$'$), then we should indeed render both as

(3) $\forall x(Gx \to Hx)$.

(c) What about our translation of (2)? The plural in 'Some logicians are wise' indicates that there is more than one wise logician. But (4) $\exists x(Gx \wedge Hx)$ says only that there is at least one. Is this minor discrepancy worth fussing about?

Almost never. When we propose something of the form 'Some Gs are H' as a premiss, or aim to derive it as a conclusion, the number of Gs that are H typically doesn't matter to us – we care about whether *any* of them are. So we can simply ignore the small translational infelicity in rendering 'Some Gs are H' as $\exists x(Gx \wedge Hx)$. In almost every context it is worth the gain in formal simplicity. Further, when we later augment our QL languages with an identity predicate, we will see how to express 'some (more than one)' with the resources of our enriched language when we really need to do so.

272

29.2   Existential import

(a)   So, putting worries about plurals aside, propositions of the form

(1)   All Gs are H,
(2)   Some Gs are H,

are standardly rendered into a QL language by corresponding wffs like

(3) $\forall x(Gx \to Hx)$,
(4) $\exists x(Gx \wedge Hx)$.

Traditionally, however, it has been supposed that a universally quantified proposition like (1) has 'existential import' – for instance, if it is true that all logicians are wise, then there must exist some logicians to be wise. Hence a proposition of the form (1) entails the corresponding proposition of the form (2). Or so the story goes. On the other hand, the wff (3) doesn't entail (4) (assuming it is possible for there to be no Gs). For suppose that there *are* no Gs. Then (3) is true: everyone x is such that (x is $G \to x$ is H) since the antecedent of the material conditional is always false. While (4) is false. Therefore (3) won't entail (4). To be sure, (3) plus the existential assumption $\exists xGx$ will entail (4). But the point is that this additional existential assumption is needed.

So the moral is this: *if* the traditional view is right, then a proposition of the form (1) entails (2), while (3) by itself doesn't entail (4) – hence the standard translations aren't fully adequate because they don't respect all logical relations.

(b)   We might well wonder, however, whether tradition gets it right. Consider for example Newton's First Law in the form

(5)   All particles subject to no net force have constant velocity.

Surely to accept Newton's Law is not to commit ourselves to the actual existence of some particles subject to no net force: doesn't the law remain true irrespective of whether there are any such particles? Another example: couldn't the notice

(6)   All trespassers will be prosecuted!

be true even if there are no trespassers? And it could well be *because* (6) is taken to be true that there are no trespassers.

(However, to complicate matters, it might be suggested that there is a subtle difference here between 'all' and 'any', with *All Gs are H* being more apt for cases where there *are* some Gs, while *Any Gs are H* leaves it open whether there are some Gs. So should we perhaps really state Newton's law with 'any'?)

(c)   We fortunately need not get entangled in such debates. We need not settle whether vernacular propositions of the form *All Gs are H* usually entail the existence of some Gs. Just regard this as one of those messy issues about ordinary language which get helpfully tidied up when we move to a formalized language.

Our policy henceforth will be to take the default rendering of *All Gs are H* (and similarly *Every/any/each G is H*) as something like $\forall x(Gx \to Hx)$, which lacks existential import. We can then always tack an explicit existential clause $\exists xGx$ onto the translation if, on a particular occasion, we think it matters.

29.3 'No'

The last two sections suggest that sparse QL languages can handle restricted 'all'/'every' and 'some' quantifiers reasonably well. But what about handling other quantifiers? Our QL languages have just two flavours of built-in quantifiers: should we, for instance, have added a built-in 'no' quantifier?

(a)   In QL_1, $\forall x \neg Hx$ means that everyone is not wise, i.e. *no one* is wise. In the same language $\neg \exists x Hx$ means that it *isn't* the case that there is someone who is wise. So this too means that *no one* is wise. Hence we already have two alternative (but equivalent) translations of that basic 'no' proposition.

The point obviously generalizes. Informally, we can recast simple, unrestricted, 'no' propositions using a quantifier prefix like '(no one/nothing x is such that)', and then recast that as either '(everyone/everything x is such that) it is not the case that' or 'it is not the case that (someone/something x is such that)', which correspond respectively to the formal expressions $\forall x \neg$ or $\neg \exists x$.

More carefully, using the same notation as in §28.8,

> Suppose we interpret the term τ as referring to o, and suppose the wff $\alpha(\tau)$ then says that o is C. Then $\forall \xi \neg \alpha(\xi)$ and $\neg \exists \xi \alpha(\xi)$ are equivalent, and say that there are no Cs (in the relevant domain).

Of course, we *could* have added a third quantifier symbol to QL languages, perhaps a – rotated! – 'N' to go with '$\forall$' and '$\exists$'. We could then express 'there are no Fs' by NxFx. This would make some translations rather smoother; the cost would be increasing the number of rules needed later for dealing with quantifier arguments. The conventional judgement is that the gain isn't worth the cost.

(b)   And what about restricted 'no' quantifications? For example, how can we render into QL_1 the calumny that

(1)   No philosopher is wise?

As with other 'no' translations, we have two options, one using a universal quantifier, one using an existential quantifier. The first option goes via the Loglish

(2)   (Everyone x is such that) if x is a philosopher, then x is not wise

to arrive at:

(3) $\forall x (Fx \rightarrow \neg Hx)$.

The second option formalizes the equivalent thought

(4)   It is not the case that (someone x is such that)(x is a philosopher and x is wise)

to get:

(5) $\neg \exists x (Fx \wedge Hx)$.

Why are (3) and (5) equivalent? $\forall x (Fx \rightarrow \neg Hx)$ is equivalent to $\neg \exists x \neg (Fx \rightarrow \neg Hx)$, and that in turn is equivalent to $\neg \exists x (Fx \wedge Hx)$, as we would expect when we recall that $\neg (\alpha \rightarrow \neg \beta)$ is equivalent to $(\alpha \wedge \beta)$.

29.4   Translating via Loglish

After those preliminaries, we now turn to tackle some translation exercises – with a general approach described in this section, and applications in the next!

As indicated in §28.8, faced with the task of translating from English to some QL language, it can help to go via Loglish as an intermediate step. And we can break down translation-via-Loglish into stages. Suppose we start, on the one side, with an ordinary-language proposition involving generality. And suppose we have, on the other side, a QL language with an appropriate glossary. Then:

Stage one   Begin by recasting our vernacular proposition by using ordinary-language quantifier prefixes linked to later pronouns, translating away any 'no' quantifiers. At a first shot, these prefixes will typically be restricted quantifiers such as '(every woman is such that)', '(someone who loves Owen is such that)' or '(some prime number is such that)'.

Stage two   Replace the vernacular pronouns with variables-as-pronouns 'x', 'y', etc., and make cross-linkings clear by explicitly tagging each quantifier prefix with the variable it is linked to, to get the likes of '(every woman x is such that)', '(someone y who loves Owen is such that)', '(some prime number z is such that)'.

Stage three   The glossary for our formal language fixes a domain for the quantifiers to range over. Now replace restricted quantifiers by using informal unary quantifiers over this domain plus conditionals/conjunctions. So, for example, '(every woman x is such that)' becomes '(everyone x is such that) if x is a woman, then ...', '(someone y who loves Owen is such that)' becomes '(someone y is such that) y loves Owen and ...', etc.

Stage four   Next, simply abbreviate the generic quantifier prefixes by '$(\forall x)$', '$(\exists y)$'. Also replace the vernacular connectives with their symbolic versions, using the standard logical symbols, and we get Loglish sentences like:

$(\forall x)(x$ is a woman $\rightarrow x$ is an adult human$)$,
$(\exists y)(y$ loves Owen $\wedge y$ is a philosopher$)$,
$(\forall z)(z$ is a philosopher $\rightarrow (\exists y)(y$ is a logician $\wedge x$ admires $y))$.

These are *still* quite straightforwardly interpretable, relying on our informal understanding of the symbols and our grasp of English.

Stage five   Finally, replace the vernacular names and predicates in Loglish sentences with symbolic counterparts using our chosen QL language's glossary, making sure that we now obey the predicates-first 'word order'. Rewrite '$(\forall x)$', '$(\exists y)$' in the formal style, without brackets, as '$\forall x$', '$\exists y$'.

Of course, it is not being seriously suggested that you have to follow this stage-by-stage plan in all its detail and in the exact order suggested! You will very quickly learn to skip lightly through these stages when translating from English to QL. Still, in our illustrative examples in the next section it will be helpful to take things very slowly and show our working, going for rather plodding explicitness with the aim of maximum clarity.

29.5 Translations into QL_2

(a) Nothing would be gained by taking (say) sober mathematical examples, and we could run the risk of making things look more difficult than they really are. So let's stick to mundane human affairs and define the following language:

In QL_2, the proper names with their interpretations are

> m: Maldwyn,
> n: Nerys,
> o: Owen;

and the predicates are

> F: ① is a man,
> G: ① is a woman,
> L: ① loves ②,
> M: ① is married to ②,
> R: ① is a child of ② and ③.

The domain of quantification: people (living people, for definiteness).

And now let's consider how to translate the following propositions into QL_2:

(1) There's someone who loves Maldwyn, Nerys, and Owen.
(2) Whoever is loved by Owen is loved by Maldwyn too.
(3) Every woman who loves Maldwyn is loved by Owen.
(4) Maldwyn loves some woman who loves Owen.
(5) Nerys and Owen love any child of theirs.
(6) Owen is Maldwyn's child.
(7) Maldwyn is married to no one.
(8) No one who loves Nerys loves Owen.
(9) Nerys is a woman everyone loves.
(10) If everyone loves Nerys then Owen does.
(11) If someone loves Nerys then Owen does.
(12) If anyone loves Nerys then Owen does.

(b) Taking our propositions in turn, we have first:

(1)   There's someone who loves Maldwyn, Nerys, and Owen
  $\simeq$ (Someone is such that) they love Maldwyn, Nerys, and Owen
  $\simeq$ (Someone x is such that) x loves Maldwyn, Nerys, and Owen
  $\simeq$ $(\exists x)(x$ loves Maldwyn $\land$ x loves Nerys $\land$ x loves Owen)
  $\simeq$ $\exists x(Lxm \land (Lxn \land Lxo))$.

We will use the sign '$\simeq$' to indicate sufficient translational equivalence. The internal bracketing of the three-way conjunction is up to you. And of course, there is nothing significant about the choice of informal variable 'x' or the formal variable 'x' – you can use any variables you like, so long as you preserve the crucial pattern of linkages from quantifier prefixes to slots in later expressions.

(2) Whoever is loved by Owen is loved by Maldwyn too
  $\simeq$ (Everyone who is loved by Owen is such that) Maldwyn loves them
  $\simeq$ (Everyone x who is loved by Owen is such that) Maldwyn loves x
  $\simeq$ (Everyone x is such that)(if x is loved by Owen then Maldwyn loves x)
  $\simeq$ $(\forall x)$(Owen loves $x \rightarrow$ Maldwyn loves x)
  $\simeq$ $\forall x(\text{Lox} \rightarrow \text{Lmx})$.

Note how the relative clause 'who is loved by Owen' is treated as a predicate restricting the quantifier.

(3) Every woman who loves Maldwyn is loved by Owen
  $\simeq$ (Every woman x who loves Maldwyn is such that) x is loved by Owen
  $\simeq$ (Everyone x is such that)(if x is a woman who loves Maldwyn, then Owen loves x)
  $\simeq$ $(\forall x)(x$ is a woman and x loves Maldwyn $\rightarrow$ Owen loves x)
  $\simeq$ $\forall x((\text{Gx} \wedge \text{Lxm}) \rightarrow \text{Lox})$.

(4) Maldwyn loves some woman who loves Owen
  $\simeq$ (Some woman x who loves Owen is such that) Maldwyn loves x
  $\simeq$ (Someone x is such that)(x is a woman who loves Owen, and Maldwyn loves x)
  $\simeq$ $(\exists x)(x$ is a woman and x loves Owen $\wedge$ Maldwyn loves x)
  $\simeq$ $\exists x((\text{Gx} \wedge \text{Lxo}) \wedge \text{Lmx})$.

(5) Nerys and Owen love any child of theirs
  $\simeq$ (Everyone x who is a child of Nerys and Owen is such that) Nerys and Owen love x
  $\simeq$ (Everyone x is such that)(if x is a child of Nerys and Owen then Nerys and Owen love x)
  $\simeq$ $(\forall x)(x$ is a child of Nerys and Owen $\rightarrow$ (Nerys loves $x \wedge$ Owen loves x))
  $\simeq$ $\forall x(\text{Rxno} \rightarrow (\text{Lnx} \wedge \text{Lox}))$.

(6) Owen is Maldwyn's child
  $\simeq$ Owen is a child of Maldwyn
  $\simeq$ (Someone x is such that) Owen is a child of Maldwyn and x
  $\simeq$ $\exists x\, \text{Romx}$.

The point of this last example is to emphasize that QL$_2$'s predicate R is determinately a *ternary* predicate, glossed as '① is a child of ② and ③'. If we want to translate 'Owen is a child of Maldywn', which involves the ordinary-language *binary* predicate '① is a child of ②', we have to use the illustrated trick of sopping up a place in the ternary predicate with a quantified variable.

Now for a couple of simple examples involving the 'no' quantifier. Remember, §29.3 tells us that 'no' propositions can be rendered in two different ways. Thus:

(7) Maldwyn is married to no one
  $\simeq$ It is not the case that Maldwyn is married to someone

$\simeq$ ¬(There is someone x such that) Maldwyn is married to x

$\simeq$ ¬∃xMmx.

Or, starting again, taking the alternative route:

$\simeq$ (Everyone x is such that) Maldwyn isn't married to x

$\simeq$ ∀x¬Mmx.

(8) No one who loves Nerys loves Owen

   $\simeq$ It is not the case that someone who loves Nerys loves Owen

   $\simeq$ ¬(There is someone x who loves Nerys and is such that) x loves Owen

   $\simeq$ ¬(There is someone x who is such that)(x loves Nerys and x loves Owen)

   $\simeq$ ¬∃x(Lxn ∧ Lxo).

Or equivalently

   $\simeq$ Everyone who loves Nerys does not love Owen

   $\simeq$ (Everyone x who loves Nerys is such that) x doesn't love Owen

   $\simeq$ (Everyone x is such that)(if x loves Nerys then x doesn't love Owen)

   $\simeq$ ∀x(Lxn → ¬Lxo).

The next proposition can also be regimented in two related ways:

(9) Nerys is a woman everyone loves

   $\simeq$ Everyone loves Nerys and Nerys is a woman

   $\simeq$ (∀xLxn ∧ Gn).

Or alternatively

   $\simeq$ (Everyone is such that) they love Nerys-who-is-a-woman

   $\simeq$ ∀x(Lxn ∧ Gn).

We will say more about why these wffs are equivalent in the next section.

Next, a conditional with complete propositions as antecedent and consequent:

(10) If everyone loves Nerys then Owen does

   $\simeq$ ((Everyone x is such that) x loves Nerys → Owen loves Nerys)

   $\simeq$ (∀xLxn → Lon).

Similarly,

(11) If someone loves Nerys then Owen does

   $\simeq$ (∃xLxn → Lon).

But now what about (12) 'If anyone loves Nerys then Owen does'? Perhaps with the right stress and/or right context we can construe this as saying 'If just *anyone* loves Nerys, then …' which is equivalent to (10). However, the more natural reading gives 'anyone' wider scope than the conditional:

(12) If anyone loves Nerys then Owen does

   $\simeq$ (Anyone/everyone is such that) if they love Nerys, then Owen loves Nerys

   $\simeq$ ∀x(Lxn → Lon).

However, can't we equally naturally read (12) as equivalent to (11) and translate it accordingly? Well, yes we can: the alternative translations $\forall x(Lxn \to Lon)$ and $(\exists x Lxn \to Lon)$ are in fact equivalent, as we will now see.

29.6 Moving quantifiers

(a) We should comment on a couple of examples from the last section where there are equivalent alternative translations.

Consider first our two renditions of 'Nerys is a woman everyone loves':

(1) $(\forall x Lxn \wedge Gn)$
(2) $\forall x(Lxn \wedge Gn)$.

To see why these are indeed equivalent, it might help to pretend there are just the three people named by 'm', 'n', and 'o' in the domain, so a wff $\forall \xi \alpha(\xi)$ amounts to $(\alpha(m) \wedge \alpha(n) \wedge \alpha(o))$ (omitting some brackets). In this special case, (1) and (2) amount to the obviously equivalent

(3) $((Lmn \wedge Lnn \wedge Lon) \wedge Gn)$
(4) $((Lmn \wedge Gn) \wedge (Lnn \wedge Gn) \wedge (Lon \wedge Gn))$.

The point about (1) and (2) generalizes. Pairs of wffs of the following forms are equivalent:

$$(\forall \xi \alpha(\xi) \wedge \beta)$$
$$\forall \xi (\alpha(\xi) \wedge \beta).$$

Or at least, this is true *so long as the wff β doesn't contain the variable ξ.* That restriction is crucial. For example, in one direction, we can't go from the wff $(\forall x Fx \wedge \forall x Gx)$ to $\forall x(Fx \wedge \forall x Gx)$ – the latter expression isn't even a wff in our syntax (why?). Similarly, we can't go in the other direction from the wff $\forall x(Fx \wedge Gx)$ to $(\forall x Fx \wedge Gx)$ – again the latter expression isn't a wff (why?).

Similar equivalences hold for the existential quantifier, and for disjunction in place of conjunction. So in summary (and do think through all these cases!):

Pairs of wffs of the following forms are equivalent:

$(\forall \xi \alpha(\xi) \wedge \beta)$ and $\forall \xi(\alpha(\xi) \wedge \beta)$
$(\exists \xi \alpha(\xi) \wedge \beta)$ and $\exists \xi(\alpha(\xi) \wedge \beta)$
$(\forall \xi \alpha(\xi) \vee \beta)$ and $\forall \xi(\alpha(\xi) \vee \beta)$
$(\exists \xi \alpha(\xi) \vee \beta)$ and $\exists \xi(\alpha(\xi) \vee \beta)$

where β doesn't contain the variable ξ. The equivalencies also hold, of course, with the order of the conjunctions/disjunctions reversed.

(b) What about moving a quantifier outside a conditional? Consider again the wff

(5) $(\exists x Lxn \to Lon)$

which is equivalent, by the definition of the material conditional, to

(6) $(\neg \exists x Lxn \vee Lon)$.

Notice the negation! By the interrelation of the quantifiers, (6) is equivalent to

(7) $(\forall x \neg Lxn \lor Lon)$.

But by the rule that we have just met for taking a universal quantifier outside a disjunction, this is in turn equivalent to

(8) $\forall x(\neg Lxn \lor Lon)$

which is equivalent to

(9) $\forall x(Lxn \rightarrow Lon)$

by the interpretation of the material conditional again. Which gives us the claimed overall equivalence between the two renditions of example (12) in §29.5.

So dragging an existential quantifier out from the *antecedent* of a conditional flips the type of quantifier. The same goes for dragging a universal quantifier out from the *antecedent* of a conditional. For example, these are equivalent (why?):

(10) $(\forall x Fx \rightarrow Gn)$
(11) $\exists x(Fx \rightarrow Gn)$.

However, since the *consequent* of a material conditional is like an ordinary, unnegated, disjunct we can pull out a quantifier as with other disjunctions. Thus, generalizing, we have the following (again, do think through these cases):

> Pairs of wffs of the following forms are equivalent:
>
> $(\forall \xi \alpha(\xi) \rightarrow \beta)$ and $\exists \xi(\alpha(\xi) \rightarrow \beta)$
> $(\exists \xi \alpha(\xi) \rightarrow \beta)$ and $\forall \xi(\alpha(\xi) \rightarrow \beta)$
> $(\beta \rightarrow \forall \xi \alpha(\xi))$ and $\forall \xi(\beta \rightarrow \alpha(\xi))$
> $(\beta \rightarrow \exists \xi \alpha(\xi))$ and $\exists \xi(\beta \rightarrow \alpha(\xi))$
>
> where β doesn't contain the variable ξ.

29.7 Summary

> Restricted universal quantifiers are translated using conditionals in the scope of universal quantifiers which run over the whole domain. Restricted existential quantifiers are translated using conjunctions in the scope of existential quantifiers which run over the whole domain.
>
> We need not add a 'no' quantifier to our QL languages, given that we can so easily render something of the form *There are no Gs* by the corresponding wff $\neg \exists x Gx$ or equivalently $\forall x \neg Gx$. And the restricted quantification *No Fs are Gs* can be rendered by either $\neg \exists x(Fx \land Gx)$ or $\forall x(Fx \rightarrow \neg Gx)$.
>
> We can ease the process of translating from English into a given QL language by going in stages via Loglish:
>
> (1) Rephrase a given English proposition using prefixed restricted quantifiers linked to pronouns (massaging away 'no' quantifiers using 'every'

or 'some' plus negation).

(2)   Replace vernacular pronouns with variables, and make cross-linkings clear by tagging quantifier prefixes with their linked variables.

(3)   Render the restricted quantifiers by using generic quantifiers (running over the whole universe) together with conditionals and conjunctions.

(4)   Use ∀ and ∃ to abbreviate quantifier prefixes, replace vernacular connectives with formal ones, giving us Loglish expressions.

(5)   Then use the glossary for the relevant QL language to render the names and predicates.

Exercises 29

(a)   Translate the following into QL_1 as best you can:

(1)   Aristotle is a pupil of Socrates and Plato.
(2)   Plato taught Aristotle only if Socrates taught Plato.
(3)   If Plato is a pupil of someone, he is a pupil of Socrates.
(4)   Some philosophers are not wise.
(5)   Not all philosophers are wise.
(6)   Any logician loves Aristotle.
(7)   No one who is a wise philosopher prefers Plato to Aristotle.
(8)   Whoever is a pupil of Plato is wise.
(9)   Not every wise logician is a pupil of Aristotle.
(10) Any logician is a wise philosopher.
(11) Aristotle prefers no philosopher to Plato.
(12) Some wise people aren't philosophers, and some aren't logicians.
(13) Only philosophers love Aristotle.
(14) Not only philosophers love Socrates.
(15) Socrates is a philosopher whom everyone wise loves.
(16) Only some logicians love Plato.
(17) No philosophers or logicians are wise.
(18) All philosophers and logicians are wise.

(b)   Which of these pairs of wffs are equivalent, which not, and why?

(1) $(\exists xFx \lor \exists xGx)$, $\exists x(Fx \lor Gx)$
(2) $(\exists xFx \land \exists xGx)$, $\exists x(Fx \land Gx)$
(3) $(\exists xFx \land \exists xGx)$, $\exists x(Fx \land \exists yGy)$
(4) $(\exists xFx \land \exists xGx)$, $\exists x\exists y(Fx \land Gy)$
(5) $\exists x\forall y(Fx \land Gy)$, $\forall y\exists x(Fx \land Gy)$
(6) $\exists x\forall y(Fx \lor Gy)$, $\forall x\exists y(Fy \lor Gx)$
(7) $(\forall xFx \rightarrow \forall xGx)$, $\exists x(Fx \rightarrow \forall yGy)$
(8) $(\forall xFx \rightarrow \forall xGx)$, $\exists x\forall y(Fx \rightarrow Gy)$
(9) $(\forall xFx \rightarrow \forall xGx)$, $\forall y\exists x(Fx \rightarrow Gy)$

(c*)   Use equivalences you now know about to outline a proof that every wff is equivalent to one in *prenex* form, where all quantifiers are at the beginning of the wff.

(d*)   We can render 'Plato and Aristotle are philosophers' by e.g. $(Fn \land Fo)$. Why can't we render 'Plato and Aristotle are classmates' by e.g. $(Cn \land Co)$? What does this sort of case tell us about some expressive limitations of QL languages?

281

30 More on translations

This chapter starts by looking at more difficult examples of translating between English and the particular formal language QL_2 from §29.5. Then we consider some issues about how to choose a QL language to use when assessing arguments.

30.1 More translations into QL_2

Let's take some more examples of translating claims into QL_2, this time ones which involve multiple quantifiers. So consider the following (mostly false!):

(1) Every man loves someone or other.
(2) Some man loves a woman.
(3) Someone Owen loves is loved by everyone Nerys loves.
(4) No woman loves every man.
(5) No woman loves any man.
(6) Anyone who is married loves someone they aren't married to.
(7) A married man only loves women.
(8) No man loves anyone who loves Nerys.

A helpful tip. In going via Loglish intermediate stages, it will be useful if we occasionally make informal use of square brackets to demarcate parts of complex expressions; then we can work within the square brackets as we move from one stage to the next. So:

(1) Every man loves someone or other
   $\simeq$ (Every man x is such that) [x loves someone or other]
   $\simeq$ (Everyone x is such that) if x is a man, then [x loves someone or other]
   $\simeq$ $(\forall x)(x$ is a man $\rightarrow$ [$(\exists y)$ x loves y])
   $\simeq$ $\forall x(Fx \rightarrow \exists y Lxy)$.

(2) Some man loves a woman
   $\simeq$ (There is some man x such that)[(there is some woman y such that) x loves y]
   $\simeq$ (There is someone x such that)(x is a man and [(there is some woman y such that) x loves y])
   $\simeq$ $(\exists x)(x$ is a man $\wedge$ [(there is someone y such that) y is a woman and x loves y])

$\simeq$ $(\exists x)(x$ is a man $\wedge$ $[(\exists y)(y$ is a woman $\wedge$ x loves $y)])$
$\simeq$ $\exists x(Fx \wedge \exists y(Gy \wedge Lxy))$.

(3) Someone Owen loves is loved by everyone Nerys loves
$\simeq$ (Someone x whom Owen loves is such that)$[x$ is loved by everyone Nerys loves]
$\simeq$ (Someone x is such that)(Owen loves x and $[x$ is loved by everyone Nerys loves])
$\simeq$ (Someone x is such that)(Owen loves x and $[($everyone y is such that$)$ if Nerys loves y then y loves $x])$
$\simeq$ $(\exists x)($Owen loves x $\wedge$ $[(\forall y)($Nerys loves y $\to$ y loves $x)])$
$\simeq$ $\exists x(Lox \wedge \forall y(Lny \to Lyx))$.

(4) No woman loves every man
$\simeq$ It is not the case that some woman loves every man
$\simeq$ $\neg$Some woman x is such that x loves every man
$\simeq$ $\neg$(Someone x is such that)$(x$ is a woman and $[x$ loves every man])
$\simeq$ $\neg$(Someone x is such that)$(x$ is a woman and $[($every y is such that$)$ if y is a man, then x loves $y])$
$\simeq$ $\neg\exists x(Gx \wedge \forall y(Fy \to Lxy))$.

Or, starting again, taking the alternative route for translating a 'no' proposition:

$\simeq$ Every woman is such that she doesn't love every man
$\simeq$ (Every woman x is such that) it is not the case that x loves every man
$\simeq$ (Every x is such that)(if x is a woman, then $\neg[x$ loves every man])
$\simeq$ (Every x is such that)$(x$ is a woman $\to$ $\neg[($everyone y is such that$)$ if y is a man, x loves $y])$
$\simeq$ $\forall x(Gx \to \neg\forall y(Fy \to Lxy))$.

Next, the stressed claim 'No woman loves *any* man' is naturally heard as saying the same as (4). But an unstressed (5) is more naturally read like this:

(5) No woman loves any man
$\simeq$ It is not the case that [some woman loves a man]
$\simeq$ $\neg\exists x(Gx \wedge \exists y(Fy \wedge Lxy))$.

Another rendition, using our other style for translating 'no' propositions, is

$\simeq$ $\forall x(Gx \to \neg\exists y(Fy \wedge Lxy))$.

And here's a third version:

$\simeq$ Every woman is such that every man is such that she doesn't love him
$\simeq$ (Everyone x is such that)(if x is a woman then [every man y is such that x doesn't love $y])$
$\simeq$ (Everyone x is such that)(if x is a woman then $[($everyone y is such that$)$ if y is a man, then x doesn't love $y])$
$\simeq$ $\forall x(Gx \to \forall y(Fy \to \neg Lxy))$.

283

Can you see why these three renditions *ought* to be equivalent to each other?

Our next example involves translating the unary predicate 'is married' into a language which only has a built-in binary predicate meaning 'is married to'. No problem! – we just rely on the obvious semantic equivalence of the unary 'is married' to 'is married to someone'. Thus we have:

(6)   Anyone who is married loves someone they aren't married to
   $\simeq$ (Everyone x who is married is such that)[there is someone y whom x isn't married to, such that x loves y]
   $\simeq$ (Everyone x is such that)(if x is married, then [(someone y is such that) x isn't married to y and x loves y])
   $\simeq$ $\forall x(x$ is married $\rightarrow \exists y(\neg Mxy \wedge Lxy))$.

Finally, we render 'x is married' using the predicate M plus an existential quantifier. What variable shall we use? Rule of thumb: when you need to introduce some variable into a wff, it is always safer to use one that doesn't already appear. That way you will avoid unintended tangles. So, choose the variable 'z':

   $\simeq$ $\forall x(\exists z Mxz \rightarrow \exists y(\neg Mxy \wedge Lxy))$.

In our next example on the list, 'A married man …' is naturally read as a universal generalization about married men. So, we can begin

(7)   A married man only loves women
   $\simeq$ (Every man x who is married is such that)(x only loves women)
   $\simeq$ (Everyone x is such that)(if x is a man and is married, then [x only loves women])

Now, 'x only loves women' is in turn naturally read as saying anyone whom x loves is a woman (but we will want to leave it open whether there *is* anyone x in fact loves). So, continuing,

   $\simeq$ (Everyone x is such that)([x is a man and is married] $\rightarrow$ [(everyone y is such that) if x loves y then y is a woman])
   $\simeq$ $\forall x((Fx \wedge \exists z Mxz) \rightarrow \forall y(Lxy \rightarrow Gy))$.

Our final example again involves that troublesome vernacular quantifier 'any-one'. As we have already seen, in some contexts, 'anyone' is replaceable by 'some-one'; (8) seems to be another case in point. The following rendition seems natural:

(8)   No man loves anyone who loves Nerys.
   $\simeq$ (Every man x is such that) it is not the case that [there is someone who loves Nerys whom x loves]
   $\simeq$ (Every man x is such that) $\neg$[(there is someone y such that) y loves Nerys $\wedge$ x loves y]
   $\simeq$ $(\forall x)(x$ is a man $\rightarrow \neg[(\exists y)(y$ loves Nerys $\wedge$ x loves $y)])$
   $\simeq$ $\forall x(Fx \rightarrow \neg \exists y(Lyn \wedge Lxy))$.

An alternative translation could be '$\forall x(Fx \rightarrow (\forall y)(Lyn \rightarrow \neg Lxy))$'. Why should these be equivalent?

And that's more than enough examples to be going on with!

284

30.2 Translations from QL₂

Translating *from* an unfamiliar language tends to be a lot easier than translating *into* that language. Once we have learnt to spot the devices which QL languages use for expressing restricted quantifications and/or 'no' quantifiers, it is often pretty easy to construe a wff straight off. And if the worst comes to the worst, and we are faced with a more dauntingly complex wff, we can always just reverse the stage-by-stage-via-Loglish procedure that we have just been using.

To illustrate this, we will take three QL₂ wffs:

(1) ¬∀x∀y((Fx ∧ Gy) → (Mxy → ∃zRzxy))
(2) ∀x(Gx → ∀y∀z(Rxyz → (Lxy ∧ Lxz)))
(3) (∀x(Gx → ¬Lxm) → ∀x((Lxm → ∃yRxmy) ∧ (∃yRxmy → Lxm))).

We now unpack these wffs in stages going via Loglish to arrive at interpretations, for example as follows:

(1) ¬∀x∀y((Fx ∧ Gy) → (Mxy → ∃zRzxy))
  ≃ ¬(For anyone x and anyone y)(if x is a man and y a woman, then if x is married to y, there is someone z who is x and y's child)
  ≃ ¬(For any man and any woman)(if they are married to each other, they have a child together)
  ≃ Not every man and woman who are married have a child together.

(2) ∀x(Gx → ∀y∀z(Rxyz → (Lxy ∧ Lxz)))
  ≃ (Everyone x is such that)(if x is a woman then [everyone y and everyone z are such that (if x is a child of y and z, then x loves y and x loves z)]
  ≃ Every woman x is such that [for anyone y and anyone z (if x is a child of y and z then x loves y and x loves z)]
  ≃ Every woman loves her parents.

(3) (∀x(Gx → ¬Lxm) → ∀x((Lxm → ∃yRxmy) ∧ (∃yRxmy → Lxm)))
  ≃ If ∀x(Gx → ¬Lxm), then ∀x((Lxm → ∃yRxmy) ∧ (∃yRxmy → Lxm))
  ≃ If no woman loves Maldwyn, then ∀x(Lxm if and only if ∃yRxmy)
  ≃ If no woman loves Maldwyn then, for any x, x loves Maldwyn if and only if x is a child of Maldwyn and someone
  ≃ If no woman loves Maldwyn, then he is loved just by any children he has.

30.3 Choosing a domain

Some QL languages are of stable and lasting interest. Two examples that you will soon meet if you continue to study logic are the language of full-blown set theory (which has just one built-in non-logical predicate, '∈' for set membership, and whose quantifiers run over sets) and the language of first-order arithmetic (which quantifies over natural numbers and which has just one built-in name for zero, and function expressions for the successor, addition, and multiplication functions – see Chapter 42). But most of the languages which we meet in this book are of *much* more fleeting interest. They are constructed entirely ad hoc, for temporary use, either for illustrative purposes (like QL_1 and QL_2), or when we want to formalize particular arguments (starting in Chapter 32). So, when rendering ordinary language into QL, how do we choose an ad hoc language?

One particular issue which arises is: how do we choose which domain to quantify over? Suppose, for example, that we want to regiment the argument

(1) Some philosophers are wise; no astrologer is wise; so some philosophers are not astrologers.

Ignoring the implication that there is more than one wise philosopher, we can regiment the argument into an ad hoc QL language along the lines of

(2) $\exists x(Px \land Wx), \forall x(Ax \rightarrow \neg Wx) \therefore \exists x(Px \land \neg Ax),$

where the predicate letters get the obvious interpretation and the domain of quantification is naturally chosen to be people.

But what if we want to regiment the equally valid argument

(3) Some philosophers are wise; no koala bear is wise; so some philosophers are not koala bears?

This time, we can't use a formal language whose quantifiers run just over people. We need a language with a more inclusive domain, one that includes both philosophers and koalas. Then we can formalize the argument like this:

(4) $\exists x(Px \land Wx), \forall x(Kx \rightarrow \neg Wx) \therefore \exists x(Px \land \neg Kx),$

where the quantifier runs over mammals, or living things, or terrestrial objects, or over any other sufficiently inclusive domain. And we *could* indeed have equally well used a more inclusive domain in regimenting (1) too.

So note then that the same premiss 'Some philosophers are wise' can, for different purposes, be equally well translated into different QL languages with different domains. The point generalizes:

> When choosing a QL language for regimenting some ordinary-language proposition(s), we will need a domain of quantification which includes everything that the informal quantifiers in the given propositions are already quantifying over. But there will in general be no uniquely correct choice of domain; it will be enough that the domain is sufficiently inclusive.

30.4 'Translation' and 'logical form'

After grappling with so many translation examples, let's finish this chapter with some rather more restful historical/philosophical reflections!

(a) Early in the last century, we find Bertrand Russell and Ludwig Wittgenstein, much influenced by Frege, being gripped by the thought that the surface look of ordinary language in some way disguises the true 'logical form' of propositions. They proposed that a central concern of philosopher-logicians should be to 'analyse' propositions to reveal this putative underlying structure. And the idea later gained ground that the now standard notation of the new quantifier/variable logic perspicuously represents real structures of 'logical form', hidden by the surface syntax of language. Is there anything in this idea?

(b)   Here's an obvious initial problem. As we have seen, if we try to render 'No woman loves Maldwyn' into a language like QL_2, we arrive at the alternatives $\neg\exists x(Gx \land Lxm)$ and $\forall x(Gx \to \neg Lxm)$. It really just doesn't seem very plausible to suggest that the first formal wff here is picking up on an existential quantifier and a conjunction somehow already hidden under the surface of the ordinary English. So should we prefer the second rendition and say instead that there is a hidden universal quantifier and a conditional? How could we possibly choose?

Note, however, that our rendition of the 'no' proposition into QL_2 involves working around two difficulties that we have imposed on ourselves. To keep our formal language sparse, we have stipulated that there isn't a 'no' quantifier built into the language, and also that the remaining quantifiers all range over a single universe of discourse with restrictions to be made by using connectives. So the particular shapes of our two formal versions of 'No woman loves Maldwyn' are really an artefact of these two optional choices we made for the sake of convenience in designing our QL languages; it would be very hard to argue that the results of *these* choices should be deeply revealing about the semantic structure of ordinary language.

(c)   Still, what about the most fundamental thing, the basic quantifier/variable idea for representing general claims? Frege and his followers are now surely onto something. For we can agree that everyday English *doesn't* vividly mark in surface syntax the deep semantic difference between a proper name like 'Maldwyn' or 'Nerys' on the one hand, and an expression of generality like 'someone' or 'nobody' on the other hand. For grammatically speaking, the two sorts of expression very often behave in much the same way – e.g. we can plug either kind into predicates like '① is Welsh' or '① loves ②' and get grammatical sentences.

Now, it would be a step too far to say that vernacular expressions of generality behave grammatically *exactly* like proper names, and can always occupy the same positions in sentences. For example, contrast 'Something wicked this way comes' with the ungrammatical 'Maldwyn wicked this way comes', or contrast 'Someone brave rescued the dog' with 'Nerys brave rescued the dog'. Or again, contrast 'Foolish Donald tweeted' with the ungrammatical 'Foolish nobody tweeted'. And so on. But still, the key point remains that the surface syntax of everyday language closely assimilates names and (some) expressions of generality, and doesn't explicitly and systematically signal the semantic divide between names and quantifiers in the way that QL syntax does.

In particular, everyday language does not mark the crucial fact that proper names are scopeless while quantifiers have scopes, and hence can generate scope-ambiguities. So, yes, it might well be said that the quantifier/variable notation represents more perspicuously aspects of underlying semantic structure which are somewhat masked by the surface grammar of English.

(d)   But we need not really press that last point. For our key claim is that it is a good strategy for logical purposes to sidestep the messy complexities of English usage – think again of 'any' vs 'every', think again of scope phenomena, etc. And we do this by (1) translating arguments involving general claims into a nicely behaved, unambiguous QL language, and then (2) evaluating the arguments in their tidily regimented form. To defend this strategy, it is *not* necessary to suppose that the artificial languages (even in part) reflect structures which are in some good sense already there 'under the surface' of English. It is enough that wffs in the formal language behave in truth-relevant ways which sufficiently respect the contents of the claims made in the original English.

Now, whenever we deploy this divide-and-rule strategy for assessing arguments – i.e. whenever we translate from ordinary language into a formal language, and then deal with the clean-and-tidy formalized arguments – we would ideally both like (i) very direct, natural, unforced translations into the relevant artificial language L, and also like (ii) an elegantly simple language L which is easy to manipulate and theorize about. But the more 'natural' we try to make the translations between English and L, the greater the number of distinctions we may find ourselves needing to mark in L, and so the more complex everything will get. And that will mean, in particular, increased complexity when we come to evaluate arguments in L.

In practice, then, we are typically faced with a trade-off between closeness of translation and ease of logical manipulation. We've seen this before when we adopted the material conditional, giving us the simplicity of truth-functional logic for PL, but at the price of some rather dubious-seeming translations of everyday 'if's. And again, in the present case, there's a trade-off. We buy the sparse simplicity of QL languages at the cost of, among other things, having to shoehorn our everyday restricted quantifications into a language where such quantifications have to be mocked up using connectives.

But arguably the price is right: the formal translations, although sometimes strained and cumbersome, do enable us to capture the logically relevant content of a wide class of ordinary claims. In particular, we can then use our formal translations in assessing the validity of a great number of arguments relying on the presence of quantifiers. And by these standards, the use of QL languages is a pretty resounding success. Or so, let's hope, the following chapters will reveal.

30.5   Summary

We have looked at examples of the translation of more complex, multiply quantified, propositions into QL, again easing the journey by going via Loglish intermediate stages.

We have also seen a few examples of the reverse journey, taking us back from QL wffs to their English translations.

In fixing on a formal language for rendering a given argument, we will need

– among other things – to assign it a sufficiently inclusive (non-empty) domain of quantification. There need be no unique way of doing this.

We do *not* claim that our renditions of e.g. restricted quantifiers reveal the underlying logical form of our vernacular propositions – so that 'All *F*s are *G*' is unmasked as really a quantified conditional. Our key claim is only that our formal translations track the (tidied-up, disambiguated) truth-relevant content of vernacular propositions well enough for the purposes of our divide-and-rule approach to logic.

Exercises 30

(a)   Translate the following into QL$_2$:

(1)   Maldwyn loves anyone who loves Owen.
(2)   Everyone loves whoever they are married to.
(3)   Some man is a child of Owen and someone or other.
(4)   Whoever is a child of Maldwyn and Nerys loves them both.
(5)   Owen is a child of Nerys and someone who loves Nerys.
(6)   Some men do not love those who they are married to.
(7)   Every man who loves Nerys loves someone who is married to Owen.
(8)   No woman is loved by every married man.
(9)   Everyone who loves Maldwyn loves no one who loves Owen.
(10) Whoever loves Maldwyn loves a man only if the latter loves Maldwyn too.
(11) Only if Maldwyn loves every woman does he love whoever is married to Owen.
(12) No one loves anyone who has no children.

(b)   Now consider the language QL$_3$ whose quantifiers range over the positive integers, with the following glossary:

n: one,
F: ① is odd,
G: ① is even,
H: ① is prime,
L: ① is less than ②,
R: ① is the sum of ② and ③.

Then translate the following into natural English (they are not all true!):

(1) $\forall x \forall y \exists z Rzxy$
(2) $\exists y \forall x Lxy$
(3) $\forall x \exists y (Lxy \wedge Hy)$
(4) $\forall x (Hx \rightarrow \exists y (Lxy \wedge Hy))$
(5) $\forall x \forall y ((Fx \wedge Ryxn) \rightarrow \neg Fy)$
(6) $\forall x \exists y ((Gx \wedge Fy) \wedge Rxyy)$
(7) $\forall x \forall y (\exists z (Rzxn \wedge Ryzn) \rightarrow (Gx \rightarrow Gy))$
(8) $\forall x \forall y \forall z (((Fx \wedge Fy) \wedge Rzxy) \rightarrow Gz)$
(9) $\forall x ((Gx \wedge \neg Rxnn) \rightarrow \exists y \exists z ((Hy \wedge Hz) \wedge Rxyz))$
(10) $\forall x \exists y ((Hy \wedge Lxy) \wedge \exists w \exists z ((Rwyn \wedge Rzwn) \wedge Hz))$

Interlude: Arguing in QL

(a) We announced in the previous Interlude that we will adopt a divide-and-rule strategy for coping with arguments involving quantifiers. We are going to sidestep the messy complexities of ordinary language by first regimenting arguments into well-behaved formal languages, and then assessing the resulting formalized arguments. We have now introduced formal QL languages. True, we haven't yet put together the whole story about the syntax of QL languages, and we have only given an informal account of how we interpret such languages. But we have said enough to be able to start discussing how to formalize a wide class of quantifier arguments.

(b) We approached questions of PL validity in two ways:

(P1) We defined tautological validity for arguments involving the PL connectives. And we gave a direct brute-force method for determining validity in this sense.

(P2) We set down some intuitively correct truth-preserving modes of inference for the connectives, guided by their intuitive meaning, and codified these rules into a natural deduction system for warranting arguments.

Soundness and completeness theorems tell us that these two approaches end up validating just the same arguments.

Similarly we can approach questions of QL validity in two ways:

(Q1) We can define a suitable notion of *q-validity* for QL arguments involving the quantifiers as well as the connectives.

(Q2) We can set down some intuitively correct truth-preserving modes of inference for the quantifiers to add to the rules for the connectives, and codify them into a natural deduction system for warranting QL arguments.

But what is q-validity? Let's have an initial sketch.

(c) Recall how things went for propositional logic. The PL logical operators are truth-functional. This means that a possible valuation of some atomic wffs will fix the truth values of all the wffs constructed from these atoms. And this motivates the definition of tautological validity. A PL inference is tautologically valid just when, for every possible valuation of its non-logical vocabulary (the relevant atoms), if its premises are true then its conclusion is true too.

Similarly, the QL logical operators – now including the quantifiers – might be said to be value-functional. What this means is that fixing the truth-relevant values of given names and predicates, plus fixing the domain of quantification, will again fix the truth values of all the wffs we can construct from those resources using the QL operators. And what are the truth-determining values of names and predicates? What are their *q-values* for short?

Exactly what you would expect from our preliminary discussions in Chapter 25! So a q-valuation will assign references to names and will assign appropriate extensions to predicates. It is these references and extensions, plus the domain of quantification, that fix the truth values of sentences in a QL language.

This motivates the definition of q-validity. A QL inference is q-valid just when, for every possible q-valuation of the building blocks of the relevant language – i.e. every way of assigning q-values to its names and predicates and every way of fixing the domain – if the inference's premises are true then its conclusion is true too.

Take, for example, the following everyday argument:

> Felix is a cat. All cats are scary. So, Felix is scary.

Obviously this is deductively valid – and moreover, it is intuitively *logically* valid, because it is valid in virtue of the meaning of the topic-neutral quantifier 'all'. Rendered into a suitable QL language, the argument becomes

> Fn, $\forall x(Fx \rightarrow Gx)$ ∴ Gn.

And this, we claim, is q-valid. It doesn't matter what domain the quantifiers are ranging over, or which object in the domain the name picks out, or which sets of objects from the domain the predicates have as extensions: on *any* such q-valuation, if the premises are true, the conclusion is true too. (Think through why this really should be true!)

(d) To backtrack, we initially characterized a (one-step) argument as being deductively valid just if there is no possible situation in which its premises are true and conclusion false. And we said that an argument is logically valid just if it is deductively valid in virtue of the way that topic-neutral notions appear in the premises and conclusion. As we noted at the time, both the idea of a possible situation and the idea of topic-neutrality are less than ideally clear.

Still, if we restrict our focus to arguments turning on the truth-functional connectives, we can trade in the general notion of logical validity for the notion of tautological validity (defined in terms of the perfectly clear notion of a valuation).

Similarly, the notion of q-validity will give us a rational reconstruction of the idea of an argument's being deductively valid in virtue of the way topic-neutral quantifiers and connectives appear in it.

However, even with what little we have said so far, you can immediately spot that there is going to be a fundamental disanalogy between assessing the tautological validity of PL arguments and assessing the q-validity of QL arguments.

In the PL case, the non-logical vocabulary of an argument comprises just the relevant atomic wffs; and each of these is assigned one of two truth values.

Given a finite handful of atoms, there is only a finite number of different possible assignments of truth-relevant values to them. *That* is why we can do a brute-force truth-table test to decide questions of tautological validity. There is only a limited number of cases to consider: so when we trudge through all the different valuations of the relevant atoms, in order to see whether a 'bad line' with true premises and false conclusion turns up, we know the process must terminate with a verdict.

In the QL case, the non-logical vocabulary of an argument comprises (say) some names and predicates; and the values we assign these are, respectively, objects on the one hand and extensions on the other. But now note that, even in the simple 'Felix' example with its one name and two predicates, there are *countless* different q-values we can potentially assign to the relevant vocabulary – countless different choices of domain, choices of references for the name, and extensions for the predicates. There is plainly no possible way of doing a brute-force search through *all* these q-valuations. And while there are tricks we can use for some simple cases, there is – perhaps unsurprisingly – no generally applicable mechanical test for q-validity.

(e) So, in general, we need to take other paths to demonstrate the q-validity of logically valid QL arguments. One possibility is to develop the truth-tree method for propositional logic which we gestured at so very briefly in §16.2. But in this book we continue to go down the natural deduction path.

We now know how to establish the tautological validity of PL arguments using Fitch-style proofs. And it turns out that this framework can be very smoothly and naturally(!) extended to give us proofs of the validity – indeed, the q-validity – of logically valid QL arguments too. In fact things can go *so* smoothly that it is very inviting to look at proofs *first*, before saying more about q-validity.

Therefore, starting in the next chapter, we will begin to explore natural rules for arguing with quantified statements, first informally, and then in a Fitch-style formal proof system.

At the outset, we just claim that our rules of inference are intuitively compelling, capturing everyday modes of inference. And given all our earlier background work on PL Fitch-style proofs, we can now go quite quickly in developing a full QL proof system. Only after we have explored this formal proof system in some detail will we return in Chapter 36 to give an official account of q-validity and explain why our proof-building rules are not just intuitively reliable but are indeed reliable for q-validity.

31 Informal quantifier rules

This chapter briskly describes four intuitively correct principles for arguing informally with the quantifiers 'every' and 'some' (when they are regimented as quantifier prefixes). Then the next chapter will explain the corresponding rules of inference for constructing arguments using formal QL quantifiers.

31.1 Arguing with universal quantifiers

(a)   Let's begin with that hackneyed old favourite,

A   Socrates is a man. All men are mortal. Hence Socrates is mortal.

This hardly needs a proof to warrant it! But consider the following derivation, where we render the second premiss using a quantifier-variable notation, with the quantifier prefix running over a sufficiently inclusive domain (see §30.3):

(1)   Socrates is a man.   (premiss)
(2)   (Everything x is such that) if x is a man, then x is mortal.   (premiss)
(3)   If Socrates is a man, then Socrates is mortal.   (from 2)
(4)   Socrates is mortal.   (from 1, 3)

The principle that is invoked to get line (3) is very straightforward: what applies to everything/everyone in the relevant domain applies to any individual thing in the domain. Using the notion of an 'instance' (introduced in §27.5), we can state the intuitively compelling principle of *universal instantiation* as follows:

From a universal generalization, we can infer any particular instance.

(b)   This first principle enables us to argue *from* a universal generalization. Our second principle will allow us to argue *to* a universal generalization. To introduce it, we will work through an example. So consider this inference:

B   Everyone likes pizza. Whoever likes pizza likes ice cream. So everyone likes ice cream.

Again, obviously valid! But how can we derive the universally generalized conclusion from the premisses with an informal proof? The trick is to consider an arbitrary representative from the domain.

Regimenting the premisses and conclusion using informal quantifier prefixes, the idea is that we can argue like this:

(1) (Everyone x is such that) x likes pizza.   (premiss)
(2) (Everyone x is such that) if x likes pizza, then x likes ice cream.
                                                                              (premiss)
  Now pick any person in the domain as an arbitrary representative, tem-
  porarily dub them 'Alex'. Then:
(3) Alex likes pizza   (from 1)
(4) If Alex likes pizza, Alex likes ice cream   (from 2)
(5) Alex likes ice cream.   (from 3, 4)
  But Alex was arbitrarily chosen, and we have appealed to no special facts
  about them; so what we can deduce about them applies to everyone:
(6) (Everyone x is such that) x likes ice cream.   (from 5)

Now, the final step here is not, repeat *not*, relying on the hopeless idea that whatever is true of some individual in a domain is true of everyone/everything. (Here's Veronika. She is – as it happens – a woman, Slovak, and plays the violin. Plainly, we can't infer that everyone is a female Slovak violinist.) Rather, the principle at stake is this 'second-level' one (compare §20.7(a), §21.3, §22.1(a)):

> Suppose, given some background assumptions, we can infer that an arbitrary representative member a of the relevant domain is F. Then, from the same background assumptions, we can infer that everything in the domain is F (where the conclusion no longer mentions the arbitrary representative a).

But when can we treat some individual as an arbitrary representative of the domain? When we rely on no special distinguishing facts about that individual. In other words, *when that individual features in no premisses or additional assumptions* – so we can only draw on general knowledge about the domain in establishing that the individual in question is F.

(c)   Let's immediately take another example of this principle of *universal generalization* at work. Consider:

  C   No horses are green. All frogs are green. So no horses are frogs.

Regimenting the premisses and conclusion, recasting the 'no' propositions using prefixed universal quantifiers and negation, we can now argue as follows:

(1) (Everything x is such that) if x is a horse, x is not green.   (premiss)
(2) (Everything x is such that) if x is a frog, then x is green.   (premiss)
  Now pick any thing in the domain as an arbitrary representative, tem-
  porarily dub it 'Arb'. Then:
(3) If Arb is a horse, Arb is not green.   (from 1)
(4) If Arb is a frog, Arb is green.   (from 2)
(5) If Arb is a horse, Arb is not a frog.   (from 3, 4)
  But Arb was arbitrarily chosen, and we have appealed to no special facts
  about it; so what we can deduce about it applies equally to anything:
(6) (Everything x is such that) if x is a horse, x is not a frog.   (from 5)

We derive (3) and (4) using our first quantifier principle. The step taking us from

(3) and (4) to (5) is just propositional reasoning. We then derive our universally generalized conclusion (6) using our second quantifier principle.

(d)   There is an old worry that goes back to George Berkeley. Think of the mathematical practice of starting a proof with, for example, 'Let Δ be an arbitrary triangle ...'. Following Berkeley, someone might jump in to ask what an arbitrary triangle could possibly be – how can it possibly be, in his words, "neither equilateral, isosceles, nor scalene; but all and none of these at once"?

However, taking Δ to be an arbitrary representative triangle in an argument, or taking Alex to be an arbitrary representative person, etc., is *not* to conjure up a peculiar sort of being which lacks specific properties or has contradictory properties. Rather, it is just to consider an individual from the relevant domain while not relying on anything distinctive about it when selecting it or when drawing a conclusion about it.

31.2   Arguing with existential quantifiers

(a)   Now we introduce two principles for arguing with 'some'. This time, it is the principle for arguing *to* a generalization which is the simple one. Consider, for example,

D   Socrates is a wise man. Therefore some man is wise.

Regimenting the conclusion with a quantifier prefix, we can render the argument as follows:

(1) Socrates is a man and Socrates is wise.   (premiss)
(2) (Something x is such that) x is a man and x is wise.   (from 1)

Call the principle being used here *existential generalization*. The idea is that, whether we are using a permanent proper name like 'Socrates' or a temporary name like our 'Alex' and 'Arb', what is true of a named individual in a domain is certainly true of *something* in the domain! We can put it this way:

We can infer an existential generalization from any particular instance of it.

Note too this similar argument:

E   Narcissus loves himself. Therefore someone loves Narcissus.

Again, a regimented proof is simple:

(1) Narcissus loves Narcissus.   (premiss)
(2) (Someone x is such that) x loves Narcissus.   (from 1)

(1) is a particular instance of the existentially quantified (2), where we replace the variable with a name; and we can again infer the existentially quantified proposition from the instance. The point of this little example is to highlight that, when we existentially generalize from a claim like (1) involving a name, we do not have to replace *all* the occurrences of the name with a variable to get a valid inference using our principle.

(b)   That was easy. But our second principle for arguing with 'some' quantifiers takes rather more explanation. Consider another obviously valid argument:

F   Someone likes pizza. Whoever likes pizza likes ice cream. So someone likes ice cream.

How can we show that the conclusion follows from the premisses?

(i)   As a warm-up exercise, pretend for a moment that there are only two people in the domain, Jack and Jill. We can then argue by cases.

Suppose, first case, Jack likes pizza. By our second premiss, he likes ice cream; hence someone likes ice cream.

Alternatively, second case, suppose Jill likes pizza. By our second premiss, she likes ice cream; hence again someone likes ice cream.

Therefore, in either case, we can conclude someone likes ice cream. Since we are given that someone likes pizza, at least one of these cases holds, so we can conclude outright that someone likes ice cream.

(ii)   Now we need to drop the pretence that there are just two people. But in general, we can't run through everyone in the domain case by case (that's probably quite impractical, even if we know who they are). What to do? We can still argue as if by cases by *arguing from a representative case*. So dub some arbitrary representative person 'Alex'.

Suppose that Alex likes pizza. Given our second premiss, it follows that Alex likes ice cream, and hence that someone likes ice cream.

Now, this conclusion that someone likes ice cream doesn't depend on who Alex is, doesn't depend on who is being supposed to be a pizza-lover. But our first premiss tells us that there *is* at least one pizza-lover to choose. Hence our desired conclusion follows outright.

To bring out the structure of the argument in (ii) clearly, we can regiment it as follows, indenting the line of proof when we make a temporary supposition:

(1) (Someone x is such that) x likes pizza.   (premiss)
(2) (Everyone x is such that) if x likes pizza, x likes ice cream.
                                                                   (premiss)
Now pick someone in the domain as an arbitrary representative, and temporarily dub them 'Alex'. Let's suppose
(3)   Alex likes pizza.   (supp)
(4)   If Alex likes pizza, Alex likes ice cream.   (from 2)
(5)   Alex likes ice cream.   (from 3, 4)
(6)   (Someone x is such that) x likes ice cream.   (from 5)
But note our interim conclusion (6) doesn't mention Alex and doesn't depend on anything special about them, other than (3) they like pizza. And premiss (1) tells us that there is someone who is, as we are supposing Alex to be, a pizza-lover. So, given (1) and the inference from (3) to (6), we are entitled to our conclusion outright:
(7) (Someone x is such that) x likes ice cream.   (from 1, 3–6)

296

Here, we get to (4) using our first principle of inference for 'every'. The step from (3) and (4) on to (5) is just a modus ponens inference. Step (6) involves our first principle for 'some'.

What makes Alex count as an arbitrary representative in this context, so that we can now make the final inference step to (7)? To repeat, the fact that we rely on no distinguishing information about Alex (other than that they like pizza) – in other words, we only draw on general knowledge about the domain in making inferences from the supposition (3).

How, then, shall we spell out the general inferential principle being used here, where we argue from a representative case?

> Suppose, given some background assumptions, (i) we can infer that something in the relevant domain is F, and (ii) from the additional supposition that a is F we can infer the claim C (where a is not mentioned in any previous assumption, and C is independent of the particular choice of a). Then, from the same background assumptions, we can infer C outright.

Note, then, that this is another 'second-level' inferential principle (i.e. another principle that tells us if one entailment holds, so does another).

(c) This principle is the most intricate of all the inference rules we will be stating in this book. But the underlying idea is simple enough: to repeat, you can think of it as a generalized version of arguing by cases.

Let's walk slowly through a second informal example, then, where we again argue from a representative case. So here is another valid Aristotelian syllogism to consider:

G Some pets are dragons. Nothing pink is a dragon. So some pets aren't pink.

Regimenting the premisses using prefixed quantifiers, we can set out a deduction of the conclusion from the premisses like this:

(1) (Something x is such that) x is a pet and x is a dragon.   (premiss)
(2) (Everything x is such that) if x is pink, x is not a dragon. (premiss)
     Now pick something in the domain as an arbitrary representative,
     and temporarily dub them 'Arb'. Let's suppose
(3)   Arb is a pet and Arb is a dragon.   (supp)
(4)   If Arb is pink, Arb is not a dragon.   (from 2)
(5)   Arb is a pet and Arb is not pink.   (from 3, 4)
(6)   (Something x is such that) x is a pet and x is not pink. (from 5)
     But note our conclusion (6) doesn't mention Arb, and doesn't depend on
     anything particular about it other than (3) it is a pet dragon. And our
     premiss (1) tells us that there is something which is, as we are supposing
     Arb to be, a pet dragon. So given (1) and the inference from (3) to (6)
     we are entitled to our conclusion outright:
(7) (Something x is such that) x is a pet and x is not pink.   (from 1, 3–6)

297

We get to (4) using our first principle of inference for 'every'. The reasoning from (3) and (4) on to (5) is elementary propositional reasoning again. Step (6) involves our first principle for 'some'. Then the final step at (7) is another application of our new principle, about which more in the next chapter.

31.3 Summary

We briskly introduced four inference rules for arguing with 'every' and 'some' in their Loglish form of quantifier prefixes. These rules are tidied-up versions of principles we already use in everyday reasoning.

Two rules are very straightforward. The rule of universal instantiation tells us that from a universal quantification you can infer any instance. The rule of existential generalization tells us that from an instance you can infer its existential quantification.

The other two rules – universal generalization, and what we called 'arguing as if by cases' – involve reasoning with 'arbitrary' instances of a universal or existential quantification, as illustrated. We will give a more careful treatment of these rules in their formal guises in the following chapter.

Exercises 31

Regiment the premises and conclusions of the following arguments using informal prefixed quantifiers and variables. Using the four quantifier principles we have met plus propositional reasoning, give informal derivations in the style of this chapter to show that the arguments are valid:

(1) If Jo can do the exercises, then everyone in the class can do the exercises. Mo is in the class, and can't do the exercises. So Jo can't do the exercises.

(2) No whales are fish. So no fish are whales.

(3) All leptons have half-integer spin. All electrons are leptons. So all electrons have half-integer spin.

(4) Some chaotic attractors are not fractals. Every Cantor set is a fractal. Hence some chaotic attractors are not Cantor sets.

(5) Some philosophers are logicians. All logicians are rational people. No rational person is a flat-earther. Therefore some philosophers are not flat-earthers.

(6) All lions and tigers are dangerous animals. Dangerous animals should be avoided. Leo is a lion. So Leo should be avoided.

Give informal derivations warranting these arguments too (a little more difficult!):

(7) There is someone who loves everyone. Hence everyone is loved by someone or other. [NB the difference between $(\exists x)(\forall y)$ and $(\forall y)(\exists x)$!]

(8) Everyone loves logic. Hence it isn't the case that someone doesn't love logic.

(9) Any philosopher who is not a fool likes logic. There is a philosopher who isn't a fool. Therefore not every philosopher fails to like logic.

32 QL proofs

We now introduce inference rules for the use of quantifiers in formal QL arguments. This is the crucial step in developing quantificational logic. However, our rules will now look familiar, because they are just formal versions of the four intuitively compelling rules we met in the last chapter.

32.1 Dummy names in QL languages

(a) We need to start, though, by asking: just what are expressions like 'Alex' doing in our informal proofs in the last chapter?

'Alex' there functions somewhat like the lawyer's 'John Roe' or 'Jane Doe'. It plainly isn't serving as an ordinary proper name which *already* has a fixed reference. On the other hand, it isn't a bound pronoun either. It is a sort of 'dummy name', or 'temporary name', or 'ambiguous name', or 'arbitrary name' – all of those labels are in use, although perhaps none is entirely happy. Another, colourless, label for the logical use is 'parameter'. We will mostly use the first and last of these labels.

When we turn to formalizing our quantifier proofs, then, we will want symbols to play the role of these dummy names or parameters. There is no one agreed policy for supplying such symbols. There are three alternatives on the market:

(A) We can use the same symbols for free-standing parameters as we already use for variables-bound-to-quantifiers (in conventional jargon, the same symbols can appear as both 'free variables' and 'bound variables').

(B) We can use the same type of symbols for dummy names as for proper names (with just some of the names getting a fixed denotation in a given language).

(C) We can use a third, distinctive, type of symbol for dummy names.

The first policy has historically been the most common one among logicians. It perhaps does conform best to the practice of mathematicians who casually move between using letters as dummy or temporary names ('Let m be the number of positive roots ...') and using letters of the same kind as quantified variables ('For any positive integer n, $(n+1)(n-1) = n^2 - 1$'), often leaving it to context to make it clear what the symbols are doing. However, when we go formal, overloading symbols like this can cause trouble unless we spell out careful rules for their double use.

The second policy can also be made to work with a bit of care. But once we have distinguished, at the semantic level, (i) the fixed-denotation names built into a particular language from (ii) its further supply of dummy names, why not highlight the distinction by using syntactically different symbols for the two styles of name?

The third policy, then, may be less economical but it does make it easier to keep track of what is going on. It conforms to the good Fregean principle of marking important differences of semantic role by using different styles of symbols. It has distinguished antecedents, particularly in the work of the great 1930s logician Gerhard Gentzen. So (C) is the policy we adopt in this book.

(b)   Given our decision, then, we now need to augment our definition of the shared logical apparatus of each QL language. Thus:

> Every QL language, as well as having an unlimited supply of *variables*, starting
>
> > x, y, z, ... ,
>
> also has an unlimited supply of *dummy names*, starting
>
> > a, b, c, ...
>
> Like proper names – and unlike variables – dummy names are also *terms*.

We will later do better than giving open-ended lists. For now, however, the crucial point is that the dummy names, proper names (§28.2), and variables (§28.6) of a language are to be sharply distinguished from each other as symbols (by using letters from the beginning, middle, and end of the alphabet).

The *syntactic* rules for wff-building introduced in §28.2(b) and §28.6(b) can remain the same, however, since we stated them as applying to terms generally. A predicate followed by the right number of terms – now proper names and/or dummy names – is an atomic wff. Hence the atomic wffs of QL_1 also include

> Fa, Gb, Lbn, Mcc, Ramc, ...

However, expressions with variables dangling free, without an associated quantifier prefix, still don't count as wffs for us, given we have adopted policy (C).

As to the *semantic* role of dummy names, just think of them for now as temporarily dubbing objects selected from the domain.

(c)   We will need some terminology to distinguish wffs with dummy names from those without. So, for future use, let's say:

> A QL wff without dummy names is a closed wff or a *sentence*.
>
> A wff with one or more dummy names in it will be called an open wff or an *auxiliary wff*.

Hence, for example,

> ∃y Mmy, ∃y∀x Lxy, ∀z(Hz → ∃y Lzy), ∀x(Lx → ∃y(Fy ∧ Rxyn)),

are sample QL$_1$ sentences; while

Lmb, ∃y May, (Ha → ∃y Lay), (La → ∃y(Fy ∧ Rbyn)),

are also wffs, but auxiliary ones as they contain dummy names.

It is the *sentences* of a given QL language which will get stable, fixed, interpretations. And when we consider formal QL arguments, we will primarily be interested in arguments from zero or more *sentences* as premisses to a *sentence* as final conclusion. Non-sentences with dummy names will mainly play the same role as the informal expressions with 'Alex' and 'Arb' in the last section, i.e. they will mainly be used in auxiliary steps in the middle of natural deduction proofs – hence our label, 'auxiliary wffs'.

(d) One comment. Swapping between the different policy options (A), (B), and (C) for handling parameters in arguments will change which expressions count as wffs by changing the allowed *non*-sentences. But the class of *sentences* – i.e. wffs without parameters/dummy names, however they are implemented – can stay constant across the options. And, as you would expect, *the logical relations between sentences will stay constant too*. Hence, although we *do* have to make a policy choice here about how we handle parameters, in the most important respect it is not a very significant choice.

32.2   Schematic notation, and instances of quantified wffs

Before proceeding, it will be useful to gather together some notational conventions, old and new, for the use of symbols in schemas (compare §28.6):

> δ (*delta*, the Greek *d*) will now be used to stand in for some dummy name.
>
> τ stands in for a term, which can be a proper name or a dummy name.
>
> ξ, as before, stands in for some variable.
>
> α(δ) and α(τ) stand in for wffs which involve one or more occurrences of, respectively, the dummy name δ and the term τ.
>
> ∀ξα(ξ) and ∃ξα(ξ) stand in for wffs which begin with a universal or existential quantifier involving the variable ξ, and where the expression α(ξ) completing the wff contains one or more occurrences of the same variable ξ.

Now, our summary versions of the four quantifier rules in the last chapter were all stated in terms of the notion of an instance of a quantified claim. So we will need a formal definition of that syntactic notion:

> Suppose ∀ξα(ξ) or ∃ξα(ξ) is a quantified wff, τ is a term, and α(τ) is the result of replacing every occurrence of ξ in α(ξ) by τ. Then α(τ) is a wff and an *instance* of the quantified wff.

For example, here are a few quantified QL$_1$ wffs with some of their instances:

301

$\forall$x Lxn: Lmn, Lnn, Lan, ... ,
$\exists$z(Fz $\wedge$ Gz):   (Fn $\wedge$ Gn), (Fa $\wedge$ Ga), (Fc $\wedge$ Gc), ... ,
$\forall$x(Fx $\rightarrow$ $\exists$yLxy): (Fm $\rightarrow$ $\exists$yLmy), (Fn $\rightarrow$ $\exists$yLny), (Fb $\rightarrow$ $\exists$yLby), ...

By contrast, the following are *not* pairs of quantified wffs and their instances:

$\neg\forall$x Fx: $\neg$Fm,
($\exists$zFz $\wedge$ Gn):   (Fn $\wedge$ Gn),
$\forall$x(Fx $\rightarrow$ $\exists$yLxy): $\forall$x(Fx $\rightarrow$ Lxm).

It is only wffs with a quantifier as the main operator which count as having instances. (And let's emphasize again: the notion of instance is defined syntactically. An instance of a true wff needn't be true – consider existential cases.)

32.3   Inference rules for '$\forall$'

(a)   After those preliminaries, we can at last turn to building a Fitch-style natural deduction system for proofs involving quantifiers. (This section and the next are pivotal: so take them slowly and carefully!)

The basic shape of proofs, the principles for column-shifting, etc., are just the same as for PL proofs. And we can re-adopt our inference rules for dealing with the sentential connectives, now applied to wffs of our QL languages. Now we add a pair of rules for constructing arguments using universal quantifiers.

Recall the first informal principle of inference we met in §31.1: from a universally quantified wff, we can infer *any* instance. As noted, this is often called 'universal instantiation'. But we will prefer the term $\forall$-*Elimination* for the formal version, in line with our previous conventions for naming rules (the idea, recall, is that an elimination rule for a logical operator o allows us to infer *from* a wff with o as its main operator). Using the obvious short-form label, then, the formal rule is very simply this:

($\forall$E)   Given $\forall\xi\alpha(\xi)$, we can derive any instance $\alpha(\tau)$.

Exactly as in PL proofs, the 'given' inputs for the application of this and other rules of inference must be *available* (in the sense of §20.6).

Using a language with a suitable glossary, we can render argument **A** from §31.1 in the last chapter as

A$'$ Fm, $\forall$x(Fx $\rightarrow$ Gx) $\therefore$ Gm.

And since we have the familiar rules for the connectives available, our sketched informal argument warranting the inference therefore becomes

(1)	Fm	(Prem)
(2)	$\forall$x(Fx $\rightarrow$ Gx)	(Prem)
(3)	(Fm $\rightarrow$ Gm)	($\forall$E 2)
(4)	Gm	(MP 1, 3)

We annotate the application of the new rule ($\forall$E) in the predictable way.

(b)   The second principle we met is the 'universal generalization' rule: what applies to an arbitrary representative in a domain applies to everything. We will prefer the label ∀-*Introduction* for the formal version. And the rule becomes this: if we have already derived a wff with a dummy name then – so long as this dummy name really can be treated as temporarily dubbing an arbitrary representative because the name features in no relevant assumptions – we can go on to derive its universal generalization from the same background assumptions (where the generalization no longer mentions that representative).

In §24.6(c) we defined the idea of the *live assumptions* for a wff in a proof – i.e. the earlier available premisses/suppositions plus the wff on that line if it is itself a premiss/supposition. Then, more formally, the rule we want is this:

Given an available wff $\alpha(\delta)$, where the dummy name δ does not occur in any live assumption for that wff, then we can universally quantify on δ, and derive $\forall\xi\alpha(\xi)$.

But note, if we quantify on δ, then that dummy name will not appear in the resulting wff $\forall\xi\alpha(\xi)$ – see §28.6(b). Hence our rule is equivalent to the following official version (think about it!):

(∀I)   We can derive $\forall\xi\alpha(\xi)$, given an available instance $\alpha(\delta)$ – so long as (i) the dummy name δ doesn't occur in any live assumption for that instance, and (ii) δ doesn't occur in the conclusion $\forall\xi\alpha(\xi)$.

Let's remark again, the variable ξ can't already appear quantified in $\alpha(\delta)$ or else $\forall\xi\alpha(\xi)$ won't be a wff.

Take, then, the argument **B** from the last chapter. Rendered into a suitable ad hoc QL language, this becomes:

B′   ∀x Fx, ∀x(Fx → Gx) ∴ ∀x Gx.

And, using our new rule, a formal proof warranting the inference here can proceed exactly like the informal argument we gave for **B**:

(1)	∀x Fx	(Prem)
(2)	∀x(Fx → Gx)	(Prem)
(3)	Fa	(∀E 1)
(4)	(Fa → Ga)	(∀E 2)
(5)	Ga	(MP 3, 4)
(6)	∀x Gx	(∀I 5)

Our way of annotating the inference to line (6) is as you would expect.

Similarly, we can formally render the argument **C** from the last chapter into a QL language like this, using an obvious glossary:

C′   ∀x(Hx → ¬Gx), ∀x(Fx → Gx) ∴ ∀x(Hx → ¬Fx).

Again, we can mirror our informal derivation with a formal one (for now, we will laboriously fill in the propositional reasoning between lines (4) and (11) below):

(1)	$\forall x(Hx \rightarrow \neg Gx)$	(Prem)
(2)	$\forall x(Fx \rightarrow Gx)$	(Prem)
(3)	$(Ha \rightarrow \neg Ga)$	($\forall$E 1)
(4)	$(Fa \rightarrow Ga)$	($\forall$E 2)
(5)	Ha	(Supp)
(6)	$\neg Ga$	(MP 5, 3)
(7)	Fa	(Supp)
(8)	Ga	(MP 7, 4)
(9)	$\bot$	(Abs 8, 6)
(10)	$\neg Fa$	(RAA 7–9)
(11)	$(Ha \rightarrow \neg Fa)$	(CP 5–10)
(12)	$\forall x(Hx \rightarrow \neg Fx)$	($\forall$I 11)

Note that the dummy name 'a' does appear in the supposition at line (5), and appears again in another supposition at line (7). However – and this is crucial – by the time we get to line (11) both these suppositions have been discharged. Hence at line (11) *there are no live assumptions involving that dummy name*. So we *are* now allowed to universally quantify on it using ($\forall$I).

32.4   Inference rules for '$\exists$'

(a)   A universal quantification can be thought of as like a big conjunction – see §28.9(b). And just as we can infer a conjunct from a conjunction by ($\wedge$E), the ($\forall$E) elimination rule says that we can infer any instance from a universally quantified wff. Similarly, an existential quantification can be thought of as like a big disjunction. And just as we can infer a disjunction from a disjunct by ($\vee$I), the ($\exists$I) introduction rule will say that we can infer an existentially quantified wff from any instance:

($\exists$I)   We can derive the wff $\exists \xi \alpha(\xi)$ from any given instance $\alpha(\tau)$.

Note, the variable ξ can't appear in $\alpha(\tau)$ or else $\exists \xi \alpha(\xi)$ won't be a wff. ($\exists$I) then formalizes our 'existential generalization' principle from §31.2. Whether we use a proper name or a dummy name, if a named individual satisfies a certain condition, we can infer that *something* satisfies that condition.

Our formal rule can now be used in the following two intuitively correct mini-proofs, which track the informal proofs for **D** and **E** from §31.2:

(1)	$(Fn \wedge Gn)$	(Prem)
(2)	$\exists x(Fx \wedge Gx)$	($\exists$I 1)

and

(1)	Lnn	(Prem)
(2)	$\exists x\, Lxn$	($\exists$I 1)

(b)   As before, the other existential quantifier rule – permitting us to argue 'as if by cases' – takes a bit more care to state. Here is the key idea again:

We are given that something is F. Pick an arbitrary instance, so suppose that a is F (making no further assumptions about a). If this supposition implies a conclusion C which is independent of our choice of representative a, then – since we are given that something is F – we can conclude C.

So there are two conditions for an application of this rule which we need to capture. (i) We need a to be an arbitrary representative – i.e. we can't invoke any distinguishing facts about a (apart from its being F). (ii) The conclusion C must be independent of our choice of representative – so C mustn't mention a.

For the corresponding formal rule, we prefer the label ∃-*Elimination* (compare ∨-Elimination), and here is a version of the rule we need:

> (∃E)   Given $∃ξα(ξ)$, and a finished subproof from the instance $α(δ)$ as supposition to the conclusion $γ$ – where (i) the dummy name $δ$ is new to the proof, and (ii) $γ$ does not contain $δ$ – then we can derive $γ$.

Strictly speaking, we could allow occurrences of $δ$ in earlier, but now completed, subproofs. However, our 'always use a new dummy name' condition (i) is memorable and is the simplest way of ensuring that $δ$ features in no prior assumptions (nor in the relevant earlier wff $∃ξα(ξ)$).

Here then is last chapter's informal argument **F** once more rendered into a suitable QL language, and now warranted using our new rule:

F'   ∃x Fx, ∀x(Fx → Gx) ∴ ∃x Gx.

(1)	∃x Fx	(Prem)
(2)	∀x(Fx → Gx)	(Prem)
(3)	Fa	(Supp)
(4)	(Fa → Ga)	(∀E 2)
(5)	Ga	(MP 3, 4)
(6)	∃x Gx	(∃I 5)
(7)	∃x Gx	(∃E 1, 3–6)

We annotate the final step by giving the line number of the existentially quantified wff which we are invoking, and then noting the extent of the needed subproof from an instance of that wff with a new dummy name to the desired conclusion. Check that this step does obey our stated rule.

By the way, don't be surprised that an application of the existential quantifier *elimination* rule ends up proving an existentially quantified wff at line (7)! Look again: the elimination rule in our example is being applied to the *earlier* existentially quantified wff at line (1) – it is *that* existential wff which we are arguing from, using the (∃E) rule.

Similarly, we can formalize last chapter's syllogistic argument **G** like this:

G'   ∃x(Fx ∧ Gx), ∀x(Hx → ¬Gx) ∴ ∃x(Fx ∧ ¬Hx).

And here is a full-dress Fitch-style proof using our rules:

(1)	∃x(Fx ∧ Gx)	(Prem)
(2)	∀x(Hx → ¬Gx)	(Prem)
(3)	(Fa ∧ Ga)	(Supp)
(4)	(Ha → ¬Ga)	(∀E 2)
(5)	Fa	(∧E 3)
(6)	Ga	(∧E 3)
(7)	Ha	(Supp)
(8)	¬Ga	(MP 7, 4)
(9)	⊥	(Abs 6, 8)
(10)	¬Ha	(RAA 7–9)
(11)	(Fa ∧ ¬Ha)	(∧I 5, 10)
(12)	∃x(Fx ∧ ¬Hx)	(∃I 11)
(13)	∃x(Fx ∧ ¬Hx)	(∃E 1, 3–12)

(c)   It is, however, getting tedious to fill in routine derivations using rules for the sentential connectives. When we can argue from some previous QL wffs to a new wff by using propositional reasoning, why don't we now allow ourselves to jump straight to that new wff? For example, here is a briefer version of the last proof, where we use 'PL' on the right to signal some PL-style inference:

(1)	∃x(Fx ∧ Gx)	(Prem)
(2)	∀x(Hx → ¬Gx)	(Prem)
(3)	(Fa ∧ Ga)	(Supp)
(4)	(Ha → ¬Ga)	(∀E 2)
(5)	(Fa ∧ ¬Ha)	(PL 3, 4)
(6)	∃x(Fx ∧ ¬Hx)	(∃I 5)
(7)	∃x(Fx ∧ ¬Hx)	(∃E 1, 3–6)

This version is not just shorter, but it highlights the quantificational part of our reasoning which is what we now care about. From now on, we will occasionally cut ourselves a degree of slack by skipping over PL reasoning like this when writing out Fitch-style proofs for arguments using quantifiers.

(d)   For another example, consider the argument:

H   Only logicians are wise. Some philosophers are not logicians. All who love Aristotle are wise. Hence some of those who don't love Aristotle are still philosophers.

This is valid (think about it!). Rendered into QL_1 this becomes

H'   ∀x(Hx → Gx), ∃x(Fx ∧ ¬Gx), ∀x(Lxo → Hx) ∴ ∃x(¬Lxo ∧ Fx).

A formal derivation to warrant the inference will therefore start

(1)	∀x(Hx → Gx)	(Prem)
(2)	∃x(Fx ∧ ¬Gx)	(Prem)
(3)	∀x(Lxo → Hx)	(Prem)

And now a general point. When premisses are a mix of universal and existential quantifications, it is a good policy to instantiate the existential(s) first. Why? Because when we use (∃E), we must always begin by instantiating the existential quantification using a dummy name *new* to the proof. So you will need to get that name into play *before* you can later use it to instantiate some relevant universal quantification.

So let's instantiate (2) with a new dummy name, and then apply (∀E) to (1) and (3):

(4)	(Fa ∧ ¬Ga)	(Supp)
(5)	(Ha → Ga)	(∀E 1)
(6)	(Lao → Ha)	(∀E 3)

Now, our target conclusion is ∃x(¬Lxo ∧ Fx), which we can derive by existentially quantifying on the dummy name in (¬Lao ∧ Fa). But *that* wff follows from what we already have by propositional reasoning (how? – fill in the proof using PL rules!). Cutting ourselves some slack and skipping the details, we can conclude:

(7)	(¬Lao ∧ Fa)	(PL 4, 5, 6)
(8)	∃x(¬Lxo ∧ Fx)	(∃I 7)
(9)	∃x(¬Lxo ∧ Fx)	(∃E 2, 4–8)

(e)   For one more initial illustration of the existential rules in action, let's give a derivation for the obviously correct inference

I   (∃x Fx ∨ ∃x Gx) ∴ ∃x(Fx ∨ Gx).

The premiss is a disjunction, so we know that the overall shape of our proof is going to be an argument by cases, like this:

(∃x Fx ∨ ∃x Gx)	(Prem)
∃x Fx	(Supp)
⋮	
∃x(Fx ∨ Gx)	
∃x Gx	(Supp)
⋮	
∃x(Fx ∨ Gx)	
∃x(Fx ∨ Gx)	(∨E)

How do we fill in the dots? In each case, we have an existentially quantified supposition, and so we will expect to use the rule (∃E). So we will start a new subproof by instantiating the quantified wff – using a new dummy name – and aiming for the conclusion ∃x(Fx ∨ Gx). Here's a completed proof:

(1)	$(\exists x\, Fx \lor \exists x\, Gx)$	(Prem)
(2)	$\exists x\, Fx$	(Supp)
(3)	Fa	(Supp)
(4)	$(Fa \lor Ga)$	($\lor$I 3)
(5)	$\exists x(Fx \lor Gx)$	($\exists$I 4)
(6)	$\exists x(Fx \lor Gx)$	($\exists$E 2, 3–5)
(7)	$\exists x\, Gx$	(Supp)
(8)	Gb	(Supp)
(9)	$(Fb \lor Gb)$	($\lor$I 8)
(10)	$\exists x(Fx \lor Gx)$	($\exists$I 9)
(11)	$\exists x(Fx \lor Gx)$	($\exists$E 7, 8–10)
(12)	$\exists x(Fx \lor Gx)$	($\lor$E 1, 2–6, 7–11)

32.5 Quantifier equivalences

We now have introduction and elimination rules for the two QL quantifiers. The good news is that *these are all the quantifier rules we need*. And if we allow ourselves to jump over merely propositional reasoning, formal quantifier proofs using these rules can often be pretty neat and natural.

We will work through more examples in the next chapter. But first, it is helpful to show that our rules are enough to prove the following fundamental facts:

(a) The choice of the variable we use when we quantify doesn't matter (so long as it is new to the wff).

(b) An initial quantifier prefix of the form $\forall\xi$ is equivalent to the corresponding $\neg\exists\xi\neg$, and $\exists\xi$ is equivalent to $\neg\forall\xi\neg$.

(c) Two adjacent initial quantifiers of the same flavour can be interchanged, and the result will be provably equivalent.

(a) First then, we warrant the trivial inference $\forall x\, Fx \therefore \forall y\, Fy$:

(1)	$\forall x\, Fx$	(Prem)
(2)	Fa	($\forall$E 1)
(3)	$\forall y\, Fy$	($\forall$I 2)

The reverse inference is of course proved the same way, showing that the wffs are equivalent. And this simple pattern of proof generalizes. For any wffs $\forall\xi\alpha(\xi)$ and $\forall\zeta\alpha(\zeta)$, where the second results from the first by swapping all occurrences of the variable ξ for a variable ζ new to the expression, there will be a derivation of the shape:

(1)	$\forall\xi\alpha(\xi)$	(Prem)
(2)	$\alpha(\delta)$	($\forall$E 1)
(3)	$\forall\zeta\alpha(\zeta)$	($\forall$I 2)

We can also warrant the trivial inference $\exists x\, Fx \therefore \exists y\, Fy$ as follows:

(1)	∃x Fx	(Prem)
(2)	Fa	(Supp)
(3)	∃y Fy	(∃I 2)
(4)	∃y Fy	(∃E 1, 2–3)

Again the pattern of proof generalizes in the obvious way.

(b)   Next, we want to warrant the inference ∀x Fx ∴ ¬∃x¬Fx. We need to derive the negation of ∃x¬Fx, so we assume that wff at (2) and aim for absurdity. And how can we now use this new existential assumption except by using (∃E)? – so we suppose an instance at (3) and continue by aiming for absurdity:

(1)	∀x Fx	(Prem)
(2)	∃x¬Fx	(Supp)
(3)	¬Fa	(Supp)
(4)	Fa	(∀E 1)
(5)	⊥	(Abs 4, 3)
(6)	⊥	(∃E 2, 3–5)
(7)	¬∃x¬Fx	(RAA 2–6)

Since the absurdity sign doesn't contain the dummy name 'a', the application of (∃E) at line (6) conforms to the stated rule.

How do we warrant the converse inference ¬∃x¬Fx ∴ ∀x Fx? To get the conclusion, we can try to prove Fa and then universally generalize. So how can we prove Fa? Let's try that frequently useful dodge: assume the opposite and aim for a reductio!

(1)	¬∃x¬Fx	(Prem)
(2)	¬Fa	(Supp)
(3)	∃x¬Fx	(∃I 2)
(4)	⊥	(Abs 3, 1)
(5)	¬¬Fa	(RAA 2–4)
(6)	Fa	(DN 5)
(7)	∀x Fx	(∀I 6)

Note, the final step is again legal, since the dummy name 'a' in (6) occurs in no live assumption, i.e. no premiss or undischarged assumption.

Now for a pair of proofs showing that we can derive ∃x Fx and ¬∀x¬Fx from each other. First, we want a proof of the following shape:

	∃x Fx	(Prem)
	Fa	(Supp)
	⋮	
	¬∀x¬Fx	
	¬∀x¬Fx	(∃E)

Since the conclusion of the subproof begins with a negation, the obvious thing to do is assume ∀x¬Fx and aim for a reductio. So we can fill in the dots like this:

(1)	∃x Fx	(Prem)
(2)	Fa	(Supp)
(3)	∀x¬Fx	(Supp)
(4)	¬Fa	(∀E 3)
(5)	⊥	(Abs 2, 4)
(6)	¬∀x¬Fx	(RAA 3–5
(7)	¬∀x¬Fx	(∃E 1, 2–6)

The derivation in the reverse direction is rather more interesting. Our premiss is ¬∀x¬Fx; how are we going to derive the desired conclusion ∃x Fx? Again, what else can we do but assume the opposite and aim for a reductio? So we have:

	¬∀x¬Fx	(Prem)
	¬∃xFx	(Supp)
	⋮	
	⊥	
	¬¬∃xFx	(RAA)
	∃x Fx	(DN)

To derive ⊥ we'll want to prove ∀x¬Fx. How can we do that? By generalizing something like ¬Fa. Let's try to prove *that* by supposing Fa and aiming for another reductio:

(1)	¬∀x¬Fx	(Prem)
(2)	¬∃xFx	(Supp)
(3)	Fa	(Supp)
(4)	∃x Fx	(∃I 3)
(5)	⊥	(Abs 4, 2)
(6)	¬Fa	(RAA 3–5)
(7)	∀x¬Fx	(∀I 6)
(8)	⊥	(Abs 7, 1)
(9)	¬¬∃xFx	(RAA 2–8)
(10)	∃x Fx	(DN 9)

(c) Finally, here are a couple of simpler proofs illustrating how we can swap the order of two initial quantifiers of the same flavour. First, universals:

(1)	∀x∀y Lxy	(Prem)
(2)	∀y Lay	(∀E 1)
(3)	Lab	(∀E 2)
(4)	∀x Lxb	(∀I 3)
(5)	∀y∀x Lxy	(∀I 4)

Next, let's warrant the inference ∃x∃y Lxy ∴ ∃y∃x Lxy. Given the existential premiss, we need to instantiate it in a supposition to prepare for an argument by (∃E). But this instance is another existentially quantified wff, so we need next to take an instance of *that*. Following this plan, we get:

(1)	∃x∃y Lxy	(Prem)
(2)	∃y Lay	(Supp)
(3)	Lab	(Supp)
(4)	∃x Lxb	(∃I 3)
(5)	∃y∃x Lxy	(∃I 4)
(6)	∃y∃x Lxy	(∃E 2, 3–5)
(7)	∃y∃x Lxy	(∃E 1, 2–6)

Do double-check that in our last two proofs (∀I) and (∃E) are used correctly!

(d)   There is, of course, nothing special about any of our particular examples in this section. To take the last case, not only does ∃x∃y Lxy imply ∃y∃x Lxy, but the same line of argument shows that, for any variables ξ and ζ, a wff of the form ∃ξ∃$\zeta\psi$ (with ψ a suitable wff-completing expression) implies the corresponding wff with the quantifiers swapped around, ∃ζ∃$\xi\psi$. Similarly, the other results in this section can be generalized.

We could therefore use these generalized results, if we want, to augment our QL proof system with *derived rules* in the sense of §23.2. For example, we could add a rule allowing change of variables as in (a). Or a rule allowing ourselves to swap around initial quantifiers of the same flavour as in (c). But probably the most useful short-cut rules to add would be this pair:

(¬∀)   Given one of ¬∀$\xi\alpha$(ξ) and ∃ξ¬α(ξ), you can derive the other.
(¬∃)   Given one of ¬∃$\xi\alpha$(ξ) and ∀ξ¬α(ξ), you can derive the other.

Exercise: use arguments as in (b) to confirm that these are correct derived rules!
However, we won't officially adopt these additional rules (though feel free to use them if you want). For remember, our principal aim is to develop an *understanding* of the core principles of our proof system. Our focus now is on understanding the quantificational part of the system (that's why we will be happy occasionally to skip over the details of PL reasoning in the middle of proofs, so as not to obscure a proof's quantificational core). But, as before, we are not particularly concerned to construct lots of ever more complicated proofs for which derived rules might frequently come in handy as short-cuts.

32.6   QL theorems

(a)   So far, all of our examples of QL formal derivations start from sentences as premises and end up with sentences as final conclusions (even if the derivations typically proceed via auxiliary wffs which use dummy names). Now for proofs which start from *no* premises to reach some sentence as conclusion. We say:

A sentence which concludes a QL proof from zero premisses is a *theorem*.

(Compare §23.1's definition of a PL theorem.) Rather unexcitingly, QL sentences which are instances of tautological schemas will be QL theorems (since the propositional rules are still in play). And equally unexcitingly, whenever we have a QL proof from α to γ (where these are sentences), there will be a corresponding theorem of the form $(\alpha \to \gamma)$. For example, the following is a theorem:

J $((\exists x\, Fx \lor \exists x\, Gx) \to \exists x(Fx \lor Gx))$.

Just suppose the antecedent, derive the consequent as in our proof for **I**, and apply the conditional proof principle (CP).

(b)   For an equally unexciting example of a different kind, consider

K $\forall x((Fx \land Hx) \to Fx)$,

which in QL_1 expresses the logical truth that whoever is a wise philosopher is indeed a philosopher. This certainly *ought* to be demonstrable just from the rules governing the logical operators. And of course it is:

(1)		
(2)	(Fa ∧ Ha)	(Supp)
(3)	Fa	(∧E 2)
(4)	((Fa ∧ Ha) → Fa)	(CP 2–3)
(5)	$\forall x((Fx \land Hx) \to Fx)$	(∀I 4)

Check that this *is* a correctly formed proof.

(c)   Here is a much more interesting example to finish the chapter. The following is another QL theorem (in any language containing a binary predicate 'L'):

$\neg \exists x \forall y(Lxy \leftrightarrow \neg Lyy)$.

Or, rather, unpacking our occasionally useful double-arrow shorthand for the biconditional, *this* is a theorem:

L $\neg \exists x \forall y((Lxy \to \neg Lyy) \land (\neg Lyy \to Lxy))$.

If we suppose this wff without its initial negation sign to be true, then we can very quickly derive absurdity:

(1)		
(2)	$\exists x \forall y((Lxy \to \neg Lyy) \land (\neg Lyy \to Lxy))$	(Prem)
(3)	$\forall y((Lay \to \neg Lyy) \land (\neg Lyy \to Lay))$	(Supp)
(4)	$((Laa \to \neg Laa) \land (\neg Laa \to Laa))$	(∀E 3)
(5)	⊥	(PL 4)
(6)	⊥	(∃E 2, 3–5)
(7)	$\neg \exists x \forall y((Lxy \to \neg Lyy) \land (\neg Lyy \to Lxy))$	(RAA 2–6)

How does this proof work? We start our subproof at (3) with an instance of the existential quantification at (2), with a view to using (∃E). We can then instantiate the quantified wff (3) with *any* term, including the term 'a' already in the wff, to get (4). But (4) tells us that Laa is true if and only it is false. And that is impossible, whatever we might be using 'a' as a dummy name for. Unsurprisingly, there is a simple PL proof of absurdity from (4) – find it! Finally, (∃E) can then be correctly applied to derive (6), and we can then apply (RAA).

Now suppose that we interpret the predicate 'L' as ① *shaves* ②, and take the domain to be *the men in some particular village*. Then **L** tells us that there is no man in the village who shaves all and only those who do not shave themselves. Sometimes this is called the Barber Paradox – but there is no genuine paradox here, just a logical theorem that there can be no such person!

Suppose instead that we interpret 'L' as ② *is a member of* ①, and take the domain to be the universe of *sets* (i.e. sets as mathematicians conceive them, treated as objects in their own right – compare §25.5). Then **L** tells us that there is no set which has as its members just those sets which are not members of themselves. Think of a set which doesn't contain itself as a *normal* set: then we have shown that there is no set of all normal sets. This is, famously, Russell's Paradox. And this time the label 'paradox' is perhaps more appropriate.

For, assuming we can understand the mathematicians' usual idea of a set as an object over and above its members, '① is a normal set' seems a perfectly sensible unary predicate. And it is a rather plausible principle that, given a sensible unary predicate, we can gather together the things that satisfy the predicate into a set. So it is a surprise to find, purely as a matter of logic, that there can be no set of normal sets – our plausible principle can't be applied across the board.

(According to most set-theorists, by the way, all genuine sets are normal – the thought being that a set newly gathers together objects that have in some sense 'already' been formed, so a set can't contain itself. On this view, our argument shows that there is no universal set of all sets.)

32.7 Summary

To formalize quantifier arguments, we need symbols in our QL languages available for use as dummy names. We take the option of using special-purpose symbols, lower-case letters from the beginning of the alphabet. Syntactically, these dummy names behave the same way as proper names, providing more terms.

Guided by the informal rules summarized at the end of the previous chapter, we presented pairs of introduction and elimination rules for the formal universal and existential quantifiers. (We will restate the formal rules diagrammatically at the beginning of the next chapter.)

Using these rules, we have found proofs for some simple syllogistic arguments, and also demonstrated some basic quantifier equivalences – we can swap variables, swap the order of quantifiers of the same kind, and swap $\forall \xi$ for $\neg \exists \xi \neg$, etc.

Exercises 32

(a) We said that if $\forall \xi \alpha(\xi)$ is a quantified wff, τ is a term, and $\alpha(\tau)$ is the result of replacing every occurrence of ξ in $\alpha(\xi)$ by τ, then $\alpha(\tau)$ is a wff. Why is that true?

(b) Revisit Exercises 31, and render the informal arguments given there into suitable QL languages, and then provide formal derivations of the conclusions from the premises. (Don't skip the propositional reasoning in these easy cases!)

(c) Also translate the following into suitable QL languages, and again provide formal derivations of the conclusions from the premises:

   (1) If Jones is a bad philosopher, then some Welsh speaker is irrational; but every Welsh speaker is rational; hence Jones is not a bad philosopher.

   (2) Everyone is such that, if they admire Ludwig, then the world has gone mad. Therefore, if someone admires Ludwig, the world has gone mad.

   (3) Jack is taller than Jill. Someone is taller than Jack. If a first person is taller than a second, and the second is taller than a third, then the first person is taller than the third. Hence someone is taller than both Jack and Jill.

   (4) Every logician admires Gödel. Whoever admires someone is not without feeling. Hence no logician is without feeling.

   (5) Either not everyone liked the cake or someone baked an excellent cake. If I'm right, then whoever bakes an excellent cake ought to be proud. So if everyone liked the cake and I'm right, then someone ought to be proud.

Also translate the following into suitable QL languages and show that they are logical truths by deriving them as theorems:

   (6) Everyone is either a logician or not a logician.

   (7) It's not the case that all logicians are wise while someone is an unwise logician.

   (8) Everyone has someone whom either they love (despite that person loving themself!) or they don't love (unless that person doesn't love themself!).

(d) Give proofs to warrant the following inferences (compare §29.6):

   (1) $(P \wedge \forall x\, Fx) \therefore \forall x(P \wedge Fx)$

   (2) $(\exists y\, Fy \vee P) \therefore \exists y(Fy \vee P)$

   (3) $\forall x(Fx \rightarrow P) \therefore (\exists x\, Fx \rightarrow P)$

   (4) $\forall x(P \vee Fx) \therefore (P \vee \forall x\, Fx)$

   (5) $(P \rightarrow \exists x\, Fx) \therefore \exists x(P \rightarrow Fx)$

(e*) Do the exercise in §32.5(d) if you haven't already done it. Now suppose we set up a QL-style logic without the existential quantifier; the universal quantifier remains, governed by the usual rules. Expressions of the form $\exists \xi \alpha(\xi)$ are then introduced simply as abbreviations for corresponding expressions of the form $\neg \forall \xi \neg \alpha(\xi)$. Show that the two familiar existential quantifier rules would then be derived rules of this system.

Alternatively, suppose we set up a QL-style language with only a 'no' quantifier, expressed using the quantifier-former 'N' (so $N\xi\alpha(\xi)$ holds when *nothing* satisfies the condition expressed by α). Give introduction and elimination rules for this quantifier. Define the universal and existential quantifier in this new language, and show how to recover their usual inference rules.

(f*) When discussing pairs of PL introduction and elimination rules, we saw that they fit together in a harmonious way, with the elimination rule as it were reversing or undoing an application of the introduction rule. Can something similar be said about the pairs of QL introduction and elimination rules?

33 More QL proofs

We continue to explore the Fitch-style system for arguing in QL languages. We start by setting out the new quantifier rules again, and stressing again the need for the restrictions on the dummy names used in applications of (∀I) and (∃E). Then we work through some more examples of quantifier proofs, commenting on various issues as we go.

33.1 The QL rules again

(a) Here are the introduction and elimination rules for the two quantifiers, now in diagrammatic form, arranged to bring out some relations between them:

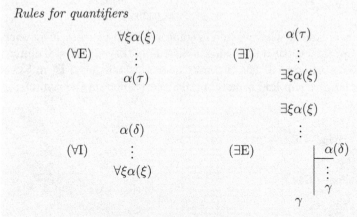

Rules for quantifiers

In all these rules, $\alpha(\tau)$ or $\alpha(\delta)$ is an instance of the corresponding quantified wff; as usual τ can be any kind of term, but δ must be a dummy name.

The following restrictions must be observed on the dummy names δ:

> For (∀I), δ must not appear in any live assumption for $\alpha(\delta)$ or in the conclusion $\forall \xi \alpha(\xi)$ (all occurrences of δ are replaced by ξ).
> For (∃E), δ must be new to the proof and must not appear in the conclusion γ.

(b) The formal rules (∀E) and (∃I) correspond to obviously correct informal inferences between propositions.

The formal derivation rule (∃E) corresponds to a surely reliable informal inference between entailments, which we spelt out and called 'arguing as if by cases' in §31.2.

Finally, the fourth rule, (∀I) corresponds to another intuitively correct second-level principle, which we spelt out and called 'universal generalization' in §31.1). Modulated into a formal key, that informal principle has become:

> Suppose, given some background assumptions, we can validly infer $\alpha(\delta)$ (where the temporary name δ doesn't appear in those assumptions). Then from the same background, we can validly infer $\forall \xi \alpha(\xi)$.

But now compare (∀I) with (RAA), (∨E), (CP), and (∀E), the other second-level rules. We have set out applications of those rules by *indenting* the relevant stretch of argument that the rule appeals to. It would be consistent to do this again when applying (∀I). In other words, instead of laying out applications of the ∀-introduction rule as in (∀I₁) below, we could instead use something like (∀I₂). We start with a blank line heading a subproof (a blank line as we are making no new supposition), then δ is introduced in the subproof and we eventually derive the required wff $\alpha(\delta)$:

$$(\forall I_1) \qquad \begin{array}{c} \alpha(\delta) \\ \vdots \\ \forall \xi \alpha(\xi) \end{array} \qquad\qquad (\forall I_2) \qquad \begin{array}{c} \vdots \\ \alpha(\delta) \\ \hline \forall \xi \alpha(\xi) \end{array}$$

This second layout is exactly what we find in some standard Fitch-style systems, often with the subproof's vertical line being additionally tagged with the dummy name which is being introduced. For example, instead of our proof **B′** in §32.3, set out as on the left, we can find something like the version on the right:

$$\begin{array}{l} \forall x\, Fx \\ \forall x(Fx \to Gx) \\ \hline Fa \\ (Fa \to Ga) \\ Ga \\ \forall x\, Gx \end{array} \qquad\qquad \begin{array}{l} \forall x\, Fx \\ \forall x(Fx \to Gx) \\ a\; \Big| \\ \quad Fa \\ \quad (Fa \to Ga) \\ \quad Ga \\ \forall x\, Gx \end{array}$$

But is the extra visual complication *really* a helpful addition, once we understand the principle underlying (∀I) proofs? This is a judgement call. We will prefer to stick to our simpler (and equally standard) style of layout.

33.2   How to misuse the QL rules

(a)   The derivation rules (∀E) and (∃I) are entirely straightforward. The rules (∀I) and (∃E) require more care, however. In the last chapter, we motivated the crucial restrictions on the use of dummy names in these rules. It will help to fix ideas if we now consider some ways derivations can go disastrously wrong if we offend against those restrictions.

So first, let's give a fake derivation from ∃x Fx to ∀x Fx:

(1)	∃x Fx	(Prem)
(2)	Fa	(Supp)
(3)	∀x Fx	(!!∀I 2)
(4)	∀x Fx	(∃E 1, 2–3)

Things go wrong at (3): from the supposition that some chosen individual is (say) a logician, we can't infer that everyone is! Formally, the hopeless move is blocked by the restriction that says we can't universally generalize on a dummy name if it features in a live assumption (e.g. an undischarged supposition).

Here's another 'proof' for the same bad inference:

(1)	∃x Fx	(Prem)
(2)	Fa	(Supp)
(3)	Fa	(Iter 2)
(4)	Fa	(!!∃E 1, 2–3)
(5)	∀x Fx	(∀I 4)

This time the gruesome mistake is at line (4). Our subproof doesn't reach a conclusion independent of our choice of instance (2) of the initial existential quantification. So we can't argue 'as if by cases'. Formally, what's gone wrong is that we have tried to apply (∃E) when the subproof ends with a wff which still contains the relevant dummy name introduced at the beginning of the subproof.

(b)   Now let's 'prove' that, if everyone loves someone, then someone loves themself – so we will argue (badly) from ∀x∃y Lxy to ∃x Lxx:

(1)	∀x∃y Lxy	(Prem)
(2)	∃y Lay	(∀E 1)
(3)	Laa	(Supp)
(4)	∃x Lxx	(∃I 3)
(5)	∃x Lxx	(!!∃E 2, 3–4)

What's gone wrong here? At line (2), we have in effect picked an individual a from the domain and we know from (1) that a loves *someone* or other. We can now go on chose a representative beloved for a at (3) – but we are not entitle to continue the argument by taking that representative to be a again!

Here's a similar case. We will 'prove' that, given first that someone is a logician and second that someone is irrational, it follows that there is an irrational logician.

Using the obvious glossary, here then is a fake derivation from ∃x Fx and ∃x Gx to ∃x(Fx ∧ Gx):

(1)	∃x Fx	(Prem)
(2)	∃x Gx	(Prem)
(3)	Fa	(Supp)
(4)	Ga	(Supp)
(5)	(Fa ∧ Ga)	(∧I 3, 4)
(6)	∃x(Fx ∧ Gx)	(∃I 5)
(7)	∃x(Fx ∧ Gx)	(!!∃E 2, 4–6)
(8)	∃x(Fx ∧ Gx)	(∃E 1, 3–7)

What's gone wrong this time? We've picked a representative logician a at line (3). Then we've picked a representative irrational person at line (4) – but we can't assume that this is a again.

Formally, in both these last two fake proofs, we have broken the rule which tells us that when we instantiate an existential quantification to start a subproof for (∃E) we must always use a dummy name new to the proof.

(c) Let's consider another pair of inferences:

∃y∀xLxy ∴ ∀x∃yLxy,
∀x∃yLxy ∴ ∃y∀xLxy.

The first is valid – why? But the reverse second inference isn't – why?
Here then is a genuine proof for the first inference:

(1)	∃y∀x Lxy	(Prem)
(2)	∀xLxa	(Supp)
(3)	Lba	(∀E 2)
(4)	∃y Lby	(∃I 3)
(5)	∀x∃y Lxy	(∀I 4)
(6)	∀x∃y Lxy	(∃E 1, 2–5)

Check that this proof is correctly formed.
And now here is a 'proof' of the reverse inference:

(1)	∀x∃y Lxy	(Prem)
(2)	∃yLay	(∀E 1)
(3)	Lab	(Supp)
(4)	∀x Lxb	(!!∀I 3)
(5)	∃y∀x Lxy	(∃I 4)
(6)	∃y∀x Lxy	(∃E 1, 2–5)

Even though the dummy name 'a' was introduced as picking out an arbitrary individual at (2), we can't now universally generalize on it to get (4). Why? Because we've made a special assumption about that individual at line (3).

(d) Let's have one last fake proof. We will 'demonstrate' that if everyone loves themself then everyone loves everyone – i.e. we will argue from ∀x Lxx to ∀x∀y Lxy:

(1)	∀x Lxx	(Prem)
(2)	Laa	(∀E 1)
(3)	∀y Lay	(!!∀I 2)
(4)	∀x∀y Lxy	(∀I 3)

We go wrong at (3). From the assumption that some arbitrarily selected individual a loves themselves, we can't infer that a loves everyone. Formally, we have offended against the rule that when we universally generalize on a dummy name, we have to replace *all* the occurrences of the name with the relevant variable. Equivalently, when we derive a universal quantification from an instance with a dummy name, that name must not appear in the quantified wff.

The moral of all our examples? Obeying those restrictions on the use of dummy names in the rules (∀I) and (∃E) is *essential* if you are to construct valid proofs.

33.3   Old and new logic: three proofs

In this section we look at three kinds of arguments which 'traditional' logicians had trouble with, to show that such arguments can be dealt with easily by our QL proof system which incorporates Fregean insights.

(a)   Take first the simple two-step argument

A   Everyone loves themself. So Maldwyn loves Maldwyn. So someone loves Maldwyn.

Why does this cause trouble for a logic of generality rooted in the Aristotelian tradition? Consider the *second* inference step. To explain its validity, the traditional logician – relying on a subject/predicate analysis of propositions – needs to discern a common (unary) predicate in its two propositions, namely 'loves Maldwyn'. But then, if 'Maldwyn loves Maldwyn' involves just *that* predicate, exactly why does it follow from the premiss of the *first* inference – which involves the quite different predicate 'loves themself'?

Formalized into a suitable QL language, however, **A** becomes this:

(1)	∀x Lxx	(Prem)
(2)	Lmm	(∀E 1)
(3)	∃x Lxm	(∃I 2)

The predicate-first notation is a mere matter of style. What is crucial is, first, that the middle proposition is now analysed at (2) as involving a *binary* predicate 'L' with two slots waiting to be filled. And second, Frege's great insight, we need to understand a quantifier as something that can be tied to different numbers of places in the same predicate. Then we can see how the very same predicate can feature in both (1) and (3).

(b)   Consider next

B   Either every wombat is a mammal or every wombat is a marsupial. Hence every wombat is either a mammal or a marsupial.

319

The main logical operator of the premiss is the disjunction. The main operator of the conclusion is the quantifier. So we need a logic that can simultaneously handle sentential connectives and quantifiers.

Ancient Stoic logic copes with some propositional reasoning; Aristotelian logic copes with some quantifier reasoning. Much later – to continue the cartoon history – George Boole in the early nineteenth century came up with a logical algebra which could be interpreted two ways. It could be read as being about 'and', 'or', and 'not' (that's why we still speak of Boolean connectives) or alternatively as being about Aristotelian syllogisms. But Boole's system still couldn't deal with both at the same time.

By contrast, our Frege-based treatment of the quantifiers combines with a logic for the connectives to allow us to argue like this (using the obvious glossary):

(1)	$(\forall x(Fx \rightarrow Gx) \vee \forall x(Fx \rightarrow Hx))$	(Prem)
(2)	$\forall x(Fx \rightarrow Gx)$	(Supp)
(3)	$(Fa \rightarrow Ga)$	($\forall$E 2)
(4)	$(Fa \rightarrow (Ga \vee Ha))$	(PL 3)
(5)	$\forall x(Fx \rightarrow (Gx \vee Hx))$	($\forall$I 4)
(6)	$\forall x(Fx \rightarrow Hx)$	(Supp)
(7)	$(Fa \rightarrow Ha)$	($\forall$E 6)
(8)	$(Fa \rightarrow (Ga \vee Ha))$	(PL 7)
(9)	$\forall x(Fx \rightarrow (Gx \vee Hx))$	($\forall$I 8)
(10)	$\forall x(Fx \rightarrow (Gx \vee Hx))$	($\exists$E 1, 2–5, 6–9)

(c) The most intractable problem for traditional logic, however, was dealing with arguments involving propositions with quantifiers embedded inside the scope of other quantifiers (as we would now put it). Consider for example

C   Every horse is a mammal. Hence every horse's tail is a mammal's tail.

To bring out the multiple generality in the conclusion, read it as 'Everything which is the tail of some horse is the tail of some mammal'. The argument is then evidently valid. Medieval logicians in the Aristotelian tradition, for all their insightful ingenuity, struggled to cope. But there's a straightforward QL proof.

Let's adopt a QL language with the following glossary:

> F: ① is a horse,
> G: ① is a mammal,
> T: ① is a tail belonging to ②;

and take the domain to be inclusive enough, perhaps all terrestrial physical objects. Then we can render **C** as

C′ $\forall x(Fx \rightarrow Gx)$ ∴ $\forall x(\exists y(Txy \wedge Fy) \rightarrow \exists y(Txy \wedge Gy))$.

Now, we will expect the conclusion to be derived by universal quantifier introduction from a wff involving some dummy name, like this:

$$\forall x(Fx \rightarrow Gx) \qquad \text{(Prem)}$$

$$\vdots$$

$$(\exists y(Tay \wedge Fy) \rightarrow \exists y(Tay \wedge Gy))$$
$$\forall x(\exists y(Txy \wedge Fy) \rightarrow \exists y(Txy \wedge Gy)) \qquad (\forall I)$$

The penultimate line is a conditional; so we will presumably want to assume its antecedent and then derive its consequent. And this antecedent is an existentially quantified wff; so the natural thing to do is to assume an instance of it, with a view to arguing by an application of ($\exists E$), giving a proof shaped like this:

$$\forall x(Fx \rightarrow Gx) \qquad \text{(Prem)}$$
$$\exists y(Tay \wedge Fy) \qquad \text{(Supp)}$$
$$(Tab \wedge Fb) \qquad \text{(Supp)}$$
$$\vdots$$
$$\exists y(Tay \wedge Gy)$$
$$\exists y(Tay \wedge Gy) \qquad (\exists E)$$
$$(\exists y(Tay \wedge Fy) \rightarrow \exists y(Tay \wedge Gy)) \qquad (CP)$$
$$\forall x(\exists y(Txy \wedge Fy) \rightarrow \exists y(Txy \wedge Gy)) \qquad (\forall I)$$

Do pause at this stage to double-check how the applications of the two rules ($\exists E$) and ($\forall I$) obey the restrictions on their relevant dummy names 'a' and 'b'.

So given that outline proof, we now simply need to join up the remaining dots:

(1)	$\forall x(Fx \rightarrow Gx)$	(Prem)
(2)	$\exists y(Tay \wedge Fy)$	(Supp)
(3)	$(Tab \wedge Fb)$	(Supp)
(4)	$(Fb \rightarrow Gb)$	($\forall$E 1)
(5)	$(Tab \wedge Gb)$	(PL 3, 4)
(6)	$\exists y(Tay \wedge Gy)$	($\exists$I 5)
(7)	$\exists y(Tay \wedge Gy)$	($\exists$E 2, 3–6)
(8)	$(\exists y(Tay \wedge Fy) \rightarrow \exists y(Tay \wedge Gy))$	(CP 2–7)
(9)	$\forall x(\exists y(Txy \wedge Fy) \rightarrow \exists y(Txy \wedge Gy))$	($\forall$I 8)

(d)   A comment on our handling of the last example. In regimenting the informal argument **C**, we chose to use a language including the predicate

T: ① is a tail belonging to ②.

You might have expected to find instead, say, the following two predicates:

H: ① is a tail,
B: ① belongs to ②.

Then instead of Txy, you would expect to use (Hx ∧ Bxy), etc.

It could be said that our predicate T is unnatural. And if we also wanted to regiment other arguments about animals and their parts, it might well be that we'll need to have predicates like H and B separately available. However, in the present context, replacing occurrences of Txy by (Hx ∧ Bxy) etc. just produces unnecessary complexity. Writing out our proof that way would make *no* use of the internal structure of this complex expression; so keep things simple.

A general principle: when we construct an ad hoc language for regimenting some argument(s), it is on the whole good policy to dig down only just as far as we need. As Quine famously puts it,

> "A maxim of shallow analysis prevails: expose no more logical structure than seems useful for the deduction or other inquiry at hand."

33.4 Five more QL proofs

Pause for breath! – and then let's work through five more examples.

(a) In §4.5, we informally showed that the following argument is valid:

D No girl likes any unreconstructed sexist; Caroline is a girl who likes anyone who likes her; Henry likes Caroline; hence Henry is not an unreconstructed sexist.

Using a QL language with a suitable glossary, and rendering the 'no' premiss with a universal quantifier, we can translate the argument like this:

D′ $\forall x(Gx \rightarrow \forall y(Fy \rightarrow \neg Lxy))$, $(Gm \wedge \forall x(Lxm \rightarrow Lmx))$, Lnm ∴ ¬Fn.

To construct a formal derivation of the conclusion, the obvious thing to do is to assume Fn and aim for a contradiction. So think through the following proof:

(1)	$\forall x(Gx \rightarrow \forall y(Fy \rightarrow \neg Lxy))$	(Prem)
(2)	$(Gm \wedge \forall x(Lxm \rightarrow Lmx))$	(Prem)
(3)	Lnm	(Prem)
(4)	Fn	(Supp)
(5)	Gm	(∧E 2)
(6)	$\forall x(Lxm \rightarrow Lmx)$	(∧E 2)
(7)	$(Gm \rightarrow \forall y(Fy \rightarrow \neg Lmy))$	(∀E 1)
(8)	$\forall y(Fy \rightarrow \neg Lmy)$	(MP 5, 7)
(9)	$(Fn \rightarrow \neg Lmn)$	(∀E 8)
(10)	¬Lmn	(MP 4, 9)
(11)	$(Lnm \rightarrow Lmn)$	(∀E 6)
(12)	Lmn	(MP 3, 11)
(13)	⊥	(Abs 12, 10)
(14)	¬Fn	(RAA 4–13)

What have we done here after line (4)? We have first disassembled the conjunction at line (2), giving us lines (5) and (6). Then we have instantiated the universal quantification at line (1) with the name 'm' to get the conditional with antecedent Gm, setting up the modus ponens inference to get line (8). We can likewise instantiate the new universal quantification at (8) in a way that links up to Fn earlier in the proof, to get (9) and hence (10).

And *now* the end is in sight. We just need to bring out the evident inconsistency between (3), (6), and (10), and we are done.

(b)   Next, we return to another silly argument that we have met before:

E   Everyone loves a lover; Romeo loves Juliet; so everyone loves Juliet.

We read the first premiss as saying: whoever x might be, then if x is a lover (i.e. if x loves someone), then everyone loves x. So, adopting a language with the obvious glossary, we can regiment this argument as

E′ $\forall x(\exists y\, Lxy \rightarrow \forall y\, Lyx),\ Lrj\ \therefore\ \forall x\, Lxj.$

And now let's replicate the informal multi-step proof we gave back in §4.1:

(1)	$\forall x(\exists y\, Lxy \rightarrow \forall y\, Lyx)$	(Prem)
(2)	Lrj	(Prem)
(3)	$(\exists y\, Lry \rightarrow \forall y\, Lyr)$	(∀E 1)
(4)	$\exists y\, Lry$	(∃I 2)
(5)	$\forall y\, Lyr$	(MP 4, 3)
(6)	Ljr	(∀E 5)
(7)	$(\exists y\, Ljy \rightarrow \forall y\, Lyj)$	(∀E 1)
(8)	$\exists y\, Ljy$	(∃I 6)
(9)	$\forall y\, Lyj$	(MP 8, 7)

Again, at each step in this proof so far, we just do the natural thing. At step (3) we will want to instantiate the quantified premiss, and the obvious option is to use the name 'r' to give us a conditional with an antecedent that connects with (2). That quickly takes us to (5), and what is the natural term to instantiate *that* with? Surely use the name 'j' this time. And so the proof continues ....

We haven't quite arrived at our target conclusion, however, as we regimented the conclusion of **E** using 'x', the first available variable for the quantification. Bother! We could retranslate that conclusion as $\forall y\, Lyj$: but that's a bit sneaky. So let's keep ourselves honest and finish up by using the variable-changing trick we met in §32.5:

(10)	Laj	(∀E 9)
(11)	$\forall x\, Lxj$	(∀I 10)

(c)   For our next example, consider the following argument (we are talking, let's suppose, about the logic class and the questions on a particular test):

F   If everyone in the class can answer *every* question, then some questions are too easy. So at least one person in the class is such that, if *they* can answer every question, then some questions are too easy.

323

That is valid. Let's show this by a QL proof.

We might be tempted to reflect all the surface structure of the premiss and conclusion, and come up with a QL translation along the following lines:

$$(\forall x(Cx \to \forall y(Qy \to Axy)) \to \exists z(Qz \wedge Ez)) \quad \therefore$$
$$\exists x((Cx \wedge \forall y(Qy \to Axy)) \to \exists z(Qz \wedge Ez))$$

Here the quantifier runs over some inclusive domain containing both people and questions, and we are using a QL language with a glossary like

    C: ① is in the class,
    Q: ① is a question,
    E: ① is too easy,
    A: ① can answer ②.

But note that the quantified structures of the subformulas $\forall y(Qy \to Axy)$ and $\exists z(Qz \wedge Ez)$ do no work at all in the argument. And since the other $\forall x/\exists x$ quantifiers are restricted to people in the class, we might as well take those people to make up the whole universe of discourse. So, following Quine's maxim of shallow analysis, let's instead take a simpler language with the following glossary:

    F: ① can answer every question,
    P: Some of the questions (in the test) are too easy.
    Domain: people in the class

Remember, we allow QL languages to have propositional letters (see §28.3(c)). And now our translated argument looks *very* much more manageable!

F′ $(\forall x Fx \to P) \quad \therefore \quad \exists x(Fx \to P).$

We've seen inferences of this form in §29.6. Here's a formal derivation (not entirely easy, but why is each step the natural one to make?)

(1)	$(\forall x Fx \to P)$	(Prem)
(2)	$\neg\exists x(Fx \to P)$	(Supp)
(3)	$(Fa \to P)$	(Supp)
(4)	$\exists x(Fx \to P)$	(∃I 3)
(5)	$\bot$	(Abs 4, 2)
(6)	$\neg(Fa \to P)$	(RAA 3–5)
(7)	Fa	(PL 6)
(8)	$\neg P$	(PL 6)
(9)	$\forall x Fx$	(∀I 7)
(10)	P	(MP 9, 1)
(11)	$\bot$	(Abs 10, 8)
(12)	$\neg\neg\exists x(Fx \to P)$	(RAA 2–11)
(13)	$\exists x(Fx \to P)$	(DN 12)

(d)   Next, here is an argument we met in the very first chapter and then informally argued to be valid in §3.1:

G   Some philosophy students admire all logicians. No philosophy student admires anyone irrational. So no logician is irrational.

We can translate the 'no' propositions using universal or existential quantifiers. Let's start by going the first way. Choosing formal predicate letters to match the English, we can then render the argument like this:

G′ $\exists x(Px \land \forall y(Ly \to Axy)), \forall x(Px \to \forall y(Iy \to \neg Axy)) \therefore \forall x(Lx \to \neg Ix)$.

Using the rule of thumb 'instantiate existential premisses first', the overall shape of the proof we are looking for is:

$$
\begin{array}{|l l}
\exists x(Px \land \forall y(Ly \to Axy)) & \text{(Prem)} \\
\forall x(Px \to \forall y(Iy \to \neg Axy)) & \text{(Prem)} \\
\quad \begin{array}{|l} (Pa \land \forall y(Ly \to Aay)) \\ \vdots \\ \forall x(Lx \to \neg Ix) \end{array} & \text{(Supp)} \\
\forall x(Lx \to \neg Ix) & \text{(}\exists\text{E)}
\end{array}
$$

Unpack the conjuncts in the supposition. And then it is natural to instantiate the second premiss using the dummy name 'a'. Which gets us painlessly to

(1)	$\exists x(Px \land \forall y(Ly \to Axy))$	(Prem)
(2)	$\forall x(Px \to \forall y(Iy \to \neg Axy))$	(Prem)
(3)	$(Pa \land \forall y(Ly \to Aay))$	(Supp)
(4)	Pa	($\land$E 3)
(5)	$\forall y(Ly \to Aay)$	($\land$E 3)
(6)	$(Pa \to \forall y(Iy \land \neg Aay))$	($\forall$E 2)
(7)	$\forall y(Iy \to \neg Aay)$	(MP 4, 6)

So the remaining task is to get from (5) and (7) to the target conclusion of the subproof, i.e. to derive $\forall x(Lx \to \neg Ix)$.

But this is relatively simple (compare **C′** in the previous chapter). We instantiate the two universal quantifiers (not with 'a' again because we want an arbitrary instance we can generalize on later). And then continue:

(8)	$(Lb \to Aab)$	($\forall$E 5)
(9)	$(Ib \to \neg Aab)$	($\forall$E 7)
(10)	$(Lb \to \neg Ib)$	(PL 8, 9)
(11)	$\forall x(Lx \to \neg Ix)$	($\forall$I 10)
(12)	$\forall x(Lx \to \neg Ix)$	($\exists$E 1, 3–11)

(e)   For a last example in this chapter, let's consider how things go if we translate the 'no' propositions in **G** using negated existential quantifiers, as in

G″ $\exists x(Px \land \forall y(Ly \to Axy)), \neg\exists x\exists y(Px \land (Iy \land Axy)) \therefore \neg\exists x(Lx \land Ix)$.

We will talk through how to discover a proof – and without using a derived rule like ($\neg\exists$) from §32.5(d).

(Though let's never lose sight of the point we first stressed in §20.5. The key thing, always, is to make sure you *understand the general principles* deployed in proofs. For us, as philosophers, proof-discovery remains secondary, even if sometimes instructive.)

In this case, given **G'''**'s negative conclusion, the obvious strategy is to assume $\exists x(Lx \land lx)$ at line (3) and aim for absurdity, so we can use a reductio argument.

We will then have *two* existential assumptions in play, at lines (1) and (3): so instantiate them in turn at lines (4) and (5). We get two conjunctions as a result. So next disassemble those. And we reach the following stage:

(1)	$\exists x(Px \land \forall y(Ly \to Axy))$	(Prem)
(2)	$\neg\exists x\exists y(Px \land (ly \land Axy))$	(Prem)
(3)	$\exists x(Lx \land lx)$	(Supp)
(4)	$(Pb \land \forall y(Ly \to Aby))$	(Supp)
(5)	$(La \land la)$	(Supp)
(6)	Pb	($\land$E 4)
(7)	$\forall y(Ly \to Aby)$	($\land$E 4)
(8)	La	($\land$E 5)
(9)	la	($\land$E 5)

What next? How do we derive $\bot$? Well, obviously we will need to use the quantified wff at (7). What shall we instantiate it with? The natural choice is 'a' as that will give us a conditional whose antecedent we will already have at line (8). So we can continue:

(10)	$(La \to Aba)$	($\forall$E 7)
(11)	Aba	(MP 8, 10)

And now the end is in sight. For we can now conjoin (11) with some earlier lines to form the conjunction

(12)	$(Pb \land (la \land Aba))$	(PL 6, 9, 11)

But this is flatly inconsistent with (2). Bring out the contradiction, and the derivation completes itself, with the Fitch-style layout beautifully keeping track of the ins and outs of the proof:

(13)	$\exists y(Pb \land (ly \land Aby))$	($\exists$I 12)
(14)	$\exists x\exists y(Px \land (ly \land Axy))$	($\exists$I 13)
(15)	$\bot$	(Abs 14, 2)
(16)	$\bot$	($\exists$E 3, 5–15)
(17)	$\bot$	($\exists$E 1, 4–16)
(18)	$\neg\exists x(Lx \land lx)$	(RAA 3–17)

Which, guided by some pretty natural strategic ideas, was not *too* hard. Just check that the two applications of ($\exists$E) are correctly done.

33.5   Summary

We have restated the formal introduction and elimination quantifier rules in a diagrammatic form. We commented on our preferred (simpler) way of laying out (∀I) inferences.

Note in particular the crucial (intuitively motivated) restrictions on the use of dummy names in the rules (∀I) and (∃E).

Pre-Fregean logic had serious difficulties coping with arguments that involve both connectives and quantifiers, or which involve propositions with multiple quantifiers. We saw how modern quantificational logic can cope smoothly and naturally with such arguments.

A bit of practical advice about proof-construction: it is usually good policy to instantiate existential quantifiers – to start subproofs for use in applications of (∃E) – before instantiating relevant universal quantifiers.

Exercises 33

Do the unstarred examples in both (a) and (b) and check your answers before returning to the starred examples.

(a)   As a warm-up exercise, consider which of the following QL arguments ought to be valid (assume the wffs are interpreted). Give proofs warranting the valid inferences.

(1) $\exists x\, Sxxx \;\therefore\; \exists x \exists y \exists z\, Sxyz$

(2) $\exists x \forall y \forall y\, Sxyy \;\therefore\; \exists x\, Sxxx$

(3) $\forall x \exists y \forall z\, Sxyz \;\therefore\; \exists x \forall y \exists z\, Sxzy$

(4*) $\neg \exists x \forall y \forall z\, Sxyz \;\therefore\; \forall x \exists z \exists y \neg Sxyz$

(5*) $\neg \exists x (Fx \wedge \exists y (Gy \wedge Lxy)) \;\therefore\; \forall x \forall y (Fx \rightarrow (Gy \rightarrow \neg Lxy))$

(b)   Render the following inferences into suitable QL languages and provide derivations of the conclusions from the premises in each case:

(1) Some people are boastful. No one likes anyone boastful. Therefore some people aren't liked by anyone.

(2) There's someone such that if *they* admire some philosopher, then I'm a Dutchman. So if *everyone* admires some philosopher, then I'm a Dutchman.

(3) Some good philosophers admire Frank; all wise people admire any good philosopher; Frank is wise; hence there is someone who both admires and is admired by Frank.

(4) Everyone loves themself if there's someone who loves them or whom they love. There's someone who is loved. Therefore someone loves themself.

(5*) Only rational people with good judgement are logicians. Those who take some creationist myth literally lack good judgement. So logicians do not take any creationist myth literally.

(6*) Given any two people, if the first admires Gödel and Gödel admires the second, then the first admires the second. Gödel admires anyone who has understood *Principia*. There's someone who has understood *Principia* who admires

327

Gödel. Therefore there's someone who has understood *Principia* who admires everyone who has understood *Principia*!

(7*)   Any adult elephant weighs more than any horse. Some horse weighs more than any donkey. If a first thing weighs more than a second thing, and the second thing weighs more than a third, then the first weighs more than the third. Hence any adult elephant weighs more than any donkey.

(c)   Why should the following QL wffs be logically true (assuming the wffs are interpreted)?

(1) $\exists x(Fx \rightarrow \forall yFy)$
(2) $\forall x\exists y(\exists zLxz \rightarrow Lxy)$
(3) $\exists x\forall y(\neg Fy \lor Fx)$

Show that those wffs are QL theorems – feel free now to use the derived rules $(\neg\forall)$ and $(\neg\exists)$ from §32.5 and to skip PL reasoning. Also give derivations to warrant the following inferences:

(4) $(\forall xFx \rightarrow \exists yGy)$ ∴ $\exists x\exists y(Fx \rightarrow Gy)$
(5) $(\exists zFz \rightarrow \exists zGz)$ ∴ $\forall x\exists y(Fx \rightarrow Gy)$
(6) $\forall x\exists y(Fy \rightarrow Gx)$ ∴ $\exists y\forall x(Fy \rightarrow Gx)$

(d*)   Although all our examples of QL proofs so far start from zero or more sentences and end with a sentence, we won't build that into our official characterization of QL proofs – they can go from wffs involving dummy names to a conclusion which may involve a dummy name.

Say that the wffs Γ (not necessarily all sentences) are QL-*consistent* if there is no QL proof using wffs Γ as premises and ending with '$\bot$'; otherwise Γ are QL-*inconsistent* – compare Exercises 22(d*).

Assuming that the terms mentioned belong to the relevant language, show

(1)   If the wffs $\Gamma, \alpha(\tau)$ are QL-inconsistent and the wffs Γ include $\forall\xi\alpha(\xi)$ then those wffs Γ are already QL-inconsistent.

and then conclude that

(2)   If the wffs Γ are QL-consistent and $\forall\xi\alpha(\xi)$ is one of them, then $\Gamma, \alpha(\tau)$ are also QL-consistent.

Show further that

(2*)   If the wffs Γ are QL-consistent and $\forall\xi\alpha(\xi)$ is one of them, then $\Gamma, \alpha(\tau_1), \alpha(\tau_2)$, ..., $\alpha(\tau_k)$ all together are also QL-consistent (for any terms $\tau_1, \tau_2, \ldots, \tau_k$ of the relevant language).

Show similarly that

(3)   If the wffs Γ are QL-consistent and $\exists\xi\alpha(\xi)$ is one of them, then $\Gamma, \alpha(\delta)$ are also QL-consistent if δ is a dummy name that doesn't appear in Γ.

Also show that:

(4)   If the wffs Γ are QL-consistent and $\neg\forall\xi\alpha(\xi)$ is one of them, then $\Gamma, \exists\xi\neg\alpha(\xi)$ are QL-consistent.

(5)   If the wffs Γ are QL-consistent and $\neg\exists\xi\alpha(\xi)$ is one of them, then $\Gamma, \forall\xi\neg\alpha(\xi)$ are QL-consistent.

34 Empty domains?

We stipulated that the domain of quantification for a QL language must contain at least one object. This might seem to be a very modest requirement – we surely don't want to be talking about *nothing*. But we need to comment.

34.1 Dummy names and empty domains

(a)   In §32.3, we considered the argument **B′**:

   $\forall x\, Fx,\ \forall x(Fx \to Gx) \therefore \forall x\, Gx$.

And we gave a formal proof warranting the inference here. It starts:

(1)	$\forall x\, Fx$	(Prem)
(2)	$\forall x(Fx \to Gx)$	(Prem)
(3)	Fa	($\forall$E 1)
(4)	$\vdots$	

At line (3), the story goes, we pick an arbitrary member of the domain and dub it with a temporary name. But hold on! *What if the domain is empty?* Then there is nothing to pick out and dub! So our derivation at this point in effect presupposes that the domain is non-empty. In its handling of dummy names, then, at least one of our (entirely standard) QL inference rules presupposes that we are dealing with non-empty domains.

In §27.3 and again in §28.8 we stipulated that domains of quantification for QL languages are always non-empty. We now see that this stipulation is a significant one: it ties in with the natural deduction rules which we have adopted.

(b)   Let's explore this link further.

Tachyons are, by definition, physical particles which are superluminal, i.e. which travel faster than the speed of light. Standard physics tells us that such particles would have deeply *weird* properties, like having more energy the slower they go. Adopting a QL language quantifying over physical particles, and with the obvious interpretations of the predicates, the following is therefore true:

(1) $\forall x(Tx \to Wx)$.

Now, given this truth, we of course *can't* use our QL inference rules to deduce

(2) $\exists x\, Wx$.

Which is just as it should be. We don't want the truth (1) – *if* something is a tachyon, *then* it has the weird property of having more energy at slower speeds – to entail a proposition that asserts that there really *are* some weird particles of this kind. So far so good.

But now consider what happens if – perhaps in the spirit of Quine's maxim of shallow analysis from §33.3(d) – we think along the following lines. The current topic is tachyons, so can't we make things simpler by taking our domain for now to be just them? (Compare our handling of argument **F** in the previous chapter where we kept things simple by taking the domain to be just students in the logic class.) Using a formal language where the quantifiers run over just tachyons, the uncontentious claim that tachyons are weird is then regimented as

(1′) $\forall x\, Wx$.

However, using our adopted natural deduction rules, we get the following proof **A**:

(1′)	$\forall x\, Wx$	(Prem)
(2′)	Wa	($\forall$E 1′)
(3′)	$\exists x\, Wx$	($\exists$I 2′)

Yet (3′) is an existential claim, only true if there *is* something which has the weird property of having more energy at slower speeds. So we seem to have deduced the existence of something truly weird from a reformulation of what was originally supposed to be an uncontroversial bit of physics.

What has gone wrong here? Again, at the second step of **A**, we take an arbitrary member of the current domain and dub it. *But we can only do that if the domain is populated.* So, in taking the domain of the relevant language to comprise just tachyons, but also assuming that we can apply our current logical apparatus, *we are already implicitly assuming that there are tachyons.*

(c) Suppose the domain of the relevant QL language is empty. Then both $\exists \xi \alpha(\xi)$ and $\exists \xi \neg \alpha(\xi)$ will always be trivially false (since nothing exists in the domain). And so the negation of the second, i.e. $\forall \xi \alpha(\xi)$, will be trivially true. (You can also look at it this way: $\forall \xi \alpha(\xi)$ is always true in the empty domain, because it is true that *if* a thing is in the domain then it satisfies the condition expressed by α – the antecedent of this generalized conditional is always false.) So, the pattern of reasoning in a proof taking us from $\forall \xi \alpha(\xi)$ to $\exists \xi \alpha(\xi)$ will take us from truth to falsehood if applied in an empty domain. Which is what happens in **A**, assuming that there are no such things as tachyons. For then the stipulated domain of quantification is empty. And that makes (1′) true and (3′) false.

(d) For a second line of argument that breaks down in empty domains, consider **B**:

(1)		
(2)	$(Fa \lor \neg Fa)$	(LEM)
(3)	$\exists x(Fx \lor \neg Fx)$	($\exists$I 2)

Our rules allow us to prove any instance of the Law of Excluded Middle from no premises. Assume we are dealing with a QL language which has the unary predicate F (expressing some property F): then in particular we will be able to prove (2) from no premises. And then (3) follows by ($\exists$I). However (3) is another existential claim; it tells us that there is something in the domain which is either F or not F. And that can only be true if there *is* something in the domain!

34.2   Preserving standard logic

Proof **A** illustrates that derivations in our natural deduction system are not always truth-preserving, *if* we allow empty domains. Proof **B** illustrates that theorems of our system are not always true, *if* we allow empty domains.

How should we respond to this observation? Some logicians argue:

An inference is logically valid if it is necessarily truth-preserving in virtue of topic-neutral features of its structure. And formal logic is the study of logical validity, using regimented languages to enable us to bring out how arguments of certain forms are valid irrespective of their subject-matter.

Now, sometimes we want to argue logically about the properties of things which we already know to exist (electrons, say). Other times we want to argue in an exploratory way, in ignorance of whether what we are talking about exists (superstrings, perhaps). While sometimes we want to argue about things that we believe don't exist, precisely in order to try to show that they don't exist (tachyons, perhaps). And we presumably want to regiment correct forms of inference which we can apply neutrally across these different cases. Hence *one* way our formal logic should be topic-neutral is by allowing empty domains. But our current QL rules – being incorrect for empty domains – are not topic-neutral. So they don't correctly capture only logical validities and logical truths. Therefore our natural deduction proof system needs revision.

Persuaded by such reasoning, some logicians do advocate the general adoption of a *free* logic – i.e. a logic free of existence assumptions, allowing empty domains (and often also allowing 'empty proper names' which don't have a reference). So how might the defender of our standard QL logic reply?

There is no One True Logic. Choosing a formal logic involves – as we have seen before – weighing up costs and benefits. And the small benefit of having a logic whose inferential principles also hold in empty domains is not worth the cost. After all, when we want to argue about things that do not/might not exist, we already have sufficient resources while still using standard logic.

First, a suitably inclusive wider domain is usually easily found (indeed, will typically be in play when engaged in serious inquiry rather than concocting artificial classroom examples). 'If in doubt, go wide' is a good motto – and see again §30.3. For example, instead of taking the domain to be tachyons and regimenting the proposition that all tachyons are weird as

∀x Wx, we can more naturally take the domain more inclusively to be, say, physical particles. We can then regiment that proposition as we initially did, as ∀x(Tx → Wx) and lose the unwanted inference to ∃x Wx.

Second, if we continue to have lingering doubts about some more inclusive domain, we can (and do) proceed in an exploratory, non-committal, suppositional mode. For example, consider mathematical inquiry which proceeds in the supposedly all-inclusive framework of full-blown set theory. What if we are sceptical about this world of sets? We can bracket our set-theoretic investigations with an unspoken 'Ok, let's take it, for the sake of argument, that there *is* this wildly infinitary universe that standard set theory talks about ...'. And then, within the scope of that bracketing assumption, we plunge in and quantify over sets in the usual way, and continue our explorations *as if* we are dealing with a suitably populated domain, to see where our investigations get to.

So yes, once we have made the supposition for the sake of further exploration that there are sets or superstrings or whatever, we might want the same logic to apply in each case, topic-neutrally. But there is no need for this logic we use, once we are working within the scope of the supposition that we *are* talking about something, to still remain neutral about whether there is anything in the domain.

The debate, predictably, will continue. But we have perhaps said enough to explain why the majority view is that, at least for our introductory purposes, it is defensible to stick with our standard logic, the logic for reasoning about non-empty domains.

34.3 Summary

Our standard natural deduction rules presuppose that we are dealing with non-empty domains.

We could revise our logic to give rules for reasoning that apply to populated and empty domains alike. But given that we almost always reason while presupposing – if only for the sake of argument – that we are indeed talking about something, the standard rules certainly apply widely enough to warrant continuing to explore them.

35 Q-valuations

In the last Interlude, we noted that we can approach questions of validity for QL arguments in two ways – semantically, by defining a notion of q-validity (on the model of tautological validity for PL arguments), and proof-theoretically, by showing how to prove conclusions from premisses by step-by-step derivations (relying on intuitively compelling inference rules for the quantifiers). We have been exploring the second approach. Now it is time to discuss q-validity.

The basic idea, as we have said before, is that a QL argument is q-valid if every relevant q-valuation which makes the premisses true makes the conclusion true too. In this chapter, then, we need to explore the idea of a q-valuation.

35.1 Q-valuations defined

In the PL case, a *valuation* of the non-logical building blocks of a language – assigning truth values to its atomic wffs – generates a unique truth value for every wff of the language. We now want an analogous story which we can apply to a QL language. What truth-relevant values should we assign to its building blocks? Given what we have said informally about reference, extension and truth in §25.7, and about domains in §26.4, §27.3, and §28.8, we know what's needed:

> A *q-valuation* for a QL language does three things:
>
> (1) It fixes some *objects*, at least one, to be the *domain* of quantification for the language. (NB, QL domains are non-empty.)
>
> (2) It assigns to each proper name some *object* in the domain to serve as the name's reference. (NB, QL proper names are non-empty.)
>
> (3) It assigns to each k-ary predicate some (possibly zero) k-tuples *of objects* from the domain to serve as the predicate's *extension*. Except that a 0-ary predicate – cf. §28.3(c)! – is simply assigned a truth value. (NB, QL predicate extensions *can* be empty.)

Let's say that the references of names and extensions of predicates on a q-valuation are their *q-values*. We can think of domains and extensions as forming sets – that's not essential, but it makes some phrasing neater (see §25.5).

The glossary for a QL language together with a given situation in the world (which determines which objects satisfy which predicates) will generate *one*

333

q-valuation for the language. When we come to define q-validity we have to take into account all the possible q-valuations. But, intuitively, the following key claim should look plausible: *any* q-valuation for a given QL language determines unique truth values for all its sentences. For many purposes, it is enough just to know that this claim is indeed true.

Still, we really should spend some time explaining *why* it is true. In the PL case, we determine the truth value of a wff by chasing truth values around its parse tree. What is the analogue for quantified wffs? We haven't yet given an official story about parse trees for QL wffs. So that's what we need to do next.

35.2 QL syntax and q-parse trees

(a) Let's review, then, our story about QL *syntax*. We saw how to construct atomic wffs in §28.2. We added connectives in §28.5 and introduced the formal quantifier/variable notation in §28.6. Then in §32.1 we introduced dummy names. Let's bring things together in one place.

First we specify again the basic building blocks of our QL languages. So:

The *logical symbols* are: $\land, \lor, \neg, \rightarrow, \bot, \forall, \exists, (,)$, $\therefore$, plus the comma.

The *variables* are: $\mathsf{x, y, z, x', y', z', x'', y'', z'', x''', \ldots}$ – i.e. a variable is a late-alphabet letter followed by zero or more primes.

The *dummy names* are: $\mathsf{a, b, c, a', b', c', a'', b'', c'', a''', \ldots}$ – i.e. a dummy name is an early-alphabet letter followed by zero or more primes.

The *non-logical vocabulary* of a particular QL language will comprise zero or more symbols for proper names (usually, mid-alphabet lower-case letters such as $\mathsf{m, n, o, \ldots}$), and one or more symbols for predicates (usually, upper-case letters such as $\mathsf{F, G, \ldots, L, M, \ldots, R, S, \ldots}$).

Each predicate will be assigned a fixed arity (a number from zero up).

The logical symbols, variables, and dummy names stay fixed across all QL languages. What can vary from case to case are the built-in names and predicates. (Let's assume there is always at least one predicate – if there were none, the resulting language could only have wffs built up from '$\bot$' and connectives!)

(b) Next, we briskly assemble the rules for constructing QL wffs which we scattered through earlier chapters, at last putting them into the same shape as our rules for constructing PL wffs in §9.1:

Assume the non-logical vocabulary of a particular QL language to be given.

The *terms* of the language are its proper names plus its unlimited supply of dummy names.

The *atomic wffs* of the language are the expressions formed by taking any k-ary predicate followed by k terms from the language.

The *wffs* of the language are then determined as follows:

(W1)   Any atomic wff of the language counts as a wff. So does $\bot$.

(W2)   If α and β are wffs, so are $(\alpha \wedge \beta)$, $(\alpha \vee \beta)$, and $(\alpha \to \beta)$.

(W3)   If α is a wff, so is $\neg\alpha$.

(W4)   If $\alpha(\tau)$ is a wff containing one or more occurrences of the term τ and $\alpha(\xi)$ is the expression which results from replacing the term τ throughout $\alpha(\tau)$ by a variable ξ new to that wff, then $\forall\xi\alpha(\xi)$ and $\exists\xi\alpha(\xi)$ are wffs.

(W5)   Nothing else is a wff.

The *sentences* of the language are the wffs which don't include any dummy names. Other wffs are *auxiliary* wffs.

We have by now seen plenty of examples of these W-rules at work. One comment, however. A QL language has unlimitedly many dummy names, and hence unlimitedly many terms. Therefore, as we construct ever more complex wffs, we need never run out of terms to quantify into, and we can form unlimitedly complex quantified wffs. Of course, *in practice*, we will rarely need more than (say) half a dozen quantifiers in a sentence. But we impose no upper limit *in principle*.

(c)   From now on, we will assume that all the dummy names of a QL language do come in some standard 'alphabetical' order (e.g. as displayed in §35.2(b)).

As we noted in §28.6, a given quantified wff can be constructed following the W-rules in more than one way. To repeat our earlier example, the QL_1 wff $\exists z(Fz \wedge Lzn)$ can be constructed by quantifying on 'm' in the wff $(Fm \wedge Lmn)$. But it also can be constructed by quantifying on 'o' in the wff $(Fo \wedge Lon)$. And now we have dummy names to play with, it can equally well be constructed by quantifying on e.g. the dummy name 'c' in the wff $(Fc \wedge Lcn)$. However, it makes things simpler if we now settle on a single possible construction history for special consideration.

We will form the *standard parse tree for a QL wff* as follows. We put the initial wff at the top, and then we apply and reapply the following rules until we reach atomic wffs or absurdity signs at the bottom of branches:

(P1)   If the wff at the current point of the tree as we work down is of the form $\neg\alpha$, write α below it.

(P2)   If the wff at the current point is of the form $(\alpha \wedge \beta)$, $(\alpha \vee \beta)$, or $(\alpha \to \beta)$, then split the tree, with the left branch going down to α and the right branch going down to β.

(P3)   If the wff at the current point is of the form $\forall\xi\alpha(\xi)$ or $\exists\xi\alpha(\xi)$, then write the instance $\alpha(\delta)$ below it – where δ is the *first dummy name in the standard order which is not in the current quantified wff*.

The first two rules are entirely familiar from forming PL parse trees. The novel tweak is in (P3), which gives us a principle for selecting a unique instance of a quantified wff, so we get a unique standard QL tree.

Here, then, are the standard QL parse trees for two wffs we've met before:

From §30.2:

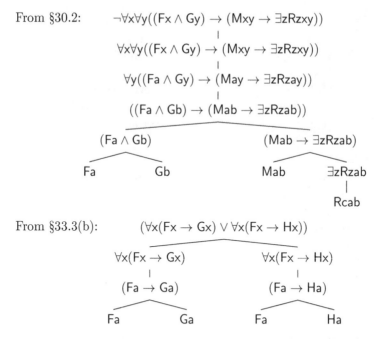

$$\neg\forall x\forall y((Fx \wedge Gy) \to (Mxy \to \exists zRzxy))$$
$$|$$
$$\forall x\forall y((Fx \wedge Gy) \to (Mxy \to \exists zRzxy))$$
$$|$$
$$\forall y((Fa \wedge Gy) \to (May \to \exists zRzay))$$
$$|$$
$$((Fa \wedge Gb) \to (Mab \to \exists zRzab))$$

$(Fa \wedge Gb)$ $(Mab \to \exists zRzab)$

Fa   Gb   Mab $\exists zRzab$

Rcab

From §33.3(b): $(\forall x(Fx \to Gx) \vee \forall x(Fx \to Hx))$

$\forall x(Fx \to Gx)$ $\forall x(Fx \to Hx)$
$|$ $|$
$(Fa \to Ga)$ $(Fa \to Ha)$

Fa   Ga   Fa   Ha

Three comments. First, note how, in the second example, the same dummy name is used on both branches – check that this is what our rule dictates.

Second, unlike a PL parse tree, a standard QL parse tree doesn't straightforwardly disassemble a wff into its *parts*. In neither of our examples is Fa at the bottom of the tree a part of – literally a subformula of – the wff at the top.

Third, if we read a standard QL parse tree from bottom to top, it represents one but only one way of constructing the top wff following rules W1 to W4. For example, 'm' could occur instead of 'a', and 'c' instead of 'b' in the first tree above, and that would give us another possible construction history of the same top wff. However, these other possible construction histories will essentially look the same (it's just that different terms will appear in place of those particular dummy names which are quantified away). So we can still think of the standard QL parse tree for a wff as essentially capturing *the* logical structure of a wff, *the* way it is built up using quantifiers-and-variables and connectives.

(d)   Now call standard QL parse trees simply *q-parse trees* for short. Since a wff has a unique q-parse tree, the following definitions – borrowed from §§9.4(a) and 9.4(d) – still work as intended:

The *main* logical operator (connective or quantifier) of a QL wff is the last operator introduced as we go up the wff's q-parse tree.

An occurrence of a logical operator (connective or quantifier) is in the *scope* of some other occurrence of an operator in a wff if the first operator is introduced *before* the second as we go *up* the relevant branch of the q-parse tree for the wff.

The core ideas here are familiar from PL so we needn't pause over them again.

We can also clarify which variables-as-pronouns get tied to which quantifier prefixes. This is not just a matter of involving the same variable – for example, the last 'x' in $(\forall x(Fx \rightarrow Gx) \vee \forall x(Fx \rightarrow Hx))$ is obviously not tied to the first occurrence of the quantifier prefix '$\forall x$'. Rather:

> An occurrence of a variable after some predicate is always introduced to-gether with an occurrence of a quantifier prefix as we go up the q-parse tree for the wff. That occurrence of the variable is then tied to – or better, is *bound* by – that particular quantifier.

35.3 Evaluating quantified wffs: the headlines

(a) A q-valuation determines the truth value of an atomic sentence in the obvious way: a predicate followed by k proper names is true if and only if the k-tuple of objects referred to by the names taken in order is in the extension of the predicate (compare §25.7). Let's leave the connectives to look after themselves just for the moment. The story gets much more interesting when we turn to the evaluation of quantified wffs. And you can immediately spot a problem. Take this simplest of quantified wffs with its q-parse tree:

Suppose we have chosen a q-valuation q for the relevant language, which in particular fixes the domain of quantification and assigns an extension to 'F'. This doesn't yet give any sort of truth-relevant value to 'a'. So there is no way yet of using something truth-relevant about the wff at the bottom of the tree to settle a value on the wff at the top. What to do?

Obviously enough, we now have to give a semantic role to the dummy name here. We first introduced dummy names to serve, mid-derivation, as temporary names to dub objects selected from the domain. So let's pursue this idea. Suppose, then, that the valuation q_a *expands* the q-valuation q by also assigning an object in the domain to the dummy name 'a' to be its q-value, i.e. its reference (note, we can do this because the domain isn't empty). Then this settles a truth value on Fa: that wff will be true on the expanded valuation q_a just if the reference of 'a' is in the extension of the predicate 'F'.

But the truth value of Fa on a single expanded valuation q_a doesn't settle the value of $\forall x\, Fx$ on the valuation q. Obviously, more is required. So *here* is the crucial new idea we need (an ancestor of the idea is already in Frege):

> $\forall x\, Fx$ is true on the valuation q iff Fa is true on *every* possible expanded valuation q_a, i.e. Fa is true no matter what object from the domain is assigned to 'a' as a temporary reference.

Look at it informally like this. 'Every woman is such that she is mortal' (where 'she' is a bound pronoun) is true just so long as 'she is mortal' is true (where 'she' is now a demonstrative), no matter which woman we are picking out using the demonstrative. Similarly, ∀x Fx is true just so long as Fa is true, *no matter which object in the domain we are temporarily picking out by* 'a'.

Careful! We need to sharply distinguish our new idea from an idea we already rejected in §27.5. We can't say, in general, that ∀x Fx is true on a valuation if each proper-name instance like Fn is true (there might not be enough proper names to name everything). Nor can we say that ∀x Fx is true if each dummy-name instance like Fa is true, even if we go round assigning all the dummy names a different reference (there might not be enough dummy names either). Unsurprisingly, we need to assign ∀x Fx a value not by generalizing over *names* (permanent or temporary) but by generalizing over *objects* in the relevant domain. To repeat, ∀x Fx is true if Fa is true *whatever object* 'a' *temporarily names*.

The corresponding principle for an existential quantifier is predictable:

∃x Fx is true on the valuation q iff Fa is true on *at least one* possible expanded valuation q_a. Or equivalently, ∃x Fx is false on the valuation q iff Fa is false on *every* possible expanded valuation q_a.

(b) So far so good. But the device of using expanded valuations really comes into its own when we are dealing with a wff with more than one quantifier. Take a simple case. Consider the following wff with its q-parse tree:

$$∀x∃y\, Lxy$$
$$|$$
$$∃y\, Lay$$
$$|$$
$$Lab$$

Assume that we are given a q-valuation q for the relevant language, which fixes the domain of quantification and assigns an extension to the predicate 'L'. As before, let q_a be a valuation which augments the q-valuation q by assigning an object in the domain as reference to the dummy name 'a'. And now let q_{ab} further expand this q_a by also assigning an object as reference to the dummy name 'b'. Then, developing our previous idea about the universal quantifier in the obvious way, we can say:

∀x∃y Lxy is true on the valuation q if and only if ∃y Lay is true on *every* possible expanded valuation q_a.

And then ∃y Lay is true on an expanded valuation q_a if and only if Lab is true on *at least one* possible further expanded valuation q_{ab}.

Hence, ∀x∃y Lxy is true just in case, no matter which object a we pick in the domain (to assign to 'a'), there is some object b in the domain (to assign to 'b') such that the ordered pair $\langle a, b \rangle$ is in the extension of 'L'. Just as we want!

35.4   The official valuational semantics

(a)   Generalizing the new ideas from the last section, we have: $\forall \xi \alpha(\xi)$ is true if $\alpha(\delta)$ is true whatever the dummy name δ denotes, and $\exists \xi \alpha(\xi)$ is true if $\alpha(\delta)$ is true on at least one assignment of reference to δ, where the dummy name is newly introduced. And we can now put these principles to work in a more careful account of how the truth values of sentences of a QL language are determined by a q-valuation for that language. (We have not made a slip here. Our prime target is indeed an account of how the value of a *sentence* – a wff without dummy names – depends on an unaugmented q-valuation. What we have just seen, however, is that this account will typically have to go via an account of how the values of wffs involving dummy names depend on expanded q-valuations.)

There will be nothing really new in this section; so don't let the now slightly more abstract mode of presentation obscure the underlying ideas.

(b)   Take a QL language. For brevity, 'q' can now denote some q-valuation for the language which perhaps has already been expanded by assignments of references to one or more dummy names. We need some shorthand notation:

> We re-use the symbol ':=' from §10.5 in assigning values to wffs. In the context where the (perhaps expanded) q-valuation q is in play, '$\alpha := V$' says that α takes the truth value V on the valuation q. When more than one valuation q is in play, we can subscript to indicate which valuation we are using, as in ':=$_q$'.

We can then present the semantic ideas already sketched in three parts. First, to evaluate the simplest wffs, i.e. atomic wffs plus the absurdity constant:

> Given a valuation q for the relevant language (possibly expanded to evaluate any dummy names currently in play),
>
> (A1)   Suppose α is an atomic wff, consisting of the k-ary predicate φ [phi] followed by k terms $\tau_1, \tau_2, \ldots, \tau_k$, for $k > 0$. Suppose q assigns the term τ_1 the object o_1 as reference, assigns τ_2 the object o_2, etc., and assigns the predicate φ the extension E. Then $\alpha := $ T if the k-tuple $\langle o_1, o_2, \ldots, o_k \rangle$ is in E; otherwise $\alpha := $ F.
>
> (A2)   Suppose α is an atomic wff consisting of a 0-ary predicate. Then q directly assigns this a truth value.
>
> (A3) $\bot := $ F.

(c)   Next, here are the rules for evaluating QL wffs whose main logical operators are the connectives (preserving their truth-functional readings):

> Take any wffs α, β. Then, on any given (possibly expanded) valuation q,
>
> (Q1)   If $\alpha := $ T, then $\neg \alpha := $ F; otherwise $\neg \alpha := $ T.
>
> (Q2)   If $\alpha := $ T and $\beta := $ T then $(\alpha \wedge \beta) := $ T; otherwise $(\alpha \wedge \beta) := $ F.

(Q3) If $\alpha := F$ and $\beta := F$ then $(\alpha \lor \beta) := F$; otherwise $(\alpha \lor \beta) := T$.

(Q4) If $\alpha := T$ and $\beta := F$ then $(\alpha \to \beta) := F$; otherwise $(\alpha \to \beta) := T$.

(d) And now for the crucial third part:

Given a valuation q (perhaps already an expanded valuation but not yet mentioning the dummy name δ), a δ-*expansion* of q now assigns some object in the domain as reference for the dummy name δ while keeping the rest of the valuation q fixed. We use 'q_δ' to symbolize a δ-expansion of q.

The rules for evaluating QL wffs whose main operators are the quantifiers are then as follows:

Let $\alpha(\delta)$ be the instance of $\forall\xi\alpha(\xi)$ or $\exists\xi\alpha(\xi)$ using the first dummy name δ new to the wff. Then for any (possibly expanded) valuation q,

(Q5) $\forall\xi\alpha(\xi) :=_q T$ if $\alpha(\delta) :=_{q_\delta} T$ for every δ-expansion q_δ; otherwise $\forall\xi\alpha(\xi) :=_q F$.

(Q6) $\exists\xi\alpha(\xi) :=_q F$ if $\alpha(\delta) :=_{q_\delta} F$ for every δ-expansion q_δ; otherwise $\exists\xi\alpha(\xi) :=_q T$.

35.5   Toy examples

(a) The last section was inevitably a bit abstract. But just keep firmly hold of the basic thought that a quantified wff $\forall\xi\alpha(\xi)$ is true just if an instance with a new dummy name $\alpha(\delta)$ is true whatever the dummy name temporarily picks out, and everything else should fall into place!

Still, it will no doubt help to work through some mini-examples. So let's take a language QL_4 with just the following non-logical vocabulary:

Proper names: m, n
Unary predicates: F, G
Binary predicate: L.

And let q be the following q-valuation for the language (we use elementary informal set notation in a lightweight way, just for tidiness):

The domain: {Socrates, Plato, Aristotle}
References,   m: Socrates
             n: Plato
Extensions,   F: {Socrates, Aristotle}
             G: ∅
             L: {⟨Socrates, Plato⟩, ⟨Plato, Aristotle⟩, ⟨Plato, Socrates⟩,
                ⟨Aristotle, Aristotle⟩}.

Here, '∅' is the standard symbol for an empty set with no members. And the members of L's extension are four ordered pairs (i.e. the pair of Socrates and then Plato, etc.) – see §25.3(c) again for the angle bracket notation.

So now let's evaluate some sentences on this q-valuation q. Take first the following sentence:

$(Fm \rightarrow \forall x\, Fx)$.

A moment's reflection shows that this has a true antecedent on q and a false consequent, so is false overall on this q-valuation. But now let's check this the hard way, working downwards though the wff's q-parse tree, appealing to our A-rules and Q-rules. So here's the tree we want:

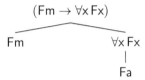

We can then reason as follows:

(1) By (Q4), $(Fm \rightarrow \forall x\, Fx) :=_q F$ iff (i) $Fm :=_q T$ and (ii) $\forall x\, Fx :=_q F$.

(2) By (A1), (i) $Fm :=_q T$, since the reference of 'm' *is* in the extension of 'F'.

(3) By (Q5), $\forall x\, Fx :=_q F$ iff there is some expanded valuation q_a where $Fa :=_{q_a} F$. Consider the expanded valuation q_a which assigns Plato to 'a'. Then on *that* valuation, the reference of 'a' is not in the extension of 'F' and so by (A1) $Fa :=_{q_a} F$. Hence (ii) $\forall x\, Fx :=_q F$.

(4) Therefore, from (i) and (ii), $(Fm \rightarrow \forall x\, Fx) :=_q F$.

(b) Next, a variant on the example $\forall x \exists y\, Lxy$ which we used earlier in motivating our semantic story about quantifiers. Here is a similar wff with its q-parse tree:

$\exists y \forall x\, Lxy$
|
$\forall x\, Lxa$
|
Lba

We evaluate this sentence on the same q-valuation q. Again working downwards,

(1) By (Q6), $\exists y \forall x\, Lxy :=_q F$ iff, for every q_a, $\forall x\, Lxa :=_{q_a} F$.

(2) For a given q_a, by (Q5), $\forall x\, Lxa :=_{q_a} F$ iff for some expanded valuation q_{ab}, we have $Lba :=_{q_{ab}} F$.

(3) We have to consider cases:

   (i) q_a assigns Socrates to 'a'. If we also assign Socrates to 'b' (and different names can name the same thing), $Lba :=_{q_{ab}} F$.
   (ii) q_a assigns Plato to 'a'. If we assign Aristotle to 'b', $Lba :=_{q_{ab}} F$.
   (iii) q_a assigns Aristotle to 'a'. If we assign Socrates to 'b', $Lba :=_{q_{ab}} F$.

(4) Hence for any given q_a, $\forall x\, Lxa :=_{q_a} F$.

(5) Hence $\exists y \forall x\, Lxy :=_q F$.

341

(c)   For a third example, take the following sentence with its q-parse tree:

$$\neg\forall x\forall y(Fx \vee Gy)$$
$$|$$
$$\forall x\forall y(Fx \vee Gy)$$
$$|$$
$$\forall y(Fa \vee Gy)$$
$$|$$
$$(Fa \vee Gb)$$

$$Fa \qquad\qquad Gb$$

Then plodding laboriously through again, we have:

(1)   By (Q1), $\neg\forall x\forall y(Fx \vee Gy) :=_q$ T iff $\forall x\forall y(Fx \vee Gy) :=_q$ F.

(2)   By (Q5), $\forall x\forall y(Fx \vee Gy) :=_q$ F iff for some q_a, $\forall x(Fa \vee Gy) :=_{q_a}$ F.

(3)   By (Q5) again, $\forall x(Fa \vee Gy) :=_{q_a}$ F iff for some q_{ab}, $(Fa \vee Gb) :=_{q_{ab}}$ F.

(4)   By (Q5), $(Fa \vee Gb) :=_{q_{ab}}$ F iff both $Fa :=_{q_{ab}}$ F and $Gb :=_{q_{ab}}$ F.

(5)   We now have to consider cases. But take the case where q_a assigns Plato to the dummy name 'a', and then go on to expand this to q_{ab} by assigning Socrates to 'b'. Then $Fa :=_{q_{ab}}$ F since Plato is not in the extension of 'F'. And $Gb :=_{q_{ab}}$ F since Socrates (along with the others) is not in the empty extension of 'G'. Hence by (4) $(Fa \vee Gb) :=_{q_{ab}}$ F.

(6)   So working back up the tree, we get $\neg\forall x\forall y(Fx \vee Gy) :=_q$ T.

35.6   Uniqueness of values

The calculations of truth values in our simple examples are already more than a little tedious! And just imagine if the domain of our q-valuation q had been a much bigger finite one. Or suppose we had started with an infinite domain and infinite extensions for predicates, and so (lacking a logical god's-eye view) we couldn't actually work through such calculations in practice. Still, trudging through our toy examples above should convince you of the following general principle which we announced before.

Recall again from §10.7(b) that a valuation of the non-logical vocabulary of a PL language uniquely determines a resulting valuation of *every* wff of the language, however complex. Similarly, and this is really the key take-away message of the whole chapter, we can now see that

A q-valuation for a QL language uniquely determines a resulting truth value of *every* sentence of the language, however complex.

Start from a q-valuation q of a given QL language. Take any sentence of the language. Form its q-parse tree. Applying our Q-rules as we go down the tree, we get an account of how the truth values of the wffs at each stage depend on the truth values of simpler wffs (perhaps the values on many expanded valuations), which in turn depend on the truth values of still simpler wffs (perhaps on many further expanded valuations), until we get to the truth values of atoms (perhaps on even more valuations). But the truth values of atoms at the bottom of branches are determinate on each relevant expanded valuation; and these values then fix the values of the wffs above them.

Note: since references and extensions (and domains) are enough to determine the truth values of all sentences, QL languages are indeed *fully extensional* in the sense of §25.7(e).

35.7   The structure of valuations

(a)   What sort of objects can feature in q-valuations? In informal logic, we frequently dream up fictional examples when imagining possible situations as counterexamples to validity claims. Are we similarly allowed to invoke fictional objects – whatever exactly they are – in building a q-valuation?

We have often used fictional examples earlier in this book. But when we move from informal logic to talking about more formal notions like tautological validity and q-validity, aren't we supposed to leave murky fictional ideas behind us?

As a step towards responding to the worry here, consider again the q-valuation q from §35.5:

The domain: $\{S, P, A\}$
References,   m: S
             n: P
Extensions, F: $\{S, A\}$
             G: $\emptyset$
             L: $\{\langle S, P\rangle, \langle P, A\rangle, \langle P, S\rangle, \langle A, A\rangle\}$.

Previously, S was Socrates, P was Plato, and A was Aristotle. But what makes Fm true on q is that the reference of 'm' (S, whatever that is) is in the extension of 'F' (is in the set $\{S, A\}$, whatever S and A are). What makes ∀x Fx false on q is that there is an object P in the domain which is not in the extension of 'F'. And so on. Which objects these objects S, P, A really *are* doesn't matter. Sellars, Putnam, and Anscombe could serve just as well for building a valuation with the same structure (if you prefer more recent philosophers) or Scarlatti, Purcell, and Albinoni (if Baroque composers are your thing).

In short: we can systematically swap around the objects used in constructing a q-valuation without changing which sentences the valuation makes true, so long as the structure of the valuation stays the same.

(b)   We can make the point more abstractly. Take a valuation q. Form a new valuation q^* by (i) swapping objects in q's domain for some other objects, the old object o being replaced by the new object o^* (different objects get different replacements). Then (ii) let q^* change references of names and extensions of predicates to match. Thus, suppose o is the reference of the name 'm' according to q; then o^* will be that name's reference according to q^*. Suppose the set $\{o_1, o_2, \ldots\}$ is the extension of the unary predicate 'F' according to q; then $\{o_1^*, o_2^*, \ldots\}$ will be the extension of that predicate according to q^*. And so on.

343

According to the q-valuation q, Fm $:=_q$ T iff o is in $\{o_1, o_2, \ldots\}$. But by design, o^* is in $\{o_1^*, o_2^*, \ldots\}$ iff o is in $\{o_1, o_2, \ldots\}$. And according to q^*, Fm $:=_{q^*}$ T iff o^* is in $\{o_1^*, o_2^*, \ldots\}$. Hence we get the key result: Fm $:=_q$ T iff Fm $:=_{q*}$ T. And it is easy to see that, quite generally, *any* sentence is true according to q if and only if it is also true according to q^*.

With only slight abuse of standard terminology, we can say that valuations related like q and q^* are *isomorphic* – i.e. have the same form. Then, in summary, isomorphic valuations make the same sentences true.

(c)   We now know, then, that it doesn't really matter what particular objects we build our valuations from – it's the structure of a valuation that matters. So a fictional example may be memorably vivid ('Consider a domain comprising Shylock, Portia, and Antonio, …'). But any isomorphic q-valuation involving a humdrum choice of uncontentious things S, P, and A will do just as well. Hence, as long as the non-fictional world is rich enough to provide materials for a q-valuation isomorphic to any fiction-based valuation we dream up, using fiction-based examples can't lead us astray. We can harmlessly take the fanciful example as a vivid proxy for a non-fictional q-valuation of the same form.

35.8   Summary

We gave a sharper account of QL syntax, and introduced the notion of a q-parse tree for a wff.

We then defined a q-valuation for a QL language. This fixes the domain of quantification, assigns an object to each proper name as its reference, and assigns a suitable extension to each predicate (except 0-ary predicates are directly assigned truth values). An expanded q-valuation in addition assigns references to one or more dummy names, as needed.

Three facts about how q-valuations fix the values of wffs:

(1)   An atomic wff formed from a predicate followed by some term(s) is true on a (possibly expanded) q-valuation just if the tuple of the reference(s) of the term(s) is in the extension of the predicate.

(2)   The connectives behave in the familiar truth-functional way in determining the truth values of wffs containing them on a q-valuation.

(3)   A wff $\forall\xi\alpha(\xi)$ is true on a (possibly expanded) q-valuation just when $\alpha(\delta)$ is true, whatever object the new dummy name δ is given as reference by a further expansion of the valuation. Similarly, $\exists\xi\alpha(\xi)$ is false on a q-valuation just when $\alpha(\delta)$ is false, whatever object the new name δ is newly given as reference.

Working up and down a q-parse tree for a QL sentence (a wff without dummy names) using these three kinds of valuation rule, a q-valuation then fixes a unique value for the sentence.

Exercises 35

(a) Take a QL language, with a couple of proper names, a couple of unary predicates, and a binary predicate, and consider the following q-valuation:

> The domain is {Romeo, Juliet, Benedick, Beatrice}
>
> m: Romeo
>
> n: Juliet
>
> F: {Romeo, Benedick}
>
> G: {Juliet, Beatrice}
>
> L: {⟨Romeo, Juliet⟩, ⟨Juliet, Romeo⟩, ⟨Benedick, Beatrice⟩,
> ⟨Beatrice, Benedick⟩, ⟨Benedick, Benedick⟩}.

Then what are the truth values of the following wffs?

(1) ∃xLmx
(2) ∀xLxm
(3) (∃xLmx → Lmn)
(4) ∀x(Fx → ¬Gx)
(5) ∀x(Gx → (Lxm ∨ ¬Lmx))
(6) ∀x(Gx → ∃yLxy)
(7) ∃x(Fx ∧ ∀y(Gy → Lxy))

(b) Now take the following q-valuation:

> The domain is {4, 7, 8, 11, 12}
>
> m: 7
>
> n: 12
>
> F: the set of even numbers in the domain
>
> G: the set of odd numbers in the domain
>
> L: the set of pairs ⟨m, n⟩ where m and n are in the domain and $m < n$.

What are the truth values of the wffs (1) to (7) now?

(c) Take the language QL$_3$ of Exercises 30(b). Consider the following q-valuation (the natural one suggested by the given glossary for the language):

> The domain is the set of natural numbers (the integers from zero up)
>
> n: one
>
> F: the set of odd numbers
>
> G: the set of even numbers
>
> H: the set of prime numbers
>
> L: the set of pairs ⟨m, n⟩ such that $m < n$
>
> R: the set of triples ⟨l, m, n⟩ such that $l = m + n$.

Carefully work out the values of the wffs (1) to (8) from Exercises 30(b).

(d*) Show that if the wff α *doesn't* contain the dummy name δ, then α is true on the valuation q if and only if it is also true on any expansion q$_δ$.

36 Q-validity

Having defined the notion of a q-valuation in the previous chapter and seen that, crucially, a q-valuation determines the truth value of every sentence of the relevant language, we can now define the notion of q-validity in the obvious way. We then draw out some parallels between q-validity and tautological validity, note that QL proofs indeed demonstrate q-validities, and also say something about how to show that an inference is *not* q-valid.

36.1 Q-validity defined

(a)   We said that

An inference step between wffs of a PL language is *tautologically valid* if and only if there is no valuation of the non-logical building blocks of the relevant language – assigning truth values to its atoms – which makes the premises all true and the conclusion false.

Remember, we quantify here over all combinatorially possible valuations (not just those that respect the meaning of atoms – see §12.4). And the companion definition for inferences in QL languages is as you would expect:

An inference step between sentences of a QL language is *q-valid* (the premises *q-entail* the conclusion) if and only if there is no q-valuation of the non-logical building blocks of the relevant language – assigning q-values to its names and predicates and fixing its domain – which makes the premises all true and the conclusion false.

Again, we quantify over all combinatorially possible q-valuations, now ignoring what the language's glossary tells us about the senses of names and predicates or about the domain. Why? Because we want to capture the idea of a QL inference being necessarily truth-preserving just in virtue of the way that connectives and quantifiers feature in the premises and conclusion. In other words, we want to characterize those QL arguments which are indeed valid but whose validity does not depend on the meaning of any non-logical vocabulary they contain or on the particular choice of domain.

(b)   To help elucidate that last point, consider a QL language whose glossary includes the unary predicates

346

F: ① is a mother,
G: ① is a parent,
H: ① is a philosopher.

Then compare

A   ∀x Fx ∴ ∀x Gx,
B   ∀x(Gx ∧ Hx) ∴ ∀x Gx.

There is no possible situation in which everyone is a mother while not everyone is a parent. So, as interpreted, **A** is valid. But the validity of this inference depends on the topics of the predicates F and G. Abstracting from the meaning of the predicates, we can obviously assign them extensions which make ∀x Fx true and ∀x Gx false. So **A** is not q-valid, and it is not *logically* valid.

Again, there is no possible situation in which everyone is both a parent and a philosopher while not everyone is a parent. So, as interpreted, **B** is valid. But this time, it doesn't matter what type of objects we are quantifying over and it doesn't matter what extensions the predicates have, the inference here will still be truth-preserving. Hence **B** is q-valid, so truth-preserving just in virtue of the meaning of the connective and the quantifier. Hence it is logically valid.

(c)   We can generalize this last point (and here we echo the point we made in §15.2 about logical validity and tautological validity). Suppose the QL inference step from some sentences Γ to the sentence γ is q-valid. Then, by definition, there is no q-valuation of the relevant language which makes Γ all true and γ false. Hence, however the world is, whatever we take the quantifiers as ranging over, and however we read the relevant names and predicates, there is no resulting combination of domain, references, and extensions which can make Γ all true and γ false. Therefore, however things are in the world, and whatever the meanings of the non-logical vocabulary, the inference is truth-preserving. In summary:

> If a QL inference is q-valid, then it is deductively valid just in virtue of the way that the topic-neutral quantifiers and connectives appear in the premisses and conclusion, and is therefore *logically* valid.

(d)   Let's add that, predictably enough, we can also say:

> A QL sentence is a *q-logical truth* if and only if it is true on all q-valuations of the language.

> One or more QL sentences are *q-consistent* if and only if there is some q-valuation which makes them all true together.

36.2   'All q-valuations'

We said that the notion of tautological validity provides a rational reconstruction of the intuitive idea of validity-in-virtue-of-the-connectives. Our claim now is that

347

the notion of q-validity can similarly serve as a neat rational reconstruction of the intuitive idea of validity-in-virtue-of-the-connectives-and-the-quantifiers for QL arguments. Or rather, it can serve *if* the idea of quantifying over *all* possible q-valuations makes sufficiently clear sense. But does it?

We saw in §35.7 that it doesn't matter which objects we build q-valuations from; it is the resulting structure that matters. Still, there can be differently structured q-valuations to consider as we look at bigger and bigger domains. Is there any determinate limit to what we need to consider? Set theorists talk about larger and larger infinities, so how far do we need to follow them in accepting their huge universes? Will what we count as a q-logical truth – a wff true on *all* valuations – depend on just which wildly infinite domains for valuations we are prepared to countenance? This would surely be an unhappy situation.

Fortunately, there is a technical result that can calm our worries here. Let's say that a q-valuation is *tame* if its domain is just some or all of the natural numbers. Then it turns out that if a QL sentence is false on some q-valuation q, then – however wild this q might be – there will also be a tame q-valuation q' which makes the sentence false. Similarly, if there is any q-valuation q which makes the premises of some QL inference true and its conclusion false, then there will also be a tame q-valuation q' which does the same job. Hence being truth-preserving on *all* valuations, whatever exactly makes for 'all', is the same as being truth-preserving on the *tame* valuations.

We will say more about this important result in the Appendix §A6. But the moral for now is simply that we needn't worry about the apparent slack in our definition of q-validity in terms of truth-preservation on all q-valuations. Yes, to be frank, we have failed to nail down what counts as quantifying over *all* q-valuations. However, when the technicalities are worked out, our definition of q-validity does turn out to capture a perfectly determinate entailment relation, one that can (surprisingly) be characterized just in terms of tame valuations.

So we can safely enough work with our current definition.

36.3   Establishing q-validity/q-invalidity: the headlines

(a)   How do we establish that a QL inference is q-valid? The principal way is to provide a QL derivation. We chose our various QL derivation rules for the very reason that they intuitively look entirely reliable, and q-validity is our regimentation for the relevant notion of reliability. So our proof system should indeed appear to be *sound* for q-validity (compare §24.6).

Still, we shouldn't just trust to appearances – so we will need to say more about soundness in the next chapter and in the Appendix. For the moment, however, let's continue to take our Fitch-style natural deduction system on trust. Then using QL proofs will be our *main* way of establishing q-validities.

(b)   What about establishing that a QL inference is *not* q-valid? The direct route is simply to come up with a *countervaluation* (compare §16.3), i.e. a q-valuation which makes the premises true and conclusion false. Take, for example,

C	Fm $\therefore$ $\forall$x Fx,
D	$\exists$x(Fx $\vee$ Gx) $\therefore$ $\exists$x Gx,
E	$\forall$x$\exists$y Lxy $\therefore$ $\exists$y$\forall$x Lxy.

To show that these hopeless arguments are not q-valid, we just need counter-valuations which make the premisses true and conclusion false. In fact the q-valuation we gave in §35.5 does the trick in each case, as is easily checked.

36.4 We can mechanically test for q-validity in simple cases

To decide whether an argument is q-valid, though, do we just have to hopefully cast around for a derivation or a countervaluation? Can we do better?

In the case of PL arguments we can mechanically test for tautological validity by a brute-force search through all the relevant valuations of the atoms in an argument (use a truth table!). But as we pointed out in the last Interlude, in the case of QL arguments we can't similarly aim to search one by one through *all* the possible q-valuations (since *any* objects can serve as the domain for a valuation, and *any* sets of them as extensions for predicates).

Still, that observation doesn't rule out there being other ways of testing for q-validity. And in some limited cases, there *are* mechanical tests available.

Take the argument

F $\exists$x(Cx $\wedge$ Ex), $\forall$x(Dx $\rightarrow$ Ex) $\therefore$ $\exists$x(Cx $\wedge$ Dx)

which involves just three *unary* predicates C, D, E. So consider any q-valuation assigning a domain of quantification and then extensions to the three predicates:

(1) Any object in the domain will either satisfy or fail to satisfy each predicate. So a domain will contain $2^3 = 8$ groups of objects (some of these groups might be empty). In one group, there are the objects which satisfy all of C, D, E. Then there are three groups, the objects satisfying C, D, the objects satisfying C, E, the objects satisfying D, E. Then there are another three groups of the objects satisfying just one predicate C, D, or E as the case may be. Finally there is the group of objects satisfying none of the predicates.

(2) Our three predicates, however, can't *further* distinguish among the objects *within* any one of these groups.

(3) It can't make any difference, then, how many objects there are in each group: so let's reduce the population of each occupied group to a single representative. That way, we can cut down the domain of our q-valuation so that it has no more than $2^3 = 8$ objects, enough to give us one object for each populated group!

(4) But we saw in §35.7 that it doesn't matter when building a q-valuation which particular objects we actually use, because isomorphic valuations (valuations which structurally 'look the same') will give sentences the same truth values. So we might as well use as our domain simply the first eight positive integers.

349

In short, to evaluate an argument like **F** (which involves just three unary predicates) for q-validity, we only need to run through the finite number of possible q-valuations for the three-predicate language with the domain $\{1, 2, 3, \ldots, 8\}$. (And it wouldn't make a difference if the argument involved some proper names too – can you see why?) Generalizing, then, in the obvious way:

> To determine the validity of a QL inference whose n predicates are all unary, we need consider no more than all the q-valuations whose domains are the numbers $\{1, 2, 3, \ldots, 2^n\}$.

Now, true enough, a search through these q-valuations does become horribly tedious as n increases, because we have to consider all the different ways of selecting some objects from the 2^n objects of a domain to form extensions for our predicates (and also permute the references of any names). But still, running through all the different combinations and checking to see if any are counter-valuations to the given QL inference *is* a finite task; it is one that a computer could happily execute even if we might get bored to tears trying to do the same. So this is the key point of principle: there does exist a brute force mechanical procedure to decide the validity of arguments with only unary predicates.

36.5 'Working backwards'

(a) Keeping our wits about us, however, informal reasoning about q-valuations can settle matters in simple cases, *without* launching on a brute-force search. For example, the argument **F** is q-invalid if there is a valuation such that

$$\exists x(Cx \wedge Ex) := T, \quad \forall x(Dx \to Ex) := T, \quad \exists x(Cx \wedge Dx) := F.$$

To ensure the valuations come out right, we need (i) the extensions of C and E to overlap, (ii) the extension of D to be included in the extension of E, and (iii) the extensions of C and D to be disjoint (i.e. non-overlapping).

Let's therefore try to build up a q-valuation satisfying (i) to (iii). We know that the domain need be no bigger than the first eight numbers. Then we can argue:

(1) Start by throwing just 1 into the extension of C and just 2 into the extension of D. So far, then, condition (iii) is satisfied.

(2) To also satisfy (ii) the extension of E must contain at least 2, and to satisfy (i) the extension of E must contain at least 1.

And we can stop here! We *already* see that the following q-valuation will in fact do the trick, making the premisses true and conclusion false (we don't need to inflate the domain further):

Domain: $\{1, 2\}$
Extension of C: $\{1\}$
D: $\{2\}$
E: $\{1, 2\}$.

(b)   Let's take another example:

G $\forall x(Fx \to Gx)$, $\forall x(Gx \to \neg Hx)$ $\therefore$ $\forall x(Hx \to \neg Fx)$.

This is q-invalid if and only if there is a countervaluation q on which

$$\forall x(Fx \to Gx) := T, \ \forall x(Gx \to \neg Hx) := T, \ \forall x(Hx \to \neg Fx) := F.$$

Suppose there is such a countervaluation q (and we can take its domain to be at most the first eight numbers):

(1)   If q is to make the conclusion false, the extensions of F and H on q need to overlap (why?). So let's begin by throwing some object – the number 1 will do as well as anything! – into the extension of both F and H.

(2)   To make the first premiss true, q requires that everything in the extension of F is also in the extension of G (why?) – hence the extension of G must contain 1 too.

(3)   But then the extensions of G and H on q both contain 1. And that makes the second premiss *false* on q (why?), contrary to what we need.

(4)   So there can be no countervaluation q which makes the premisses of **G** true and its conclusion false. Hence **G** is q-valid.

Note, then, we have here established an inference is q-valid by a different method than producing a QL natural deduction proof. Instead, we have supposed the inference isn't q-valid and found that this supposition leads to contradiction.

(c)   In short, when dealing with sufficiently simple arguments – like Aristotelian syllogisms which involve only unary predicates – it can be quite easy to find a countervaluation or show that there can't be one. The plan is to suppose the argument is *not* valid, i.e. to suppose there is a there *is* a countervaluation, then 'work backwards' to see what this q-valuation must look like. Either you'll find one (showing the argument is not q-valid) or discover that there can't be one (showing the argument is q-valid). This 'working backwards' strategy can then be systematized, becoming the so-called *truth tree* method (compare §16.2(b)).

36.6   The *Entscheidungsproblem*

(a)   Things get more interesting, however, as soon as we consider arguments involving binary predicates. Take, for example, an argument which includes these premisses:

H   (i) $\forall x \exists y\, Rxy$, (ii) $\forall x((Rxy \wedge Ryz) \to Rxz)$, (iii) $\forall x \neg Rxx$.

Arguing informally, we can see that these premisses can only be true together in an infinite domain. Why?

(1)   Pick an object #1 in the domain. Then by (i) there is some object #2 in the domain such that #1 is R to #2. And by (iii) this object can't be #1 again. So we need a new distinct object #2 in the domain.

(2)   By (i) there is some object #3 in the domain such that #2 is R to #3. By (iii) this object can't be #2 again. And it can't be #1 again, or else

we would have both #1 is R to #2 (by our previous assumption) and now #2 is R is #1, and hence by (ii) #1 is R to #1 – which is ruled out by (iii). So we need a new distinct object #3 in the domain.

(3) Keep on going. The domain must contain (at least) some objects #1, #2, #3, #4, #5, ..., all distinct.

Moral, as soon as we have a binary predicate like R in play, we may need to think about q-valuations with infinite domains. By itself, this observation still doesn't rule out there being some decision method for determining the validity of arguments with binary predicates. But if we need to deal with infinite domains, it does suggest that a decision method, if one exists, is going to require more sophisticated techniques than anything we have touched on so far.

(b) The situation, then, is this. We want to know whether a QL argument is q-valid. We can't just blunder through a search across every possible q-valuation of the relevant language, though we now know that a limited search procedure can be used to decide validity in *some* special cases. So what about the *general* case? Is there a suitably sophisticated mechanical decision procedure that can always be applied to determine whether a QL argument is q-valid, even when we have to tangle with the infinite? This is the so-called *Entscheidungsproblem* (decision problem) first posed by David Hilbert and Wilhelm Ackermann in their 1928 book *Grundzüge der Theoretischen Logik*. (This short but hugely influential classic, later translated as *Principles of Mathematical Logic*, is the first recognizably modern logic book, and still worth reading.)

The decision problem was soon solved in the negative by Alonzo Church and Alan Turing, working independently in 1935–36. Once we have a clear analysis of the notion of a mechanical decision procedure, and a resulting clear analysis of some of the limitations of mechanical computing procedures, we can show that there can indeed be no such procedure to decide all questions of QL validity.

The arguments for this bit of metatheory (theory *about* QL logic) are beautiful and not too hard: but sadly they go beyond what we can cover in this book.

36.7   Generalizing again

A simple point to conclude this chapter. Claims about tautological validity are implicitly general: as we put it before, buy one tautological entailment and you get indefinitely many of the same form for free. It is the same with q-validity, because an argument is q-valid merely in virtue of its logical form, a form that can be displayed using a purely logical schema.

For example, we have just shown that

G $\forall x(Fx \rightarrow Gx), \forall x(Gx \rightarrow \neg Hx) \therefore \forall x(Hx \rightarrow \neg Fx)$

is q-valid. But then we can see that any argument of the same shape

$$\forall \xi(\alpha(\xi) \rightarrow \beta(\xi)), \forall \xi(\beta(\xi) \rightarrow \neg \gamma(\xi)) \therefore \forall \xi(\gamma(\xi) \rightarrow \neg \alpha(\xi))$$

has to be q-valid too.

Why? Suppose an instance of that schema were *not* q-valid. Then there would be a q-valuation which made its premisses true and conclusion false. This countervaluation will fix a domain, and fix extensions for the relevant α, β, and γ (i.e. settle which objects these expressions are respectively true of). So carry this q-valuation over to **G**, assigning the same domain, and assigning F, G, H respectively the extensions of the relevant α, β, and γ and it would a countervaluation for **G**. But we know that there is no such thing.

36.8 Summary

Q-validity is defined in the predictable way: a QL inference between sentences is q-valid if it is truth-preserving on all q-valuations.

Our QL proof system is sound: so a proof in the system from given sentences as premisses to a sentence as conclusion shows that the inference from the premisses to the conclusion is q-valid.

We can show a QL inference is q-invalid by finding a countervaluation, a q-valuation which makes the premisses true and conclusion false. But note, q-invalidity doesn't prove plain invalidity; a q-invalid argument will not be valid in virtue of the way that quantifiers and connectives appear, but it can be valid for some other reason.

In some simple cases, we can mechanically test a QL inference for q-validity – in particular, when it just involves unary predicates. There is, however, no general method for deciding questions of q-validity.

Exercises 36

(a) Find countervaluations to show that the following inferences are not q-valid:

(1) $\forall x Lxx$ ∴ $\forall y \forall z Lyz$
(2) $\forall x(Fx \lor Gx)$ ∴ $(\forall x Fx \lor \forall x Gx)$
(3) $\forall x \exists y \forall z\ Rxyz$ ∴ $\forall z \exists y \forall x\ Rxyz$

Use informal reasoning in the style of §36.4 to decide which of these inferences is q-valid:

(4) $\exists x\ Fx$, $\forall y(Gy \to \neg Fy)$ ∴ $\exists z \neg Gz$
(5) $\neg\exists x(Px \land Mx)$, $\neg\exists x(Sx \land \neg Mx)$, ∴ $\neg\exists x(Sx \land Px)$
(6) $\forall x(Fx \to Gx)$, $\forall y(\neg Gx \to Hx)$ ∴ $\forall z(\neg Hz \to Fx)$
(7) $\exists x(Rx \land \neg Px)$, $\forall x(Rx \to Sx)$, ∴ $\forall x(P \to \neg Sx)$
(8) $\forall x(Px \to Mx)$, $\exists x(Sx \land \neg Mx)$ ∴ $\exists x(Sx \land \neg Px)$
(9) $\forall x(Lxm \lor \neg Lxn)$, $\neg Lnm$ ∴ $\neg\exists x Lxn$
(10) $(\exists x\ Lox \to Ho)$, $(\exists x\ Lxn \to Lon)$, Lmn ∴ Ho

(b*) Find out more about systematically looking for countervaluations and perhaps discovering that there can't be one by looking at the online supplement on quantifier truth trees.

37 QL proofs: metatheory

When discussing PL inferences, we tackled questions of validity twice over. We first defined a notion of tautological validity for such inferences. Next we developed a Fitch-style proof system. We then noted the soundness and completeness theorems which show that these two approaches to validity end up warranting the same inferences. It is important that you understand what these theorems say, and why they are non-trivial: however, their proofs, though not particularly difficult, have been left to an Appendix.

Similarly, in discussing QL inferences, we have tackled questions of validity twice over. This time, we developed a Fitch-style proof system first, since it is quite straightforward to extend our PL proof system. But we now also have in place a suitable reconstruction of the notion of logical validity for QL inferences, namely q-validity. Unsurprisingly, we want there to be soundness and completeness theorems to show that here too our two approaches march in step.

Our discussion can be quite brisk, however, both because some key ideas are already familiar from the PL case, and because the main proof sketches again will be left to the Appendix. What matters for now is just that you understand what the central metatheorems actually claim.

37.1 The QL proof system reviewed

Our discussion of the metatheory of propositional logic started by codifying the principles for constructing PL proofs. We will want to similarly codify the principles for constructing QL proofs. But once we have specified that we are now working with QL wffs, the story can go in three quick stages.

First, we simply carry over to our QL proof system the very same inference rules for the *connectives* that we used in PL proofs.

Second, we add our four new *quantifier* rules to the list of QL inference rules. Here they are again in summary:

($\forall$I) We can derive $\forall \xi \alpha(\xi)$, given an available instance $\alpha(\delta)$ – so long as (i) the dummy name δ doesn't occur in any live assumption for that instance, and (ii) δ doesn't occur in the conclusion $\forall \xi \alpha(\xi)$.

($\forall$E) Given $\forall \xi \alpha(\xi)$, we can derive any instance $\alpha(\tau)$.

(∃I)   We can derive the wff $\exists \xi \alpha(\xi)$ from any given instance $\alpha(\tau)$.

(∃E)   Given $\exists \xi \alpha(\xi)$, and a subproof from the instance $\alpha(\delta)$ as supposition
to the conclusion γ – where (i) the dummy name δ is new to the
proof, and (ii) γ does not contain δ – then we can derive γ.

Third, our QL inference steps get put together to form complete proofs in
just the same column-indenting style as for PL proofs. So we needn't repeat the
general proof-building rules.

One comment. All our sample QL proofs so far start from zero or more *sentences* as premises and end with a *sentence* as conclusion. This is the important
case. But we will not actually *ban* derivations which start and finish with wffs
with dummy names. In fact, it is useful for metatheoretical purposes to allow
such cases.

37.2   Generalizing QL proofs

Here, though, is an initial point worth pausing over. In §24.4 we showed that
there is an important sense in which PL proofs generalize. The same goes for QL
proofs, as noted briefly in §32.5. Thus compare:

$\forall x\, Fx$	$\forall \xi \alpha(\xi)$	$\forall z(\exists y Rzy \wedge Hz)$
$\forall x(Fx \to Gx)$	$\forall \xi(\alpha(\xi) \to \beta(\xi))$	$\forall z((\exists y Rzy \wedge Hz) \to \forall x\, Sxz)$
Fa	$\alpha(\delta)$	$(\exists y Rcy \wedge Hc)$
$(Fa \to Ga)$	$(\alpha(\delta) \to \beta(\delta))$	$((\exists y Rcy \wedge Hc) \to \forall x Sxc)$
Ga	$\beta(\delta)$	$\forall x Sxc$
$\forall x\, Gx$	$\forall \xi \beta(\xi)$	$\forall z \forall x\, Sxz$
(1)	(2)	(3)

On the left, (1) is the simple proof we met in §32.3. In (2) we use schemas to
reveal the general pattern of argument in (1). And then it doesn't matter what
we substitute for α and β, it doesn't matter which variable ξ we choose, and
it doesn't matter which previously unused dummy name δ we choose; we will
always get an argument with the same structure as in (1).

For example, take $\alpha(\xi)$ to be $(\exists y R \xi y \wedge H \xi)$ and $\beta(\xi)$ to be $\forall x\, Sx\xi$. Then replace
ξ in (2) with 'z' and δ with 'c', and we get the array (3) which has the same
structure as (1) and hence is another proof.

We can generalize the point:

(i)   Take any QL proof. Systematically replace its predicates, variables,
names, and dummy names with suitable schematic expressions. In particular, replace a predicate followed by a variable or name or dummy
name by a schema like $\alpha(\xi)$ or $\alpha(\tau)$ or $\alpha(\delta)$ as appropriate. Call the
result a QL *proof schema* – compare the idea of a PL proof schema we
met in §24.4. This proof schema reveals the structure of the original

proof: it reveals all the relationships between the constituents of the original proof which make it a correctly formed derivation.

(ii) Now systematically fill in such a schema to get another array of wffs. The wffs in this array follow the same pattern of derivation, so the array will be another correctly formed derivation.

In summary then, and in parallel to the claim about generalizing PL proofs, we have:

Any substitution instance of a QL proof schema is also a proof.

So, as with claims about PL proofs, the claim that a given QL proof is valid is doubly general. First, it isn't language-specific: i.e., another proof that is syntactically the same but which is framed in a different language (where the names and predicates have different interpretations) will also be valid. Secondly, within a language, a claim about validity generalizes to other syntactically different proofs in the way just explained.

37.3   Two turnstiles again

In §16.4 and §24.5 we introduced two turnstile symbols to use as shorthand in our English metalanguage. Let's quickly remind ourselves!

The single turnstile '⊢' ('proves') is the *syntactic* turnstile, and $\Gamma \vdash \gamma$ says that there is a formal proof using premisses Γ and finishing with γ as conclusion. In the earlier context, the proof system in question was our Fitch-style PL natural deduction system for propositional logic. We can now use the same single turnstile symbol again in the present context, where the proof system in question is our Fitch-style QL system for quantificational logic. When we want to be explicit about which proof system is in question, we can subscript the turnstile: thus '⊢$_{PL}$' vs '⊢$_{QL}$'.

The double turnstile '⊨' ('entails') is the *semantic* turnstile, and $\Gamma \vDash \gamma$ says that any semantic valuation of the relevant type which makes Γ all true also makes γ true. In the earlier context, the relevant semantic valuations were those appropriate to a PL language, assigning truth values to its atoms. We can now use the same double turnstile symbol again in the present context, where the kind of semantic valuation in play is a q-valuation for a QL language, assigning q-values to its non-logical constituents. When we want to be explicit about which semantics is in question, we can subscript the turnstile: thus '⊨$_{PL}$' vs '⊨$_{QL}$'.

37.4   Soundness

In §24.5, we noted a sequence of matching pairs of claims about the relations ⊨$_{PL}$ and ⊢$_{PL}$. You can easily check that the same matching pairs hold for ⊨$_{QL}$ and ⊢$_{QL}$. We could add further matching pairs specific to QL. But there is limited interest in listing off particular parallels between the relations expressed by the syntactic and semantic turnstiles since we have Two Big Metatheorems, ensuring that the two relations *always* march in step.

So let's turn to the first key result. In §24.6, we highlighted that

Our PL proof system is sound: for any wffs Γ and γ, if $\Gamma \vdash_{PL} \gamma$ then $\Gamma \vDash_{PL} \gamma$.

As you would now hope, especially given our earlier remarks about soundness in general, there is a parallel soundness result for quantificational logic:

Our QL proof system is sound: for any sentences Γ and γ, if $\Gamma \vdash_{QL} \gamma$ then $\Gamma \vDash_{QL} \gamma$.

In other words, our QL proof system really does work as we have advertised, and its derivations are genuine proofs. A correctly formed derivation starting from premisses Γ and finishing with γ does indeed warrant the claim that the conclusion is logically entailed by the premisses, and more specifically warrants the claim that the conclusion is q-entailed by the premisses.

Despite its great importance, a soundness proof for our QL proof system is relatively straightforward; in fact, we can use the same overall strategy as we used in proving soundness for PL. In other words, we first define what it is for a line on a QL proof to be *good* – it is good if any (possibly expanded) q-valuation which makes true the live assumptions at the line also makes the wff at that line true. Then we show that our QL proof-building rules make every line of a properly constructed proof good (because applying a rule always takes us from good lines to another good line). Then we conclude that the last line is good, so the proof's conclusion q-validly follows from the premisses.

The devil – only a minor one! – is in the details. QL proofs can feature auxiliary wffs along the way, as we introduce dummy names. So the expanded q-valuations we need to look at as we go through a proof line by line can change, as relevant dummy names come into play or leave the field. But handling this is pretty easy. For more, see the Appendix §A2.

37.5 Completeness

(a) In §24.7, we met the other Big Metatheorem about our propositional logic, a companion to the soundness theorem:

Our PL proof system is complete: for any wffs Γ and γ, if $\Gamma \vDash_{PL} \gamma$ then $\Gamma \vdash_{PL} \gamma$.

Which suggests an obvious question: can we prove a parallel completeness result for quantificational logic? In other words, can we establish the following?

Our QL proof system is complete: for any sentences Γ and γ, if $\Gamma \vDash_{QL} \gamma$ then $\Gamma \vdash_{QL} \gamma$.

In Frege's work in the nineteenth century, and again in Bertrand Russell and A. N. Whitehead's epoch-making *Principia Mathematica* (1910–13), what is now standard quantificational logic is not clearly separated off from a considerably richer logical framework. It was Hilbert who first isolated something equivalent to our QL proof system, albeit in a very different style. He didn't have our fully formed notion of q-validity; but still, it was Hilbert who was first able to raise something close to the question whether our proof system for quantificational logic is complete for q-validity – again, the question is posed in his 1928 book with Ackermann.

They didn't have to wait long for an answer. In his dissertation of 1929, Kurt Gödel – the greatest logician of the twentieth century – gave the first completeness proof. It can be adapted to show our QL proof system already has enough rules of inference to enable us, in principle, to provide a suitable formal proof to warrant any q-valid inference.

(b)   A completeness proof for QL sits just over the threshold that marks the beginning of a serious study of mathematical logic. You don't need to be able to cross the threshold in an introductory first encounter with formal logic. However, in the optional Appendix for enthusiasts who want a glimpse beyond, we *will* sketch a really rather elegant completeness proof (different from Gödel's), following the same kind of strategy we use to prove the completeness of our PL system.

We will also see there that a simple corollary of our completeness proof will give us the theorem promised in §36.2 which settles any worries we might have about the definition of q-validity quantifying over an apparently indeterminate range of valuations.

37.6   Summary

QL proofs allow new quantifier rules of inference, but otherwise their structure is just as for PL proofs.

Like PL proofs, we can generalize from a particular QL proof to get a whole family of proofs structured in the same way.

Our QL proof system can be proved to be sound using a similar strategy to our soundness proof for the PL proof system.

Our QL proof system is also complete. There is more than one way of establishing this, but again the proof we will outline in the Appendix runs in parallel to the completeness proof we give for the PL proof system.

However, actual proofs of the metatheorems go beyond what we really need in a first introduction to formal logic: understanding the content of the soundness and completeness theorems is what matters.

Interlude: Extending QL

(a)   Let's pause for a brisk review of our explorations since the last Interlude:

We considered some informal rules of inference involving quantifiers, noting the role played by parameters or dummy names. We need some way to handle parameters in our formal languages. There are various options, but it is clearest to introduce a new category of symbols to do the job, our formal dummy names.

We then adopted formal versions of those informal quantifier rules to give us a natural deduction system for QL derivations.

Our earlier discussions of translating to and from QL languages had involved the interpretation of the vocabulary of a language via a glossary. We then moved on to consider the valuational semantics for such languages – i.e. we explored how the truth values of sentences of the language are determined by a q-valuation which fixes the domain, the references of names, and the extensions of predicates. The key new idea to grasp here, to take the simplest of illustrations, is that $\forall x\, Fx$ is true on a q-valuation q if and only if Fa is true on every expansion of q which assigns some object in the domain as temporary reference to the dummy name 'a'.

Once we have the notion of a q-valuation for a QL language in play (compare the notion of a valuation for a PL language), we can readily define the notion of a q-valid inference (compare the notion of a tautologically valid inference). The inference from given QL sentences (wffs without dummy names) as premisses to some sentence as conclusion is q-valid if and only if every q-valuation of the relevant language which makes the premisses true makes the conclusion true.

We now have two relations that can hold between premisses and a conclusion. The conclusion can follow from the premisses via some derivation in our Fitch-style QL proof system. And the inference from the premisses to the conclusion can be q-valid. The two relations march in step: if one holds, the other holds. Our formal proof system is sound and (perhaps more surprisingly) is complete.

(b)   It would, however, be odd to stop our introductory logical enquiries at this point. For QL languages, as they stand, are still missing a very important class of expressions. Take, for example, that simple arithmetical truth

$$2 + 7 = 3 \times 3.$$

Syntactically, the addition and multiplication signs here each combine with two terms to form another term. Semantically, they each express a binary function, which maps two numbers to their sum or product respectively. In short, both signs are *function symbols*.

As so far characterized, QL languages lack function symbols. So these languages can't be used simply and directly to express functions. This is surely a major shortcoming for languages advertised as being appropriate for regimenting deductive reasoning in general and rigorous mathematical reasoning in particular! So one further step we will want to take is to allow function symbols into our formal languages. This is cheeringly straightforward.

What about the equality sign in the equation? It works like a binary predicate, combining with the two functional terms to make a complete arithmetical proposition. What is this sign used to say? In our example, that the number which is the result of adding 2 and 7 *is the very same number as*, i.e. is none other than, the number which is the result of multiplying 3 and 3. But now compare the claims that George Orwell is Eric Blair, the tallest mountain is Mount Everest, the set of unicorns is the empty set, and so on. These again deploy the notion of a given thing a being one and the same identical thing as b. This notion of identity has the kind of generality and topic-neutrality that makes it of central interest to logic. So, to go along with introducing function symbols, we will also want to handle the special identity predicate.

(c)   These, then, will be the focal topics of the remaining chapters: function expressions and the identity predicate. We will explore how to add them to our QL languages to get what we will call QL$^=$ languages.

We take the more interesting topic of identity first. Of course, we can assign any meaning we like to a *non-logical* predicate in a QL language. So we can already set up a QL language to have a predicate which is intended to express identity. To be clear, then, the proposal now is to look at languages which have a *logical* identity predicate – a built-in predicate whose meaning is as fixed as the meanings of the connectives and quantifiers, and which is governed by inference principles which stay fixed across QL$^=$ languages in the same way as our already familiar principles stay fixed across QL languages.

(d)   Quine famously said "To be is to be the value of a variable", meaning that regimenting a theory using a quantifier-variable notation is our best way of making it clear what the theory commits us to, forcing us to be explicit about what we are quantifying over. And he argued that *any* worthwhile theory ought to be susceptible to being regimented in a QL$^=$ framework for the sake of definiteness.

We don't have to buy those Quinean doctrines in a full-strength version. But this much is right: with suitable choices of predicates and function expressions, QL$^=$ languages indeed have *very* wide application. Which is why understanding their logic matters.

360

38 Identity

As just noted in the Interlude, the idea of identity has the kind of generality and topic-neutrality that makes it an appropriate subject for logical inquiry. In this chapter, we say more about the identity relation.

38.1 Numerical vs qualitative identity

Compare two types of cases:

(A) Jill and her twin sister Jane are (as we say) identical; we cannot tell them apart. You and I have identical scarves. Simultaneously in London and Paris, Jack and Jacques are wrapping up identical bottles of Chanel No. 19 to send to their respective beloveds.

(B) Since Jill and Jane are twins, Jill's mother is identical to Jane's mother (she is one and the very same person). There are two scarves, but you and I bought them from the identical branch of Marks and Spencer. And as luck would have it, Jack's beloved is one and the very same as Jacques's; the identical woman is the object of both men's desires.

Type-(A) cases are instances of what is often called *qualitative identity.* Jill and Jane are distinct beings sharing the same intrinsic properties (well, in the real world, maybe not strictly speaking all the same properties: but let's pretend that they are perfect duplicates). Likewise for the two distinct but identically similar scarves and the two bottles of perfume. In type-(B) cases, however, we have instances of *numerical identity.* It is one and the very same entity – the very same mother, the very same shop, the very same beloved – that is in question each time. Our topic in this chapter is the notion of identity in this latter sense of strict numerical identity.

It is tempting to say that our concern is with the idea of 'one object being the very same thing as another'. But that cannot possibly be quite the right way to put it. If there really is 'one object' and 'another object' then there are two of them, and so then they of course cannot be numerically identical after all!

38.2 Equivalence relations

The identity predicate '① is one and the very same as ②' expresses a binary relation. Rather more specifically, it expresses an *equivalence* relation. More specifically still, it expresses what can be thought of as the *smallest* equivalence relation. This section explains.

(a)   We first need to define three features a binary relation R can have.

(1)   A relation R is reflexive iff, for any appropriate a, a has relation R to a. Examples: 'is as tall as', 'has a parent in common with', 'drives the same make of car as' express reflexive relations. For a logical example, single-premiss entailment is reflexive – a proposition entails itself.

(We want a to be 'appropriate' in the sense of being an object that can possibly stand in the relation R. We don't want to deny that *being as tall as* is a reflexive relation, just because it is nonsense to say e.g. that the number seven is as tall as itself. *Being as tall as* is reflexive in its appropriate domain of application.)

(2)   A relation R is symmetric iff, whenever a has R to b, then b has R to a. Examples: 'is married to', 'is a different gender to', 'adjoins' express symmetric relations. For a logical example, *being inconsistent with* is symmetric – if A is inconsistent with B then B is inconsistent with A.

(3)   A relation R is transitive iff, whenever a has R to b, and b has R to c, then a has R to c. Examples: 'is heavier than', 'is an ancestor of', and 'is part of' express transitive relations. For a logical example, single-premiss entailment is transitive – if A entails B and B entails C, then A entails C. (Compare (5) and (5') in §24.5.)

(b)   Relations can have these features in various combinations. As just noted, (single-premiss) entailment is reflexive and transitive; but it is *not* symmetric. 'Is heavier than' is transitive, but neither symmetric nor reflexive. Again, 'has a parent in common with' is reflexive, symmetric, but non-transitive, while 'is at least as tall as' is reflexive, transitive, but non-symmetric.

We are interested now, though, in relations which have all three features:

An equivalence relation is one which is transitive, symmetric, and reflexive.

Examples: 'is the same age as', 'has the same surname as', 'is a full sibling of', 'is parallel to', 'is truth-functionally equivalent to' all express equivalence relations. So too does 'is qualitatively identical to'.

(c)   Suppose now we have some domain of objects and an equivalence relation R defined over those objects. Because of reflexivity, every object in the domain is R to something, if only itself. Note too that if a is R to b and a is R to c then, by symmetry, b is R to a; and so by transitivity b is R to c. In other words: if a is R related to two things, they are also R related to each other. It follows that

An equivalence relation R carves up its domain into non-overlapping groups of things, where the members of each group all stand in relation R to each other. These are R's *equivalence classes*.

For a simple illustration, take the domain of UK citizens, and take the equivalence relation *having the same legal surname as*. This carves up the domain into equivalence classes of people who share the same surname. Everyone is in one such class, and no one is in more than one class. Some of these classes are large: there are a lot of Smiths. Others might contain just one or two members.

For another example, take the domain of natural numbers and consider the relation *differs by a multiple of 3 from*. This is an equivalence relation (its symmetry and transitivity are obvious; and for reflexivity, note that a number differs from itself by zero times three). This relation carves up the numbers into the equivalence classes $\{0, 3, 6, 9, \ldots\}$, $\{1, 4, 7, 10, \ldots\}$, and $\{2, 5, 8, 11, \ldots\}$.

38.3   Identity as the smallest equivalence relation

(a)   Let's now add some informal symbolism to English.

When a is indeed one and the very same thing as b, then we will write '$a = b$' (read 'a is identical to b').

Note that it is perfectly appropriate to borrow the familiar mathematical symbol here. For when in ordinary arithmetic we write, say, '$2 + 3 = 10 - 5$' we are claiming that the number which is the result of adding 2 and 3 is the very same as the number which results from subtracting 5 from 10. The left-hand and the right-hand of the equation aren't just picking out qualitatively similar things; the expressions on either side pick out the very same number. Similarly for fancier mathematical uses of the sign '$=$'.

What '$=$' expresses is evidently reflexive, symmetric, and transitive. Play along with the familiar fiction again. Then, first, Clark Kent is, of course, one and the very same as Clark Kent. More generally,

(1)   For any a, $a = a$.

Second, if Clark Kent really is none other than Superman, then Superman must be none other than Clark Kent. Generalizing:

(2)   For any a and b, if $a = b$ then $b = a$.

And third, if Clark Kent is one and the very same as Superman, and Superman is one and the very same as the Superhero from Krypton, then Clark Kent is one and the very same as the Superhero from Krypton. Generalizing again:

(3)   For any a, b, and c, if $a = b$ and $b = c$, then $a = c$.

(b)   As with any equivalence relation, the identity relation therefore carves up a domain of objects into equivalence classes.

But of course, in this case, the equivalence classes will contain precisely one item each. For example, the only being related to Clark Kent by the identity relation is that very person (however we name him). The identity relation, then, is the equivalence relation which partitions a domain into the smallest possible equivalence classes, with each member of the domain in its own separate class.

(c)   The extension of a relation, recall, comprises the ordered pairs which satisfy the relation. So the extension of the identity relation defined over some domain comprises just the ordered pairs $\langle a, a \rangle$, $\langle b, b \rangle$, $\langle c, c \rangle$, ... (running through each object in that domain). But any other equivalence relation defined over the same domain *also* has those pairs in its extension (as well as other pairs), because every equivalence relation is reflexive. What is distinctive about the identity relation, then, is that the extension of the identity relation is the common core contained in the extension of *every* equivalence relation defined over the relevant domain. In other words, the identity relation will have the smallest extension of any equivalence relation defined over the domain. In that sense, identity is always the smallest equivalence relation on a domain.

(d)   The identity relation does not make a real connection between distinct things: so some (like Wittgenstein in his *Tractatus*) would argue that identity is not a *genuine* relation at all. But again, as in §25.3(b), we will set aside philosophers' worries, and follow the logicians' usual generous practice, and allow what is expressed by the binary identity predicate to count as a relation.

But if the identity relation always holds between a thing and itself, how can true identity propositions be informative? It was news to the Babylonians that the Morning Star is the very same thing as the Evening Star. It is news to the beginning geometry student that the centre of the circle drawn through a triangle's vertices is the very same point as the one where the perpendicular bisectors of its sides meet. It will be news to Lois that Clark Kent is none other than Superman. How can identities like these be news?

A Fregean will argue that what we need here is the sense/reference distinction again. In true identity statements, we twice pick out the same object as reference (and yes, it is trivial that an object has to be identical to itself). But in the informative cases we pick out the same object by using terms with two different senses which give two different 'modes of presentation' of the same thing (and it may not be at all trivial that these modes of presentation arrow in on the same target).

38.4   Leibniz's Law

(a)   The crucial principle governing strict numerical identity is *Leibniz's Law*:

(LL)   If $a = b$ (i.e. a and b are one and the same thing), then whatever property a has, b has.

There can be no exceptions to this. If the object a is one and the very same thing as the object b, then a's having the property P just is one and the very same state of affairs as b's having the property P.

Hence, if Superman is Clark Kent, then whatever properties Superman has, Clark has. If Superman can fly, then so can Clark (though you might not realize it!). If Superman loves Lois, so does Clark.

Likewise, if Jill's mother is one and the very same person as Jane's mother, then Jill's mother and Jane's mother have the same properties. If Jill's mother is a logician, so is Jane's. If Jill's mother has three children, so does Jane's.

Leibniz's Law is also often called the *Indiscernibility of Identicals* – if a and b really are the same thing, then of course you can't tell 'them' apart. And this is trivially equivalent to another uncontroversial principle, which we can call the 'Diversity of the Dissimilar':

(DD) If a has some property that b lacks, then a is not identical to b.

If Superman can fly and Clark (in any guise) can't, then Clark isn't the superhero after all. If Jill's mother has red hair and Jane's mother hasn't, then they are different people.

(b)   Don't confuse the correct principle of the Indiscernibility of Identicals with the converse principle of the *Identity of Indiscernibles*.

Leibniz himself held that if a and b share all the same properties – so are not discernibly different in kind – then they must be one and the very same thing. If we are generous enough about what counts as a 'property' (to include for instance the property of being located in a particular place) this *may* be defensible.

However, the metaphysical principle of the Identity of Indiscernibles looks false if we mean ordinary intrinsic qualities. For example, it seems that two atoms can be duplicates in each and every intrinsic respect, can be qualitatively perfectly identical, yet still be two distinct things, differing only in their spatial locations and in their relations to other things.

(c)   Finally, let's stress that Leibniz's Law in the form (LL) is a statement about *things* (it is a metaphysical principle): if a and b are the same thing, then a and b have the same properties. But it implies a claim about *language*, and the interchangeability of referring expressions:

(LL′) Suppose that in the sentence $C(n)$, the context C attributes some property to the object referred to by the term n (the same property whichever term n completes the sentence). Then if a and b are co-referential terms and $C(a)$ is true, then $C(b)$ is also true.

How is (LL′) consistent with the fact that we cannot exchange the co-referential names 'Superman' and 'Clark Kent' in the context 'Lois believes that ① can fly' salva veritate? Because, as we explained in §25.7, the gappy context here does *not* straightforwardly express a property.

38.5   Summary

We must distinguish qualitative from strict numerical identity. Qualitative and strict numerical identity are both transitive, symmetric, and reflexive relations, i.e. are both equivalence relations. But strict numerical identity is the 'smallest' equivalence relation – it relates an object to nothing other than itself.

The key principle governing identity is (LL) Leibniz's Law: if a and b are identical then whatever property a has, b has.

There is a linguistic version of this principle, (LL'): if a and b are functioning as co-referential singular terms in the claims $C(a)$ and $C(b)$, and also the context C expresses the same property in each case, then these claims must have the same truth value.

Exercises 38

(a)   In addition to the properties of relations already defined, we say

   (i)   A relation R defined over a given domain is Euclidean just if, whenever a has R to b and a has R to c, then b has R to c;
   (ii) R is asymmetric if, whenever a has R to b, then b does not have R to a;
   (iii) R is irreflexive if no object has R to itself.

Give examples of relations which are neither reflexive nor irreflexive, and neither symmetric nor asymmetric. Which of the following are true?

   (1)   If R is asymmetric, it is irreflexive.
   (2)   If R is transitive and irreflexive, it is asymmetric.
   (3)   If R is transitive and symmetric, it is reflexive
   (4)   If R is an equivalence relation, it is Euclidean.
   (5)   If R is asymmetric and Euclidean, it is irreflexive.
   (6)   If R is Euclidean and reflexive, it is an equivalence relation.

Give QL proofs for examples of the true claims.
   Take the domain containing just the five numbers $0, 1, 2, 3, 4$. How many different equivalence relations can be defined over the domain? (For this purpose, count relations as the same if they have the same extensions.)

(b)   (LL') is quite understandable as it is. But give a version which might satisfy a logician who is *very* pernickety about the use of quotation marks.

(c*)   Which, if any, of the following arguments involving identity claims are valid? How do they relate to Leibniz's Law?

   (1)   Tubby is so-called because of his size. Tubby is none other than Dr Jones. Hence, Dr Jones is so-called because of his size.
   (2)   Few people have heard of Besarionis dze Jughashvili. Jughashvili is in fact Stalin. Therefore few people have heard of Stalin.
   (3)   George Orwell is a well-known author. George Orwell is Eric Blair. So Eric Blair is a well-known author.
   (4)   Necessarily, nine is nine. The number of planets is nine. So, necessarily, the number of planets is nine.

39 QL⁼ languages

We now add a special symbol for the identity relation to our QL languages. Then we explore the additional expressive power of the resulting QL⁼ languages.

39.1 '=' as the identity predicate

(a)   We could, of course, pick a letter like 'I', and use this as a binary identity predicate in the usual way. So 'I' would then take two terms to form an atomic wff such as Imn, and would say of the object(s) picked out by the terms that they are one and the same. However it is standard to use the familiar identity sign '='; and we will allow this symbol to be written *between* a pair of terms to form a new kind of atomic wff.

However, the choice of a special symbol and the departure from the predicate-first arrangement is, of course, not the important thing. What matters is that this identity sign is now going to be treated not as a regular predicate (whose interpretation can vary from q-valuation to q-valuation) but as a new logical constant (which retains a fixed interpretation on every valuation).

We will call a QL language with a built-in, fixed-meaning, identity predicate a QL⁼ language. The syntax of such a language can, for the moment, be defined by taking QL syntax as summarized in §35.2, and adding:

> The *logical symbols* of a QL⁼ language also include $=$.

> The *atomic wffs* of a QL⁼ language also include every wff of the form $\tau_1 = \tau_2$ where τ_1 and τ_2 are terms.

So $m = n$, $a = b$, $m = a$, etc., count as atomic QL⁼ wffs. The rest of our official syntactic rules can stay the same as for unaugmented QL languages. However, for reasons of aesthetics and readability, we will adopt a familiar shorthand:

> We abbreviate expressions like $\neg m = n$, $\neg a = b$, $\neg x = n$, $\neg y = z$, etc., by respectively $m \neq n$, $a \neq b$, $x \neq n$, $y \neq z$, etc.

What about the semantics for our new symbol? We can read '=' as meaning ① *is identical to* ②, or ① *is none other than* ②. And we add to the semantic rules given in §35.4 the following truth rule for evaluating one of the new atomic wffs on a (possibly extended) valuation q:

(A4) Suppose α is an atomic wff of the form $\tau_1 = \tau_2$. And suppose q assigns the term τ_1 the object o_1, and assigns the term τ_2 the object o_2. If o_1 is one and the same object as o_2, then $\alpha := \text{T}$; otherwise $\alpha := \text{F}$.

From now on, when we talk about q-valuations for QL= languages, we will mean valuations which are governed by this new rule in addition to our old evaluation rules for QL languages.

(b) The general principles about the reflexivity, symmetry, and transitivity of identity can now be expressed as QL= wffs like this:

(Ref) $\forall x\, x = x$,
(Sym) $\forall x \forall y (x = y \to y = x)$,
(Trans) $\forall x \forall y \forall z ((x = y \wedge y = z) \to x = y)$.

It is easy to see that these are in fact q-logical wffs of our QL= languages, i.e. they are true on any q-valuation.

For example, (Sym) is true on a q-valuation q just if $(a = b \to b = a)$ is true on every extended valuation q_{ab} assigning temporary q-values to the two dummy names. But, if the antecedent of this conditional is true on q_{ab}, that must be because q_{ab} assigns the dummy names the *same* q-value, which will make the consequent true as well: so the conditional is indeed true on any q_{ab}.

(Ref), (Sym), and (Trans) will also turn out to be easy *theorems* when we introduce suitable natural derivation rules to handle identity in a QL= proof system in Chapter 41.

39.2   Translating into QL=

Having an identity sign in our language gives us a surprisingly rich extension to our expressive resources. Let's run through some first simple examples, taking a variant of QL2 extended with the identity predicate:

In QL=₁, the proper names with their interpretations are

> m: Mrs Jones,
> n: Nerys,
> o: Owen;

and the predicates are

> F: ① speaks Welsh,
> G: ① is a woman,
> L: ① loves ②,
> M: ① is taller than ②.

The domain of quantification: people (living people, for definiteness).

We'll translate the following:

(1)   Nerys is none other than Mrs Jones.

(2)   If Nerys speaks Welsh, and Mrs Jones doesn't, then they are different people.

(3)   Everyone except Nerys loves Owen.

(4)   Someone other than Owen is taller than Nerys.

(5)   Only Mrs Jones loves Owen.

(6)   Only Nerys and Owen love Mrs Jones.

(7)   Nerys only loves people who love her.

(8)   Nerys is taller than at most one person.

(9)   At most one woman speaks Welsh.

(10)   Whoever loves Mrs Jones loves no one else.

First, 'is none other than' is naturally read as simply an assertion of identity (so we don't always have to translate 'none' by a quantifier). While 'are different people' is a denial of identity. So here are our first three simple translations:

(1) $n = m$

(2) $((Fn \land \neg Fm) \rightarrow \neg n = m)$, or more readably $((Fn \land \neg Fm) \rightarrow n \neq m)$

(3)   Everyone except Nerys loves Owen
  $\simeq$ (Everyone is such that) if they are not Nerys, they love Owen
  $\simeq$ $\forall x(\neg x = n \rightarrow Lxo)$, or more readably $\forall x(x \neq n \rightarrow Lxo)$.

Someone who says 'Everyone except Nerys loves Owen' perhaps *implies* that Nerys *doesn't* love Owen. But they do not actually *assert* that by (3). For it would be consistent to add '... and maybe Nerys does too: I just don't know.'

(4)   Someone other than Owen is taller than Nerys
  $\simeq$ (Someone is such that) they are not Owen and they are taller than Nerys
  $\simeq$ $\exists x(x \neq o \land Mxn)$.

(5)   Only Mrs Jones loves Owen
  $\simeq$ Mrs Jones loves Owen and no one else loves Owen
  $\simeq$ $(Lmo \land \neg \exists x(x \neq m \land Lxo))$.
  Or equivalently,
  $\simeq$ Mrs Jones loves Owen and anyone who loves Owen is Mrs Jones
  $\simeq$ $(Lmo \land \forall x(Lxo \rightarrow x = m))$.

(6)   Only Nerys and Owen love Mrs Jones
  $\simeq$ Nerys loves Mrs Jones and Owen loves Mrs Jones, and anyone who loves Mrs Jones is either Nerys or Owen
  $\simeq$ $((Lnm \land Lom) \land \forall x(Lxm \rightarrow (x = n \lor x = o)))$.

Some uses of 'only', then, get translated using the identity predicate. But keep your wits about you, and don't forget that many uses of 'only' in quantified sentences do *not* require the identity predicate to render them. For example,

(7)   Nerys only loves people who love her
  $\simeq$ (Everyone is such that) if Nerys loves them, then they love her
  $\simeq$ $\forall x(Lnx \rightarrow Lxn)$.

369

Next we note that the *universal* quantifier plus the identity predicate can be used to render 'there is at most one'. So:

(8) Nerys is taller than at most one person
   ≃ Take any people x and y: if Nerys is taller than x, and Nerys is taller than y, then x is none other than y.
   ≃ $\forall x \forall y ((\mathsf{Mnx} \land \mathsf{Mny}) \to x = y)$.

The translation is compatible with there being no one whom Nerys is taller than – but that is how it should be! Similarly,

(9) At most one woman speaks Welsh
   ≃ $\forall x \forall y ([(\mathsf{Gx} \land \mathsf{Fx}) \land (\mathsf{Gy} \land \mathsf{Fy})] \to x = y)$.

(10) Whoever loves Mrs Jones loves no one else
   ≃ (Everyone x is such that) if x loves Mrs Jones, then x loves no one other than Mrs Jones
   ≃ (Everyone x is such that)(if x loves Mrs Jones, then [(everyone y is such that) if y isn't Mrs Jones, then x doesn't love y])
   ≃ $\forall x (\mathsf{Lxm} \to \forall y (y \neq \mathsf{m} \to \neg \mathsf{Lxy}))$.
   Or equivalently
   ≃ $\forall x (\mathsf{Lxm} \to \forall y (\mathsf{Lxy} \to y = \mathsf{m}))$,
   or equivalently again (as we can always use a negated existential quantifier to render a 'no one')
   ≃ $\forall x (\mathsf{Lxm} \to \neg \exists y (\mathsf{Lxy} \land y \neq \mathsf{m}))$.

39.3 Numerical quantifiers

(a) We have just seen how to render something of the form 'there is at most one F' by a corresponding QL⁼ wff:

(1) $\forall x \forall y ((\mathsf{Fx} \land \mathsf{Fy}) \to x = y)$.

And of course we know how to translate 'there is at least one F':

(2) $\exists x \mathsf{Fx}$.

Putting these together, then, we can translate 'there is exactly one F' (i.e. there is at least one and at most one F) by the conjunction:

(3) $(\exists x \mathsf{Fx} \land \forall x \forall y ((\mathsf{Fx} \land \mathsf{Fy}) \to x = y))$.

Here's an alternative, simpler, translation that will do equally as well:

(4) $\exists x (\mathsf{Fx} \land \forall y (\mathsf{Fy} \to y = x))$

which says that something is F, and anything which is F is that same thing again. And, helping ourselves to the shorthand for the biconditional, here's an even brisker version:

(5) $\exists x \forall y (\mathsf{Fy} \leftrightarrow y = x)$.

Why is this again equivalent? (5) says that there is something x such that (i) any F thing is identical to x, while (ii) anything identical to x, and hence x itself, is F. Later, when we have some deduction rules for working with the identity predicate, we will be able to derive (3), (4), and (5) from each other.

(b)   Now consider the following wffs:

(6) $\exists x \exists y ((Fx \wedge Fy) \wedge x \neq y)$

(7) $\forall x \forall y \forall z (((Fx \wedge Fy) \wedge Fz) \rightarrow ((x = y \vee y = z) \vee z = x))$.

The first says that there is an F and also another, distinct F. So (6) says that there are at least two Fs. While (7) says that if we try to pick three things which are all F, then at least two of the Fs will be identical – i.e., there are at most two Fs. The conjunction of (6) with (7) will therefore say that there are at least two Fs and at most two Fs, or in other words that there are *exactly* two Fs.

Or – if you think about it! – we could more neatly translate that by

(8) $\exists x \exists y (\{(Fx \wedge Fy) \wedge x \neq y\} \wedge \forall z \{Fz \rightarrow (z = x \vee z = y)\})$.

(c)   An aside. We can now fulfil a promise made in §29.1(c). We noted there that the English plural in 'Some logicians are wise' surely indicates that there is more than one wise logician. But a standard translation along the lines of $\exists x(Gx \wedge Hx)$ says only that there is at least one. Usually, we said, the difference isn't worth fussing about. But we added that when we augment our QL languages with an identity predicate, we can then express 'some (more than one)' with the resources of our enriched language, if and when we really need to do so. We now know how. For using the same idea as in (6), we can translate 'Some logicians are wise' into $QL^=$ while now making explicit the indication that there is more than one wise logician, by writing something like

(9) $\exists x \exists y (((Gx \wedge Hx) \wedge (Gy \wedge Hy)) \wedge x \neq y)$.

(d)   To continue with our numerical quantifiers. Consider next

(10) $\exists x \exists y \exists z (\{((Fx \wedge Fy) \wedge Fz) \wedge ((x \neq y \wedge y \neq z) \wedge z \neq x)\} \wedge$
$\forall w \{Fw \rightarrow ((w = x \vee w = y) \vee w = z)\})$

(using 'w' instead of 'x'). This says that you can find three Fs, all different, and any F you choose is one of them – in other words there are exactly three Fs.

We can obviously keep going in a similar vein, expressing numerical quantifications of the kind 'there are at least n Fs', 'there are at most n Fs', 'there are exactly n Fs' using just the familiar quantifiers, the connectives, and identity.

(e)   The link between logic and elementary arithmetic is closer, however, than a mere point about QL's capacity to express numerical quantifiers. Suppose we abbreviate (4), saying that there is exactly one F, as $\exists_1 x Fx$. (By the way, you should also note the frequently used alternative notation $\exists! x Fx$). And suppose we abbreviate the version of (8) with G replacing F, saying that there are exactly two Gs, as $\exists_2 x Gx$.

Now take the version of (10) with $(Fx \vee Gx)$ instead of Fx (and $(Fy \vee Gy)$ instead of Fy, etc.). This says that there are exactly three things which are either F-or-G. Abbreviate it $\exists_3 x (Fx \vee Gx)$.

Then consider the long wff which we can then abbreviate

(11) $(\{(\exists_1 xFx \wedge \exists_2 xGx) \wedge \neg\exists x(Fx \wedge Gx)\} \rightarrow \exists_3 x(Fx \vee Gx))$.

What does this say? That if there is one F and two Gs (and nothing is F and G), then we have three things that are F-or-G. For example, as we teach the toddler, if there is one thing in my left hand, and two things in my right, then there are three things in my hands altogether.

So we have found that a simple *proposition* of applied arithmetic is *expressible* in QL$^=$. But more than that, not only is this truth expressible in purely logical terms, but *it is in fact a q-logical truth*: it can be shown, with a bit of effort, to be true on all q-valuations, and it can be proved as a *theorem* in a proof system for QL$^=$.

Which raises an intriguing, deep, and difficult question: just how much elementary arithmetic is, so to speak, just logic in disguise?

39.4 Existence claims

We want (Ref), (Sym), and (Trans) to be q-logical truths. And on reflection we want the likes of (11) in the last section to be q-logical truths too. In this section, however, we comment on some perhaps unwanted cases.

(a) Work in our language QL$^=_1$. Then consider the following sentence which says that there is at least one person:

(1) $\exists x\, x = x$.

This is true on any q-valuation q of the language. For there is always at least one expanded valuation q_a on which a = a is true, because the domain always contains at least one object which can be assigned to 'a' as temporary reference.

Consider now the following sentence of QL$^=_1$ which says that there is someone who is Nerys (so Nerys exists!):

(2) $\exists x\, x = n$.

This is true on a q-valuation q if there is some extension q_a on which a = n is true. But again this is always the case, because we can always take the extension which assigns to 'a' the same reference as 'n', and names always get a reference on a q-valuation.

So both (1) and (2) come out as q-logical truths. But is it true as a matter of mere logic that at least one person exists or that Nerys in particular exists? Surely not! So (1) and (2) are examples of q-logical truths which are *not* logical truths in the intuitive sense. How should we respond?

(b) Start with the second example. Ordinary language has 'empty names', names which fail to pick out an object, yet which have a role in the language and don't produce mere nonsense. In the Fregean terminology of §25.6, it seems that ordinary names can have sense even if they lack reference. That is why it is contentful to be told that Lois Lane or Santa Claus don't really exist, but that there is such a real person as Donald Trump.

It might seem natural, then, to extend our formal logical languages by similarly allowing names to be non-denoting. And then a wff like (2) can be sometimes true, sometimes false, depending on whether 'n' has a reference. This will require us to adopt a version of *free logic*, i.e. a logic free of certain existence assumptions. But adopting a free logic does involve significant revisions and complications.

So, rightly or wrongly, we will cling to the simplicity of QL/QL$^=$ languages and standard logic as they stand. We will continue to ban empty names (forcing (2) above to be true) rather as we ban empty domains (which forces (1) to be true) – compare the discussion of Chapter 34. The issues aren't quite the same, but the debates about whether to accommodate empty domains and empty names can have similar contours, so we won't rehearse similar arguments pro and con again. The standard line is to note that there is, after all, a sense in which non-denoting names are linguistically defective when used in serious, fact-stating discourse, and by default we normally argue on the background assumption that what we are talking about exists: our standard formal logic can then aim to capture how we should argue given that assumption. And the q-logical truths of our formal languages are then the truths that are guaranteed *once the assumption of non-empty domains and non-empty names is in place.*

(c)   A quick final remark. Apprentice philosophers often come across the slogan 'Existence isn't a predicate'. If this is read naively as saying that a language can't have a predicate-like expression (i.e. an expression with one slot waiting to be filled up by a term) which, just in virtue of its meaning, necessarily applies to just those things which exist but not otherwise, then the slogan misleads. Even in formal languages like ours, the gappy expression $\exists x\, x = \text{①}$ does the job perfectly well (and is indeed very useful in a free logic).

Still, if the philosophical slogan is intended to bring out the close relation between vernacular talk of existence and the use of something fundamentally different from an ordinary predicate, namely the operation of existential quantification, then the slogan is indeed apt.

39.5   Summary

We add to QL the identity sign, governed by the syntactic rule that a term followed by '=' followed by a term is an atomic wff.

The identity sign is governed by the semantic rule that an atomic wff of the form $\tau_1 = \tau_2$ is true on the valuation q iff the terms τ_1 and τ_2 have the same reference according to q.

With an identity predicate now built in, QL$^=$ languages can now express basic laws like the reflexivity, symmetry, and transitivity of identity, and capture a form of Leibniz's Law.

QL languages have the resources to express more complex quantifiers like 'Everyone other than Nerys', 'Exactly three people', etc.

Simple applied arithmetical truths of the kind 'one F and two Gs makes three F-or-G's (assuming no overlap between F and Gs)' are not only expressible using quantifiers, connectives, and identity, but are q-logical truths of QL$^=$.

The likes of $\exists x\, x = n$ also – perhaps less happily – come out as q-logical truths. But this reflects the fact that the q-logical truths of QL$^=$ languages are the truths that are guaranteed once the assumption of non-empty domains and non-empty names is in place.

Exercises 39

(a)   More Welsh affairs! Render the following into QL$_1^=$:

(1)   Someone other than Owen loves Nerys.
(2)   Only if Nerys is Mrs Jones does she love only Owen.
(3)   Exactly one Welsh speaker loves Owen.
(4)   Mrs Jones loves everyone except Owen.
(5)   Some women other than Nerys only love Owen.
(6)   Some women only love people who love them.
(7)   Only if she loves Owen is Nerys loved only by him.
(8)   There are exactly two women who love exactly two people.

(b)   The language QL$_2^=$ has two proper names

m: zero,
n: one,

and two predicates

M: ① succeeds ② i.e. ① immediately follows ② in the natural numbers,
R: ① is ② plus ③.

And its domain of quantification is the natural numbers (integers from zero up). Translate the following wffs from QL$_2^=$ into natural English:

(1) $(\forall y \exists x Mxy \land \forall x \forall y \forall z((Mxz \land Myz) \to x = y))$
(2) $\forall x \forall y \forall z((Mxy \land y = z) \to Mxz)$
(3) $\forall x \forall y(Rxym \to x = y)$
(4) $\forall x \forall y(Rxyn \to Mxy)$
(5) $\forall x \forall y \forall z((Rxyz \to Rxzy) \land (Rxzy \to Rxyz))$
(6) $\exists x(Rxxx \land \forall y(Ryyy \to y = x))$
(7) $\forall x \forall y \exists z(Rzxy \land \forall w(Rwxy \to w = z))$
(8) $\forall z \forall x((Mxz \land \forall y(Myz \to y = x)) \land Rxnz)$
(9) $\exists x \exists y(\{[((Mxm \lor Mxn) \land (Mym \lor Myn))] \land \forall x = y\} \land$
$\qquad\qquad\qquad \forall z\{(Mzm \lor Mzn) \to (z = x \lor z = y)\})$

The notation we have chosen here is evidently somewhat unhelpful! For a start, we could avail ourselves of the permission to use non-letter symbols in QL languages so that we could instead use, e.g., '0' and '1' to denote zero and one. And rather than Rzxy we will want to be able to use something that looks more like $(x + y) = z$. In Chapter 42 we will see how to do this.

40 Definite descriptions

In this chapter, we extend our discussion of the expressive resources of QL$^=$ with its built-in identity predicate by considering how so-called 'definite descriptions' can be rendered using Russell's famed Theory of Descriptions.

40.1 The project

Consider the expressions 'the man in the corner drinking a martini', 'the oldest woman in the world', 'the Queen of England', 'the smallest prime number', 'the present King of France', 'the largest prime number'. Such expressions – more generally, expressions of the type 'the F' – are standardly called *definite descriptions*. A definite description aims to designate a particular thing. But as the last two cases remind us, definite descriptions can easily fail to pick out any entity: there may be nothing which is F, and so nothing which is *the F*.

Now, imagine we are at a party. I tell you that a number of people from different disciplines are here, and say 'The physicist is over there, talking to George'. Then, assuming what I said is true, it certainly seems that you can correctly conclude, for a start, that there is a physicist present (and indeed, as we'll remark in a moment, that there is just one physicist present).

Generalizing, if a claim of the form *The F is G* is true then, for a start, so is the corresponding claim of the form *There is at least one F* (set aside rogue cases, as when G is filled by the likes of 'non-existent' or 'fictitious'). How can we reflect *this* sort of logical entailment inside our formal languages? We can't treat '*the F*' like a name with no internal structure. We need a theory of descriptions.

40.2 Russell's Theory of Descriptions

(a)   Take again the proposition

(1)   The physicist (present at the party) is talking to George.

How could we render this, as best we can, into a QL$^=$ language?

Using the predicate 'F' for *physicist*, and quantifying over people at the party, we can express the proposition that there is exactly one physicist at the party as follows – compare §39.3 (4):

(2) $\exists x(Fx \land \forall y(Fy \to y = x))$.

Suppose we now add a clause inside the scope of the existential quantifier, using the predicate 'G' for *is talking to George*, like this:

(R) $\exists x((Fx \wedge \forall y(Fy \rightarrow y = x)) \wedge Gx)$.

Arguably, this is an acceptable rendition of (1):

> If (R) is true – if there is one and only one physicist (here at the party), and they are talking to George – then surely (1) holds: it is true that *the physicist here is talking to George*. And conversely, if (1) *the* physicist is talking to George, then there is a physicist here; there is only one physicist here (otherwise there would be no one who is *the* physicist); and moreover, this person is talking to George. Which makes (R) true.

Which suggests the following general proposal:

> A proposition of the kind *The F is G* can be rendered into $QL^=$ by a corresponding wff like (R) which is true or false in the same circumstances.

And note that (R) elementarily entails $\exists x\, Fx$; so this rendition does, as wanted, capture the simple entailment from *The F is G* to *there is an F*.

(b) Instead of (2), we could equally well use

(3) $\exists x \forall y(Fy \leftrightarrow y = x)$

to render the proposition that there is one and only one physicist; compare §39.3 (5). Hence, instead of (R), we could equally well use the slightly snappier

(R') $\exists x \forall y((Fy \leftrightarrow y = x) \wedge Gx)$

to render the proposition that the physicist is talking to George.

And a third equivalent way of saying the same is the more long-winded

(R'') $(\{\exists x Fx \wedge \forall x \forall y((Fx \wedge Fy) \rightarrow x = y)\} \wedge \forall x(Fx \rightarrow Gx))$

which renders 'There is at least one physicist and there is at most one physicist and whoever is a physicist is talking to George'. In the next chapter we will develop the resources to give natural deduction proofs that (R), (R') and (R'') do entail each other: but for the moment let's take this intuitively correct claim on trust.

(c) The proposal that we can formally render an ordinary-language proposition of the kind *The F is G* by (R) or one of its equivalents is due to Bertrand Russell. It is part of his *Theory of Descriptions*. However, does (R) really get the truth conditions of the ordinary-language proposition right?

Plausibly, as we said, if (R) is true, then *The F is G* is true. But, on second thoughts, do the two really match on falsehood? Suppose that there is no *F*. Then (R) is straightforwardly false. But do we want to say the same, however, about *The F is G*? Russell himself uses the example 'The present King of France is bald'. Is *this* straightforwardly false? Some might argue:

> Since France isn't a monarchy, 'The present King of France is bald' does not even make it to the starting line for being true or false, since the definite description fails to pick out anything.

376

Compare 'Mr Brixintingle is bald', where the apparent proper name 'Mr Brixintingle' is just a fake, invented to look vaguely name-like, but in fact attached to no one. That sentence fails to make any determinate claim, and so surely lacks a truth value. Non-referring names like this create truth-value gaps (which is why we have banned non-referring names from QL/QL= languages where we want sentences to be determinately true or false on a valuation). Non-referring descriptions create truth-value gaps too.

In sum, *The F is G* is neither true nor false when there is no *F*. However, the corresponding (R) is plain false. Hence *The F is G* is not adequately rendered by (R).

What are we to make of this line of argument?

Certainly, a claim of the form *The F is G* can fail to be true in more than one way. It can fail (a) because there isn't an *F*; it can fail (b) because there are too many *F*s (so we shouldn't talk of *the F*); it can fail (c) when there is a unique *F* but it isn't *G*. The Russellian will claim that his rendition in the version (R″) captures this very nicely: *The F is G* can be false in three different ways, depending on which of the three conjuncts in (R″) isn't satisfied. The anti-Russellian disagrees, and will instead say that only in case (c) is the claim actually false; in cases (a) and (b) *The F is G* is neither true nor false.

But what does this disagreement really come to? How do we decide such issues? Even the principles that should guide debate here are very unclear. We certainly can't pursue these matters any further in this book. We just have to note that there is a minefield hereabouts!

Fortunately, we can move on with a good conscience. Because all we need for *our* current purposes is the following claim, and *this* is uncontroversial:

Given the limited resources of bivalent QL= languages, wffs modelled on the Russellian form (R), or its equivalents (R′) and (R″), are the best options available for rendering propositions involving definite descriptions like *The F is G.*

40.3 Descriptions and existence

Take a QL= language with the glossary

K: ① is a king of France,
B: ① is bald,

The domain: presently existing people.

Then, following Russell, we can render his favourite example 'The present King of France is bald' by

(1) $\exists x((Kx \land \forall y(Ky \to y = x)) \land Bx)$.

This is *false* because

(2) $\neg\exists x(Kx \land \forall y(Ky \to y = x))$

377

is *true*. It indeed isn't the case that there exists one and only one present King of France. In other words, (2) tells us that

(3) The present King of France doesn't exist!

Now compare the true (2) with a formal wff of the shape

(4) $\neg \exists x\, x = n$

involving a proper name. As we noted in §39.4, in QL$^=$ languages, a claim such as (4) is always *false* (since QL names always have a reference). Therefore the likes of (4) can't be used to regiment true informal non-existence claims involving names – like 'Santa Claus doesn't exist' – into standard QL$^=$ languages.

The (controversial!) moral that Russell drew was that – in order to correctly handle true non-existence claims involving names – we should treat ordinary proper names as disguised definite descriptions. So we should treat 'Santa Claus doesn't exist', for example, as saying 'The *S* doesn't exist' (where *S* is a predicate like '...is a bearded red-coated worldwide distributor of Christmas presents'). And then *this* can be rendered as a true claim along the lines of (2), using a suitably Santa-describing formal predicate S in place of K.

40.4   Descriptions and scope

(a)   Set aside the Russellian doctrine that names are disguised descriptions, and get back to definite descriptions themselves. Let's next note that, just as ordinary-language quantifiers mixed with negation can produce scope ambiguity (see §26.3(c)), so ordinary-language definite descriptions mixed with negation can produce ambiguity.

Suppose we are discussing famous baldies. You challenge me to name ten. I reel off a list beginning

> The Dalai Lama is bald,
> Bruce Willis is bald,
> The actor who plays 'Captain Picard' in Star Trek is bald,
> The King of France is bald, ...

and you interrupt, saying

> No! That last one is not right. (A) The King of France isn't bald – he doesn't even exist!

Your protest is surely correct, and the way you have phrased it seems natural enough.

But now compare a second occasion. We are discussing people who *aren't* bald. So this time I reel off a list of famous non-baldies:

> The Queen of England isn't bald,
> Bill Clinton isn't bald,
> Gwyneth Paltrow isn't bald,
> (B)   The King of France isn't bald, ...

And again you interrupt, this time saying

No! That last one is not right. You can't say that – he doesn't even exist!

Again, you are surely right. But how can it be that my assertion (B) is flawed, when you, using exactly the same words in (A), can be understood as saying something correct?

We will have to discern an ambiguity. 'The King of France isn't bald' can be used to express two different claims, one true, the other false. And Russell's Theory of Descriptions gives us a very natural diagnosis of the apparent ambiguity here; it treats it as a straightforward scope ambiguity.

So, to capture the truth you intended to assert using (A), the negation must be understood as having wide scope, governing the whole sentence, giving a true message we can render like this:

(1) $\neg\exists x((Kx \wedge \forall y(Ky \rightarrow y = x)) \wedge Bx)$.

On the other reading of the sentence, the one appropriate to the false occurrence (B), the negation has narrow scope, governing just the predicate 'bald'; and the resulting false message can be rendered

(2) $\exists x((Kx \wedge \forall y(Ky \rightarrow y = x)) \wedge \neg Bx)$.

(b)   Here is another case of a scope ambiguity involving a definite description, a modal case worth mentioning even though it takes us beyond the resources of $QL^=$. Suppose the President is actually a Republican. Then consider:

(3)   The President might have been a Democratic.

This again has two readings. Are we saying there's a possible scenario in which the election goes differently, leading to someone else winning who is a Democrat? Or are we saying of the actual President that this very person might have been a Democrat – contemplating a different personal trajectory? If we imagine adding to QL languages a modal operator $\lozenge$ to be read as 'It might have been the case that', then we can represent the two readings of (3) by alternatively giving $\lozenge$ wide or narrow scope, along the following lines:

(4) $\lozenge\exists x((Px \wedge \forall y(Py \rightarrow y = x)) \wedge Dx)$
(5) $\exists x((Px \wedge \forall y(Py \rightarrow y = x)) \wedge \lozenge Dx)$.

(c)   This much seems clear, then: an operator forming a definite description from a predicate is *like* a quantifier in giving rise to questions of relative scope. But Russell claimed significantly more. He held that the appropriateness of the regimentation of *The F is G* by (R), and the way it accounts for the scope behaviour of descriptions, shows that the 'the' here really *is* another genuine quantifier, though a binary one (compare §26.1). Indeed, the claim goes on, the formal rendition (R) somehow reveals the true underlying semantic structure of vernacular claims involving definite descriptions.

But again, it is quite unclear exactly what that last claim comes to. And for our limited purposes in this book, we can happily avoid another minefield by simply leaving it as an open question whether a more fully Russellian position on descriptions is defensible.

40.5 More translations

What *is* defensible, to repeat, is the claim that wffs like (R) or their equivalents are the best options we have for rendering propositions of the form *The F is G* into QL-type languages. Let's see this core of Russell's Theory of Descriptions put to work in a few more examples.

So we will translate the following into the language $QL_1^=$ of §39.2.

(1) The Welsh speaker who loves Mrs Jones is Owen.
(2) Owen loves the woman who loves him.
(3) Owen only loves the woman who loves him.
(4) The tallest woman speaks Welsh.
(5) The woman who loves Owen loves the Welsh speaker who loves Nerys.

Take these in turn. The informal 'x is a Welsh speaker who loves Mrs Jones' can be rendered by $\{Fx \wedge Lxm\}$. So following the Russellian model (R), the complete translation of the first proposition will run

(1) $\exists x((\{Fx \wedge Lxm\} \wedge \forall y(\{Fy \wedge Lym\} \rightarrow y = x)) \wedge x = o)$.

If we follow the simpler model (R'), we'd get the slightly brisker

(1') $\exists x \forall y((\{Fy \wedge Lym\} \leftrightarrow y = x) \wedge x = o)$.

The second example is similar. The definite description this time is 'The woman who loves Owen', and 'x is a woman who loves Owen' is translated by $\{Gx \wedge Lxo\}$. So following the models (R) and (R'), we arrive at the alternative translations

(2) $\exists x((\{Gx \wedge Lxo\} \wedge \forall y(\{Gy \wedge Lyo\} \rightarrow y = x)) \wedge Lox)$.
(2') $\exists x \forall y((\{Gy \wedge Lyo\} \leftrightarrow y = x) \wedge Lox)$.

To translate the third example, we need to add to our translation of (2) that for anyone other than the woman who loves Owen, Owen doesn't love them – or equivalently, anyone Owen does love is none other than that woman again. Which gives us

(3) $\exists x[((\{Gx \wedge Lxo\} \wedge \forall y(\{Gy \wedge Lyo\} \rightarrow y = x)) \wedge Lox) \wedge \forall z(Loz \rightarrow z = x)]$.

Next, note that the tallest woman is the woman such that she is taller than all other women. Now, 'y is a woman who is taller than all other women' can be rendered by $\{(Gy \wedge (\forall z(Gz \wedge z \neq y) \rightarrow Myz))\}$. Using the brisker (R') style of translation, we therefore get

(4') $\exists x \forall y([\{(Gy \wedge (\forall z(Gz \wedge z \neq y) \rightarrow Myz))\} \leftrightarrow y = x] \wedge Fx)$.

Our last example involves two descriptions. For a moment, abbreviate 'loves the Welsh speaker who loves Nerys' by 'C'. And to keep things slightly simpler, let's again use (R') as our template. Then we have, as a half-way translation,

The woman who loves Owen is C
$$\simeq \exists x \forall y((\{Gy \wedge Lyo\} \leftrightarrow y = x) \wedge Cx).$$

And then unpacking C, we have

$$Cx \simeq \exists z \forall w((\{Fw \wedge Lwn\} \leftrightarrow w = z) \wedge Lxz).$$

So, if we plug the one into the other, we get

(5) $\exists x \forall y((\{Gy \wedge Lyo\} \leftrightarrow y = x) \wedge \exists z \forall w((\{Fw \wedge Lwn\} \leftrightarrow w = z) \wedge Lxz)).$

Now, the last translation gets the truth conditions right, at least if we have set aside the possibility of truth-value gaps. However, the messiness of this $QL_1^=$ rendition compared to the relative simplicity of the original English surely casts some doubt on the stronger Russellian thesis that the Theory of Descriptions captures the true underlying 'logical form' of the vernacular claim.

40.6 Summary

Propositions of the form *The F is G* are best rendered into $QL^=$ Russell-style, by corresponding wffs like (R) $\exists x((Fx \wedge \forall y(Fy \rightarrow y = x)) \wedge Gx)$, or like (R') $\exists x \forall y((Fy \leftrightarrow y = x) \wedge Gx)$.

This uncontentious claim, part of Russell's Theory of Descriptions, should be distinguished from Russell's much more contentious claims that this sort of rendition gets the truth conditions of *The F is G* exactly right, and moreover in some sense reveals the true logical form of vernacular statements involving descriptions.

However, Russell's analysis does plausibly diagnose certain apparent ambiguities involving descriptions as being scope ambiguities.

Exercises 40

(a)   Yet more Welsh affairs! Translate the following into $QL_1^=$:

(1)   There is one and only one Welsh speaker who loves Mrs Jones.
(2)   The Welsh speaker who loves Mrs Jones is either Nerys or Owen.
(3)   The woman who loves Nerys does not love anyone but Owen.
(4)   Someone other than the woman who loves Owen is taller than Nerys.
(5)   The one who loves Nerys is the one she loves.
(6)   Only if she loves him does Owen love the woman who speaks Welsh.
(7)   Owen loves the shortest Welsh speaker.
(8)   The shortest Welsh speaker loves the tallest Welsh speaker.

(b)   Using Russell's Theory of Descriptions – following the template (R') for definiteness – translate the following into $QL_2^=$ from Exercises 39:

(1)   The (i.e. *the* one and only) successor of zero exists.
(2)   The successor of the successor of zero doesn't equal one.
(3)   The sum of zero and one is one.
(4)   The sum of zero and the successor of zero is one.

And for masochists:

(5)   The sum of zero and the successor of zero is the successor of zero.

These examples show how we can render informal *function* expressions (e.g. for the successor function) using formal relational *predicates* and Russell's Theory of Descriptions. But at a considerable cost in unnaturalness. For more on this, see §42.4.

41 QL= proofs

Inference rules for arguing with identity propositions in a Fitch-style natural deduction system are very straightforward. One rule just reflects the trivial fact than any object is identical to itself. The other rule is a version of Leibniz's Law.

41.1 Two derivation rules for identity

(a) How are we going to argue to and from wffs of the form $\tau_1 = \tau_2$?

On any q-valuation, whatever object it assigns the term τ as its reference, it will be true that $\tau = \tau$. So the following introduction rule is certainly safe!

> (=I) At any point in a derivation, we can add a wff of the form $\tau = \tau$, where τ is any term.

Compare the rule (LEM) from §23.3: like that rule, (=I) allows us to add a line to a derivation without appealing to input(s) given at previous steps. Simple!

(b) As for arguing from a wff $\tau_1 = \tau_2$, evidently what we need is some version of Leibniz's Law. In §38.4, we met this in the form that tells us that, if $a = b$, then whatever holds of a holds of b. We now reflect this principle as a rule of inference (in a first version):

> (=E) Given $\tau_1 = \tau_2$ and $\alpha(\tau_1)$, we can derive $\alpha(\tau_2)$ – where $\alpha(\tau_1)$ contains at least one occurrence of the term τ_1 and $\alpha(\tau_2)$ is the result of replacing some or all of those occurrences with τ_2.

This is truth-preserving however many occurrences of τ_1 we replace with τ_2.

(c) Let's immediately show that we can use these rules to derive as theorems the three principles (Ref), (Sym), and (Trans) that we stated in formal versions in §39.1(b). Proving the reflexivity principle (Ref) is trivially easy!

(1)		
(2)	$a = a$	(=I)
(3)	$\forall x \, x = x$	(∀I 2)

Just remember that dummy names are terms, so we are allowed to introduce (2) by (=I). And the dummy name here doesn't occur in a premiss or temporary supposition, so we are then allowed to universally generalize on it.

Now, consider the following little proof, annotated in the obvious way:

(1)	m = n	(Prem)
(2)	m = m	(=I)
(3)	n = m	(=E 1, 2)

To see what is going on here, think of (1) as the wff $\tau_1 = \tau_2$, and (2) as the wff $\tau_1 = m$. Then we use Leibniz's Law to replace τ_1 by τ_2 in (2) to derive (3).

The same idea can be used to establish the general symmetry principle (Sym):

(1)		
(2)	a = b	(Supp)
(3)	a = a	(=I)
(4)	b = a	(=E 2, 3)
(5)	(a = b → b = a)	(CP 2, 4)
(6)	∀y(a = y → y = a)	(∀I 5)
(7)	∀x∀y(x = y → y = x)	(∀I 6)

Next, as a step towards proving the transitivity principle, we can first note this little proof:

(1)	m = n	(Prem)
(2)	n = o	(Prem)
(3)	m = o	(=E 2, 1)

Here, we take (2) to be the wff $\tau_1 = \tau_2$, and (1) to be the wff $m = \tau_1$. Then we use Leibniz's Law to replace τ_1 by τ_2 in (1) to derive (3). And we can now establish the general principle (Trans) using the same idea:

(1)		
(2)	(a = b ∧ b = c)	(Supp)
(3)	a = b	(∧E 2)
(4)	b = c	(∧E 2)
(5)	a = c	(=E 4, 3)
(6)	((a = b ∧ b = c) → a = c)	(CP 2–5)
(7)	∀z((a = b ∧ b = z) → a = z)	(∀I 6)
(8)	∀y∀z((a = y ∧ y = z) → a = z)	(∀I 7)
(9)	∀x∀y∀z((x = y ∧ y = z) → x = z)	(∀I 8)

(d)   Consider next the argument 'Bertie is none other than Lord Russell. Lord Russell co-wrote *Principia Mathematica*. Hence Bertie co-wrote *Principia Mathematica*'. Rendered into a suitable QL⁼ language, this becomes

m = n, Fn ∴ Fm.

Intuitively, this inference is just a simple one-off application of Leibniz's Law. But annoyingly, with our formal inference rule (=E) as stated, we need *two* applications of the Law (and we need to invoke the reflexivity principle too):

383

(1)	$m = n$	(Prem)
(2)	Fn	(Prem)
(3)	$m = m$	(=I)
(4)	$n = m$	(=E 1, 3)
(5)	Fm	(=E 4, 2)

Our current rule says that given $\tau_1 = \tau_2$ and $\alpha(\tau_1)$, we can derive $\alpha(\tau_2)$. In this case, $\alpha(\tau_1)$ is instantiated by Fn, so τ_1 is 'n'. Hence the identity wff we need for applying (=E) must be of the form $n = \tau_2$, and that isn't the premiss we are given at (1). We therefore need the little two-step dance through (3) and (4) to get us an identity wff with the terms swapped the right way round.

It isn't hard work to reverse the terms in (1). But equally it isn't particularly natural to set things up so that we need to use Leibniz's Law twice to get from $m = n$ and Fn to Fm. This last thought motivates liberalizing (=E) so that we can appeal to identity premisses with the terms in either order, like this:

(=E)   Given $\tau_1 = \tau_2$ or $\tau_2 = \tau_1$, and $\alpha(\tau_1)$, we can derive $\alpha(\tau_2)$ – where $\alpha(\tau_1)$ contains one or more occurrences of the term τ_1 and $\alpha(\tau_2)$ is the result of replacing some or all of those occurrences with τ_2.

Our official Fitch-style QL= proof system will therefore be the QL system augmented by the rules (=I) and our liberalized version of (=E).

41.2   More examples

(a)   We will work through some more examples in turn. Start with

A   The author of *Emma* wrote *Persuasion*. Jane Austen wrote *Emma*. Hence Jane Austen wrote *Persuasion*.

Put 'E' for *wrote Emma*, 'P' for *wrote Persuasion*, and let 'j' denote Jane. Then, handling the definite description Russell-style, we can render the argument

A′ $\exists x((Ex \wedge \forall y(Ey \rightarrow y = x)) \wedge Px), Ej \therefore Pj$.

And a formal derivation is a straightforward proof by ($\exists$E):

(1)	$\exists x((Ex \wedge \forall y(Ey \rightarrow y = x)) \wedge Px)$	(Prem)
(2)	Ej	(Prem)
(3)	$((Ea \wedge \forall y(Ey \rightarrow y = a)) \wedge Pa)$	(Supp)
(4)	$(Ea \wedge \forall y(Ey \rightarrow y = a))$	($\wedge$E 3)
(5)	Pa	($\wedge$E 3)
(6)	$\forall y(Ey \rightarrow y = a)$	($\wedge$E 4)
(7)	$(Ej \rightarrow j = a)$	($\forall$E 6)
(8)	$j = a$	(MP 2, 7)
(9)	Pj	(=E 8, 5)
(10)	Pj	($\exists$E 1, 3–9)

(b) Next, consider the argument

B   Bertie is the only Nobel-prize-winning logician. Bertie is Lord Russell. So Lord Russell is the only Nobel-prize-winning logician.

Putting 'N' for *is a Nobel-prize-winning logician*, 'm' for Bertie and 'n' for Lord Russell, we can formally render the argument

B′ $(Nm \land \forall x(Nx \to x = m))$, $m = n$ ∴ $(Nn \land \forall x(Nx \to x = n))$.

And the corresponding one-step formal proof is then immediate:

(1)	$(Nm \land \forall x(Nx \to x = m))$	(Prem)
(2)	$m = n$	(Prem)
(3)	$(Nn \land \forall x(Nx \to x = n))$	(=E 2, 1)

This trite example is just to illustrate a case where we use the identity at (2) to replace more than one occurrence of 'm' at the same time by Leibniz's Law.

(c) Now take the argument

C   If anyone loves Angharad, it is Meurig or Ninian. Some Welsh speaker loves Angharad. So either Meurig or Ninian speaks Welsh.

Following Quine's maxim of not exposing unnecessarily much structure, let's use the simple predicate F to render ① *loves Angharad*, and G for ① *speaks Welsh*. So the argument can go into QL$^=$ as

C′ $\forall x(Fx \to (x = m \lor x = n))$, $\exists x(Fx \land Gx)$ ∴ $(Gm \lor Gn)$.

And a formal proof can then unfold like this:

(1)	$\forall x(Fx \to (x = m \lor x = n))$	(Prem)
(2)	$\exists x(Fx \land Gx)$	(Prem)
(3)	$(Fa \land Ga)$	(Supp)
(4)	Fa	($\land$E 3)
(5)	Ga	($\land$E 3)
(6)	$(Fa \to (a = m \lor a = n))$	($\forall$E 1)
(7)	$(a = m \lor a = n)$	(MP 4, 6)
(8)	$a = m$	(Supp)
(9)	Gm	(=E 8, 5)
(10)	$(Gm \lor Gn)$	($\lor$I 9)
(11)	$a = n$	(Supp)
(12)	Gn	(=E 11, 5)
(13)	$(Gm \lor Gn)$	($\lor$I 12)
(14)	$(Gm \lor Gn)$	($\lor$E 7, 8–10, 11–13)
(15)	$(Gm \lor Gn)$	($\exists$E 2, 3–14)

We make the obvious supposition at line (3), and then immediately disassemble the conjunction. How are we going to instantiate the universal quantifier at (1)?

Obviously by using the dummy name 'a' to set up the modus ponens inference leading to (7). Now we have set out to use the disjunction (7) in a proof by (∨E) to get (Gm ∨ Gn). The steps after (7) then almost write themselves.

(d) In §40.2, we noted two different ways of translating the claim 'There is exactly one philosopher', there labelled

(2) ∃x(Fx ∧ ∀y(Fy → y = x)).

(3) ∃x∀y(Fy ↔ y = x).

Let's give a proof that the first of these entails the second (leaving a proof of the reverse entailment as an exercise). So, now unpacking the shorthand for the biconditional, we aim to warrant the inference

D   ∃x(Fx ∧ ∀y(Fy → y = x)) ∴ ∃x∀y((Fy → y = x) ∧ (y = x → Fy)).

Evidently, we need a proof of the following overall shape

$$
\begin{array}{ll}
∃x(Fx ∧ ∀y(Fy → y = x)) & \text{(Prem)} \\
\quad (Fa ∧ ∀y(Fy → y = a)) & \text{(Supp)} \\
\quad \vdots & \\
\quad ∃x∀y((Fy → y = x) ∧ (y = x → Fy)) & \\
∃x∀y((Fy → y = x) ∧ (y = x → Fy)) &
\end{array}
$$

The penultimate line will presumably be derived by existentially quantifying ∀y((Fy → y = a) ∧ (y = a → Fy)); and *that* will be have to be derived by universally generalizing something like ((Fb → b = a) ∧ (b = a → Fb)). So let's join up the dots:

(1)	∃x(Fx ∧ ∀y(Fy → y = x))	(Prem)
(2)	(Fa ∧ ∀y(Fy → y = a))	(Supp)
(3)	Fa	(∧E 2)
(4)	∀y(Fy → y = a)	(∧E 2)
(5)	(Fb → b = a)	(∀E 4)
(6)	b = a	(Supp)
(7)	Fb	(=E 6, 3)
(8)	(b = a → Fb)	(CP 6–7)
(9)	((Fb → b = a) ∧ (b = a → Fb))	(∧I 5, 8)
(10)	∀y((Fy → y = a) ∧ (y = a → Fy))	(∀I 9)
(11)	∃x∀y((Fy → y = x) ∧ (y = x → Fy))	(∃I 10)
(12)	∃x∀y((Fy → y = x) ∧ (y = x → Fy))	(∃E 1, 2–11)

Similar proofs will show that the wffs labelled (R), (R'), and (R″) in §40.2 – the three Russellian versions for rendering a proposition of the form *The F is G* – are also provably equivalent. That is to say, from any one of them as premiss there are QL= derivations of the other two. Checking that claim can be left to the end-of-chapter Exercises!

41.3   One and one makes two

We will finish this chapter by showing, in outline, that the following inference can be shown to be valid by a $\mathsf{QL}^=$ proof:

$\exists x(Fx \wedge \forall y(Fy \rightarrow y = x))$, $\exists x(Gx \wedge \forall y(Gy \rightarrow y = x))$, $\neg\exists x(Fx \wedge Gx)$ $\therefore$
$\exists x \exists y(([\{Fx \vee Gx\} \wedge \{Fy \vee Gy\}] \wedge \neg x = y) \wedge \forall z[\{Fz \vee Gz\} \rightarrow \{z = x \vee z = y\}])$.

Look at this carefully! It renders

There is exactly one F, there is exactly one G, and nothing is both F and G; so there are exactly two things which are F or G.

Roughly, then, it expresses a bit of applied arithmetic: one thing and another different thing makes two things altogether.

Now, at the *beginning* of our proof there will be the three premisses. Two of them are existential quantifications, so we will want to make two suppositions with a view to ($\exists$E) inferences from those premisses.

At the *end* of the proof, we will have our target doubly existentially quantified conclusion. And how will be derive that? Presumably by getting to an instance which we can then existentially quantify twice.

So that suggests the overall shape of the proof we want will be like this:

$\exists x(Fx \wedge \forall y(Fy \rightarrow y = x))$	(Prem)
$\exists x(Gx \wedge \forall y(Gy \rightarrow y = x))$	(Prem)
$\neg\exists x(Fx \wedge Gx)$	(Prem)
$(Fa \wedge \forall y(Fy \rightarrow y = a))$	(Supp)
$(Gb \wedge \forall y(Gy \rightarrow y = b))$	(Supp)
Fa	($\wedge$E)
$\forall y(Fy \rightarrow y = a)$	($\wedge$E)
Gb	($\wedge$E)
$\forall y(Gy \rightarrow y = b)$	($\wedge$E)
$\vdots$	
$(([\{Fa \vee Ga\} \wedge \{Fb \vee Gb\}] \wedge \neg a = b) \wedge$ $\forall z[\{Fz \vee Gz\} \rightarrow \{z = a \vee z = b\}])$	(?)
$\exists y(([\{Fa \vee Ga\} \wedge \{Fy \vee Gy\}] \wedge \neg a = y) \wedge$ $\forall z[\{Fz \vee Gz\} \rightarrow \{z = a \vee z = y\}])$	($\exists$I)
$\exists x \exists y(([\{Fx \vee Gx\} \wedge \{Fy \vee Gy\}] \wedge \neg x = y) \wedge$ $\forall z[\{Fz \vee Gz\} \rightarrow \{z = x \vee z = y\}])$	($\exists$I)
$\longleftarrow$	($\exists$E)
$\longleftarrow$	($\exists$E)

Here, to avoid repetitious clutter, the long arrows at the end just indicate bringing down the previous long wff to the next line.

And how do we fill in the dots? There are four conjuncts in the wff just after the gap which we now need to establish. How do we derive them?

(1) We derive {Fa ∨ Ga} immediately from the earlier Fa.

(2) We derive {Fb ∨ Gb} immediately from the earlier Gb.

(3) We derive ¬a = b by supposing a = b and getting a contradiction. How? Note that a = b together with Fa gives Fb which together with Gb implies (Fb ∧ Gb). But that entails ∃x(Fx ∧ Gx), which contradicts the third premiss. (It is this stage of the proof, then, which uses Leibniz's Law.)

(4) It just remains to prove ∀z[{Fz ∨ Gz} → {z = a ∨ z = b}]. But this too is now quite straightforward. For note that we have already derived ∀y(Fy → y = a) and ∀y(Gy → y = b), and these together fairly obviously imply what we want, as we will now show.

Here then is the required proof-fragment demonstrating that last implication, which we can then insert into our outline proof above:

∀y(Fy → y = a)	(already derived)
∀y(Gy → y = b)	(already derived)
{Fc ∨ Gc}	(Supp)
Fc	(Supp)
(Fc → c = a)	(∀E)
c = a	(MP)
{c = a ∨ c = b}	(∨I)
Gc	(Supp)
(Gc → c = b)	(∀E)
c = b	(MP)
{c = a ∨ c = b}	(∨I)
{c = a ∨ c = b}	(∨E)
[{Fc ∨ Gc} → {c = a ∨ c = b}]	(CP)
∀z[{Fz ∨ Gz} → {z = a ∨ z = b}]	(∀I)

You can now assemble together all the described ingredients to get a completed proof, as claimed. True, the proof isn't very short! – but it is not very difficult, and only a little strategic thinking is needed to get the proof done.

41.4 Metatheoretical headlines

(a) That's enough examples of proofs using the identity predicate!

We should note, for the record, that the predictable metatheorems obtain for our Fitch-style QL= system. In particular, it is sound and complete.

In other words, a correctly formed derivation from zero or more sentences as premisses to some conclusion always yields a q-valid inference – i.e. every q-valuation which makes the premisses true (meaning every QL= valuation which handles the identity predicate according to the semantics we gave in §39.1), makes the conclusion true.

And conversely, every such q-valid inference involving the identity predicate can be warranted by a corresponding proof in our system.

The metatheorems are proved by relatively minor tweaks on the corresponding proofs for our QL proof system. We need not pause over them in this book.

(b) We can usefully finish, though, with a quick additional note. You might wonder whether our informal version of Leibniz's Law in §38.4 in fact invites formalization in a way rather different way to our inference *rule* (=E). Why don't we express the Law using a single generalized *proposition* such as the following:

(LL$_2$) $\forall x \forall y (x = y \rightarrow \forall X(Xx \rightarrow Xy))$?

Here, we are not only quantifying (lower case) over *objects* but also quantifying (upper case) over *properties*. So we read (LL$_2$) as saying that for whatever objects x and y might be, if x is none other than y then any property X had by x is had by y too. Isn't this what we want?

Note, however, that (LL$_2$) is *not* well-formed in our quantificational languages. For these languages have just a first 'order' of quantifier, i.e. they can only generalize over objects in the domain, using little-'x' type variables which can occupy positions where names can occur. These languages do *not* have big-'X' type variables which can occupy positions where property-expressing predicates can occur; and so they can't have a second 'order' of linked quantifiers generalizing over properties. (Or at least, that will do as a first headline summary.)

It is because QL and QL$^=$ languages only have the first order of quantifiers that they are standardly called *first-order languages*, and their logic is therefore called *first-order logic*, or *first-order quantification theory*. The contrast is with *second-order* languages, where we can also quantify into predicate position.

So, since (LL$_2$) is not available, we have to resort to something like our inference-rule version of Leibniz's Law. But note that our version in effect only commits us to the claim that identical objects share every feature *expressible in the relevant language* (it tells us that when $\tau_1 = \tau_2$ we can deduce $\alpha(\tau_2)$ from $\alpha(\tau_1)$ for any suitable expression α). And it doesn't matter how rich the language is, this will be a weaker claim than the full-strength intuitive version of Leibniz's Law which says that identicals share *every* feature.

This of course raises the question of why we don't move to a second-order logic so we can have a full-strength version of Leibniz's Law. But that turns out to be a tricky issue, one that takes us well beyond what we can treat properly in an introductory text.

41.5 Summary

Our proof system for arguing in QL$^=$ is the old QL system augmented by two new derivation rules for the identity predicate, which we can put in diagrammatic form like this:

$$\tau_1 = \tau_2 \ \ or \ \ \tau_2 = \tau_1$$

$$\vdots$$

(=I) $\qquad \vdots \qquad\qquad\qquad$ (=E) $\qquad\qquad \alpha(\tau_1)$

$$\tau = \tau$$

$$\vdots$$

$$\alpha(\tau_2)$$

The τs can be any terms. $\alpha(\tau_2)$ is the result of replacing some or all occurrences of τ_1 in $\alpha(\tau_1)$ by τ_2.

Exercises 41

(a)   Use QL$^=$ derivations to show the following inferences are valid:

(1)   Mrs Jones isn't Kate. So Kate isn't Mrs Jones.

(2)   No one who isn't Bryn loves Angharad. At least one person loves Angharad. So Bryn loves Angharad.

(3)   If Clark Kent isn't Superman, then Clark isn't even himself. Superman can fly. So Clark can fly.

(4)   The goods were stolen by someone. Whoever stole the goods knew the safe combination. Only Jack knew the safe combination. Hence Jack stole the goods.

(5)   Take two people (perhaps the same): if the first is taller than the second, the second is not taller than the first. Therefore, if Kurt is taller than Gerhard, they are different people.

(6)   There is a wise philosopher. There is a philosopher who isn't wise. So there are at least two philosophers.

(7)   Anyone who loves Jo is a logician. Why? Because only one person loves Jo. And some logician loves Jo.

(8)   For any number, there's a larger one. There is no number which is larger than itself. So for any number, there's a distinct number which is larger than it.

(9)   Exactly one person admires Frank. All and only those who admire Frank love him. Hence exactly one person loves Frank.

(10)   The present King of France is bald. Bald men are sexy. Hence whoever is a present King of France is sexy.

(11)   Someone is a logician. But no one is the only logician. Therefore there at least two logicians.

(b)   Take the wffs (R), (R'), and (R'') from §40.2. We claimed that from each wff we can derive the other two using a QL$^=$ proof. Give at least three of the six required proofs. Remember, for us an expression of the form $(\alpha \leftrightarrow \beta)$ simply abbreviates the corresponding expression $((\alpha \to \beta) \land (\beta \to \alpha))$.

(c)   Outline a proof that 'one and two makes three' in the style of §41.3

42 Functions

Once we leave behind toy examples, we quickly find ourselves wanting to use formal languages which involve expressions for functions. For example, the standard formal language of arithmetic – as you would expect – has symbols for the addition and multiplication functions. We don't want to finish our introduction to quantificational logic without saying just something about how to add expressions for functions to QL$^=$ languages. But we will be brief.

42.1 Functions, informally again

(a) A function, in the most general sense, maps some input(s) to zero, one, or many determinate output(s). Here are some non-mathematical examples to add to those we gave before in §12.2:

(1) The function which maps a PL wff to the wff which is its negation.
(2) The function which maps someone alive at the first moment of 2020 to their age in days at that moment.
(3) The function which maps a person to their oldest biological child.
(4) The function which maps a latitude and longitude to a location on the Earth's surface.
(5) The function which maps a PL wff and a valuation of its atoms to a truth value (the value the wff takes on that valuation).
(6) The function which maps a country and a date to the reigning monarch(s) of that country at that date.

The first example is a unary function which takes a single input (or as mathematicians would say, has a single *argument*), and it always gives a unique output (yields a *value*) of the same kind. While the second example reminds us that unary functions can also map inputs of one kind to outputs of some quite different kind – in this case every person is mapped to an integer. The first function can sensibly be reapplied to one of its own previous outputs; the second function can't be.

The third example is, by contrast, a partial function: it does not yield a value for some of its possible inputs.

The fourth example is a binary function mapping two inputs of the same general kind (numbers) to an output of a different kind.

The fifth example takes two inputs of very different kinds.

The final example is a partial binary function which takes two inputs of quite different kinds and sometimes – for instance, in cases of a dual monarchy – yields more than one output of a third kind.

And all of these functions are defined as applying to some limited range of things, *much* less than everything! For example, we can't apply the first function to people, or the second function to wffs.

(b)   As we now go formal, however, we are going to set aside partial functions and multi-valued functions. In other words, we are going to deal only with *total* functions that always deliver a *unique* output for every input of the right type. Indeed, we are only going to consider functions that can sensibly be applied to *every* object in the domain of the relevant language, without restriction of type. This means we can always re-apply a function to its own output, or apply it to the output from some other function.

This involves a quite radical narrowing of focus:

(i)   Setting aside multi-valued functions is perhaps a minor loss (indeed, many mathematicians and logicians do not want to count multi-valued functions as genuine functions at all).

(ii)   Many functions are partial – beginning with the school-room division function (we learn early on that you can't divide by zero). Sometimes we can conveniently make an informal partial function total by 'completing' it, by sending inputs that aren't ordinarily associated with a value to some artificial default value. But this tactic has significant limitations (e.g. it's an early theorem of computability theory that computable partial functions need not have a computable completion).

(iii)   As we noted in §27.3, it is typical mathematical practice to work with more than one domain of objects at the same time (and to quantify over the different domains using different sorts of variables). Related to this, we very often use functions that take arguments from one domain to deliver values in another (sending lines to lengths, say). It is always rather artificial to work with a single all-inclusive domain; and it is even more artificial to restrict ourselves to working with functions all defined over a common domain, functions which always give values in the same domain.

However, despite the narrowing of focus, it will still be useful to say something about how to handle those functions that *do* take one or more objects (*any* objects) from the current domain as input(s), and then always map these inputs to a single determinate object in the same domain as output. So that's our topic.

42.2   Function symbols, syntax

(a)   The syntactic headlines: by default, we use lower case letters like 'f' and 'g' – letters which are not otherwise in use! – to express functions. A function symbol will then combine with one or more terms to form another term denoting an object in the same domain. And we will take it that each function symbol has its own fixed arity, i.e. it always combines with a fixed number of terms to form another term (just as each predicate symbol has a fixed arity, i.e. combines with a fixed number of terms to form a wff).

And how do function symbols combine with terms? The default arrangement in our formal languages is that *a k-ary function symbol followed by k terms is a new term* (just as a k-ary predicate followed by k terms is a wff). Call such a complex term a *functional term*.

(b)   Suppose that we have, for example, a language with the two proper names 'm', 'n', and with the unary function symbol 'f' and binary function symbol 'g'. Then the following will count as terms (since the formation rule allows a function symbol to be combined with terms that are already functional terms, and remember dummy names are also terms):

fn, ffn, fffn, gmn, gaa, fgmn, gmfn, fgbfn, ggmnn, gffngmfn, ...

This notation is in fact quite unambiguous, once we have fixed the arity of the function symbols (it is worth pausing to convince yourself of this).

However, although it works in principle, an officially bracketless notation like this quickly becomes quite hard to read in practice. One way of improving readability is to introduce brackets, and write g(m, n) rather than gmn, write g(g(m, n), n) rather than ggmnn, and so on. Similarly, suppose 'h' is a ternary function symbol; then h(fm, g(m, n), fn) is surely a lot more readable than hfmgmnfn.

Another useful dodge is to write binary function symbols *infix* rather than *prefix*. In other words, instead of putting the function symbol before the terms it applies to, we write the symbol between them, and put brackets round the result. For example, suppose we borrow '+' for formal use to express the addition function; then instead of writing expressions like +mn or +m+nn or even +++mnmn we can write comfortably familiar (and readable!) expressions like (m + n) and (m + (n + n)) and (((m + n) + m) + n).

(c)   However, let's keep things simple for the moment. Let's stick to the austere bracketless prefix style as our official notation, while having a relaxed policy of unofficially 'pencilling in' brackets and/or using infixed symbols when it makes for readability.

So, with that by way of explanation, we can now augment our formal account of QL$^=$ syntax to allow for the presence of function symbols. Using 'θ' (*theta*) to stand in schematically for a function symbol, the story begins like this:

Assume the non-logical vocabulary of a particular QL$^=$ language to be given, i.e. zero or more names, zero or more predicates of various given arities (to add to the built-in logical identity predicate), plus zero or more function symbols of various given arities.

Then the *terms* of the language are now defined as follows:

(T1) Any proper name is a term.
(T2) Any dummy name is a term.
(T3) If θ is a k-ary function symbol, and $\tau_1, \tau_2, \ldots, \tau_k$ are k terms, then $\theta\tau_1\tau_2\ldots\tau_k$ is a term.
(T4) Nothing else is a term.

(d)   The rest of the $\mathsf{QL}^=$ syntactic story – the account of how to form wffs from predicates, terms, and logical operators – can remain *exactly* as before. In other words, functional terms (built from function symbols plus terms) can appear wherever other terms can appear, expressions with functional terms will count as instances of quantified wffs, and so on.

For example, suppose that, alongside the names 'm' and 'n', the unary function symbol 'f', and binary 'g', our $\mathsf{QL}^=$ language has the unary predicate 'F' and binary predicate 'L' . Then the following will now be atomic wffs:

$$\mathsf{Ffa,\ Fffm,\ Fgmn,\ Lafb,\ Lfmfn,\ Lgmnfn,\ fm = n,\ fa = gmb.}$$

Then, by the usual construction of quantifying on some term, we can form further wffs, such as

$$\mathsf{\forall y Ffy, (\forall y Ffy \to Fgmn), \exists x \forall y Lxfy, \exists x fx = n, (\exists x fx = n \lor \forall y Ffy).}$$

And instances of the simple quantified wff $\forall x Fx$ will now include

$$\mathsf{Fm,\ Ffm,\ Ffa,\ Fffffm,\ Fgab,\ Ffgmfn,\ Fgffngmfn, \ldots.}$$

Though, to repeat, such austere wffs without brackets to help the eye quickly become hard to parse.

42.3   Function symbols, semantics

(a)   Already back in §12.2, we distinguished the *sense* of an expression for a function from its *extension*.

Compare our distinction between the sense and extension of predicates (§25.4). The sense is what is grasped by someone who understands the predicate; but it is the extension which fixes the truth values of sentences involving the predicates (if we forget about non-extensional contexts). Similarly here: the sense of a function expression is what you have to grasp in order to understand it. We can typically think of this as a rule or procedure for correlating some object(s) as input with some unique output. This rule will set up ordered tuples linking the inputs and their outputs: it is these tuples which form the function expression's extension.

For the simplest of examples, let's consider an arithmetic language whose domain is the natural numbers, and which has one unary and one binary function symbol, with the following glossary entries:

> s: the successor of ① (i.e. the next number after ①)
> +: the sum of ① and ②.

For readability, we will use infix notation for the addition function.

To grasp the sense of the unary 's' as just introduced, you need to understand the rule that the function returns as value the next number after its input. This rule then determines pairings of inputs and outputs as follows:

$$\langle 0, 1 \rangle, \langle 1, 2 \rangle, \langle 2, 3 \rangle, \langle 3, 4 \rangle, \langle 4, 5 \rangle, \ldots$$

These ordered *pairs* form the extension of 's'.

And it is the extension which fixes the truth values of wffs containing the function symbol. How? By fixing the reference of any functional term $s\tau$, where τ is some term. And how does 's's extension do this? As follows: if the term τ refers to the number m, then the term $s\tau$ refers to the unique n such that the pair $\langle m, n \rangle$ is in the extension of 's'. (Think about it!)

Hence the sequence of functional terms s0, ss0, sss0, etc., refer respectively to 1, 2, 3, ...

Similarly, to grasp the sense of the formal symbol '+' as just introduced, you need to understand the rule that the function returns as value the sum of its first input and second input. This rule then determines pairings of any two inputs with a unique output; so we can take the extension of '+' to be all ordered *triples* of the form $\langle j, k, j + k \rangle$:

$$\langle 0, 0, 0 \rangle, \langle 0, 1, 1 \rangle, \langle 1, 0, 1 \rangle, \langle 0, 2, 2 \rangle, \langle 1, 1, 2 \rangle, \langle 2, 0, 2 \rangle, \langle 0, 3, 3 \rangle, \langle 1, 2, 3 \rangle, \ldots$$

And how does this extension fix the reference of a term formed by applying '+' to two terms? Like this: if the terms τ_1 and τ_2 refer to the numbers m_1 and m_2 respectively, then the term $(\tau_1 + \tau_2)$ refers to the unique n such that the triple $\langle m_1, m_2, n \rangle$ is in the extension of '+'. (Again, think about it!)

(b)   To continue with the example, suppose next that our arithmetical language also contains the unary predicate

F: ① is odd.

Then the following wffs will render the given informal arithmetical claims:

$(s0 + ss0) = sss0 \simeq$ the sum of one and two is three,
$\simeq$ one plus two equals three.
$Fs0 \simeq$ one is odd.
$F(s0 + ss0) \simeq$ the sum of one and two is odd.
$\forall x(x + 0) = x \simeq$ adding zero to any number gives the same number.
$\forall x \forall y\, (x + y) = (y + x) \simeq$ adding a second number to a first one is
   the same as adding the first to the second.
$\forall x(Fx \to F(x + ss0)) \simeq$ an odd number plus two is an odd number.
$\forall x(\exists y\, x = (y + y) \to Fsx) \simeq$ the successor of any number which equals
   some number plus itself is odd.

(c)   The stated extensions of the function symbols 's' and '+' are the ones fixed by the intended senses of the symbols. But when we turn to consider questions of validity for arguments involving those function symbols, we will of course need to consider other possible extensions the symbols can take on alternative q-valuations. So, generalizing:

A q-valuation q for a language with function symbols assigns to a unary function θ the following q-value: a set of ordered pairs of objects from the domain such that for every object o_1 in the domain there is one and only one pair $\langle o_1, o_2 \rangle$ in the set. This is the extension of θ.

If the term τ refers to the object o_1 on (a perhaps expanded) q, then the term $\theta\tau$ refers to the unique o_2 such that the pair $\langle o_1, o_2 \rangle$ is in the extension of θ.

Similarly, for the binary case we have:

A q-valuation q assigns to a binary function θ a set of ordered triples of objects from the domain such that for all objects o_1 and o_2 in the domain there is one and only one triple $\langle o_1, o_2, o_3 \rangle$ in the set. This is the extension of θ.

If the term τ_1 refers to the object o_1 on (a perhaps expanded) q, and τ_2 refers to the object o_2, then the term $\theta\tau_1\tau_2$ refers to the unique o_3 such that the triple $\langle o_1, o_2, o_3 \rangle$ is in the extension of θ.

We can generalize further in the obvious way to deal with the q-values of k-ary functional symbols. You can fill in the details!

42.4   Functions, functional relations, and definite descriptions again

It is very instructive to pause to compare two approaches to handling functions in a formal setting – the natural direct method of using function symbols of the kind which we have just been introducing, and a rather unnatural indirect method using Russell's Theory of Descriptions.

(a)   Think informally for a moment. To repeat, the extension of a (total, single-valued) unary function f is a set of ordered pairs of objects of the relevant kind such that for every object o_1 there is one and only one pair $\langle o_1, o_2 \rangle$ in the set.

Now suppose that the binary relation R is such that every relevant object is R to one and only one thing. In that case, the extension of R is *also* a set of pairs satisfying just the same condition that for every object o_1 in the domain there is one and only one pair $\langle o_1, o_2 \rangle$ in the set. Call this kind of binary relation *functional*.

A unary function f and a binary functional relation R can therefore have identical extensions. In such a case, we'll say that the function and the functional relation *correspond* to each other. (Similarly, a binary function can correspond to a ternary functional relation, etc.; but we won't labour to spell this out.)

Let's again have a really simple example. Take the relevant domain to be the natural numbers. Then consider the unary *successor* function and the binary functional relation *is succeeded by*. The function and the relation – unsurprisingly! – correspond to each other. Both have the extension

$$\langle 0,1\rangle, \langle 1,2\rangle, \langle 2,3\rangle, \langle 3,4\rangle, \langle 4,5\rangle, \ldots$$

And now note that we can simply *define* the function in terms of the relation: for *the successor of n* is, of course, *the number such that n is succeeded by it*.

The point generalizes. Suppose that the one-argument function f corresponds to the two-place functional relation R. Then instead of using a functional expression like *f(n)* to refer to some object, we could instead use a definite description applied to R to speak of *the object x such that n is R to x* and we will still be talking of just the same thing.

(b) Now carry all this over to our formal languages. Take our language where the unary function symbol 's' expresses the successor function. But now add to the language the relational predicate 'S' meaning ① *is succeeded by* ② (equivalently, ② *succeeds* ①).

Then we can express the claim that the successor of zero is odd by

Fs0.

But we can also render the same claim by translating 'The number such that it succeeds zero is odd'. Handling the description Russell's way, we'll get

$$\exists x((S0x \land \forall y(S0y \to y = x)) \land Fx).$$

That's manageable, though it does introduce two quantifiers. But here's another simple truth: three is odd, which we can neatly express like this:

Fsss0.

But if we try to express that three is odd using the successor relation and Russell's Theory of Descriptions, we need to formalize

> The number such that it succeeds the number such that it succeeds the number such that it succeeds zero is odd.

And to render this takes three applications of Russell's Theory of Descriptions, one inside another, leading to quantifiers buried six deep!

So yes, in principle, everything you can do in a $QL^=$ language with symbols for total functions you can in principle do in a $QL^=$ language without functions: just use functional relations plus Russell's Theory of Descriptions. But even our very simple example already shows something of the cost of trading function expressions for relational predicates; every time we try to mirror the application of a function by using the corresponding functional relation plus Russell's Theory of Descriptions we will introduce quantifiers embedded inside the scope of other quantifiers. Things get very messy very fast!

Moral? Don't *always* try to do without built-in function expressions!

42.5   Proofs involving functions

When included in a $QL^=$ language, function symbols enable us to form new terms. These new terms can then be used in derivations. We can apply our existing quantifier rules exactly as before. Note, in particular, that the rules ($\forall$E) and ($\exists$I) – which talk of 'terms' in general – still obviously remain correct when we allow functional terms (why?). So there is going to be no real novelty in proofs involving functional expressions. Still, let's have a simple example, to illustrate what we can do now we have functional terms in play.

(a) Continue to work in our language for a fragment of arithmetic, with a name '0' denoting the number zero, a one-place function symbol 's' for the successor function, and a two-place function symbol '+' (used infix) expressing the familiar addition function. As we noted, our language can form terms $0, s0, ss0, sss0, ssss0, \ldots$, and can this way denote each of the natural numbers: these terms can therefore be said to be our language's *numerals*.

Here, then, are four *very* basic principles of the arithmetic of the natural numbers, recast in our formal language:

(A1) $\forall x \,\neg 0 = sx$
(A2) $\forall x \forall y (sx = sy \rightarrow x = y)$
(A3) $\forall x \,(x + 0) = x$
(A4) $\forall x \forall y (x + sy) = s(x + y)$.

Informally: zero is the first natural number, it isn't the successor of any number. Distinct numbers have distinct successors; or equivalently, if two numbers have the same successor then they must be the same. Adding zero makes no difference. And finally we have a formal counterpart of the basic principle that $x + (y+1) = (x + y) + 1$.

Let's say that these four principles together – these basic *axioms* of arithmetic, if you like – form *Theory A*. Then we can use Theory A to prove some simple arithmetic truths. Let's first formally show that $3 + 2 = 5$ by deriving the sentence $(sss0 + ss0) = sssss0$:

(1)	Theory A	(Premises)
(2)	$(sss0 + 0) = sss0$	($\forall$E A3)
(3)	$\forall y (sss0 + sy) = s(sss0 + y)$	($\forall$E A4)
(4)	$(sss0 + s0) = s(sss0 + 0)$	($\forall$E 3)
(5)	$(sss0 + s0) = ssss0$	(=E 2, 4)
(6)	$(sss0 + ss0) = s(sss0 + s0)$	($\forall$E 3)
(7)	$(sss0 + ss0) = sssss0$	(=E 5, 6)

At lines (2) and (3), we use the term $sss0$ to instantiate the quantifier in A3 and then the initial quantifier in A4. At line (4) we use 0 to instantiate the universal quantifier in (3), then at (6) we use s0 to instantiate the same universal quantification. And so on.

This kind of proof can be used prove any correct equation involving just numerals and addition, such as $7 + 6 = (4 + 5) + 4$. So theory A can be used as a calculator for the addition of numerals. If you are masochistic enough.

(b) Theory A can also be used to prove some quantified truths. For example: there is no natural number x such that $x + 3 = 2$. Let's derive the corresponding formal statement $\forall x \neg (x + sss0) = ss0$ from the theory:

(1)	Theory A	(Premisses)
(2)	$(a + sss0) = s0$	(Supp)
(3)	$\forall y(a + sy) = s(a + y)$	($\forall$E A4)
(4)	$(a + sss0) = s(a + ss0)$	($\forall$E 3)
(5)	$s(a + ss0) = s0$	($=$E 4, 2)
(6)	$\forall y(s(a + ss0) = sy \rightarrow (a + ss0) = y)$	($\forall$E A2)
(7)	$(s(a + ss0) = s0 \rightarrow (a + ss0) = 0)$	($\forall$E 6)
(8)	$(a + ss0) = 0$	(MP 5, 7)
(9)	$(a + ss0) = s(a + s0)$	($\forall$E 3)
(10)	$0 = s(a + s0)$	($=$E 8, 9)
(11)	$\neg 0 = s(a + s0)$	($\forall$E A1)
(12)	$\perp$	(Abs 10, 11)
(13)	$\neg(a + sss0) = s0$	(RAA 2–12)
(14)	$\forall x \neg(x + sss0) = ss0$	($\forall$I 13)

Check through to make sure you understand the steps here.

(c) Our arithmetical theory A is a *terribly* weak theory. It is interesting to see *how* weak.

   To reduce clutter, let's now abbreviate the numerals $0, s0, ss0, sss0, ssss0, \ldots$ as simply $0, \bar{1}, \bar{2}, \bar{3}, \bar{4}, \ldots$. And start by noting that Theory A can easily prove each of $0 + 0 = 0, 0 + \bar{1} = \bar{1}, 0 + \bar{2} = \bar{2}, 0 + \bar{3} = \bar{3}, \ldots$ (pause to convince yourself of this). Therefore, using standard $QL^=$ logic, this theory can prove each numeral *instance* of the generalization $\forall x(0 + x) = x$. But *Theory A can't prove that generalization itself* (contrast the theory's axiom A3).

   How do we show this? Suppose we can find some *countervaluation* which makes the combined premisses of Theory A true and yet makes $\forall x(0 + x) = x$ false. Then this shows that there can't be a $QL^=$ derivation from Theory A to that wff. For the soundness of $QL^=$ logic tells us that a properly constructed derivation would be truth-preserving on all valuations, i.e. couldn't have countervaluations.

   Here's how to construct one artificial – but still legitimate! – countervaluation which does the trick:

(1) Take the valuation's domain to be the natural numbers together with two new 'rogue' elements a and b (these could be Albert Einstein and his friend Kurt Gödel). Let '0' still refer to zero.

(2) But now take 's' to pick out the successor* function s^* which is defined as follows: $s^*n = n + 1$ for any natural number in the domain, while for our rogue elements $s^*a = a$, and $s^*b = b$. You can immediately check that A1 and A2 are still true on this valuation.

(3) We now have to interpret the addition function symbol '+' as a function defined over our new extended domain. Suppose we take this to pick out the addition* function. This behaves as before applied to natural numbers: so $m +^* n = m + n$ for any natural numbers m, n in the

domain. And $a +^* n = a$ and $b +^* n = b$ for any natural number n. Further, for any x (whether number or rogue element), $x +^* a = b$ and $x +^* b = a$. It is easily checked that interpreting '+' as addition* *still* makes Axioms 3 and 4 true.

(4) But by construction, $0 +^* a \neq a$, so this makes $\forall x(0 + x) = x$ false on our interpretation.

42.6 ω-incompleteness!

A formal theory of arithmetic is said to be omega-complete or ω-*complete* if, for any context α, whenever it can prove all the sentences $\alpha(0)$, $\alpha(\overline{1})$, $\alpha(\overline{2})$, $\alpha(\overline{3})$, ..., it can prove the corresponding universal generalization $\forall x \alpha(x)$. Otherwise, the theory is ω-*incomplete*. We have seen, then, that our Theory A is ω-incomplete: it can prove $0 + 0 = 0$, $0 + \overline{1} = \overline{1}$, $0 + \overline{2} = \overline{2}$, $0 + \overline{3} = \overline{3}$, ..., but can't prove $\forall x(0 + x) = x$.

Evidently, we need to beef the feeble theory A. What we want is a richer bunch of axioms to start from, in order to give us an ω-complete theory of (at least) addition and multiplication and other simple arithmetical functions. However – to give a tantalizing glimpse ahead – in an epoch-making paper in 1931, Kurt Gödel showed that we can't ever get what we want. It turns out that *any* formal theory of arithmetic satisfying some very modest and entirely desirable conditions will remain ω-incomplete somewhere. There will *always* be some α (in fact, a not-very-logically-complicated α, though different ones for different theories) for which the theory proves all the truths $\alpha(0)$, $\alpha(\overline{1})$, $\alpha(\overline{2})$, $\alpha(\overline{3})$, ..., but can't prove the corresponding truth $\forall x \alpha(x)$. Astonishing!

42.7 And where now?

The last couple of sections have given us a very fleeting first glimpse of how we can start to formally regiment a theory in a first-order QL$^=$ language. We set down a bunch of fundamental assumptions, principles, or *axioms* of the theory. We can then derive various consequences from these axioms by (more or less strictly and completely developed) formal QL$^=$ proofs. And we can also seek to show that various other possible consequences don't follow from these axioms by conjuring up countervaluations where the axioms would be true but the conjectured consequence is false.

The first two serious theories usually studied by apprentice logicians are *Peano arithmetic* (a very much richer and more competent theory than our cut-down miniature Theory A, of course, though still ω-incomplete), and standard *set theory*. We can think of these as, respectively, core theories of the mathematically finite and of the mathematically infinite. And in these next stages of the logical journey, we very quickly get to wrestle with really fascinating issues, both technical and philosophical.

But, for now, we have to pause at the threshold ...

42.8 Summary

We can extend formal QL$^=$ languages to include expressions for functions. The simplest extension only allows expressions for total single-valued functions from the domain to itself.

Syntactically, a k-ary function symbol followed by k terms forms another term. Semantically a valuation will assign a k-ary function a suitable extension (a set of $k + 1$-tuples reflecting the condition that any k objects as inputs are mapped by the function to a unique value as output).

Adding built-in function symbols allows for a much more economical treatment of functions compared with using functional relations and the Theory of Descriptions.

In formal proofs, terms constructed by applying and re-applying function symbols can be used just like other terms, to instantiate quantifiers, feature in uses of Leibniz's Law, etc.

We gave examples of formal proofs using functional terms in a simple theory of arithmetic.

Exercises 42

(a) Take the QL$^=$ language with the names, predicates and function symbols as described in §42.2. For each of the following wffs give, where possible, a q-valuation which makes the wff true and a q-valuation which makes it false:

(1) fm $=$ fn
(2) $\exists y \forall x\, fx = y$
(3) $\forall x \exists y\, fx = y$
(4) $\forall x\, ffx = fx$
(5) $\forall x \forall y\, gxy = gyx$
(6) $\forall x \forall y\, gfxfy = fgxy$
(7) $(\exists xFx \wedge \forall x \neg Ffx)$
(8) $((Fm \wedge \forall x(Fx \to Ffx)) \to \forall x\, Fx)$

(b) Add the infix function symbol '$\otimes$' to mean multiplication (circled to distinguish it from letter 'x') to the arithmetical language of §42.5, and add to Theory A the axioms

(A5) $\forall x\, (x \otimes 0) = 0$
(A6) $\forall x \forall y\, (x \otimes sy) = ((x \otimes y) + x)$.

Use this augmented theory to prove the following arithmetical truths:

(1) $(0 \otimes ss0) = 0$
(2) $(sss0 \otimes ss0) = ssssss0$
(3) $(ss0 \otimes (s0 + ss0)) = ssssss0$.

Also show that

(4) If $\bar{n}$ is a numeral, we can derive $(0 \otimes \bar{n}) = 0$
(5) If $\bar{n}$ is a numeral, we can derive $(\bar{n} \otimes s0) = \bar{n}$.

Can the augmented theory prove $\forall x(0 \otimes x) = 0$?

Appendix: Soundness and completeness

In this Appendix, we outline soundness proofs for our PL and QL natural deduction systems, and then go on to outline completeness proofs for both systems. (Extending the proofs to cover the QL$^=$ system doesn't involve any particularly exciting new ideas; so we won't do that here.)

Two comments. First, we will indeed only give *outlines*, explaining the Big Ideas. There is nothing to be gained in an introductory book by giving all the details; doing that would just obscure the overall shapes of the arguments.

Second, the proofs don't presuppose any specific knowledge of mathematics. But they *are*, necessarily, a couple of degrees more abstract and mathematical in flavour than the few metatheoretical proofs earlier in the book. Still, allowing for their abstractness, they are quite approachable – if you take things slowly!

A1   Soundness for PL

(a)   Here is a general definition that we've seen before, in §32.3:

> The *live assumptions* at a line of a Fitch-style proof are (i) the wff at that line, if it is a premiss or temporary supposition, plus (ii) any earlier premisses and undischarged (i.e. still available) suppositions.

And now here's another version of a definition we met when first discussing PL soundness in §24.6(c):

> A line in a PL proof is *good* if and only if the wff on that line (if there is one) *is* tautologically entailed by the live assumptions at that line.

However, at the *last* line of a completed proof, no suppositions will still be available. So to say that the last line of a proof is good is just to say that the wff on that line – i.e. the conclusion of the proof – is tautologically entailed by the premisses, if any (as a special case, a theorem deduced from no premisses is a tautology). Hence the claim that our PL proof system is sound is equivalent to the claim that the *last* line of any complete proof is good.

(b)   We will now argue as follows:

> (1)   The *first* line of any PL proof is good.
> (2)   If each line in a PL proof before line n is good, so is line n.
> So (3)   *Every* line of a PL proof must be good.
> So (4)   The *last* line of a PL proof must be good.

(1) is trivial: if there is a wff on the first line of a proof, it must be a premiss and it is tautologically entailed by the premiss at that line. Next, we chose our proof-building rules precisely because they look intuitively truth-preserving: so applying a rule to add another line to a proof ought to take us from some previous good line(s) to another good line. Hence (2) *ought* to be true too. But with the premisses (1) and (2) in place, we know the first line of a proof is good, so the second line is also good, so the third line is also good, and so on through the proof. Hence (3) follows, giving us the soundness theorem in the form (4).

To fill out this argument, we just(!) have to check the claim underlying (2), i.e. we need to check that an application of a PL proof-building rule always preserves goodness when we add a new line. Which is not difficult, just tedious.

For how can we extend a proof? Let us count the ways. We can add a new premiss or a new temporary supposition. But obviously doing *that* gives us a new good line – for the wff we've added will be entailed by the live assumptions which include the newly added one. Or else we can apply one of the eleven rules of inference (iteration, ex falso quodlibet, four pairs of introduction/elimination rules, plus the outlying double negation rule). And now there is nothing for it but to hack through all the different ways of extending a proof, to show that each does indeed keep our proof virtuous.

(c)   Before looking at this task, we need a couple of useful facts.

Ask yourself: at a given line, which previous assumptions (premisses and suppositions) *are* live in the sense defined, i.e. are available? Well, start from the given line and walk up the current column. If and when you get to a temporary assumption, step one column left. Go up again. If and when you get to another temporary assumption, step another column left. Keep on going until you find yourself in the home column and proceed to the top of the proof. Then every premiss or supposition you pass en route counts as a live assumption. (Draw a skeletal diagram of a Fitch-style derivation or two, and think about it!)

This implies our two useful facts:

If the *wff* at the earlier line j is still available at the later line k, all the assumptions that are live at line j are still live at line k.

If the *subproof* starting with a temporary supposition at the earlier line i and finishing at line j is still available at the later line k, then all the assumptions that are live at line j except for the supposition at the top of the subproof at line i are still live at line k.

The first is obvious; the second only takes a little more thought (draw more skeletal diagrams!).

(d)   With those useful facts to hand, let's consider just two ways of extending a proof by using a rule of inference. We'll take one 'first-level' rule where we infer a wff from two previous available wffs in the proof, and one 'second-level' rule where we use an available subproof to infer a new wff.

(MP)   Suppose we have α at the good line i, and $(\alpha \to \beta)$ at the good line j, and suppose both these wffs are still available at the later line k. Because

403

those earlier lines are good, the live assumptions at i tautologically entail α, and the live assumptions at j tautologically entail $(\alpha \rightarrow \beta)$. Combine those earlier live assumptions, and those pooled assumptions must then tautologically entail β. But by our first useful fact, those pooled assumptions are still among the live assumptions at line k. So if we use (MP) to infer β at line k, this will indeed give us another good line, with β entailed by the live assumptions of that line.

(RAA)   Suppose we have a subproof starting with α and finishing with $\bot$ at the good line j. And suppose this subproof is still available at line k. By the goodness assumption, the live assumptions at line j, which include α, tautologically entail $\bot$. So the live assumptions at line j apart from α tautologically entail $\neg\alpha$. But by the second useful fact, the live assumptions at line k will be the live assumptions at line j apart from α. So if we use (RAA) to infer $\neg\alpha$ at line k, this will indeed give us another good line.

Another nine arguments like this (exercise: find them!) will complete the demonstration that (2), *every* legitimate way of extending a proof whose lines are good up to now gives us a proof with one more good line. Then we are done.

A2   Soundness for QL

(a)   We prove soundness for QL by using an exactly parallel argument. We start by re-defining the appropriate notion of goodness:

A line of a QL proof is *good* if and only if the wff at that line (if there is one) is true on every relevantly expanded q-valuation which makes the live assumptions at that line true.

By a 'relevantly expanded' q-valuation for a line we mean a q-valuation (of the current language) that is expanded to assign values to any dummy names that appear in the wff and/or in any assumption which is live at that line.

As with the argument for PL's soundness, we can then argue that every line of a properly constructed QL proof is good, and hence that the last line is good, which establishes QL's soundness. And how do we show that every line of a QL proof is good? As before, by noting (1) that a proof (trivially) must start with a good line. And then showing that (2) every legitimate way of extending a QL proof whose lines are good up to now gives us a proof with one more good line.

(b)   Again showing (2) is not difficult, though tedious. We just have to go through all the different ways of extending proofs. We will consider one of the new quantifier rules of inference:

($\forall$I)   Suppose that we have a wff $\alpha(\delta)$ at the good line j. Suppose the live assumptions at that line are Γ. And to keep things simple to start with, suppose the wffs Γ and the wff $\alpha(\delta)$ involve *no* dummy names except for the occurrence(s) of δ in $\alpha(\delta)$.

Take some q-valuation q of the language. Since by assumption line j is good, any expansion q_δ which makes Γ true makes $\alpha(\delta)$ true too. But since δ

doesn't appear in the wffs Γ, the assignment of a value to that dummy name can't affect the truth values of those wffs – see Exercises 35(d*). Hence q_δ makes Γ all true if and only if the original unexpanded q makes Γ all true. So the goodness of line j means: for any q which makes Γ all true, any expansion q_δ will make $\alpha(\delta)$ true, and therefore (by the rule for evaluating universally quantified wffs) q will make $\forall\xi\alpha(\xi)$ true too!

Hence, if we move to a line which still has Γ as live assumptions, and where the wff on that line is $\forall\xi\alpha(\xi)$, this line will be a good one.

We can now easily generalize this line of thought to allow for cases where some other dummy names are being carried along for the ride. We then get a demonstration that an application of ($\forall$I) universally generalizing on a dummy name which doesn't appear in the live assumptions for a line takes us from a good line to another good line.

We can give similar arguments that the other three ways of extending proofs by applying quantifier rules of inference are goodness-preserving. We also need to check that the eleven propositional rules shared with PL are still goodness-preserving. Dotting every 'i' and crossing every 't' and putting everything together will take some rather tedious pages. But we can excuse ourselves from the further work. Rounding out our soundness proof for QL can be left as an enterprise for masochistic enthusiasts.

A3 Completeness: what we want to prove

Here are a couple of definitions, from §15.6 and Exercises 22(d*):

The PL wffs Γ are *tautologically consistent* if and only if there is a valuation of the relevant atoms which makes the wffs all true together.

The PL wffs Γ are PL-*consistent* if and only if there no PL proof of $\bot$ using (some of) those wffs as premises.

And now note the following:

(1) $\Gamma \vDash \gamma$ if and only if $\Gamma, \neg\gamma$ are tautologically inconsistent.

(2) $\Gamma \vdash \gamma$ if and only if $\Gamma, \neg\gamma$ are PL-inconsistent.

Both of these should by now look obvious. For the first, see §15.6 again. For the second, note that if Γ prove γ, then Γ plus $\neg\gamma$ will yield absurdity. And if you can get from Γ plus $\neg\gamma$ to absurdity, then you can use a reductio proof to get from Γ to $\neg\neg\gamma$ and hence γ.

So take the PL completeness theorem (with Γ finite in number, as in §24.5):

(C$_P$) If $\Gamma \vDash \gamma$, then $\Gamma \vdash \gamma$.

We can then use (1) and (2) and contrapose to get the equivalent claim

If $\Gamma, \neg\gamma$ are PL-consistent, then $\Gamma, \neg\gamma$ are tautologically consistent.

But now note that *this* is just a special case of the slightly more general claim that, for any finite number of wffs Δ,

(*) If Δ are PL-consistent, then Δ are tautologically consistent.

So in the next section we set out to prove (*), and thereby secure our complete-ness theorem (C_P) for PL. (And similarly, in §A5, we will use an analogue of (*) to secure the completeness theorem for QL: more about that shortly.)

A4 PL completeness proved

(a) Our proof for (*) will take two stages:

(S) We show that the PL-consistent wffs Δ can be beefed up into a bigger collection Δ^+ which is PL-consistent and *saturated*.

(V) We show that there is always a valuation which makes the wffs in a PL-consistent and saturated collection all true.

By (V), then, there is a valuation which makes all the wffs Δ^+ in (S) true. But this valuation will of course make all the original PL-consistent wffs Δ true together. Which proves (*).

(b) So what do we mean by saying that a set of wffs is saturated? We mean it is *saturated with truth-makers*. And what do we mean by *that*? We mean that for every complex wff in the set (every wff that isn't an atom or negated atom) there are one or two simpler wffs also in the set such that, if the simpler ones are true, so is the more complex one. Thus:

Some wffs Γ form a *saturated* collection if they satisfy the following seven conditions, for any wffs α, β:

(i) If $\neg\neg\alpha$ is one of the wffs Γ, so is α;

(ii) if $(\alpha \wedge \beta)$ is one of the wffs Γ, so are α and β;

(iii) if $\neg(\alpha \wedge \beta)$ is one of the wffs Γ, so is at least one of $\neg\alpha$ and $\neg\beta$;

(iv) if $(\alpha \vee \beta)$ is one of the wffs Γ, so is at least one of α and β;

(v) if $\neg(\alpha \vee \beta)$ is one of the wffs Γ, so are $\neg\alpha$ and $\neg\beta$;

(vi) if $(\alpha \to \beta)$ is one of the wffs Γ, so is at least one of $\neg\alpha$ and β;

(vii) if $\neg(\alpha \to \beta)$ is one of the wffs Γ, so are α and $\neg\beta$.

By inspection, we see in each case that, if the simpler wff(s) on the *right* of the conditional are true, so is the complex wff on the *left*. And note that these seven clauses cover every form of wff that isn't an atom or negated atom.

It is more or less immediate from our cunning definition that (V) is true. Suppose wffs Γ taken together are PL-consistent and saturated. Since they are PL-consistent, they can't contain an atom and its negation, so we can consis-tently choose the valuation which makes all the naked atoms true and makes any other relevant atoms false (and so makes any negated atoms true). This chosen valuation therefore makes the *basic* wffs among Γ all true (recall, in Exercises 13 we defined a basic wff to be an atom or the negation of an atom).

We can easily assign numerical degrees of complexity such that a wff always counts as more complex than its truth-makers (as given by (i) to (vii)). Now look at the wffs Γ in order of increasing complexity. So after the basic wffs, the atoms and negated atoms, the next simplest wffs are all true on the chosen valuation – since by saturation these wffs have basic truth-makers among Γ, and these basic truth-makers are true on the chosen valuation. Then, going up another level of complexity, the next simplest wffs are also all true on this valuation – since by saturation these wffs too have simpler truth-makers among Γ, and we've just seen that those are true on the chosen valuation. Keep on going. *Truth on the chosen valuation percolates upward through more and more complex wffs, eventually making all of Γ true on the chosen valuation.*

(c)   Now to prove (S). Recall the results of Exercises 20(b*), 21(b*), and 22(c*). There are seven of them, neatly matching (i) to (vii) in our definition of saturation. And each result has the same shape: it tells us that *if some wffs are PL-consistent and contain a complex wff of such-and-such form, then we can always add truth-makers for that wff while keeping our collection of wffs PL-consistent!*

So given the PL-consistent wffs Δ, arrange them in some order. Imagine, if you like, a logical demon walking along the list of wffs.

(1)   Every time they encounter a wff of kinds (i), (ii), (v), or (vii), they add the appropriate truth-maker(s) to the end of the list, which we know that they can do while maintaining PL-consistency.

(2)   Every time they encounter a wff of kinds (iii), (iv), and (vi), they also add a truth-maker while maintaining PL-consistency. Again we know that they always *can* do this (which is the important point – there always exists an appropriate extension of the list). Imagine, then, that the demon uses their demonic powers so as always to choose the truth-maker which preserves consistency.

As the demon walks along the list, every complex wff will have simpler truth-makers added to the list, and these truth-makers (if complex) will have their still simpler truth-makers added, and so on. Since the additions get simpler and simpler, if the initial Δ are finitely many, the walk eventually terminates. So the demon will arrive at a still PL-consistent but fully saturated collection Δ^+ where there are no more truth-makers which they need to add. Which establishes (S).

Of course, the demon is just a fancy for vividness. The point is that a suitably saturated collection Δ^+ *exists*, there's a process for constructing it in principle. (And – just for the record – the argument for (*) can in fact be tweaked to cover the case where we start with an infinite initial collection of wffs Δ.)

A5   QL completeness proved

(a)   The QL completeness theorem tells us that

(C$_Q$)   If $\Gamma \vDash \gamma$, then $\Gamma \vdash \gamma$,

where Γ and γ are some QL sentences, finitely many. For reasons exactly parallel to those given in §A3, we can prove (C$_Q$) by showing

(**)   If Δ are QL-consistent, then Δ are q-consistent,

where again Δ are finitely many QL sentences, and some wffs are QL-consistent just if there is no QL proof of absurdity from them. And the shape of the two-stage proof of (**) is the same as that of our proof of (*):

(qS) We show that the QL-consistent sentences Δ can be beefed up into a bigger – this time perhaps infinite – collection Δ^+ of wffs which is QL-consistent and *q-saturated* (to be defined!).

(qV) We show that there is always an expanded q-valuation which makes the wffs in a QL-consistent and q-saturated collection all true.

By (qV), there is an expanded q-valuation q^+ which makes all the wffs Δ^+ in (qS) true (expanded, because as we will see, Δ^+ will involve dummy names). But q^+ will of course make all of the smaller original Δ true. By assumption all of Δ are sentences, so q^+'s assignments of values to dummy names which don't occur in Δ are irrelevant. So ignoring those assignments, we are left with a q-valuation q which makes all of Δ true. Which proves (**).

That, at any rate, is our strategy. We need to start with a definition of q-saturation.

(b) Say that a collection of wffs Γ from a QL language is q-saturated if it satisfies the conditions (i) to (vii) for being saturated, and it also satisfies the following conditions:

(viii) If $\forall \xi \alpha(\xi)$ is one of the wffs Γ, so is $\alpha(\tau)$ for any term τ that appears in any wff from Γ (and there is at least one such term);

(ix) If $\exists \xi \alpha(\xi)$ is one of the wffs Γ, so is $\alpha(\tau)$ for some term τ;

(x) If $\neg \forall \xi \alpha(\xi)$ is one of the wffs Γ, so is the corresponding $\exists \xi \neg \alpha(\xi)$;

(xi) If $\neg \exists \xi \alpha(\xi)$ is one of the wffs Γ, so is the corresponding $\forall \xi \neg \alpha(\xi)$.

In cases (ix) to (xi), if the wff given on the right of the conditional is true, so is the original wff on the left; so again these three clauses give truth-makers. In the special case of (viii), the truth of all the added wffs given on the right will make the quantified wff on the left true if (but only if) the domain contains no more objects than those named by the terms appearing in Γ.

So next we need to show (qV) is true. We use the same basic trick as before, i.e. choose an expanded q-valuation which makes the basic wffs – atomic wffs and negated atomic wffs – in a QL-consistent set of wffs Γ all true. And then show that if Γ taken together are q-saturated, all of them must be true on this chosen q-valuation. How, then, we do choose the needed expanded q-valuation?

(c) Assume Γ are QL-consistent and q-saturated. Remember there are only a finite number (maybe zero) of different proper names in any QL language, and hence occurring in Γ. So now proceed as follows:

(1) Take all the different terms that appear in Γ, and line them up, proper names first $\tau_0, \tau_1, \ldots, \tau_k$ (finitely many), followed by the dummy names $\tau_{k+1}, \tau_{k+2}, \tau_{k+3}, \ldots$ (perhaps unlimitedly many of them). (Fine print: if there are no terms at all occurring in Γ, that can only be because there are no quantified wffs in Γ, so we would in effect be back dealing with propositional logic – we can safely ignore that boring case.)

(2) Set the domain for our chosen q-valuation to be the natural numbers from zero up, one for each of the terms τ_j that actually appear in Γ (so perhaps that's *all* the natural numbers).

(3) Let the reference of the term τ_j be the number j. So note, we are dealing with the special case where every object in the domain is the reference of some term on our chosen q-valuation.

(4) And now for the clever trick: suppose φ is a unary predicate. Say that the number j is in the extension of φ if and only if the atomic wff $\varphi\tau_j$ is among Γ! Then that makes all the unnegated wffs of the form $\varphi\tau_j$ in Γ true. And if $\neg\varphi\tau_j$ is among Γ, then by QL-consistency $\varphi\tau_j$ is *not* among Γ, so j is not in the extension of φ, and hence $\varphi\tau_j$ is false and $\neg\varphi\tau_j$ is true. In short, all basic wffs formed from unary predicates will come out true on our chosen q-valuation.

(5) Say that the pair of numbers $\langle i, j \rangle$ is in the extension of the binary predicate ψ if and only if the atomic wff $\psi\tau_i\tau_j$ is among Γ! By the same reasoning as is in the unary case, all basic wffs (atoms and negated atoms) formed from binary predicates will come out true on our chosen q-valuation. Handle predicates of other arities, including zero, similarly.

So, we have arrived at our chosen q-valuation which makes the simplest wffs from among Γ all true together.

Now we just need to show that, as in the PL case, a valuation which makes the simplest wffs in a q-saturated collection of wffs true makes all of them true.

By definition, in a q-saturated collection, every complex wff has truth-makers in the collection. In particular, note that if $\forall\xi\alpha(\xi)$ is among Γ, then so is $\alpha(\tau)$ for every term τ which appears somewhere in the wffs Γ. But then if those instances are all true on the chosen q-valuation, then since each number in the domain is named by one of those terms, $\forall\xi\alpha(\xi)$ is true on that valuation too. So, as in the PL case, truth can percolate up from the simplest truth-makers to more and more complex wffs, eventually making *all* the wffs in Γ true. Which establishes (qV) – and moreover, we see that to find a q-valuation which makes all the wffs in the QL-consistent q-saturated collection true we need look no further than valuations constructed out of natural numbers.

(d) It remains to prove (qS). Again, we use the same basic idea as in the proof of (S). So given the QL-consistent wffs Δ, finitely many, arrange them in some order. Imagine again a logical demon walking along the list of wffs. Then:

(1) Every time they encounter a wff of kinds (i), (ii), (v), (vii), (x), or (xii), they add to the end of the list the appropriate truth-maker(s), which we know they can do while maintaining QL-consistency (obvious for the new last two cases).

(2) Every time they encounter a wff of kinds (iii), (iv), and (vi), they have to choose a truth-maker to add, but again we know that they always *can* do this while maintaining QL-consistency. Imagine that they use their demonic powers to jump the right way!

(3) When they encounter a wff of the kind (viii), a universal quantification $\forall \xi \alpha(\xi)$, they add every instance $\alpha(\tau)$ where τ is any term that appears somewhere in the wffs in their list so far (or if no term appears yet, then use the first dummy name). This is easily seen to maintain QL-consistency, as we in effect noted in Exercises 33(d*).

(4) When they encounter a wff of the kind (ix), an existential quantification $\exists \xi \alpha(\xi)$, they add the instance $\alpha(\delta)$ where δ is the first dummy name that doesn't appear anywhere in the list of wffs so far. Then, with this new term in play, they revisit every universally quantified wff encountered so far, and now also instantiate it with this new term. Again, doing all this maintains QL-consistency, which follows from another point noted in Exercises 33(d*).

And the demon keeps on going.

But note that this time – in contrast with the PL case – the demon's task can be an infinite one, even if they start from only finitely many Δ. Why? Take the case where the original Δ_0 comprises just the single sentence $\forall x \exists y Lxy$. First following the instruction (3) and then repeatedly following (4) as new existential quantifications are popped onto the end of the list, the demon's list will start growing in the following stages:

Δ_0: $\forall x \exists y Lxy$
Δ_1: $\forall x \exists y Lxy, \exists y Lay$
Δ_2: $\forall x \exists y Lxy, \exists y Lay, Lab, \exists y Lby$
Δ_3: $\forall x \exists y Lxy, \exists y Lay, Lab, \exists y Lby, Lbc, \exists y Lcy$
Δ_4: ...

and there is no end to the process. What to do?

There is a standard mathematical trick to use. Our logical demon, starting from a given initial (finite) collection Δ, will build up a perhaps infinite sequence of (still finite) collections $\Delta_0, \Delta_1, \Delta_2, \ldots$, each one extending the previous one, and all QL-consistent. *We can now define our desired Δ^+ to be the union of all these Δ_j* (so a wff is in Δ^+ if and only if it is in some Δ_j). Though it is rather more fun to imagine a demon who can go faster and faster and so complete the infinite task of building Δ^+!

So the QL-consistent Δ get beefed up to a collection Δ^+ which is q-saturated. (Why? Because every complex wff acquires truth-makers along the way). And the wffs Δ^+ are still QL-consistent. (Why? Because if they were not, there would be a proof of absurdity using premisses from among Δ^+ – finitely many premisses, since proofs are finite. Hence all these premisses would be in some finite Δ_j: but that would contradict the QL-consistency of Δ_j.) Which establishes (qS).

Or at least, it establishes (qS) if we can cash out the metaphor of the demon making a perhaps infinite sequence of choices through a branching tree of options. But in fact it is not hard to tell a slightly more abstract version of the story, as any more advanced book on mathematical logic will do.

So let's leave things here, except for one final observation.

A6   A squeezing argument

(a)   Let's say that a q-valuation whose domain is some or all of the natural numbers (integers from zero up) is a *tame* valuation. And using this notion, let's introduce a third turnstile symbol:

> We will use $\Gamma \vDash \gamma$ to abbreviate the claim that there is no tame valuation which makes all Γ true and makes γ false.

Now, we have just seen that if some wffs are QL-consistent, then there is not just a *q*-valuation which makes them all true, but more particularly there is a *tame* valuation which does the job. Which by the sort of equivalences we met in §A3 tells us that

(1)   If $\Gamma \vDash \gamma$, then $\Gamma \vdash \gamma$.

But the soundness theorem

(2)   If $\Gamma \vdash \gamma$, then $\Gamma \vDash \gamma$

seems quite secure (you can check that the key steps in its proof don't depend on exactly which valuations we are quantifying over in defining q-validity). And we certainly have

(3)   If $\Gamma \vDash \gamma$, then $\Gamma \vDash \gamma$.

For if there is no q-valuation at all which makes all Γ true and makes γ false, then there can't in particular be a tame valuation tidily built from the natural numbers which makes Γ true and γ false.

(b)   We offered the notion of q-validity as a rational reconstruction of the idea of logical validity for QL arguments. But in §36.2 we worried whether the idea of quantifying over *all* possible q-valuations makes sufficiently clear sense – what counts as 'all' of them? Could it make a difference just which wildly infinite domains for valuations we are prepared to countenance?

We can now see that we needn't worry – a point that seems to have been first explicitly emphasized by the logician Georg Kreisel. Going round the circle of implications in (1), (2) and (3), the relations symbolized by the three turnstiles must be equivalent in the sense that, if any one holds between Γ and γ, so do the other two. So yes, our original definition of q-validity was perhaps somewhat slack in not fixing the universe of valuations we are quantifying over; but it characterizes a relation $\vDash$ which is 'squeezed' between the relations $\vDash$ and $\vdash$. And those two sharply defined relations are provably equivalent; one holds if and only if the other does. So there is no wriggle room: despite the apparent slackness in our initial definition, that definition is in fact rigorous enough, it says enough to ensure that the relation $\vDash$ has a sharp extension, the same as the extension of $\vDash$ and $\vdash$. Which is a relief, and a happy note to end on.

The Greek alphabet

Upper case	Lower case	Name	English equivalent
A	α	alpha	a
B	β	beta	b
Γ	γ	gamma	g
Δ	δ	delta	d
E	ϵ, ε	epsilon	e
Z	ζ	zeta	z
H	η	eta	(long) e
Θ	θ, ϑ	theta	th
I	ι	iota	i
K	κ	kappa	k
Λ	λ	lambda	l
M	μ	mu	m
N	ν	nu	n
Ξ	ξ	xi	x
O	o	omicron	o
Π	π	pi	p
P	ρ	rho	r
Σ	σ, ς	sigma	s
T	τ	tau	t
Υ	υ	upsilon	u (or y)
Φ	ϕ, φ	phi	ph
X	χ	chi	ch (as in 'loch')
Ψ	ψ	psi	ps
Ω	ω	omega	(long) o

Thus, with conventional accents, Σωκράτης, Πλάτων, Ἀριστοτέλης (*Sōcratēs, Platōn, Aristotelēs*) name the Greek philosophers.

The word *logic* derives from λόγος (*logos*), which has multiple meanings, including *word, reason,* and *account.* Thus *psychology* is a late coinage derived from Greek roots, for an account of the *psychē,* ψυχή.

In Aristotle, a συλλογισμός (*syllogismos*) is an inference. In Euclid, a θεώρημα (*theōrēma*) is a proposition to be proved.

One of the Greek words for love is φιλία (*philia*); and wisdom is σοφία (*sophia*). Hence a lover of wisdom is a φιλόσοφος, a *philosophos.*

Further reading

Parallel reading

If asked to recommend just one text to read alongside this book, I would choose

Nicholas J. J. Smith, *Logic: The Laws of Truth* (Princeton UP, 2012).

This is very clearly and engagingly written in a similar spirit.

Smith's book also, in parts, takes an interestingly different approach since it has chapters exploring logic by the tree method, before it later turns to a brief treatment of natural deduction. We can argue about the pros and cons of the two approaches, trees vs natural deduction, as an introduction to formal logic: ideally you should know something about both. Indeed, the first edition of this present book was tree-based. As an alternative to Smith's chapters, then, you will find revised versions of my earlier tree chapters at logicmatters.net.

Since Fitch's own 1952 book, there have appeared over thirty introductory texts using his style of proof system. No two seem to agree at *all* the main choice points – for example, do we use an absurdity constant, do we use dummy names, do we indent proofs when using the ∀-introduction rule? However, for a friendly introduction with a similar enough system see:

Paul Teller, *A Modern Formal Logic Primer* (Prentice Hall, 1989).

Teller's book also covers trees, has a particularly approachable, relaxed style, and is freely available at the book's website, tellerprimer.ucdavis.edu. Alternatively, see the brisker open-source text

P. D. Magnus et al., *forall x*, forallx.openlogicproject.org.

Philosophical matters arising

We have inevitably touched on a number of philosophical issues which we couldn't pause to discuss at length – starting with worries about the nature of propositions and about the very idea of necessity. A wonderful resource which has many entries on general topics like these, and entries too on the particular logicians and philosophers mentioned in this book, is

The Stanford Encyclopedia of Philosophy, plato.stanford.edu.

However, some of these entries will be rather tough going for a real beginner, so here are a few more suggestions. First, two books:

A. C. Grayling, *An Introduction to Philosophical Logic* (Blackwell, 3rd edn. 1997),

Mark Sainsbury, *Logical Forms: an Introduction to Philosophical Logic* (Blackwell, 2nd edition 2000).

Read Grayling Chs. 2 and 3 on the nature of propositions, and on the ideas of necessity and analyticity. And read Sainsbury Chs. 1, 2, 4 and 6 on logic and the project of formalization, on truth-functionality, and on quantification. Sainsbury discusses conditionals in his Ch. 2 (and in his Ch. 3 too). For more on troubles with conditionals, see the introduction and some of the papers collected in

Frank Jackson, ed., *Conditionals* (OUP, 1991).

Jackson himself proposes the neat story about the meaning of indicative 'ifs' sketched in §19.5(c).

Our logical system in this book is 'classical', containing the rule (DN), or equivalently (LEM). For more on constructivist doubts about the legitimacy of these rules see

Stephen Read, *Thinking About Logic* (OUP, 1995), Ch. 8.

Richard Zach et al., *The Open Logic Text*, openlogicproject.org, first chapter of Part XI, Intuitionism.

We have helped ourselves to a basically Fregean distinction between sense and reference. For an approachable discussion of Frege's own views see

Harold Noonan, *Frege: A Critical Introduction* (Polity, 2001), Chs. 4 and 5.

Going further in formal logic

There is a very extensive annotated Study Guide available at logicmatters.net. But two good places to start are

David Bostock, *Intermediate Logic* (OUP, 1997),

Ian Chiswell and Wilfrid Hodges, *Mathematical Logic* (OUP, 2007).

Despite their titles, neither book goes a great deal beyond this one. But Bostock is very good on the motivations for and interrelations between various styles of logical system, and on explaining some key metatheorems. Also see his last chapter for some discussion of empty names, empty domains, and free logic. Chiswell and Hodges are also very clear and their book provides an excellent basis for more advanced formal work.

Our final chapter hinted that there is much of interest in formal theories of arithmetic, and in Gödel's famed incompleteness theorems in particular. If those hints piqued your interest, then I can't resist suggesting that you soon dive into

Peter Smith, *An Introduction to Gödel's Theorems* (CUP, 2nd edition 2013; now freely available at logicmatters.net).

Index

Entries for *symbols, rules of inference,* and *concepts* give the principal location(s) where you will find them introduced. *Names* are not indexed when they are merely used in examples.

CPSIA information can be obtained
at www.ICGtesting.com
Printed in the USA
BVHW022343240423
662942BV00003BA/48

9 781916 906327